CONSTRUCTION FUNDING

The Process of Real Estate Development, Appraisal, and Finance

FOURTH EDITION

Nathan S. Collier
Courtland A. Collier
Don A. Halperin

BICENTENNIAL
1807
WILEY
2007
BICENTENNIAL

JOHN WILEY & SONS, INC.

This book is printed on acid-free paper.♾

Published by John Wiley & Sons, Inc., Hoboken, New Jersey
Published simultaneously in Canada.

Wiley Bicentennial Logo: Richard J. Pacifico

For general information about our other products and services, please contact our Customer Care
Department within the United States at (800) 762-2974, outside the United States at (317) 572-3993
or fax (317) 572-4002.

Wiley also publishes its books in a variety of electronic formats. Some content that appears in print
may not be available in electronic books. For more information about Wiley products, visit our web
site at www.wiley.com.

Library of Congress Cataloging-in-Publication Data:
Collier, Nathan S., 1952-
  Construction funding : the process of real estate development, appraisal, and finance / Nathan
S. Collier Courtland A. Collier Don A. Halperin.—4th ed.
    p. cm.
  Includes index.
  ISBN 978-0-470-03731-7 (cloth)
1. Construction industry–Finance. 2. Mortgage loans. 3. Leases. 4. Real estate development.
I. Collier, Courtland A. II. Halperin, Don A. III. Title.
  HD9715.A2C59 2007
  690.068'1–dc22

                                                                        2007006908

Printed in the United States of America

10 9 8 7 6 5 4 3 2 1

Contents

Preface

> When we mean to build,
> We first survey the plot, then draw the model;
> And when we see the figure of the house,
> Then must we rate the cost of the erection,
> Which if we find outweighs ability,
> What do we then but draw anew the model
> In fewer offices, or at last desist
> To build at all?
>
> —William Shakespeare,
> *The Second Part of Henry IV* (Act I, Scene 3)

This book takes the reader through the real estate development process in an easy-to-understand format, starting with land acquisition and ending with permanent financing, emphasizing the financing and appraisal aspects.

An understanding of the basics of the real estate development and financing process is of tremendous benefit to anyone whose life or livelihood is impacted by the real estate sector. The authors' guiding principle in this text was to give a concise synopsis of the real estate funding and development process to aid anyone working with a developer to understand the developer's point of view. Whether you are an engineer, architect, surveyor, general contractor, or potential investor or developer, this book will broaden and deepen your understanding of every developer and development project.

Following an actual 260-unit apartment community through the development process, this book explains all aspects of the process in easy-to-understand terms with real-life examples and anecdotes.

To give the reader a front-row seat at the unfolding of the development process, the appendices, illustrations, and examples include loan documents used by major financial institutions and exhibits drawn from actual appraisals.

Written by Nathan S. Collier, a highly successful developer and owner-operator of multifamily communities, this edition is an extensive revision of a classic textbook favorite. In addition to his success as a multifamily developer, Collier, who holds a BS in Finance, an MBA, and a JD degree, also is a registered real estate broker, licensed building contractor, member of the Florida Bar, and a certified public accountant (CPA).

At a time when the simultaneous pass rate for all four parts of the CPA exam hovered below 25 percent, Collier passed on his first sitting, scoring among the top ten individuals in the state of Florida. He has served as an expert witness on behalf of the Florida Department of Professional Regulation, been an instructor for a nationwide LSAT (Law School Admission Test) preparatory course, and taught graduate and undergraduate courses for the University of Florida's Warrington College of Business. He is a life member of the University of Florida Foundation, which oversees a billion-dollar portfolio.

Collier is on the Board of Directors of the National MultiHousing Council (NMHC) and a member of the Real Estate Roundtable and World Presidents' Organization. His property management and development firm is Paradigm Properties, Inc., whose Web site may be found at www.teamparadigm.com.

The book is divided into three major parts, which, although related, are largely independent. Part I, "Background," is introductory.

Chapter 1, "Characteristics of Real Estate," gives an overview of the real estate sector and several of its unique aspects.

Chapter 2, "Different Types of Business Organizations," outlines the fundamentals of various types of business organizations and is intended to acquaint those without a business background with the various types of business organizations they may find in the real estate field and the pros and cons of each.

Chapter 3, "Negotiation," rapidly covers the fundamentals of negotiation. After having been virtually ignored by academia, the field of negotiation is now a topic of serious study at many top business and law schools. Perhaps because every piece of real estate is unique and the development process is so chaotic, successful negotiation is a vital part of every successful development. Therefore, an understanding of the fundamentals of negotiation contributes largely to the success of any development project.

Part II is the heart of the book, dealing with the development process itself, from start to finish.

Chapter 4, "The Development Process: An Overview," gives a brief insight into the development process and includes an excellent outline of the process.

Chapter 5, "Market Studies, Site-Feasibility Analysis, and Selection," covers the factors involved in determining the proper market-selection techniques to apply to find the perfect site and the elements of a correctly conducted feasibility study to verify that the conditions conducive to the success of the project exist.

Chapter 6 is titled "Creating the Project Pro Forma." A pro forma is a projected operating statement for the development project and includes forecasts of income and any preconstruction appraisal of the project.

Chapter 7 is "The Appraisal." The appraiser's report plays a key role in determining the amount of money that a financial institution will lend to finance the construction of a development project. Understanding the appraisal and how it is formatted is a major key to understanding the financing of real estate.

Chapter 8, "Sources of Financing, the Loan Application Process, and Term Sheets," discusses the various lending institutions that are traditional capital sources for the real estate industry. Common terms are discussed and defined, and the loan application process is reviewed. The chapter also presents an in-depth analysis of a bank term sheet.

Chapter 9, "The Commitment," reviews in detail a loan commitment letter for a $15-million construction project, taking the reader through common clauses and requirements.

Chapter 10, "Closing the Loan," goes through the documents required to close a major construction loan, including the note, mortgage, loan agreement, unconditional guarantee, and closing statement.

Part III delves into two interesting and timely aspects of real estate finance and development in greater detail.

Chapter 11, "Joint Ventures," explores possible joint-venture deal structures between an operating partner (hands on, sweat equity) and a financing partner (institutional, deeper pockets), outlining various common deal points that are discussed in depth. The acquisition of an existing income-producing property is emphasized, but the arrangements have universal application.

Chapter 12, "Condominiums and Condominium Conversions," is a behind-the-scenes look at the actual sale of an existing 168-unit rental community to a condominium converter. Marketed by an acclaimed national brokerage firm, the offering generated significant response. The reader has the unique opportunity of following the bid and sale process from the perspective of the owner of a major real estate investment.

Part IV deals with some of the more mathematical and technical aspects of the construction phase, covering cash flow and funding disbursement, including the draw schedule, the time value of money, net-present value, future worth, and minimum attractive rates of return.

Chapter 13, "How to Forecast Cash Needs During Construction," explains how to plan all project expenditures; while Chapter 14, "Basic How-to-Do-It Time Value of Money Calculations," focuses on how time, interest, and the nature of repayment affect cash flow and defines total project financing and cash requirements.

Foreword

I am a developer. I develop for many reasons, the most important is that I out-and-out love it. It stirs my soul, fires my passion, captures my interest, enthralls and grips me at the most visceral level.

Development is an intense, consuming process; it also can be one of the most creative processes on this earth. Staring at a plot of land and visualizing what could be, what might be, what should be, is an exciting way to exercise the imagination.

The pleasure is in sitting down with your engineer and architect and trying to create the best project while dealing with what seems like a million and one constraints, while maximizing and optimizing those constraints. In my wilder flights of fancy, I compare project development to Michelangelo staring at a piece of marble and visualizing within the stone the statue of David.

The constraints are many: from regulatory, zoning, political, permitting, and ever-more complex building codes to the financial, marketplace, site, topographic, and surrounding infrastructure, to name a few. Sometimes it seems as though development is not so much design as it is patiently assembling a giant jigsaw puzzle.

The rewards, however, also are many. Nothing beats the feeling of watching that building come up out of the ground, slowly taking form, and eventually being occupied. I drive by projects that I completed years ago and still take pride in their beauty and the resolution of the myriad problems involved in bringing them to fruition.

Development, done right, can be quite remunerative. It is also a double-edged sword: A development project that goes south can provide a hard lesson and many sleepless nights when the full impact of a personal guarantee on a construction loan becomes all too real.

To be specific, I am an apartment developer or, as we often say in the industry, a multifamily developer. Typically, I like to develop 200-plus units at a density of 12 to 16 apartments per acre; I have developed as few as 8 units per acre (practically single-family units) and as many as 50-plus units per acre.

Like many developers, I also invest in my projects. Occasionally, I have been the builder or general contractor as well. I am atypical as a developer in several respects, at least for the size of the projects I do. First, I am an individual. Although, for many years, it was the norm for developers to be private individuals (and often eccentric ones at that), the trend today is toward corporate developers, particularly in the larger developments that I prefer. I also am atypical in that many times I am the sole investor in my projects, and I mostly keep what I develop. Many developers bring in or sell out to equity partners who build, stabilize, and flip a property. Although some people confuse the terms, and roles sometimes overlap, being a developer of real estate is very different from being a builder or an investor.

I came up through the ownership and management side of the real estate business. I simply enjoy real estate. It has a certain solidness to it that has always attracted me. I read *Gone with the Wind* as a youth, and one scene has stayed with me: Scarlett O'Hara clutches the soil of Tara, the family plantation, and realizes that land is the foundation of everything. She vows never to be separated from the land, to always own land. It seemed like an eminently sensible philosophy to me then, and still does.

In my experience, most developers come into the business from either the construction side or the financial side, and a few come from architecture or land planning. Although the field is changing rapidly, few universities offer degrees or courses of study in development. It is a complex profession that requires an interesting variety of skills that are frequently learned on the job.

I received a bachelor's degree in finance, spent another couple of years getting an MBA with an accounting concentration, and I am a registered real estate broker as well as a licensed building contractor. And, in what now seems like another life, I also became a CPA and an attorney; I maintain my currency in both professions. I do not practice any of these professions per se, but I use the knowledge of each daily as a developer. More than anything else, I negotiate, which is why this book has an entire chapter on negotiation.

I do not do retail, office, or industrial development. Each of these is an arcane specialty in and of itself, with its own precepts, nuances, submarkets, and area-specific requirements. Although I hold a building contractor's license, it is not a primary area of expertise, and I typically hire a general contractor to do the actual construction.

Nathan S. Collier

Acknowledgments

My thanks to University of Florida Masters in Real Estate students Garritt Bader, Patrick Boileau, Jess J. Johnson, and Marc K. Nakleh, and their professor, Mark Monroe, for providing learning points, definitions, summaries, and questions and answers for each chapter, which are new to this edition.

And special thanks and much gratitude to my tireless assistants, the esteemed Evan Weber and Jackie Proveaux, whose energy and many abilities are invaluable to me.

PART I
Background

1

Characteristics of Real Estate

REAL ESTATE'S TRADITIONAL, CYCLICAL NATURE

Real estate has traditionally been a cyclical business, and that characteristic has fundamentally shaped the industry. The basic real estate cycle, illustrated in Figure 1-1, proceeds as follows: economic expansion, robust construction, rising occupancy and increasing rents, good times, easy money, abundant financing at good rates, and boom times, resulting in overbuilding, oversupply, and a glut that may take years to absorb. A real estate recession results when new-construction starts come to a virtual halt but, because of long planning and construction time frames, completions continue to come on line. Occupancy as well as rents fall, particularly after adjusting for inflation, specials, incentives, and discounts. Eventually, as the overcapacity is worked off, occupancy and rents begin to rise again, and the final recovery phase begins. Boom followed by bust has long been a hallowed real estate tradition.

Many argue that increasing sophistication in the industry, more institutional ownership with accompanying oversight, increased accounting transparency, and greater financial discipline imposed by the involvement of Wall Street capital markets will dampen, if not eliminate, real estate cycles. Computerization and the Internet are revolutionizing the flow of information in the industry, and only time will tell the full impact of all these changes.

Transparency refers to how easy it is for the investing public to view a company's books (financial statements and operating results). Traditionally, many real estate developers operated within privately-held companies that disclosed little, if any, financial information. Mistakes and missed forecasts or overoptimistic projects could be hidden from the public eye. Today, the larger number of REITs (Real Estate Investment Trusts) and other publicly-held companies that are involved in construction and development help provide information that increases investor confidence and knowledge of the industry. Still, even publicly-held companies may legally make accounting choices relevant to how much detail they wish to report. A company may cite the need not to give out vital proprietary information to its competitors and may choose to report total expenses and income from operations without further breaking down the information by region, property class, or individual property.

In addition to the basic real estate cycle, shown in Figure 1-1, we will look at three other cycle types that affect the real estate industry:

1. United States national economic cycle
2. Capital market cycles, including liquidity and interest-rate cycles
3. Property market (or occupancy) cycles

Within *capital market cycles*, we will look at both *liquidity* and *interest-rate cycles*. Within *property market (or occupancy) cycles*, we will look at how various real estate sectors move through the real estate cycle at different times and how, even within one real estate sector, different parts of the country will be in different phases of the real estate cycle at the same time. We will then look briefly at how the rental-rate growth cycle impacts occupancy.

UNITED STATES NATIONAL ECONOMIC CYCLE

It is important to remember that there are many types of business cycles. The most widely followed is the U.S. national economic cycle, traditionally marked by the quarterly reporting of the expansion (or contraction) of the GNP (gross national product), with a recession defined as two consecutive quarterly contractions of the GNP. There are also global economic cycles and regional economic cycles, all of which, through imports and exports, affect investor confidence and America's national economic cycle. Obviously, new projects are more likely to be undertaken during an upswing and at the top of an economic cycle than on a downswing.

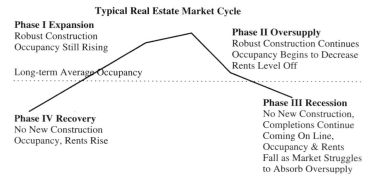

FIG. 1-1   Typical Real Estate Market Cycle.

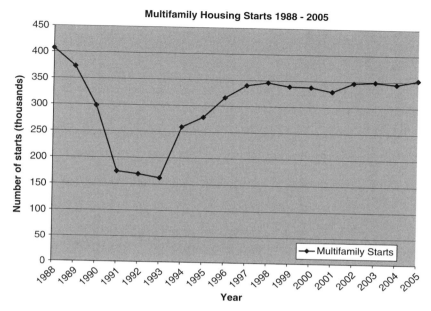

FIG. 1-2 Multifamily housing starts, 1988–2005. (*Source*: U.S. Bureau of the Census, *Construction Reports*, Series C-20, Housing Starts.)

Figure 1-2 depicts multifamily housing starts from 1988 to 2005. The impact of the real estate recession of the early 1990s is clearly shown in the multiyear decline in housing starts beginning in 1990 and continuing until 1994. The recovery phase occurs in 1995, and for the next ten years multifamily housing starts oscillate roughly between 340,000 to 350,000 per year.

The excessiveness of the robust 1988 and 1989 multifamily housing starts of 407,000 and 373,000, respectively, is highlighted by the fact that almost twenty years later multifamily housing starts are still significantly lower (345,000 in 2004 and 353,000 in 2005) in spite of a population growth of roughly 50 million people from 1990 to 2005.

CAPITAL CYCLES: LIQUIDITY AND INTEREST RATES

Compared with other sectors, real estate is a capital-intensive sector of the economy. Real estate requires a significantly greater investment of capital for every dollar of revenue generated than may be required for a less capital-intensive sector such as the service sector, hence, real estate's sensitivity to the capital markets. *Capital cycles* are affected by both liquidity and interest-rate cycles. *Liquidity cycles* reflect fluctuations in the *availability* of capital; whereas *interest-rate cycles* reflect fluctuations in the *cost* of capital. Although related, these concepts are very different. It is quite possible for interest rates to be favorable (when the cost of capital is affordable), but for one reason or another capital is not available—its availability is constrained. The opposite also is often true: When interest rates are high, money is often very available and the markets are liquid; but the cost of the money is so high that few projects will pencil out because the cost of the capital is higher than the intrinsic return of the project. Consequently, the use of debt capital would represent negative leverage.

A classic example of a liquidity crisis occurred in the conduit lending market in the fall of 1999 when Nomura (a very large Japanese bank with a major American real estate lending portfolio) abruptly shut down its real estate lending operations, shocking the *commercial mortgage backed securities* (CMBS)/*conduit lending market* (see Chapter 8) and virtually shutting the conduit lending door for many months.

At other times in the past, real estate has simply been out of favor as a sector of the economy, either because analysts or economists did not foresee favorable prospects or because a recent real estate downturn had left painful memories of loan losses in the minds of lenders.

Interest rates move in cycles that, although related to and with impact on national economic cycles, move somewhat independently, at times lagging and at times leading the national economic cycle. The Federal Reserve (the Fed) will tend to attempt to move interest rates higher if it thinks the economy is overheating and lower interest rates if it believes that the economy is in need of stimulation. However, the Federal Reserve can directly change only short-term interest rates. The Fed affects short-term rates by lowering the discount rate (the interest rate at which the Federal Reserve lends money to banks), but longer-term rates are set by investor expectations about inflation and the necessary return on capital.

Most ten-year term, commercial real estate loans are written at a spread (i.e., the additional amount of interest charged over a given index) over the matching 10-year U.S. Treasury note rate. Spreads are quoted in basis points or 100ths of a percentage point. Spreads over the Treasury note rate will typically be 75 to 250 basis points, or .75% to 2.5%. For instance, if the Treasury rate is 5.5%, the commercial real estate rate may vary from 6.25% to 8.0% (5.5% + 0.75% = 6.25% to 5.5% + 2.5% = 8%). The spread varies according to market conditions, the type and grade of real estate, and the amount of leverage (that is, the ratio of loan to value).

Loans to the U.S. government are generally defined as risk free, shorthand for noting that there is no risk of default (an inflation risk remains, though). Because default risk is the probability that the principal lent will not be repaid, defining loans to the U.S. government as risk free is either a vote of faith in the strength of the U.S. economy on which the taxes are levied to raise the money used to repay the loans or a tacit recognition that, if the need arose, one of the powers of a national sovereign is the ability to order that money be printed to pay its bills. Of course, printing money to pay national debts is only a temporary solution. When the supply of any good, including money, exceeds demand, the price drops. Inflation is what happens when the "price" (or value) of money drops. History has shown that rampant inflation is the inevitable result of expanding the money supply faster than the growth rate of the underlying economy. The Confederacy found this out during the Civil War in the 1860s, as did Germany during the Great Depression in the 1930s. The bitter joke in Germany at the time was that you used to be able to go shopping with your money in your purse and take your purchases home in your cart, but the hyperinflation was so bad that you had to use your cart to carry your money to market and you could take home your resulting purchases in your purse.

Because it is considered free of default risk but not free of inflation risk, the rate at which the marketplace is willing to lend money to the U.S. Treasury is considered the true cost of money plus a premium for anticipated inflation over the period of the loan. Economists have long debated the true cost of money (the rate the market would demand in the absence of risk or inflation), but it is generally considered to be about 2% to 3%.

The spread over the Treasury rate represents the risk premium the marketplace puts on commercial real estate loans. Fluctuations in interest rates charged to real estate borrowers are a result of variations in both the amount of spread over the 10-year Treasury rate demanded by the marketplace and variations in the underlying 10-year Treasury rate. This topic is covered in greater detail in Chapter 8 in relation to sources of financing.

PROPERTY MARKET CYCLES

Property market cycles, sometimes called occupancy cycles, refer to the balance of demand and supply of real estate itself. Yet, absent NASA making great strides in interplanetary exploration, because the supply of real estate is fixed, property market cycles refer to the balance of supply and demand of the buildings that sit on the real estate. Property cycles occur both in various real estate sectors and geographically within any one sector; that is, at the same time, different regions of the country will be in various stages of the cycle. In all cases, they are impacted by the rental-growth rate cycle.

Real Estate Sectors

Real estate is a vibrant, fragmented, and evolving economic sector that at times defies easy analysis. Real estate can be divided into Institutional (governmental or nonprofit: schools, museums, city halls, police stations, public hospitals, etc.), Private (owner-occupied homes), and Commercial sectors. Commercial real estate can be further divided into different sectors and subsectors. Office, Retail, Industrial and Warehouse, and Multifamily constitute a common division. The Office sector is often subdivided into suburban and central-city business districts. Retail can be divided many ways, but it is commonly divided into Regional Malls, first and second tier; Strip Malls; Factory Outlets; and Power Centers (sometimes called "big boxes" because a power center is a retailer strong enough to draw customers to a stand-alone location, to just one big box). Other types of real estate that are not as large but defy easy categorization in one of the major sectors include Senior

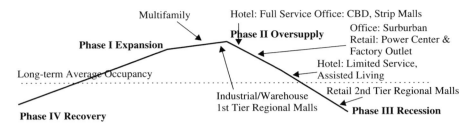

FIG. 1-3   Typical national real estate market cycle by property type.

Housing (with subsectors for active retirees, assisted living, and full service) and Hotels (full service, extended stay, limited service, and resort are potential categories), as well as specialty retail such as outlet malls and multiuse mixes of retail and entertainment. Sometimes new subsectors emerge. The trend toward miniwarehouses is an example of a sector that took off in the 1990s. "Telco hotels," that is, large equipment farms, buildings, or parts of buildings that house the transmission gear for phone, data, and Internet companies, emerged in the mid to late nineties. More recently, the residential condominium sector exploded (both new construction and conversions of existing projects; see Chapter 12) and then contracted within roughly a five-year period.

Obviously, all of these sectors and subsectors are very different and respond differently to various economic stimuli; thus, they are at any given time at different phases in the real estate cycle. Figure 1-3 illustrates a typical national real estate cycle by various types of property.

Geographic Variations Within a Property Type

Remember that although there are national cycles, by the very nature of real estate, product and occupancy cycles are local or regional in nature. Capital can flow across borders and from region to region to find the highest return; real estate, however, is immobile. If a particular region becomes overbuilt (i.e., oversupplied), it is not possible to pick up a building and ship it to a region where there is an undersupply. To a certain extent, even though the buildings do not move, it is possible for the people who occupy and use those buildings to move. However, this can be a slow, costly, and disruptive solution. Figure 1-4 shows a typical distribution of where various cities may be in a multifamily (apartment) cycle.

Typically, rental-growth rate cycles are a primary driver of occupancy cycles. Figure 1-5 illustrates a rental-growth rate cycle as stagnant to negative rent growth, characterized by the recession portion of the cycle, giving way to modest rent growth during the recovery, followed by strong rent growth during the expansion phase that justifies new construction. Equilibrium occurs at the top of the cycle but is generally recognized only in retrospect. The oversupply phase of the real estate cycle features declining but still positive rent growth.

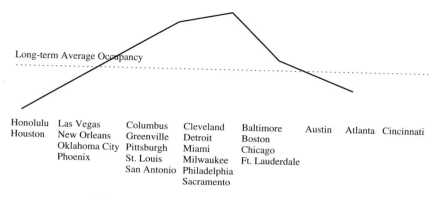

Honolulu	Las Vegas	Columbus	Cleveland	Baltimore	Austin	Atlanta	Cincinnati
Houston	New Orleans	Greenville	Detroit	Boston			
	Oklahoma City	Pittsburgh	Miami	Chicago			
	Phoenix	St. Louis	Milwaukee	Ft. Lauderdale			
		San Antonio	Philadelphia				
			Sacramento				

FIG. 1-4 Geographic occupancy cycle analysis.

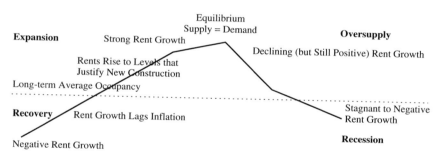

FIG. 1-5 Rental-growth rate cycle.

Although analysts attempt to define what the long-term average occupancy rate is for a given sector, the vagaries of the marketplace defy easy categorization, as illustrated by Figures 1-6 and 1-7. Figure 1-6 shows nationwide industrial vacancy (availability) rates ranging from 5.5% to more than 10.5% for the period 1981 to 2004, illustrating how difficult it is to determine a long-term average occupancy rate for a sector. Was the peak in vacancies that occurred during the recessionary years of the early 1990s an aberration to be discounted or part of a normally occurring cycle for which one must plan? What about the vacancy peak in 2002 to 2004? Is there a long-term upward trend in vacancy? Or are recent trends an aberration? And can a reversion to the long-term mean be forecasted? How can one tell the difference among random fluctuations, "normal" cycles, and long-term structural changes in the marketplace? No easy answers exist and opinions among intelligent professionals differ, which, in turn, is what creates markets.

Figure 1-7 shows the ten highest and lowest Central Business District (CBD) office rents for North America as of 2001. These numbers probably represent close

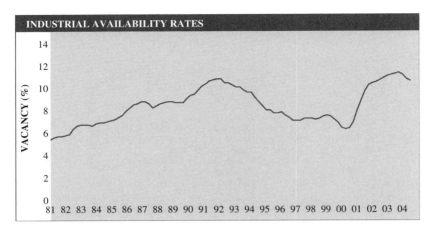

FIG. 1-6 Nationwide industrial vacancy (availability) rates, 1981–2004. (*Source*: Torto Wheaton Research, published online at www.tcasset.com.)

HIGHEST CENTRAL BUSINESS DISTRICT RENTS

CITY	RENTS PER SQ. FT.
1. San Francisco, CA	$69.00
2. Boston, MA	$60.00
3. Silicon Valley, CA	$54.00
4. Manhattan, NY	$49.51
5. Seattle, WA	$39.00
6. Washington, D C	$36.48
7. Toronto, ON (Canada)	$34.00
8. Chicago, IL	$32.10
9. W. Palm Beach, FL	$31.01
10. Sacramento, CA	$30.00

LOWEST CENTRAL BUSINESS DISTRICT RENTS

CITY	RENTS PER SQ. FT.
1. Edmonton, AB (Canada)	$12.00
2. Vancouver, BC (Canada)	$18.00
3. Philadelphia, PA	$18.08
4. Raleigh-Durham, NC	$18.75
5. Memphis, TN	$19.25
6. Nashville, TN	$19.50
7. St. Louis, MO	$20.00
8. Wilmington, DE	$20.00
9. Winston-Salem, NC	$20.00
10. Montreal, QC (Canada)	$20.05

FIG. 1-7 Highest and lowest central business district rents. (Copyright © 2001 by Institutional Real Estate Inc. All Rights Reserved.)

to the peak of CBD rents during the great Internet run-up of the stock market. Markets softened after the tech bubble burst, and it took roughly five years for the office market to completely recover, that is, for 2006 rents to approximate 2001 rents.

It is important to note that these numbers, like many numbers in real estate, are only approximations. Rent numbers are generally gathered from brokers who specialize in office leases, and since there is generally no legal requirement to report such numbers nor penalty for inflating or providing selective disclosures, all numbers must be taken with a grain of salt. It is not unusual to see different sources reporting significantly different numbers at the same time for supposedly the same market, with variations arising from the source of their data, their definition of the market, and their chosen methodology.

Furthermore, there are many submarkets within any given market, and rents may vary greatly even within a submarket, depending on building quality and the desirability of the location. For instance, even in Manhattan (which is a submarket of New York City itself), there is substantial variation between office rents downtown (Wall Street) and midtown (Rockefeller Center). In addition, office locations exist on the Upper West Side, Harlem (the location of former U.S. President William J. Clinton's official office), the Upper East Side, and on and on.

Even the ranges within the top ten and bottom ten rents are great. The range on the high side is $69 to $30 per square foot and on the low side, $12 to $20 per square foot. Applying national averages to local markets can be a recipe for disaster.

The problem of real estate cycles is exacerbated by the long lead times necessary for development, which are being further lengthened by an increasingly complex regulatory environment. A New York City rezoning can easily take five years or more; the CEO of a major apartment REIT (Real Estate Investment Trust) that specializes in infill development and redevelopment said several years ago that the company faces court battles in approximately 30% of its projects, and that percentage is no doubt higher today. At the time of the original conception of a development, market conditions may be favorable. By the time the land has been tied up, approvals secured, and a great deal of time and capital invested, the outlook may not be so rosy. By this time, the project has tremendous momentum, and many firms and people (and their egos and pocketbooks) are committed to it. These enterprises are rarely cut and dried. Signs of downturn are often hard to read, and although hindsight is usually 20/20, the crystal ball is often murky when one tries to look ahead. Moreover, there is a strong tendency to believe that "this project" is different because of "the unique site," "our extraordinary architecture," "the strength of our development team," "the wonderful marketing plan," "the financial strength of our backers," or some other factor.

If the project's conception is basically sound, forecasters may be right. There is a philosophy that every development over a given 50-year life will have its up and down times, and if the first down time happens to come up front, well, those are the breaks of the business: If you do not have the deep pockets to ride it out, you should not be in the business.

Another philosophy of development holds that the time to start thinking about a development is during a down cycle, because by the time you get through the lengthy planning, permitting, and regulatory approval process, the market will have recovered. As someone once said, all real estate makes money, it is just a question of who owns it when it does. Another common saying among those in the real estate field who urge caution at the top of the cycle is that "in the long run, it's the deals you *don't* do that make you the money."

LIQUIDITY AND EXIT STRATEGY

Every investment should have an exit strategy—that is, a plan indicating how long the investment will be held, and when and how it will be sold, and specifying the criteria for determining when it is time to sell. This is especially true of real estate. By its nature, real estate is not a liquid investment. Unlike a Treasury bill or the stock of a Fortune 500 company, real estate cannot be quickly sold and converted to cash. Thus, it is important for an owner to have given significant thought on how best to liquidate an investment. Some developers and investors are "flippers": Build it, stabilize it, and sell it. While this is the time of greatest risk, it is also the time that yields the greatest profit. In apartment development, returns on equity in the high teens to mid-20s can be achieved with regularity by sophisticated players. Other developers and investors can be long-term holders, but even a long-term holder tends to sell after ten years.

Real estate is illiquid for several reasons:

- Unlike shares of stock, real estate is not fungible. Each site and structure is unique in design, age, maintenance, location, and market, among other variables.
- Financing is generally required. The dollar amounts tend to be large, at least relatively. Existing financing is often not readily assumable, and even if the purchaser wishes to pay cash, there may be existing financing that has pre-payment penalties.
- Tax consequences tend to be significant, and sophisticated tax avoidance strategies—such as a Section 1031 exchange—may be required.
- Ownership can be complex: Title insurance and surveys are generally required, easements and covenants must be reviewed, lien searches must be done.
- Environmental liability issues must be carefully investigated; a current owner can be held liable for cleaning up environmental contamination caused by prior owners.
- Due diligence must be performed for deferred maintenance as well as zoning and code compliance.
- On income property, existing leases must be analyzed and verified, credit reports run on existing tenants (sometimes), and expenses verified.

To use a term of art from economics, real estate tends to be inelastic on the downside; that is, factors that tend to create upward rises in prices, when reversed, tend to create less downward pressure on prices. The reason is simple: Most holders of real estate are wealthy, with other available resources, and tend to wait out downward price cycles. This is not always a successful strategy in terms of real inflation-adjusted dollars. Sometimes a potential seller simply ends up waiting until inflation has increased the "value" of the subject property to the asking price.

Historically, nationwide real estate cycles tend to occur in a seven- to ten-year wave. Although values in some real estate sectors are relatively stable (such as apartments), others (such as office, hotel, and retail sectors) tend to rise and fall with greater volatility. Astute investors may attempt to time sales and purchases so as to catch these fluctuations in value. Furthermore, maintenance requirements for real estate increase with time and operational requirements may also increase. Many investors prefer to stay with top-grade portfolios and regularly cull their holdings of properties over a desired age.

A ten-year investment in an apartment development can yield returns in the low to mid teens. This return is a blend of the "pop" in value created by the development process and the lower underlying return that comes from the operation of the project. Obviously, the return pop created by development is not available in a straight purchase, unless some value is added through repositioning or renovating the property.

There are several ways in which apartments (and most real estate) may deliver value. The first is from the capitalization (or cap) rate, which is the rate of return required by the market (see Chapter 6). The cap rate is a measure of the income produced from the day-to-day operation of the property.

Cap rate is simply the Net Operating Income (NOI) produced by the real estate divided by the price paid for the real estate. For example, a property that was purchased for $10 million, which produces $500,000 of NOI, has a cap rate of 5% (e.g. $500,000/$10,000,000 = 5%).

Another way that apartments may deliver value is through appreciation. Real estate has a good historical track record of delivering appreciation. However, (1) the past is no guarantee of the future, (2) good maintenance and frequent capital expenditures are often required, (3) appreciation must always be measured against inflation, and (4) it is difficult for a real estate asset to appreciate if the surrounding area does not progress as well—i.e., demographic and economic trends may overwhelm the efforts of even the most capable property managers.

The third way that property may deliver value is through leverage. Leverage refers to the use of debt to "lever" the return on investors' equity investment. Leverage should be *positive*. The interest rate on the debt must be less than the cap rate of the property or, in other words, less than the return on the operation of the property.

Obviously, debt with an interest rate of 6% on a property with a cap rate of 5% results in negative leverage and a negative cash flow at any meaningful loan-to-value ratio. To put it mildly, negative cash flow is generally considered bad! Most financial institutions will not make loans that result in negative cash flow and, indeed, most require a positive debt-coverage ratio (discussed later). Alternately, debt of 6% on a property with a cap rate of 7% would result in positive leverage.

Amortization and the resulting mortgage constant must be taken into account, too. Most loans require not only the payment of interest but of principal as well. Dividing the amount of the total loan payment (interest AND principal) by the total amount of the remaining loan yields the mortgage constant. Since the amount of remaining loan is constantly being reduced for an amortizing loan, the mortgage constant is constantly increasing. Also, the shorter the amortization period, the higher the mortgage constant.

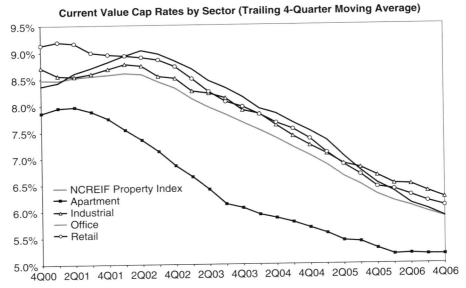

FIG. 1-8 Declining cap rate trend. (*Source*: NCREIF; Prudential Real Estate Investors (U.S.), published online in Prudential Financial October 2004 newsletter, www.prudential.com/prei.)

Warning: A mortgage constant higher than the cap rate will result in negative leverage and may yield a negative cash flow at a higher loan to value.

Cap rates fell drastically in the first five years of the twenty-first century (see Figure 1-8). In 2000, cap rates of 8%–9% were available; in 2006, cap rates of 5%–6.5% were more the market norm. Theories abound for the decline, with the most-mentioned culprits being the fall in the 10-year Treasury rate and the decline of the stock market, which combined with globalization, created pools of capital in search of a resting place. Others believe that the financial markets have come to accept real estate as a stable asset class deserving of greater capital allocation. Still others believe that investors have relatively short memories, and the lack of a significant real estate downturn since the early 1990s has led to complacency about risk evaluation and insufficient risk premiums being required by the marketplace in the pricing of real estate returns.

Factors such as grade, property age, and geographic region all impact capitalization rates. California and the heavy urban corridors of the northeast, such as Boston, Manhattan, and Washington, DC, tend to have some of the lowest cap rates in the nation. Presumably California compensates for its lower capitalization rate with greater price appreciation, security, and glamour. Likewise, the urban corridors are valued for the depth and breadth of their markets and their higher international profile. Perhaps there is security in increased market data and thus with lower risk, making a lower return acceptable.

Because apartments tend to be one of the more stable real estate sectors, most other sectors offer higher operational returns as the marketplace demands additional compensation for added volatility.

There are several reasons to sell a real estate project, including the desire to maintain a certain average age of properties, to realign toward a new strategic investment philosophy, or to raise capital for new investment. However, the most obvious reason to sell is to harvest profit. This may be motivated by both economic reasons and the requirements of financial reporting. Publicly-held corporations operate under GAAP (generally accepted accounting principles), which are based on historical costs and transactions. Generally, investments in real estate must be carried at historical costs less depreciation, regardless of market value. Therefore, under GAAP, the only way a publicly-held company can show the increase in value of an investment in real estate on its books is to sell it.

SUMMARY

Traditionally, real estate is cyclical and is characterized by four phases: *expansion*, characterized by robust construction and rising occupancy; *oversupply*, where robust construction continues as occupancy begins to decline and rents level off; *recession*, during which no new construction is begun, but projects in the pipeline are completed and begin operating amid falling occupancy and rents; and *recovery*, characterized by increasing occupancy and rents as the market absorbs oversupply. Historically, nationwide real estate cycles tend to occur in seven- to ten-year waves.

Real estate cycles are affected by the U.S. national economic cycle; capital market cycles, including liquidity and interest rate cycles; and property market (or occupancy) cycles. The U.S. national economic cycle traditionally is marked by the expansion or contraction of GNP. As real estate is a capital-intensive sector of the economy, it is sensitive to fluctuations in the capital markets. Capital cycles are affected by both liquidity cycles and interest rate cycles. Property market cycles are also called occupancy cycles, and these terms refer to the balance of demand and supply of real estate itself. These cycles occur both in various real estate sectors and geographically within any single sector, so that at the same time different regions of the country will be in various stages of a real estate cycle. Finally, every investment should have an exit strategy, and this is especially true of real estate because of its illiquid nature.

KEY TERMS AND DEFINITIONS

Basis point: 1/100 of a percent, e.g., 25 basis points = .25%.

Default risk: The probability that the lent principal will not be repaid.

Exit strategy: How long an investment will be held, when and how it will be sold, and what criteria determine when it is time to sell.

Federal Reserve discount rate: The rate at which the Federal Reserve lends money to banks, a short-term interest rate.

GNP: Gross national product, the sum of all goods and services produced by a country.

Interest rate cycles: Fluctuations in the cost of capital.

Liquidity: The ease with which an asset can be converted to cash.

Liquidity cycles: Fluctuations in the availability of capital.

REIT: Real Estate Investment Trust, a publicly-held firm that invests in real estate.

Spread: The additional amount charged over a given index, normally given in basis points; it reflects the risk premium placed on a loan by the market.

Transparency: How easy it is for the investing public to view a company's financial statements and operating results.

KEY LEARNING POINTS

- Understand the traditional real estate cycle
- Understand how liquidity and interest rates affect capital cycles
- Identify different real estate sectors and give examples in each sector
- Understand the role of the Federal Reserve, inflation, and spreads in setting commercial real estate loan interest rates
- Understand that real estate markets are local or regional while capital can flow across borders
- Understand why real estate is illiquid

QUESTIONS

1. Explain the traditional real estate cycle by detailing its phases and how the cycle affects construction, occupancy, and rents.
2. What are the aspects of capital markets that are described by liquidity cycles and interest rate cycles?
3. You are working to secure a 10-year commercial real estate loan. The current 10-year Treasury note rate is 5.00%. If your bank is willing to lend to you at a spread of 125 basis points over the Treasury note rate, what is the interest rate of your loan?
4. What are the three primary real estate sectors? Give examples in each.
5. What is the primary driver of occupancy cycles?
6. Give seven reasons why real estate is considered illiquid.
7. Explain how "real estate tends to be inelastic on the downside."

2
Different Types of Business Organizations

FORMS OF COMPANY ORGANIZATIONS

There are many forms of company organizations. Most are creatures of state law, and several spring from special provisions in the Internal Revenue Code. Because every state can set the ways in which a business can be organized under its jurisdiction, the potential variety of business forms is quite great. However, many states adopt "uniform statutes" that represent a consensus on the best-drafted statutes and are designed to encourage uniformity among state commercial codes. States do profit from additional jobs and economic activity when businesses are headquartered within them, and states often vie to speedily pass statues that codify the most modern or efficient forms of business organization. Delaware is widely known to have a legal system that greatly favors the modern corporation and, as a result, many Fortune 500 firms are incorporated under Delaware law.

The following company organization forms cover the vast majority of those in existence in the United States today:

- *Sole Proprietorship:* individual owner; that is, a single person only
- *Partnership:* any number of partners, often called a general partnership
- *Limited Partnership:* general partner(s) and any number of limited partners
- *Limited Liability Company:* managing member(s) and any number of members, a new form
- *C Corporation:* shareholders, board of directors, president, and other employees
- *S Corporation:* corporation and partnership hybrid, used for small businesses

There are also two specialized forms of business:

- *REIT (Real Estate Investment Trust):* a specially-taxed corporation for real estate
- *Joint Venture:* a temporary partnership (see Chapter 11)

The business forms are listed in roughly ascending order of complexity; most major business organizations are corporations, although they may have had their beginnings in other forms. Each of these forms of business has certain advantages and disadvantages with regard to the authority and responsibility of the principals (owners and operators). In addition, each form of business has an effect on the ability to raise any funds (i.e., debt or equity capital) needed for the operation and growth of the company.

REITs and S corporations are forms of business organizations modeled to comply with specific provisions of the Internal Revenue Code; indeed, the name S Corporation comes from the fact that it is based on Subchapter S of the Federal Income Tax Code.

SOLE PROPRIETORSHIP—UNLIMITED LIABILITY

A *sole proprietorship* is the simplest of business organizations to form. An individual just starts conducting business and instantly he or she is a sole (or individual) proprietorship. No documentation is required to create this form of business organization. No filing of organizational papers with the state is generally required. Anyone can start a business, and undoubtedly the construction and development industry offers some of the greatest opportunities for the ambitious and hardworking. Many now-successful developers and contractors started out on a shoestring, using savings, trade credit, capital borrowed from friends and family, or even personal credit cards as startup capital.

Local authorities should be consulted to ensure that all proper licenses are obtained and the proper fees paid to conduct business. To hold oneself out as a contractor or builder in most jurisdictions requires a special license attesting to a certain educational background, experience level, and often the passing of some sort of certification exam, as well as the possession of certain minimum levels of insurance.

To hold oneself out as a developer usually requires no license per se, other than perhaps the general occupational license required of anyone setting up a business in a particular jurisdiction.

Legal advice should be obtained about protecting your business name and other aspects of the business, and an accountant should be consulted about insurance needs, income tax considerations, and estimated tax payments. If employees are hired, an accountant should advise about employment tax payments and reporting requirements, retirement and health programs, unemployment benefits, and workers' compensation programs.

Although a sole proprietorship is the simplest form of business organization, a sole proprietor business shares with a general partnership a huge negative: unlimited personal liability for the business owner. This means that a business owner operating as a sole proprietor may lose not only his or her initial investment in the business but virtually every other personal and professional asset, as well as savings, cars, home—everything.

Loss may occur not only because of the debts incurred during the normal operation of business but also as a result of liens or judgments resulting from personal injuries arising from the operation of the business. In today's litigation-prone climate, the list of possibilities for which a business owner can potentially be held liable is virtually endless: The classic slip and fall and a serious or fatal car accident involving an employee driving on company business are just two examples. Liability can exist not only for negligent or insufficient performance of a contract but also for any one of an ever-increasing number of forbidden employment practices, regardless of the owner's personal knowledge.

Insurance can offer some protection, but insurance comes with a substantial cost. And every policy has its payment limitation and fine print, with myriad policy coverage exceptions. Federal bankruptcy laws offer some final level of protection, and many state laws protect some minimal level of assets; however, these are of limited comfort when a business owner realizes that a relatively simple change in the form of business organization could have afforded greatly increased liability protection.

The life of a sole proprietorship is obviously limited by the life of its owner. Although the assets, tangible and intangible, of the business may transfer to the owner's estate upon his death, the business form ceases.

PARTNERSHIP—UNLIMITED LIABILITY

Benefits of a Partnership

Running a business can be a daunting task, and partners can be of great help. The next simplest form of business is a *partnership*, often called a *general partnership* to distinguish it from a *limited partnership*, which will be discussed shortly. Partners bring many different resources to the table. Often just a different personality can be of great assistance; one partner is the detail person, the other is the grand visionary. One partner handles the inside, the other partner handles the outside. One partner brings construction skills, the other partner knows development. Sometimes one partner brings the capital to the table, and the other partner brings operational skills, the ability to get the job done.

A partnership can consist of any number of people or entities greater than one (there is a minimum of two parties). The partners do not have to be people; business entities can be partners and form partnerships. No filing of organizational papers with the state is generally required. In most partnerships, every one of the partners has some job to do to help the business prosper. In this case, they are all active partners. In some partnerships, one or more of the partners take no part in the operation of the business and are partners in name only. In this case, they are silent partners. Usually, a partner who contributes nothing but cash will be a silent partner. If the financing partners know little or nothing about construction, they may prove to be a handicap to operations, and the company would benefit if the financiers will accept the silent-partner role. However, the financier's capital may provide the funds that are essential to the survival of the firm, at least while the firm is young and growing and has not yet built up, to any substantial degree, liquid assets of its own.

As in the sole proprietorship described earlier, in a general partnership there is unlimited liability. Any partner may be held liable for the debts of the entire partnership. As a practical matter, creditors will make a beeline for the most available and affluent partners.

Partnership Formation by Holding Oneself Out as a Partnership

Although many partnership agreements are and should be in writing, a written agreement is not necessary to form a partnership. All that is necessary is that you agree to become partners and hold yourself out as such to the world. Indeed, if you act in such a way that a reasonable person would assume you are partners, then you may be held liable for the acts committed by your "partner(s)" in the normal course of business.

Suppose, for example, you are sitting down at lunch with a supplier with whom you have a history of doing business and an account to which your employees make frequent charges. A third person joins you, begins repeatedly to call you his partner, and waxes long and eloquently about your fantastic partnership and the grand project you are commencing together shortly. You sit quietly and do nothing to indicate disagreement. The next day your "partner" wanders into the supplier's warehouse, effusively greets the supplier, makes a reasonable purchase, and asks that it be charged to your account, referring back to yesterday's lunch conversation and his partnership with you. A judge and jury may find that the supplier, as a reasonable man, acted properly in assuming that this person was your partner, that therefore the charge was correct, and that you are liable for payment.

If there is no agreement to the contrary, the partnership automatically becomes an equal partnership, wherein every partner has an equal share in the rewards, losses, and liabilities of the company. However, all partners do not have to be equal. Indeed, partnership interests can be sliced and diced in as many ways and levels as the creative legal mind can conceive: Voting interests do not have to have equal-income interests; partners can have different interests in operating income than they do in capital assets, or they can have different interests in different projects; partners can draw salaries in addition to the income or loss from their partnership interests. Income can even be split differently at different levels—for instance, the first million dollars is split 80/20, the next million 60/40, and everything thereafter 50/50. Although it would not be binding on the outside world (because any one partner can be held liable for all the debts of the partnership, and that is the meaning of unlimited liability), partners can even agree to split losses differently from income.

Unlimited Liability of a Partnership

Regardless of the percentage share owned by each partner, each and every partner remains liable for all debts of the company. For example, if a partnership loses $1,000,000 on a construction contract and all of the partners except one disappear, that sole remaining partner is responsible for the entire $1,000,000, even if she only owned 10% of the firm. And, as in the case of a sole owner, the debts of the firm can reach back to the personal assets of the individual. The advantages and disadvantages of a partnership operation are therefore quite similar to those of an individual operation. The increased ease of capitalization and the ability to tap into the entrepreneurial energy of multiple owners is a big advantage for the partnership form of business, but the unlimited liability for the actions of partners over whom little or no control can be exercised is a more than counterbalancing factor, especially because better forms of business organization are readily available.

The comments regarding personal injury liability, insurance, and bankruptcy protection laws for a sole proprietorship apply to a partnership as well.

Because the traditional partnership is a voluntary association of individuals, new partners must be voted in—that is, approved by the partners of the existing partnership. Technically, the partnership dissolves and reforms every time a partner is added or departs (including by death). Obviously, this may present problems when a partner wishes to retire or pursue other investments. Although partnership agreements have attempted to address this issue in various ways, by outlining procedures to be followed and requirements to be met, and (at times) creating mutual obligations among the partners in regard to buy-and-sell agreements, and restrictions on the transfers of partnership interests, the nature of traditional partnerships remains a fundamental drawback of the general partnership form of business organization.

It should be noted that for many years, numerous large legal and accounting firms were partnerships. These days most have morphed into various types of professional corporations.

LIMITED PARTNERSHIP—LIMITED LIABILITY

Two Classes of Partners: General Partner(s) and Limited Partners

A *limited partnership* is somewhat similar to a *general partnership*, except that there are two classes of partners: (1) the *limited partners*, who are investors contributing funds in hope of returns and who have *limited liability*, and (2) the *general partner(s)*, who make policy and manage the firm and have *unlimited liability*. Unlike a sole proprietorship or a general partnership, a limited partnership must have an agreement in writing that is filed with the secretary of state in the state in which the limited partnership is formed and a tax must be paid; generally, an annual renewal must be made and an additional tax paid. The tax is usually based on the amount of capital contributed to the limited partnership and can range from a very nominal amount to thousands of dollars. Generally, the renewal tax is significantly less than the original filing tax.

Failure to file annually with the state will generally result in the dissolution of the limited partnership and its treatment as a general partnership with unlimited liability. Most limited partnerships have a set life selected at the time of creation; 30 years is a typical life span chosen at formation.

Limited Liability of Limited Partners

Each limited partner is financially liable only to the extent of his financial investment in the company. Suppose, for example, that a company is started with six
limited partners, and each of them contributes $100,000 for a total of $600,000.
In case of failure or bankruptcy of the company, or a court suit that is settled
against the company, the total loss will be limited to the original $600,000 already
contributed plus whatever other assets the limited partnership may have acquired
since its founding. In other words, no one of the six limited partners will have to
dig into a personal bank account or other personal assets, such as stocks or bonds,
to cover the indebtedness of the company. The only loss will be the original cash
investment of $100,000 each. Of course, if the company is successful up to the
time the catastrophe occurs and has accumulated $1,000,000 in assets, it could
lose all of that. However, each individual would lose no more than the original
contribution already paid into the limited partnership.

Limited Authority of Limited Partners

The limited partners are prohibited from participating in management or policy
making for the company. Only the general partner can perform management and
policy-making functions, such as determining what to buy and what to sell, whom
to hire and whom to fire. Obviously, the general partner must be selected with
great care because the limited partners, by necessity, put great trust in the general
partner. A limited partner who involves himself in the operations of the partnership
risks losing his limited liability.

General Partner—Unlimited Liability

In a limited partnership, there must be one or more persons or entities who are the
general partners. The liability of the general partner(s) is unlimited in a manner
similar to that of the sole proprietorship or regular partnership. However, in many
states, a corporation or other entity may be the general partner. This allows an
individual who wishes to be a general partner to gain protection against unlimited liability by forming a corporation of which she may be the sole owner, thus
effectively retaining control while having the protection of a corporate shield.

Piercing the Corporate Veil of a Corporate General Partner

Although a corporation should protect against personal liability, under certain relatively rare circumstances, the corporate veil may be pierced, and the individual
owners may be held personally liable. Thus, when a corporation serves as general
partner, it is advisable that the form and substance of a corporation be rigorously
observed. If a judge or jury decides that the corporation was a sham, it may be
disregarded. Failure to maintain insurance or a certain minimal capitalization may
lead to attacks on the corporate form. Treating the corporate bank account like a
personal account or failing to respect the corporate form in other ways also gives

a plaintiff's attorney an edge to try to strip away corporate protection. In short, the argument goes: If the defendant did not treat the corporation as an actual, real entity, why should the courts? The risks and expenses of litigation being what they are, as a practical matter, a good attorney does not have to win: To get to the settlement table, the attorney merely has to create a reasonable possibility that she might win.

Interests in a Limited Partnership

Interests in a limited partnership can be divided in any reasonable way, just as the interests in a general partnership can be divided. For example, with 41 partners, the 40 limited partners may each have a 2.25% share, for a total of 90%, while the general partner has a 10% share. The general partner makes all management decisions, including the sale of the company's assets, regardless of how many shares the general partner holds. Of course, the general partner can usually be removed by a majority vote of the limited partners; in some instances, a limited partnership agreement may call for a supermajority vote to remove the general partner.

Restrictions on Transfer of Interest, Number of Partners

Although generally not a legal requirement, limited partnerships have tended to retain the requirement for the general partner to approve the transfer of interests. This requirement is rarely withheld, but it does reflect the general use and reputation of a limited partnership as a vehicle for a smaller business organization. There are generally no legal restrictions on the number of limited partners; however, because of the roots of their legacy in the historical traditions of general partnerships, limited partnerships are generally used for businesses with fewer owners and corporations used for larger, more widespread ownership. Whereas a large public corporation could easily have hundreds of thousands of owners, if not millions, most limited partnerships typically have a half dozen to, at most, a few hundred limited partners. However, there are now publicly-traded limited partnerships. Obviously, as both professionals and the public become more familiar and comfortable with various types of business organizations, creativity and initiative in their use increases and the distinctions between the forms begin to blur, as they seem to morph with each new innovation.

Fewer limited partners generally make life easier for the general partner. If enough capital can be raised with just a few limited partners, so much the better. However, more limited partners generally means that more equity capital can be raised. If the price per share is too high, not all the shares may be sold. As a result, the initial capital raised may not be sufficient to finance the proposed business. On the other hand, if the capital is raised by the sale of a large quantity of individual shares at a low price per share to a large number of limited partners, a great deal of paperwork can be expected. There will be an extraordinary amount of record keeping required as shares change hands, additional correspondence and phone calls to answer inquiries and complaints from the larger number of partners, and an increase in the general busywork that inevitably accompanies large groups of owners from a wide variety of backgrounds and differing outlooks.

The sale of interests may be subject to the rules of the Securities and Exchange Commission (SEC), a federal agency, as well as state blue-sky laws, and the counsel of a competent attorney is required.

LIMITED PARTNERSHIPS AND REAL ESTATE SYNDICATORS: PARTNERSHIPS WITH A TARNISHED REPUTATION

Limited partnerships have a long and somewhat checkered history in the real estate field. Limited partnerships were very popular in the heydays of real estate tax shelters prior to the passage of the Tax Reform Act of 1986. During that era, limited partnerships were the vehicles of choice for real estate syndicators who used a network of brokers to raise funds for the real estate ventures they were promoting. A brief review of that period offers a deeper understanding of some of the potential pitfalls of the development process and provides an introduction to the tax implications of real estate.

Marriott Corporation, the big hotel company, was a major user of limited partnerships to raise capital during the 1980s. An article in the April 1, 1991, issue of *Business Week* titled "Marriott is Smoothing Out the Lumps in Its Bed" describes Marriott's extensive use of limited partnerships as financing devices and illustrates several key aspects of the real estate cycle—from the excess of the boom times to the negative pricing pressures and the halting of new construction during bust times—together with the length of time necessary for the market to absorb overbuilding.

Few companies were as sorry to see the supercharged '80s come to an end as Marriott Corp. The giant hotelier used last decade's financial fads—*leverage, limited partnerships, and tax-driven real estate deals*—to become one of the nation's most profitable developers. It all worked so swimmingly: Marriott would develop a hotel site, sell the lodge for a nice profit to investor groups, and then collect lucrative fees to manage the property. Over the decade, the $8.3 billion lodging and food-service concern expanded its rooms sixfold, to 150,000... *With the real estate market in a blue funk, the company is paying a steep price for last decade's joyride.* Its balance sheet is now carrying roughly $1.5 billion worth of mortgages on hotels and other properties it hasn't yet been able to unload. What's more, *a nationwide glut of rooms has led to cutthroat pricing* in the industry, placing enormous pressure on Marriott hotels...Marriott's years of 20% earnings growth are over. Still, the hotel giant has moved quickly to shore up its tattered balance sheet and bolster profits. Bill Marriott *suspended virtually all new hotel construction* last September—a move that will help relieve debt pressure... *Its profits depended too heavily on tax loopholes that made the purchase of newly built hotels attractive to investment partnerships. But such tax-motivated real estate deals were discouraged after the Tax Reform Act of 1986.* Suddenly, Marriott had to guarantee returns of up to 10%—sometimes out of its own pocket—to keep investors coming...Then, *after the real estate market collapsed in 1990, Marriott had a hard time attracting investors.* Though the company has unloaded some hotels such as its Atlanta property, Marriott is now stuck with about 150 others—including a $300 million hotel in San Francisco's Yerba Buena district. *Analysts figure it could take up to two years to unload all of these properties.* (Emphasis added.)

A developer's job is to find land suitable for development, tie up the land, oversee the design of a viable project, obtain the required regulatory approvals, find a suitable general contractor able to complete the project for the budgeted amount, and then line up both debt and equity capital. Debt capital means a financial institution, most frequently a commercial bank; equity capital requires an investor. Equity capital has always been tougher to find than debt capital.

The syndication of limited partnerships was one way of solving the need for equity capital. If you needed a million dollars, it was often easier to form a syndicate of one hundred investors with ten thousand dollars each than to find one investor with a million to spare for your project. This was especially true prior to the Tax Reform Act of 1986.

Syndication: Hefty Commissions, Hefty Promotes, Lofty Valuations

A real estate syndicator usually wore several hats, acting both as developer and general partner of the limited partnership, which would own the completed development. A network of brokers sold shares of the limited partnership to individuals, generally taking 5% to 10% commissions. The syndicator would also generally take a share of the limited partnership as a hefty *promote*, often in the 10% to 20% range. (A promote is the fee for putting the deal together.) The individual investors tended to be numerous and relatively unsophisticated, giving the syndicator/general partner a significant advantage. Because of the hefty fees charged up front, the valuation of the real estate involved was often suspect and many owners of real estate–related limited partnerships found that the true market valuation of the underlying assets did not support the price they paid for their limited partnership interests.

Additional Income Streams for the Syndicator/General Partner

In addition to compensation for putting the deal together, syndicators often collected separate fees for such services as brokering the purchase of the land, arranging the financing, overseeing the construction process, and sometimes the property's lease up. Other sources of income included fees for the management of the underlying real estate, either through the general partner or through a wholly-owned captive management company. In addition, an "ambitious" syndicator might form various companies to perform services (janitorial, landscaping, laundry equipment, etc.) for or to sell supplies to the real estate operations.

Of course, if such services and supplies were of high quality and competitively priced, no harm was done. However, the normal checks and balances of an arm's-length business relationship did not exist and abuses frequently occurred.

Exit Strategy and Roll Ups

The exit strategy for most real estate limited partnerships was intended to be the sale of the underlying real estate when market conditions were fortuitous, usually intended to be within a ten-year period. Often such forecasted market conditions never arrived, and many deals floated in that never-never land: enough cash flow to carry the debt, not enough to generate a sale sufficient to cover the debt plus a return on the initial investment, to say nothing of achieving the much hyped appreciation potential. Often the general partner was not highly motivated to sell the real estate because it would mean, at a minimum, the end of his management contract and the related lucrative and risk-free income stream. Indeed, over the years, more than one entrepreneur, noting that many limited partnership interests were selling in the secondary market at significant discounts to the NAV (Net Asset Value) of the underlying real estate, attempted a roll up, that is, attempted to buy a controlling interest in a limited partnership, vote the general partner out, and sell the real estate (they hoped) for a net price greater than the total of the discounted partnership interests.

Although this objective was occasionally successfully and quite lucratively accomplished, general partners (much like their Fortune 500 CEO counterparts when targets of hostile takeover offers) frequently adopted a scorched-earth policy, vehemently fighting the change of management. Lawsuits were not infrequent.

Limited Partnership Interests Generally Nonliquid

Investors in limited partnership interests who wanted to liquidate their interests found that they had few options. No liquid market existed for their interests. Over the years, a few brokers attempted to create "clearinghouses" for limited partnership interests, but the discount to NAV, much less the original purchase price, tends to be steep. The advent of the Internet has led to efforts to create an electronic marketplace in limited partnership interests, but the ultra-microcapitalizations (e.g. $1,000,000 to $25,000,000) and the uniqueness of each real estate deal makes a robust marketplace difficult.

In the absence of a public marketplace, often the only market for resale was other existing owners and the general partner. Occasionally the general partner would not be thrilled to provide the names and addresses of other limited partners, citing "privacy issues." And, in any case, because many limited partners tended to be relative real estate novices investing for the first time, the idea of putting more capital, even at a hefty discount, into an already troubled deal was not appealing.

Limited Partnerships and Tax Shelter Abuses

Prior to the Tax Reform Act of 1986, real estate offered significant tax advantages that at times led to abuses. At that time, the owner of real estate could recover the value of the depreciable assets (i.e., the buildings), by means of a depreciation allowance over a 15-year depreciable life. Depreciation is a method of allocating the cost of a capital asset to an income stream. One of the challenges of accounting as a profession is matching expenditures with revenue: Which resource outlays result in which revenue? One function of accounting is to serve as an information system that lets investors and managers know how effectively resources are being used. Some costs, such as utilities, janitorial services, and landscape maintenance, are clearly short-term expenses and, therefore, allocated to the current period. They help generate revenue at the time they are spent and should be charged against the rental revenue. Obviously, the cost of a $5-million apartment building is related to the rental revenue received and, equally obviously, it will also generate revenue for some time in the future. That period of time is known as the *depreciable life*, and most of the time the depreciable life chosen is dictated by the Internal Revenue Code rather than by any true attempt in the field to estimate the remaining useful life of the building. Either straight-line depreciation or an approved form of accelerated depreciation may be used. Accelerated depreciation may be thought of as akin to a new car; although a car may have a useful life of 10 years or more, most of the value loss occurs in the first few years. Because use of accelerated depreciation generated more immediate tax shelter, it was generally the method of choice. During the first few years of ownership this accelerated depreciation allowance would generally exceed the net rental income. The result was a theoretical, net "paper" loss, which constituted a tax shelter for any outside income up to the amount of the excess depreciation.

Leveraged Depreciation

If an investment of $1 million of equity by 100 limited partners at $10,000 each (leveraged with $4 million in debt) resulted in a development with depreciable assets of $5 million, then under certain accelerated methods of depreciation—such as the double declining balance method—as much as $665,000 of depreciation could be taken in the first year. At a tax rate of 50%, then, in effect this would result in tax savings of $332,500 per year for the entire limited partnership, or $3,325 per 1% limited partner, or a return of more than 33% on a $10,000 investment for the first year based on tax benefits alone. Of course, with accelerated methods of depreciation, the amount of depreciation available (and thus the available tax benefits) decline each year. However, the use of leverage (debt) allowed limited partnerships to take depreciation several times the actual amount of the equity investment.

The Day of Reckoning: Facing the Tax Man at Time of Disposition

Limited partnerships were frequently sold primarily on the basis of tax benefits by salespeople working on commission, whose interests were not always exactly aligned with those of their clients, to say the least. Although the initial tax benefits were very real, what was rarely discussed was what happened when either the partnership interest or the underlying real estate was sold. Presuming that the sales price exceeded the depreciable basis or tax basis (original cost less depreciation allowed or allowable), the limited partner would then need to pay taxes on all the depreciation previously taken. The silver lining was that most of the tax would be paid at lower capital gains rates; however, the gain due to the excess of accelerated depreciation over straight-line depreciation was taxed as ordinary income. The longer a property was held, the more closely accelerated depreciation and straight-line depreciation converged. It was possible for the mortgage on the real estate to exceed the tax basis, particularly when the property was held a while and appreciation was harvested via refinancing. The good news was that mortgage proceeds (either the original financing to acquire or construct, as well as any subsequent refinancing at higher debt levels to take advantage of property appreciation) were not taxable inasmuch as they represented debt that had to be repaid.

The bad news was that when a property was sold and the level of debt exceeded the tax basis, there was *phantom income*, that is, the tax gain exceeded the amount of cash proceeds. For example, after several years of accelerated depreciation, a property with an original cost basis of $5 million and a $4 million mortgage could have depreciated to $3.5 million. Although the sellers would receive only $1 million of net proceeds on the sale (the $5 million sales price less $4 million of the mortgage debt), they would owe taxes on $1.5 million ($5 million sales price less $3.5 million tax basis)—that is, they would have a half million dollars of *phantom income*.

Because of the use of leverage and depreciation, the amount of taxes owed by a limited partner in many cases equaled or exceeded the amount of the original equity investment in the limited partnership. Although the taxpayer had received tax benefits over the years exceeding the amount of tax due, most had viewed it as a return on their investment, and few had put aside the funds to deal with such a contingency. The outcome could have been seen by any competent tax professional, but the lure of immediate benefit led many to unduly discount or to totally ignore the distant day of reckoning. Furthermore, the mood of the time was buoyant, and the unspoken assumption was that another tax shelter could be found when the time came—a most unwise assumption in light of the events that actually unfolded.

Current Tax Law More Restrictive

Several factors combine to greatly reduce current real estate tax benefits:

- The time period over which assets may be depreciated has been greatly increased; that is, residential real estate is now depreciated over 27.5 years, almost double the previously allowed 15 years.

- Only straight-line depreciation is allowed for real estate; accelerated depreciation is no longer allowed.
- The Alternative Minimum Tax (AMT) now exists, limiting the total amount of tax benefits any one taxpayer can obtain. The AMT is a very complicated tax, because it interacts with many potential tax benefits. Some say that it is so complex that it could not have been enacted prior to the widespread availability of computerized income tax preparation programs.
- The top tax bracket has been lowered from up to 70% to the current maximum of 35%. The lower maximum tax bracket makes tax shelters less attractive, particularly those tax shelters whose underlying economic rationale was eclipsed by their tax-benefit aspects.

CORPORATION—LIMITED LIABILITY, PERPETUAL LIFE, EASE OF TRANSFER OF INTEREST

The chief advantages of a corporation lie in its limited liability, ease of share transferability, and perpetual life. A corporation typically requires a president and a secretary as the minimum number of officers for formation. Frequently, the offices of treasurer and vice president are included as well. Anyone can form a corporation, it is really quite easy. Standard forms and handbooks are readily available, and filing fees and reporting requirements can be fairly minimal. There are services that will set up a corporation in any state for a nominal fee. To raise needed capital, the corporation sells shares in the ownership of the corporation. The buyers of the stock become part owners of the corporation and are called stockholders or shareholders.

Limited Liability of Shareholders

One advantage of a corporation lies in the limitation of liability of shareholders. Every shareholder of a corporation is protected against any financial loss exceeding the investment already made to purchase the share of stock. The only loss that can come to any owner of shares in a corporation is limited to the loss of the capital already paid to buy the shares in the company. No one can attempt to collect from any shareholder of the company because of the corporate debts. For this reason, when some small corporations with marginal financial resources seek loans, the lenders may require one or more officers or major shareholders of the corporation to personally endorse the loan notes to provide additional security for the loans. A personal endorsement involves an agreement to be personally liable for the amount of the indebtedness in case of default by the corporation. However, the loan endorsers would be liable only for those loans on which they signed and would not be liable for other debts incurred through the daily operations of the corporation. A corporation may issue as many shares of stock as it cares to, subject to the approval of the shareholders and certain legal requirements. The shareholders of a corporation vote in an election, usually held at a shareholders' meeting, to elect a board of directors, and the board of directors in turn elects the officers of the corporation. Traditionally, the officers of a company are the president, the vice president, the secretary, and the treasurer, although the titles of chief executive officer (CEO), chief operating officer (COO), and chief financial officer (CFO) are more commonly used today. There may also be a CIO, meaning a chief information officer or chief investment officer. Shareholders are normally entitled to one vote per share (though different classes of stock can exist with different rights, including varying voting rights), so the holders of the majority of the stock can generally control the corporation.

Perpetual Life and Ease of Transferability of Shares

Unlike most other forms of business organizations, corporations are set up for perpetual life; that is, in the absence of a voluntary or involuntary dissolution, a corporation exists forever. Corporations are creatures of statute and did not exist under common law; indeed, prior to the enactment of enabling statutes, to form a corporation required a specific legislative act. Thus, from a historical perspective, the widespread popularity of corporations is relatively recent. As a practical matter, the risks of business and the recentness of the industrial revolution are such that relatively few business organizations of any kind exist that are more than 100 years old. These days corporations merge, acquire, and then spin off divisions with such frequency that after a while, the genealogy of any one corporation can become quite complex.

Corporate stocks, which represent shares of ownership in a corporation, are among the easiest forms of business ownership to transfer. This ease of transferability is partially a result of stock's legal status as a negotiable instrument, but it is also in large measure the result of the widespread prevalence of markets and institutions that exist to facilitate trading in stock and the traditions and expectations that have grown up around stock markets in our business culture. Familiarity goes a long way toward reducing perceptions of risk and thus inducing investors to part with their capital.

In a corporation, the board of directors is responsible for formulating policies for the firm, including the hiring and firing of the chief executive officer, who also typically sits on the board in order to foster closer ties and communication. The CEO then hires the rest of the firm's employees and operates the firm in accordance with the policies of the board of directors. An astute CEO consults with the board on her choice of top officers, some of whom may be chosen to sit on the board (they would be known as inside directors, in contrast to an outside director who has no other direct business relationship with the corporation). A strong and independent board of directors is an important component in the success of a corporation; thus, inside directors should be kept to a minimum and only outside directors should sit on the audit and compensation committees. A board of directors has a significant fiduciary responsibility to the shareholders.

Not all corporations are publicly held, that is, registered on a public exchange and actively traded. Stock can be sold via private placement—a limited offering to a select group of sophisticated individuals or entities of high net worth. The laws regarding corporations are rigorous, and offerings for sales of shares must be handled in accordance with the rules of the Securities and Exchange Commission.

Control of the Corporation—Some Caveats

With one vote per share, one would think that the owner of the majority of a corporation's stock holds unquestioned control of the company, inasmuch as this owner holds the majority of votes at shareholders' meetings. Yet, although usually the majority rules, if the corporate bylaws call for the board of directors to be elected at the annual meeting of shareholders and make no provision for special meetings to be called at the request of the shareholders, legally the owner(s) of a majority of the stock may simply have to wait until the next annual meeting to elect a board of directors of their own choosing.

Furthermore, the terms of the board of directors of many corporations are staggered. For instance, directors may serve for five-year terms, with only two members of a ten-person board coming up for election each year. Thus, it can take several years to put a new majority on the board.

These rules may be changed, but the process is often time-consuming and cumbersome; sometimes a supermajority may be required to make certain changes. The rights of minority shareholders must be kept in mind, as these rights are protected by law and cannot be overlooked.

There are many instances of companies being controlled by holders of less than a majority of the outstanding stock where the majority of the shares are widely distributed in small lots, and the majority shareholders have difficulty in reaching a consensus. This minority control is usually possible when shareholders of small lots are widely dispersed. Being out of touch with the corporation and not fully aware of the issues, they often do not attend shareholders' meetings, or they abstain from voting their shares. In addition, the controlling minority shareholder may persuade absentee shareholders to proxy enough votes to constitute a majority of those shares being voted.

Priorities of Payment upon Liquidation

A shareholder is a part owner of the firm and, therefore, in time of financial trouble stands last in line for distribution of the assets. If the firm is forced to liquidate, government tax claims are usually paid first, employees' salaries next, then specific lien holders, commercial debts, bonds by class, and, finally, the owners (shareholders) divide what is left, if anything. Each class of creditor is paid in full before the next class gets anything, with lien holders given first priority with respect to the asset liened.

DOUBLE TAXATION OF DIVIDENDS ON C CORPORATIONS

Most major corporations are known as C corporations (sometimes called "C corps"), because they are structured so as to be taxed under Subchapter C of Chapter 1, Subtitle A, Article 26 of the United States Code. Article 26 is more commonly known as the Internal Revenue Code, and Subtitle A deals with income taxes (as opposed to estate and gift taxes, employment taxes, miscellaneous excise taxes, and alcohol and tobacco taxes). Chapter 1 is titled "Normal Taxes and Surtaxes," and Subchapter C deals with the taxation of corporations.

A major drawback of the corporate form of business organization is the double taxation of dividends. Corporate income is taxed twice before it reaches the owner. Federal income taxes are first paid at the corporate level, and then the income is taxed again at the individual level when the income is distributed to owners in the form of dividends. Of course, if the corporation chooses not to distribute any income as dividends, the shareholder is not subject to any income tax, unless she chooses to sell her stock and there is a resulting capital gain.

Although general and limited partnerships and limited liability companies must file tax returns, these returns are for informational purposes only. Both types of business entities are treated as *flow through* entities for federal income tax purposes. Income generally just flows through the entity, for tax purposes, to the underlying partners and is taxed only once.

C corporations have remained the business organizations of choice for large firms mainly because they are well known and understood by the marketplace. When people are investing capital, it is hard to underestimate the importance of the familiar in getting them to part with funds. The slightest degree of uncertainty can raise the cost of both debt and equity capital. The swings in stock prices that can occur when a company is off its earnings projections (the so-called whisper number) by just pennies, bear mute testimony to this truth. Furthermore, the significant financing infrastructure oriented toward C corporations that exists to raise both debt and equity capital does not exist for other business forms: It is not called the New York Stock Exchange for nothing.

SUBCHAPTER S CORPORATIONS

Subchapter S corporations were created by Congress (before the popularity of limited partnerships and limited liability companies, or LLCs, solved many of the same issues) under Subchapter S of the Internal Revenue Code to address the issue of double taxation of dividends on behalf of that perennial American icon, the small businessperson.

Simply, an S corporation, or "S corp," is a regular corporation that is taxed as a partnership; that is, its income is taxed only once. The income of an S corporation is not taxed at the level of the business entity, rather it is taxed only at the individual level. An S corporation must meet certain requirements in Subchapter S of the Internal Revenue Code and must make a voluntary election in favor of S corporation status. Originally limited to corporations with no more than 15 owners, the availability of the election has been expanded over the years to allow as many as 75 individual owners.

Moreover, there is some flexibility in the definition of what constitutes a single owner. For example, a husband and wife count as one. Furthermore, Congress did not think it just that an S corporation already at its maximum legal limit of owners should lose its tax status if distribution of an owner's estate upon her death created additional owners. Therefore, an exemption was created to treat an estate as a single owner. Because the S corporation was designed to help individual with certain complex exemptions related to certain types of trusts and charitable organizations, shareholders are limited to individuals who are legal residents of the United States; nonresident aliens cannot be owners. Furthermore, there can be only one class of stock. However, because variations in voting rights are specifically excluded by the statute as creating a different class of stock, presumably the intent of Congress was to forbid variations in order of priority of payment upon dissolution.

With the advent of limited partnerships and limited liability companies, the popularity of S corporations as a business form has declined. The primary reason for the continued popularity of S corporations among small business owners over limited liability companies (discussed in the next section) is the reduction of self-employment taxes; the dividends from a S corporation are not subject to self-employment taxes. With a limited liability company, income flows through to the ultimate taxpayer, retaining its original characteristics.

LIMITED LIABILITY COMPANIES

Limited liability companies (LLCs) are a relatively recent legislative creation and are based on the concept of freedom of contract. That is, the statute pretty much authorizes carte blanche in terms of structuring the form of the business organization. The result allows the fascinating and exciting blend of many of the best aspects of sole proprietorships, limited partnerships, and corporations—in short, a businessperson's dream.

The first LLC statute was enacted in Wyoming in 1977 in order to attract business development and spur economic development. In 1982, Florida was the first large state to enact legislation enabling LLCs, but even then little use was made of LLCs due to a lack of Internal Revenue Service (IRS) rulings on how LLCs would be treated for tax purposes.

In 1988, IRS Revenue Ruling 88–76 was promulgated, clarifying that LLCs would be treated as partnerships for federal income tax purposes. Since then most states have enacted statutes authorizing the creation of LLCs. In Florida, LLCs remained largely unused until the legislature decided in 1998 to treat LLCs as partnerships for state income tax purposes, effectively removing LLCs from the burden of the state's corporate income tax.

LLCs were created to address several issues that current business forms did not address. For example, limited partnerships require at least two people, a limited partner and a general partner, and the general partner had to assume liability. Although many businesses got around this requirement by forming an S corp to be the general partner, it added a level of complexity: Two entities to maintain, two tax returns to file, the corporation tended to have a board of directors and required officers and an annual meeting, both the business and the S corporation had to file annual reports with the state in which they where formed, records and minutes of meetings had to be kept, and so forth. Furthermore, only those who were willing to risk personal liability, the general partners, could be active in the business. Many limited partners chafed at this restriction.

C corps provided limited liability and unlimited owners, but the double taxation of income made them exceedingly unpopular with smaller businesses that had the flexibility to choose different business forms.

S corps solved the double taxation issue, but the limitation on the number of owners and the complexity of some of the tax issues were ongoing irritants. Furthermore, certain aspects of the business organization were mandated: It had to have officers (generally a president and a secretary as a minimum) and a board of directors; in many states (though not Florida), multiple people were required to form and run the organization.

There had to be a simpler, more efficient way to organize a business, one that was easy to create and maintain with minimal constraints on form. LLCs were created as the answer. As the name implies, the liability of the owners, called members, is limited to the assets of the firm. No member is required to assume liability. All members (owners) are permitted to actively engage in the business; the members in charge of running the business are known as "managing members." There need be only one member—in most states, an individual can set up, own, and run an LLC, and the manager need not be a member. There is no requirement for the typical corporate structure of a board of directors or multiple officers, and there is tremendous flexibility as to the operating structure.

Like corporations and limited partnerships, LLCs do require initial and annual filings with the state in which they were formed.

Unlike C corporations, which result in double taxation via the federal income tax on income both at the corporate level and again at the individual level when income is distributed in the form of dividends, LLCs, like partnerships and S corps, are flow-through entities. There is no income taxation at the entity level; income is taxed only once, at the individual level.

REIT: REAL ESTATE INVESTMENT TRUST

Created by Congress in 1960, Real Estate Investment Trusts (REITs) were designed to provide the public with a means to participate in the equity ownership of commercial real estate. In essence, a REIT is a regular corporation that has made a tax election: In return for a requirement that 95% of its taxable income be distributed annually to its shareholders, Congress allowed the taxable income of a REIT to flow directly through to its owners and be taxed only once, at the shareholder level. Thus, REITs, like partnerships and limited liability companies, are exempt from taxation at the business-organization level.

Several other restrictions apply: REITs must receive virtually all their income from the ownership of real estate, and there are limitations on how much real estate can be sold in any given year. The requirement to distribute virtually all taxable income results in a high dividend rate, which makes them popular with some investors. However, it is also a double-edged sword: Because they are not allowed to retain any earnings, REITs are always in need of additional capital if they are to grow. When conditions are favorable in the Wall Street capital markets, this is not an issue; investment banks find underwriting secondary stock offerings extremely lucrative. However, the ups and downs of the real estate cycle and the peculiarities of the stock market are such that it is not unusual for the Wall Street capital access window to be closed.

Although REITs were allowed to own real estate, originally they were forbidden to operate or to manage real estate. As a result, for many years REITs were further constrained by the requirement that they hire third-party operating companies. This added layer of complexity limited the amount of entrepreneurial energy that REITs, as owners, were able to bring to bear on the property they owned.

In 1986, as part of the Tax Reform Act, Congress greatly loosened the restriction and allowed REITs to provide "customary" services associated with real estate ownership. As a result, in the early 1990s, REITs reached maturity and became a true investment vehicle. Figure 2-1 shows the growth, both in absolute numbers and in market capitalization of REITs, from 1971 to 2005. The effects of the real estate recessions of the early 1970s and of 1990 can be seen in the reduction of the total market capitalization of REITs for those years. Although most REITs are equity REITs—that is, they have direct equity in and ownership of real estate—REITs are also allowed to invest in and own mortgages on real estate. Those REITs that do invest in mortgages are known as mortgage REITs; a REIT that has both equity and mortgage holdings is known as a hybrid REIT. Obviously, the vast majority of REITs are equity REITs.

Additional recent developments include the rapidly increasing professionalization of management, conservative use of dividends, increased independent monitoring, and the UPREIT structure.

The Umbrella Partnership REIT, or UPREIT, structure is an interesting innovation that emerged in the early 1990s as a way to postpone tax consequences. Normally, when an individual or partnership sells property to a REIT, substantial income taxes can result. The UPREIT postpones those taxes. With an UPREIT, instead of selling real estate directly to a REIT, the preexisting partnership contributes the real estate to a new partnership, known as the operating partnership, with the REIT as the general partner. In exchange, the partners in the preexisting partnership receive shares in the new operating partnership, or UPREIT, known as units. Under the Internal Revenue Code, the contribution of property at the time of the formation of a partnership is generally a tax-free event.

Units of the UPREIT receive distributions equal to the dividends paid by the REIT, and the units can be redeemed, generally one for one, for stock in the general partner REIT. In other words, the units of the UPREIT are the equivalent to stock in the REIT in all but name and thus also appreciate (or depreciate) in lockstep with the REIT stock. Generally, the partners hold the UPREIT units until they are ready to liquidate, and at that time they redeem their units for stock and sell the stock. It is at that time that the Internal Revenue Service collects its due.

Annual Equity Market Capitalization
(Millions of dollars at year end)

Year	Composite Number of REITs	Composite Market Capitalization	Equity Number of REITs	Equity Market Capitalization	Mortgage Number of REITs	Mortgage Market Capitalization	Hybrid Number of REITs	Hybrid Market Capitalization
1971	34	1,494.3	12	332.0	12	570.8	10	591.6
1972	46	1,880.9	17	377.3	18	774.7	11	728.9
1973	53	1,393.5	20	336.0	22	517.3	11	540.2
1974	53	712.4	19	241.9	22	238.8	12	231.7
1975	46	899.7	12	275.7	22	312.0	12	312.0
1976	62	1,308.0	27	409.6	22	415.6	13	482.8
1977	69	1,528.1	32	538.1	19	398.3	18	591.6
1978	71	1,412.4	33	575.7	19	340.3	19	496.4
1979	71	1,754.0	32	743.6	19	377.1	20	633.3
1980	75	2,298.6	35	942.2	21	509.5	19	846.8
1981	76	2,438.9	36	977.5	21	541.3	19	920.1
1982	66	3,298.6	30	1,071.4	20	1,133.4	16	1,093.8
1983	59	4,257.2	26	1,468.6	19	1,460.0	14	1,328.7
1984	59	5,085.3	25	1,794.5	20	1,801.3	14	1,489.4
1985	82	7,674.0	37	3,270.3	32	3,162.4	13	1,241.2
1986	96	9,923.6	45	4,336.1	35	3,625.8	16	1,961.7
1987	110	9,702.4	53	4,758.5	38	3,161.4	19	1,782.4
1988	117	11,435.2	56	6,141.7	40	3,620.8	21	1,672.6
1989	120	11,662.2	56	6,769.6	43	3,536.3	21	1,356.3
1990	119	8,737.1	58	5,551.6	43	2,549.2	18	636.3
1991	138	12,968.2	86	8,785.5	28	2,586.3	24	1,596.4
1992	142	15,912.0	89	11,171.1	30	2,772.8	23	1,968.1
1993	189	32,158.7	135	26,081.9	32	3,398.5	22	2,678.2
1994	226	44,306.0	175	38,812.0	29	2,502.7	22	2,991.3
1995	219	57,541.3	178	49,913.0	24	3,395.4	17	4,232.9
1996	199	88,776.3	166	78,302.0	20	4,778.6	13	5,695.8
1997	211	140,533.8	176	127,825.3	26	7,370.3	9	5,338.2
1998	210	138,301.4	173	126,904.5	28	4,916.2	9	6,480.7
1999	212	145,387.1	175	136,014.3	27	6,885.0	10	2,487.8
2000	189	138,715.4	158	134,431.0	22	2,652.4	9	1,632.0
2001	182	154,898.6	151	147,092.1	22	3,990.5	9	3,816.0
2002	176	161,937.3	149	151,271.5	20	7,146.4	7	3,519.4
2003	171	224,211.9	144	204,800.4	20	14,186.5	7	5,225.0
2004	190	305,025.1	150	273,629.0	33	24,774.1	7	6,622.0
2005	197	330,691.3	152	301,491.0	37	23,393.7	8	5,806.6

Market capitalization equals price of shares multiplied by the number of shares outstanding.

FIG. 2-1   Growth of REITs in numbers and capitalization, 1971 to 2005. (*Source*: National Association of Real Estate Investment Trusts (NAREIT), 2007, www.nareit.com.)

The UPREIT structure has allowed REITs essentially to purchase properties whose owners would otherwise be reluctant to sell because of tax considerations. The property owners are relieved of the burdens of property management and gain the security of what are essentially dividends, as well as the benefits of liquidity. Real estate generally requires a significant period of market exposure to ensure a good price and cannot usually be sold piecemeal. UPREIT units can be sold at any time, and a person's holdings can be converted and sold off a bit at a time if so desired.

Figure 2-2 shows an early 2001 ranking of the top 50 REITs by implied equity market capitalization and illustrates both diversity of the property focus of the REITs and the high degree of concentration of market capitalization in the top percentile of the universe of approximately 200 publicly-traded REITs. Implied market capitalization combines the value of the common stock of the REIT and the additional value of the UPREIT units discussed earlier—that is, what the total market

TOP 50 REITs by Implied Market Cap (includes common stock and operating units)

REIT NAME	Symbol	Property Focus	2/14/01 Price $	1 Yr Total Return %	Equity Mkt Cap (Millions)	Implied Mkt Cap (Millions)
1 Equity Office Properties Trust	EOP	*Office*	29.938	31.4	9,189.80	10,449.00
2 Equity Residential Prop Trust	EQR	*Residential*	51.172	35.2	6,735.50	7,365.00
3 Simon Property Group Inc	SPG	*Retail*	25.875	14.9	4,365.90	6,046.90
4 Boston Properties Inc	BXP	*Office*	40.703	42.7	3,526.10	4,497.40
5 Spieker Properties Inc	SPK	*Office*	52.813	37.5	3,474.10	3,940.20
6 Host Marriott Corporation	HMT	*Hotel*	12.984	55.3	2,868.50	3,689.10
7 ProLogis Trust	PLD	*Industrial*	20.891	20.6	3,453.00	3,559.20
8 Apartment Invest & Mgmt Co	AIV	*Residential*	42.656	23.8	3,043.00	3,398.80
9 Vornado Realty Trust	VNO	*Div/Other*	36.047	23.8	3,130.60	3,392.90
10 Duke-Weeks Realty Corp	DRE	*Office*	22.906	23.9	2,930.40	3,365.20
11 Public Storage Inc	PSA	*Self-Storage*	25.563	19.8	3,280.80	3,286.90
12 AvalonBay Communities Inc	AVB	*Residential*	45.953	41.3	3,087.70	3,118.50
13 Crescent Real Estate Equit Co	CEI	*Office*	21.625	49.2	2,335.80	2,942.30
14 Archstone Communities Trust	ASN	*Residential*	23.594	24.8	2,898.20	2,920.60
15 Kimco Realty Corporation	KIM	*Retail*	41.25	28.2	2,601.10	2,601.10
16 General Growth Properties, Inc	GGP	*Retail*	34	25.4	1,773.90	2,443.60
17 AMB Property Corporation	AMB	*Industrial*	23.859	26.7	2,007.50	2,146.60
18 CarrAmerica Realty Corp	CRE	*Office*	29.547	47.6	1,921.10	2,101.00
19 Liberty Property Trust	LRY	*Industrial*	26.5	23.4	1,807.60	1,925.60
20 Mack-Cali Realty Corporation	CLI	*Office*	27.203	20.8	1,581.80	1,799.20
21 Rouse Company	RSE	*Retail*	26.125	23.8	1,795.60	1,795.60
22 Plum Creek Timber Co Inc.	PCL	*Land*	26	19.5	1,782.90	1,782.90
23 Post Properties Inc	PPS	*Residential*	37.359	5.8	1,479.70	1,673.30
24 Highwoods Properties Inc	HIW	*Office*	24.656	24.6	1,440.30	1,635.90
25 Charles E Smith Resi Rlty Inc	SRW	*Residential*	45.406	35.6	995.2	1,608.30
26 Health Care Property Invest Inc	HCP	*Health Care*	30.641	37	1,558.80	1,582.10
27 Arden Realty Inc	ARI	*Office*	23.625	23.6	1,503.70	1,555.00
28 First Industrial Realty Trust Inc	FR	*Industrial*	33.016	33.3	1,275.70	1,513.20
29 Reckson Associates Realty Corp	RA	*Industrial*	22.984	29.3	1,290.20	1,467.10
30 FelCor Lodging Trust Inc	FCH	*Hotel*	23.938	47.5	1,256.90	1,462.70
31 Hospitality Properties Trust	HPT	*Hotel*	25.813	48	1,457.70	1,457.70
32 Regency Centers Corporation	REG	*Retail*	24.047	34.5	1,368.20	1,408.20
33 BRE Properties Inc	BRE	*Residential*	28.656	35.6	1,315.20	1,380.70
34 Mission West Properties Inc	MSW	*Industrial*	13.984	80.1	238.1	1,380.10
35 New Plan Excel Realty Trust Inc	NXL	*Retail*	14.953	6.9	1,310.70	1,332.80
36 Camden Property Trust	CPT	*Residential*	31.75	30.4	1,237.90	1,318.60
37 Franch Finance Corp of America	FFA	*Restaurant*	22.875	2.8	1,293.80	1,293.80
38 Cousins Properties Incorporated	CUZ	*Div/Other*	26.094	13.1	1,284.10	1,284.10
39 United Dominion Rlty Trust Inc	UDR	*Residential*	11.453	26.5	1,170.70	1,256.20
40 Weingarten Realty Investors	WRI	*Retail*	41.797	27.1	1,120.50	1,120.50
41 MeriStar Hospitality Corp	MHX	*Hotel*	21.703	53	999.3	1,095.80
42 Westfield America Inc	WEA	*Retail*	14.172	14.6	1,039.60	1,083.20
43 HRPT Properties Trust	HRP	*Office*	7.906	1.5	1,043.20	1,043.20
44 Essex Property Trust Inc	ESS	*Residential*	49.797	52.7	929.00	1,035.30
45 CBL & Associates Properties Inc	CBL	*Retail*	27.438	38.5	687.80	1,016.60
46 Home Prop of New York Inc	HME	*Residential*	26.984	9.2	581.90	1,009.80
47 Chateau Communities Inc	CPJ	*Residential*	31.25	36.2	890.50	1,004.20
48 CenterPoint Properties Trust	CNT	*Industrial*	46.016	30.9	956.00	956.00
49 Prentiss Properties Trust	PP	*Office*	24.813	23.6	907.70	949.30
50 Taubman Centers Inc	TCO	*Retail*	11.453	9.3	583.90	948.50

FIG. 2-2 Ranking of top REITS by market capitalization, February 14, 2001. (*Source*: SNL Financial, Charlottesville, VA (434) 977-1600, www.SNL.com.)

capitalization would be if all the UPREIT units were redeemed. These REITs focus on a wide range of property types: Office, Residential, Retail, Industrial, Hotel, Self-Storage, Land, Restaurant, and Health Care. The ultimate in miscellaneous classifications falls to Vornado Realty Trust, number 9 on the list, and Cousins Properties, number 38, whose property-type focus is given as "Diversified/Other." Residential is the most common property-type focus (with 12 REITs), closely followed by Office (with 11 REITs) and Retail (with 10 REITs so classified). Industrial attracts 7 REITs, and Hotel 4 REITs. It is interesting to note that the two largest REITs, Equity Office Properties Trust and Equity Residential Property Trust, were founded by the same man, real estate investor Sam Zell, who at the time served both as chairman of the board.

Figure 2-3 is the March 5, 2007, ranking of the top 50 REITs. What in 2001 was called Residential, here is called Multifamily, and what was Retail is now divided into Regional Mall and Shopping Center. Note on this more-recent ranking,

TOP 50 REITs by Implied Market cap (includes common stock and operating units)

	Company Name	Ticker	Property Focus	Closing Price ($) as of 3/5/2007	1 Year Total Return (%)	Market Value ($M)	Implied Market Cap ($M)
1	Simon Property Group, Inc.	SPG	Regional Mall	104.15	31.37	23,077.1	29,235.0
2	Vornado Realty Trust	VNO	Diversified	117.36	33.43	17,791.9	19,601.6
3	General Growth Properties, Inc.	GGP	Regional Mall	58.06	22.16	14,153.3	17,224.1
4	Public Storage, Inc.	PSA	Self-Storage	94.60	23.64	16,356.5	16,461.8
5	ProLogis	PLD	Industrial	61.36	21.13	15,722.7	16,038.0
6	Boston Properties, Inc.	BXP	Office	113.73	43.13	13,527.5	15,954.3
7	Equity Residential	EQR	Multi-Family	46.70	10.11	13,730.5	14,660.6
8	Archstone-Smith Trust	ASN	Multi-Family	52.81	15.76	11,638.3	13,196.9
9	Host Hotels & Resorts, Inc.	HST	Hotel	24.20	27.08	12,675.6	13,130.5
10	Kimco Realty Corporation	KIM	Shopping Center	47.11	34.40	11,832.3	12,156.1
11	AvalonBay Communities, Inc.	AVB	Multi-Family	125.46	26.37	9,954.6	9,972.8
12	SL Green Realty Corp.	SLG	Office	137.15	59.54	8,115.2	8,484.6
13	Macerich Company	MAC	Regional Mall	88.45	28.89	6,363.5	7,531.0
14	Health Care Property Investors, Inc.	HCP	Health Care	35.04	36.44	7,199.1	7,407.7
15	Developers Diversified Realty Corporation	DDR	Shopping Center	61.71	28.23	7,105.6	7,159.4
16	Plum Creek Timber Company, Inc.	PCL	Specialty	37.75	7.90	6,693.3	6,693.3
17	Duke Realty Corporation	DRE	Office	42.45	26.34	5,809.4	6,336.1
18	Apartment Investment and Management Company	AIV	Multi-Family	54.88	31.02	5,355.1	5,911.3
19	AMB Property Corporation	AMB	Industrial	56.45	9.96	5,583.1	5,846.7
20	Regency Centers Corporation	REG	Shopping Center	79.93	28.32	5,530.9	5,590.1
21	CBL & Associates Properties, Inc.	CBL	Regional Mall	43.61	9.67	2,858.1	5,076.0
22	Federal Realty Investment Trust	FRT	Shopping Center	86.94	28.93	4,819.0	4,851.8
23	Liberty Property Trust	LRY	Industrial	48.58	14.73	4,440.4	4,643.9
24	Ventas, Inc.	VTR	Health Care	42.71	45.44	4,538.8	4,538.8
25	Taubman Centers, Inc.	TCO	Regional Mall	55.02	40.46	2,948.8	4,497.4
26	Douglas Emmett, Inc.	DEI	Office	26.51	NA	3,048.8	4,374.9
27	United Dominion Realty Trust, Inc.	UDR	Multi-Family	30.53	19.61	4,138.2	4,344.5
28	Weingarten Realty Investors	WRI	Shopping Center	46.51	22.13	4,019.2	4,159.1
29	Camden Property Trust	CPT	Multi-Family	68.09	9.32	3,867.1	4,123.2
30	Mack-Cali Realty Corporation	CLI	Office	48.46	13.88	3,285.2	4,028.7
31	Hospitality Property Trust	HPT	Hotel	41.72	8.07	3,914.8	3,914.8
32	New Plan Excel Realty Trust, Inc.	NXL	Shopping Center	33.12	38.47	3,427.8	3,521.0
33	Essex Property Trust, Inc.	ESS	Multi-Family	126.12	30.40	3,052.7	3,367.4
34	Rayonier Inc.	RYN	Specialty	42.77	4.21	3,303.6	3,303.6
35	Digital Realty Trust, Inc.	DLR	Specialty	37.23	41.85	2,069.8	3,187.8
36	BRE Properties, Inc.	BRE	Multi-Family	61.10	18.94	3,096.1	3,154.8
37	Health Care REIT, Inc.	HCN	Health Care	42.85	28.69	3,136.3	3,136.3
38	Brandywine Realty Trust	BDN	Office	33.53	18.97	2,970.8	3,103.6
39	Alexandria Real Estate Equities, Inc.	ARE	Office	100.89	16.69	2,968.7	2,968.7
40	Kilroy Realty Corporation	KRC	Office	77.34	7.03	2,528.9	2,708.2
41	Nationwide Health Properties, Inc.	NHP	Health Care	29.82	43.31	2,634.2	2,634.2
42	Realty Income Corporation	O	Retail: Other	26.07	20.73	2,633.2	2,633.2
43	Corporate Office Properties Trust	OFC	Office	47.31	17.36	2,180.1	2,580.3
44	HRPT Properties Trust	HRP	Office	12.18	23.81	2,570.7	2,570.7
45	Home Properties, Inc.	HME	Multi-Family	53.59	12.73	1,779.5	2,506.0
46	Colonial Properties Trust	CLP	Diversified	43.59	−5.21	2,016.8	2,477.9
47	Highwoods Properties, Inc.	HIW	Office	40.59	30.52	2,282.7	2,474.8
48	Crescent Real Estate Equities Company	CEI	Office	18.84	−1.59	1,935.7	2,366.3
49	First Industrial Realty Trust, Inc.	FR	Industrial	44.44	23.80	1,996.2	2,287.7
50	Lexington Realty Trust	LXP	Diversified	20.02	5.35	1,406.1	2,116.9

Source: SNL Financial LC

FIG. 2-3 Ranking of top REITS by market capitalization, March 5, 2007. (*Source*: SNL Financial, Charlottesville, VA (434) 977-1600, www.SNL.com.)

the rise, fall, and demise of REITs named in 2001. Office is the most common property-type focus (with 12 REITs), followed by Multifamily (with 9 REITs) and Shopping Center (with 6 REITs so classified). Regional Mall attracts 5 REITs, and Health Care 4 REITs. The 2001 top REIT, Sam Zell's Equity Office Properties Trust, recently was purchased by The Blackstone Group, a private investment and advisory firm, after Blackstone went head to head in a takeover battle for Equity Office with Vornado Realty Trust (on both the 2001 and 2007 rankings). Particularly striking is that the implied market capitalization of the 2007 top REIT, Simon Property Group, is almost three times what it was six years earlier. And as a group, the implied market cap rates of the Top 50 have more than doubled.

JOINT VENTURES

It is possible to form a company by combining various types of the company structures previously described into a joint venture (sometimes referred to as a syndicate). For example, several individual construction companies could band together into a joint venture partnership for the purpose of taking on a particular job too large for any one of them to handle alone. The company so formed could be a partnership, limited partnership, limited liability company, or corporation, with each of the individual companies having a mutually agreed upon share. Each of the individual firms would retain its company characteristics, so that the joint venture company might be composed of two corporations and one limited partnership, and those three together would form a new corporation with temporary life for the duration of the construction project. The combined corporation could also be made up of three separate partnerships or any other combination. The entire organization is usually disbanded and dissolved at the end of the job, when each of the member companies would again go about its own business. The purpose of a joint venture is generally to accomplish a single task or project as opposed to establishing an ongoing business relationship. Sometimes a joint venture is used to raise sufficient operating capital and to combine enough other company resources (such as experienced personnel and specialized equipment) to take on a large job without straining or exceeding the resources of any individual member; sometimes one participant provides the capital and another provides the personnel and the on-site operating knowledge and resources. See Chapter 11 for a closer look at joint ventures.

SEPARATE ENTITIES UNDER COMMON OWNERSHIP

Sometimes a single company or a person will own several separate subsidiary corporations that are not coupled in a joint venture. This often occurs in a design-build operation, which provides engineering, architectural, and construction services to any outside owner. Under common ownership, one company designs the project and another builds the project for a client-owner. One of the reasons for doing this may stem from a desire to protect one subsidiary company from the debts and liabilities of the other subsidiary company. There could be, for example, a bid made too low by the construction corporation, resulting in heavy losses and consequent liabilities. If the construction corporation should go bankrupt, the design firm would not be seriously affected because it would not be liable for the debts of the other firm. This relationship depends on points of law to be successful and should be established with the help of a competent attorney. A second reason for establishing a separate company is for simplicity of management and control. If a contractor has difficulty determining whether a particular segment of the firm is profitable because all costs are not fully allocated where they should be, then a possible solution is to set up that segment of the firm as a separate, independent firm with its own management, keeping its own set of books. For example, some contractors set up a separate firm to own and maintain their heavy equipment, renting it out to jobs constructed by affiliated firms. Separate firms allow the benefit and convenience of tailoring more specific incentive plans for employees.

SUMMARY

These are the common types of company organizations, each providing different benefits:

Unlimited Liability

- *Sole Proprietorship* (individual owner, i.e., one person only)
- *Partnership* (any number of partners, often called a general partnership)

Unlimited Liability for General Partner, Limited Liability for Limited Partners

- *Limited Partnership* (a general partner(s) and any number of limited partners who are not allowed to be active in the business)

Limited Liability

- *C Corporation* (income taxed at corporate level and at shareholder level if distributed as dividends; requires board of directors, annual meeting, and at least two individuals, generally a president and secretary).
- *Limited Liability Company* (or LLC; managing member(s) and any number of members; one person can form; very flexible).
- *S Corporation* (limited to 75 shareholders; requires board of directors, annual meeting, and at least two individuals, generally a president and secretary).

Two Specialized Forms of Business

- *Joint Venture* (essentially a temporary business association)
- *REIT: Real Estate Investment Trust* (a special corporation for real estate ownership; must distribute 95% of taxable income and own only real estate; income taxed only at shareholder level)

Remember that even with business forms that provide for limited liability, if the company has insufficient net worth, banks and other providers of capital may require that the owners of the business personally guarantee the repayment of any loans. In that case, the owners of the business retain personal liability for the debt they guarantee. Still, because of the general statutory limitation of owner's liability to the assets of the business that are provided by limited partnerships, limited liability companies and corporations would grant some protection against a lawsuit, such as for personal injury or employment law violation.

KEY TERMS AND DEFINITIONS

C corporation: Overseen by a board of directors that hires a chief executive officer and other staff to run the firm. Owners who purchase shares in the company are called shareholders, who enjoy limited liability. C corporations are so named because their structure is outlined in Subchapter C of Chapter 1, Subtitle A, Article 26 of the United States Tax Code. Income is taxed at the corporate level and at the individual level through taxes on dividends.

Flow-through entity: A business organization in which income is taxed at the individual owner level rather than at the corporate level.

Limited liability company (LLC): Business organization that has a managing member and any number of members. This form of organization allows tremendous flexibility as to the operating structure. Taxable income is not taxed at the corporate level and flows through to owners.

Limited partnership: Made up of one or more general partners who make policy and manage the firm and any number of limited partners who are investors seeking return. The general partner(s) has unlimited liability and limited partners have limited liability. Taxable income is not taxed at the corporate level and flows through to owners.

Managing members: Members of a LLC who are actively engaged in the running of the firm.

Partnership (or general partnership): Two or more partners (people or entities) share unlimited liability.

Promote: A fee charged for putting a real estate deal together.

REIT: Real Estate Investment Trust, a publicly-held firm that invests in real estate.

S corporation: Similar in structure to a C corporation except that income is not taxed at the corporate level. S corporations are so named because their structure is outlined in Subchapter S of the Internal Revenue Code. S corporations may include up to 75 owners.

Sole proprietorship: Has an individual owner with unlimited liability, and it is the simplest of business organizations.

UPREIT: Umbrella Partnership Real Estate Investment Trust, a form of a REIT in which a preexisting partnership can contribute real estate into a new partnership called the operating partnership of which the REIT is the general partner.

KEY LEARNING POINTS

- Know the advantages and disadvantages of the various business organizations
- Understand the implications of liability and how it differs among business organizations
- Understand the differing roles of owners and managers within each business organization
- Understand the specialized forms of business used in real estate: REITs and joint ventures

QUESTIONS

1. For each of the following criteria, choose the business form described that fits best:
   a. Provides the most flexibility in terms of the structure of the business
   b. Is the simplest form of business ownership
   c. Must distribute 95% of its taxable income annually to its shareholders
   d. Made up of a managing member and any number of members who can actively participate in the management of the business
   e. Is a temporary business entity formed for the completion of a single project
   f. Income is taxed at both the corporate level and individual owner level
   g. Any number of partners who share unlimited liability
   h. Managed by a board of directors, holds annual meetings, and income flows through to individual owners for taxation

2. What is the limit on how many people can hold shares of an S corporation?

3. Which business form enjoys the most significant financing infrastructure for the raising of debt and equity capital due to the market's familiarity with it?

4. What changes in tax law have greatly reduced the tax benefits of owning real estate?

5. List some common fees sometimes collected by syndicators or general partners in putting together real estate deals.

6. What is the primary difference in terms of liability between the two classes of partners in a typical limited partnership?

3
Negotiation

One man gives freely, yet grows all the richer; another withholds what he should give, and only suffers want.—Proverbs 11:24

Negotiation: To deal or bargain with another or others as in the preparation of a treaty or in the preliminaries to a business deal.—*Webster's Encyclopedic Unabridged Dictionary of the English Language*

INTRODUCTION

All life involves negotiation. Whether you realize it or not, from the moment you wake up until you lay your head down for eve's rest, you will negotiate: with your spouse, those who report directly to you, your boss, the driver of the car whose eye you catch and who nods to let you into a lane of traffic. They have something you want, you have something they want. The exchange must be negotiated, decisions made. Clearly, not all negotiations are about capital. A negotiation may be for just a few minutes of your time, where to go for dinner, what movie to see, permission for your teenager to buy a certain product; it may simply be for your emotional approval or it may be a change in attitude that is desired. But you do negotiate. All day long you evaluate the strength of your position, the depth of your attachment to whatever is being offered or requested, the strength of the other party's position, the importance you place on the relationship, the value you place on satisfying yourself versus satisfying the other party. That is negotiation.

Negotiation can and should be studied; there are principles, strategies, and gambits involved. It is a skill that can be acquired and honed. Negotiation is an incredibly valuable ability to have at your command. After having been ignored as a separate field of academic study for many years, negotiation is now the subject of course study in some of the finest business and law schools in America.

There is a tendency by the participants in a negotiation to assume a certain inevitability as to the achieved outcome, particularly in less complex, single-point negotiations. This is what happened, therefore this is what had to happen. When I teach negotiation, I enjoy breaking the class into teams of one-on-one and doing a simple used-car sale negotiation. People are generally astounded by the wide range of outcomes; it helps them realize how much people's mindsets and the interaction of personalities can impact outcome.

Negotiation is a crucial skill for a developer; a developer must negotiate with banks, contractors, regulatory bodies, neighborhood groups, equity partners—the list goes on and on. Every development is unique, there is no formula that can be followed ad infinitum that will guarantee success for a developer; each development requires balancing the interests of many parties, interests that are often in tension. The developer must negotiate a solution. It is for this reason that this chapter on negotiation is included as a brief overview of a fascinating subject.

In essence, a good negotiation is finding out what is worth $1.00 to you and $1.25 to the other party and trading that for something that is worth $2.25 to you but only $2.00 to that party. Negotiation in its highest form is about finding all the value in a given situation. Different outcomes have different values to different people. A good negotiation is *not* about winning or losing or ego fulfillment, it is about finding what is of low value to me and of high value you, and vice versa, and finding some basis on which to make an exchange.

You can think of the possible outcomes of a negotiation as being the area beneath a curve between an *x* axis and a *y* axis, with *x* being you and *y* being the other party. If the outcome is on the *x* axis, *x* got everything, if the outcome is on the *y* axis, *y* got everything. Coordinates between represent various possible permutations of potential outcomes. Outcomes that lie on the curve mean that, regardless of how it was distributed, all the value in the negotiation was realized. Outcomes at points beneath the curve mean that not all of the possible value in the situation was realized.

To find all the value in a situation, the parties must be willing to communicate reasonably honestly and intensively about their true desires, wishes, expectations, and the actual value they place on various outcomes. This does not mean that you should necessarily put all your cards on the table up front; business is a competitive environment. It does mean that the full and often subtle benefits of cooperation are often undervalued and that cultivating an atmosphere of trust, a culture of reliability, and a reputation for dependability can create much greater prosperity than being

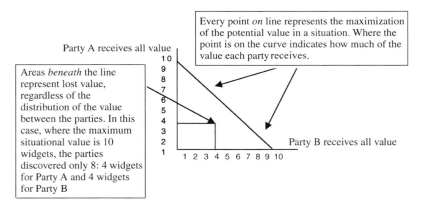

FIG. 3-1

known as a stonewall, tough guy, hard-nosed negotiator. A hard-style negotiator will frequently win the first time, even the first few times. However, everyone will be actively looking for alternatives to whatever good or service the hard-style negotiator provides and will breathe a sigh of grateful relief when it is inevitably found. This is becoming all the more true as the world economy is increasingly dominated by service- and knowledge-based sectors in which human initiative and creativity are the value drivers.

Our perceptions of the world and of the proper way to approach negotiation can be self-fulfilling prophecies. I once attended an excellent weeklong hands-on seminar on negotiation at the Harvard Law School in Cambridge, Massachusetts. During the seminar we spent about a third of the time in lectures, a third of the time in work groups of about 20 people with two teaching assistants, and a third of the time doing mock negotiations, starting out one-on-one and progressing during the week to more complex multiparty negotiations.

In the negotiations, each party was given a sheet of paper outlining his position and what he knew about the situation. Although all parties' papers dealt with the same situation, the perspectives and facts available to each party obviously varied. It was an interesting series of exercises, partly because the wide variety of outcomes reached by different negotiators from the same situation of facts was astounding and partly because each party gave the other a postnegotiation debriefing in which he revealed how he reacted to and felt about various statements, assertions, and strategies employed by the other party. This was a unique feedback opportunity that rarely happens in the real world, and it was invaluable in honing skill sets.

Several colleagues attended the seminar at the same time, and one of them related an interesting story about self-fulfilling prophecies that occurred in his work group. Although the seminar included many valuable strategies and techniques for dealing with hard-style negotiators, one of its basic premises was that the greatest value could be found through the establishment of trust, communication, and cooperation. Notwithstanding this ubiquitous message, the personality of a participant in my colleague's workshop was such that he repeatedly chose hard-style negotiation: presenting high initial demands with little if any willingness to move thereafter, demanding concessions without willingness to reciprocate, belittling the other person's position, exhibiting minimal if any respect for the relationship.

This person's reputation quickly spread, and one by one the other participants in the work group adapted to his style when dealing with him. Parties dealing with him quickly hardened their positions, and people began to enter into negotiations with this individual "loaded for bear," sometimes hitting him hard before he even began, moving to claim more territory in anticipation of needing more bargaining chips to trade to get back to where they felt they needed to be. These negotiations took longer and were more tumultuous. A significant number of his negotiations deadlocked—a rare outcome in this process. In group negotiations, the others on his side tended to freeze him out and discount his input.

This is a classic case of expectations creating reality, a self-reinforcing system. This individual's worldview probably was that it was a tough world so you had to be a hard-style negotiator. The world responded to his attitude, and that is how the world treated him; he now had plenty of evidence to support his belief. Even if he tried to adopt a softer, more cooperative style of negotiation, in any case where his reputation preceded him, he would have to work harder and longer to establish an atmosphere of trust. In addition, because anyone learning new behaviors is often awkward in the beginning, it may take him even longer to fully internalize a cooperative mindset and learn how to express himself in ways that create and establish trust and facilitate communication.

The good news is that people usually sense good intentions and honest, sincere effort and respond in kind. The longer you are willing to persist in your efforts to establish communication, build trust, and develop the relationship, the greater the chances that the sincerity of your efforts will be realized and appreciated. In cases where trust and communication have broken down between the parties at a deep level, but there is still interest in reaching an agreement, a mediator can often serve as a buffer to facilitate settlement.

We will be dealing primarily with negotiation in high to medium trust situations where the maintenance of an ongoing relationship, as well as reputation, is important. Most business negotiations, we can hope, fit into this framework.

ALWAYS KNOW YOUR BATNA,
TRY TO DISCOVER YOUR ZOPA

Always know your alternatives. Continuously update yourself on your BATNA. What is your BATNA? Your BATNA is your Best Alternative To a Negotiated Agreement. Believe it or not, intelligent, educated people have gotten so wrapped up in a negotiation, so focused on the outcome directly in front of them, that they have negotiated outcomes that were worse, more problematic, than those that could have been achieved by simply walking away from the table or bringing other parties to the table. Call it the power of inertia!

ZOPA is the Zone of Potential Agreement: If you are asking $100,000 but are willing to settle for $80,000 and, the other parties are offering $70,000 but are willing to go as high as $90,000, the range between $80,000 and $90,000 represents the Zone of Potential Agreement. If they were willing to go only as high as $75,000, then there would be no Zone of Potential Agreement—that is, your lowest figure of $80,000 is above their highest number of $75,000. Of course, we are treating this as a one-dimensional negotiation, and the best negotiators know that such is rarely the true case and that the greatest value in any situation can best be found by exploring all the attributes through intensive communication and finding creative ways to add value. Interestingly enough, sometimes parties with a meaningful ZOPA do not reach agreement. For one reason or another they fail to discover that there is a price or range of price on which they can both agree. Usually, communication breaks down and one or the other party fails to persist, to continue negotiating. ZOPA may also be thought of as the overlap of the two parties' BATNAs.

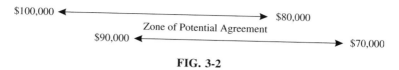

FIG. 3-2

FOUR PRINCIPLES OF NEGOTIATION

The following four principles can serve as guidelines for the negotiator:

1. Focus on the *why*, not the *what*.
2. Find third-party standards, use respected authority, understand the power of precedents.
3. Separate personalities from issues.
4. Get creative, find additional value, search for the third alternative.

Focus on the Why, Not the What

Too often parties spend too much time and energy arguing about the positions they have chosen to take without adequately exploring the interests behind the positions; that is, they focus on *what* the other party wants without understanding the *why* behind the *what*. Often, other means can be found to satisfy those interests. Just because other parties' positions are in opposition to ours does not necessarily mean that their interests are also in opposition. Quite frequently, the parties to a negotiation have many interests in common.

As a developer, I have frequently met with neighborhood groups concerned about development near their homes. Usually, their positions can be characterized as anti-development and mine as pro-development. At the same time, we have many interests in common: We both want stable or rising property values and a safe, attractive area that is a pleasant place to live. Frequently, we all have strong ties to the community at large. We hold common social and human values. We all want the respect of our peers and the love of our families. The interests that bind and unite us often far outweigh the things that divide us.

Occasionally, taking the time to emphasize and reiterate shared interests can lay a positive groundwork for negotiations, building and maintaining trust. It is easy to project our fears and to demonize the other side. As we are reminded of the interests and values we have in common, we once again see the other party as human, more like ourselves and thus easier to work with and trust.

I once attempted to rezone a large wooded, unused parcel of agricultural-zoned land for multifamily use. I controlled the land under an option contract but did not own it. A large, well-organized, rather affluent adjacent neighborhood was not thrilled at the possibility of rezoning. The residents had enjoyed living next to the woodlands for many years and would have liked that reality to have continued indefinitely. However, they were astute enough to realize that the existing agricultural zoning was no longer realistic; all the land around it had been developed, no true agricultural use existed for quite some distance out into the countryside. The land was entitled to be rezoned. The question at debate was to what use and at what intensity. As a practical political matter, the two possible land uses were multifamily or single family.

The neighborhood group's position was, fine, if it must be rezoned, then rezone it single family and let's be done with it. We can live with single-family zoning; after all we are single-family property owners. As the developer, I thought I could prevail on the merits of land planning, and after meeting with the commissioners, I thought I had a decent chance to get a majority of votes. However, voting in opposition to a well-organized neighborhood group is never a politically popular step for any elected official, and I was reluctant to risk losing the rezoning vote if a negotiated solution was possible.

Find Third-Party Standards, Use Respected Authority, Understand the Power of Precedents

In conjunction with my development team, I spent a lot of time listening to the group, getting a sense of their leadership, both formal and informal, their values and perceptions. I formed an understanding of what they visualized as single-family zoning. Using a *respected third-party authority* (crucial to the credibility of the information being given, particularly if the information is not welcomed), we explained exactly how broad a classification single-family zoning was, that it could include zero-lot-line, cluster housing, affordable housing, and a possible density of up to eight units per acre—a far cry from their half-acre-minimum lot sizes. We pointed out that many of the things they liked about their neighborhood were the result of private deed restrictions rather than public zoning. We explained that structures could be built within 30 feet of their backyards with no requirement of a fence or buffer. We further explained that it was virtually impossible to legally restrict affordable housing from any area.

We were leading them to the conclusion that although their *position* was single-family zoning, their true *interest* was an upscale, single-family *look* in the area immediately adjacent to their neighborhood.

We chose to downplay their *position* and address their *interest* by offering to make the buildings facing their subdivision look as much like large upscale homes as possible. We agreed to the following restrictions on the buildings directly facing their neighborhood:

- No buildings higher than two stories (there were many two-story homes in the neighborhood); we would build three stories only in the interior of the apartment community out of the line of sight of the single-family neighborhood.
- We agreed to build no more than eight units per building on the buildings facing the neighborhood.
- We agreed to certain architectural standards for the buildings facing the neighborhood to give them more of a single-family look—i.e., a required minimum number of changes of roof elevation, individual entrances, no breezeways, etc.

- We further agreed to build a fence, to install a 50-foot greenspace buffer, and to build no structure within 100 feet of their subdivision.

Separate Personalities from Issues

Although a viable neighborhood association existed, it had no power to bind its members and individual homeowners were free to state their personal opinions regardless of any "deal" struck by the association as a whole. The vast majority of the neighbors were committed to a civilized, diplomatic interchange, but there were several rather strong personalities that on occasion bordered on the hostile and were capable of inspiring resentment. In our group planning sessions and in all our internal interactions, I very consciously refused to allow any negative venting or expressions of animosity. I refused to allow any statement to be made internally that we could not stand by publicly. I did not believe that you could demonize anyone privately and then *effectively* negotiate in good faith. Indeed, I always insisted that we spend some time in our negotiating sessions "walking a mile in their shoes," seeing the issues from the other parties' perspective, both emotionally and intellectually, with emphasis on what they must be feeling and perceiving and how that would lead them to act.

Get Creative, Find Additional Value, Search for the Third Alternative

Several factors complicated the negotiation. Although everything we were offering was feasible, based on our vision of the potential development, we were offering substantial concessions. Indeed, we were negotiating on several fronts: The landowners were not to pleased with the concessions that we were willing to make, and they were concerned that in the event we did not exercise our option to purchase, they would be stuck having to live with any agreement we had made.

Furthermore, a portion of the property lay within the city and a portion was in the county. So we were dealing with two sets of government staff and two zoning boards. The city portion (suitable for about 85 units only) lay behind the county portion (suitable for about 250 units) and was accessible only through the county portion. Thus, if the county portion was not developed, the city portion could not be developed.

The good news was that the city portion was already zoned for multifamily; the bad news was that it was zoned for affordable housing, which did not fit into our development vision. We knew we needed to get creative. We approached the city staff and pointed out that given the parcel's out-of-the-way location, the dearth of developers for affordable housing in general, much less those of this parcel's uneconomical size, and the long time the parcel had lain fallow, it was unlikely that the parcel would be developed as affordable housing. Left unsaid but likely noted by all present was that even if such an affordable development were proposed, the site plan would face substantial opposition by the very neighborhood with which I was negotiating.

My proposal to the city was, basically, that a bird in the hand was worth two in the bush. I offered to host 85 units of affordable housing for a five-year period, after which my obligations would cease. I also offered another benefit to the city that was of no cost to the development and perhaps even a benefit. Because affordable housing often carries a social stigma, I offered to scatter the affordable housing units throughout the entire development (all the units were to be built to the same standard—it was the lower rent amount that made them affordable, not any reduction in quality—thus, there would be nothing else to distinguish them from other units). Because the affordability criterion would expire after five years, the financial penalty could be borne.

After suitable discussion, ruminations, and a correct assessment that some affordable housing now was better than none, the city graciously accepted my proposal. The neighborhood group (which was in the county and thus had limited ability to impact the city) was basically happy with my deal with the city. I believe they liked the idea of the five-year burn off of the affordable housing zoning, which many of them had been surprised to find was so close to their neighborhood. However, no agreement had yet been reached about the county parcel, and the date of the zoning hearing was rapidly approaching.

The neighborhood group, the property owners (two brothers representing their family), county staff, a few attorneys, and I met the night of the zoning hearing in a conference room next door to the hearing room; there was standing room only. The core of the neighborhood group (represented by the official homeowners association) and I had reached agreement; a few individual neighbors were holding out, but their requests, although reasonable from their point of view, were such that I did not feel that the commission would give them much legal weight. My biggest problem was that although one of the owners was inclined to go along with the deal, the other was hanging back. I lay low and let the pressure build; I had no cards left to play, and I was banking on the power of momentum to carry the day. It had taken almost a year and more than $100,000 in outlays to get to this point. The owners were developing the retail property in front of my optioned multifamily land, and our project would give their development a boost. I was trusting that when it came to the moment of decision, the tide of forward progress would provide the final push. I wish I could say I had more up my sleeve than that, but I did not. As time dragged on without agreement, my attorney asked if I wanted to request a postponement of the hearing. I declined; I knew the power of a deadline to compel movement. If we did not reach an agreement tonight, it was unlikely that we ever would. Eventually, our time came, and we were called into the zoning hearing. We had the outline of an agreement but no closure.

The staff and engineering professionals who represented me as the developer requesting the zoning change, laid out the facts for the hearing board and responded to their questions. The board then opened the hearing for public comment. The president of the neighborhood association outlined the arrangement that we had spoken of and said it was acceptable to that group. I walked up to the podium and waxed eloquent about how the agreement was a fine example of neighborhood and developer working hand in hand to create a better living environment for all concerned. However, even as I spoke I was not sure whether I had my owners on board yet. I halfway expected to hear an objection from the back of the room as I spoke.

Few in the room realized how crucial the next few moments were. At the conclusion of my remarks, I turned to the brothers and publicly asked for their assent. To my relief, they both nodded (or at least one said yes and the other did not object—it was that close). I rushed over and shook their hands in front of the commission, staff, citizens, lawyers, and reporters. The agreement was not legally binding until we signed the documents, but these were men of their word and I would trust their handshakes over some people's contracts.

This negotiation illustrates several very important things, including the four principles of negotiation described earlier:

- The power of addressing underlying interests versus stated positions.
- The power of creative solutions, of thinking outside the box.
- The power of a deadline.
- The power of persistence.
- The power of momentum (which can be particularly important in multiparty negotiations).
- The power of using *respected authority.* Using credible, authoritative *third-party professionals* to explore how the interests behind positions could be better served was crucial to the success of the negotiation. And, indeed, I, too, was educated and sensitized as a developer to the power and concerns of a well-organized neighborhood group.

THE IMPORTANCE OF CLEAR COMMUNICATION AND CONSCIOUSLY WORKING TO BUILD TRUST

Trust is crucial; it must be consciously earned and maintained, and it can be easily destroyed. Staying in contact and keeping your commitments are vital to building and sustaining trust. When I was first starting out and still operating on a wing and a prayer, a fine gentleman once agreed to sell me a nice piece of property on very favorable terms, including owner-provided secondary financing. All I had to do was get primary bank financing. Achieving such financing turned out to be a bit harder than I had expected, and the process dragged on longer than I had anticipated, and I had to request an extension of the contract, which the seller was kind enough to grant.

He would call frequently, asking for updates and following up on progress points that I had mentioned earlier. Returning those calls promptly when I had no good news to report (which was virtually always) was an act of courage. I so badly wanted to put those bad news calls off until I had good news or to somehow sugarcoat the situation. But I knew that this gentleman's faith and trust in me was the best thing I had going for me in this deal, and I would not, could not, let him down. I made sure he was always at the top of my call list. When I saw the pink message slip with his name on it, I would visualize that I was calling back the lottery to accept my million-dollar prize so that I would make the call with the same speed and enthusiasm (I seriously thought this deal could easily bring in a cool million eventually, and that was how I had to approach it.)

There was only one time that I delayed returning his call. One day at about 4:30 I received a message to call him and simultaneously, a message that the loan committee had once again kicked back the loan, asking for more information for what seemed like the umpteenth time. I was whipped, and my body language showed it: slumped shoulders, hanging head. I was afraid that my voice would convey my discouragement and that the seller would lose faith in my ability to pull off the deal. I got a good night's sleep, and with fresh energy I returned the call by nine o'clock the next morning.

I did pull off that deal, and it was a sweetheart. I still own the property today, and the cash is flowing as in the land of milk and honey. The deal was originally set up as a nothing-down deal. The owner would hold a 25% second mortgage behind a bank's 75% primary mortgage. The bank was protected, and the owner got a good price and a quick sale. I took the deal to my primary bank on an informal basis and they passed on it; nothing-down deals went against their grain, particularly those of this size. I took it to a second commercial bank that I did business with, and they said "Sure!" Or at least the local folks did. And eventually their regional office okayed it as well, after much sniffing around trying to find the nonexistent flaw. Then it went up to national headquarters, where it slowly got committeed to death. They never said no (I think they did not want to upset their local staff, who were strong proponents—they knew me, and they knew the property was prime); they just asked question after question. They got their answers, waited a few days, and then came up with more questions. Meanwhile, time was slipping away. The property owner had already granted one extension; I was told no more would be forthcoming as the owner already had an offer in hand for $100,000 more than our contract. True or not, it was motivational. It was the morning of December 22, and I had to present to the seller a loan commitment from a lending institution by midnight, December 31, or the deal was kaput. And all I had in hand was yet another request for more information from the bank loan committee.

I decided to walk away from "the loan committee from developer hell." I called up the loan officer of my first-choice bank and said those fateful, magic words that a banker loves to hear and a developer hates to say: "Would you do the deal if I put some money into it?"

The answer was a resounding yes, and I will owe this loan officer for the rest of my days. He polled his loan committee by phone, ran around on Christmas Eve and collected signatures, and on the 27th of December, a mere five days later, he presented me with a loan commitment; 30 days later we closed. And I still had to put only about 5% down into the deal.

PERCEPTIONS CAN BE REALITY

Perception is important, and how the bargaining process unfolds can add or detract from perceived value. We have a saying in our marketing department: "Our customer's perception is our customer's reality." That is, if someone believes something and acts on that belief, it is his reality. If a potential customer thinks that a competing community offers more value for less capital, even if this is not true, then that is the belief that he will act upon unless we introduce information to create a new belief system.

The best illustration of perception is the story about the hiker who sees a shadowy form looming ahead in the dusk of the evening, shuffling forward with an ambling gait. "Bear!" shouts the hiker as he scrambles back up the path, running for dear life. In truth, the menacing beast was merely a large, shaggy, friendly dog in search of a pat on the head and a scratch behind the ear. Yet our hiker perceived a bear, and that was the "reality" to which he responded.

We are all familiar with the store that heavily advertises a few specials, creating the image of overall low prices, when the reality is that most of its prices are higher than the competition's. Yet because few consumers in today's fast-paced world have the time to do extensive comparison shopping, especially on small-ticket items, many shoppers will act on the false "reality" created by a clever marketing campaign.

To successfully negotiate, it is important to have an ongoing awareness of people's perceptions and to impact them as positively as possible. The following story illustrates how the process of negotiation can affect perceptions regardless of the outcome.

A gentleman walks into an antique store. A beautiful grandfather clock sits in a corner. The detailing is exquisite, the tones of the chimes divine. The price approaches the heavens: $2,000. The gentleman knows that it is the perfect present for his wife for their upcoming anniversary. But the price is well outside his budget. He does some quick figuring: A thousand dollars would be a bargain, he would like to spend $1,200, and his maximum is $1,400. He approaches the proprietor a little hesitantly, compliments him on his fine store, and wonders whether the price of the grandfather clock is open for discussion. The aged store owner looks him over closely, asks him a few questions to ascertain whether he is a serious buyer, and then allows as how he could let it go for a mere $1,750. The buyer thanks the seller for the concession and states that although the clock is truly magnificent, his budget for the purchase is only $1,000. The seller turns and walks away a few steps, turns again and suggests that the purchaser is a jokester. The buyer tells the story of his upcoming anniversary, of his wife's love of antique clocks, and remarks on what a fine specimen of its genre the clock is. The store owner listens in bemused silence and then interrupts with, "Sixteen hundred, and that's my final offer!" The buyer says that he may be able to squeeze out $1,200 by postponing a few purchases. The back and forth continues, and finally a deal is struck: "Twelve hundred fifty dollars, delivery included!"

A successful negotiation, two happy parties. Now suppose the same scenario, same clock, same parties, up to the point when the buyer had offered $1,000. Suppose the seller had said, "No, but you can have it for just $1,250." The buyer would have instantly suffered tremendous remorse and become beset by doubts as to the perceived value of the clock even though the price was well within his range.

Regardless of the outcome, the seller's behavior via a rapid price capitulation would have conveyed a message as to the potential lack of value of the article being sold, and that message would have induced extensive postcognitive dissonance in our buyer.

An intelligent negotiator is patient and allows the process of a negotiation to unfold, always aware of the importance of perceptions and unspoken expectations, of hidden assumptions and the small, often subtle, but vital rituals of human interaction.

SIX CRUCIAL STRATEGIES OF NEGOTIATION

1. *Know your desired outcome.* Sounds incredibly simple, doesn't it? Yet you would be surprised how many times otherwise intelligent people enter into a negotiation with no other goal than to simply win without having a clear idea of what they want to accomplish. Ask yourself the question, "If they say yes, then what?" It is important that you know *specifically* what it is you want the other parties to do. In contract situations, I find it helpful to draw up as simple a contract as possible and bring it with me or, if appropriate, send it to the other parties in advance for their review. It is amazing how the process of drawing up the agreement clarifies my thoughts, brings out additional points that need to be covered, and focuses my mind.

2. *Listen!.* Listening is the easiest, cheapest concession you can make. Listening shows respect and gives others a sense of being understood and valued. Practice listening to ideas that go against your normal grain. Subscribe to a magazine whose editorial content is 180 degrees from your political beliefs. As simple as it may seem, listening is the most important skill a negotiator has at his command. Closely allied are observation and patience. In a book I strongly recommend, *Seven Habits of Highly Effective People*, Stephen Covey deals with the extraordinary potential impact of listening, summarized succinctly in the phrase "Seek first to understand, then to be understood."

3. *Knowledge is power.* Always know as much about the other party's business as you can. To developers, capital is oxygen, the fuel their business runs on. When I was starting out as a developer, I joined the Mortgage Banker's Association just to be able to attend its conventions, listen in on the seminars ("Finding the Hidden Risk in a Developer's Loan Package: A Banker's Guide to a Lender's Minefield"—that's a seminar topic sure to perk up a developer's ears), get a feel for its members' thought processes, and receive its internal publications. (Membership was restricted to mortgage bankers—I was able to join only because my status as an attorney let me become an associate member—and the dues were stiff. I dropped out after a few years when I felt the learning curve had begun to flatten.)

4. *Go to the balcony, visit the mountaintop.* Occasionally call a time out and image yourself standing on a balcony overlooking the negotiation. Become a

fly on the wall. Emotionally detach yourself. What new insights are available? Imagine how other people whose knowledge, maturity, and skills you respect would view the situation. Breathe deeply. What additional perspectives have you gained? Sometimes I call taking this time out "going to the mountaintop." It is a powerful visualization for me in terms of clearing my head and taking the long view, the overall perspective. To me, "going to the mountaintop" invokes memories of times when I was skiing or hiking where the air was crisp, the view incredible, and the mind relaxed. Those memories help to induce that calm mindset in times of pressure and stress and thus infuse me with fresh energies and confidence.

Faced with a difficult question, consider sleeping on it. This is one of my favorite tactics to lessen the urgency of the situation, avoid being stampeded, and gain needed perspective. Things frequently look different in the morning. Many fears are born of fatigue.

5. *Beware of deadlines.* Some call it the 90/10 rule: Often 90% of a negotiation takes place in the final 10% of the time available. Protect your internal or real deadline with a cushion so that you will not be pressured.

I once had to refinance a 260-apartment community. Negotiations with our first-choice lender, after getting off to a great start, fell apart at the last moment. I was 30 days away from default on two loans (i.e., a first and second mortgage) for which I was personally liable. I turned to a second lender and started the process again. The deadline loomed before us, motivating everyone. People worked extra hours and pulled off miracles. Through it all, I stayed calm and assured and held firm on several deal points even as the clock ticked down.

Why? Not because I was superhuman or had nerves of steel. Rather, it was because I had something up my sleeve: Unbeknownst to anyone but me and the other principals involved, I had negotiated 90-day extensions on both notes. It was not cheap; if I were to take that option, I would have to pay a loan point up front plus the normal interest rate (steep interest for just 90 days). But it did extend my deadline, a bit of news I shared with no one. I had managed to better my BATNA, and I slept better as a result.

6. *Understand the interests behind the position.* Avoid positional bargaining. There is a reason for the other party's position, some interest that must be satisfied. Is there any other way to satisfy that need? People are human and creatures of emotion.

A case in point: A builder was trying to buy out a small competitor, a gentleman well past the age of retirement. The builder knew the seller well, knew that he was a motivated seller, knew him as a pleasant, intelligent, reasonable, and generally excellent businessperson. Negotiations had stalled over the seller's firm price—$10,000,000, a number that simply could not be justified by any reasonable valuation method.

Finally the buyer stopped arguing with the seller, stopped trying to convince him that he was wrong, stopped shoving spreadsheets at him that "proved" that his business, his work of a lifetime, was not worth what he was asking. Taking a break over lunch, the buyer picked a relaxed moment and asked a very simple and seemingly obvious question: "Why $10,000,000?"

Back shot the answer: "Because that's what my brother-in-law got when he sold his business." Ouch!

This negotiation was not about logic, or spreadsheets, or even money, really. It was about pride, prestige, self-image, and family bragging rights. Knowing what truly motivated the seller, the buyer was quickly able to structure a deal to buy the business over time with a face price of $10,000,000 but with future performance clauses and sweetheart seller financing (a low down payment and an exceedingly low interest rate) that made the deal work for the buyer as well.

COMMON TACTICS

Cherry Picking

Cherry picking is what you do when you have multiple bids or offers and you attempt to pick out the best points of each and combine them into one. Depending on the nature of the negotiated subject, this is done either by making separate purchases of each subpoint or by using the best points of the other bids as precedent or authority for your chosen winner to match.

Playing the Bargaining Chips versus Blue Chips Game

Playing the Bargaining Chips versus Blue Chips Game means deliberately asking for more than you need (including in your initial position throwaway items as bargaining chips as well as nonnegotiable or highly-valued items—blue chips). If you are making the initial offer, this is sometimes called "lowballing." Why do it?

- You may get it.
- It gives you room to negotiate.
- By anchoring high, you give the other party a chance to "win" by getting you to lower your requirements.
- It makes whatever you are offering in exchange seem more valuable.

Lowballing also tends to make the negotiation last longer, thus consuming more resources, and may undermine your credibility. In the future, other parties may pad their positions to counter anticipated padding on your part.

The Nibble

If "the nibble" is done intentionally and to excess, this tactic can undermine a relationship and a reputation. You have struck a deal, the broad outlines of which are clear. Or are they? The nibble is used when a party goes back to the table and asks for more. And more. And more. In complex deals there are often many minor points that arise that must be settled and clarified, and it is not unusual to have to have continuing mini-negotiations. That is fine and normal if the spirit of the original deal is maintained. The nibble is an intentional tactic that plays against the goodwill of the other party and her unwillingness to jeopardize the entire deal over a relatively minor point. The nibble depends on the forward momentum of the deal for its success; overuse of the nibble will kill forward progress. Avoid the nibble, or at least use it sparingly.

Points of Personal Privilege

Some deal points assume importance out of all proportion to their real or monetary value. I have cheerfully granted parking privileges adjacent to campus to a seller's nephews and granddaughters, allowed a seller's wife to take home a favorite computer, even paid for leasing a Lexus for a year. All these concessions were *de minimis* in terms of the multimillion-dollar deals involved, and all involved the personal status/prestige of the deal maker on the other side of the table. I call these points of personal privilege, and as long as there is full disclosure to all interested parties, I delight in granting them as a means of showing respect for and interest in the personal concerns of the other party.

The Flinch

The flinch is a signal of resistance. On the buy side, the flinch is used, voluntarily or not, as a signal to the seller that the price is too high. On the sell side, using the flinch means that the seller keeps going until he sees the other party blink. Basically, the seller keeps adding on, asking for more until she gets resistance, that is, the flinch. The flinch can be as subtle as an involuntary widening of the iris of the eye or a delicately raised eyebrow, or as telling as a twitch of the head or a full-body wince. Of course, some negotiators flinch automatically at any opening number. However, the wise negotiator knows that the flinch is a two-way signal that can send a meaningful message, and if overdone, loses its power to convince the other party that he has gone far enough and needs to back off.

The flinch in action: "Ah, yes. The watch you are asking about is $1,000 (*no flinch*). That price is for the basic model. You are looking at the deluxe model that sells for $1,500 (*no flinch*). However, we only have the superdeluxe model in stock, which goes for $2,000 (*no flinch*). Perhaps you might want to look at the solid gold model, preferred by some of our most discriminating customers, for only $5,000? (*flinch!*)." The seller has now learned the buyer's price range.

The Higher Authority: The Mother-in-Law Rate

This is a classic. You own a hotel, a restaurant, anything for which good friends and not such good friends will call you up and ask for a discount or even a freebie. Your well-rehearsed reply is, "I'll be glad to give you the rate I give my mother-in-law." The mother-in-law rate may or may not be much of a deal, but the social customs and well-understood family obligations of our culture make it a powerful precedent and difficult to ask for any greater discount or better deal.

The Fading Offer

The fading offer is evident when the other party takes things off the table or raises the price, lowers the terms, or otherwise removes value from the bargaining table. This is a power move and is typically used as a bluff or by someone who perceives herself as having a strong bargaining position and/or attractive alternatives. In the absence of a credible rationale such as outside events truly beyond her control, the party using the fading offer demonstrates that a minimum of value is placed on a continuing relationship. The best response to the fading offer is to ignore it and reaffirm the validity of the last positions on the table. If you succumb to the fading offer ploy, expect more hardball tactics.

The Missing Person Stall

The authority figure necessary to consummate the deal or confirm a critical point cannot be found. The missing person stall is usually used to keep you at the table while the other party figures a way to increase her BATNA.

Take It or Leave It

The take-it-or-leave-it approach is a power move and an indication that the party views this as a one-shot relationship. If you have no BATNA, take the offer but start developing your alternatives.

KEY POINTS TO REMEMBER

Objections are a gift—use them! They give incredible insight into the other parties' thought processes and decision criteria. Any good salesperson will tell you that it is rarely the first or even the second objection that is the true motivator. Often it is the last reason people mention that is the most important issue.

Always let the other side save face. Don't box the other party into a corner. People have long memories: always leave them a graceful way out.

Always leave something on the table. Push until you find the point of resistance, and then back off. It is a courtesy that will be remembered and an investment in relationships and reputation that will reap a bountiful return.

Never ask for what the other party cannot give you; know the limits of his authority. Make sure the person you are talking to has the authority to make a deal. "If we were to reach an agreement today, can you bind your organization?" If this person cannot give you what you want, ask who can. It is very frustrating to have invested energy and time in a negotiation only to find that the party with whom you are communicating does not have the power to give you what you are after.

Practice multilevel thinking: Double and triple think. You must be aware of what you want (think), what they want (double think), and what they think you want (triple think).

Continuously discipline yourself to separate the people from the problem. Practice standing back from your emotions; visualize yourself standing outside yourself and your feelings. Do not let your fears color your analysis of the other party's motivations. When I need to separate myself from my emotions, I ask myself, "How would an alien view this situation?" The humor of imaging a "little green woman from Mars" stepping out of a flying saucer and trying to make heads or tails of the human drama puts things in perspective and allows me time to remember the relative importance of earthly issues.

Always ask for what you want; they can't say yes unless you ask.

The amount and frequency of the concessions from the other side can speak volumes.

Making an offer you think the other person will refuse will tell you volumes about his interests as he explains why your offer is unsatisfactory. Your offer must be good enough not to be insulting, that is, to be seen as a display of bad faith. Moreover, your offer may be seen as a precedent, so be sure that you can live with the precedent you are setting.

Understand that the other party has his problems too.

Be wary of multiple constituencies.

Simplify, simplify, simplify.

Preparation is vital, planning is crucial.

Whoever cares least about a successful outcome has the strongest bargaining position; therefore, always develop your BATNA. BATNAs do not have to be static. Use the time spent in a negotiation to improve your BATNA. Develop alternatives, create allies, gain additional knowledge.

Use the power of precedent; look for objective criteria.

The best way to get a larger slice of the pie is to find a way to enlarge the pie before trying to divide it up. The more options you have, the more potential solutions you have. A choice between something and nothing is no choice at all. Invest energy in creating new win/win options for mutual gain.

Think of negotiation as a process, not an event.

There are many kinds of power, but they break down into two kinds: external (positional) power and internal (personal) power. Capital is external power; self-confidence is internal power. The degree on the wall from an Ivy League institution may convey positional power; the knowledge you carry in your head is personal power. The title of CEO is positional power; the ability to stay cool, calm, and collected is personal power. Positional power is conferred by others and may be removed by others. Personal power is yours as long as you claim it. To paraphrase Ecclesiates, "The race does not always go to the swift nor the battle to the strong." The ability to listen empathetically is one of the greatest and most powerful sources of personal power.

Behavior has consequences. Your reputation is important. You cannot repeatedly talk your way out of what you have repeatedly behaved yourself into. If you pick up one end of a stick, you pick up the other end as well.

IMPORTANT QUESTIONS TO ASK

In any negotiation process, there are a number of important questions to ask. Ask about the process: "Can you explain your organization's internal decision-making process?" is a much better question than, "Who can make a decision?"

Ask about the other party's goals: "Specifically, what is it that you want to achieve?" "What is your ideal outcome?" "What is your expected outcome?" "What is your bottom line?" "If you were to have it all your way, what would it look like?"

After you have listened to the person's explanations of her goals, test her understanding of your goals: "What do you think I want?" "What do you think motivates me?" "What do you think a likely outcome of this negotiation will be?"

Continue to gently ask questions throughout the process: "How much flexibility do you have?" (Notice that this is a slightly different question from "Do you have any flexibility?" in that the question assumes that flexibility exists; the only issue is how much flexibility.)

Do not hesitate to push: "What is your rock-bottom price? (This is a slightly different question from "Is that your rock-bottom price?" in that it contains the hidden assumption that a lower price does exist.)

Be prepared to ask for closure: "If we could resolve this issue, would you be ready to sign now?" "Is there anything else you would like to discuss before we commit?"

MASLOW'S HIERARCHY

It is important never to forget that in any negotiation, you are dealing with human beings, human beings driven by many, often conflicting, emotions and whose motivations are complex and often evolving. To keep that foremost in my mind, I keep an illustration of Maslow's hierarchy on my wall (Figure 3-3).

Abraham Harold Maslow (1908–1970) was an American psychologist who put forth a theory of needs-based motivation, whereby humans mature from basic survival-oriented needs such as hunger, thirst, shelter, and sex through intermediate safety needs such as protection, comfort, and stability on to higher love-based needs such as affection and acceptance, eventually facing even more advanced needs such as one's self-worth. The highest need of all was what he called self-actualization—the fulfillment of one's greatest human potential. It is a wise negotiator who maintains in the forefront of her mind an ongoing awareness of the full range of needs of the other party.

ETHICS AND NEGOTIATION:
LYING VERSUS PUFFING VERSUS BLUFFING

What is ethical in negotiations? Where is the dividing line? Everyone is expected to "put his best foot forward," but when does stating things in their most favorable light cross over into overstating your qualifications? And then into outright lying?

FIG. 3-3   Maslow's hierarchy of needs.

Do you have an obligation to correct misapprehensions of which you are aware? Even if you did not deliberately create them? Does the level of materiality matter? Is there such a thing as a white lie? Does the depth of the relationship factor in? Does the level of experience and sophistication of the other party enter into the equation?

Although these are questions that individuals and organizations must ask and answer for themselves, for me and those who work for me the guiding principle is clear: Honesty is always the best policy. As the poet said, "Oh, what a tangled web we weave, when first we practice to deceive!"

SUMMARY

We engage in negotiation every day. We must evaluate and reevaluate our desires, bargaining positions, and the positions of others. Negotiation is a hallmark of human interaction, and it is a skill that should be studied, acquired, and honed. Perception is reality in negotiation, and clear communication is essential to successful interaction and the building of trust. The *four principles of negotiation* are:

- Focus on the why, not the what
- Find third-party standards, use respected authority, understand the power of precedent
- Separate personalities from the issues
- Be creative, find additional value, search for the third (or, for that matter, fourth and fifth) alternative

Those with whom you negotiate may use tactics to influence your perceived bargaining power or how you perceive them. Do not be fooled by these actions;

instead, remember the four principles. These principles will guide you to *six crucial strategies for negotiation:*

- Know your desired outcome
- Listen
- Knowledge is power
- Go to the balcony, visit the mountaintop
- Beware of deadlines
- Understand the interests behind the position

Remember to ask thoughtful questions that reveal the interests behind your partner's position. Listen carefully, and always remember that you are dealing with humans who have basic needs that must be met in order for them to walk away from the table feeling that they found all the value to be made in a deal.

KEY TERMS AND DEFINITIONS

BATNA: Best Alternative To a Negotiated Agreement.

External (positional) power: Power derived from the position, office, or title held and the ability to control rewards and punishments; external power is conferred by others and can be taken away.

Internal (personal) power: Power derived from natural ability, the respect of others, and the ability to influence others; internal power exists within the individual and cannot be taken away.

Maslow's Hierarchy: A theory of needs-based motivation, whereby humans mature from survival-oriented needs through intermediate safety needs on to higher love-based needs, advanced by Abraham Maslow (1908–1970), an American psychologist.

Multilevel thinking: Awareness of what you want (think), what the other party wants (double think), and what they think you want (triple think).

ZOPA (Zone of Potential Agreement): The overlap of two parties' BATNAs.

KEY LEARNING POINTS

- Learn to discover your BATNA and your ZOPA.
- Know the Four Principles of Negotiation.
- Know the Six Crucial Strategies of Negotiation.
- Understand the common tactics used in negotiation.
- Understand that negotiation deals with human emotions and needs, and know Maslow's Hierarchy.

QUESTIONS

Understand your negotiating partner. For each of the following situations, name the negotiation tactic used by your partner and describe how to counter it.

1. You are negotiating to purchase a 26-foot fishing boat. The sticker price is $35,000. The seller agrees to throw in four world-class fishing poles if you take the deal today. You tell her that you want to think about it overnight. When you call the next day to agree to the terms, the seller seems disinterested in the negotiation and says that the fishing poles are no longer part of the deal.

2. You run a small pizza-delivery franchise and have just hired a new deliveryman. You have agreed to start his salary at $6.50 per hour plus tips and 20 cents per mile. He accepted the terms last week, but he came back today with a story about how his car is getting old and is in need of many repairs. Twenty cents per mile may not cover the wear on his car, and he would like 30 cents per mile.

3. You are closing on a 200-unit apartment community that is across the street from a large state university. You and the seller have agreed to all the terms of the contract, and the close should be smooth sailing. At the closing, the seller tells you that his son will be a freshman at the university next fall and needs a place to park for class. He asks if his son will be able to park at the apartment complex.

4. You are purchasing an office building in the central business district of a major city. As you are negotiating the terms of the sale contract, the property manager, who is needed to confirm important parts of the contract, is unavailable. The seller says you will need to meet again to make sure everyone is at the table.

PART II
The Development Process
Start to Finish

First Union National Bank Becomes Wachovia

In discussing the Hidden Lake project, we refer to First Union as the lender. In September 2001, however, Wachovia Corp. and First Union Corp. completed a $14.3 billion merger. First Union was the larger, acquiring institution but chose to use the Wachovia name for the merged company. With the merger, Wachovia became the nation's fourth-largest bank. Its New York Stock Exchange ticker symbol is WB, and the merged company's base is Charlotte, North Carolina.

4

The Development Process: An Overview

INTRODUCTION

Development begins with a vision; an idea coupled with the skills, desires, and resources necessary to bring the vision to fruition. The process of development is long and complex, and although it is hard to do the process justice in a single checklist format, the following provides an excellent, if brief, outline of the development process:

- Concept: Product identification and establishment of development criteria
- Identify seed capital
- Assemble internal team: Site acquisition, financial analysis, marketing, negotiation
- Market area identification
- Location possibilities
- Feasibility study
- Marketing study
- Site analysis: Preliminary environmental study, suitability for desired purpose; identifying potential obstacles and opposition
- Preliminary pro forma: Use of market knowledge to estimate cost, potential income and expenses, possible operating profit and project final sales value; estimating value added by development process; ascertaining available financing
- Land acquisition: Optioning the land, securing control
- Obtain environmental Phase I report and soil borings analysis of site
- Preliminary contacts with possible debt and equity sources
- Assemble external team: Architect, engineer, land planner, landscape architect, surveyor, legal team; line up possible general contractors; sign contracts with major professionals; detail levels of responsibility; clarify areas of involvement
- Design process: Site, structures, and specifications

- Begin formulating marketing and leasing plan
- Select property manager, sign contingent contract
- Estimating and preliminary bidding process: Ongoing interaction with potential contractors with respect to cost estimates, design suggestions, and specifications
- Regulatory approval process: Zoning versus site plan approval
- Obtain final construction documents and site plan
- Release final construction documents to possible contractors
- Raise equity capital, finalize deal structure, form of ownership entity
- Debt capital, the construction loan: Send out project loan packages, receive term sheets, submit loan application, expedite required third-party reports, obtain commitment letter
- Receive preliminary bids, value engineering, and final bids
- Negotiate contractor contract and project schedule
- Risk/Reward analysis: Review pro forma and assumptions therein, assess available debt and equity capital, review general contractor contract; make go/no-go decision
- Sign construction contract
- Obtain building permit
- Close on land option, close construction loan, file notice of commencement, give notice to proceed to contractor
- Break ground
- Begin oversight of construction process, exercise quality control
- Manage marketing and leasing program, fine-tune interior design issues
- Field visits and progress reports, approve construction drawings and change orders
- Punch lists
- Certificate of occupancy
- Substantial completion
- As-built survey
- Lease up
- Occupancy and grand opening
- Stabilization
- Convert construction loan to short-term permanent loan
- Depending on exit strategy (flip vs. hold), either
  - Begin or intensify marketing for sale, or
  - Circulate updated permanent loan packages
- Start or intensify search for new development opportunity

Many of these steps will overlap or run concurrently. This chapter gives a brief overview of the development process and certain key points and definitions. The following chapters focus on certain major points in the process, including site selection and site-feasibility analysis, the creation of a project pro forma, and an in-depth analysis of the project appraisal; several subsequent chapters discuss the process of obtaining a construction loan.

DEFINITIONS

These definitions set the framework for the respective roles of the various players in the development process:

Developer: An individual, firm, or other entity that locates and secures control of a parcel of land, conceives an appropriate project to be built on that land, and obtains the needed regulatory approval for that project. The developer typically provides the seed capital necessary to get a project to the point where all development rights are vested. This amount is often several percentage points of the total forecasted value of a project; that is, a $10 million project can easily require several hundred thousands of dollars to be fully permitted and quite possibly substantial additional funds. These funds are usually reimbursed at the start of construction or at the close of the construction loan by the investor providing equity for the project. The developer also usually receives a "promote" or return for the time he has invested and risk he has taken in putting together or *promoting* the project.

Builder: The general contractor who does the actual construction of a project, generally by bidding the job out to a variety of subcontractors. The builder typically must "bond" a project, that is, provide assurances from a third-party insurer, guarantor, or surety that the builder will provide the funds to finish the project for the contracted price if the builder does not perform as agreed. The contract may be cost plus a fee or a fixed price.

Investor (owner): An individual, firm, or other entity that provides the equity capital necessary to build a project. Frequently investors do not commit themselves until the project is fully vested with development rights. The investor must often assume personal or corporate liability for the construction loan.

Lender: An individual, firm, or other entity that provides the debt capital necessary to build a project. The lender will not commit until the project is fully vested with development rights.

Property Manager: Typically, an individual, firm, or other entity who handles property management once the project is completed and who also may handle the marketing and management of the lease-up and stabilization phase of the project.

THE CONCEPT: PRODUCT IDENTIFICATION AND ESTABLISHMENT OF DEVELOPMENT CRITERIA

Most developers tend to specialize within a particular sector of development: e.g., suburban office, strip mall, big box, regional mall, single family, multifamily, assisted living, industrial warehouse, or central business district (CBD) high-rise

office. Even within a particular sector, there is a tendency to further subspecial-
ization. For instance, within the multifamily residential sector, developers tend to
pick subcategories in which to specialize: affordable housing, tax credit, luxury,
market rent, student housing, condominium, low rise, high rise, garden style.

Thus, selection of the development concept, product identification, and establishment of development criteria are often a matter of strategic preselection based
on the developer's prior track record and the company's chosen focus. Although
some expansion is normal and even expected—that is, into an adjacent state or
subsector (e.g., from market rent to luxury housing)—a developer choosing to stray
too far from his field of expertise will find it more difficult to attract debt and equity
capital. For example, a developer with a strong track record in ministorage may
have trouble getting a construction loan to build a regional mall, and a developer
who has specialized for 20 years in building tract housing in Arizona may find it
difficult to attract support for a 60-story high-rise condominium on Manhattan's
Upper East Side.

SEED CAPITAL AND ASSEMBLING THE TEAM

Most developers have existing sources of seed capital, internal or external, that can
be tapped for projects. Almost as a matter of definition, a developer without access
to some sort of capital is not a developer. Most experienced developers also have
a well-vetted team, both internally and externally, with whom they have worked
over the years. In that case, assembling the team may be as simple as gathering the
veterans of prior developments together and reviewing the development criteria,
alerting them to block out time on their work schedules as appropriate, and receiving
feedback as to changing market or regulatory conditions.

If the developer is venturing into a new market or sector, he may choose to
assemble a new team with experience in that area. There are many ways to find
out who the respected professionals are in any given area. A developer may inquire of his bank the name of the bank's local real estate loan officer, who is
usually knowledgeable about the players in her local market. Because most developers maintain multiple banking relationships, multiple inquires can be made
and answers cross-checked. Local regulatory officials can be excellent sources of
information, and if they are prohibited from giving direct recommendations, astute
questions—such as "Which engineering firms' site plans get through the review
process the fastest?" "Which architects' building plans are approved with the fewest
review comments?" or "Which general contractor has the highest percentage of
first-time passed inspections?"—will yield valuable information. Visiting ongoing
or recent job sites and determining which professionals are responsible can also
give a feel for who the best players are in any given market. Appraisers, real
estate brokers, title companies, and real estate lawyers also are good sources of
information. In addition, every profession has a national organization, such as the
American Institute of Architects or the National Home Builders Association, that
often tracks activity by marketplace within its respective profession and frequently
will rank local participants by size. Although biggest is not always best, this is

a good place to start. Moreover, most developers have a network of relationships within the field that they can call upon for recommendations.

MARKET AREA IDENTIFICATION

Although major institutional investors choose to limit their direct real estate investments in the United States to the top 60 or so markets in terms of size, each of those markets has multiple submarkets, and there are many viable, profitable markets within the smaller markets. All real estate is local, and because there is a finite limit to how many markets one can maintain adequate knowledge of and supervisory presence in, many developers tend to specialize geographically (e.g., southeastern United States, southern California, the eastern seaboard, north-central Florida). Thus, the search for the best combination of specific site and overall suitable market would typically be limited, at least initially, to markets with which the developer is familiar.

An interesting question is raised as to which is better: a fantastic site (great visibility, choice demographics, excellent drive-by traffic) in a so-so market (mediocre occupancy, slightly below average rents, lethargic job formation) or a so-so site (nearby power lines, bad sight lines, questionable surrounding area) in a fantastic market (robust rent growth, booming economy, tight and rising occupancy). Unless there is reason to believe that the so-so market conditions are permanent (rather than just a phase in a normal business or real estate cycle), choosing the best site over the best market is the prevailing choice, in theory, because markets recover but sites cannot move. Although the theory is a simplification, in that the factors that make a site great can change (traffic patterns evolve and demographics are not set in stone), site characteristics do tend to be more stable than market conditions.

MARKET REPORTS

Detailed reports on the top 50 to 60 markets are readily available, often over the Internet, most of them fee based. The quality and quantity of the information are improving rapidly, and an increasing number of markets are being followed. Good-quality data is now being reliably collected and archived for the top 75 to 80 markets, and information that was very difficult to come by is now at the tip of your fingers.

Major institutional players (developers and investors) generally prefer to stay in markets where information is readily available from several reliable sources to allow cross-checking. This generally restricts them to the top 50 to 60 markets. The general rule of thumb for developers is: Never propose an investment in a market that the investment committee or board of directors must use a map to locate. Unlike regional developers, who tend to be more flexible and entrepreneurial, major institutional players (large life insurance companies, pension funds, topflight REITS) tend to be most comfortable in markets where other investors like themselves are already present; it creates a sense of security and assures them of an exit strategy.

Every builder or developer produces a product or service designed to meet a particular market need. To improve one's chances of success, it is wise to select a market that is not already saturated by the competition, a market that needs a product that can be produced at a competitive price with good quality and workmanship, a market that is stable and shows signs of future growth and improvement.

An aggressive developer should select from the widest possible geographic market area; the wider the selection, the greater the opportunity to find superior building sites at reasonable prices. If the developer's interest extends outside the limits of his corporate home base, then potential target markets should be identified. Probably every urban area needs some kind of construction, but whether it needs apartments, shopping centers, offices, or industrial buildings depends on the current status of each local market. A good indication of current market needs can be found by determining the present vacancy rate, current construction activity, and a forecast of growth in demand.

For instance, for the residential market, if the vacancy rate is less than 5%, there may be a demonstrated need for additional residential rental units, unless a large amount of apartment construction is already on the drawing boards or under way, or the population count is declining instead of growing. Furthermore, adjustments should be made for discounts—e.g., rentals in which landlords give a bonus for signing a lease, such as two months' free rent included in a one-year lease, or any other marketing specials. If all rentals are firm and without giveaways, then a hard market prevails. Given a 95% or better occupancy ratio and a hard market as described, it is still necessary to determine the type of unit to build.

Occupancy rates for offices tend to fluctuate more than apartment occupancy rates and are generally lower than for apartments, with anything greater than a 90% to 92% rate considered acceptable. Office rents also tend to be higher per square foot than apartment rents of similar construction (three-story, low-rise, or high-rise buildings), perhaps reflecting a market-required premium for the lower occupancy and higher volatility. Office markets are typically divided between suburban and CBD or downtown. Central-business district offices tend to be high-rise projects.

Market reports come in many forms, including brief summaries. As examples, here are synopses prepared by Reis, Inc. (Used with permission from Reis, Inc. and reis.com) of four sectors of the Orlando, Florida, market as of September 30, 2006:

Orlando Apartments: The market continues to benefit from a host of favorable trends. While demand for condominiums has been very strong, robust population growth through in-migration has continued to support strong demand for rentals as well. Also supporting rental demand is the combination of low household incomes and high single-family prices, the latter resulting from the recent run-up. In addition, the condo sector with its higher profit margins has been no less attractive to developers than to residents. Rental development, thus, slowed as developers exercised their preferences. This only tightened the rental market. So has rampant condo conversion. In a trend that peaked in 2005, according to Reis, more than 17,600 Orlando area rental units switched to condo status that year. This compares dramatically with the 2,494 apartments that completed construction during the period. Apartment vacancy, as a result, has fallen to multiyear lows. The rate for third quarter was 4.7%, down 10 basis points since midyear, down 30 points since third quarter 2005. Rental growth rates, meanwhile, continue to run high. The gains of 6.6% and 7.1% projected by Reis, respectively, for the asking and effective averages for 2006 all told would be the largest single-year increases reported by this source for this market since 1996. Respective averages for third quarter were $863 and $807 per month, up 1.8% and 1.6% since midyear. With the condo market cooling generally, the national apartment market as a whole finds itself in a period of transition as developers refocus on rental projects. Data for Orlando, however, tell a slightly different story. While the condo conversion trend has eased up a bit, it remains significant, its volumes continuing to exceed same-term apartment construction completions by substantial margins. Thus, the 5,467 rental units that defected to the for-sale market during the first three quarters of the year alone compare strikingly with the 1,040 new apartments projected for completion for the entire year (the smallest single-year delivery total seen here since coverage commenced in 1980). While conversion activity has slowed, demand remains vibrant. Indeed, noted Southeast Real Estate Business in a November 2006 report, "The Orlando market continues to lead the state in condominium sales due to a strong job market, wide range of product and price ranges attracting first-time homebuyers, move-up buyers, second home buyers, empty nesters and investors." Looking ahead through 2010, Reis expects the pace of apartment construction to remain slow for this fast-growing MSA, the rate of vacancy to remain within a few basis points of 5.0% through 2010, and rent growth to proceed at favorable though diminishing rates.

Marcus & Millichap Real Estate Investment Brokerage Company, reporting in October, projects a year-end vacancy rate of 4.6%, down 20 basis points for the year. A 6.8% increase, to $875 per month, is forecast for the average asking rent for the year. Effective rents will increase 7.5%, to $822, as concessions diminish.

Orlando Industrial: Relocations into the market by national companies, states Grubb & Ellis Company in its third quarter report on the local market, confirm Central Florida's role as "the logistics and distribution hub of the state." It's not merely logistics that drives this market, however; but also raw population growth with all it requires for the warehousing of materials required for housing construction and goods related to growth generally. In addition, suburban areas support a significant, if small, tech-related flex market. In its analysis of the multi-tenant, non-manufacturing space sector, Reis reports consistently active development extending without interruption as far back as 1997. The 1.35 million square feet that completed construction in 2005 were a near-identical match to the average maintained over the previous four years. For 2006 all told, 1.6 million square feet, the largest single-year sum since 2001, are expected to deliver; similar volumes are anticipated year by year through 2010. Demand, meanwhile, maintains an advantage over same-term new supply, a trend seen here since 2003 and not expected to abate throughout the forecast period. Net absorption for 2005, accordingly, was 1.6 million square feet, with a net of 1.85 million projected for 2006. Accordingly, the vacancy rate, heading downward from its 11.1% 2002 peak, will continue its descent at a more or less steady pace. Reis expects a year-end 2006 rate of 9.3%, down 40 basis points for the year. By the close of 2010 the firm expects to be reporting vacancy at 7.9%. This steady improvement has been favorable for landlords. Rent growth, while not spectacular, returned in 2004 (in small measure) in the wake of three years of loss. For 2005 Reis reports respective increases of 2.1% and 2.2% for the asking and effective averages. Gains of 2.5% and 2.7%, to $4.95 and $4.86 respectively, are forecast for 2006, with slightly larger year-over-year increases expected for the remainder of the firm's five-year forecast period. While its numbers differ from Reis's due to criteria for measurement, Grubb & Ellis also reports significant lease rate growth, a trend reflecting in part increased land and construction costs (see Special Real Estate Factors for additional commentary on factors affecting industrial rents). For the larger, more inclusive market tracked by Grubb & Ellis, 1.4 million square feet were reported under construction per the close of third quarter, with activity heaviest in southeast and southwest Orange County and Seminole County. CB Richard Ellis reports about a million square feet under construction at year-end 2006, with 3.5 million square feet of additional product in planning stages.

Grubb & Ellis reports third quarter overall industrial vacancy at 6.2%, down 50 basis points since mid-year and down 60 since third quarter 2005. Rates by property type are recorded at 5.9% for warehouse and 7.4% for flex. Respective average asking rents of $6.43 and $10.54 psf resolve to an overall average of $8.48 psf.

Orlando Office: Strong population and employment growth, including strong growth in Professional and Business Services with related impact on office demand, makes for a strong market. This, of course, is not one of the nation's major high-rent Class A* markets nor is it a top choice for Fortune 500 company headquarters, but is dynamic nonetheless. That said, absorption has been running head over heels over new supply as developers have been unable to keep up with demand. Indeed, at 9.1% according to Reis, vacancy as of third quarter, down fully 430 basis points from a year earlier, had become sufficiently low as to suggest inadequate supply. Consider: the 546,000 square feet projected to deliver in 2006 all told (only 230,000 of which had arrived on line by the close of third quarter) amount to less than half of the 1.25 million square feet of projected net absorption (most of which had been achieved as of quarter-end). This huge excess of demand over new supply, moreover, has ruled this market since 2004: net absorption and construction completion totals over the two-year span 2004-2005 are calculated, respectively, at 2.16 million and 767,000 square

---

Class A Buildings are always the highest-quality space in a given market. Finishes, services and amenities, and systems are top of the line. Rents are above market. *Class B*: Buildings with average services, appearance, image, location, and rents for a given market. *Class C*: Generally older buildings with minimal services, frequently with structural obsolescence, in secondary locations.

feet, with construction consisting, generally speaking, of small- to medium-size projects. Looking ahead, Reis expects demand and new supply to swing into better balance. Net absorption and construction completion totals for the four-year span 2007 through 2010 are forecast at 3.22 million and 3.32 million square feet. Vacancy, accordingly, will stabilize at its present level, more or less; by the end of its five-year forecast period the firm expects to be reporting a rate of 8.8%. Demand, thus, will be challenged continually by shortages of suitable space. Rents flourish. For 2006 Reis is projecting respective increases of 4.4% and 8.0% for the asking and effective averages, which would be the largest single-year increases recorded by this source for this market since 1996. Respective averages for third quarter 2006 are given as $20.61 and $17.75 psf, up 1.7% and 2.7% since mid-year. According to a January 2007 report in Southeast Real Estate Business, however, rents will need to increase "significantly" to keep up with the increases in development costs. In its latest forecast, Reis expects to see yearly gains in the range of 3.5% to 5.0%, roundly stated, through 2010. For investment in office properties, meanwhile, Southeast cites "the most significant sales activity ever experienced in Central Florida...In 2005, transaction volume totaled more than 5.7 million square feet, more than double the previous record set in 2002. In 2006, sales activity reached more than 3.7 million square feet, the second highest yearly total ever posted." Among recent deals reported by this source is America's Capital Partners' $96.25 million ($228.51 psf) acquisition of downtown's Class A Bank of America Tower.

CB Richard Ellis puts fourth quarter metro area vacancy at 7.0%, down 130 basis points over six months. The average asking gross lease rate is given as $20.94 psf, up from $20.52 psf at midyear.

Orlando Retail: Few of the nation's cities can provide ground as fertile for retailing and retail real estate development than Orlando, with its extraordinary population growth and robust residential development profile. "Retail development booms across Orlando," proclaims the headline of a January 2007 report in The Orlando Sentinel. Indeed, according to a recent report by International Council of Shopping Centers (ICSC) cited by this source, Orlando has become Florida's leading market for investment in retail development. Reis, reporting on the community and neighborhood center market, projects a 2006 construction completion total of 700,000 square feet (about half of which had finished by the close of third quarter), most in a single year since 1992. Net absorption, meanwhile, will fall a little short in 2006, taking 524,000 square feet, 220,000 of which have been achieved year-to-date. It would, however, be incorrect to infer weakness in the community-neighborhood center market from this instance of supply overhang. Net absorption enjoyed substantial margins over same-year supply over the preceding three years. After new supply retains the advantage in 2007, construction completion and net absorption totals should proceed in rough tandem over the 2008 to 2010 period. Vacancy, meanwhile, is low. The rate for third quarter is reckoned at 5.1%, down 10 basis points since mid-year, up 30 year-over-year. Little change is expected for year-end, and while a small rise will place the rate close to, but not above, the 6.0% mark in 2007, this will be followed by flat vacancy through the remainder of the firm's five-year term of forecast. Occupancy, accordingly, will not suffer from the projected small excesses of new supply over same-term demand. Nor will rent growth. The increases of 4.9% and 4.5% projected for the asking and effective averages for 2006 will be followed by per annum increases in the range of 3.5% to 4.5%, roundly speaking, through 2010. Respective averages for third quarter were $18.11 and $16.34 psf. For the larger, more inclusive market that it covers, CB Richard Ellis's mid-year report (its latest) cited 2.1 million square feet of construction underway metro-wide. Reis, meanwhile, reports 1.2 million underway in regional-scale projects, all in the Winter Park at Fowler Groves regional mall in northwest suburban Fowler Groves, due on line in 2007; 414,700 square feet in power centers; and more than 3.4 million square feet under construction in mixed-use developments. In south suburban Kissimmee, Loop West, a 400,000 square feet-square-foot power center, is under construction for 2007 delivery. In addition, planning is complete for SoDo (South of Downtown), a $100 million, 700,000-square-foot mixed-use project from Kimco Developers and North American Properties intended for a site on S. Orange Avenue in Orlando.

In its most recent report, CB Richard Ellis reported second quarter retail vacancy at 6.5%, down from 7.9% a quarter earlier. Rates by property type were 9.1% for neighborhood centers, 8.5% for community centers, 2.1% for power centers, and 3.0% for specialty centers. The weighted average lease rate was given as $16.00 psf with a high-end rate of $40.00 psf.

The following snapshots of the San Jose, California market (Used with permission from Reis, Inc. and reis.com,) provide contrast to the Orlando market and illustrate the amount of regional diversity that can exist within the national market. See also Tables 4.1 and 4.2.

San Jose Apartment: Strange to behold. While apartment vacancy during the recent period of local economic collapse never rose higher than 6.0%, the market nonetheless fell into a period of severe turmoil in the grip of huge rental losses and steep landlord concessions. It was but the other side of the coin that had visited unprecedented rental growth upon San Jose apartments in 2000. And while vacancy has remained at ostensibly favorable levels, vacancy before the economic bust was nearly nonexistent. Landlords, apparently, were having their rugs pulled from beneath them by the precipitous vacancy increase, the almost immediate population out-migration, and competition from new units coming on line, including new condo units. With the economy now on the mend and developers adding only small volumes of new apartment inventory, the market has settled into recovery. Reis reports third quarter vacancy at 3.7%, down 40 basis points from a quarter earlier, down 70 year over year. Little change is expected for the next several years as net absorption maintains small same-year margins over the modest volumes of new construction expected to deliver. Thus, only 631 new apartments will arrive on line this year, the smallest single-year total recorded by this source for this market since 1996. The most recent significant

**TABLE 4.1   Orlando Vacancy and Rents,
Q3 2006 vs. Q3 2005**

Vacancy

Sector	3Q06	3Q05	Chg
Office	9.1%	13.4%	−430 bps
Multifamily	4.7%	5.0%	−30 bps
Retail	5.1%	4.8%	30 bps
Industrial	9.7%	10.2%	−50 bps

Rents

Sector	3Q06	3Q05	Chg
Office	$20.61 pef	$19.59 pef	5.2%
Multifamily	$863 month	$808 month	6.8%
Retail	$18.11 pef	$16.99 pef	6.6%
Industrial	$4.83 pef	$4.73 pef	2.1%

Source: Reis Observer, Reis, Inc.

**TABLE 4.2   San Jose Vacancy and Rents,
Q3 2006 vs. Q3 2005**

Vacancy

Sector	3Q06	3Q05	Chg
Office	15.7%	19.0%	−330 bps
Multifamily	3.7%	4.3%	−60 bps
Retail	2.8%	3.7%	90 bps
Industrial	15.7%	16.4%	−70 bps

Rents

Sector	3Q06	3Q05	Chg
Office	$26.15 pef	$25.00 pef	4.6%
Multifamily	$1.395 month	$1.294 month	7.8%
Retail	$30.12 pef	$28.40 pef	6.1%
Industrial	$6.67 pef	$6.43 pef	3.7%

Source: Reis Observer, Reis, Inc.

completion according to Reis was the 289-unit second phase of The Redwoods at North Park in northeast San Jose. A November date of delivery was cited in the firm's third quarter report.

While the trend now is slowing, condo conversion activity also has helped with the tightening of the market. Reis counted nearly 1,000 units making the switch last year; none, however, have converted year-to-date in 2006. Rent growth also has returned. Huge losses over the period 2001 through 2004 were followed by gains of 3.2% asking and 3.8% effective in 2005. With confidence regained, landlords are expected to impose respective increases in 2006 on the order of 7.6% and 8.2% with per annum gains in the range of 3.0% to 5.0% expected, roundly speaking, thereafter through 2010. That said, even this series of impressive increases will not come close to redeeming the severe losses suffered post-2000. Average asking and effective rates for third quarter are given as $1,395 and $1,325 per month, up 2.6% and 3.0% since mid-year. Helping landlords to some extent are metro San Jose's exceedingly high single-family home prices, the resumption of significant population growth, and the local market's chronic shortage of affordable housing.

Marcus & Millichap forecasts year-end vacancy at 3.1%, down 150 basis points for the year. An 8.5% increase in the average asking rent, to $1,445 per month, is expected. Effective rents will show a 10.2% gain, to $1,385.

Note the strong contrast with the Orlando apartment market, with average asking rents of $1,445 in San Jose versus $875 for Orlando and asking rents up 8% in San Jose versus 6.8% in Orlando. Not only are average residential rents higher in California but the rate of rent growth is higher as well. Furthermore, the vacancy rate in California is lower: a projected 3.1% versus a projected 4.6%. Why are San Jose's rents so much higher? Higher costs, starting with per-unit land costs, account for some of the difference. The scarcity of developable sites and the restrictive regulatory climate also restrain development activity. The result drives up rents as consumer demand bids up the price of the limited available supply of housing stock. It should be noted that Orlando rents have held up strongly over the last five years while San Jose rents dropped sharply after the 2001 dot-com stock market bubble burst and the corresponding recession. In spite of higher rents, cap rates (i.e., going-in returns) in California tend to be meaningfully lower than in Florida, with the possible exception of south Florida. Presumably, this means that while rents are higher, costs also are higher.

San Jose Industrial: It will take a long while for the industrial market with its wounded R&D-flex sector to reach favorable rates of vacancy and to redeem the rental losses suffered during the recent period of hardship. But progress clearly is underway. The robust cycle of development that turned the market into a wasteland of oversupply upon the disappearance of demand and the contraction of the user base has yielded to a period of relative inactivity. Including the 301,000 square feet of new multi-tenant non-manufacturing space added to the market in 2005, the three year period then ending delivered only 652,000. With demand, meanwhile, slowly returning to positive ground, the vacancy rate has been edging downward. From its 16.5% year-end 2003 peak, the rate had drifted to 15.7% by the close of 2005. While Reis reports construction activity picking up slightly in 2006, the 650,000 square feet expected to deliver all told this year will be overmatched two-to-one by net absorption, projected at 1.35 million square feet. The vacancy rate, accordingly, will shed 40 additional basis points to close the year at 15.3%. While construction completion volumes will slowly increase, increases in net absorption will allow demand to maintain its lead over new supply. By the end of 2010, then, vacancy is expected to be running at a little above 13.0%. Rent growth mirrors the progress in demand and occupancy. Four years of substantial loss were followed by substantial gains—3.7% asking, 3.8% effective—in 2005. Increases of similar proportion are anticipated for 2006 with slightly larger year-over-year gains expected thereafter. Year-end 2006 asking and effective averages are projected at $6.92 and $6.72 psf. With expansion, albeit subdued, returning to tech employment, signs of improvement have emerged in the R&D real estate sector. According to regionally-based BT Commercial Real Estate, which tracks this large, 154-million square foot market, vacancy, while still high, is moving convincingly downward. At 18.2%, the third quarter rate is down from 19.4% only a quarter earlier (vacancy here peaked above 23.0% in 2003). Construction of this property type, meanwhile, has ceased, according to BT (Grubb & Ellis, however, reports 196,000 square feet of R&D-flex space underway all told in two projects in San Jose). Neither the speculative nor build-to-suit segments, reports BT, have seen any new deliveries since a small spec sum delivered in third quarter 2005. Net absorption exploded during third quarter 2006, meanwhile, growing occupancy by 1.8 million square. This is precisely the kind of demand-over-supply dynamic required if healthy occupancy is to return to the market. Among third quarter transactions contributing was Boston Scientific's 226,000 square foot lease in Baytech Business Park in San Jose, Silicon Graphics' 128,000 square foot deal in Arques Technology Center in Sunnyvale, and a 117,500 square foot sublease by Rackable Systems at 46555 Landings Parkway in Fremont.

Grubb & Ellis reports third quarter overall greater Silicon Valley vacancy at 12.2%, down 30 basis points from a quarter earlier and down 300 since third quarter 2005. Average asking rents by property type are $11.64 psf for R&D-flex, $8.16 for general industrial, and $5.40 for warehouse-distribution, each up notably since mid-year.

Note that industrial rental rates are much closer than apartment rental rates, with San Jose having a warehouse per square foot rate of $5.40, lower than Orlando's $6.40 rate and San Jose's flex-space rate only slightly higher, $11.64 versus Orlando's flex rate of $10.54 per square foot per year.

San Jose Office: Few of the nation's markets can tell a story as woeful as the one told here regarding the collapse of the telecom-dotcom sector early in the decade. From 2.5% at year-end 2000, the vacancy rate leapt to 16.8% only a year later—on its way to the 21%-plus rates that tyrannized the market for several years thereafter. Rents, meanwhile, suffered cataclysmic losses. Now the story is one of recovery. First came the requisite halt to construction. Only 17,000 square feet will arrive on line this year (all during fourth quarter), a negligible addition preceded by only 80,000 square feet all told over the preceding two years. Net absorption for 2006, meanwhile, is forecast at 1.3 million square feet, most of which had been accomplished by quarter-end. Indeed, with absorption running positive in substantial volume since 2004, the vacancy rate has enjoyed consistent downward movement. By the close of the latest quarter the rate had fallen to 15.7%, down 10 basis points since mid-year, down 330 since third quarter 2005. If possible, the recent history of San Jose office rents is even more dramatic. Two years of per annum losses greater than 20% (and near 30% for effective rents) kicked off a five-year decline that left prices at less than half what they were in 2000. Only in late 2005 did small, quarterly increases reappear. For 2006, though, Reis is expecting substantial gains. While the redemption of all preceding losses seems impossible for the foreseeable future (and for a while beyond as well), asking and effective averages are expected to show increases of 5.1% and 8.2% all told this year. With effective rates maintaining the lead, yearly growth rates in the range of 3.0% to 5.0%, roundly speaking, are anticipated for the remainder of the firm's five-year forecast period. As improbable as it may have seemed during the recent period of crisis, a new construction cycle places substantial volumes of new space on the horizon. Beginning with more than 900,000 square feet next year, Reis expects nearly 3.7 million of additional new product to deliver by the end of 2010. Demand, however, will rule. Including the 1.7 million square feet projected for 2007, net absorption for the period 2008 through 2010 will run to nearly 6.3 million square feet. The downward movement in vacancy, accordingly, will continue. Reis's latest analysis calls for a rate of 9.3% by the close of 2010. CB Richard Ellis reports no major projects expected to break ground over the next several quarters. Grubb & Ellis Company, on the other hand, reports 1.8 million square feet presently underway metrowide, virtually all of it in the seven-building Moffett Towers project in suburban Sunnyvale, due to deliver by the end of 2007.

"The pieces are becoming aligned for landlords to further reduce concessions and ratchet up rents," states Grubb & Ellis. The firm reports third quarter Class A and B asking averages of $32.64 and $25.92 psf full-service gross. Quarter-end vacancy is given as 11.1%, down from 12.6% a year earlier.

While San Jose's office rents are as much as 50% higher than Orlando's, San Jose's vacancy rate at 11.1% is more than 50% higher than Orlando's 7% vacancy rate. While office space is obviously more economical in Orlando than San Jose, it is difficult to make a direct comparison because the markets appeal to such different commercial demographics, as firms chose to be based in California to be near concentrations of certain technological and human capital.

San Jose Retail: Retail has been an oasis of stability and good health. Neither the prodigious employment losses nor the outright losses in population through net out-migration were able to inflict harm upon this resilient sector. Persistent consumer confidence and high household incomes clearly have been positive factors. But so, too, has been the county's characteristically low development profile. The market was well-positioned to manage the recent economic troubles, because, for one thing, it is notoriously difficult to build here. Thus, despite occasional bouts of quarterly negative net absorption (and a negligible positive total recorded for all of 2005), vacancy has remained exceedingly low. With demand now improving and construction activity remaining minimal, the rate has fallen even farther. Reis reports third quarter 2006 community and neighborhood center sector vacancy at 2.8%, down from 3.2% at the end of 2005. Rates in the neighborhood of 3.0% are expected to prevail through 2010. On the supply side, meanwhile, only 152,000 square feet are expected to complete construction this year, all during fourth quarter in a single project, the Hacienda Gardens Shopping Center community center in San Jose, to which Reis assigns an October completion date. Indeed, large projects are few and far between here. Among the few in planning stages are the 900,000 square foot Forum at Sunnyvale planned for Sunnyvale and the 600,000 square foot second phase of Westfield Shoppingtown Valley Fair proposed for Santa Clara. With the retail sector running at virtual full occupancy amid all the surrounding travail, landlords have not evinced great concern. Apart from a small loss in the average effective rent in 2002, which was redeemed promptly in 2003, rent growth has proceeded at favorable rates. Average asking and effective rates for community and neighborhood space each increased 4.4% in 2005; respective gains of 5.0% and 4.2% are forecast for 2006 with yearly increases in the range of 4.0% to 4.5%, in round figures, expected for the remainder of Reis's five-year forecast period. Prices, moreover, are very high by U.S. retail market norms. Third quarter asking and effective averages are reported at $30.12 and $27.62 psf, up 1.5% and 1.1% since midyear.

Reporting earlier in the year, Marcus & Millichap projected a 10-basis-point decline in vacancy, to 3.7%, 2006 all told. With "vacancy low, rents [are] set to rise," stated this source in its 2006 outlook report. A 3.8%, increase, to $30.09 psf, was forecast for the average asking price while the average effective rate was projected to grow 3.7% to $27.72.

Once again, San Jose's retail rents are significantly higher than Orlando's, though Orlando has had a significant increase in higher-end retail in the last five years.

For a look at Reis, Inc.'s Orlando and San Jose market reports from five years ago, see Exhibit A-5 in Appendix A.

We have briefly looked at the amount of variation that occurs in rents, vacancy, and rent-growth rates that occur on the national level; it is important to understand, further, that a similar amount of variation can occur even within a given metro market. Even with a given submarket and subtype, the variation between the high and low rents can be substantial. Factors such as age, design, trends, and microlocation all play major roles.

Most market reports follow a standard format—an overview of the local economy with a focus on nonfarm employment trends and population growth. This makes sense: People and jobs create the economic activity that development requires. Frequently, the rate of household formation is also reviewed, particularly in the retail and residential market reports. After giving an overview of the local economy, the typical market report then looks specifically at factors impacting the specified sector, including occupancy, completion and absorption rates, and rent rates and rental-growth rates, often tracking the various factors over a 5- to 10-year time frame via a graph or chart.

Chapter 5 discusses site analysis and selection in greater detail, and Chapter 6 deals with the project pro forma.

LAND ACQUISITION:
OPTIONING THE LAND, SECURING CONTROL

After initial investigations indicate that there is a reasonable probability of success for the proposed project on a given site, several important steps must be taken. The land on which to construct the project must be secured, regulatory approvals must be obtained, and capital commitments for both the equity and debt portions of the financing must be received.

Most developers prefer to gain control of the land via an option to purchase the land. An option on the land is the right, for a limited period of time, to purchase the land at an agreed-upon price and terms. This option minimizes the loss of capital if for any reason construction does not go forward. More than one project has been stymied because of a last minute building moratorium, interest rate hike, construction cost jump, or other market change.

Options may be structured in as many ways as a creative developer or his lawyer can devise, but frequently there is an up-front monetary payment and additional monthly payments. These may or may not be applied to the purchase of the land. Often a landowner will give a reputable developer a free, 45- to 90-day "look see"; that is, the developer puts up soft capital (refundable) to show good faith and that he is serious (not just window shopping), and in return the landowner agrees to take the property off the market. During this period, a cautious developer will do a quick title search to ensure that the purported landowner has a good, marketable title with no undisclosed defects or quiet partners who might surface at the last moment with additional complications.

Conversations should be conducted with the appropriate planning officials to discuss the viability of the proposed project from a regulatory point of view.

The option should include full rights to go onto the property, conduct studies (environmental audits, etc.), do tests (soil borings, etc.), and generally do all the tasks and obtain all the permits necessary for development. The option should clearly state that the developer has the right to apply in the owner's name for all permits and necessary regulatory approvals, including zoning changes if needed. It is cumbersome to have to go back to the landowner and obtain her signature to initiate the various permitting processes. Some jurisdictions even require a specific power of attorney for anyone other than the landowner to sign documents regarding the land.

To protect the landowner, the option should state with some degree of specificity the intended land use. For example, a project may fail to proceed late in the game, and a surprised landowner may suddenly find herself with land zoned for single-family residences that was formerly zoned for retail. Too much specificity can be counterproductive. Concepts evolve; a project that was originally intended to be all offices may come to include a retail component, and a condominium project may work out better, from a cost perspective, than a multifamily project.

In hot markets or for a top-grade site, a landowner may adopt a take-it-or-leave-it approach and insist on immediate purchase. In that case, the initiative and advantage lies with the developer who has access to ready capital and whose local market knowledge makes him comfortable in taking the plunge prior to full vesting of all development rights.

Sometimes a landowner is willing to contribute her land in return for an interest in the development or provide a long-term lease. Such a lease would have to convey full development rights, automatically be subordinate to any financing, and typically be for a minimum term of 30 years; 99-year leases are not uncommon.

REGULATORY APPROVALS: LAND USE AND ZONING

Local governmental regulations covering the allowable uses of a development fall into two broad categories: land use and zoning. Land use is the highest category, including broad headings such as residential, agricultural, retail, industrial, institutional, office, and mixed use. Zoning is an exercise of police power by a municipality or county to regulate and control the character and use of property, that is, a set of laws, codes, and rules that determine what kind of building or development can be built in certain areas. Zoning implements the land-use category and is more detailed. For instance, a parcel of land with a residential land use may have multifamily zoning specifying 8 to 12 units per acre. Zoning is easier to change than the underlying land use.

Each zoning district typically regulates the following:

- Permitted use
- Size (bulk) of the building permitted in relation to the size of the lot
- Required open space for residential uses on the lot or the maximum amount of building coverage allowed on the lot
- Number of dwelling units permitted on the lot
- Distance between the building and the street
- Distance between the building and the lot line
- Amount of parking required
- Size and placement of signs

The purpose of zoning is to protect property values by separating and regulating incompatible land uses. The nation's first zoning laws were implemented in New York City in 1916 in response to the rapid development occurring in lower Manhattan, including the 42-story Equitable Building built in 1914 on lower Broadway. The use of steel beam construction had removed the common constraints on building heights imposed by previous methods of construction. The shadow cast by the Equitable Building's structure deprived neighboring areas of light, and merchants on fashionable Fifth Avenue were concerned about the intrusion of loft warehouses and factories.

Revolutionary for their time, New York City's first zoning regulations basically separated what were perceived as incompatible uses, such as factories and residential areas, and set up height restrictions and setback requirements. New York City was portioned into three basic zoning districts—residential, commercial, and manufacturing—that remain in force today. The three top-level categories are further subdivided by intensity of use into retail or manufacturing categories, and parking, building bulk, or residential density. Public parks are exempt from zoning laws. The regulations became a template for other cities' ordinances, as the concept of zoning spread across the nation. In 1926, the United States Supreme Court upheld the concept of zoning against a due-process challenge in *Village of Euclid v. Ambler Realty*, 272 U.S. 365, 389–90 (1926).

Houston, the fourth largest city in the United States, is famous for not having zoning. Indeed, in November 1993, voting for the third time in a half century (the previous votes were in 1948 and 1962) on the issue, Houston voters narrowly rejected a referendum to establish zoning. All property owners must comply with land use regulations, which primarily deal with life, health, and safety issues, and extensive "private zoning" exists in the form of deed restrictions binding homeowners in a given development.

Zoning has been criticized as exclusionary, designed to keep out "undesirables," a tool wielded by the "haves" to keep out various racial subsets or economic classes deemed unfit by those in power. Another criticism of zoning is that it is fundamentally unfair, because it grants special status to one group (property owners with property with existing uses) over another group (property owners of undeveloped or underdeveloped real estate). Both of these criticisms are embodied in the concept of NIMBYism (Not In My Back Yard) and its even more extreme relative, BANANA (Build Absolutely Nothing Anywhere Near Anything). Another variant of the criticism of zoning is that it favors the politically well connected who know how the system works over outsiders and political neophytes. One of the more interesting criticisms of zoning is that it has eliminated many vibrant multiuse communities and institutionalized the need for an automobile; that is, in most cases it is no longer possible to walk or bike from one's residence to engage in the necessary daily rituals of commerce such as grocery shopping or dining. Nevertheless, zoning is a reality of the development process and here to stay.

If a parcel lacks the proper land use designation and/or zoning, an assessment must be made of the likelihood of obtaining the desired change. This process has increased geometrically in complexity in the last decade or two, and the required commitment of time, energy, and capital can be substantial. At the same time, the increase in value also can be substantial. Because of the long-term commitment required, when the highest and best use of the land is clear, it is frequently the property owner who goes through the rezoning process before bringing the land to market. When it is uncertain as to what the most profitable use of the land will be, a landowner may wait for a developer to come along with a vision for the land. Because of the complexity and large number of meetings to attend, most developers will not attempt a rezoning unless they already have a substantial presence in the vicinity; that is, the logistics favor the local developer over the out-of-town developer. Many zoning rights are vested to the property owner to one degree or another, and many lawsuits have been successfully filed by landowners characterizing an undesired downzoning as an unlawful taking. Of course, a significant number of such suits have been lost as well, particularly by landowners who sat on their zoning for long periods of time while the regulatory climate become more restrictive.

Sometimes, when the peculiar shape or unusual topography of a lot will cause unnecessary hardship if full compliance with all the applicable zoning regulations is required, a variance may be granted, but only to the extent necessary to allow reasonable use of the real estate in question.

SITE PLAN APPROVAL

Once the proper land use designation and zoning are obtained, the next step is usually to develop a site plan that shows where the buildings and parking will be located on the site. It generally shows how the developer intends to hook into the necessary utilities (water, sewer, electricity); comply with various regulations such as building height, lot-coverage ratios, floor-area ratio, and landscaping; and demonstrate compliance with local transportation plans and water management.

The needed documents generally require several disciplines to prepare—at a minimum, an architect and an engineer. Frequently, a land planner and a landscape architect are needed as well. In theory, the granting of a site plan is based strictly on compliance with applicable zoning rules and regulations and should be pretty much a matter of fact. As a practical matter, many elements of judgment and interpretation are often encountered. In some jurisdictions, site plan approval is done by governmental staff, who generally do not hold public hearings; in other jurisdictions, there is a plan board consisting of appointed citizens, a public hearing, and a related input process

Once the site plan is completed, usually only minor changes (e.g., moving a building up to a maximum 10 feet or a 5% increase in square footage) are permitted without reentering the entire process. Although zoning and land use are typically permanent unless changed via legislative act, the period of time a site plan remains valid varies with the jurisdiction. Some site plans expire after just a year. Extensions may be requested and are usually granted, but they are not a matter of right.

As a practical matter, if it seems that a developer needs more time to bring to fruition other parts of the project, it is possible to slow down the approval process near the 80% to 90% completion point, secure in the knowledge that there is high probability that a burst of effort should be able to secure the needed approvals in a matter of weeks. A developer endeavors to hire professionals who not only have excellent technical skills but who also have developed good relationships and reputations with local officials and governmental staff, so as to be able to give good informal readings on the probability of success of various possible alternatives. Included in these informal readings should be a heads up if the political or regulatory winds are about to shift.

PLANNED DEVELOPMENTS

Planned developments (PDs) are hybrids of the site planning and rezoning process. Many jurisdictions favor PDs because a straight rezoning enables a relatively wide variety of potential subuses within a category. With a PD you know exactly what you are getting when you rezone, because you essentially do the site plan at the same time as the rezoning. In effect, you are rezoning to a specific site plan. Moreover, because—unlike site planning—rezoning is not a matter of right, the granting of a rezone in conjunction with a PD confers upon the permitting body a fair amount of negotiating power.

Many developers are ambivalent about the PD process. Yet PDs are often able to get permission for a rezoning that would not otherwise be obtainable. On the other hand, it is a much longer, more expensive, and drawn-out process. Furthermore, because a PD is a zoning ordinance, changes can be made only by returning to the legislative body (usually the city or county commission) and asking for a change to the ordinance, which is a difficult and time-consuming process. As a development or construction project unfolds, it is not unusual to discover opportunities to improve the project or save capital that were not readily apparent earlier. The PD process makes it more difficult to implement any desired modification.

Some of the better PD ordinances have language that delegates to staff the right to make minor changes "consistent with the PD," but this is by no means universal. Astute developers can ask for alternatives to be preauthorized for their PD, certain aspects to be made optional, or for staff to be preauthorized to make a certain level of minor changes.

BUILDING PERMIT

The length of time necessary to obtain a building permit is a critical factor in project development. It may take weeks or months between the initial submission of completed plans and the receipt of approval to commence construction. Often a site-clearing permit or even a foundation permit can be obtained in advance of the full permit, allowing substantial progress to be made and helping a fast track project stay on time.

DEBT CAPITAL

For an experienced developer with a proven track record of successful building, in a strong market, with a good site, and equity capital equal to at least 20% of cost, debt capital is generally relatively easy to obtain. Indeed, there are usually many sources of construction financing for strong developers. As the adage goes, banks are in the business of lending capital to people who do not need it.

A developer will find it essential to develop a general familiarity with the financial markets that have the capability to fund such projects. In addition, a developer must develop access to key people within those markets (such as bank loan officers and mortgage brokers). One or more possible sources of funding for the project should be located early on, either by sending out preliminary project packages or by phone calls to lenders with whom the developer has an established relationship. Potential lenders may respond with a *term sheet*, a nonbinding, highly-qualified letter stating the dollar amount and the terms under which they could lend on the project as presented.

Typically, a bank will charge an up-front fee ranging from a half point to a full point (a point being 1% of the amount lent) for an interest-only variable-rate construction loan that will run for one to two years. Often a bank will issue what is called a *mini-perm* (short for mini-permanent)—that is, a two-year interest-only construction loan, followed by a three-year term, 25-year amortization loan. (The payments of principal and interest are structured so as to pay the loan off over 25 years, but the entire outstanding principal balance is due at the end of three years: The amortization is for 25 years, but the term is for three years.)

Typically, the project will have to have stabilized (met its projected income and expense budget) before the bank will roll the loan over from the construction loan to the mini-perm loan. Because much of the risk has been eliminated, the mini-perm will often offer the investor-owner a lower interest rate, usually a choice of a longer-term variable rate (yearly instead of monthly) or a fixed rate. Often, an additional fee is due at the rollover point, which is a major motivation of the bank to keep the loan on its books.

If the developer so desires, banks will often make a *par loan*— that is, no points are charged up front. However, there is no free lunch: The interest rate will be slightly higher to make up for the loss of the up-front fee. A classic case of "pay me now or pay me later."

Construction loans are made by a commercial real estate loan department and are generally portfolio loans. Such loans, unlike many other loans, are retained on the bank's books, and the bank can bundle and resell portfolio loans in packages and thus obtain new funds to relend. Because banks obtain much of their funds through short-term deposits, it makes sense that they shy away from long-term loans. A bank will generally make a longer-term loan only when it thinks it can resell the loan through its capital markets department. When a bank resells a loan, it typically makes capital on the up-front fees charged the borrower and on a spread between the interest rate at which the loan was made and the rate at which it is sold.

Because the market can change rapidly, the sooner a bank can resell a loan, the less risk it runs that interest rates will fall during the bank's holding period and that the bank will have to suffer a loss on the sale or hold the loan to maturity or until interest rates rise. Of course, if rates rise between the time the bank makes the loan and the time it sells the loan, the bank will make money. Typically, banks will attempt to alleviate the risk of interest rate change by buying interest rate swaps (a simple explanation is swapping—for a fee—a floating rate for a fixed rate).

The 360-Day Year

How many days in a year? Most people would say 365 days, with a 366-day leap year every four years. Ask a banker, and she most likely will tell you 360 days. Why? Because that way the bank can earn more money. Buried in most notes is a provision that interest is supposed to be calculated as if there are 360 days in a year but paid every day for 365 days. Do the math. Most people would assume that if you borrowed $10,000,000 for exactly one year at 10%, you would pay $1,000,000. However, under the 360-day rule you would calculate that $1,000,000 in interest per year at $2,777.78 per day if there were only 360 days in a year: $1,000,000 ÷ 360 = $2,777.78 per day. And when you pay $2,777.78 per day for 365 days, you end up paying $1,013,888.89 in interest, or an extra $13,900. Make enough loans and it starts to add up.

EQUITY

An investor provides the equity capital necessary for actual construction. The developer usually provides the seed equity necessary to get to the point of construction. Investors can be individuals of high net worth, insurance companies, pension plans, investment banks, or REITs. A developer may have an established working relationship with an investor or group of investors. A track record of successes tends to attract a following, and a successful developer may accumulate the funds to make a significant investment in his own projects.

Developers have a reputation for being fond of financial leverage and having a bit of a cavalier attitude toward debt. One wit is reported to have said that an individual developer's definition of equity is "debt that he has not personally guaranteed" and a corporate developer's definition of equity is "debt that comes due after the project bonus check has been cashed."

DESIGN

During the conception stage of the original idea, the project's form and substance may have been somewhat fuzzy and indistinct, and perhaps it actually consisted of a range of alternative proposals. During the feasibility stage, the project outline begins to take on a more definite shape. By the time the design stage is reached, the project, by necessity, has arrived at clear-cut fruition. The developer confers with the designers, usually a professional land engineer and an architect, and describes all the functions the project is supposed to perform as well as its budget limitations and general appearance. The designer translates those thoughts into design concepts and then into plans, specifications, and contract documents. These design services are typically provided by professionals under contract and can account for as much as 6% to 10% of the total project cost for a complex design or as little as 1% to 2% for an apartment community without complicating factors. Architectural fees also can vary greatly, depending on the amount of design responsibility assumed (and attendant liability) and how actively the architect is asked to participate in the construction-management process.

DESIGN-BUILD AND CONSTRUCTION

A developer may choose the desired builder early in the process and have that builder work closely with the architect in designing the project, providing on-going feedback on best construction methods and materials. This is known as design-build.

After the design is completed, the financing committed, the land secured, the permits obtained, and decisions reached on any other consequential details, the contract is awarded for construction of the project. The construction contract may be of any variety of standard forms or a progressive modification thereof. The construction contract may be awarded as a result of competitive bidding or ne-gotiations or both, as discussed in later chapters. The construction period may consume several months to several years, depending on the size and complexity of the project.

During the construction period, the investor must be extremely vigilant. Cash outflows are large and continuous, and regular visits to the project to monitor progress and inspect for quality are essential. The monthly draws (incremental dispersals of the construction loan funds) must undergo careful analysis to prevent overdrawing by subcontractors or the general contractor. Although the contractor may have contracted to build for a fixed price, usually the developer is personally liable for the construction loan, and the lender will look only to the developer for repayment if anything goes amiss. Even a fixed price contract may have various exceptions, exemptions, and allowances that could leave the investor liable for additional contributions of capital.

In addition, if completion is late, interest charges to cover the construction loan still continue. And even a contract with a firm completion date and liquidated damages will contain an exception clause for acts of God, weather delays, and other circumstances beyond the control of the contractor.

SUMMARY

Development is a complex process requiring organization and knowledge of many aspects of the real estate development industry. Checklists and project plans that include timetables will assist in achieving the requisite level of organization and efficiency. Before actual construction can begin, a developer must determine (a) what type of property he plans to develop and (b) in which market area should such development be sought. At the minimum, the developer must research vacancy, rental-growth rates, and competing projects for the proposed development to determine if there is a development opportunity in that market. Professional market reports can easily be purchased for the top 50 to 60 markets in the United States. Once a desirable market area and property type is identified, a developer must start assembling an external team that includes architects, engineers, contractors, attorneys, surveyors, and land planners. At the same time, the developer should have enough seed capital to initiate the development project. The developer's seed capital is used in the beginning of the project to pay for the necessary items used to determine project feasibility as well as to finance initial costs to launch the project.

Developers favor using an option contract to secure control of the land while they evaluate their development plans. There are numerous ways to structure an option contract, provided the requirements of both developer and landowner can be met. Use of an option contract minimizes the loss of capital should the project fail to launch.

Land use and zoning are critical issues that may constrain what can be built on a particular site. A developer must be acquainted with the appropriate regulating agencies and their particular processes for getting a land use or zoning change.

Once a developer has selected a market and identified a site to develop, the development team works to develop a site plan. The site plan depicts placement of buildings and parking on the site, how the improvements connect to utilities, and how the project expects to comply with various governmental regulations, and it must be approved by the local regulatory body. Typically, only minor changes are permitted to the site plan without restarting the whole process. For a planned development (PD), the rezoning and the site plan are usually completed simultaneously. Some developers find the PD process best for obtaining desired rezoning while other developers may have concerns if they think the process could be expensive and time consuming.

The developer's knowledge of financial markets is essential. He must be aware of the sources capable of funding the type of project being worked on. Initially, a lender may issue a "term sheet"—i.e., a nonbinding, highly-qualified letter, stating the dollar amount and terms the lender might offer to finance the proposed project. A common type of loan given by banks to developers is a mini-permanent (or "mini-perm"), which often includes a two-year interest-only construction loan followed by a three-year term, 25-year amortization loan. Due to their short life, construction loans are generally portfolio loans and retained on the issuing bank's books. Along with financing, the developer must secure equity capital to fund the project. Equity capital can come from the developer, individuals of high net worth, insurance companies, pension funds, investment banks, or REITs.

After the land, financing, rezoning, and site plan approvals are secured, the developer works with an architect and an engineer to resolve all design issues and come up with project construction documents. These construction plans can range from 1% to 10% of the total project cost, depending on the complexity of the plan and site conditions.

KEY TERMS AND DEFINITIONS

Builder: General contractor who does the actual construction of the project for the developer.

Developer: An individual or firm that locates and secures control of a parcel of land, obtains necessary approvals, and adds improvements to the land to increase its value.

Equity investor: Individual or firm that provides equity capital necessary to build a project.

Land use: Highest category of governmental regulation concerning allowable uses of a development. Headings include residential, agricultural, retail, industrial, office, and mixed use.

Lender: Individual or firm that provides debt capital necessary to build a project.

Market area: Geographic area in which property lies.

Market report: Report with detailed information about the market area. This report can contain information on demographics, vacancy rates, rental rates, and growth rates, along with other pertinent information.

Option contract: Contract giving the developer the right but not obligation to purchase a piece of property at a specified price within a specified time period.

Project pro forma: Cash flow forecast for a specified project.

Property manager: Individual or firm who handles property management once a project is completed.

Seed capital: Capital needed in the beginning of a project to get the project off the ground.

Site plan: Plan that shows where buildings and parking are to be located on a site.

Term sheet: Nonbinding letter from a lender stating the terms under which the lender could lend on a project.

Zoning: An exercise of police power by a municipality or county to regulate and control the character and use of a specific piece of property. Zoning implements the land-use category and is more detailed than the land-use category.

KEY LEARNING POINTS

- Explain the general process of development.
- Identify the professional consultants who are part of a developer's team.
- Explain how a developer would locate respected professionals to join the team.
- Explain what a developer would research in trying to determine if there is an opportunity for development in a certain area.

- Explain why a developer would use an option contract to secure control of a piece of property.
- Explain the difference between land use and zoning laws.
- Define a site plan.

QUESTIONS

1. Identify some of the professional consultants who will be a part of a developer's external team.
2. Why would a developer require a project to be bonded by a builder?
3. When would a typical investor commit to a project?
4. Why would a developer normally pick a fantastic site in a so-so market over a so-so site in a fantastic market?
5. Why do institutional investors tend to be more comfortable in markets where other institutional players are already present?
6. What research may help a developer determine if a market has the demand for a certain type of project?
7. Why do developers prefer the option contract to a purchase and sale agreement at the initial stage of the development process?
8. What is the reason for having zoning laws? Provide some criticisms of these laws.
9. What is the general purpose of a site plan and who is needed to help put it together?
10. Why would a bank choose to use a 360-day year method for its financing?

5
Market Studies, Site Feasibility Analysis, and Selection

FACTORS AFFECTING SITE DESIRABILITY

The various factors that make one site superior to alternative sites within the same area are all relative to the selected market, be it luxury high end, mid-market, or affordable. They include the following:

- Location
- Adaptability
- Accessibility
- Transportation and commuting time
- Shopping
- Schools and churches
- Recreation

Not all of these factors will always apply to all projects, and for each project their relative importance may vary. However, to guard against forgetting or overlooking an important factor, each factor should always be at least considered. Any nonapplicable factors may then be discarded. A few additional factors may apply to some out-of-the-ordinary sites, such as public improvements and environmental amenities. When considering public improvements, pay particular attention to paving, sewers, and municipal water, gas, and electric lines servicing the property. Environmental amenities include scenic views and proximity to an ocean, a lake, mountains, a desert, or even some human-made point of great interest, such as a historic district or a university. These environmental amenities constitute intangible but real influences within the general framework of location. At the same time, negative influences should also be taken into account, as one serious negative factor can offset several positive features. Consider noise levels, odors, crime and vice activities, and the general reputation of the area. Areas with even one serious negative factor that for any reason appear to be on the decline or on the brink of decline, should be avoided as poor risks. Figure 5-1 is an example of a site evaluation checklist.

CHECKLIST FOR SITE EVALUATION

Site_____ Zoning _____

Date visited_____By_____

Executive Comments/Suggested Development:_____

_____

_____

<u>OWNERSHIP AND DESCRIPTION</u>

Owner_____
(if business entity, include officers)

Address:_____

Phone/Fax/Cell/E-mail: _____

Agent_____

Address:_____

Phone/Fax/Cell/E-mail: _____

Tract address: _____
        (street)   (city)   (county)

Legal description: _____

_____

_____

Deed restrictions/restrictive covenants: _____

Subdivision/Owners Association regulations: _____

FIG. 5-1 Site evaluation checklist.

IMPORTANCE OF LOCATION

After determining the product (for example, apartments) and the market area (what part of what town), the next big task is to pick a site. The time-honored philosophy of real estate is that the three most important criteria for real estate are "location, location, location." The term "location" includes most other factors of importance in selecting a suitable site for a proposed project. When considering alternative sites, a developer should be fully convinced of the suitability of each proposed site. Any sites that do not warrant this conviction should be discarded out of hand.

Easements on land?_____

Area Master Plan/Historic District, etc.?_____

Tract size: dimensions: _____x_____x_____Acres_____

Adjacent landowner(s): _____Zoning _____

Address/Phone/Fax/Cell/E-mail: _____

Adjacent landowner(s): _____Zoning _____

Address/Phone/Fax/Cell/E-mail: _____

Adjacent landowner(s): _____Zoning _____

Address/Phone/Fax/Cell/E-mail: _____

Adjacent landowner(s): _____ Zoning _____

Address/Phone/Fax/Cell/E-mail: _____

LAND USE AND VALUES

Asking price: Per acre_____Total_____Option price_____

Purchase price: _____Date:_____

Debts against tract: _____Held by: _____

Pre-payment/other restrictions: _____

Special assessments: _____

Buildings on tract: _____Sq. Ft:_____

Est. value: _____Conforming land use? _____

Tax assessor's value: _____Tax rate used_____

Value est.: Pending development _____For development _____

Comments:_____

List recent sales of similar tracts:_____

_____

_____

List recent or proposed developments in area; include distance, if proposed, site source:

FIG. 5-1   Continued.

_____

_____

TOTAL LOCATION

Describe frontage road(s): _____

Traffic counts: _____

Nearest four-lane highway: _____

Nearest limited access freeway: _____

Nearest public airport: _____

Major airlines serving: _____

Flights per day: _____

Nearest international airport: _____

Nearest executive/private airport: _____

List all Retail outlets within:

0.25-mile radius: _____

0.5-mile radius: _____

1-mile radius: _____

List major retail stores within:

3-mile radius: _____

5-mile radius: _____

List all office developments within:

1-mile radius: _____

3-mile radius: _____

5-mile radius: _____

List major activity centers (malls, universities, office parks > 250,00 sq. ft.) within: 10 miles:

_____

List neighborhood shopping centers: _____

FIG. 5-1   Continued.

List closest entertainment centers, movie theaters: _____

Nearest childcare: _____

Nearest elementary school: _____

Nearest middle school:_____

Nearest high school:_____

Provide 1-, 3-, & 5-mile radius demographic data: age, sex, income, education level, est. retail sales:

Nearby communities:_____

_____

Describe/evaluate nearby employment centers; include distance in time/miles: _____

_____

Distance from central business district: miles_____Minutes by car: _____

Describe/evaluate local public transportation: _____

Comment on surrounding highways, local streets, including approach to land: _____

_____

Describe and evaluate surrounding development; provide map. If single-family, list prices of homes; if office or multifamily, give rental rates and list as A, B, or C.

_____

_____

HAZARDS, NUISANCES, ENVIRONMENTAL
Environmental audit available? — If so, attach or state how may be obtained. If not, explain why not and list any potential environmental issues, including asbestos, radon, underground tanks, plumes, etc.:_____

_____

Is the tract free from existing or likely:

    Heavy and frequent rail traffic?   Yes   No   _____

    Heavy highway or street traffic? Yes   No   _____

    Airport noise and hazards?   Yes   No   _____

FIG. 5-1   Continued.

High-power electric lines?	Yes	No	_____
Other unusual noise, vibrations?	Yes	No	_____
Unusual crowds, heavy parking?	Yes	No	_____

Is there adequate distance and buffer between the tract and:

Likely sites of fire?	Yes	No	_____
Smoke sources?	Yes	No	_____
Chemical or other odors?	Yes	No	_____
Dust or dirt sources?	Yes	No	_____
Unsightly views?	Yes	No	_____
Areas prone to flooding?	Yes	No	_____
Polluted bodies of water?	Yes	No	_____
Dilapidated structures?	Yes	No	_____

Observations:_____

TOPOGRAPHY

Is the tract characterized by or are there large areas of:

Swamp or marsh?	Yes	No	_____
Steep ravines or grades?	Yes	No	_____
Rock outcroppings?	Yes	No	_____
Soil erosion?	Yes	No	_____
Rocky or sandy soil?	Yes	No	_____
High water table?	Yes	No	_____
Poor surface drainage?	Yes	No	_____

About how much of the tract is:

Hilly? _____%   Rolling?_____%   Level?_____%

What is the average elevation of the land?_____

High point?_____   Low point? _____

FIG. 5-1   Continued.

Heavy cutting needed:

For streets?_____For building site?_____For other purposes?_____

Heavy fill-in needed: For streets? building site?_____swampy areas?_____ other? _____

Is the tract adequately drained?_____Type of soil: _____

Special drainage provisions needed:_____

Trees: Woods Sparse Woods____ Scrub____ Open____

Comments:_____

UTILITIES

Are utilities present or readily available?

Public water supply by:_____Contact person:_____

Address/Phone/Fax/Cell/E-mail: _____

Distance to main_____Size of main_____Private irrigation well possible?_____

Remarks_____

Public sewage by:_____Contact person:_____

Address/Phone/Fax/Cell/E-mail: _____

Distance to main_____Size, invert _____Capacity available?_____

Electric by:_____Contact person:_____

Address/Phone/Fax/Cell/E-mail: _____

Phone by:_____Contact person:_____

Address/Phone/Fax/Cell/E-mail: _____

Cable by:_____Contact person:_____

Address/Phone/Fax/Cell/E-mail: _____

Internet access : _____

Street lighting?_____Storm sewers? _____

LOCAL GOVERNMENTAL JURISDICTION
Governing authority: (county/city, etc.): _____

FIG. 5-1 Continued.

Contact person:_____Address:_____

Phone/Fax/Cell/E-mail: _____

Police protection by: _____Garbage removal by:_____

Fire protection by: _____Nearest station: _____

Impact fees/permit fees:_____

Development climate:_____

COMMUNITY FACILITIES

Churches:_____

Parks: _____

Playgrounds/swimming pools:_____

Lakes, streams, outdoor sports areas: _____

Major sports teams:_____

Golf courses: _____

Performing arts center/ other cultural facilities:_____

Libraries:_____

Other: _____

FIG. 5-1   Continued.

SITE SELECTION

The goal of good site selection is to choose and secure the best available parcel of land for the type of development to be erected. The following discussion on how to select a site uses an apartment project as an example, but with slight modifications the approach is equally applicable to many other types of developments, such as an industrial park, an office building complex, a shopping center, a warehouse, or a motel.

ADAPTABILITY

Although the location may be fantastic—for example, it is 400 yards from an expressway and well sited on a mountainside, with a clear trout stream running through it and overlooking an 18-hole championship golf course with the ocean beyond, it may still be worthless to the developer if it is not developable or in any other way not adaptable to the project. Adaptability includes deed covenants, zoning, and land use laws, as well as natural geography. Researching for adaptability includes examining deed covenants or restrictions. These documents can be found in the abstract of title or in the deed and are recorded at the county clerk's office. If, for example, the land is restricted by deed to the building of single-family homes, then no one can build apartments, even if the zoning is favorable. Covenants against race or religion are no longer valid by court decree, but covenants on minimum areas of dwelling units and maximum heights can be enforced. If these covenants are violated, any property owner in the same subdivision can bring suit in civil court and have the project enjoined and stopped. Zoning laws and building codes also control adaptability; they are found in local and state ordinances. These laws are passed for the benefit of the community as a whole, to prevent potential damage to the value of surrounding properties as the result of spot zoning or incompatible land use.

Otherwise promising developments are frequently prohibited by zoning laws designed to protect the value of existing homes and other property. For example, a desirable piece of land may appear to a developer as an ideal location for a high-rise building, but local ordinances may limit the height or density (number of units to the acre). Or building within a fire zone (usually a high-density downtown zone with special restrictions) may require methods and materials of construction that are prohibitively expensive. Or requirements governing setbacks, side yards, and off-street parking may combine to make a proposed walk-up apartment project unfeasible. The seasoned developer does not purchase land with the optimistic (and usually unfounded) hope that the zoning restriction against the expected use can be changed. The process of zoning change is long and arduous and usually unsuccessful. Even if the zoning can be changed, the time and expense involved often make the effort unreasonable if alternative sites are available.

Finally, the term "geography" embraces both topography and subsoil, both of which are significant influences on construction costs. If a visual inspection of the site discovers swampy or marshy land, steep ravines, rock outcroppings, or poor surface drainage, the site preparation will probably require a significant amount of work and expense before any buildings can be started, thus, in effect, increasing the land acquisition cost for the project. Similarly, if preliminary inspection reveals a high water table or pockets of muck beneath the topsoil, the construction cost will probably be increased. To compensate for the increased construction cost, the seller of the property should be expected to accept a correspondingly lower selling price for the land purchase. Excessive excavation and other site preparation costs should not come as a surprise after financing is arranged. If there is any doubt regarding the cost of dealing with the geography of a site, the land should be placed under an option to purchase until test borings or test pits reveal the true nature of the subsurface condition. Test borings are not expensive, and competent testing laboratories are widely available.

ACCESSIBILITY

An otherwise fine piece of land is worthless if there is no easy way of getting to it, or if access is unreasonably restricted or otherwise inadequate. In most cases, potential renters or buyers look for a place with easy access and like to drive their automobiles right up to the front door. Good locations for residential use should have frontage on a local street, a short distance from an arterial. Of course, it is possible to build successful apartment projects alongside six-lane expressways, providing that proper buffering is installed. Accessibility does not preclude building out in the country, provided that a major highway passes nearby. Most people (except in Manhattan and a few other exceptional places) habitually rely on the automobile as their major mode of transportation, and a site with inadequate access should be avoided. Access through a blighted, run-down area or by way of a stretch of dirt road or a congested thoroughfare greatly diminishes the desirability of a site. Of course, there are exceptions. For instance, if the project is within a short, pleasant walk to work, shopping, or mass transit, it may prove to meet the needs of a significant rental market even without good accessibility for autos. The meaning of "accessibility" will vary somewhat, depending on the particular market selected, and a common sense evaluation is advised.

TRANSPORTATION

Although nearby public transportation (bus, train, subway) running on frequent schedules can be an important means of providing accessibility, both public and private transit are considered in computing commuting time from the apartment to work. Either private or public means of travel may be used, or the two may be joined, but in any case, the resulting time from dwelling to work should not be excessive. Travel time usually is considered to be of greater importance than travel distance, because people generally regard time as the governing factor and do not mind traveling longer distances if it can be done at higher speeds within a reasonable time. There is usually a greater selection of desirable dwelling sites farther away from an employment center. A 10-mile drive on an expressway may actually take less time than a 2-mile ride on a local bus, and there is a much greater selection of desirable sites within a 10-mile radius than within 2 miles. In some areas bicycling is coming into favor, so accessibility to bikeways should also be considered.

Public transportation assumes greater importance in densely-populated urban areas. Even in low-density urban areas, public transportation is helpful to many potential renters and is necessary for some. Because bus routes are flexible and buses can be routed to where potential riders live, a large enough rental project may generate an extension of a bus route to the new development. Of course, the prospect of such extensions cannot be relied on, but may serve to further enhance the value of an already feasible project. An ideal site is located within a short walk of existing bus or commuter train lines on routes as direct as possible between home and work so that people do not have to make transfers on their way to and from the workplace.

COMMUNITY FACILITIES

The availability of community facilities should also be considered. These include shopping, schools, churches, and recreation—parks, playgrounds, and entertainment centers. It is preferable to be within walking distance of such community facilities, but this is not mandatory. With a good transportation network available and easy access by automobile, physical proximity, although desirable, is not essential. Short travel times and low travel costs are the real criteria for determining "closeness" to community facilities of all types.

Reserving the Site

Once a promising site is finally located, the site should be reserved by option so that no one else can buy it while the financing and other preliminaries are being arranged. Standard option agreement forms are available, which provide that the owner of the land gets a sum of capital that binds the owner to selling or leasing the land to the buyer if the buyer so desires, and prevents the owner from selling or otherwise encumbering the land to anyone else. In other words, the buyer pays for and gets, for a specified length of time, an option to buy or lease the land. The price of the option depends on the terms. For instance, if farmland suitable for a proposed development is selling for $20,000 per acre, but the proposed development project would actually support a land cost of up to $100,000 per acre, a farmer may well accept $1,000 per acre for a one-year option to sell his farmland for, say, $80,000 per acre in the event that a viable project can be put together. In this case the real value received by the farmer for the option is the chance to sell the land at a higher than normal land-sale value if the project goes through. The farmer takes a low price for the option in exchange for a chance at a high price for the land sale. On the other hand, if the option were written to purchase the land at a lower price of, say, $25,000 per acre (equal to the current market price as farmland), the farmer would be justified in asking a much higher price for the option because the farmer is relinquishing for one year any opportunities to sell at current rates and does not realize any special benefit from the project. In this case, from the farmer's viewpoint, the break-even price may be the lost interest had the land been sold and the funds invested. If lost interest is calculated at 12% on $20,000 per acre, then the farmer might ask for at least $2,400 per acre for an option for one year.

At the expiration of the option period, if the buyer decides not to exercise the option to buy, the landowner keeps the option capital and the land. If, after obtaining the option, it is found that the project will not work to full satisfaction, the buyer must be prepared to drop the option and lose the cost of purchasing the option. For instance, if sufficient financing is not available at a reasonable rate, or construction costs should suddenly increase, or the market collapses, the buyer must be mentally and financially prepared to forfeit all the option capital. That option capital is considered an unavoidable ordinary expense of carrying on the business of land development.

SUMMARY

Whatever type of property you plan to develop, site selection is a cornerstone of the development process. Remember the old axiom: The three most important criteria for real estate are "location, location, location." But implied in the term "location" are many factors that make a land parcel more or less desirable, including:

- Geographical location with respect to public improvements and environmental amenities
- Adaptability
- Accessibility
- Available transportation options and acceptable commuting times
- Availability of community facilities such as shopping, schools, churches, and recreation

A comprehensive checklist, such as the one included in this chapter, should be used to assess the feasibility of a site for a particular type of development. Factor in negatives such as noise levels, odors, and the presence of crime or vice, which often can outweigh positive site factors. Once a promising site is located, reserve it through an option to buy. That will give you time to finalize your site analysis and line up financing and other preliminaries.

KEY TERMS AND DEFINITIONS

Accessibility: The ease with which one can travel to and from a property.

Adaptability: The ability of a parcel of land to be used for various purposes, which is influenced by zoning, deed covenants, land use laws, and natural geography.

Community facilities: Places such as shopping centers, schools, churches, and recreational facilities that meet the needs of people.

Environmental amenities: Factors influencing the desirability of a site that exist outside of it, such as scenic views, proximity to an ocean, a lake, the mountains, a desert, or a human-made point of interest.

Option to buy (or lease): An agreement that in exchange for a sum of capital or other consideration, a landowner will sell (or lease) the land to a buyer if the buyer chooses to exercise the option by an agreed-to date.

Public improvements: Factors that influence the desirability of a site and are provided by the government, such as paving, sewers, and municipal services such as water, gas, and electricity.

Restrictive covenants (in a deed): Terms in the deed to a property that outline the ways in which a property can or cannot be used, what can be built on the property, and the intensity of development allowed. Sometimes referred to as private zoning.

Setbacks, side yards: Terms usually found in the zoning code that restrict building within a certain distance of the property line.

KEY LEARNING POINTS

- Understand the factors that affect site desirability.
- Be able to conduct a site evaluation and feasibility analysis.
- Know how to reserve a site by placing it under an option to buy.

QUESTIONS

1. You are considering the purchase of a property that has certain restrictive covenants contained in the deed, one of which precludes members of a certain religious faith from living on the property. Should you be concerned with legal liability if members of that faith eventually desire to take up residence on the subject property?

2. You are considering purchasing a property but have some questions about the soil conditions and water table at the site that may add considerable cost to preparing the site for development. This property seems to fit your other acquisition criteria for purchase perfectly, and you don't want to risk losing the acquisition to another buyer. What should you do?

3. Give several examples of "community facilities."

4. Which is generally more important to potential tenants regarding transportation options, physical proximity to their destination or travel time to the destination?

5. What are the factors that make a site more or less desirable for development?

6
Creating the Project Pro Forma

INTRODUCTION

Every development project requires a pro forma. A pro forma is a projected operating statement, that is, a forecast of how the project will perform. Of necessity, it involves assumption piled on top of assumption. Rents, lease-up rates, occupancy rates, operating expenses, and interest rates must all be forecasted. Relatively slight changes in any of these assumptions, particularly when projected for three, five, or ten years, can result in major differences in the bottom line.

Also very difficult to forecast are construction costs. Although a developer who is in the business on a regular basis, or who has built a similar project recently in the area presently under consideration, has a rough idea of what construction costs will be, but until the architectural plans are completed and let out for hard bid, the cost of construction is at best an estimate. Shortages of labor or building materials (lumber, drywall, etc.) or unexpected site or soil conditions can play havoc with even the best-laid plans. Certain types of buildings—mini-warehouses, standard industrial storage facilities, three-story garden apartments at medium density—are relatively easy to estimate. High-rise and multistory mixed-used (office, retail, and residential) buildings are much more complex, with interacting codes creating geometric increases in difficulty.

Many developers form a working relationship with a builder, often called a design-build relationship, whereby the builder is chosen up front without any bidding process because of the developer's confidence in the builder, based on the builder's reputation and past performance. The builder has continuous input during the design phase and is often able to suggest cost savings that would be more difficult to achieve later in the process.

Upon selecting a suitable site, a project pro forma should be created to determine the level of profit, if any, the proposed project will return. A pro forma will include an operating statement forecasting income, expenses, and net operating income (operating profit). It also will include a forecast of the project's total cost, including the cost of land, hard construction costs, and such soft costs as marketing expenses, surveys, architectural and engineering fees, legal fees and financing costs, which covers loan fees, appraisals, and interest during construction and lease up. The pro forma also will include certain assumptions as to the probable loan amount and applicable interest rates, both during construction and for the permanent take-out loan.

A thorough and successful pro forma is important to the investor/developer for two reasons: (1) the pro forma provides assurances that the investor/developer is embarking on a venture with a high probability of success, and (2) the pro forma is needed later as part of a presentation to lenders when applying for financing for the project. The lenders will study the project pro forma to determine the soundness of the project and to be sure that their loan funds will be well secured by a viable and profitable project.

A preliminary pro forma may contain just a single number for project operating costs and a per-square-foot number for construction costs (these numbers can be approximated quite closely by experienced industry veterans, and early in the process they are just professional estimates), but detailed line item numbers backed up by satisfactory documentation will be expected prior to loan closing.

To a certain extent, the numbers in a pro forma are looped: There is a *market capitalization rate*, which a developer can do very little about; a given return on investment must be achieved and X dollars in rent will only carry Y dollars in costs. Costs and rents are juggled, tradeoffs discussed and made. The developer strives to find the location, the materials, the builder, the theme, the marketing plan, the ambiance, the designer, the architect, the project, and the overall team that will allow her to attract the maximum amount of income for an acceptable level of costs. Much professional judgment is involved, much guesswork in deciding what the marketplace will reward; frequently, it is a mixture of sizzle and steak, of form and substance, of marketing plan and hard construction processes that make a given project a success.

Over the long run, a pro forma represents a sort of a self-fulfilling prophecy of the market. The rents must justify the development and construction costs or development will not proceed. If rents are too low, no housing or offices or retail or hotels will be built. If development fails to occur in an area where there is a need (population growth, increasing disposable income, job formation, increasing economic activity), then rents (or occupancy) will rise to the level necessary to justify development costs.

If construction costs, for labor or materials, are too high, development will taper off until either rents rise or costs fall and development delivers the necessary return to motivate investors/developers to move forward. Markets are complex, and many factors affect them; no developer wants to be caught overextended during an "adjustment" phase of the market. There is a real estate saying to the effect that "all real estate eventually makes money, the key is to own it when it does."

At the same time, there is pressure to continue developing even in an uncertain market. Projects may have been on the drawing board for a long time, and certain approvals and permits may expire, as may land options. Furthermore, no one can predict the future, and there is frequently good reason to believe that better times lie ahead in the near future or that a certain project's characteristics are such that it will prosper where others may falter. In addition, developers have spent considerable time and effort forging internal teams that must be either compensated or dismantled. If a smoothly functioning team is laid off, not only does a developer lose the benefit of their services and the resources spent assembling the team, her competition, who many see the economic situation differently, may hire her best people.

The following form the core of a project pro forma:

- Forecasted Operating Statement, showing Income, Expenses, and Net Operating Income
- Forecasted Project Costs, showing Land Costs, Hard Construction Costs, and Soft Costs
- Forecasted Financing: Requested Loan Amount, Required Equity Contribution, Final Project Value

FORECASTED OPERATING STATEMENT SHOWING INCOME, EXPENSES, AND NET OPERATING INCOME

The example shown in Figure 6-1 involves Hidden Lake Apartments, an actual project, but the form of the presentation would be quite similar for any other real estate venture, such as a motel, a strip center, a warehouse, or an office building, provided that certain modifications were made as applicable. This example is particularly interesting in that the 260-unit total community being developed involves the renovation of 39 existing apartment homes simultaneously with the construction of 221 new apartments. A third of the 221 new apartments (74) are three-bedroom/three-bath units, and two-thirds (147) are two-bedroom/two-bath units. The 39 existing units include 5 three-bedroom/two-bath units, 29 two-bedroom/two-bath units, and five one-bedroom units.

It is important to remember that development is a process with a large number of variables and unknowns. This project began with a potential of 300 units, in that it was a parcel of approximately 20 acres, with a base zoning of 10 units to the acre with an additional 5 units per acre allowed if certain bonus points were earned. These bonus points generally dealt with energy conservation issues such as building orientation, internal and external storage for bicycles, ventilation patterns that would encourage turning off the HVAC (heating, ventilation, and air-conditioning) systems during days of mild weather, and extra landscaping, including planting shade trees to reduce the heat sink effect of the parking lot and to shade the buildings. In addition, bonus points could be awarded for providing affordable housing, defined as setting rents for as many as 20% of the units at a level that would not exceed 40% of the income of a family below certain HUD (United States Department of Housing and Urban Development) income levels that defined poverty.

Relatively few zoning categories offered such bonus points, so there was not much history or precedent to guide the developer and the planning professionals. During the regulatory and permitting process, as information was received, processed, analyzed, and responded to, the number of potential units that would constitute the final project seemed to vary continuously. Because every bonus point

KEY INDICATORS		SQ. FT.	TOT. APTS.	TOTAL SQ. FT.	AVG. RENT	PER SQ. FT.	MONTHLY FIGURES	ANNUAL FIGURES	PER UNIT FIGURES
Project Configuration:									
3 Bedroom/3 Bath		1306	74	96,644	1045	.80	77,330	927,960	
2 Bedroom/2 Bath		949	147	139,503	855	.901	125,685	1,508,220	
3 Bedroom/2 Bath		1200	5	6,000	875	.729	4,375	52,500	
2 Bedroom/2 Bath		1000	29	29,000	675	.675	19,575	234,900	
1 Bedroom/1 Bath		800	5	4,000	525	.656	2,625	31,500	
Clubhouse/Office				4,519					
Total Base Rent			260	279,666			229,590	2,755,080	10,596
Other Income							7,418	89,016	
Gross Potential Income (GPI)							237,008	2,844,096	10,939
Vacancy/Collection Loss	7%						(16,591)	(199,087)	
Effective Gross Income (EGI)							220,417	2,645,009	
Operating Expenses	31.9%	of EGI					(70,313)	(843,758)	(3245)
Net Operating Income							50,104	1,801,251	6,928
Debt Service							(110,065)	(1,320,776)	(5,080)
Debt ServiceCoverage Ratio (DCR)	1.39								
Pre-Tax Cash Flow							40,040	480,475	1,848

VALUATION INDICATORS	CAP RATE			TOTAL VALUATION	PER-UNIT VALUE
Value at cap rate of:	8.50%			$21,191,192	81,504
Value at cap rate of:	8.75%			$20,585,729	79,175
Value at cap rate of:	9.00%			$20,013,904	76,976

FIG. 6-1   Forecasted operating statement: Income, expenses, and net operating income for Hidden Lake Apartments.

for which the project qualified had an associated cost, new figures were constantly being inserted into the pro forma to determine the impact on the bottom line. To complicate matters, the bonus points were grouped into several categories, and an additional bonus was given for reaching a certain level in each category.

In the final analysis, the developer chose to pass on the bonus dealing with affordable housing and thus qualified for 13 of the potential 15 units per acre, or a total of 260 units on a 20-acre parcel.

Another interesting facet of this particular project was that it was an urban infill project.

Much apartment development occurs at the edge of urban sprawl, where large tracts of land are available with no assemblage issues and land costs are still relatively low. This parcel was close to the city center, surrounded by existing developments, and had been assembled almost serendipitously by the developer over a seven-year span as adjacent parcels of land had come available. Theoretically, infill apartment projects are preferred by both city planners and environmental-ists because they put housing near major activity centers, sometimes even within walking distance, reduce the number and length of trips requiring the use of an internal combustion engine, and generally consume fewer resources and require less infrastructure than urban sprawl projects.

Although bordered on the west by commercial zoning, much of the surrounding land was of an unusual configuration: low-density multifamily zoning that had been developed as single-family detached housing. During the regulatory and permitting process, these surrounding neighborhoods expressed strong opposition. The land had never been developed and it was still attractively wooded, a nice mini-forest in the middle of an urban setting. In essence, the surrounding homeowners had had the benefit of a private-sector-provided park for lo these many years and they wanted that arrangement to continue indefinitely.

Because the land already possessed the requisite multifamily zoning, eventual approval was virtually certain. However, the opposition grew to eventually include both a lawsuit against the permitting governmental body and an administrative ap-peal. Both lacked merit on their substance. Yet even when lacking a substantive case, our society chooses to grant substantial procedural rights in our legal system that can create significant delays. The lawsuit was eventually thrown out on sum-mary judgment. (A summary judgment is a judgment of the court which says that even if all the facts are as you allege, you still lose as a matter of law, so there is no point in holding a trial.)

Legally overturning the decision of a quasi-legislative body such as a devel-opment review board is difficult; the burden of proof is on the plaintiff, and the standard to be met is high. The judge is not allowed to substitute his judgment for that of the development review board; it is not enough for the judge to disagree with the decision of the board or for the plaintiff to convince the judge that the decision was a bad one or even that it was a wrong decision. The plaintiff may convince the court of the wrongness of the decision and still lose. The burden of proof a plaintiff must carry is to convince the judge that no reasonable person could come to that decision and that competent evidence did not exist in the record to support the decision of the board. It does not matter that contradictory evidence supporting another outcome also exists; the board's job is to weigh and choose among the points of evidence presented. If there were no opposing sides with opposing views, there would be no dispute. The developer is generally well represented by com-petent professionals with excellent credentials who are very careful to make sure that sufficient facts and evidence are presented to the board to support the ruling the developer seeks.

Thus, once a development review board grants approval for a development, it is extremely difficult to overturn its holding. However, in addition to site plan approval from the local city, to proceed with the development also required the approval of the state water management district. The project received a recommen-dation for approval from the district staff and was moving forward promptly until a nearby landowner filed a protest. This resulted in delays and additional hearings and attorneys' fees, but eventually the project was granted preliminary approval.

At this point the protest evolved into an appeal of the approval and a request for an administrative hearing.

The bad news was that by this time the project had been delayed a year or more. The good news was twofold: (1) eventual approval on the merits was virtually certain, and (2) it was at about this time that the lawsuit was finally thrown out. This served to alert the opposition to the weakness of their substantive case and to the benefits of negotiation. Several members of the staff of the state water management district served as mediators, and eventually an agreement was reached whereby the appeal was dropped in return for several concessions by the developer, including moving the building nearest to the closest neighbor to the other edge of the development. The developer was willing to negotiate in order to save three to six months; the neighbors were willing to negotiate because they had come to realize that they would eventually lose on the merits and that although their chief bargaining chip was removal of the delay they were causing, each day that passed devalued their position.

As is so often the case, nothing was agreed to that could not have been agreed to a year earlier; the passage of a year merely served to convince the parties of the need to negotiate. The result was the loss of literally thousands of man-hours on all sides, preparing for and participating in numerous mind-numbing hearings, along with the loss of hundreds of thousands of dollars in opportunity costs, carrying costs, and attorney and other professional fees. The result was a development that was slightly different but not significantly better. This outcome is not unique. As our society becomes ever more litigious, more developments are being actively opposed. The result is increased housing costs as developers pass on their costs to the ultimate consumer.

In retrospect, it is easy to say that more attention should have been paid to neighborhood interaction. The developer was an experienced developer who had a successful track record in securing zoning changes, in part because of his understanding of the political process. To a certain extent, the developer was complacent because the required zoning was already in place and his legal background was such that he knew that everything requested for the development was according to statute. Yet he clearly underestimated the amount of opposition the project would receive and the cost and time involved in overcoming procedural delays during the process of enforcing property rights.

Choosing the Project Configuration

The number and mix of the units should be optimized to obtain the greatest return from the project. Frequently, the number of units is determined by local zoning code, and the developer simply does her best to maximize the total number of units allowed. The "mix" means the types of units that will be built, that is, the relative percentages of four-, three-, two-, and one-bedroom apartments, plus studio or no-bedroom units. The mix can be further varied by the number of bathrooms and the addition of dens, studies, solariums, porches, balconies, and the like. Units may be flats or townhouses; garages, attached or not, may be offered.

The developer of the project in the preceding example decided on this balance after studying the local market, looking at trends in the area, and considering national trends. This ratio must be decided only after careful consideration. It constitutes one of the more important decisions affecting operating management that the developer makes for a project.

Two bedrooms/two bathrooms is the predominant floor plan currently being built because it represents the best mix of construction costs, rents, and market penetration in a developer's estimation. Although one-bedroom units generally represent the highest rent per square foot, they usually cost most per square foot to develop and build. From a construction cost point of view, the cost of the kitchen does not vary much from a one-bedroom to a three-bedroom, but the rent typically more than doubles. Each unit, regardless of size, requires only one HVAC assembly, one water heater, one electric panel, and so forth. Although there may be some increase in costs due to such things as more air-conditioning tonnage or a 40- or 50-gallon hot water heater instead of a 30-gallon heater, the marginal cost increase is less then the marginal rent increase. Bedroom space is some of the most economical space to create, and the average cost of back-to-back bathrooms is less than the cost of a stand-alone bathroom.

Furthermore, although one-bedroom units or studios may yield the highest rents per square foot, they do not yield the highest total rent per unit. Because most sites are constrained by the number of units per acre that the zoning allows and most developers build the maximum number of units allowed per acre, in the absence of other constraints, every one-bedroom or studio unit that is built is built at the cost of a larger unit that could yield greater total rent.

Site Coverage Ratio

Site coverage ratio refers to the percentage of a site that can be covered with impervious surfaces—building, sidewalk, parking lot. Lot coverage may be thought of as that portion of a lot which, when viewed directly from above, is or would be covered by a building or any part of a building or any impervious surface. In nonurban environments, a 50% restriction is not unusual—that is, no more than 50% of the site may be covered; the rest must be "green space." In Central Business Districts, where there may be 100% impervious surface, the same concept may be expressed in terms of "open space", that is, a certain percentage of the land area must be reserved for plazas, fountains, gardens, and the like.

Floor Area Ratio

The floor area ratio is the ratio of the total *building* square footage (as opposed to the *impervious surface* square footage for the site coverage ratio) to the total site square footage. In the case of Hidden Lake, the ratio is about 1 to

1. The three-story buildings cover about one-third of the site. In the case of single-family units, floor area ratios of .25 or .33 to 1 are common, that is, a one-story house may cover a quarter to a third of the lot. In Manhattan, floor area ratios of 25 or 50 to 1 are not unheard of; a 25- to 50-story building that covers the entire lot would yield such ratios.

Furthermore, although there may be floor area ratio (FAR) and site coverage restrictions, the critical restriction generally applied by zoning in the multifamily arena is units per acre, usually with no distinction between one-bedroom apartments and four-bedroom apartments. Obviously, there is a tremendous difference between 200 one-bedroom apartments (200 bedrooms) and 200 four-bedroom apartments (800 bedrooms). So given these facts and that the larger (i.e., more bedrooms) the apartment, the lower the average construction cost per square foot, why doesn't a developer build all units as four-bedroom apartments? The answer is that it would be more difficult, if not impossible, to rent up a community with such a lopsided floor plan mix as opposed to a community with a more varied, market-oriented mix of floor plans.

From a marketing perspective, the more floor plans the better (at least to the point of confusing the customer with too many choices), but too many floor plans increases construction complexity and thus construction costs. Many communities are built with only two to four basic floor plans, with variety sometimes being added with simple-to-construct tack-on dens or screened-in porches. End or corner units with additional windows often add beneficial variety. Frequently, top floor units will have vaulted ceilings or gables as relatively low-cost architectural features.

Similarly, the top floor of a multistory building costs more to construct than a lower floor and therefore must yield a higher rent if each rental unit is to earn a rent comparable to its cost. Top-floor apartments are also more desirable—the view is better, it is quieter, and there is less disturbance from people going by. For these reasons, a unit on a higher floor often commands a higher rent.

As soon as the site has been selected and an option to buy has been established, an architect should be engaged. Of course, an architect cannot work without input from the developer. The architect will need a topographic survey showing the size of the plot, the relative elevations of the land, the location of the street and all pertinent utilities, and so on. But the developer makes the basic decisions on the type of project to build and the amenities it will contain, such as a swimming pool, laundry building, utility building, clubhouse, tennis courts, and so on. The architect also must be told the approximate size of each apartment unit in terms of bedrooms and square feet. This is part of the original decision-making process of the developer. The architect then puts all these parts of the program together and attempts to satisfy the client, the building codes, and other regulatory and site constraints while designing a handsome building.

If the price of the land is fixed (some contracts for land purchase may be denominated in terms of apartments per acre allowed or, in the case of retail/office, square footage permitted), maximizing the number of apartments decreases the proportional cost of land per apartment.

For certain selected markets, however, it may be desirable to disregard density as a goal and purposely cut down on the number of units that can be built. Lower density can lead to larger open spaces and perhaps to a more attractive and more marketable community. The final decision on density depends on the cost of the land, the type of competition in the area, existing zoning regulations, off-street parking requirements, building height restrictions, and side yard and setback rules, as well as which segment of the rental market is being courted. Acceptable density for an urban infill location (20, 30, or 40 apartments per acre or even more) is very different for a suburban location (12 to 16 apartments per acre), and single-family density is typically two to six homes per acre.

Many very attractive high-density urban infill communities are being developed on the heavily populated eastern seaboard, particularly in the metropolitan areas that form the urban swath from Boston to Washington. California, boasting some of the highest residential land costs in the United States, has many higher-density apartment developments. In the South, garden-style apartment developments (three-story walk-ups—no elevator) with a density of 12 to 16 apartments per acre are very popular.

When height exceeds three stories, although land cost per apartment drops, construction costs begin to rise. Building codes become stricter (e.g., most codes mandate that electrical wiring must be in conduit for residential property of more than three stories), elevators must be added, and lower floors must be strengthened to handle the extra weight of additional upper floors. Moreover, parking spaces generally must be found for the cars associated with the additional apartments. Surface parking is often not feasible in areas where land costs justify midrise and high-rise apartments, and parking structures can easily run well north of $10,000 per parking space in construction costs.

However, low-density development (e.g., less than 12 apartments per acre) can also have additional construction costs. Infrastructure costs for such necessities as interior roads, water, sewer, and electric lines can rise rapidly as density drops. Land costs will obviously be higher as well.

Setting Rental Rates

The schedule of rental rates is the next major decision that must be made by a developer. Before any project is begun, a survey of the local market is needed to determine what amenities should be included, what rent per square foot is being charged against those amenities and the raw rentable space, and how the local rental trends compare with regional and national trends. If, for example, all existing apartments in a general location have two bathrooms, then any proposed apartments will either have to provide two bathrooms or must have a reduced rent to remain competitive if they are to have only one bathroom. On the other hand, any additional features that are not provided by the competition will call for a higher rent than that charged by others. If the competition simply offers living space but the proposed project will have a swimming pool and a clubhouse, the projected rent can be higher than that of the competition. Further amenities could well include vaulted ceilings, built-in bookcases, fireplaces, eat-in kitchens, dens, whirlpool tubs, and sauna baths, but it is well to remember that additional mechanical gadgetry demands increased maintenance and that the increased rent may not prove to be worthwhile with these higher maintenance costs.

Another consideration is future replacement of equipment as it wears out, which can prove expensive and troublesome. Amenities do not always pay for themselves. Their inclusion depends entirely on the market for which the project is being built. A good feasibility study or appraisal will include a detailed analysis of the surrounding communities, the amenities offered, the square footage of the apartments, and a rental rate comparison.

In choosing an amenity package, it is important to bear in mind that certain amenities may be added later in the life of project, during a renovation, to revitalize the project if market conditions so require, whereas others must be provided in the beginning or not at all. It is possible, 10 or 20 or 30 years down the road, to upgrade a community by switching from vinyl flooring to ceramic tile, or to enlarge the clubhouse, or add a tennis, volleyball, or basketball court, install ceiling fans, screen in existing porches, add landscaping, upgrade the quality of carpet, add chair rail molding to the dining room or crown molding to the living room, provide a painted accent wall, build a playground, install appliances with higher energy efficiency, or even upgrade kitchen cabinets.

Some upgrades, such as going from 8-foot to 9-foot ceilings or adding a second bathroom, are virtually impossible except during initial construction. Given that the trend over the last few decades has been to ever larger and more luxurious apartments with ever growing amenity packages, an investor/developer who intends to hold the community for the long term will focus on the "now or never" amenities. It should be noted that many developers are "flippers"; that is, they build 'em and they flip (sell) 'em. Much like Wall Street's short-term focus on quarterly earnings results, developers have a strong incentive to focus on the immediate; the result is a tendency to spend "splash cash," to put discretionary capital where it will create the greatest immediate visual marketing impact, not necessarily the most long-term value or quality.

Location within a project may also affect the rent schedule. In an office building, a corner office is more desirable than an interior space; in an apartment, a unit with a better view or in a prestige location will carry a higher dollar value. Thus, balcony units bring more rent than ground-floor units, units with direct pool access are sometimes more valuable, and those overlooking a valley are worth more than those facing a parking lot.

When estimating future costs and income, we have ignored the effects of inflation, assuming either benign inflation rates or that in the case of significant inflation, rents will rise to cover increases in operating expenses. Because apartments tend to have short lease terms, they can react quickly to inflationary pressures. This is not always the case with retail and office spaces, which tend to have longer-term leases that may or may not be indexed to the Consumer Price Index. Generally, inflation favors the property owner by increasing the owner's equity, and this is particularly so if debt has been locked in at a favorable rate. In this case, if a proposed project is feasible with constant, noninflated dollars, then it should be even less risky should inflation occur. Thus, the examples shown in this chapter appear in terms of constant dollars.

Exceptions to using constant dollars will occur. Whenever investors believe that inflation is predictable, they begin investing with that assumption. One of the important by-products of inflation in real estate is the appreciation of property values rather than depreciation as the years pass. If inflation causes real estate prices to rise by 4% per year, then a typical project purchased a year ago for $10,000,000 is now worth $10,400,000. If the project was purchased for a $2,000,000 down payment, then the buyer made a profit on the appreciation of $400,000, or 20% on a $2,000,000 investment. This is in addition to any operating profit that may have occurred.

The next chapter deals again with the project's potential income stream in reviewing the project appraisal. The numbers in Figure 6-1 are drawn from the developer's original pro forma upon which the decision was made to go forward with the project. The rent shown in the developer's original preliminary pro forma and the appraiser's final report differ slightly, as we will see shortly. This is not unusual, partly because of the time gap that often separates the initial decision to proceed and the final appraisal.

Note that the rental rates for the 39 existing units are substantially below those of the new units, both in absolute terms and in rent per square foot. The developer did a market study of communities in the surrounding area that were comparable to the intended development in terms of amenities and unit size. For the new units, that market study was used to select a rent of $1,045 per month, or 80 cents per square foot for the 1,306-square-foot three-bedroom/three-bathroom unit and a rent of $855 per month, or 90.1 cents per square foot, for the two-bedroom, two-bathroom unit. The rent for the existing 39 units was determined on the basis of the existing rent structure with an allowance for the improvements to be made.

Multiplying the monthly rent for each floor plan by the number of units specified for that floor plan yields a monthly base rent total of $229,590, and annualizing that monthly number by multiplying by 12 months yields an annual potential income from a base rent of $2,755,080.

Other Income

The main income stream of an apartment community is the base rents. However, apartment communities also generate other or auxiliary income from sources such as application fees, pet rent or nonrefundable pet deposits, redecoration fees, and retained deposits. Income above standard rents may also be generated by premium locations, such as pool or lake views rather than a parking lot view, or by corner apartments that may be larger or have more windows, or by top floors with better views and no impact noise caused by upstairs neighbors. Extra charges for short-term leases can also constitute extra income.

There are opportunities for obtaining income from still other sources, such as laundry machines, vending machines, or covered parking. It is not necessary for the project to actually own any vending or laundry machines. They can be owned and serviced by another company that pays a royalty or fee to the project. Some communities offer cable, Internet, or even basic phone services, buying at bulk rates and reselling at a slight profit.

In this case, because this market has a strong student component, the "Other Income" number will also include roommate rent for occupancy in excess of the number of bedrooms if students decide to double up in a bedroom. Although at times there are attempts to specify the expected amounts of auxiliary income to be derived from each specific source, it is also very common to see a lump sum number used, as is done here.

The developer has allowed for an additional $7,418 per month, or $89,016 per year, for "Other Income."

Gross Potential Income

The rents from each floor plan and the estimated income from all other auxiliary sources are summed to one number representing the maximum possible income to be received from the project. This number is known as the Gross Potential Income (GPI). In Figure 6-1, the summation of the base rent, $2,755,080, and the Other Income of $89,016 yields a Gross Potential Income of $2,844,096.

Vacancy and Collection Loss

The next item shown in Figure 6-1 after Gross Potential Income is Vacancy and Collection Loss. This is included to account for the fact that the maximum possible gross annual rental income is based on 100% occupancy for an entire year. It would be very nice if 100% occupancy could be achieved, but in all likelihood there will be some vacancies, and at least some income will be lost in turnaround time between the time one resident moves out and the next one moves in. Furthermore, a small percentage of residents will leave without paying a current bill, and there may be some bad checks that cannot be collected.

When the two factors, that is, the vacancy ratio and the bad debts, are added together, 7% is a commonly-used figure for vacancy and collection loss. Obviously, rates vary geographically and over time. Residential markets such as Manhattan and San Francisco are famous for having 1% or 2% vacancy rates; rent control, exceedingly high land costs, and the infamous regulatory hurdles are all factors. Even outside those markets, lending underwriters have occasionally accepted a 5% vacancy and collection loss figure with compelling justification and substantial market documentation. Regional economic conditions can affect rental markets. For instance, Houston, during the oil bust, and Detroit, during the early heydays of the initial Japanese auto import success, both experienced abnormally low occupancy rates as mobile workers picked up and left in search of jobs elsewhere.

The entire rent schedule must be realistic, and the prudent developer is cautious about being too aggressive when setting it. Once the lender accepts the rent schedule submitted by the developer and makes a commitment based on that schedule, the developer will be held to it. That stipulated amount of income will have to be produced before the construction loan can be rolled over into a mini-perm or the project taken out into the lending marketplace in search of permanent financing. If the rents are too high, the apartments will remain empty or be leased slowly and the forecasted income will never be realized without adjustments in the rent schedule or the marketing plan. The developer will perhaps then lose the project, as well as the equity in it. In addition, much more can be lost. The developer who signs personally for any loans will be held responsible for their payment. Therefore, the developer's decision to adopt a rental schedule must be very carefully considered, as it is a most important one. However, there are pros and cons on both sides: Lower rents mean a lower mortgage loan amount, but a lower mortgage loan means that the owner must provide more equity cash.

Traditionally, investors and developers have attempted to minimize their equity investment by maximizing their debt, for several reasons:

- They are capital constrained. This is a polite way of saying that they do not have enough money, that their vision exceeds their means. Many developers frequently push the edge of the envelope, trying to develop the largest projects their resources will allow and then some.
- The higher the leverage, the greater the return on the equity that is invested.
- Debt is generally cheap equity, that is, debt capital costs a lot less than equity capital. Or at least the difference between a 70% loan to value (LTV) rate and an 80% rate is relatively mild. Mezzanine debt (so called because it is the "second floor" of debt) generally goes up to a 90% LTV rate and is significantly more expensive; for a percentage higher than that, you are paying equity rates for capital and will frequently have to give up an equity position. Many lenders these days forbid secondary financing, therefore most "mez" debt, as it is colloquially known, is secured by a lien on the entity that owns the real estate, rather than the real estate itself.

Many investors in real estate have an aversion to debt; REITs, for example, have often eschewed debt, at times having an LTV rate at or below 50%. The added security of a low LTV rate can boost a stock and result in a higher bond rating or more favorable credit line terms. Generally, the easier it is for REITs to raise equity (i.e., if the Wall Street secondary offering window is open), the more they avoid debt.

Some real estate sectors, such as retail, hotel, and office, tend to be more volatile than others, such as apartments. The reason is evident: During recessionary times people may stop shopping and retail will "go dark" (i.e., the lights are turned off); jobs may be lost and office projects may become "see through" (i.e., no one is occupying them so you can see through them from one side to the other). But everyone still has to sleep somewhere every night, which means that even in recessionary times, apartments will rent. The stable income stream afforded by apartments means that both lenders and investors are more comfortable with higher levels of debt for apartments than for other types of real estate.

On the other hand, higher rents, which lead to a higher mortgage loan, may lead to so many vacancies that the owner cannot meet the financial obligations, and the entire project may be lost. The power of leverage works in both directions and must be very studiously balanced. The rent must be at just the right level to maximize the profit with the greatest possible occupancy, and this rental rate will produce the maximum greatest possible amount of mortgage capital with the least owner's capital.

A 7% Vacancy and Collection Loss on a Gross Potential Income of $2,844,096 gives a $199,087 deduction from GPI for vacancy and collection losses.

Effective Gross Income

When Vacancy and Collection Losses are subtracted from Gross Potential Income, the result is Effective Gross Income, or the amount of gross income that the project can reasonably be expected to generate. In this case, the Effective Gross Income for the project is $2,645,009, or Gross Potential Income less Vacancy and Collection Losses, or $2,844,096 − $199,087 = $2,645,009.

Operating Expenses

After a realistic total income is computed, the net operating expenses for the year must be determined. For ease of computation and because the developer owned and operated numerous other communities in the immediate area and was comfortable with the local cost structure, the developer's initial pro forma estimated operating expenses as a percentage of income, in this case 31.9% of Effective Gross Income, or $3,245 per unit. Various industry-related institutions collect national and regional data on operating expenses, and these numbers are well within normal parameters.

At the time of actual loan application, the financing institution will typically request more detailed line item estimates on operating expenses. The result will be a breakdown of the cost of operation of the project into several broad categories:

1. Utilities
2. Payroll
3. Maintenance, supplies, and repairs
4. Replacement reserve
5. Management
6. Taxes
7. Miscellaneous

1. The utilities to be listed are those that must be paid by the project. These include lights in common areas such as the parking lot, clubhouse, and pool areas, as well as hallway lights etc. Frequently water, sewer, and trash collection fees are included in the rental rate. Although it is rare, some communities

pay all resident electric and gas bills, and others may include heat and air-conditioning in the rent, all of which are utility costs. Today, utilities may also include such things as cable or Internet access or even local phone service.

2. The payroll of the project covers the on-site leasing and management staff, as well as cleaning, grounds upkeep, and maintenance employees. The payroll includes payroll taxes, insurance, and any fringe benefits offered by the company.

3. Maintenance and repairs for an apartment community include all items that are the responsibility of the owner. In retail and office projects, the owner takes care of the exterior and the tenant is responsible for everything inside the building shell. Although it is the owner's responsibility in retail and office projects to take care of all exterior maintenance, including both capital (roof replacement, etc.) and operating (lobby cleaning, parking lot litter control, lawn care) costs, it is common for leases to assess a Common Area Maintenance (CAM) charge in order to pass back to the tenant the costs of ongoing exterior operational maintenance. This charge can be a flat fee with an inflation rider, or it can be based on actual costs and allocated, usually on the basis of square footage, to all the occupants of a development. In apartments or motels the owner must take care of the interior and the exterior, including everything that would be included in normal wear and tear, such as repairing a faulty toilet. Owners of apartments typically try to recover costs or damages due to resident carelessness or abuse from the residents.

4. A well-run business always maintains liquid reserves to cover emergencies, unforeseen events, and needed capital investments or renovations. Real estate operations are no exception to the rule, but some owners neglect to put capital aside, preferring to operate on a day-to-day basis without adequate provision for future capital needs. They mistake cash flow for profit, not sufficiently aware that some of that cash flow represents a return of capital, that is, the gradual aging of the building and the appliances therein.

   A time will come when the roof must be replaced, the parking lot resurfaced, the exterior repainted, or the project renovated in order to stay competitive. At that time the capital must be found to replace thousands of yards of carpeting, or to buy 100 new refrigerators, or whatever else is needed.

   As a result, many lenders require a replacement reserve to be set aside with monthly payments into a separate bank account. This amount may range from $225 per year per apartment for a newer apartment community to as much as $400 per year per apartment for an older community with much deferred maintenance.

5. Management expenses are those strictly associated with the costs of management and marketing. They include the costs of collecting rents, showing and leasing apartments, needed accounting services and programs, as well as any home office overhead and expenses directly associated with the project.

6. Taxes include licenses, fees, and ad valorem (according to value) real estate taxes, in addition to any income taxes paid by the company before any capital is transferred into the hands of the owners. Some prefer to include payroll taxes in this category, but it seems more logical to put payroll taxes into item 2, since they constitute a direct cost.
7. The miscellaneous category covers everything else. It is a catch-all for anything that does not fall into the first six categories of expense items. It may include, for example, advertising, accounting, and legal costs.

Expenses for the pro forma should actually be estimated as accurately as possible, and they should be based on existing costs and conditions insofar as they can be determined at the time the project is proposed, for much the same reasons as given for income prediction. If the expenses are set too high, the mortgage will not be as large as it should be and the owner will have to invest an undue amount of cash. Every dollar that can be saved on expenses will add a dollar to the net income, because expenses are subtracted from gross income to obtain net income. On the other hand, if the expenses have been underestimated, the mortgage may be so large that the payments on the inflated amount may prove to be an imposing burden. Once the development is a reality, it will become necessary to meet all bills. If all the capital has gone to make mortgage payments so that none is available for maintenance, for example, then either the residents will move out because of the resulting deferred maintenance and reduced service or the creditors may force the owner into bankruptcy. There must be enough income to pay both the expenses and the mortgage, and the income cannot be increased without destroying a very carefully balanced rental schedule.

Operating expenses do not include payments on the note and related mortgage as they are not an expense of the project itself but rather of the debt financing on the project, that is, the chosen capital structure. Every payment on the mortgage includes both principal and interest. The part that goes to pay off the principal is not a tax-deductible expense but is a reduction in debt and therefore an increase in equity.

Net Operating Income

Net Operating Income (NOI) is the result of subtracting operating expenses from effective gross income. In this case, $2,645,009 of effective gross income less $843,758 of operating expenses yields $1,801,251 of projected net operating income.

Debt Service

A $15,000,000 loan with an 8% interest rate and a 30-year amortization yields a monthly loan payment or Debt Service (DS) of $110,065 and an annual debt service of $1,320,776. The terms *debt service*, *mortgage payment*, and *loan payment* can typically be used interchangeably; *debt service* is the more commonly used terminology in the financial arena.

Debt Service Coverage Ratio

Lenders are quite interested in making sure that there is enough money, that is, Net Operating Income (NOI), to cover the required debt service. To gauge the margin of error involved, a debt service coverage ratio is calculated. The debt service coverage ratio (DSCR or, often, DCR) is simply the Net Operating Income divided by Debt Service, or DCR = NOI/DS. In this case, the DCR is $1,801,251 of NOI divided by $1,320,776 of annual debt, yielding 1.36.

A DCR of 1.20 to 1.25 is generally considered the minimum acceptable ratio for apartments; the more volatile the income stream, the stronger the desired DCR. In other sectors of real estate with less stable income streams, lenders often require higher DCRs. Obviously, the DCR can be impacted by many factors. The numerator, NOI, is sensitive to rent rates, occupancy rates, and variations in expenses. The denominator, Debt Service, is sensitive to interest rates, the amount of the loan, and the amortization of the loan—the amount of principal payment that is required with each loan payment. Varying the different inputs and observing the result on the DCR gives an idea of the DCR's sensitivity to change.

Remember that the pro forma is attempting to forecast the market interest rate at which the project will be able to obtain permanent financing, which is often two years after the date of the pro forma. So, accurate forecasts of interest rates requires an extremely clear crystal ball. A change of 0.5% in the interest rate will increase the annual debt payment by more than $63,000 and lower the 1.36 DCR, calculated earlier, to 1.30. Furthermore, because loans on real estate are generally quoted at a spread over a given market interest rate, such as the London Inter Bank Offered Rate (LIBOR) or the ten-year T-bill rate, and that spread also changes with market conditions, one is, in essence, also attempting to forecast what spread is going to be required by the marketplace. This particular project would break even at an interest rate of 11.5%; that is, with a $15,000,000 loan and a 30-year amortization the income of the project would just carry the debt. Of course, times of high interest rates are usually times of high inflation, resulting in large rent increases.

Although lenders cannot control interest rates, they can control the amortization of the loan. In the example in Figure 6-1, the debt service was calculated based on a 30-year amortization. Reducing that to 25 years (while maintaining the original 8% interest rate) will increase the annual debt service payment by more than $68,000 and decrease the DCR again to 1.30. Decreasing the amortization further to 20 years results in a total increase in debt service of almost $185,000 per year and a debt service coverage ratio of 1.20. Attempting to pay off the loan in just 15 years would result in extra debt payments of almost $400,000 yearly and a DCR of 1.05. The pre-income-tax cash flow would be a mere $81,000 per year.

If the loan amount were to be reduced by a half million dollars to $14,500,000 and all of the other original assumptions held constant, the debt service would be reduced by $44,026 annually and the DCR would rise to 1.41. Of course, any reduction in the loan amount would require additional equity participation by the developer/investor/owner.

Project Cash Flow

Subtracting the Debt Service from the Net Operating Income yields the cash flow from the project. This is the immediate return that the investors will receive. In this case Net Operating Income of $1,801,251 less Debt Service of $1,320,776 yields an annual cash flow of $480,475.

Capitalization Rate

The question now is, "What is the value of a project that produces a yearly net operating income of $1,801,251?" It is assumed that this amount or greater will be forthcoming until the project is sold for its original cost plus capital appreciation. In every year from now on until sold, the business should have a net operating income of at least $1,801,251 after expenses are deducted from gross income. This preliminary example does not consider inflation or deflation, since we are assuming only constant-value dollars.

The value of the project can be found by dividing the yearly net operating income by a capitalization rate, or cap rate. The cap rate represents the desired return by the marketplace for an investment of similar characteristics. The value thus found is the worth of the project as an investment. It is not an attempt to value the buildings or of the land per se, but the value of the project as an income stream produced by the operation of the buildings and land as a business.

NOI/Cap Rate = Value

Capitalization rates are set by the marketplace and are generally deductively determined based on the sale of similar projects. For example, if nearby apartment projects of comparable age and features with a yearly net operating income of $1 million are selling for $10 million, then the prevailing capitalization rate for projects of that quality is 10%: $1,000,000/ $10,000,000 = 10%. Net Operating Income (the income stream) divided by cap rate (the desired return) equals value (what the free marketplace will pay); NOI/cap rate = value.

Values and cap rates move inversely; that is, if cap rates go up, then values go down. If cap rates go down, values go up.

This makes intuitive sense if you think about it. Cap rates represent the desired rate of return in the marketplace. If the market demands a higher rate of return, a given income stream is worth less. If the market decides it will accept a lower rate of return, a given income stream is worth more. Let's take our real estate project with its $1,000,000 per year net operating income (the income stream) and find the value at cap rates of 5%, 10%, and 20%:

Net Operating Income	Divided by Cap Rate	Equals Value
$1,000,000/	5%	= $20,000,000
$1,000,000/	10%	= $10,000,000
$1,000,000/	20%	= $ 5,000,000

During a period of inflation, or at times when there is a high demand for capital, the cap rate will rise along with interest rates. This makes sense, because interest rates are simply the desired return on money, which is really just another good in the marketplace, and the cap rate represents the desired return on money after it has been converted into real estate. All other things being equal, a rising cap rate results in a decrease of the value of the project, which is equal to the annual net operating income divided by the cap rate. The larger the denominator, the smaller will be the resulting value:

$$\text{Investment market value} = \text{Net Operating Income/cap rate}$$

A smaller denominator will produce a larger investment value. In our case, dividing the $1,320,776 of NOI by three different capitalization rates gives three different project valuations:

Capitalization Rate	Valuation	Per Unit Valuation @ 260 Units
0.085	$21,191,192	$81,504
0.0875	$20,585,729	$79,175
0.090	$20,013,904	$76,976

We will deal with capitalization rates further in Chapter 7, "The Appraisal."

We now turn from examining the operating statement to the second of the three portions of the pro-forma, Forecasted Project Costs.

FORECASTED PROJECT COSTS SHOWING HARD CONSTRUCTION COSTS, LAND COSTS, AND SOFT COSTS

Project costs fall into three general categories: land costs, hard costs, and soft costs:

- *Land costs* represent the fair market value of the raw land.
- *Hard costs* represent actual construction costs to erect the buildings, including site preparation.
- *Soft costs* refer to all architectural, planning, engineering, permitting, financing, and marketing costs.

Figure 6-2 shows the total project costs laid out by hard costs, land costs, and soft costs.

Hard Construction Costs: Value Engineering

In our pro forma, total hard construction costs of $12,733,836 were initially estimated using a per square foot number plus a 5% allowance for the building contractor's fee, a 5% contingency, and a $12,800 per apartment renovation estimate for the existing 39-unit apartment community. A small amount for site clearing

HARD COSTS:

KEY INDICATORS		SQ. FT.	TOTAL APTS.	TOTAL SQ. FT.	PER NEW UNIT COST	TOTAL COST	PER-SQ. FT. COST
HARD COST					@ 221 Units		@ 221 Units
3 Bed / 3 Bath		1,306	74	96,644	58,770	4,348,980	45.00
2 Bed / 2 Bath		949	147	139,503	45,552	6,696,144	48.00
Clubhouse/Office				4,519		Included	
Totals			221	240,666	49,978	11,045,124	45.89
Contractor Fee	5%				2,499	552,256	2.29
Contingency	5%				2,499	552,256	2.29
Upgrade Existing Units			39	39,000		499,200	
Site Work (clearing)					385	85,000	.35
Totals			260	279,666	55,361	12,733,836	50.83
LAND COSTS							
LAND: 20 +/− acres			@ 260		8,642	2,200,000	9.32
HARD COSTS + LAND					64,003	14,933,836	60.15
SOFT COSTS							
Architecture and Engineering							
Architecture					656	145,000	
Engineering – Permitting and Civil					271	60,000	
Engineering – MEP and Structural					68	15,000	
Interior Design					34	7,500	
Landscape Architecture					68	15,000	
Blueprints and Renderings					34	7,500	
Contingency			10.0%		113	25,000	
					1,244	275,000	
Fees, Deposits, Permits, and Surveys							
Construction Lender's Fee @			0.5%	15,200,000	344	76,000	
Water/Sewer/Electric Fees			$1,571/apt	221 units	1,571	347,191	
City: Plan Review Fees					271	60,000	
Building Permits and Inspections			$100/apt	221 units	100	22,100	
Bank Construction Inspections					68	9,000	
Surveying					23	15,000	
Contingency					41	5,000	
					2,418	534,291	
Closing Costs							
Legal					68	15,000	
Documentary Stamps and Intangible Tax			0.0055		378	83,600	
Title Insurance			0.002		138	30,400	
					584	129,000	

FIG. 6-2   Cost summary for Hidden Lake Apartments.

was included beyond the other amounts simply because it had been separately bid in anticipation of the need to get an advance start on the project. The local jurisdiction would issue a clearing permit well in advance of the other permits, and this was preliminary work that could be done while the developer was still in the process of selecting the general contractor.

The per-square-foot numbers used in the pro forma were derived from the developer's recent experience and consultation with builders in the area. In spite of a developer's best efforts, it is not unusual to have hard bids coming in over

Interim Property Taxes:			226	50,000
Marketing and Lease Up:			588	130,000
Furnishings:				
Clubhouse and Pool			566	125,000
Models			158	35,000
Miscellaneous			90	20,000
			814	180,000
Construction interest:				
3/4 yr. @.75 Av. Bal.@ 8.5%	0.75	0.75	3,288	726,750
Developer's Fee:	4.0%		3,091	683,119
TOTAL SOFT COSTS			12,254	2,708,160

SUMMARY:

Hard Costs		12,733,836	57,619
Land		2,200,000	8,642
Soft Costs		2,708,160	12,254
Total Project Cost @ 221 New Units		$17,641,996	79,828
80% of Cost Construction Loan		$14,113,597	63,862
Equity Required		$3,528,399	15,966
Project Value @ 8.75 Cap Rate @ 260 Units		$20,585,729	79,180

FIG. 6-2 Continued.

acceptable construction costs. In that case, a process is begun, called value engineering, whereby selective reductions and changes are made that, it is hoped, will not significantly affect the viability of the project for its intended use.

Less expensive materials may be chosen, a more economical method of construction selected, features eliminated, and so on. Real-life examples abound. An office building designed with a marble lobby ended up with ceramic tile, a multistory auxiliary building at a major teaching hospital was built without windows, an apartment community designed with French doors onto a balcony ended up with French doors and no balcony—just a railing flush with the building (and, yes, it does look a little strange).

If the project is an income-producing project, careful value judgments must be made so that the value engineering does not produce cost savings that result in a reduction of income; that is, value real or perceived, in excess of the costs saved. A way to reduce costs must be found that will not reduce the value of the project. For example, an income project may be forecasted to return 10% "cash on cash"—for example, for every million dollars spent, rent of $100,000 is expected to be generated, and based on that forecasted rent, capital may be borrowed, first short-term to fund the construction and then, later, when the project has stabilized, long-term, so-called permanent financing. If a $10,000 cost savings results in a $500 annual loss of income, then it might well be implemented for it is yielding only a 5% cash on cash (or cash on cost) return. That is, the $10,000 reduction in cost will result in only a $5,000 reduction in value ($500/10% = $5,000). If the same $10,000 cost savings results in a $2,000 annual loss of income, then it would be rejected because the particular feature is generating an excellent 20% cash on cash return. Of course, in reality, such numbers are rarely, if ever, known with certainty and professional judgment calls must be made repeatedly, the correctness of which is not known until the marketplace renders its final judgment.

Sometimes cost is reduced where it is not immediately apparent, but may show up later in increased maintenance costs or user satisfaction: Block walls become two-by-four wood walls, sound proofing is reduced, one coat of paint is used instead of two. Some changes are relatively minor. In a large project, even a simple thing like painting the trim the same color as the walls instead of an accent color can result in a cost savings of tens of thousands of dollars.

Other means of reducing costs run the gamut. Eliminate chair railing or crown molding, choose less expensive appliances or a less efficient air-conditioner, lower-grade carpet, sinks of synthetic materials instead of china or stainless steel, fiberglas tubs and shower stalls instead of ceramic tile, single-glazed glass instead of double-glazed, sliding glass doors instead of double colonial doors. Heat pumps may be used instead of gas heat, perhaps completely eliminating the need for a gas contractor on-site, a savings of capital and perhaps time as well as complexity. Heat strips may be used instead of heat pumps. Landscaping may be reduced or simplified, PVC pipe used instead of copper, ceiling fans eliminated, porches open instead of screened in, a 6-foot instead of 8-foot fence ($9 a linear foot vs. $15), a smaller pool installed ($50 per square foot for a pool vs. $20 per square foot for decking), standard roofing shingles used instead of the more three-dimensional architectural grade. Skylights can be reduced or eliminated, spray on "popcorn" ceilings used instead of plastered ceilings, less expensive surfacing material used on the building such as hardboard instead of brick, vinyl siding instead of stucco.

In this case, three large general contractors were approached, given plans, and asked for pre-hard-bid final estimates. This was done because the time constraints of the marketplace required a quick start in order to reach completion in time to catch the market's seasonal peak and a full bidding process would have consumed an inordinate amount of time. Two of the general contractors chose to go to their favorite subcontractors and get quick, nonbinding numbers for the major portions of the work. The resulting numbers came in extremely close. After adjusting the bids to compare apples to apples, the high bid and low bid were within $300,000, or 2.2%, of each other, and the third bid came in almost exactly in the middle.

Unfortunately, even the lowest estimate was more than three-quarters of a million dollars over the pro forma number of $12,733,836. Value engineering was vigorously employed. The first thing to go was the first-story brick overlay (brick wainscoting on the clubhouse was retained, and brick was used in the entryway signage and fence columns); next was the stucco that was to wrap the interior courtyard walkway columns; hardboard was substituted. The plans called for concrete drainage pipes to handle the stormwater runoff from the parking lots to the retention areas; a form of plastic pipe was substituted. Transoms above the entrance doors were eliminated (the walkways would have blocked out much of the light anyway), several allowances were trimmed. That created net savings sufficient to get the project cost down to $11,935,000 including the contractor fee, leaving approximately $800,000 left over to cover renovation costs on the existing units of $499,200 and the original desired contingency fund of $552,256. It was decided to leave the renovation costs at $499,200 and seek a financing institution that would accept a lower contingency number of approximately $300,000.

Land: Cost versus Value

In this pro forma, the land is valued at $2,200,000, or $8,642 per unit, or $110,000 per acre. For purposes of the pro forma, the land is generally carried at its fair market value regardless of the cost to the developer, whether that number is higher or lower. It is not unusual for a developer to acquire land at an economical price and increase its value through rezoning or to astutely buy raw land in the path of development or new road construction and benefit from the increase in value. Although future road construction plans are generally part of the public record, few are willing to wade through the minutiae in order to determine the potential for increased land values. In addition, such plans are subject to change and few investors have the resources or the patience to wait the three, five, or even ten years required to harvest the investment. Land value can also be enhanced through assemblage. Smaller parcels may increase in value when assembled into a larger parcel. A developer who is able to obtain land below its fair market value may include it in his cost estimates at fair market value and obtain a portion of the equity needed for the project in that manner.

It is also possible for a developer to overpay for land. This can happen simply because of an incorrect assessment of the value of the land. Sometimes events that were relied upon to provide value, such as surrounding developments or the addition of an interstate interchange, can be delayed or canceled. Local government agencies can impose moratoriums on the issuance of new permits, or a desired zoning change may be denied. Additional regulatory burdens may be imposed; impact fees may be implemented or raised significantly.

Impact fees are taxes levied by local or county government, purportedly to pay for a new development's share of the local infrastructure: roads, parks, schools, and so on. In the Orlando area in the year 2000 impact fees were approximately $5,000 per apartment unit; thus, a 240-unit apartment would pay a $1,200,000 up-front tax just to be allowed to come into existence. This is in addition to the annual property tax bill of roughly $350,000. In addition, because the property tax value of a construction project is minimal, some local governments assess a "municipal services fee" during construction to more closely track the property tax revenue that would be received if the project were completed.

Furthermore, if the land is purchased at the height of a boom cycle that has crested by the time the regulatory, permitting, bidding, and financing process is completed, the developer must hold the land until the market once again firms up. This creates an associated carrying or holding cost. There are several ways to evaluate holding costs. If a purchase is 100% financed, with no corporate or personal liability, the holding costs may be considered equal to the interest costs. If there is liability for nonrepayment beyond loss of the land, a cost must be assigned to the risk assumed. If cash or a combination of cash and debt is used to pay for the land, a cost must be assigned to the cash. The cost could simply be the developer's actual direct cost of capital, that is, the developer borrowed the capital on a credit line at the one-year Treasury bill rate plus 225 basis points (a basis point is 100th of 1% — 100 basis points equals 1% and 225 basis points is 2.25%). Or the developer could have withdrawn capital from a capital market account and used the rate it was earning there as her cost of capital. The developer may use a blended cost of capital; she may know what her average cost of capital is and apply that rate. Or the developer may have a hurdle rate that she applies. For instance, if an investment does not return a minimum of 15%, then she is not interested. She may apply an opportunity cost approach. For example, the best alternative investment on the horizon returns 14%, so this investment must equal that return.

Soft Costs

At $2,708,160 the total soft costs exceed the raw land value of $2,200,000. The largest of the soft costs is construction interest of $726,750, followed by the developer's 4% fee of $683,119, and water, sewer, and electric fees of $347,191. Together these three items make up almost two-thirds of the total soft costs.

Architecture and Engineering   Architecture and engineering costs are among the few costs that can be determined up front with some degree of accuracy. Although such services can be purchased on an hourly ad hoc basis, most developers will negotiate a contract based on a fixed price, an hourly rate with a not-to-exceed number, or a percentage fee. Costs can vary widely, depending on the type of project, the area of the country, the scope of the services desired, and the related degree of liability assumed. Frequently, the architect takes the lead role and his scope of services can be expanded to include an active role in the oversight and management of the construction process. Some firms provide the full range of services in-house, others farm out certain areas such as structural engineering or land planning. Some developers prefer to take a very active role in the management of both the preconstruction and construction processes and limit the architect's role to preparing the plans and certifying percentage of completion to the financing institution for draws during construction. However, given the complexity of the actual construction process, virtually any set of architectural drawings will require some modification, enhancement, clarification, or realignment to reflect unforeseen code issues, a need for greater detail, change orders, and the like, so the architect will remain involved at some level throughout the construction process.

It is interesting to monitor how costs evolve from the initial estimates of the pro forma to the final, actual, real-world expenses. Although the total amount for architectural and engineering services for the project stayed within the total estimated

$275,000, amounts for the line items did shift around. The total for the architect was substantially less; the amounts for the engineers, both structural and permitting/civil, were higher. In regard to the civil engineering site-planning process, the increase was due to greater than anticipated opposition during the permitting process. In regard to the MEP (mechanical, electrical, plumbing) and structural engineering, it was due to several factors: a last-minute change of engineering firms because of scheduling issues and compliance with new, tougher codes imposed as post-Hurricane Andrew wind shear and tie down issues became part of the inspection process.

Fees, Deposits, Permits, and Surveys

Construction Lender's Fee   Lenders typically charge between ½ and 1 full point for a loan (a point is 1% of the amount of the loan); the more speculative the project or the more desperate the developer (i.e., the less competition for the loan), the higher the points.

Some government programs, such as HUD (the federal cabinet-level Department of Housing and Urban Development) Section 236 loans, have fees that can add up to 4% to 5% of the loan amount. There are several reasons for this, including that the loan amounts tend to generous, at times requiring no equity other than the developer's fee, require no personal or corporate guarantee of repayment, and are both construction loans and true permanent loans. The loans do require a guarantee that the construction will be completed, but that is a risk the investor/developer can assign to a bonded contractor. The loans are expensive in another way as well: They are generally for a term of 30 years, and the interest rate charged for that entire time is a blend of the market's higher construction period interest rate and the generally lower stabilized interest rate on permanent financing. As a result, the owner ends up paying a slightly higher-than-market rate for possibly as long as 29 years in return for having a lower interest rate for the 1- to 2-year construction period. Of course, prepayment is allowed and the project is assured of permanent, 30-year financing at its inception, unlike most construction or mini-permanent loans, which have a 2- to 5-year maximum term.

The creator of the pro forma must estimate both the amount of the loan that can be obtained and the fee the financing institution will charge. Estimating the fee is the simpler task in this case because the developer had a strong track record and a recent history of loan dealings. Plus, the financing of multifamily apartments of this quality is as close to a commodity as is possible in the development business, i.e., apartments as a class are more alike than other real estate products. Estimating the loan amount is more involved because the dollar amount lent is based on the value of the final project and the cost of the project, both of which involve significant variables. In this case a loan of $15,200,000 was estimated with a ½-point fee of $76,000, and, in the final analysis, a loan of $15,000,000 with a ½-point fee of $75,000 was obtained.

Water, Sewer, and Electric Fees   In this example, the water, sewer, and electric fees were charged by the local utility company, Gainesville Regional Utilities, as a capital facility charge for the cost of hooking up to the local system. This cost brings utilities to the site edge; actual site utility costs are included in the hard construction costs. Because the local utility company is owned by the local municipality, these fees may be thought of as akin to impact fees.

City Plan Review Fees, Building Permits and Inspections, Bank Construction Inspections, Survey and Contingency Costs   Every governmental body charges to review plans, issue building permits, and conduct inspections; the amounts vary widely by jurisdiction and must be simply accepted as a cost of doing business. The bank financing the project required an independent inspection with every monthly draw at $750 per inspection. The pro forma allows for a full year of inspections; mostly likely only nine or ten will be required. The survey fee of $15,000 is for any survey work required during construction and the final as-built survey; additional survey costs are built into the architecture and engineering costs. The contingency number is tight but proved to be adequate.

Closing Costs

Legal, Documentary Stamps, Intangible Tax, and Title Insurance   Legal refers to the cost of the bank's attorney at the loan closing, in this case $15,000. This is a fixed cost set by the lender up front, usually in the term sheet or commitment letter. Documentary stamps and intangible tax are fees set by the state for recording deeds and mortgages in the official records of the local county. In this case the fee is $.55 per $100 of mortgage amount, or $83,600 for a $15,200,000 loan. Title insurance assures the lender that the borrower possesses good title to the land; in this case the title insurance fee includes the cost of the borrower/developer's attorney for the work performed in the loan closing. Some states set title insurance rates by statute, others allow the free market to do so. Florida recently moved to a free market pricing system; the amount shown, $30,400 is based on the old set price system, so substantial savings were achieved based on a negotiated premium.

Interim Property Taxes

Governing authorities that rely on property taxes as a revenue source appraise real estate at a fixed point in time, usually at the end of each year, and assess a tax based on the value at that time. In the past, construction projects were often valued at mere land value until completed, leading to occasional situations in which final inspections would be deliberately postponed until after the new year in order to save a full years' tax. Valuing only the land had a certain logic: If the value of a commercial project is dependent on its income stream and it has yet to produce income, then there is no value to be assigned. The fallacy in this logic lies in the fact that the marketplace values not only current income streams, but the possibility of future income as well. In these more sophisticated, revenue-hungry times it is not unusual to see local government property appraisers base valuation on cost or a percentage of completion. Indeed, some authorities even choose to levy a municipal service fee in lieu of property taxes during construction, ostensibly for providing police and fire protection. In this case relatively little new construction was in place on the first of the year, so the $50,000 shown for interim property taxes is based on the prior years' taxes plus an adjustment for the expected increase in the Consumer Price Index.

Marketing and Lease Up

Marketing and lease up constitute an incredibly important part of the process. After all, what good is an empty building no matter how well designed or built? Typically, the number for this item will include the cost of a marketing trailer and related setup and landscaping costs—in this case, one site marketing director, one full-time leasing agent, and a part-time leasing agent for weekend coverage. Occasionally, the contractor is able to advance the construction of a clubhouse sufficiently so as to eliminate the need for a marketing trailer, but that is the exception, particularly because the clubhouse would also have to be located so that it could be separated from the rest of the construction project. Marketing trailers may be rented from an incredibly wide selection of choices, ranging from a very basic "construction office" style up to several-thousand-square-foot modular buildings with upscale exterior trim that mimics the appearance of a permanent building. A marketing trailer typically goes on site an absolute minimum of three to four months before the first apartment will be available for occupancy; it is not unusual to see trailers on site six months in advance with a prior "teaser" ad campaign to spark interest and create a profile. Brochures must be prepared and marketing displays created, showing floor plans and materials used in order to give potential residents a feel for the project in advance of actually having apartment models to show. The amount shown here, $130,000, or $588 per unit, is probably on the low side, reflecting the developer's strong presence in the local market and familiarity and comfort with that market. Farther away from home base, there is a tendency to spend more "insurance" money. Economy of scale has a direct impact on marketing costs: Brochure design is a fixed cost no matter how many are printed, display ad costs are fixed, and the cost of a marketing trailer does not vary tremendously whether it serves 100 apartments or 400 apartments. Although labor costs may go up as leasing agents are added to cover additional shows, there are significant times of the day and weekend that are slow, when labor costs are simply going for minimal phone coverage.

Furnishings

Clubhouse, Pool, Models, and Miscellaneous   The clubhouse and model apartments are very important marketing tools and must be professionally decorated to reflect the intended ambiance of the community and attract the target resident profile. The pool area must project a relaxing, luxurious image that welcomes the customers home and sparks the imagination, allowing them to envision themselves using and enjoying the amenities. Included in the furnishing budget number are the exercise equipment for the clubhouse workout room, as well as office equipment needed for the on-site management and leasing office to function: computers, copier, fax, desks, chairs, and so forth. Sometimes the furnishings and equipment for the marketing trailer are selected to fit into the decorative scheme of the clubhouse. The $180,000 shown here in the pro forma is an adequate but by no means generous number. Creativity, innovation, and ingenuity will be required to achieve the desired results within the budget given.

Construction Interest

The construction interest amount can be estimated with a fair degree of accuracy if it is based on projected loan draw schedules. However, for a preliminary analysis, a rough approximation will suffice. The amount of construction interest shown in the pro forma was based on several assumptions. It was assumed, first, that the job would take nine months to complete, that the average outstanding loan balance would be 75% of the total loan balance, and that the average interest rate would be 8.5%. The loan balance starts at zero and ends up at 100%. If draws occurred evenly throughout the project, then the average outstanding balance would be only 50%, the average of zero and 100%. There is much about development and construction that is more an art than a science; the assumption of the interest rate amount in the initial pro forma is at best an educated guess, based on the consensus forecast of economists whose track record for accuracy in foretelling the future is dubious at best.

The time line is rather aggressive for a project of this size, but achievable. The average outstanding balance was chosen to be on the high (conservative) side, and as the project started, short-term interest rates were falling in response to rate cuts by the Federal Reserve, so the developer had hopes of coming in well under the $726,750 number given for construction interest. An initial saving of $10,000 was achieved, inasmuch as the loan amount of $15,000,000 was $200,000 less than the estimate used in the pro forma. A drop in interest rates of 0.5% over the nine-month life of the project would save approximately $42,000, and a reduction in the average amount of the loan outstanding from 75% to 65% would yield an additional saving in excess of $100,000. Obviously, the more patient the subcontractors, and thus the general contractor, are in regard to payment, the better it is for the project's interest costs.

If the interest estimate is inadequate, the investor/developer will be required to fund the balance as it comes due in the final stages of the project. In a large project such as this, buildings will obviously come on line over time and it is possible that the early buildings will be generating rental income in time to help with any interest shortage or other minor cost overruns in the later stages. A wise developer does not count on this, but merely knows that it is a possible silver lining.

Developer's Fee

The developer's fee is sometimes called a "promote," because a portion of it is a fee for promoting or sponsoring the project. The developer's fee covers the developer's costs and overhead in putting the project together and carrying it forward; it is also compensation for the risks involved. This fee must not only cover the costs and risks of the current project, it must also cover the forfeited costs and related risks in the projects that did not go forward: the dead ends explored looking for the right site, the right market conditions, and an amenable zoning board. The fee of 4%, or $683,119, shown here is probably on the low to moderate side, particularly given the fact that the developer ran the additional risk of purchasing the land prior to obtaining full development rights and assumed personal liability on the construction loan.

Summary of Forecasted Project Costs

Total soft costs of $2,708,160 combined with a total land value of $2,200,000 and total hard construction costs of $12,733,836 yield a total project cost of $17,641,996 for the construction of 221 new apartments and the renovation of 39 existing apartments. If the $499,200 to renovate the existing apartments is backed out, the cost per apartment for the new construction is $77,569.

FORECASTED FINANCING: REQUESTED LOAN AMOUNT, REQUIRED EQUITY CONTRIBUTION, FINAL PROJECT VALUE

We now turn to the final and shortest of the three major portions of the pro forma: forecasting the financing. Typically, most institutional lenders will not lend in excess of 80% of the cost of a project. In this case, that is $17,641,996 total project costs × 80% = $14,113,597.

The difference between the total project cost and the maximum potential loan amount is the required equity, which in this case is $3,528,399. The astute reader may already have noticed that the loan amount of $15,000,000 received on this project is in excess of the 80% maximum of total project cost calculated in the preceding paragraph. That is because the loan covered both the new and existing units, and since the developer had equity in the existing units, he was able to borrow on them to obtain a higher loan amount.

The developer was able to close the project construction loan without having to make any significant additional outlay of cash, obtaining the required equity of $3,528,399 from three sources:

1. Ownership of the raw land free and clear, a $2,200,000 value
2. Borrowing approximately $885,000 against equity in the existing apartment community
3. Contributing the developer's 4% overhead and profit fee of $683,119 to the project

The numbers add up to more than the required amount, partly because the land that the existing apartments sat on had to be deducted from the total land value, and partly because the bank desired slightly more equity because of the non-direct-cash nature of the equity contributions. Banks prefer to recognize any developer fee either at the end of a project or prorated over the life of the construction in the monthly loan draws. The contribution of the developer's 4% fee represents a very real cost in terms of salaries, office expense, and overhead spread over the several years from project conception to final stabilization. The land value of $2,200,000 represented substantial appreciation over the developer's purchase price in prior years because of land parcel assemblage, normal appreciation due to the passage of time, as well as astute purchases in prior down periods of the real estate cycle. The equity in the existing apartment community was due to repositioning the property through capital improvements and marketing efforts, aggressive property management, and normal price appreciation, as well as mortgage paydown over time.

In this particular case, although the developer was required to put in little or no cash at loan closing, it was solely because he was able to bring to the table substantial equity in other forms, much of it representing prior cash outlays. The strength of the development team and the general contractor chosen to build the project contributed to the financing institution's willingness to proceed.

Based on the NOI and an 8.75% capitalization rate, the project is projected to have a final valuation of $20,585,729. Of that final valuation, approximately $1,445,000 can be attributed to the existing project in its original form, so the projected increase in final project value over the total project cost is $1,500,000, or approximately 8.5% of the total project cost.

SUMMARY

A *pro forma* is a projected operating statement that forecasts how a project will perform. To create a pro forma, a developer must determine a project's expected income, costs, and financing structure.

A developer begins by first determining how many rental units can be constructed according to local regulatory and zoning codes through the use of site coverage and floor area ratios. Once the site is under contract, an architect is usually hired to develop formal plans for the site. Rental rates are then established in an effort to determine expected income. Amenities provided in the development measured against those found in competing properties are the primary foundation for determining a rate. In addition to base rent, income may also be derived from auxiliary sources, including application and service fees.

Once *gross potential income* has been determined, vacancy and collection losses are deducted to discover the project's *effective gross income*. Vacancy is deducted to reflect the loss in potential income associated with a project that may not be 100% leased upon completion. Subtracted from *effective gross income* are the project's *operating expenses*, which typically include common area utilities, on-site management, maintenance, replacement reserves, and taxes. At this point, the developer has developed the project's projected *net operating income*. Once a developer determines the project's financing structure, the mortgage constant can be subtracted from *net operating income* to produce the *project cash flow*, the immediate return project investors expect to receive.

Development costs are classified according to *hard costs, land costs*, and *soft costs*. Hard costs are those associated with the actual building construction; they are estimated at a dollar amount per rental unit or per square foot and include contractor fees and contingencies. Land costs reflect the fair market value of the raw land; this value is largely dependent on the regulatory environment and local zoning codes. Most of the remaining costs associated with development are considered soft costs, and include construction interest, architectural and engineering fees, surveys, building permits, and developer's fee.

KEY TERMS AND DEFINITIONS

Auxiliary income: Project income from sources other than base rent.

Debt coverage ratio: A ratio used to determine if a project's income stream is sufficient to cover mortgage payments; it is equal to net operating income divided by the debt service.

Effective gross income: Gross potential income less vacancy and collection losses.

Floor area ratio: The ratio of the total building square footage to the total site square footage.

Gross potential income: The sum of base rental income and total auxiliary income.

Net operating income: Effective gross income less operating expenses.

Operating expenses: Net annual project expenses, including utility and management fees, maintenance costs, replacement reserves, and taxes.

Pro forma: A projected operating statement that forecasts how the project will perform.

Project cash flow: The immediate return that investors of the project expect to receive.

Site coverage ratio: The percent of a site that can be covered with impervious surfaces.

Vacancy and collection loss: A deduction of gross potential income based on the likelihood that the development will not be 100% occupied.

KEY LEARNING POINTS

- Know how a developer determines the amount of rentable space that can be constructed on a site.
- Identify how base rental revenues are determined.
- Understand how vacancy and collection loss affect a property's gross potential income.
- Define the multiple operating expense categories.

- Understand how a project's rental revenue and capitalization rate can affect project financing.
- Define the three types of project costs that are included in a pro forma.
- Understand how to assemble a pro forma.

QUESTIONS

1. A pro forma makes multiple assumptions in order to forecast how a project will perform. List four.

2. Construction costs are one of the most difficult pro forma items to estimate. Why?

3. List the two primary methods employed to determine the maximum amount of development that can be constructed on a site.

4. When determining a site's development potential, why is maximizing a site not always the best alternative?

5. Which type of development is considered less risky based on inflationary concerns: retail, office, or apartment?

6. List some of the auxiliary income that can be generated in a project.

7. List the seven groups of operating expenses that are deducted from effective gross income to yield net operating income.

8. How is the debt coverage ratio calculated, and how does a lender use this value?

9. What is the name of the process by which selective changes in project scope are undertaken to reduce project cost? What is the goal of this process?

10. Why must a developer carefully assess the value of a site?

11. List the fees that, when combined, typically account for two-thirds of all project soft costs.

12. List some of the additional costs that need to be considered with project completion.

7
The Appraisal

INTRODUCTION

The appraiser plays a key role in the development process. It is upon the appraiser's report that the financing institution places its primary reliance in determining the ultimate value of the development project. Although the appraiser's report will be reviewed by internal experts in the bank, the value placed on the development by the appraiser's report forms the foundation for determining the amount of capital the bank will lend for construction.

Federal lending laws require the lender to initiate the appraisal. The lending institution has the final say in who the appraiser for the project will be, but it is not unusual for the developer to be consulted as to his opinion on the qualifications and suitability of various possible candidates. Furthermore, the bank will bid out the appraisal, and different appraisers will come back with a range of bids and, at times even more important, promised delivery dates. Because the cost of the appraisal is typically borne directly by the developer and it is rare for the best price to be accompanied by the best delivery date, the developer will once again be contacted for input as to whether he would prefer speed or economy.

The astute developer forms a good relationship with the leading appraisers in the area who specialize in his real estate sector and consults them on an informal basis to check the validity of the myriad assumptions that are made in putting together a project pro forma. It is a mutually advantageous relationship, as the appraiser also needs knowledgeable sources in the real estate community.

Cautionary Note: The Hidden Lake Apartments appraisal studied here is for a market that has a strong student component. Thus, we will see much greater emphasis on per-bedroom data than we may expect to see in an appraisal for a non-student-oriented community. In a standard (often called "market rent") community, generally only one family occupies each apartment, whether it is a one-income or a two-income household. In a student-oriented community, each bedroom is usually occupied by a separate economic unit and thus represents a separate potential income stream. This is why student-oriented communities tend toward the larger three- or four-bedroom apartments in their overall unit mix. With market rent communities, more bedrooms per apartment does not necessarily mean more household

income; indeed, somewhat the opposite. More bedrooms generally means more dependent children and, all other things being equal, less household income available
for rent.

Definition: An appraisal is an opinion of value supported by market research. It
is an attempt to establish a probable sales price or "market value" for an existing or
proposed facility. Market value is generally defined as the price a willing seller and
a willing buyer would reach in an arm's-length transaction with both having full
knowledge of the situation and adequate exposure to the market. The government
definition of market value is the one most often used:

> The most probable price which a property should bring in a competitive and open
> market under all conditions requisite to a fair sale, the buyer and seller each act-
> ing prudently and knowledgeably and assuming the price is not affected by undue
> stimulus. (*Federal Register* 12 CFR 563.17-1a)

Implicit in this definition is the consummation of a sale as of a specified date
and the passing of title from seller to buyer under conditions whereby:

- Buyer and seller are typically motivated.
- Both parties are well informed or well advised and each acting in what they
  consider their own best interest.
- A reasonable time is allowed for exposure in the open market.
- Payment is made in terms of cash in U.S. dollars or in terms of financial
  arrangements comparable thereto.
- The price represents the normal consideration for the property sold unaffected by special or creative financing or sales concessions granted by anyone
  associated with the sale.

ORGANIZATION OF AN APPRAISAL

The following outline taken from the Hidden Lake Apartments appraisal gives an
idea of what is included in an appraisal:

Part I: *General Organization*
Letter of Transmittal
Salient Facts and Conclusions
Certification

Part II: *General Appraisal Information*
Introduction
Purpose of Appraisal
Intended Use of Report
Definition of Appraisal Problem/Scope of Analysis
Definitions
Assumptions and Limiting Conditions
Special Appraisal Assumptions

PROJECT BACKGROUND

Obviously, an appraisal contains a tremendous amount of information; the Hidden Lake appraisal was just fewer than 300 pages and weighed several pounds. The purpose of all this information is to support the conclusion of value reported in the appraisal. Several of the exhibits contained in the appraisal are worthy of special note and can give a sense of the overall nature and scope of the project.

Figure 7-1 shows the apartment projects completed or planned for the local market for a six-year period; this may give the reader a sense of the size and the ebb and flow of the market and potential competition.

Figure 7-2 is a detailed Site Location Map; the size of the surrounding lots gives a clear indication that the project is in an infill location, surrounded by existing single-family properties.

Figure 7-3 is the Site Plan, showing the new construction, the existing buildings, and the extensive water retention basins.

Figure 7-4 shows elevations of Building 3, one of the smaller buildings but still typical of the architectural style. This elevation shows brick on the ground floor, which was eventually eliminated in the process of value engineering. In an oversight due to the fast-tracking of the project, the plans were never amended to remove the additional width of foundation required by the brick façade over the

Anticipated Supply Analysis Gainesville, Florida

Project No	Estimated Completion Date	Property	Location	Number of Units	Number of Bedrooms	Location City/ County	Status
	1996						
1	Aug-96	Royal Village Apartments	Depot Avenue @ 8th Street	105	235	City	Completed
2	Aug-96	The Landing Apartment Project	3800 Block S.W. 13th Street	80	320	City	Completed
3	Aug-96	University Place Apartments	3700 Block S.W. 27th Street	176	480	County	Completed
4	Aug-96	Melrose Place Apartments Phase II	1000 S.W. 62nd Blvd.	58	232	County	Completed
5	Aug-96	Lexington Park Apartments Phase 1	3900 Block S.W. 27th Street	168	552	County	Completed
6	Aug-96	Lake Crossing Apartments	5300 Block N.W. 39th Avenue	264	452	County	Completed
7	Aug-96	College Park Apartments	211 N.W. 16th St. and 2nd Ave.	45	135	City	Completed
8	Aug-96	Arbor East Apartments	2335 S.W. 35th Place	35	70	County	Completed
			Sub-Total	931	2,476		
	1997						
9	Jan-97	Campus Club Apartments	4000 S.W. 37th Blvd.	252	924	County	Completed
10	Aug-97	The Gables Apartments Phase 1	5600 S.W. Archer Road	80	192	County	Completed
11	Jan-97	Pebble Creek Apartments	2307 S.W. 16th Place	168	264	City	Completed
12	Aug-97	Museum Walk Apartments	3500 Block S.W. 19th Avenue	105	244	County	Completed
13	Aug-97	Lexington Parke Apartments Phase 2	3900 Block S.W. 27th Street	132	468	County	Completed
14	Aug-97	Stoneridge Apartments Phase 2	3800 S.W. 34th Street	36	108	County	Completed
15	Aug-97	Hidden Village Phase 2	2725 S.W. 27th Avenue	60	80	County	Completed
			Sub-Total	833	2,280		
	1998						
16	Jan-98	Madison Cove Apartments	5500 S.W. Archer Road	96	n/a	County	Completed
17	Jan-98	Huntington Lakes Phase 3 Apartment	5800 Blk. N.W. 39th Avenue	198	n/a	County	Completed
18	Mar-98	The Reserve At kanapaha	4400 S.W. Archer Road	272	n/a	County	Completed
19	Jun-98	The Gables Apartments Phase 2	5600 S.W. Archer Road	88	n/a	County	Completed
20	Aug-98	Paddock Club Apartments	1200 Blk. Ft. Clark Blvd.	264	528	County	Completed
21	Aug-98	Tivoli Apartments	2900 Blk S.W. 13th Street	144	384	City	Completed
22	Aug-98	The Links at Haile Plantation	Haile Plantation Development	200	n/a	County	Completed
23	Aug-98	The Cottages at Old Archer	2800 Blk Old Archer Road	36	72	County	Completed
24	Aug-98	Stoneridge Apartments ,Phase 3	3800 S.W. 34th Street	24	96	County	Completed
25	Aug-98	Arlington Apartments ,Phase 3	200 S.E. 2nd Place	13	38	City	Completed
			Sub-Total	1,335	1,118		
	1999 (Approx.)						
26	Aug-99	Aspin Ridge of Gainesville	3800 Blk. S.W. 34th Street	72	120	County	Completed
27	Aug-99	Legacy at Fort Clark Apartments	1500 Blk. Ft. Clark Blvd.	348	n/a	County	Completed
28	Aug-99	Stoneridge Apartments ,Phase 4	3800 S.W. 34th Street	48	150	County	Completed
29	Dec-99	Union Street Station Apartments	100 Blk. S.E. 2nd Avenue	51	n/a	City	Under Construction
30	Aug-99	Countryside at the University	4000 S.W. 23rd Street	72	288	County	Completed
31	Aug-99	University Club Townhouses	2900 Blk. S.W. 23rd St.	90	360	County	Completed
32	Dec-99	Pinewood Terrace Apartments	4800 Blk N.W. 43rd St.	152	292	City	Completed
33	Aug-99	Country ManorApartments , Phase 2	2701 N.W. 23rd Blvd.	56	144	City	Completed
			Sub-Total	889	1,354		

FIG. 7-1 Potential apartment projects/competition table.

replacement siding. As a result, a significant extra amount of concrete went into the foundation, and the building sports a small concrete lip around its perimeter.

Figure 7-5 gives the unit floor plans of both the two- and three-bedroom apartments. The foyer entry into the three-bedroom units, along with the juxtaposition of the large kitchen and the living room, combine to give them a greater open feeling than the more linear layout of the two-bedroom floor plan.

TRIANGULATION: THREE APPROACHES TO VALUE—COST, INCOME, AND MARKET

In order to assure that the appraisal process reflects an accurate estimate of market value, value is calculated based on three different methods and the numbers

Project No	Estimated Completion Date	Property	Location	Number of Units	Number of Bedrooms	Location City/ County	Status
	2000						
	(Approx.)						
34	Aug-00	Bellamay Plantation Apartments	2600 Block S.W. 75th Street	360	n/a	County	Completed
35	Aug-00	University Town Apartments	3245 S.W. Archer Road	264	820	County	Completed
36	Aug-00	Sterling University Glades	3443 S.W. 39th Blvd.	120	432	County	Completed
37	Aug-00	Sante Fe Pointe Apartments	9100 Blk N.W. 83rd St.	168	672	County	Completed
38	Aug-00	Campus Lodge Apartments	2800 Blk. S.W. Williston Rd.	360	1016	County	Completed
39	Aug-00	Countryside at the University -P 2	3800 S.W. 23rd Street	72	288	County	Completed
40	Aug-00	Barrington Ridge Apartments	7000 Blk. W. University Ave	66	148	County	Completed
			Sub-Total	1,410	3,376		
	2001						
	(Approx.)						
41	Aug-01	Kensington Park Apartments	3800 Blk S.W. 20th Avenue	110	220	County	Planned
42	Aug-01	Homestead Phase 3	3600 Blk S.W. 34th Street	180	380	County	Planned
43	Aug-01	Stoneridge Apts. Phase 5	3800 S.W. 34th Street	108	324	County	Planned
44	Aug-01	Victoria Station Apts.	3000 Blk. S.W. 35th Place	65	130	County	Planned
45	Aug-01	Hidden Lake Apts.	1015 N.W. 21st Avenue	221	516	County	Planned
46	Aug-01	Fairfield Apartments	3600 Blk. S.W. 20th Avenue	396	1044	County	Planned
			Sub-Total	1,080	2,614		

Anticipated Supply Analysis

Year	Units	Bedrooms	Average Bedrooms Per Apartment
1996	931	2,476	2.66
1997	833	2,280	2.74
Total 1996/97	1,764	4,756	2.70
1998	1,335		
1999	889		
2000	1,410		
2001	1,080		
Total	4,714		

Total Projects	46	
Average per Project	141	n/a

Building Permit Summary

Year	SFR	MF	Total
1991	892	436	1,328
1992	1,055	588	1,643
1993	962	521	1,483
1994	1,062	520	1,582
1995	924	1,047	1,971
1996	1,040	813	1,853
1997	1,059	606	1,665
1998	1,082	1,138	2,220
Sub-Total	8,076	5,669	13,745
1999 (1)	597	838	1,435
Total	8,673	6,507	15,180
Average/Year 1991-98	1,010	709	1,718

(1) 1999 Permits Through June (6 Months)

SFR = Single Family Residential ; MF = Multiple Family

Updated 1/2000

FIG. 7-1 Continued.

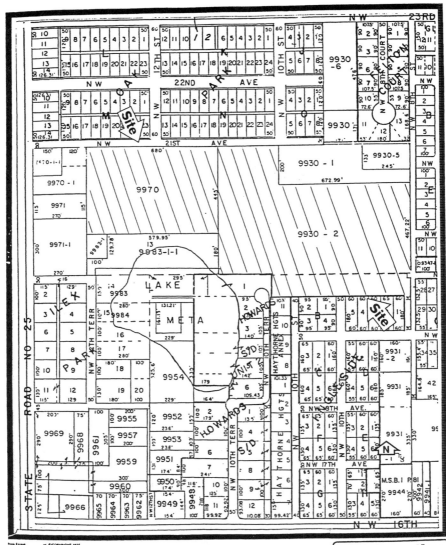

EMERSON APPRAISAL COMPANY
Appraisers, Consultants & Market Analysts

FIG. 7-2 Site location map.

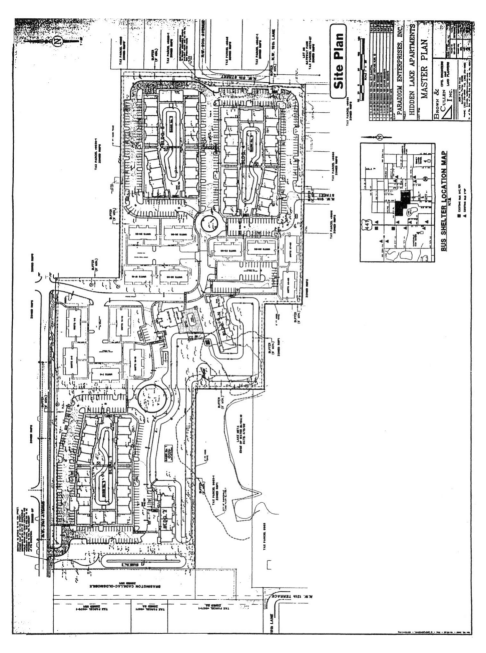

FIG. 7-3 Site plan.

145

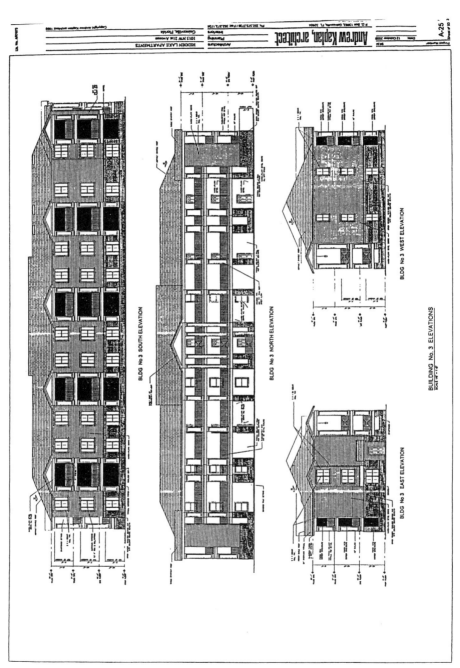

BLDG No 3 SOUTH ELEVATION

BLDG No 3 NORTH ELEVATION

BLDG No 3 WEST ELEVATION

BLDG No 3 EAST ELEVATION

BUILDING No. 3 ELEVATIONS

FIG. 7.4 Building elevations.

146

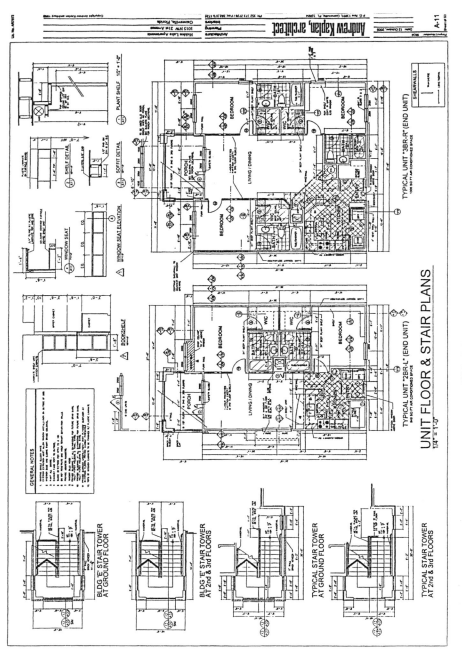

FIG. 7-5 Floor plans.

Comparable Land Sales

Apartment Land Sales Gainesville, Florida

Sale No.	Date	Property	Address	Size SF	Acres	Apt. Units	Density Apartment Units/Acre	Bedrooms	Density Bedrooms Per Acre	Average Bedrooms Per Apt. Unit	Zoning	Sale Price	Time Adj Sale Price Jan-02 5.00%	Per SF	Per Acre	Per Bedroom	Per Apt. Unit
1	Jul-99	Campus Lodge Apts. Lot	2800 Blk. Williston Road	1,463,616	33.60	360	10.7	1016	30.2	2.8	PUD	$2,476,800	$2,776,080	$1.90	$82,621	$2,732	$7,711
2	Aug-97	Paddock Club Apts. Lot	1200 Blk. Ft. Clark Blvd.	1,742,400	40.00	264	6.6	528	13.2	2.0	PUD	$1,800,000	$2,190,000	$1.26	$54,750	$4,148	$8,295
3	Oct-99	Brighton Park Apts. Lot	3100 S.W. 44th Avenue	194,278	4.46	69	15.5	138	30.9	2.0	R-3	$275,000	$304,792	$1.57	$68,339	$2,209	$4,417
4	Nov-95	Campus Club Apts. Lot	4000 S.W. 37th Blvd.	1,132,124	25.99	252	9.7	924	35.6	3.7	R-3	$1,293,875	$1,687,429	$1.49	$64,926	$1,826	$6,696
5	Jan-97	Cottages at Old Archer	2800 Blk. SW Archer Rd.	168,142	3.86	36	9.3	72	18.7	2.0	R-3	$275,000	$342,604	$2.04	$88,757	$4,758	$9,517
Sales Analysis																	
		Low		168,142	3.86	36	6.6	72	13.2	2.0		$275,000	$304,792	$1.26	$54,750	$1,826	$4,417
		High		1,742,400	40.00	360	15.5	1016	35.6	3.7		$2,476,800	$2,776,080	$2.04	$88,757	$4,758	$9,517
		Average		940,112	21.58	196	10.4	536	25.7	2.5		$1,224,135	$1,460,181	$1.65	$71,879	$3,135	$7,327
Subject	Nov-00	Hidden Lake Apartments Proposed	1015 N.W. 21st Avenue	881,665	20.24	260	12.8	594	29.3	2.3							

FIG. 7-6 Land sales table.

Cost Approach Summary

Proposed Hidden Lake Apartment Project
"Stabilized" Market Value
1015 N.W. 21st Avenue Gainesville,Florida

Replacement Cost New,Less Depreciation

Apartment Buildings

Existing Units - Five 3B-1B-2B Buildings	16,050	SF @	$43.97 Per SF	=	$705,719
Existing Units - Eight 2B-2B-2B Buildings	25,440	SF @	$44.50 Per SF	=	$1,132,080
Proposed Units- 2 Bd/2 Bath Units / 147 Units	139,503	SF @	$51.41 Per SF	=	$7,171,849
Proposed Units- 3 Bd/3 Bath Units / 74 Units	96,644	SF @	$49.88 Per SF	=	$4,820,603
	277,637		$49.81 Average		

Sub-Total Apartment Buildings   **$13,830,250**

Other Buildings

Clubhouse Building	2,029	SF @	$85.00 Per SF	=	$172,465

Sub-Total Other Buildings   **$172,465**

Site Improvements and Indirect Costs

Asphalt Parking Lot and Sidewalk Area	594	Spaces. @	$600 Per Space	=	$356,400
Swimming Pool and Decking					$75,000
Landscaping, Lighting,Drainage System,Site Work,Utilities and other misc. Site Improvements					$780,000
Indirect Costs					$1,750,000
Professional fees,Lease-up Costs,Typical Financing Costs,Utility Connection Fees, Etc.					

Sub-Total Site Improvements and Indirect Costs   **$2,961,400**

Furniture,Fixtures and Equipment (F.F. & E.)

Apartment Units (Unfurnished - none)	260	Apt. Units. @	$0 Per Unit		$0
Clubhouse and Common Areas					$180,000

Sub-Total Furniture,Fixtures and Equipment   **$180,000**

	Sub-Total Improvements and F.F. & E. Cost (IC)		**$17,144,115**
Typical Developer/Entrepreneurial Profit	$17,144,115	IC. @ 10.00%	$1,714,412
	Estimated Replacement Cost New (RCN)		**$18,858,527**

Less: Depreciation

Physical Curable	Repairs/Deferred Maintenance	$0
	New Construction/Remodeling - None noted	
Physical Incurable-Real Estate	Simple Effective Age/Economic Life Method	

	45 Yr. Eco. Life -		1.0 Yr. Eff. Age.	2.22%	$414,678
	$18,858,527	RCN			
	$-0	Less: Physical Curable Depreciation			
	($198,000)	Less: F,F & E RCN			
	$18,660,527	Depreciation Base			
	$18,660,527	Dep. Base @	2.22%		

Physical Incurable-F.F. & E.	Simple Effective Age/Economic Life Method	

	8 Yr. Eco. Life -		0 Yr. Eff. Age.	0.00%	$0
	$198,000	RCN X	0.00%	Depreciation	
Functional Depreciation	None noted				$0
External Depreciation	None noted				$0

Total Depreciation   **$414,678**

Depreciated Improvement Value   **$18,443,849**

Add : Land Value   **$1,850,000**

Indicated Value by Cost Approach   **$20,293,849**
Rounded   **$20,290,000**

(1) See attached Marshall & Swift Cost Tabulation Sheet.

FIG. 7-7 Cost tabulations.

Rental No.	Apartment Project	Apt. Unit Type	Unit Rental Per Mo.	Unit Size SF	Unit Rental Per SF	Unit Rental Per BR	Utilities & Services Included in Rent	Reported Occupancy	Amenities/Comments
1	**The Landings Apts.** 3801 S.W. 13th Street	2Br/2.5 Bath	$845	1,100	$0.77	$423	Refuse & Pest	99.0%	Project Built in 1996;92 Units; Good Condition. Unfurnished Apartment Units. Clubhouse,Swimming Pool,Tennis Court. Washer and Dryer hookups in units.
		3Br/3Bath	$1,050	1,226	$0.86	$350			
2	**Colonial Village Apartments** (Formerly Polo's Apts.) 2330 S.W. Williston Road	1Br/1Bath	$595	640	$0.93		Refuse & Pest	99.0%	Project Built in 1989-94;560 Units; Good Condition. Unfurnished Apartment Units. Clubhouse,Swimming Pool,Tennis Court. Washer and Dryer Appliances included in rent.
		2Br/2Bath	$735	903	$0.81	$368			
		3Br/3Bath	$895	1,093	$0.82	$298			
3	**The Laurals Apts.** 4455 S.W. 34th Street	1Br/1Bath	$640	623	$1.03		Refuse & Pest	100.0%	Project Built in 1989-91;254 Units; Good Condition. Unfurnished Apartment Units. Clubhouse,Swimming Pool,Tennis Court. Washer and Dryer Appliances included in rent.
		2Br/2Bath	$795	984	$0.81	$398			
		3Br/3Bath	$999	1,444	$0.69	$333			
4	**Museum Walk Apartments** 3500 S.W. 19th Avenue	2Br/2Bath	$850	1,053	$0.81	$425	Refuse & Pest	94.8%	Project Built in 1997;105 Units; Good/New Condition. Clubhouse,Swimming Pool,Tennis Court. Washer and Dryer Appliances included in rent.
		3Br/3Bath	$1,065	1,344	$0.79	$355			
5	**Oxford Manor Apts.** 2777 S.W. Archer Road	1Br/1Bath	$549	560	$0.98		Refuse & Pest	95.0%	Project Built in 1986-88;366 Units; Good Condition. Unfurnished Apartment Units. Clubhouse,Swimming Pool,Tennis Court. Washer and Dryer Appliances included in rent.
		2Br/2Bath	$724	976	$0.74	$362			
		3Br/3Bath	$960	1,371	$0.70	$320			
6	**Cobblestone Apartments** 2801 N.W. 23rd Blvd.	2Br/2Bath	$855	1,275	$0.67	$428	Refuse & Pest	98.6%	Project Built in 1986-88;366 Units; Good Condition. Unfurnished Apartment Units. Clubhouse,Swimming Pool,Tennis Court. Washer and Dryer Appliances included in rent.
		3Br/3Bath	$1,015	1,407	$0.72	$338			
	Minimum		$549	560	$0.67	$298		94.8%	
	Maximum		$1,065	1,444	$1.03	$428		100.0%	
	Average		$838	1,067	$0.81	$366		97.7%	

Subject - Estimated Rental (January 2002)
Hidden Lake Apartments

		Apt. Unit Type	Unit Rental Per Mo.	Unit Size SF	Unit Rental Per SF	Unit Rental Per BR	Utilities & Services Included in Rent		Amenities/Comments
Existing Units		1Br/1Bath	$575	770	$0.75		Refuse & Pest		Project Proposed for 2001; 260 Units; Good Cond. Washers & Dryers in Units
		2Br/2Bath	$750	1,060	$0.71	$375			
		3Br/2Bath	$925	1,380	$0.67	$308			
Proposed Units		2Br/2Bath	$855	949	$0.90	$428			
		3Br/3Bath	$1,045	1,306	$0.80	$348			
Average					$0.77	$365			

January 2002

Hidden Lake Apartments (Proposed) Gainesville,Florida

	Annual	%	Per Month	Per Sq.Ft. (277,637)	Per Apartment Bedroom (594)	Per Apartment Unit (260)
APARTMENT RENTAL INCOME						
5 - 1 Bedroom/1 Bath Apt. Units						
5 Apartment Units X 12 months X $575/Mo.	$34,500					
29 - 2 Bedroom/2 Bath Apt. Units						
29 Apartment Units X 12 months X $750/Mo.	$261,000					
5 - 3 Bedroom/2 Bath Apt. Units						
5 Apartment Units X 12 months X $925/Mo.	$55,500					
147 - 2 Bedroom/2 Bath Apt. Units						
147 Apartment Units X 12 months X $855/Mo.	$1,508,220					
74 - 3 Bedroom/3 Bath Apt. Units						
74 Apartment Units X 12 months X $1,045/Mo.	$927,960					
TOTAL APARTMENT RENTAL INCOME (ARI)	$2,787,180		$232,265	$10.04	$4,692	$10,720
OTHER INCOME						
Vending,Pet fees, Late fees & Misc. Income - 3.0% ARI	$83,615					
TOTAL OTHER INCOME	$83,615		$6,968	$0.30	$141	$322
TOTAL GROSS INCOME (GI)	$2,870,795		$239,233	$10.34	$4,833	$11,042
LESS VACANCY AND COLLECTION LOSS- 7 %	($200,956)		($16,746)	($0.72)	($338)	($773)
EFFECTIVE GROSS INCOME (EGI)	$2,669,840	100.00%	$222,487	$9.62	$4,495	$10,269
OPERATING EXPENSES						
Real Estate Taxes and Insurance						
Real Estate Taxes	$238,000	8.91%	$19,833	$0.86	$401	$915
Personal Property Taxes	$7,450	0.28%	$621	$0.03	$13	$29
Property Insurance	$38,000	1.42%	$3,167	$0.14	$64	$146
Misc. Taxes, Licenses & Fee's	$2,000	0.07%	$167	$0.01	$3	$8
Sub-Total R.E. Taxes and Insurance Exp.	$285,450	10.69%	$23,788	$1.03	$481	$1,098
Maintenance						
Building Maintenance	$75,000	2.81%	$6,250	$0.27	$126	$288
Yards and Grounds Maintenance	$24,000	0.90%	$2,000	$0.09	$40	$92
Sub-Total Maintenance Expense	$99,000	3.71%	$8,250	$0.36	$167	$381
Utilities Expense						
Common Area - Electricity,Water,Sewer & Refuse	$50,000	1.87%	$4,167	$0.18	$84	$192
Sub-Total Utilities Expense	$50,000	1.87%	$4,167	$0.18	$84	$192
Administrative Expenses						
Management -Base Fee 3.5%	$93,444	3.50%	$7,787	$0.34	$157	$359
On site Management Personal (Manager & Staff)	$180,000	6.74%	$15,000	$0.65	$303	$692
Advertising	$24,000	0.90%	$2,000	$0.09	$40	$92
Bookkeeping,Auditing and Legal Expense	$18,000	0.67%	$1,500	$0.06	$30	$69
Management Supplies and Other Misc. Exp.	$30,000	1.12%	$2,500	$0.11	$51	$115
Sub-Total Administrative Expenses	$345,444	12.94%	$28,787	$1.24	$582	$1,329
Reserves For Replacement						
Appliances, Finishes,Mech. Systems,Misc. 2.5% EGI	$66,746	2.50%	$5,562	$0.24	$112	$257
Sub-Total Reserves for Replacements	$66,746	2.50%	$5,562	$0.24	$112	$257
TOTAL OPERATING EXPENSES	$846,640	31.71%	$70,553	$3.05	$1,425	$3,256
NET OPERATING INCOME (NOI)	$1,823,199	68.29%	$151,933	$6.57	$3,069	$7,012

FIG. 7-9 Stabilized operating statement.

arrived at are compared as a cross check to see how well they converge. The three methods are the Cost Approach, the Income Approach, and the Sales Comparison or Market Approach.

The Cost Approach: Value = Current Land Value + (Cost of Improvements − Depreciation)

Cost of Land   The cost approach is based on the assumption that one measure of value of a real estate project is the cost to duplicate the project less any loss of value due to depreciation. Depreciation may be physical, functional, or external. Physical

Proposed Hidden Lake Apartment Project

"Stabilized" Market Value
1015 N.W. 21st Avenue Gainesville, Florida

Sale Number	Apartment Project	Net Operating Income (% OF EGI)	Operating Expenses (% OF EGI)	Operating Expenses Per Unit	Operating Expenses Per Bedroom	Operating Expenses Per SF
	Gainesville					
1	Camelot Apartments	59.51%	40.49%	$2,621	$1,511	$2.83
2	Lexington Park Apartments	59.46%	40.54%	$6,194	$1,801	$4.95
3	Avenues At College Park	64.40%	35.60%	$3,106	$1,553	$3.62
4	Polos Apartments	56.80%	43.20%	$3,351	$1,700	$3.85
	Other Area Sales					
5	Burmuda Dunes Apts.	63.45%	36.55%	$3,797	$2,170	$3.75
6	Cameron Lakes Apts.	64.71%	35.29%	$2,709	$1,521	$2.52
7	Knights Krossing I & 2	58.15%	41.85%	$6,306	$1,843	$4.92
8	River Walk/River Club	67.26%	32.74%	$3,856	$1,236	$3.14
	Analysis					
	low	**56.80%**	**32.74%**	**$2,621**	**$1,236**	**$2.52**
	High	**67.26%**	**43.20%**	**$6,306**	**$2,170**	**$4.95**
	Average	**61.72%**	**38.28%**	**$3,993**	**$1,667**	**$3.70**
Subject	**Hidden Lake Apartments Proposed**	68.29%	31.71%	$3,256	$1,425	$3.05

FIG. 7-10 Income and expense comparison.

Apartment Market Sales

Apartment Sales Gainesville,Fl./Other Areas

Sale No.	Date	Project	Address	Sale Price*	Year Built	Condition	Total Units	Bed-Rooms	NRA Size SF	GIM	OAR	Avg. Unit Size SF	Avg. Size/BR	Time Adj. Jan-02 3.0%	Time Adj. Price Per/Unit	Time Adj. Price Per/Bed-Room	Time Adj. Price Per/SF
Gainesville Sales																	
1	Jul-99	Camelot Apartments	3425 S.W. 2nd Avenue	$4,900,000	1968/69	Good/Avg.	128	222	118,574	5.56	10.1%	926	534	$5,255,300	$41,057	$23,673	$44.32
2	Nov-98	Lexington Park Apartments	3700 S.W. 27th St.	$30,278,000	1996	Good	300	1,032	375,600	6.28	9.0%	1,252	364	$33,078,700	$110,262	$32,053	$88.07
3	Nov-96	Avenues At College Park	111 N.W. 15th Terrace	$1,500,000	1995	Good	25	50	21,445	6.54	9.4%	858	429	$1,728,800	$69,152	$34,576	$80.62
4	Aug-94	Polos Apartments	2330 S.W. Williston Rd.	$26,820,000	1989-94	Good	560	1,104	478,912	5.86	9.2%	855	434	$32,787,500	$58,549	$29,699	$68.46
Other Area Sales																	
5	Jun-97	Burmuda Dunes Apts.	Orlando , Florida	$25,500,000	1994	Good	336	588	340,602	6.85	8.7%	1,014	579	$29,006,300	$86,328	$49,330	$85.16
6	May-97	Cameron Lakes Apts.	Jacksonville,Florida	$15,869,700	1995	Good	302	538	323,916	5.79	9.5%	1,073	602	$18,091,500	$59,906	$33,627	$55.85
7	Nov-98	Knights Krossing I & 2	Orlando , Florida	$44,043,500	1995-97	Good	456	1,560	583,920	6.03	9.1%	1,281	374	$48,117,500	$105,521	$30,845	$82.40
8	Aug-99	River Walk/River Club	Athens , Georgia	$32,800,000	1996-98	Good	366	1,142	448,822	7.23	8.8%	1,226	393	$35,096,000	$95,891	$30,732	$78.20
		Sales Analysis				Low	25	50		5.56	8.7%	855	364		$41,057	$23,673	$44.32
						High	560	1,560		7.23	10.1%	1,281	602		$110,262	$49,330	$88.07
						Average	309	780		6.27	9.2%	1,061	464		$78,333	$33,067	$72.89
Subject	Jan-02	Hidden Lake Apartments Proposed	1015 N.W. 21st Avenue		2001	Good	260	594	277,837			1,068	467				

* Cash equivalent basis

FIG. 7-11 Market sales table.

depreciation is evidenced by wear and tear, deferred maintenance, or structural decay. Functional depreciation, sometimes called functional obsolescence, may be due to poor floor plan layout or another inadequacy. Functional depreciation often occurs as a result of changes in market demands or in customer expectations or needs over time; for instance, older buildings may lack the upgraded wiring to handle modern communication needs, and various architectural styles fall in and out of grace. Office buildings built before the 1950s were rarely air-conditioned; now it would be unthinkable to build without air-conditioning. Other examples of functional obsolescence abound in the single-family market. There was a time when a three-bedroom, one-bath house with a single garage was the norm. Now two or two and a half baths are de rigueur and double garages the minimum. Compliance with the Americans with Disabilities Act creates interesting issues of obsolescence, as do increasingly complex fire, health, and safety codes. Environmental issues also raise interesting issues of functional obsolescence; even trace amounts of nonfriable asbestos can create marketing issues even where no true health issues exist. External obsolescence is a loss in value due to conditions outside the property, such as an oversupply or other condition that usually affects a broad class of properties.

The cost approach begins with the value of the land and moves on to determine the cost of construction. A search is made for recent, comparable sales of vacant land. The sales are adjusted to compensate for any favorable financing and for market conditions at a rate of 5% per year. Five comparable land sales were found for this property (see Figure 7-6).

Land Sale 1 is 2 miles southwest of the University of Florida and represents the 33.6-acre Campus Lodge Apartments lot, which was developed with 360 apartments and 1,016 bedrooms. The lot sold in July 1999 with an adjusted price to January 2002 (the estimated stabilization date of Hidden Lake Apartments) of $82,621 per acre, $2,732 per bedroom, and $7,711 per apartment.

Land Sale 2 is the 264-apartment, 528-bedroom Paddock Club Apartments lot, which is a larger 40-acre plot that sold in August 1997 for $1,800,000. This yields a time-adjusted price of $54,750 per acre, or $4,148 per bedroom, and $8,295 per apartment.

Land Sale 3 is the Brighton Park Apartments lot, a smaller 4.46-acre parcel of land that sold in October 1999 for $275,000 and was improved with 69 two-bedroom units. The time-adjusted purchase price was $68,339 per acre, $2,209 per bedroom, and $4,417 per apartment.

Land Sale 4 is the Campus Club Apartments 25.99-acre parcel, which contains 252 apartments and 924 bedrooms. The lot sold in November 1995, which yields a time-adjusted purchase price of $64,926 per acre, $1,826 per bedroom, and $6,696 per apartment.

Land Sale 5 is the Cottages at Old Archer, a smaller 3.86-acre lot that sold in January 1997 for $275,000, yielding a time-adjusted purchase price of $88,757 per acre, $4,758 per bedroom, and $9,517 per apartment unit, based on proposed improvements of 36 two-bedroom units.

The range of prices per acre is from $54,750 to $88,757, with an average per acre price of $71,879. The per-bedroom price ranges from $1,826 to $4,758, with an average price of $3,135 per bedroom. The price per apartment sale varied from a low of $4,417 to $9,517, with $7,327 the average.

The subject property will contain 20.24 acres and have a density of 260 apartment units and 594 bedrooms. The appraiser considered the most comparable land sales to be the larger apartment tracts of land with similar locational characteristics in regard to the major activity centers in the Gainesville area; thus, he estimated the subject tract of land "to have a land value towards the middle upper end of the range as indicated by the available comparable sales."

Thus, the following value estimates were arrived at:

$$\text{Price per Acre Method: } 20.24 \text{ acres} \times \$87,500 \text{ per acre} = \$1,771,000$$
$$\text{Price per Bedroom Method: } 594 \text{ BDs} \times \$3,250 \text{ per BD} = \$1,930,500$$
$$\text{Price per Apartment Method: } 260 \text{ Apts.} \times \$7,000 \text{ per Apt.} = \$1,820,000$$

$$\text{Final Estimate of Land Value} = \$1,850,000$$

Note that this estimate is about 15% less than the $2,200,000 value that the developer placed on the land in his preliminary pro forma.

Cost of Improvements Figure 7-7 shows how the appraiser calculated the cost of the four main components of the improvements: Apartment Buildings, the Clubhouse, Site Improvements/Indirect Costs, and Furniture, Fixtures, and Equipment.

Apartment Buildings: Using Marshall and Swift cost data, the appraiser estimated the reproduction (replacement) cost of the existing 39 units at between $43.97 and $44.50 per square foot and a cost to complete the new apartments at between $49.88 and $51.41 per square foot, yielding a total cost for the apartment buildings of $13,830,250.

The Clubhouse: The clubhouse was estimated at $85 per square foot, for a total of $172,465.

Site Improvements/Indirect Costs: The parking lot and sidewalks were estimated at $600 per space (one per bedroom), for a total of $356,400, and the swimming pool and decking came in at $75,000. Landscaping, lighting, drainage system, site work, and other miscellaneous site improvements were estimated at $780,000. Indirect costs, such as professional fees, lease up costs, typical financing costs, utility connection fees, and so on, were estimated at $1,750,000.

Furniture, Fixtures, and Equipment: Furniture, fixtures, and equipment for the clubhouse were estimated at $180,000. This represents the cost to professionally decorate the clubhouse to make it a marketing showplace for the apartment community, outfit the gym area with high-quality exercise machines, and equip the appropriate portions as functioning offices complete with desks, computers, copier, and so forth.

The appraiser then ran a subtotal, getting $17,114,115. To this the appraiser added a typical developer/entrepreneurial profit of 10%, or $1,714,412, for a total estimated Reproduction Cost New (RCN) of $18,858,527.

Less: Depreciation   Depreciation represents the loss of value over time due to wear and tear and any obsolescence. Because this 260-apartment development has a 39-unit existing component and $18,858,527 is the cost to replace the entire 260 apartments when brand new, the appraiser had to address the issue of depreciation on the existing 39 apartments. There are several types of depreciation to assess.

Physical Curable Depreciation: Physical curable depreciation is essentially deferred maintenance, repairs that should be done but have not been done. The appraiser determined that there was no curable physical depreciation; the 39 units had been well taken care of and there were no outstanding maintenance issues that would detract from value.

Physical Incurable Depreciation: The components of a building's furniture, fixtures, and equipment (FF&E), do not last forever; doors may have to be replaced, doorknobs will not work forever, a refrigerator may have a useful life of 15 years before needing to be replaced. At any given point in time these components do not need to be replaced (i.e., they are not yet ready to be cured), but sooner or later they will have to be replaced and an allowance must be made for the loss of value today represented by that future cost.

Functional Depreciation: Depreciation can also occur as a result of obsolescence internal to the property. Tastes change, technology advances. Buildings built in the 1950s and 1960s prior to the widespread advent of central air-conditioning suffered functional obsolescence until they were renovated. Office buildings that are not rewired to handle today's high-speed data requirements run the risk of functional obsolescence. Fifty years ago single-bathroom homes were the norm; today multiple bathrooms are a must. Room sizes have increased. Properties that do not reflect these current standards are examples of functional depreciation. External obsolescence also is taken into account.

The appraiser determined that the total depreciation was $414,678. This number was subtracted from the estimated RCN to obtain a Depreciated Improvement Value of $18,443,849. To this number was added the Land Value of $1,850,000, for a total Indicated Value by Cost Approach of $20,293,849, or $20,290,000 rounded.

The Income Approach

The premise of the income approach is that the value of a commercial real estate property lies in the income stream it generates. The income stream is simply income less operating expenses, or net income. It is important to note that the income stream we use to determine value is before debt service. The method used to finance the acquisition of real estate, although it may impact the rate of return on equity invested, is separate from the value of the underlying real estate.

The appraiser estimates the net income from the operation of the real estate and then capitalizes it at a rate that is commensurate with the risk involved and the life expectancy of the improvements on the real estate. As discussed in Chapter 6, capitalization rates (or cap rates) are set by the marketplace and reflect the marketplace's desired return on a particular product type, given its current income and future outlook. Cap rates are generally determined deductively, based on the sales of similar projects. For example, if similar projects with a yearly net operating income of $1 million are selling for $10 million, then the prevailing capitalization rate for projects of that quality is 10%: $1,000,000/$10,000,000 = 10%. Net operating income (the income stream) divided by cap rate (the appropriate market return) equals value (what the free marketplace will pay): NOI/cap rate = value.

The income approach has three main steps:

1. Estimate income.
2. Estimate expenses.
3. Determine the capitalization rate.

Estimating Income   When the appraiser is asked to estimate fee simple market value, market rent should be used. This is the rent that could be obtained if the improvements on the real estate were occupied and rented at market levels. Market rent can be above or below actual rents. In office buildings, for example, credit tenants may have signed long-term leases during vibrant economic times agreeing to rents that exceed current market rents in a more subdued business environment.

On the other hand, it is not unusual for apartment rents for existing residents to slightly lag market rents as management's inducement for existing residents to renew.

The appraiser assumes that the real estate will be operated in a competent manner and to the standards of professional property management, and this assumption will guide the estimates of operational expenses, occupancy, and rental income.

As in the approach for determining land value, comparables are sought. Existing apartment communities whose characteristics are thought to be sufficiently similar to the subject property are examined to determine the appropriate rental structure.

In this case, the appraiser chose six available apartment communities as comparables (see Figure 7-8) and reviewed the one-, two-, and three-bedroom rental rates. From this data, minimum, maximum, and average numbers for Unit Rental per Month, Unit Size in Square Feet, Unit Rental per Square Foot, and Unit Rental per Bedroom were tabulated. Applying those numbers to Hidden Lake and adding some professional judgment, elaborated on in the narrative of the appraisal, the appraiser came up with the following potential rental income for Hidden Lake Apartments as of January 1, 2002, the expected stabilization date for the project. (See Fig. 7-9.)

$$
\begin{aligned}
&5 \text{ one-bedroom/one-bath units @ } \$575/\text{month} \times 12 \text{ months} = \$ \quad 34{,}500 \\
&29 \text{ two-bedroom/two-bath units @ } \$750/\text{month} \times 12 \text{ months} = \$ \quad 261{,}000 \\
&5 \text{ three-bedroom/two-bath units @ } \$925/\text{month} \times 12 \text{ months} = \$ \quad 55{,}500 \\
&147 \text{ two-bedroom/two-bath units @ } \$855/\text{month} \times 12 \text{ months} = \$1{,}508{,}220 \\
&74 \text{ three-bedroom/three-bath units @ } \$1{,}045/\text{month} \times 12 \text{ months} = \$ \quad 927{,}960
\end{aligned}
$$

Total estimated apartment rental income $2,787,180

The appraiser also allowed an additional 3% of total apartment income, or $83,615, as "Other Income." Other Income is non-direct-rent money received, such as application fees, pet fees, premium view or location charges, retained damage deposits, late fees, vending machine income, and so forth. Adding the Other Income to the Estimated Apartment Rental Income yielded an estimated Gross Potential Income (GPI) of $2,870,795 for the community.

Based on his knowledge of local market conditions and the operational experience of similar communities, the appraiser selects an appropriate vacancy and collection loss rate for the community. In the case of Hidden Lake, the appraiser selected a vacancy rate of 7% of Gross Potential Income, or $200,956, for the community. Subtracting the vacancy rate from the GPI yielded an Effective Gross Income (EGI) of $2,669,840 per year.

Estimating Expenses   Lacking historical operating statements that would be available for an appraisal of an existing project, an appraiser for a proposed construction project must again make estimates based on the experiences of similar projects in the same geographic area.

For the purposes of this appraisal, operating expenses are divided into five major groups: Real Estate Taxes and Insurance, Maintenance, Utilities Expense, Administrative Expenses, and Reserves for Replacement.

Real Estate Taxes and Insurance: Real estate taxes and insurance include ad valorem property taxes, personal property taxes, and casualty insurance, together with miscellaneous licenses, fees, and minor taxes. Because jurisdictions vary in regard to methods and levels of assessment of real property, a detailed knowledge of local custom and practice is very helpful in determining the appropriate amount of assessed valuation for real estate tax assessment. The assessed value of real estate for purposes of taxation is generally less than valuation for sale or financing. Just as the Federal Income Tax Code has spawned a subindustry of specialized interpretations, definitions, experts, and unique applications, so also, to a lesser extent, has the area of real property taxation. A review of the assessment of three similar projects resulted in a determination that the most probable amount of real estate taxes for the project would be $238,000.

In addition to levying an annual tax on the value of real property, the State of Florida also allows for the levy of a tax on the value of personal property used in a business. Detachable items, such as refrigerators, ovens, and the like, that can be removed without doing structural harm to the building are considered personal property and subject to separate taxation. Again, a survey of similar projects resulted in an estimated personal property valuation for purposes of tax assessment of $1,058 per apartment or $463 per bedroom, or a total of $275,000 for the entire apartment community. The estimated tax millage rate is 27.1 mills or 27 cents of tax per $1,000 of assessed valuation. The amount of $275,000 of personal property valuation taxed at a rate of $.27 per thousand equaled an estimated personal property tax of approximately $7,450.

Casualty insurance costs may be estimated based on prevailing costs at similar properties, or an insurance company quoting rates in the region may be asked for a quote. The annual insurance cost estimate arrived at by the appraiser is $38,000. Miscellaneous taxes and fees were estimated at $2,000 per year. The total for real estate taxes and insurance is $285,450 per year or $23,788 per month, or $1.03 per square foot of building area, $481 per bedroom, $1,098 per apartment, or 10.69% of effective gross income.

Maintenance: Maintenance covers the care of the buildings, exterior and interior, care of the yards and grounds, pool service, maintenance supplies, and pest control. Building maintenance includes heating and air-conditioning repairs, plumbing and electrical repairs, and any needed maintenance to the exterior surface of the building.

Yards and grounds maintenance is generally contracted out to a service; a fee of $2,000 per month, or $24,000 per year, is typical. Building maintenance and supplies can cost from 15 to 50 cents per square foot even for new construction, with building design, floor plan and site layout, as well as materials used all impacting potential costs. This project is well designed, with only two floor plans and no elevators, and is located in an area with reasonable labor costs; therefore, a maintenance expense of 27 cents per square foot is chosen. This amount is calculated to be about $75,000 per year, or $6,250 per month. Combining the yard maintenance and building maintenance numbers gives an annual number of $99,000, or $8,250 per month, 36 cents per square foot, $167 per bedroom, $381 per apartment, or 3.71% of effective gross income.

Utilities Expense: Utilities expense covers garbage collection and electric, water, and sewer for the common areas. The costs of lighting an apartment community at night along with normal utility costs for the clubhouse and pool area, can be significant. Residents are expected to bear the costs of electric, water, and sewer for their own units. Utility expenses are estimated at $50,000 per year, or $4,167 per month, 18 cents per square foot, $84 per bedroom, $192 per apartment, or 1.87% of effective gross income.

Administrative Expense: Administrative expenses include any management fee charged by a professional management firm hired to oversee the operation of the property, as well as the costs of the normal office and clerical functions required to run an apartment community. These expenses include office and leasing staff payroll, marketing and advertising expenses, bookkeeping costs, the costs of office supplies, telecommunication costs, and miscellaneous expenses.

Management fees range from 3% to 5% of the rents collected for large, high-end projects and as much as 12% to 15% for a stand-alone single-family rental. Generally, the more upscale the community, the lower the management fee: 3% of $1,000 in rent yields close to the same management fee as 7% of $450 in rent. The larger the community, the lower the management fee: Three hundred apartments in one location imposes significantly less than three times the administrative workload of 100 units. Economies of scale certainly exist in the operation of apartment communities and are greatest in apartment communities of 200 to 300 or 400 units, and are significantly better toward the high end of that scale. In communities of more than 300 or 400 units the economies of scale begin to taper off sharply.

A very loose rule of thumb in the apartment industry is a minimum of one service person and one office person per one hundred apartments. With fewer than 100 units this staffing level works against you. You either have to staff at levels that make your per-unit labor costs higher than your larger competitors or you have to use part-time help and run the risk of losing marketing leads when you are not open or not there when your residents seek help.

One hundred units can be staffed one and one, office and service; however, there is no slack for vacation, sick leave, or the busy first week of the month when rents come in to be processed. Furthermore, each person must be the classic jack-of-all-trades and master of none. The service person must either possess the skills to handle all repairs across the board, such as electrical, plumbing, and carpentry, or the expense of an outside vendor must be borne. The office person must be skilled in leasing, customer service, bookkeeping, and other administrative tasks.

At 200 units, you can have a professional on-site manager and afford to hire a slightly less skilled and less expensive leasing agent. They may alternate taking a morning off during the week in order to keep the office open half days on Saturdays and Sundays. The same goes for service personnel: A more skilled supervisor can oversee the work of a handyman.

In the mid-200 unit range (for instance, at the 260-unit level of Hidden Lake Apartments), staffing can be adjusted by using part-time help to achieve a level of 2.5 full-time equivalents (FTE), or you can average out to 2.5 FTE for the year by staffing with three people during busy seasons and dropping down to two persons during off-peak times. These numbers apply to both office and service staffing.

At 300 units, even greater economies of scale and administrative ease are possible by fine-tuning skill levels to position needs, along with establishing a certain critical mass of people to form a true operations team capable of performing extensive backup.

For Hidden Lake, the management fee is put at 3.5% of effective gross income, or $93,444. It is estimated that $180,000 in payroll costs, including benefits, will cover on-site personnel. This includes the manager and the leasing and service staff. Other administrative costs, including marketing and advertising, are estimated at $24,000 per year. Bookkeeping and legal are estimated at $18,000 per year. Miscellaneous administrative is put at $30,000 per year, for a total administrative expense of $345,444, or $28,787 per month, $1.24 per square foot, $582 per bedroom, $1,329 per apartment, or 12.94% of effective gross income.

Reserves for Replacement: The final expense category is Reserves for Replacement, which covers such capital items as roof replacement, replacement of major appliances, parking lot resurfacing, air-conditioning and heating replacement, and the like. Reserves for replacement typically run from 2% to 5% of effective gross income, or $200 to $500 per apartment per year.

Because this is a newly constructed project, a reserve for replacement of 2.5% of effective gross income, or $66,746, will be used. This is $5,562 per month, or 24 cents per square foot, or $257 per apartment.

Net Operating Income   This project is estimated to have total operating expenses of $846,640, which is 31.71% of gross effective income, or $70,553 per month, $3.05 per square foot, $1,425 per bedroom, or $3,256 per apartment.

When the total operating expenses of $846,640 are subtracted from the project's effective gross income of $2,669,840, an annual net operating income (NOI) of $1,823,199 is achieved. This is the annual operating income stream that we will attempt to value via a capitalization rate. Figure 7-10 shows how Hidden Lake Apartments' income and expenses compare with those of eight other apartment communities on both a percentage of effective gross income, and on a per unit, per bedroom, and per square foot basis.

Determining the Capitalization Rate   Two common methods for valuing proper-ties based on their net income streams are an analysis of discounted cash flows (DCF), with a revision factor and appropriate property yield rate, and direct capi-talization. The discounted cash flow method is used most often when dealing with uneven income streams or going through an initial lease up. Apartment projects at stabilized occupancy typically put out a very steady income stream, so discounted cash flow analysis will be forgone in favor of the direct capitalization method.

Apartments generally enjoy a steady income stream for several reasons. One is that the large number of leases for the project mean that the loss of any one lease has minimal impact, unlike the loss of an anchor tenant for a regional mall. Another reason for the stable income stream is the very nature of apartment communities and their market: Population tends to be either stable or growing within a given geographic area. Also contributing to the stability of apartment income streams is the high priority people give to obtaining shelter.

Capitalization rates to be applied to the net operating income stream of real estate can be derived through a market analysis of comparable apartment sales. If we know the sales price of comparable apartment communities and we know their net operating income, then simple division of net operating income, as of the date of sale, by the sales price will yield the proper capitalization rate. After evaluating recent sales, the appraiser picked a capitalization rate of 8.75% for this project.

Final Value by the Income Approach   Dividing Hidden Lake's estimated net operating income of $1,823,199 by a capitalization rate of 8.75% yields, via the income approach, an indicated value of $20,836,560, or $20,840,000 when rounded.

Note that this value is very close to the valuation of $20,290,000 reached via the cost approach. We now have one final method of valuation to examine, the market or sales comparison approach.

The Market Approach

The premise of the market approach is that the recent open market sales of similar projects provide guidance as to the valuation of the project at hand.

A sales search of the Gainesville market showed four recent sales of apartments within the area; only three of which were for relatively new projects (see Figure 7-11,

Apartment Market Sales): Sale 2, Lexington Park Apartments; Sale 3, The Avenues at College Park Apartments; and Sale 4, The Polos Apartments. Sale 1, Camelot Apartments, is an older apartment community included because of its size, but it is not representative of the prices obtained for newer apartment communities.

Because of the dearth of recent sales of newer and larger apartments in the Gainesville area, the appraiser expanded the sales search to North Central Florida and other university towns in the southeastern United States. This expanded search turned up two sales in the Orlando urban area: Sale 5, the Bermuda Dunes Apartments, and Sale 7, the Knights Crossing Apartments located near the University of Central Florida. Sale 6 is the Cameron Lake Apartments in Jacksonville, Florida, home of the University of North Florida. Sale 8 is the River Walk/River Club Apartments in Athens, Georgia, home of the University of Georgia.

The table in Figure 7-11 summarizes the information obtained from the sales search (NRA stands for Net Rentable Area). The information in this table is used to support two methods of arriving at value using the market comparison approach. The first is the Gross Income Multiplier method and the second is the Physical Comparison method.

Gross Income Multiplier   The Gross Income Multiplier (GIM) is obtained by dividing the sales price by annual gross income (GPI) derived from a project. For example, if Hidden Lake sold for the $20,840,000 valuation given by the income approach, its GIM would be 7.27 (GIM = sales price/GPI or 7.27 = $20,840,000/$2,870,795).

GIM is a quick way of comparing projects. The strength of this method is its ease of use; it does not require any knowledge of the actual operating expenses, actual vacancies, or actual income for a project. You simply need to know the market rent amounts for the given unit mix of a community, and you can quickly calculate Gross Potential Income. The weakness of the GIM method is related to its strength, in that use of GIM makes three important assumptions:

1. That all projects have market vacancy rates (or that the project can quickly reach market vacancy rates with professional management)
2. That actual rents are close to market rents for all projects being compared (or that the project can quickly reach market rents under professional management)
3. That there are uniform expense characteristics among the projects being compared

The last assumption can be the most crucial. Assuming cost uniformity is a dangerous practice unless you are an experienced professional; cost structures can change significantly between geographic regions and project type and design. The first two assumptions really repeat basic assumptions underlying the appraisal process—that market rents and vacancies rates are obtainable—because that is inherent in defining them as the market rates. If they were not achievable, they would not be the market rates.

In essence, the GIM for a property is that property's price-earnings ratio and implicitly compensates for variations in property condition, age, unit mix, location, and other factors. The table shows GIM ranging from a low of 5.56 to a high of 7.23, with an average of 6.27. As new construction, the subject property should have a GIM in the range of 6.5 to 7.0, and the appraiser chose to apply a GIM of 6.9. Gross income multipliers are not adjusted for time because it is assumed that sales prices and GPI move in conjunction and thus no adjustments are necessary.

Physical Comparison   The physical comparison method involves comparing the price per square foot and the price per bedroom provided by the sales comparison data obtained from the sales comparison search. Note that the prices are time adjusted at the rate of 3% per year.

The table shows a time-adjusted price per bedroom ranging from $23,673 to $49,330, with an average of $33,067. When prices at the lower and upper ends of the range are removed (similar to Olympic judging), a relatively tight range of values remains: $29,699 to $34,576. The appraiser determined that the characteristics of the project put it at the high end of the range, and a price per bedroom of $34,000 was chosen.

The table shows a time adjusted sales price per square foot of $44.32 to $88.07, with an average of $72.89. When sales prices at the lower and upper ends of the range are removed, the range of values becomes $55.85 to $82.40 per square foot. The appraiser determined that the characteristics of the Gainesville market and the nature of the subject project called for a price per square foot of $70 to $74, with a final value of $72 per square foot chosen from the middle of that range.

We now have three values given by the market approach:

1. A GIM of 6.90
2. A price per bedroom of $34,000
3. A price per square foot of $72

Applying those values to the subject project yields the following results:

Gross Income Multiplier Method:

Gross Potential Income of $2,870,795 × GIM of 6.90 = $19,808,488 or
$19,810,000 (rounded)

Price per Square Foot Method:

279,666 square feet @ $72 per square foot = $20,135,952 or
$20,140,00 (rounded)

Price per Bedroom Method:

594 bedrooms @ $34,000 per bedroom = $20,196,000 or
$20,200,000 (rounded)

Taking a middle value from the range of indicated values for the market approach, the appraiser arrived at an Estimated Stabilized Market Value via the market approach of $20,000,000.

SUMMARY

The three approaches to determining value, cost, income, and market, have given the following three values:

Value by cost approach	$20,290,000
Value by income approach	$20,840,000
Value by market approach	$20,000,000

The appraiser concluded by considering all the elements (quantity and quality of the data in each approach) and giving the most weight to the income approach, and ended up toward the upper middle end of the value range with an Estimated Market Value on a Stabilized Basis (at about January 2002) of $20,600,000, allocated as follows:

Land	$ 1,850,000
Improvements	$18,570,000
Furniture and equipment	$ 180,000
Total	$20,600,000

The *appraiser* is a vital player in the development process, as the appraisal forms the basis for establishing a project's value. According to federal lending laws, the lender of a proposed development hires an appraiser to provide an opinion of a project's value and, subsequently, the amount of financing that is likely to be extended.

By definition, an appraisal is an opinion of value supported by market research. It attempts to define a probable sales price, or *market value*, for a facility that a willing buyer and seller would reach in an arm's-length transaction in a competitive and open market.

A typical appraisal will contain six sections: *general organization, general appraisal information, background information, property data, value conclusion*, and *addenda*. These sections highlight basic facts about the project and its location, the purpose and scope of the appraisal, complete property data and property history, the overall estimate of value, and supplemental information, such as the credentials of the appraiser.

There are three ways that an appraiser can estimate market value, the *cost approach*, the *income approach*, and the *market approach*. The cost approach assumes that the value of the subject property equals the cost to duplicate the project today; it is equal to the current value of land plus the cost of improvements less depreciation. Depreciation can be accounted for in three ways: *physical depreciation, functional obsolescence*, and *external obsolescence*. The income approach uses the net income stream generated by the property divided by the capitalization rate to achieve an estimate of value, and it is usually done in one of two ways: *direct cash flow analysis* or *direct capitalization*. The market approach estimates value by using recent open-market sales of similar projects, and it is typically conducted using either a *gross income multiplier* or *physical comparison*.

KEY TERMS AND DEFINITIONS

Appraisal: An opinion of value supported by market research.

Competitive and open market: Condition for the sale of a property where buyer and seller are both informed and motivated and where the price paid represents the normal consideration for the property, unaffected by special financing or sales concessions.

Cost approach to value: Estimates market value of a property based on the cost to duplicate the project today; equal to the current value of land plus the cost of improvements less depreciation.

External obsolescence: Loss in value due to conditions outside the property; this form of depreciation is largely incurable.

Functional obsolescence: Loss in value due to changes in market demands and/or customer tastes over time; it may be curable or incurable.

Gross income multiplier: A way to estimate the value of the subject property by multiplying it by the property's income stream; it is found by dividing the sales price by the annual gross income derived from the project.

Income approach to value: Estimates market value of a property based on the income stream that it generates.

Market approach to value: Estimates market value of a property by comparing it to recent open-market sales of similar properties.

Market value: Price that a willing buyer and seller would reach in an arm's-length transaction in a competitive, open market.

Physical depreciation: Loss in value due to general wear and tear that normally occurs over time.

KEY LEARNING POINTS

- Understand what an appraisal attempts to define.
- Define how a typical appraisal report is organized.
- Name and define the three types of depreciation estimated when using the cost approach to value.
- Understand how a project's income stream is used to estimate value using the income approach.
- Understand how value is estimated using the market approach.

QUESTIONS

1. To a lender, how does the appraised value of a project affect the amount of financing available?
2. What does an appraisal attempt to define?
3. Name the six sections included in a typical appraisal. In what section is one likely to find information about whether the site is located in a floodplain?
4. Briefly define these items found within an appraisal: site-location map, site plan, and floor plan.
5. On what method does the cost approach base a project's estimated value?
6. The value of depreciation is estimated three ways in the cost approach; name and briefly describe each.
7. In the income approach, name the five typical operating expenses that are subtracted from a project's income stream to produce net income.
8. How does the market approach estimate the value of a property?

8

Sources of Financing, the Loan Application Process, and Term Sheets

INTRODUCTION

In this chapter we discuss the difference between a mortgage broker and a mortgage banker. We talk briefly about construction financing versus permanent financing and then discuss various types of commercial real estate lenders and their market shares. We focus in detail on one of the largest and newer types of lender: commercial mortgage backed securities (CMBS), or CMBS/conduit loans. We then discuss the loan application process and compare two actual term sheets issued on a construction loan application.

BANKER, BROKER: WHAT'S THE DIFFERENCE?

It is important to clearly understand the difference between a mortgage *broker* and a mortgage *banker*. A mortgage broker brings together a lender and a borrower and facilitates the transaction for a fee. Mortgage brokers will often perform some underwriting services as well. They may screen the borrower and the property for financial strength and suitability, and they may also oversee the gathering of the reports and documents necessary to constitute a complete loan application and perform the required analysis of the financial information and reports generated by the property and borrower.

A mortgage banker is the actual lender who makes a loan secured by a mortgage on real estate from his own capital with the intention of selling the loan to another at a later date. This lender is in contrast to a portfolio lender, who makes a loan with the intention of keeping it to maturity. In essence, a mortgage broker provides services, a mortgage banker provides capital.

For a long time prior to regulatory reform, it was exceedingly difficult, if not impossible, for banks in the United States to operate across state lines. As a result, lending was primarily local in nature. That is, a local bank would gather in funds as deposits and then lend them out as loans in the area. If deposits exceeded loan demand or if loan demand exceeded available funds, the local bank was not in a position to easily transfer funds from areas of capital surplus within the country to areas in need of capital. At that time, allocating capital from one area of the country to another was one of the valuable services provided by the mortgage banking industry. Today, with the advent of lending institutions of nationwide scope and the use of commercial mortgage backed securities (CMBS) that act as loan "conduits" between Wall Street and Main Street, the free market reallocates capital as needed virtually automatically.

MORTGAGE BROKERS VS. DIRECT APPLICATION

If visions of development projects are to become realities, the successful investor or developer must find reliable sources of funding. Mortgage brokers can be used, but some lenders maintain their own network of loan officers who can be approached directly. In either case, a good loan package should be prepared containing all pertinent information on the borrower, the site, and the project, along with a pro forma. Mortgage brokers perform somewhat the same function as internal loan officers for a commercial bank. They service and maintain the borrower relationship during the transaction, act as a connection point and as a conduit of information, and do some independent verification of the information contained in the loan package. They may also oversee the gathering of the vast amounts of paperwork, certifications, and reports that are involved in the loan process.

The mortgage broker can serve as an experienced guide through this paperwork maze, as he should be familiar with each lender's preferences and idiosyncrasies. And the broker can not only select an appropriate lender for any given project but potentially expedite the request for funds directed toward that lender. Mortgage brokers typically give the borrower an estimate of the amount of funds that may be borrowed and the terms available. These will vary greatly, depending on the type of lender approached. For example, insurance companies and pension funds have a reputation for offering the lowest rates, but they usually want the lowest loan to value—that is, fewer loan proceeds for the borrower. Commercial bank loans are typically the fastest and most flexible; but they usually require a personal and/or corporate guarantee (depending upon the size and quality of their respective balance sheets), have loan terms of five years or less, and have a variable interest rate. (Although a locked rate can be purchased easily in the financial markets, it will typically be a higher fixed rate than that offered by a CMBS/conduit loan. For example, in early 2007, a 10-year interest rate swap to fix a variable loan to a fixed rate over a given index, for an 80% loan to value, class B multifamily loan in excess of $10 million dollars, cost approximately 55 basis points. Remember, a basis point is 1/100 of a percent—that is, 100 basis points = 1. The price of a swap varies greatly with market conditions and the specifics of any loan. Furthermore, it is a bit of a misnomer to say that a swap spread to fix a loan was such and such on a given day, as the rates vary throughout the day and typically only the last quote of the day is given as the rate for the day). Obviously, the options are many, and a borrower must know her priorities.

Mortgage brokers may be able to shop a loan to a greater variety of sources than the borrower can, and they are in constant touch with the market. Sometimes a mortgage broker may be able to stimulate a lender's interest by vouching for the borrower to the lender. A mortgage broker's reputation with his lenders is one of the important assets that a broker brings to the transaction. Typically, each lender has a slightly different format for providing the information required for approval of a loan application, and each lender may turn down a request if incorrect or insufficient data is presented or if the data is not presented in a form approved by the institution.

The same lender may use internal loan officers for construction lending and brokers for its capital markets/permanent lending group. Indeed, as the result of mergers and the legacy of ongoing operations and relationships, the same lender may use both internal loan officers and brokers to make the same type of loan, giving the borrower the choice of how to proceed. Indeed, because a given lender may maintain relationships with many mortgage brokers, it is not unheard of for different mortgage brokers to quote to a borrower different loan terms from the same lender. This is because they essentially are estimating, based on their prior experience (which may vary from the stated policies), what a lender will be willing to do with a given property and a given borrower. This quote is sometimes called a term sheet, a nonbinding statement about the terms and conditions under which the loan will be granted. When dealing with a mortgage broker, particularly for the first time, a cautious borrower may inquire as to whether the term sheet proffered is based upon a written term sheet from the lender, a verbal conversation, or simply past dealings. It is not unheard of to have a conference call that includes the borrower, the lender, and the mortgage broker to gauge the extent of the lender's interest and the depth of his knowledge of the real estate in question. A lender who issues a term sheet without delving deeply into the loan package is to be avoided, as he is likely to issue a commitment letter substantially at variance with his term sheet. An interesting question to ask of any lender or mortgage broker is what percentage of term sheets issued lead to commitment letters and what percentage of commitment letters lead to loan closings.

Although it is not a frequent occurrence, an astute borrower should be wary of a bait-and-switch offering whereby a lender and/or mortgage broker promise terms better than they can deliver. There are many unknowns in borrowing, and fully exploring an option to the point of reasonable certainty takes time and money. Given these uncertainties, a borrower, having invested much time, energy, and money pursuing a given loan opportunity, may choose to proceed even if the final terms are not as generous as originally stated. In all fairness, the vast majority of lenders and mortgage brokers do their best for their clients and care sincerely about their own reputations.

Although some mortgage brokers may also serve as mortgage bankers, making loans out of their own capital and then selling them, mortgage brokers per se do not provide their own funds for any project. They are professionals whose job it is to be middlemen between borrower and lender, collecting a fee for matching would-be borrowers with appropriate lenders. The broker's job is to arrange the loan, and that is all. After the loan is closed, the broker has no more interest in it. The broker's fee usually is about .5% to 2% of the loan amount. In most states, mortgage brokers are licensed by the state after passing a written examination.

CONSTRUCTION AND PERMANENT FINANCING

Usually, two major loans are required to finance a project, although some lenders will combine these into one. The two loan types are:

1. *Short-term financing* to finance the construction stage.
2. *Long-term, permanent financing* of a mortgage loan obtained upon completion of construction and stabilization, used to finance the project over its normal operating life. Stabilization is the point at which a project has fully leased up to the market level of occupancy and has been in operation long enough to have a solid track record of income and expenses on which a lender can rely in making a permanent, long-term loan.

Construction Financing

Occasionally a developer may obtain some sort of preconstruction short-term financing such as land purchase loans, land development loans, "front" capital, or "gap" financing; however, these types of loans are relatively rare and expensive for the simple reason that there is inadequate collateral to secure the loan. Although the land itself can serve as collateral, loans on raw land are typically at 50% or less of market value because raw land is illiquid (it cannot be readily converted into cash), and raw land does not produce an income stream with which to service the loan. Lending funds to cover development costs prior to the start of construction is highly speculative, and the rates charged on such a loan, if it could be obtained at all, would reflect those risks.

The construction loan is usually the first institutional-quality loan involved in a development project. Construction loans are most commonly made by commercial banks; however, many other institutions are players in the construction loan arena, including life insurance companies and various finance companies. Construction loans are meant to be replaced with permanent financing when the project is completed. Obviously, the construction lender is in an undesirable position if the developer is unable to obtain permanent financing at the end of construction. The degree of assurance that the construction lender requires so that permanent financing will be available at the end of construction varies according to the type of project.

At one end of the spectrum, a construction lender may require a take-out commitment (a promise of permanent financing) from a lending source that it considers credible before it is willing to lend on certain types of office or retail developments that have not presigned any major tenants. On the other hand, a construction loan for a well-sited apartment community by an experienced developer and investor team would not typically require any commitment from a permanent lending source. This is because the market for the permanent financing of apartments is well established and loans are readily available.

In intermediate situations, a construction lender on a condominium project may require a certain percentage of presales (50% is a common number) before authorizing the start of construction. A strip center or mall may need signed leases from several anchor tenants to proceed.

Permanent Financing

There are several sources from which a developer can obtain permanent financing for a project. The source to approach depends on the size and nature of the project. In some instances, a particular lending institution can handle any type and size of real estate venture. But there are some financial institutions, such as insurance companies and pension funds, that will not lend less than a million dollars. On the other hand, all banks are restricted to lending no more than 5% of their equity capital on any one loan, and for certain smaller or regional commercial banks this may mean they cannot lend on larger projects. However, even when a small bank is incapable of handling a larger loan, it can join forces temporarily with another bank or banks, all participating in a given loan, thus forming a financing joint venture. In that case, the originating bank handles the details involved in getting the total sum requested by the developer. The developer usually has no contact at all with the other participating banks, because all of the joint loan arrangements with the other banks are worked out by the originating bank. However, the process of lining up the other participating institutions may delay processing the loan, particularly if there is anything unusual about the project, loan application, or borrower.

The term *permanent financing* is a bit of a misnomer because much so-called permanent financing, although amortized over 25 or 30 years, is for a term of just 10 years. Remember, *amortization* refers to the length of time it will take for a given periodic payment of principal and interest to extinguish a debt, whereas *term* refers to the length of time the debt is to be owed. When the period of the term is shorter than the period of the amortization, then the debt is said to balloon, and a single large payment of principal is due to repay the loan at the end of the term. There are several reasons that the term for permanent financing is often shorter than the amortization:

- Lenders wish to avoid lending too far into a distant and murky future.
- Borrowers frequently expect their properties to appreciate and believe that significant tax-free capital may be obtained by refinancing at periodic intervals.
- The owners intend to sell within the 10-year time period and are aware that new owners typically refinance the properties anyway.

If lenders are willing to lend beyond 10 years, they typically charge a premium of 10 to 50 basis points, a premium that, from the borrower's point of view, is wasted money if the property is refinanced earlier.

Permanent, fixed rate financing frequently has prepayment penalties. Prepayment penalties range all the way from a basic yield maintenance formula designed to maintain the lender's expected return in case a borrower decides to refinance because of falling interest rates, to high set fees that seem to be structured more as profit centers for the lender than to address any true cost involved or compensate for lost profits.

LENDER TYPES

Although all of the various institutions that lend long-term capital for real estate projects at times may be referred to as banks, there are five leading sources of lending in the commercial real estate field:

1. Commercial mortgage backed securities (CMBS), or conduit loans
2. Insurance companies
3. Quasi-governmental corporations such as Fannie Mae (Federal National Mortgage Association, FNMA) and Freddie Mac (Federal Home Loan Mortgage Corporation, FHLMC) and governmental agencies such as the Federal Housing Administration (FHA)
4. Commercial banks
5. Pension funds and other trusts, credit companies, private investors

Although the market shares of various types of commercial real estate lenders fluctuate according to market conditions, Figure 8-1 illustrates the breakdown of loan origination by lender type and property type for the first quarter of 2000. Note that these tables refer to the ultimate source of the funds, not the front organization with which the borrower may deal during the process of obtaining the loan. For example, a life insurance company will frequently use a mortgage broker to solicit and screen its loan applications, and a borrower may never have direct contact with the true source of the funds.

Each of the aforementioned lender types offers certain advantages and disadvantages, and within each type there are a number of individual firms doing business.

Because commercial mortgage backed securities (CMBS/conduit loans) have become such an important factor in the commercial real estate lending market, we will discuss them in some detail with an occasional comparison or reference to the characteristics of other lender types and then discuss, in general, the loan application process and term sheets.

CMBS: COMMERCIAL MORTGAGE BACKED SECURITIES, OR CONDUIT LOANS

Commercial mortgage backed securities (CMBS/conduit loans) constitute a specialized form of mortgage banking that has emerged as a major source of real estate lending in the last few years. Institutions make hundreds of separate real estate loans, bundle the loans, and use them as collateral for a bond offering that is then sold on Wall Street. They are called conduit loans because the lender is

Lender Type	$ Amount (000s)	%
CMBS or Conduit Loans	$3,248,282	29.0%
Life Insurance Company	$2,833,969	25.3%
Fannie Mae, Freddie Mac, FHA	$2,455,805	21.9%
Commercial Banks	$1,193,108	10.6%
Pension Fund	$187,614	1.7%
Credit Company	$156,942	1.4%
Other	$1,132,315	10.1%
TOTAL	11,208,035	100.0%

Loan Origination by Property Type

Property Type	$ Amount (000s)	%
Multifamily	$5,143,600	45.9%
Office Building	$2,958,997	26.4%
Retail	$1,148,997	10.2%
Industrial	$828,162	7.4%
Health Care	$353,314	3.2%
Hotel/Motel	$243,937	2.2%
Other	$531,258	4.7%
Total	11,208,036	100.0%

FIG. 8-1 Loan origination by lender and property type. (*Source*: Mortgage Bankers' Association, published *in Florida Real Estate Journal*, October 16–31, 2000, page 9.)

acting as a conduit between the real estate market and Wall Street, and the result is called a commercial mortgage backed security.

Lenders strive to use uniform documents and common underwriting standards for all loans so as to reduce the complexity of the loan packages and achieve greater marketability of the resulting offering. It is not unusual for the stack of documents required for a conduit closing to be quite thick and the mortgage itself to run dozens and dozens of pages.

Single-Purpose Entity

Conduit lenders generally require that the owner of the property to be mortgaged be a single-purpose entity, that is, it should own no assets other than those incidental to the operation of the property. This is to simplify matters in case of a default and subsequent foreclosure.

Nonrecourse Loans and Carve-Outs

Conduit loans are typically nonrecourse loans to the borrower; that is, in the event of default, the lender can look only to the loan for repayment. This is obviously a major benefit for the borrower. Such loans generally have carve-outs, which means that some liability exists for certain eventualities, such as fraud in the application, failure to pay income taxes or insurance, misapplication of rent, environmental transgressions, and so forth.

Loan Quality and Rating Agencies

The larger the offering and the better the quality of the loans within it, the better the interest rate the lender achieves. Sometimes a lender purchases loans from other lenders (generally lenders too small to put together their own CMBS) in order to achieve a critical mass for their offering, although this may create issues concerning the uniformity of loan documentation and underwriting standards. Independent rating agencies, much like bond rating agencies, will rate the quality of the loans within the CMBS prior to sale. Real estate loans are typically ranked by sector and then by the quality of the property for which the loan is made within that sector. For instance, apartments are generally considered the lowest risk of all real estate sectors because of the steadiness of the income stream. Office property generally follows apartments, and retail and hotel developments are considered among the more volatile sectors (restaurants fail with regularity, hotel occupancies fluctuate significantly according to economic activity as business travel and vacation plans are among the first things to be put off in an economic downturn). Within each sector, loans are rated according to the quality of the properties that secure them. A brand new office building fully occupied with grade A, Fortune 50 tenants, at market rents, with long-term leases tied to Consumer Price Index escalator clauses, in midtown Manhattan, generally ranks much higher than a 30-year-old suburban office complex with no-name tenants who have so-so credit histories in Tulsa. Commercial mortgage backed securities are sold in layers, or tranches, with buyers able to choose the degree of risk in which they wish to participate. Figure 8-2 illustrates how the CMBS tranche process works.

Escrowed Funds

All conduit loans, as well as most other permanent real estate loans, require that funds be escrowed for certain purposes, generally property taxes, insurance, and, frequently, reserves for replacement. Typically, no interest is paid to the borrower for these funds, and the use of the capital represents a profit center for the lender and/or escrow agent. A fair amount of paperwork is involved in the monthly transferring of these funds and the annual payment of the related expenses. Because the funds involved rarely exceed a couple of percentage points on the original loan, logically it would be much more efficient if lenders offered a no-escrow option for a point or two lower loan-to-value ratio.

In refinancing an existing building, an engineering report is generally ordered to assess the quality of the building structure. It is not unusual for the report to find a few items of deferred maintenance, for which the lender will escrow 125% of the amount estimated to make the repairs.

Loan Spreads

Conduit loans are generally priced at a spread over the 10-year Treasury bill rate in existence at the time the loan was made. In the high-liquidity, easy-money era of 2006 and 2007, apartment loans typically went for between 80 to 125 basis

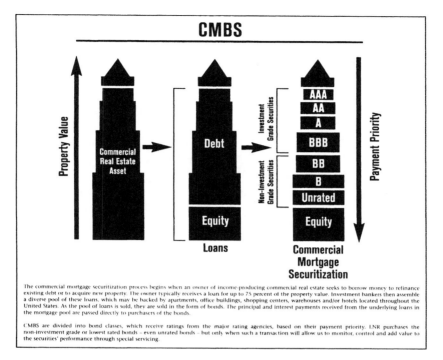

FIG. 8-2   Illustration of commercial mortgage–backed securities tranche process. (*Source*: LNR Property Corporation, *Annual Report* (1999).)

points over the 10-year Treasury rate, depending on the quality of the property, the loan-to-value ratio, and the tightness of the market. However, in past decades, there have been times when risk premium over the 10-year Treasury rate has been in the range of 125 to 240 basis points, again depending on the quality of the loan and other related factors.

The lower the loan-to-value, the better the spread. Loan-to-value ratios offered on apartments are often higher than those offered on other property types, again because of the relative stability of the income stream as compared with those of other sectors of real estate inasmuch as volatility equates to risk.

Note: Distribution/Warehouse refers to larger industrial buildings primarily used for distribution with 20-foot ceiling heights, truck-high loading dock facilities, easy access to major highways or rail, and minimal office space. R&D (Research and Development)/Flex refers to versatile space intended for basic office, assembly, laboratory, or other high-tech use; typically one- or two-story buildings with some office finishes and only basic loading facilities. Industrial refers to manufacturing space with heavy power availability, reinforced flooring for heavy machinery, some truck-high loading facilities, and ceiling heights of less than 20 feet, with less than 20% office space.

Current Fixed Spread Range

	Low Leverage	High Leverage
Anchored Retail	85	100
Strip Center	90	120
Multi-Family	80	100
Distrib./Whse.	95	130
R&D/Flex/Ind'l	90	125
Office	85	110
Hotel	100	125

LIBOR Floating Spread Range
L +100–250, plus fees

FIG. 8-3   Range of basis point spreads over the 10-year Treasury bill for real estate sectors as of early 2007. (*Source*: L. J. Melody & Company, *Market e-News*, March 16, 2007.)

Figure 8-3 illustrates the basis point spread range over the 10-year Treasury bill for various product classes as of early 2007. The chart is intended for 10-year fixed-rate CMBS/conduit loans, but because conduit loans are the largest sector of the commercial real estate lending market, it serves as a guideline for other types of real estate lenders and clearly shows how loan spreads vary for different real estate product classes.

Figure 8-4 presents spreads for 10-year commercial mortgages (an average of loan spreads for all commercial real estate sectors) from January 1996 to January 2006 and shows how loan spreads can vary significantly over time.

Portfolio Risk

Although the ability to make loans and then sell them eliminates certain risks for the lender, other risks still exist. The major risk is that it takes a significant period of time to make enough loans in order to take a CMBS offering to the marketplace, and interest rates may move between the time a lender begins making the loans and the time the lender takes them to market. Of course, if interest rates rise, the lender makes capital because the marketplace will pay a premium for above-market returns. However, if interest rates fall, the lender must sell the loans at a sufficient discount so as to give CMBS buyers market rates of return.

MATCHING SOURCES AND USES OF FUNDS: PORTFOLIO LOAN VS. MORTGAGE BANKING

When a lender intends to hold a loan until maturity, it is called a portfolio loan. When a lender intends to resell the loan, that lender is involved in mortgage banking. A prudent lender matches the terms of the sources and uses of its capital. That is, if the source of your capital is subject to being withdrawn in the short term (e.g., commercial bank deposits), you do not lend it out long term. This is why

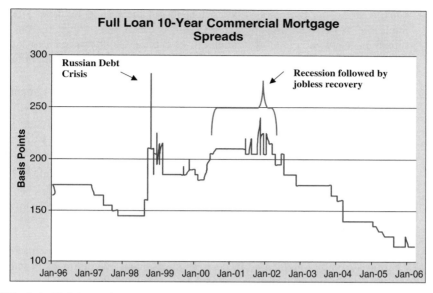

FIG. 8-4   Full-loan 10-year commercial mortgage spreads. (*Source*: Fantini & Gorga, *Observations*, June 2006, www.fantinigorga.com.)

commercial banks (whose funds come primarily from short-term deposits that can be withdrawn at will) make shorter-term construction loans for their portfolio (i.e., to keep) but act as mortgage bankers only when it comes to permanent financing.

An insurance company or pension fund that has secure long-term funds is an appropriate institution to make permanent loans. Commercial banks, with their extensive ties in the real estate community and large networks of loan officers, are in a prime position to originate real estate loans, both construction and permanent, and then resell the longer-term loans to other institutions with different capital structures that lack their extensive networks. Thus, commercial banks' aversion to long-term loans gives them a natural affinity for mortgage banking.

QUALIFYING THE BORROWER

Qualifying the prospective borrower involves comparing the characteristics of the prospective borrower with the criteria established by the lending institution. Qualifying basically involves checking into assurances that the borrower possesses the three fundamental C's of a good borrower:

1. *Character:* The borrower has the desire to repay and has habitually repaid all obligations in the past. If a borrower is reluctant to repay her just debts, the high cost of forcing collection can make loans at normal interest rates unprofitable for any lender.

2. *Competence:* The borrower is competent to put the loaned funds to a profitable use. A borrower making a good profit is much more likely to repay on time than one who is incompetent and loses capital. Competence ensures that the capital loaned will not be squandered or wasted because of ineptitude, thus decreasing the risk to the lender.
3. *Collateral:* The borrower has sufficient resources to guarantee repayment of the loan. The lender needs assurance that the mortgage loan capital will be invested in the construction or purchase of a sound, well-built structure in a good location that will encourage preservation and appreciation of value and will protect against rapid deterioration or depreciation. This also assures the lender that if foreclosure should become necessary, the borrower's equity in the property is sufficient to cover the defaulted loan.

LEVERAGE

Traditionally, a developer strives for maximum financial leverage, because the highest profit is usually obtained on projects using as much leveraging as possible. Leveraging means using as little as possible of one's own cash to control as much property as possible through the use of borrowed capital. This is sometimes referred to as getting rich using OPM (other people's money).

The maturing of the development field and the emergence of larger, deeper-pocketed developers have tempered, to a certain extent, the maximum use of leverage in development, but the use of debt and leverage remains a fundamental portion of the development equation.

TRANSFERABILITY OF OWNERSHIP

Unless the mortgage stipulates to the contrary, lenders are free to sell a mortgage to whomever they desire, and borrowers are free to sell the property with the new buyers assuming the obligations of the old mortgage. However, most loans have a due-on-sale clause prohibiting new buyers from assuming the old mortgage without permission from the lender, which may include qualifying the new owner. Sometimes there is a fee for this service, often 1% of the loan amount, though it is not unusual for the lender to allow the first transfer with only a nominal fee to cover costs.

IMPORTANCE OF THE LOAN APPLICATION

A well-organized loan application, which is complete, logical, and neatly presented, gives the impression that the loan applicant is a skilled professional. Every loan involves some judgment calls, and a well-planned and well-documented presentation by the borrower may persuade the lender to make those calls in favor of the borrower, assuming that the entire project is as well planned as the presentation and will have less than ordinary risk. The form of presentation thus influences a lender both directly and indirectly.

Items Included with a Loan Application

An application for a loan should have full plans, including a site plan; engineering specifications; cost estimates; a rendering (sketch) of the completed project; a marketing and feasibility study; full maps, including aerial maps; complete estimates of operating expenses and income (as discussed in prior chapters); and the qualifications and financial statement of the borrower. The bank may furnish a standard form for the borrower's financial statement. The architectural plans should be fairly complete and drawn by an architect (for a single-family residence, many states permit builders to draw the plans). The term "plans" includes specifications, and the more complex the building, the more precise and extensive the required specifications.

In addition, a surveyor will be needed to obtain field measurements and to draw the plot plan showing the legal description of the land, the lot and block number, name of the subdivision, and other required data.

Local Presence, Loan Committee, Sign-Offs

It is frequently wise to make the loan application to a lender with a local presence in the same area as the project. Thus, the lender will already be familiar with the geography, demography, and other factors affecting the neighborhood of the project and perhaps even with the borrower, either personally or by reputation. Such a lender will have a far greater "feel" for the project than an out-of-town lender far removed from the project. With this familiarity, a lender can make a decision on the loan much more rapidly. Some lenders use loan committees that meet once or twice each week to decide on all applications; other lenders use a sign-off process whereby loan applications require the sign-off of two or three individuals, including at least one from the credit department and the head of the commercial-loan group. Different individuals will have different levels of dollar amounts they can sign off on, and the higher the loan amount the greater the associated internal prestige of possessing such authority.

Application Fees

When a loan application is formally submitted, it typically includes a loan-application fee, which may include funds to cover the bank's internal costs. It may also include the bank's best estimate of the external reports it will have to order to process the loan, such as appraisals, environmental studies, and the like.

Term Sheet

It is common for a lender to informally vet the loan application and indicate its degree of interest. If the lender has a high degree of interest, it will issue a nonbinding term sheet, which will list the terms on which it is interested in making the loan, provided everything checks out as presented. If the borrower is pleased with the term sheet, she may proceed with the formal application or may choose to attempt to negotiate some of the items on the term sheet.

A good loan officer knows the internal workings of his organization and the thought processes and criteria of the key decision makers; thus, if the project is as advertised, every loan application submitted to the lender should be approved according to the term sheet provided, with no additional conditions. As a matter of diplomacy, lenders often will not turn down a loan; they will merely add conditions to it that make it untenable. A well-documented request for a loan may receive a response in as short a time as one week; it is the process of gathering all the documentation, particularly those reports that come from third parties, that takes time.

To show a cross section of responses, at the end of this chapter are term sheets from two different banks for the same proposed Hidden Lake Apartments construction loan, dated within two weeks of each other. The first is from First Union, then ranked sixth in U.S. banks according to asset size. The second term sheet is from Compass Bank, a regional bank ranked in the top 40 banks in the United States in terms of asset size, and a member of the S&P 500 Index.

Although each term sheet uses its own unique language and order, they cover essentially the same information: Borrower, Estimated loan amount, Purpose, Collateral, Term, Interest rate, Fees, Guarantors, Equity required, and Additional requirements.

Borrower: The listed name of the borrower is somewhat perfunctory. Business entities frequently are formed for the sole purpose of doing a development, and names are chosen almost whimsically; the key is the fiscal strength of the guarantor and the amount of the equity required.

Estimated loan amount: Note that the loan amounts offered are within $100,000 of each other or with a variance of only two-thirds of 1%. Because the numbers were arrived at independently, it is either an astounding coincidence or, more likely, an indication of the uniformity of underwriting standards and industry norms.

Purpose: To construct 221 new units and renovate 39 existing units.

Collateral: Both term sheets call for a first mortgage on the land and all improvements. A part of the land being used for this development was on a 99-year lease with 67 years remaining. That is why the First Union appraisal refers to a "leasehold mortgage." (Although the loan could have been closed on the land lease, the borrower was able to negotiate the purchase of the land lease for $70,000 virtually simultaneously with the loan closing and thus to simplify the title.) Note that both banks also require an assignment of rents, leases, and contracts in order to obtain a security interest. It is not unusual for a residential apartment lease to have a clause that makes it subordinate to the permanent financing on the development.

Term: The two term sheets vary slightly in regard to term. The First Union term sheet offers a two-year construction lease up and a one-year mini-perm, or a two-year construction lease up and a three-year mini-perm. Compass Bank offers an 18-month construction lease up and an 18-month mini-perm period. The construction lease-up period is interest only, and all the mini-perm loans call for payments to be based on a 25-year amortization. Compass Bank makes a pitch here for getting the permanent loan business, touting the expertise of their capital markets group. First Union makes its move for additional business at the end of its term sheet, explaining the various permanent loan options it offers.

Interest rate: Both term sheets offer a floating interest rate determined by a spread over the 30-day LIBOR (London Interbank Offered Rate). The LIBOR is the rate at which banks can borrow capital, and thus the spread over LIBOR represents the profit a bank makes after it pays its expenses; it is also the premium it earns for the lending risk it incurs. Compass Bank calls for 2.00% over LIBOR and notes that LIBOR is currently at 6.62%, thus the starting interest rate would be 8.62%. Note that the First Union term sheet calls for a spread of 195 basis points over the LIBOR, or 1.95% over LIBOR. First Union also offers to reduce the spread by 10 basis points, to 185, if the borrower elects to enter into an interest rate swap. This would, in effect, fix the interest rate, thus reducing risk. It also has the side benefit of generating business for First Union's in-house swap desk. As luck would have it, the borrower chose to fix, and interest rates dropped rather precipitously during the construction period.

Interest-rate swap: Both banks are offering a floating rate; that is, the rate could go up, it could go down. An interest rate swap means giving up the potential benefits of a decline in interest rates in return for being protected against a rise in interest rates. In effect, it is buying a fixed rate. This is done quite frequently, and there is a substantial market for this type of financial instrument. Because it is for a short period of time, the cost of an interest rate swap is relatively nominal.

Fees: Both banks require a 21-point loan origination fee, or approximately $72,500. This is a competitive fee under the current market conditions, reflecting the size of the loan, the attractiveness of the project, and the quality of the borrower. Fee income is obviously a lucrative source of income for financial institutions. Although a given loan officer may discuss hundreds of loan possibilities during a year, review any number of written packages a year, and issue many term sheets, perhaps only 1 of every 10 term sheets actually closes. Thus, a loan officer, even one working for a large bank, may book only $50 to $100 million worth of loans a year.

Guarantors: This is the shortest line on the term sheet and is deceiving in its simplicity, for it is one of the most vital. The quality and financial strength of the borrower or the borrower's guarantor is one of the most crucial elements of the loan underwriting process. It matters not how fine the project, nor how excellent the location, nor how attractive the pro forma, you must have a financially strong guarantor. The only possible alternative is substantial cash equity, far above and beyond the norm, and if a developer has access to funds of that magnitude, she generally has access to a person or entity capable of being a guarantor.

Initial equity requirement: Both banks state essentially the same thing in mirror language: First Union requests equity equal to the greater of 15% of costs or the difference between the stated loan amount and cost; Compass states that it will fund up to the lesser of 85% of cost (excluding developer profit) or the stated loan amount. Thus, if costs are $17,000,000 and the loan amount is $14,500,000, $2,550,000 of equity would be required (15% of the $17,000,000 of costs) and only $14,450,000 of the loan would be funded ($17,000,000 of costs less $2,550,000 of equity). If, on the other hand, the project cost turned out to be higher than expected at $17,200,000, the entire $14,500,000 loan amount would be funded, but $2,700,000 of equity would be required ($17,200,000 of costs less $14,500,000 of loan amount). First Union limits the loan amount to 75% of value and Compass to 80% of value.

Additional requirements: Both banks require an appraisal and verification of zoning. First Union is more specific as to reviewing the construction contract, the general contractor, and bonding.

At this stage in the process, the borrower sits down with each lender separately and negotiates to see what terms are flexible and whether there is any additional value to be discovered. When all alternatives have been fully negotiated, a formal loan application is made and a final loan package is submitted. Because this is a construction loan, final cost figures will be required by the bank at this time. Paralleling the financing process, the developer has also been negotiating with various general contractors and, if all has gone well, is by this point very close to reaching an agreement, which will be the basis for the construction cost numbers submitted to the bank. The development process requires extensive multitasking skills.

Once the loan application is submitted and approved, the bank will issue a commitment letter, which is the subject of the next chapter.

SUMMARY

Securing the best loan is essential to having a successful project for a developer. Mortgage brokers and bankers are instrumental in helping the developer obtain the right loan. A *mortgage broker* brings together a lender and borrower and facilitates the transaction for a fee. A mortgage broker is constantly in touch with the market and can shop a loan to a wide variety of sources. The broker serves as the contact point for the borrower and helps with some preliminary underwriting of the loan. A *mortgage banker* is the actual lender who makes the loan with the intention of selling the loan to another institution at a later date. As a loan is shopped around, interested lenders will issue a "term sheet," which is a nonbinding statement about the terms and conditions under which the loan will be granted.

Two types of loans are generally required to finance a project: *short-term financing*, to finance the construction stage, and *long-term financing*, to be used when the building is complete and stabilized. Construction loans are generally provided by commercial banks and, at times, will require a take-out commitment from a credible permanent-lending source. Permanent financing can be secured through several sources depending on the size of the project.

There are five leading sources of lending in the commercial real estate field: *commercial mortgage backed securities (CMBS), insurance companies, governmental agencies* and *quasi-governmental corporations, commercial banks*, and *pension funds*. CMBS act as a conduit between the real estate market and Wall Street, helping bring more loan dollars to the real estate market. CMBS are sold to investors in layers, or tranches, with buyers able to choose the degree of risk in which they wish to participate. The price of a CMBS/conduit loan is typically quoted as a spread over the 10-year Treasury-bill rate at the time the loan was made. As the lending risk of the property type increases, so does the spread over the Treasury.

In trying to determine if a borrower is qualified, the lender checks to ensure the borrower possesses the three C's: Character, Competence, and Collateral. The lender wants to know if the borrower has the desire to repay, the ability to repay, and the resources to guarantee repayment of the loan.

Organizing a complete, logical, and neatly presented loan application can show the bank that the borrower is a skilled professional. The application should include full project plans, engineering specifications, cost estimates, an artist's rendering of the completed project, marketing and feasibility studies, maps and aerial maps, estimates of income and operating expenses, and the qualifications and financial statement of the borrower.

The term sheet offered to an applicant will indicate the terms by which a lender will make a loan, provided all information presented checks out. While each lender uses its own format, the items on a typical term sheet will include borrower's name, estimated loan amount, purpose, collateral, term, interest rate, fees, guarantors, equity required, and additional requirements.

KEY TERMS AND DEFINITIONS

Amortization: Refers to the length of time it will take for a given periodic payment of principal and interest to extinguish a debt.

Carve-outs: Stipulation in a nonrecourse loan that liability will exist for certain events, such as fraud in application, failure to pay taxes or insurance, misapplication of rent, etc.

Commercial mortgage backed security (CMBS): A pool of real estate loans that serve as collateral for a bond offering that will be sold on Wall Street.

Construction financing: Short-term financing provided to fund a project's construction.

Mortgage banker: Actual lender who makes a loan secured by a mortgage on real estate from his own capital with the intention of selling the loan to another institution at a later date.

Mortgage broker: A broker brings together lender and borrower and serves as a connection point and conduit of information throughout the transaction.

Nonrecourse loan: Type of loan that in the event of default, the lender can only look to the loan for repayment.

Permanent financing: Long-term financing obtained upon completion of construction and stabilization.

Portfolio loan: Loan made where the lender has the intention of holding it until maturity.

Portfolio risk: The risk a lender endures in the period of time it takes for a lender to issue the necessary amount of loans to take a CMBS offering to the market. During this time, interest rates may move higher or lower, which may benefit or hurt the lender.

Term: Length of time a debt is to be owed.

Term sheet: A nonbinding document issued by a potential lender describing the terms under which the lender would make a loan. A term sheet typically spells out the borrower, estimated loan amount, purpose of the loan, collateral, term, interest rate, fees, guarantors, equity required, and additional requirements.

Three C's—Character, Competence, and Collateral: Three items a bank must ensure the borrower possesses to be classified as a "good" borrower.

KEY LEARNING POINTS

- Explain the difference between a mortgage broker and a mortgage banker.
- Identify the five leading sources of commercial real estate lending.
- Explain the two major loan types required to finance a project and what type of institution generally makes these loans.
- List and define the three fundamental items a lender looks at when qualifying a buyer.
- Explain in detail items that should be included in a loan application.

QUESTIONS

1. Define what is a mortgage broker and what are the broker's responsibilities.
2. What are the two major loan types required to finance a project and what type of institution generally makes these loans?
3. Describe the difference between a mortgage banker and portfolio lender.
4. When would a development be considered stabilized?
5. What are the three primary reasons that the term for permanent financing is often shorter than amortization?
6. What are the five leading sources of commercial real estate lending?
7. Describe what a lender looks into when qualifying a buyer.
8. List the items that should be included in a loan application.
9. What is a term sheet and list the items that it typically includes.

TERM SHEET - CONSTRUCTION
September 29, 2000

This term sheet is not a commitment, nor is it intended to be a commitment, on the part of First Union to provide financing. No commitment to lend will be binding on First Union unless set forth in writing and executed by an officer of First Union and accepted by the borrower in writing. The proposed conditions have been based on information provided and are a basis for discussion. If you wish to proceed, please notify Andy Hogshead so that we may further underwrite and respond to your request.

BORROWER: Collier Venture One, LLC

ESTIMATED LOAN AMOUNT: $14,525,000 construction/mini-perm loan, subject to Loan-to-Value and Debt Service Coverage constraints.

PURPOSE: To finance land and existing improvements consisting of 39 units known as Bailey Gardens Apartments plus the construction of 221 Class A apartment units and amenities on approximately 20 acres of land located on NW 21st Street in Gainesville, Florida.

COLLATERAL: First mortgage and first leasehold mortgage on land and improvements plus an Assignment of Rents, Leases, and Contracts.

TERM: Option 1: 24-months' construction/lease up period.
1-year mini-perm based on a 25-year amortization.
Option 2: 24-months' construction/lease up period.
3-year mini-perm based on a 25-year amortization.

INTEREST RATE: 30-day LIBOR + 195 basis points, floating without an Interest Rate Swap. The spread may be reduced to 185 basis points in the event the Borrower elects to enter into an Interest Rate Swap.

FEES: 1/2% of the loan amount, payable at closing.
The Borrower shall be responsible for plan review fee and inspection fees during construction.

GUARANTORS:	Nathan S. Collier.
INITIAL EQUITY REQUIREMENT:	Minimum of 15% of the total project costs or the difference between the stated loan amount and total costs, whichever is greater.
ADDITIONAL REQUIREMENTS:	1) The construction contract shall reflect a guaranteed or fixed maximum price and shall be subject to the review and approval by Lender from a General Contractor acceptable to the bank. 2) Subject to an appraisal, acceptable to the Lender, supporting a maximum loan to value of 75%. 3) Verification of the appropriate zoning, permits, and governmental approvals for a development of this nature. 4) The General Contractor shall be bonded as to payment and performance. 5) Loan may be closed on Construction-Permanent Convertible loan documents.
PERMANENT LOAN OPTION:	The Borrower may exercise the Permanent Loan Option through the Construction/Permanent "Convertible" loan program. The loan as described above will be closed on Construction/Permanent loan documentation which will provide, at Borrower's option, for a long-term permanent loan at any time during the Construction Term or Extensions. The permanent loan structure, forward fixed interest rate, and conversion requirements will not be defined until such time as the Borrower requests this option. This option feature is provided to the Borrower for no additional cost or fee; however, a fee may be charged for the permanent loan when delivered. A "Conversion Agreement" will be attached to the construction loan documentation in blank and will be negotiated at the time the Borrower requests the Permanent Loan Option. The Conversion Agreement will detail the permanent loan structure, forward fixed interest rate, and the loan/project conversion requirements. The Permanent Loan Agreement will detail the loan requirements for the permanent loan.

⊛ Compass Bank

Paradigm Group
Attention David Materna, President
Via Hand Delivery

David C. Wilson
Vice President

Term Sheet for Paradigm
October 12, 2000

Borrower:	Paradigm Properties or a to be formed entity satisfactory to Compass Bank
Guarantor:	Nathan S. Collier
Amount:	$14,425,000
Purpose:	Construction-mini perm of a 221-unit apartment complex (new units) and the refinancing and rehabilitation of 39 existing units now known as Bailey Gardens to be located at NW 21st Ave., Gainesville, Alachua County, Florida
Interest Rate:	30-Day LIBOR + 2.00% floating. Today the 30-Day LIBOR is 6.62%. There will be no prepayment penalty associated with this loan.
	Should you wish to insulate yourself from interest rate risk, we would appreciate the opportunity to provide proposals on providing you with a cap or a no cost collar.
Term:	A maturity of three years after the loan closing. The construction and lease up period, during which time interest only will be paid, will be limited to 18 months. After the construction and lease up period ends, the loan will be repaid with monthly payments of principal and interest based upon a twenty-five year amortization. Should you decide to phase the project we will be glad to adjust our terms to adapt our term sheet to that type of structure.

We anticipate that the project will be moved to a permanent loan upon reaching stabilized occupancy. We have a very capable capital markets group and would like to be able to offer you various proposals for the placement of the loan with a permanent lender.

Loan Organization Fee: 1/2 %

Collateral: We will require a first mortgage on the real property and all improvements. In addition to the real property, the mortgage and security agreement will encumber any personal property used in conjunction with the real property. Borrower shall execute an assignment of leases, rents, profits and contracts granting lender a first security interest in same. Lender shall not exercise the right to collect said rent or closing proceeds until a default exists under the terms of the loan documents.

A real property appraisal will be required from an appraiser approved and engaged by Lender, in a form satisfactory to Lender. The appraisal will set forth, among other things, the use of the property upon which the appraisal is based, a legal description of the property appraised, the existing zoning classification of the property, detailed information concerning comparable sales, the use of the property compared, the fair market value of the estate of the Borrower, the value of the proposed improvements and the projected market value of the original property as improved.

We will extend funding to the extent of $14,425,000 or to the extent that we have a maximum Loan to Value of 80% or 85% of cost (*existing Developer Profit*), whichever is less.

Funding: There will need to be adequate equity and loan funds available at inception and throughout construction for the completion of the building shell. The Bank will utilize the services of a construction inspection company. The construction inspection company will perform a "plans and spec" review to determine if, in their opinion, the project can be built in the time frame set forth and within the budget set forth. They will be required to make periodic inspections of the property prior to each draw request. If in our opinion, the project cannot be completed within the agreed upon budget, you will be required to inject additional equity in an amount sufficient that when combined with the undisbursed loan proceeds, the project can be completed.

Loan Closing Costs: All of the costs of making this loan including, but not limited to, title insurance, appraisal fees, surveys, UCC searches, inspection fees, insurance premiums, attorney's fees, recording fees, documentary stamps and intangible taxes, are to be paid by the Borrower.

This term sheet is for discussion purposes only and is issued at a time when Compass Bank has not completed its credit review of the project, the Borrower or the proposed collateral. All terms of a credit facility, if later approved, will be outlined in a detailed commitment letter delivered to the Borrower.

Please do not hesitate to call me at 367-5038 should you have any questions.

Sincerely,

David C. Wilson
Vice President

9
The Commitment

At this stage, the application for a mortgage loan has been submitted to a potential lender either directly or through a mortgage broker, and the developer is waiting for a response from the lender. If the lender's criteria are met and capital is available, then, after careful consideration, the loan committee of the lender will probably approve the application. However, no money will change hands yet. Instead, the lender will issue a formal document that commits it to lending a specified sum of capital to a specified borrower, provided the borrower fulfills the numerous conditions set forth in the statement, including the ominous and vague requirement that there be no material adverse change in the financial condition of the borrower or guarantor prior to closing. The document is called a commitment or commitment letter, as shown at the end of this chapter.

COMMITMENT LETTER AND CLOSING CONDITIONS SCHEDULE

This commitment letter, together with its related closing conditions schedule shows a form that is used by one particular major commercial bank. It is not universal. Each company devises its own form, but this form is representative and contains the information and data normally provided in most commitments. Once the commitment is accepted and signed by the borrower, it becomes a binding contract, obligating the borrower to borrow the capital and construct the project according to the plans submitted and any stipulations contained in the commitment. The lender is similarly obliged to furnish the stipulated sum of capital at the stated interest rate for the stated period of time.

Many of the items in a commitment letter duplicate or reaffirm in slightly greater detail what was originally set forth in the term sheet; however, because it is intended to be a legally-binding contract, the language of the commitment is more formal, mildly more legalistic than that of the term sheet.

THE COMMITMENT LETTER

Loan Type

The Loan Type is formally noted to be a Real Estate Construction Loan.

Principal Loan Amount

The Principal Loan Amount shown in the commitment letter is approximately 3% or $500,000 higher than the Principal Loan Amount shown in the term sheet. This is mainly the result of a favorable appraisal and, to a lesser extent, the result of negotiations between the lender and the borrower, and the borrower's willingness to reduce risk by using an interest rate swap to go to a fixed-rate loan. The loan still has a cap of 75% of the market value as per an appraisal acceptable to First Union.

A Sources and Uses of Funds Budget is attached, which will dictate how funds are released by the bank. Each line item must stand alone; that is, just because one item was completed for less than the budgeted amount does not automatically mean that the funds will be available to fund cost overruns on another line item. Such a switch would be a matter of negotiation with the bank and at its discretion.

Borrower

The Borrower is the same as in the term sheet, Collier Venture One, L.L.C., a limited liability company formed especially for this venture and the legal owner of the raw land.

Guarantor

The Guarantor is the same as in the term sheet; a copy of an Unconditional Guaranty is shown in Exhibit A-4 in Appendix A. In addition to the standard terms of default such as failure to make prompt payment, the Guaranty also includes as events of default both the death of the Guarantor and material misrepresentation: "Any warranty, representation or statement made or furnished to FUNB [First Union National Bank] by or on behalf of Customer or Guarantor, in connection with this Guaranty or to induce FUNB [First Union National Bank] to extend credit or otherwise deal with either Customer or Guarantor proving to have been false in any material respect when made or furnished." Personal and professional ethics and the value of reputation and relationships should be sufficient to insure honesty; if not, the above clause should provide additional motivation.

Purpose and Property

The purpose is the same as that given in the term sheet: "To provide financing for the land and existing improvements consisting of 39 units known as Bailey Gardens plus the construction of 221 Class A apartment units and amenities on approximately 20 acres of land plus parking spaces and appurtenances ('Improvements')." The property clause also closely follows the original term sheet: "Approximately 20 acres of land located on N.W. 21st Avenue, being more particularly described as Gainesville, Alachua County, Florida (the above land, all Improvements, and other collateral, are collectively the 'Property')."

Interest Rate and Required Hedge

At 1.9% over the one-month LIBOR rate, the interest rate offered is a blend of the rates originally offered in the term sheet. The required hedge clause takes the interest rate swap option offered in the term sheet and makes it a requirement while giving more transaction detail. The interest swap is for two years, the construction period of the loan. The borrower was not required to obtain an interest rate swap for the third year, the mini-perm conversion year, that was contingent upon the borrower's achieving a 1.25 debt coverage ratio as detailed under the Special Conditions clause.

Prepayment, Repayment, Maturity Date, and Construction Period

The Prepayment, Repayment, and Maturity Date clauses spell out the details necessary to effect the deal. The Collateral and Commitment Fee faithfully follow the term sheet. The Construction Period sets forth ten months from closing but in no event later than August 31, 2001. This puts into writing verbal understandings with the lender and clarifications that occurred during the loan application and review process. The lender's concern regarding a firm completion date reflects the leasing dynamics of the target rental market, in this case the start of school at the University of Florida, which is the dominant economic mover in Gainesville. The completion date is aggressive but doable, particularly because the developer, in an effort to keep the project on track, had taken the calculated risk of obtaining a clearing permit and hiring a site contractor to prep the site, even to the extent of digging footers—all prior to closing the loan and signing the final contract with the general contractor.

The Prepayment clause states that the loan may be repaid at any time. However, because there is an underlying interest rate swap agreement for two years, any prepayment would involve having to pay to unwind the swap agreement. If interest rates were to fall during the term of the loan (and they did), the cost of unwinding the interest rate swap could be substantial. On the other hand, if interest rates where to rise, the borrower would not be motivated to pay off a lower fixed rate loan early. If the borrower chose to go into permanent financing, using the capital markets arm of the construction lender (remember that both term sheets touted their respective capital markets skill and permanent financing abilities), the lender would typically be more flexible than if third-party permanent financing was used.

As a practical matter, because the construction will take a good 10 months and any refinancing requires a good 6 months of stabilized operating results, the earliest the property could conceivably be refinanced into a permanent loan (which would, in effect, provide funds for the repayment) would be 16 months into the 24-month interest rate swap. That time frame assumes that the property is stabilized upon completion, which is rare in a normal market rent community but quite possible in a university town when, as in this case, the completion date coincides with the start of the school year.

The Repayment clause states that payments are due on the 10th of the month, the loan is interest only for the first 24 months, and then monthly consecutive payments of principal are due based on a 25-year amortization until the Maturity Date. Most owners of apartments prefer to have the payment due on the 1st of the month, particularly for the permanent financing, because that is when rents are due. It may seem like a small thing, but ten days' interest on $15,000,000 at 8% is $32,877.

The Maturity Date is three years from the closing date of the loan, and that is when all the principal and accrued interest will be due and payable in full.

Collateral

The Collateral is a first mortgage on the property, including all improvements presently located or subsequently constructed. The need for the first leasehold improvement mortgage was eliminated when the borrower purchased the 99-year ground lease that encumbered a portion of the property. As additional collateral, the lender wished a first priority assignment of all leases, rents, profits, and contracts, as well as a first priority interest in all personal property attached, affixed, or used in connection with the construction or operation of the property.

Commitment Fee

The Commitment Fee is $75,000, or ½ of 1% of the loan amount. This is simply a charge the bank levies for making the loan and covers its cost of maintaining a commercial real estate loan department and processing the loan (versus the interest that covers the cost of the funds themselves and the related risk of nonpayment). The commitment fee is a significant source of profit and year-end bonuses. The half point is a good rate; negotiations frequently start at a full point, and at times some institutions require an additional quarter to half point when the loan transfers from its interest-only construction phase to the amortizing mini-perm phase of the loan. The half point charged reflects the length and depth of the relationship of the borrower and lender as well as the credit quality of the borrower and the quality of the site and project. Some institutions give the option of rolling the commitment fee into the interest rate (i.e., they will forgo the commitment fee in return for a higher interest rate). It is even possible to go the other way: Buy down the interest rate by paying greater points. It is always a tradeoff. Rolling the commitment fee into the interest rate may reduce the required cash up front, but frequently the bank charges a small premium for the service.

The original version of the commitment letter specified that the commitment fee, although *payable* at closing, was *earned* by the bank at the time the borrower accepted the commitment. Because many things can go wrong between the commitment and the closing, it is quite possible that the loan could fail to close for no fault of the borrower, thus leaving the borrower liable for payment and still without a construction loan. Thus, this clause was changed to read that the commitment fee was not earned until closing. Although it is stating the obvious, loan documents can not be read too carefully. One institution's documents read that once the bank wired the funds, the borrower was liable for repayment. Although it was not explicitly stated, the wording made it clear that the borrower's obligation to repay existed regardless of whether the borrower ever received the funds that were wired. It is exceedingly rare for funds to be lost in the transfer system, but it certainly has happened. Even FedEx loses an occasional package. In this case, the borrower objected and pointed out that the bank had a lot more clout to deal with any discrepancies that might arise. After some polite discussion, the bank offered to limit the borrower's liability to one day's interest, provided it was promptly notified of the failure of the funds to arrive. Although the borrower was still of the opinion that there should be no liability where there was no fault or receipt of funds, the possibility was remote and the downside risk acceptable, so the offer was accepted and the closing proceeded apace.

Payment and Performance Bonds, General Contract, and Closing Date

The General Contract is the contract between the developer/borrower and the general contractor, and it must be of a form and substance that are acceptable to the bank and must include a guarantee of completion and an absolute right for the bank to step into the borrower's shoes vis-à-vis the general contractor in the event of a default by the borrower. In this case, a highly-modified AIA (American Institute of Architects) contract was used.

The bank required that prior to closing, either the general contractor be credit qualified or that the borrower furnish both payment and performance bonds issued by a surety acceptable to the bank. The bonds are simply a guarantee that the project will be completed according to the contract between the general contractor and the developer. The guarantee is given by an individual or institution (the surety, generally some type of insurance or bonding company) with sufficient net worth and liquidity to make the guarantee meaningful. In this case the general contractor was of sufficient financial strength to credit qualify, that is, the bank waived the bond. The bond fee would have been a half a percentage point of the hard construction cost or approximately $65,000 in this case. Although the absolute dollar amount is significant, as a percentage of the amount guaranteed the bond fee was on the low side of the industry standard; it is not unheard of for bond fees to be several percentage points of the contract amount guaranteed. The bond fee in this case was low because of the financial strength and excellent track record of the general contractor. In the past, when using smaller general contractors who lack the strong balance sheet necessary to credit qualify, the developer has chosen to post a bond in the form of a certificate of deposit of 10% to 20% of the contract amount in order to forgo having the general contractor pay high performance bond fees and pass the cost onto the developer.

The commitment letter specifies November 30, 2000, as the closing date, which is only 15 days after the date of the official issuance of the commitment letter on November 15, 2000. The tight time frame was specified because the bank was concerned about the project's being done in time to catch the start of the school year at the University of Florida in August 2001. In actuality, the loan was closed on November 17, 2000, just two days after the official issuance of the commitment letter. This was physically possible only because all the material terms had been prenegotiated while waiting for the final official loan approval, and all the required documents had been reviewed extensively prior to the commitment and prepositioned at the closing attorney's office. It is also a tribute to the high level of initiative and customer service displayed by J. Andrew Hogshead and Susan Beaugrand of the Jacksonville, Florida, commercial real estate lending department of First Union National Bank, without whose yeoman efforts Hidden Lake Apartments' completion date could have been seriously delayed.

Environmental and Appraisal

The Phase 1 environmental assessment and the appraisal report (see Chapter 7) are two very critical reports that must be furnished. Because they can take a substantial amount of time to prepare, it is vital that they be ordered very early in the loan application process. The appraiser must be approved and engaged by the lender, but at the borrower's expense. Note that the commitment letter provides the option to purchase a type of insurance for $1,400 from the Lender's Collateral Protection and Liability Program in lieu of obtaining an environmental report. Because the cost was at or below the cost of an environmental report and the process faster and simpler with no downside risk (there is always a chance an environmental report can come back with problems, but insurance is insurance is insurance), the borrower chose to take this option.

Closing Conditions Schedule, Representations and Covenants

In addition to the terms and conditions set forth in the commitment, the borrower must also comply with the closing conditions schedule attached to the commitment. The closing conditions schedule, which is as long and detailed as the commitment, is discussed later in this chapter.

The borrower must provide proof of such things as access to public streets and utilities as well as proper zoning approvals. The borrower must also make promises as to when the project will commence and when it will be complete and that the proceeds of the loan will be properly applied. The borrower must provide proof of title insurance on the land, proper surveys, plus hazard insurance. The borrower must show that there are no liens on the land and provide documentation that the contractor, architect, engineer, and leases all provide that any claim they have will be subordinate to the claims of the lender. Many of these areas are addressed in the closing conditions schedule in greater depth and detail. By now the reader may accurately surmise that banks, like lawyers, view redundancy in verbiage as a best defense against the possibility of omission of a critical issue.

Administration and Disbursement Requirements, Costs, and Required Reports

The borrower agrees to "comply with any additional loan administration and disbursement requirements as to periodic and final draw requests, retentions, inspections, up-front equity, equity calls and indemnification of First Union." Basically, the borrower agrees to do it the bank's way.

The borrower agrees to "pay all costs, expenses and fees (including, without limitation, flood hazard determination, acceptable appraisals, acceptable environmental assessments, inspection fees of $550 per inspection and plan and cost review of $1,500, all parties' attorney's fees, transfer taxes, tax service fees, documentary stamps and recording fees) associated with closing the loan, which shall be payable at Closing or when billed, as determined by First Union."

The borrower agrees to provide, upon request, such reports and information relating to the property securing the loan as the bank may require, including, without limitation, acquisition information, information regarding potential or actual development, information for third-party agencies, rent rolls, leases, and operating reports. The boilerplate language of the commitment goes on to reserve the right to require several reports that are applicable only to commercial projects: tenant estoppel certificates, franchise agreements, service contracts, liquor or other licenses, and equipment leases.

Special Conditions

The commitment lists three special conditions:

1. Full review of the land lease by bank counsel, a requirement that was made moot by the last-minute purchase of the underlying ground lease by the borrower.
2. Verification of the appropriate zoning, permits, and government approvals for a project of this nature.
3. That the conversion of the loan to the one-year mini-perm at the end of the two-year interest-only construction loan is subject to a 1.25 times the debt coverage ratio; that is, the net operating income of the property at the time of the conversion must be sufficient to cover one and a quarter times the mortgage payment (interest at the then-prevailing rate plus amortization of principal based on 20 years); that is, NOI/debt service = 1.25.

The commitment goes on to say that the preceding terms and conditions are "not exhaustive and that the Commitment is subject to other terms and conditions customarily required by First Union for similar loans"; a very flexible, wide-open statement that significantly favors the lender. As a sage once said, sometimes the Golden Rule is that he who has the gold, makes the rules.

Once again the borrower "represents and agrees that all financial statements and other information delivered to First Union are correct and complete." Furthermore, "No material adverse change may occur in the business or financial condition of Borrower or any Guarantor prior to Closing Date. First Union's obligations under this Commitment are conditioned on the fulfillment, to First Union's *sole satisfaction* [emphasis added], of each term and condition referenced by this Commitment." Although the language of the commitment strongly favors the lender, the robust free market tends to equalize the relationship, at least for strong borrowers. The bank is in the business of making loans and needs quality customers, preferably those who do repeat business. The bank values its reputation as a good lender, for such a reputation is an important asset in attracting top-tier borrowers. Banks can always find borrowers, but no bank wants to be a lender of last resort. Banks want to lend money to borrowers and projects to which other banks want to lend money.

A loan officer spends much of her working hours trying to source good loans and strong borrowers with successful track records. As a practical matter, as long as the project goes well, most of the contract language is irrelevant. The lender and the borrower have a common goal: a successful project that generates a strong income stream.

The commitment goes on to state that it "supersedes all prior commitments and proposals with respect to this transaction, whether written or oral. . .[and that this] Commitment is not assignable *by Borrower* [emphasis added], and no party other than Borrower shall be entitled to rely on this Commitment. . . [and this] Commitment shall not survive Closing." It is interesting to note that although the bank restricts the borrower from assigning the commitment, it, by implication, reserves the right to do so inasmuch as the general rule of law is that all contracts (except those for personal services) are assignable unless specifically stated otherwise. In all likelihood, the bank would have removed the clause if requested by the developer; the probability of the bank's assigning the contract was so low as to make the point moot.

The phrase "This Commitment shall not survive Closing" simply states the general rule of law. Every closing generates many documents, some of them contradictory as positions and the deal evolve. Thus, the law takes the position that no agreement or document survives closing unless it specifically states otherwise. In other words, the documents signed at closing supersede all others prior in time; it is presumed that all issues are worked out at closing and the closing documents are those that are intended to govern the agreement.

CLOSING CONDITIONS SCHEDULE

The closing conditions schedule forms a part of and supplements the commitment and lists general descriptions of certain conditions that must be satisfied prior to closing.

Loan Documents

The loan documents include the note, mortgage, loan agreement, financing statements, assignments of rent, guaranties, and other such instruments that evidence or secure the loan. These instruments are discussed in greater detail in the next chapter, which will deal exclusively with the closing. The loan documents must be in form and substance acceptable to the bank. Annual interest during the loan term occurs on a per diem (per day) basis on the assumption that a year contains 360 days. This convoluted way of calculating interest results in the bank's collecting a slightly higher rate of interest than the stated rate. The folklore of the banking industry is that this method has its roots as a shortcut in the days before the advent of calculators in order to make hand calculations simpler and faster and has never changed because the banks have no incentive to make such a change, and the marketplace has never rebelled sufficiently to compel a change.

The loan documents include a due on sale and a due on encumbrance statement, prohibiting a sale or encumbrance of the property without the bank's prior written consent, which may be granted or withheld at the bank's sole discretion. The definition of a sale includes, but is not limited to, any transfer of partnership interests in or stock of the borrower.

Preconstruction Review

The bank has no obligation to close the loan until it has completed a review of the plans and specifications and site plan, the environmental report, the geotechnical report, the general contractor's contract, the architect's contract, the developer's cost breakdown, the contractor's cost breakdown, the final project budget, and such major subcontracts as the bank may require. The bank must be satisfied at its sole, but reasonable, discretion with each and every aspect of the preconstruction review.

Construction Advances

The procedures and conditions for the bank to issue advances on the loan (i.e., draws) will be in accordance with the loan agreement, a document signed at closing. The loan agreement is a kind of housekeeping document; it covers many of the details of the day-to-day relationship between the bank and the borrower, including the procedures and conditions under which construction advances will be made and the amount of retention the bank will require.

Survey

The borrower must deliver a current survey, certified to the bank and to the title insurer, with a form of surveyor's certificate acceptable to the bank. A current survey usually means one within 90 days of closing. "Certified to the bank and to the title insurer" basically means that the surveyor is acknowledging that the survey is prepared for the benefit of the bank and the title company and that they are entitled to rely on it; in essence, that they are parties to the contract. The general rule of contract law is that if you are not a party to the contract, you are not entitled to rely on the contract. For example, if you were an adjacent property owner who happened to get a copy of the survey and you relied on the survey to establish the boundary of your property (i.e., you used it to determine the proper setback for new construction) and it turned out to be incorrect, you would have no recourse against the surveyor, because you were not a party to the contract, you were not an intended beneficiary of the survey/contract. The surveyor's liability is generally restricted to those with whom he has privy of contract.

There are different kinds of surveys and seemingly infinite levels of detail that can be required. The sanctioning body for surveyors sets standards for the different types and levels of surveys; the surveyor's certificate states to what level the survey was conducted. The bank reserves the right to set the level of the survey performed; as a practical matter, it is the level required by the title company to underwrite the title.

The bank reserves the right to modify the commitment if the improvements are shown to be in a special flood hazard area. This is usually determined through consulting Federal Emergency Management Agency (FEMA) flood zone maps, which are based on large-scale aerial surveys, which, of necessity, lack the accuracy of an on-ground survey. In addition to land elevations, flood zone determinations are the result of calculations as to the anticipated amount and rate of precipitation, water percolation rates (1 inch of rain in an hour may cause some local flooding, whereas 6 inches spread over 24 hours may be absorbed without problem), upstream conditions, and local soil conditions (sand obviously drains faster than clay), all of which are subject to professional judgment and on-the-ground verification. In short, in certain circumstances flood zones can be challenged and modified.

Title Commitment and Policy

A title commitment is a commitment from a title insurance company that it will issue a title insurance policy showing the borrower to be vested with marketable fee simple title to the property, free and clear of all defects, liens, encumbrances, or exceptions, except for property taxes for the current years and such matters as may be acceptable to the bank. Acceptable exceptions include utility easements and the like.

If you deal in real estate long enough, no matter how careful you are, you will run afoul of a title issue. A case in point occurred several years ago when a developer purchased a small ($50' \times 50'$) land parcel containing a dilapidated rental dwelling for $50,000 to complete a site for an apartment community, obtaining both title insurance and a warranty deed. The seller was a finance company, which had obtained title via a foreclosure. The finance company also happened to own a subsidiary that was a title company, and because the seller generally gets to pick the title company that issues the title policy, it naturally chose its own subsidiary.

During the foreclosure, the finance company had been unable to obtain service of process on the record holder of title to the land and so gave notice via publication in the local newspaper, which is legally acceptable after a duly diligent search has been made for the owner. When time came to close the loan on the much larger overall development, an application was made to purchase a new title insurance policy with another, larger title insurance company. This company's search of the public records turned up a death certificate for the owner of the small out parcel that was dated during the period of time that notice via publication was under way. Suffice it to say, the law takes notice of the fact that few dead people read newspapers and requires instead that the estate of the deceased be notified or, if there is no formal probate proceeding, that the heirs of the deceased be notified. It did not matter that the finance company had no knowledge and perhaps no reasonable way of knowing contemporaneously that its service of process was invalid: The lack of legal notice meant that the entire foreclosure proceeding was subject to challenge.

This was a problem, as the developer was ready to proceed with the development and the cloud on the title of a portion of the land was a serious impediment. The good news was that the developer had obtained title insurance when the land was purchased; however, the title insurance was for only the amount of the purchase price of the land, $50,000, and the developer stood to loose substantially more than that if the project failed to proceed or even if it was substantially delayed. Because the title company's limit of liability was $50,000, it could simply pay off at the policy limit and walk away, forcing the developer to sue the finance company under the covenants of the warranty deed. However, because the finance company that was liable under the warranty deed was also the parent of the title company, the title company chose to stay on the case longer than it might normally.

Long term, there were three potential solutions, along with various permutations of each:

1. Get quit claim deeds from the heirs, which would convey their interest in the land.
2. Refile the foreclosure suit.
3. File a suit to quiet title, which would resolve claims to the land.

There was a fourth option that was not considered viable but eventually turned out to have an impact: Wait seven years for the curative statute to run. Curative statute are laws passed by every state (and thus vary from state to state) that cure various title problems by setting a statute of limitations on when various claims against a title must be raised. Florida statute provide for three main curative periods: 7, 20, and 30 years. For various reasons, including a very strong claim of title on the public record and being in possession of the land and paying property taxes thereon, the shortest curative period of 7 years applied.

Getting a quit claim deed from the heirs was the simplest solution, but they could not be readily found. The problem with refiling the foreclosure suit, this time against the heirs, was that in addition to delaying the project, it would open up the remote possibility that the defendants would somehow find the money to pay off the debt and reclaim title to the land. The suit to quiet title was eventually the option chosen.

However, that was a slow, long-term solution, and the developer was looking for a solution that would allow a rapid start to the project. The current site plan called for part of the building to rest on the parcel in question. The developer applied for an amendment to the site plan that simply flipped the building so that only parking lay upon the disputed land, thus greatly reducing the downside risk of the developer. The change was able to be made at the staff level and thus went through rapidly. The developer and his attorney then approached the title company from which they wished to obtain a title policy to give to the construction loan lender and began discussions on the willingness of the title company to "write over" the title defect. In essence, the developer was attempting to assess the willingness of the new title company to insure the risk that the title defect could not be cured. This involved an evaluation of the strength of the underlying legal case as well as the financial strength of the finance company that remained liable under the warranty deed. The title policy was of a good size and highly profitable to the title insurance company, and the developer and his attorney had a enjoyed a good ongoing relationship with the principal decision makers of the title company. Still, the initial answer was an out-and-out negative, bordering on disbelief that the question had even been asked.

The developer persisted, and educated, and discussed options. Just getting the title company to discuss the request on a "what if" basis was a victory, because it elevated it to the level of a possibility. It was a close call to the end, but eventually the title company agreed to write the policy if the developer was willing to give a personal guarantee to indemnify the title company for any losses due to the title defect in question. The loan closing proceeded with only a few weeks' delay, and the project was completed in a timely manner.

Eventually the heirs, a brother and a sister, were found. The sister was willing to sign the required documents. The brother was easy to find once the private investigator discovered where to look: The brother was incarcerated. However, he was in no hurry to sign anything, and it seemed as though this case became a source of amusement and a chief occupation as he whiled away the idle hours serving time. The case dragged on for years, and eventually it was the running of the seven-year curative statute that persuaded the brother to settle with the original title company for a four-digit sum just a year or so before his claim became moot.

The moral of this story is that title problems will crop up no matter how intensive your due diligence and that at times it requires extreme creativity and persistence to solve them. A good developer must be a superb negotiator and a persistent optimist.

Lien Search

There must be a Uniform Commercial Code (UCC) search on the chattel and other personal property covered by the bank's agreement, showing clean title, and there must be no judgment liens outstanding in the public records in reference to the borrower, the property, or the guarantor. Personal property is any property that is not real property (i.e., land). *Chattel* is an archaic word for personal property that some lawyers still like to use, perhaps because it sounds important and mysterious and justifies legal fees. Property can be transformed from personal property to real property. When lumber is delivered to a site, it is personal property. When it is incorporated into a building, it becomes real property. In essence, a building is personal property that has been converted to real property. If something can be removed from a building without causing damage to the building, it is generally considered to be personal property. Thus, a built-in range is considered to be real property, but a free-standing stove is still personal property. A free-standing refrigerator is personal property, the compressor for a central air-conditioning system is real property. The furniture in an office or an apartment is considered personal property. When land is in a raw state, there typically is no personal property thereon; thus, this clause is intended to cover the personal property that will be on premise and owned by the developer/project when the apartments are completed, and the personal property owned by the developer in the existing 39 units.

Insurance, Architect's Contract, Subdivided Lot, Legal Requirements, Utilities, and Taxes

The borrower must furnish insurance policies that are acceptable in form and substance to the bank, with coverage acceptable to the bank from companies acceptable to the bank. The bank must receive a copy of the architect's contract, and it must be assigned to the bank and contain a clause holding that the bank has the right to step into the borrower's shoes in the event of default and use the plans and specifications to complete the project, and the contract and assignment thereof must be in form and substance acceptable to the bank. The borrower must provide satisfactory evidence that the lot is taxed as a single lot for real estate purposes and complies with applicable zoning, subdivision laws, ordinances, and regulations, including without limitation, the Americans with Disabilities Act, and that the borrower's use does not violate any easement, covenant, or condition affecting the property. The borrower must furnish the bank with satisfactory evidence that all applicable utilities are available at the property boundaries in adequate quantities and that all real estate taxes are current as of closing.

Closing Certificate

The borrower is required to deliver to the bank at closing a sweeping, comprehensive certificate indicating that all financial statements and other information delivered to the bank are correct and complete, that there has been no material adverse change in the business or financial condition of the borrower or guarantor, that all the borrower's and guarantor's representations and warranties remain true, and to the best of the borrower's and guarantor's knowledge, information, and belief, that all conditions to closing have been satisfied and no fact, condition, or circumstances exist that would entitle the bank to terminate the commitment.

Opinion of Counsel

The borrower is also required to furnish an opinion from the borrower's and guarantor's counsel that the loan is not usurious (i.e., that the loan does not violate any state or federal law in regard to excessive interest rates) and that the borrower and guarantor are fully authorized to execute the loan documents (this is important where the borrower or lender is not a natural person, i.e., a corporation, partnership, or limited liability company, and a specific authorization to enter into a loan may be required under the empowering papers creating the entity). Said counsel must further opine in writing that each of the loan documents has been duly executed and constitutes a valid, enforceable, legally-binding obligation of the borrower and guarantor and that no action, suit, or proceeding is pending against either the borrower, guarantor, or the property, and that the zoning of the property permits its contemplated use.

Signs, Entity Resolutions, and Additional Information

The borrower agrees to allow the bank to post signs on the property announcing the bank as the provider of the construction financing. As to any nonnatural borrower or guarantor, the borrower agrees to furnish to the bank the appropriate resolutions and satisfactory evidence of authority documenting the right of individuals acting on behalf of the borrower or guarantor to act and bind them together with evidence that both are duly organized, validly existing, in good standing, and duly qualified to conduct business in the jurisdictions where they are organized and/or qualified and where the property is located.

The borrower further agrees to furnish any and all other information, documentation, opinions, and assurances with respect to this transaction as the bank or its counsel reasonably requires.

November 15, 2000

Mr. David Matema
Collier Venture One, L.L.C.
P.O. Box 13116
Gainesville, Florida 32604

Re: Real Estate Construction Loan Commitment—Hidden Lake Apartments

Dear Dave:

First Union National Bank ("First Union") is pleased to offer you this commitment ("Commitment") to lend on the following terms and conditions:

LOAN TYPE:
Real Estate Construction Loan (the "Loan")

PRINCIPAL LOAN AMOUNT:
Not to exceed the lesser of U.S. $15,000,000 or 75% of market value reflected in an appraisal acceptable to First Union.

The Loan will be allocated in accordance with the Sources and Uses of Funds Budget attached to this Commitment.

BORROWER:
Collier Venture One, L.L.C.

GUARANTOR(S):
Unconditional guaranty/guaranties of payment and performance in form acceptable to First Union from Nathan S. Collier (each a "Guarantor").

PURPOSE:
To provide financing for the land and existing improvements consisting of 39 units known as Bailey Gardens plus the construction of 221 Class A apartment units and amenities on approximately 20 acres of land plus parking spaces and appurtenances ("Improvements").

PROPERTY:
Approximately 20 acres of land located on N.W. 21st Avenue, being more particularly described as Gainesville, Alachua County, Florida (the above land, all improvements, and other collateral, are collectively the "Property").

INTEREST RATE:

Interest shall accrue on the unpaid principal balance at an annual interest rate equal to the one-month LIBOR Contract Rate plus 1.90%. The LIBOR-based rate shall be determined in accordance with First Union's adjusted LIBOR Rate formula.

REQUIRED HEDGE:

The Borrower shall hedge the floating interest expense of the Loan for the full term of the Loan by maintaining one or more interest rate swap transactions with the Lender (or with another financial institution approved by the Lender in writing) in an aggregate notional amount equal to the outstanding principal balance of the Loan, with the Borrower making fixed rate payments and receiving floating rate payments to offset changes in the variable interest expense of the Loan, all upon terms and subject to such conditions as shall be acceptable to the Lender (or if such transaction is with another financial institution, all upon terms and subject to such conditions as shall be approved by the Lender in writing).

PREPAYMENT:

The Loan may be prepaid in whole or in part at any time. Any prepayment shall include accrued interest and all other sums then due under the Loan. No partial prepayment shall affect an obligation of Borrower to pay principal or interest otherwise due under the Loan or Swap Agreement.

REPAYMENT:

Payable in consecutive payments of accrued interest only, commencing on the 10th day of the second month after closing, and continuing on the 10th day of each subsequent month for 24 months. Commencing on the 10th day of the 25th month after Closing and on the 10th day of each subsequent month, consecutive payments shall be due consisting of principal plus accrued interest based upon a 25 year amortization, until the Maturity Date.

MATURITY DATE:

In any event, all principal and accrued interest shall be due and payable in full 3 years from the Closing ("Maturity Date").

COLLATERAL:

A first mortgage and first leasehold mortgage on the Property, including all Improvements presently located or subsequently constructed. The legal description of the Property and the condition of title must be approved by First Union.
A first priority assignment of leases, rents, profits and contracts.
A first priority security interest in all personal property attached, affixed or used in connection with the construction or operation of the Property.

COMMITMENT FEE:

Borrower shall pay First Union U.S. $75,000 as a non-refundable commitment fee, which is deemed earned at the time Borrower accepts this Commitment and is payable at Closing.

CONSTRUCTION PERIOD:
10 months from Closing, but in no event shall construction completion occur later than 8/31/01.

INITIAL EQUITY REQUIREMENT:
In addition to Borrower's contribution of land, prior to Closing, Borrower shall deposit with First Union equity funds in cash or shall submit to First Union acceptable evidence of equity contributions previously made or evidence of equity contributions committed and readily available in an aggregate amount not less than $843,391.

PAYMENT AND PERFORMANCE BONDS:
Prior to Closing, The General Contractor shall be credit qualified or the Borrower shall furnish First Union with both payment and performance bonds (collectively the "Bonds") regarding the General Contract (defined below) issued by a surety acceptable to First Union naming the Borrower and First Union as dual obligees thereunder.

GENERAL CONTRACT:
Prior to Closing, First Union must receive an acceptable guaranteed maximum fixed price contract ("General Contract") with a general contractor acceptable to First Union.
("General Contractor"). The General Contractor shall include a guarantee of completion. The General Contract must be assigned to First Union and the General Contractor must undertake in writing to perform under the General Contract on behalf of First Union in the event of a default by Borrower. The General Contract, the assignment of contract, and undertaking to complete must be in form and substance acceptable to First Union in all respects.

CLOSING:
The Loan shall be closed on a mutually agreeable date, but no later than 11/30/00 the actual date of closing being "Closing" or "Closing Date".

ENVIRONMENTAL:
Borrower shall, at Borrower's expense, engage an environmental consultant previously approved by First Union for the purpose of conducting an acceptable Phase I environmental assessment of the Property.
In lieu of obtaining the Phase I report, Borrower may satisfy this condition by completing a questionnaire regarding the environmental condition of the Property. If the Property is determined to qualify for the Lender's Collateral Protection and Liability Program, Borrower shall pay an environmental assessment fee in the amount of $1,400, which shall be due and payable at Closing.

APPRAISAL:
First Union must receive an acceptable appraisal of the Property. Appraiser shall be approved and engaged, at Borrower's expense, by First Union.

CLOSING CONDITIONS SCHEDULE:
In addition to the terms and conditions set forth in this Commitment, Borrower shall comply with the Closing Conditions Schedule for a real estate construction loan attached to this Commitment.

REPRESENTATIONS AND COVENANTS:
Borrower will provide additional construction loan representations as to access and utilities, zoning and approvals, construction criteria, use of proceeds and notice of commencement, all to be set forth in the Loan Documents. Borrower will also provide additional construction loan convenants as to commencement and completion, title insurance, survey, hazard insurance, liens and lien waivers, permanent loan commitment, subordination of claims of contractor/architect/engineer, leases and advertising, all to be set forth in the Loan Documents.

ADMINISTRATION AND DISBURSEMENT REQUIREMENTS:
Borrower will also comply with additional construction loan administration and disbursement requirements as to periodic and final draw requests, retentions, inspections, up-front equity, equity calls and indemnifications of First Union, all to be set forth in the Loan Documents.

COSTS:
Borrower shall pay all costs, expenses and fees (including, without limitation, flood hazard determination, acceptable appraisals, acceptable environmental assessments, inspection fees of $550 per inspection and plan and cost review of $1,500, all parties' attorneys' fees, transfer taxes, tax service fees, documentary stamps and recording fees) associated with closing the Loan, which shall be payable at Closing or when billed, as determined by First Union.

REQUIRED REPORTS:
Borrower shall provide, at First Union's request, such reports and information relating to the Property securing the Loan as First Union may require in the loan documents or otherwise, including, without limitation, acquisition information, information regarding potential or actual development, information regarding residential development, information for third-party agencies, rent rolls, estate leases, operating reports, tenant estoppel certificates, franchise agreements, service contracts, liquor or other licenses, and equipment leases.

SPECIAL CONDITIONS:
1. Full review of land lease by bank counsel.
2. Verification of the appropriate zoning, permits, and government approvals for a project of this nature.
3. The mini-perm conversion is subject to a 1.25x debt coverage ratio.

The preceding terms and conditions are not exhaustive, and this Commitment is subject to other terms and closing conditions customarily required by First Union for similar loans (including without limitation late charges, default interest, financial covenants, restrictions on transfers of all or part of the Collateral or any interest in the Collateral or in Borrower, and restrictions on further liens or encumbrances on the Collateral).

Borrower represents and agrees that all financial statements and other information delivered to First Union are correct and complete. No material adverse change may occur in the business or financial condition of Borrower or any Guarantor prior to the Closing Date. First Union's obligations under this Commitment are conditioned on the fulfillment, to First Union's sole satisfaction, of each term and condition referenced by this Commitment.

This Commitment supersedes all prior commitments and proposals with respect to this transaction, whether written or oral, made by First Union or anyone acting with its authorization. No modification to this Commitment shall be valid unless made in writing and signed by an authorized officer of First Union. This Commitment is not assignable by Borrower, and no party other than Borrower shall be entitled to rely on this Commitment. This Commitment shall not survive Closing.

Please indicate your acceptance of this Commitment and the terms and conditions contained herein by signing below and returning one executed copy of this Commitment to the undersigned. This Commitment shall expire unless the acceptance is received by the undersigned on or before November 21, 2000 time being of the essence.

Thank you for allowing First Union to be of service. Please do not hesitate to give me a call if I can be of further assistance.

Very truly yours,

FIRST UNION NATIONAL BANK

J. Andrew Hogshead
Vice President

Cc: Susan Beaugrand

ACCEPTANCE OF COMMITMENT:
Accepted and Agreed:

COLLIER VENTURE ONE, L.L.C.

By: _____   _____
              Nathan S. Collier   Date
              Managing Member

GUARANTOR(S)

By: _____   _____
              Nathan S. Collier   Date

ATTACHMENTS:
Closing Conditions Schedule
Sources and Uses of Funds Budget

This Closing Conditions Schedule forms a part of, or supplements a Real Estate Construction Loan Commitment from First Union. Listed below are general descriptions of certain conditions that must be satisfied prior to closing the Loan contemplated by the Commitment. All surveys, title reports, certificates, and other materials required to be delivered by Borrower to First Union prior to Closing shall be delivered not later than 10 days before the Closing Date. All terms not otherwise defined in this Closing Conditions Schedule shall have the meanings assigned to them in the Commitment.

LOAN DOCUMENTS:
The note, security instrument (mortgage, deed to secure debt, deed of trust), loan agreement, financing statements, assignments, guaranties, and such other instruments and documents that evidence or secure the Loan (collectively, the "Loan Documents") shall be in form and substance acceptable to First Union. Certain of the terms and conditions that will be included in the Loan Documents are described in this Closing Conditions Schedule. However, the Commitment is not intended to set forth all of the terms or conditions of the Loan Documents.

Annual interest during the term of the Loan shall accrue on a per diem basis on the assumption that a year contains 360 days. The Loan Documents will also contain due on sale and due on encumbrance clauses which prohibit any sale or encumbrance of the Property without the prior written consent of First Union, which consent may be granted or withheld in First Union's sole discretion. A "sale" shall include, but not be limited to, any transfer of partnership interests in or the stock of Borrower.

PRECONSTRUCTION REVIEW:
First Union shall have no obligation to close the Loan until First Union has completed a preconstruction Loan review of the Improvements, which review shall consist of, without limitation, a review of the following: (i) plans and specifications and site plan; (ii) environmental report; (iii) geotechnical report; (iv) general contractor contract; (v) architect's contract; (vi) developer cost breakdown; (vii) contractor cost breakdown; (viii) final project budget; and (ix) such major subcontracts as First Union may require. As a condition to Closing, First Union must be satisfied in its sole but reasonable discretion with each and every aspect of the preconstruction Loan review.

CONSTRUCTION ADVANCES AND LENDER INSPECTIONS:
The procedure for and conditions to all construction advances, including provision for First Union inspections, will be set forth in a loan agreement between Borrower and First Union. The Loan will be disbursed in accordance with First Union's standard policies and procedures. Loan disbursements for the costs of deposits required by manufacturers or fabricators of building materials, furnishings, fixtures or equipment for Improvements will not be made. Borrower shall pay the costs of Loan inspections as provided in the Loan Documents.

SURVEY:
Borrower shall furnish for First Union's approval a current survey of the Property. Such survey shall be prepared in accordance with First Union's standard policies

and procedures, and shall be certified to First Union and First Union's title insurer using a form of surveyor's certificate acceptable to First Union. Such survey shall include evidence that the Improvements are not located within a Special Flood Hazard Area. First Union will also obtain, at Borrower's expense, a certificate of flood hazard determination for the Property. If the Improvements (or any portion of the Improvements) are located in a Special Flood Hazard Area or if the Property (or any portion of the Property) is located in a wetlands area, First Union reserves the right to terminate the Commitment or to modify the Commitment and request from Borrower such other agreements, covenants and documentation as First Union may require.

TITLE COMMITMENT AND POLICY:
A title insurance company selected by Borrower and approved by First Union shall be prepared to issue unconditionally to First Union at Closing an ALTA standard form, full coverage Mortgagee's Title Policy, as evidenced by a title commitment delivered to First Union prior to Closing. The title policy shall (i) show Borrower to be vested with valid marketable fee simple title to the Property, free and clear of all defects, liens, encumbrances or exceptions, except for ad valorem taxes for the current year and such other matters as may be acceptable to First Union; (ii) insure the mortgage, deed of trust, or deed to secure debt to be a valid first lien on the fee simple title to the Property in the full amount of the Loan; (iii) contain no exception for mechanic's and materialmen's liens, survey matters or any other matters not acceptable to First Union; (iv) include such endorsements and provide such coverages as First Union may require including, without limitation, coverage for future advances prior to the completion date under a pending disbursements clause acceptable to First Union; and (v) insure all access and other easements necessary for the use of the Property. Legible copies of all easements, rights-of-way, and other matters affecting title to or use of the Property shall be submitted to First Union prior to Closing for its review, and all such matters must be acceptable to First Union.

LIEN SEARCH:
There shall be performed (i) a UCC search on the chattels and other personal property covered by First Union's security agreement, and such search shall have revealed no prior financing statements on such chattels and personal property; and (ii) a search for all judgment lien and lis pendens records with respect to Borrower, each Guarantor, and the Property.

INSURANCE:
Borrower shall furnish First Union from insurance companies acceptable to First Union such policies of insurance in form and substance and with coverages acceptable to First Union in all respects.

ARCHITECT'S CONTRACT:
First Union must receive a copy of the contract between Borrower and the architect for design and supervisory services. The contract must be assigned to First Union and the architect must agree that First Union may use and copy the plans and

specifications in the event of a default by Borrower. The architect's contract and assignment of contract and consent to use of plans and specifications all must be in form and substance acceptable to First Union.

SUBDIVIDED LOT:
Borrower shall deliver to First Union satisfactory evidence that the Property constitutes a separate subdivided lot for purposes of and in accordance with applicable zoning, subdivision laws, ordinances and regulations, and that the Property is taxed as a single lot for real estate tax purposes.

LEGAL REQUIREMENTS:
First Union shall receive satisfactory confirmation of Borrower's representation that the zoning of the Property allows the uses planned for the Property, and that the Property is in compliance with all applicable zoning laws, ordinances and regulations (including without limitation, the Americans with Disabilities Act) and with the zoning classification applicable to the Property and that Borrower's proposed use does not violate any easement, covenant, or condition affecting the Property. Borrower shall furnish First Union with satisfactory evidence that all governmental laws, regulations, and requirements applicable to the construction and use of the proposed Improvements on the Property have been complied with and that the plans have been prepared in accordance with such laws, regulations, and requirements.

UTILITIES:
Borrower shall furnish First Union with satisfactory evidence that all applicable utilities, including, without limitation, water and sewer service, are permanently available at the boundaries of the Property in adequate quantities.

TAXES:
Payment of all real estate taxes and assessments applicable to the Property shall be made at Closing and, if the Property is purchased at Closing by Borrower, shall be appropriately prorated.

CLOSING CERTIFICATE:
Borrower shall deliver to First Union at Closing a certificate acceptable to First Union indicating (i) all financial statements and other information delivered to First Union are correct and complete; (ii) there has been no adverse change in the business or financial condition of Borrower or any Guarantors, from that set forth in the financial information submitted to First Union; (iii) all of Borrower's and each Guarantor's representations and warranties remain true; and (iv) to the best of Borrower's and each Guarantor's knowledge, information, and belief, all conditions to Closing have been satisfied and no fact, condition, or circumstance exists that would entitle First Union to terminate the Commitment.

OPINION OF COUNSEL:
In addition to any other opinions or assurances requested by First Union, Borrower shall furnish to First Union at Closing, and in draft form prior to Closing, an opinion of Borrower's and Guarantor's counsel (acceptable to First Union) to the

effect that (i) the Loan from First Union to Borrower is not usurious; (ii) Borrower and each Guarantor are fully authorized to enter into and perform all of the terms and obligations of the Loan Documents; (iii) each of the Loan Documents has been duly executed and constitutes the valid and legally binding obligation of Borrower and each Guarantor, as the case may be, and is enforceable in accordance with its terms; (iv) no action, suit, or proceeding is pending against Borrower, the Property or any Guarantor; (v) such counsel has no knowledge of any laws, regulations, requirements, or information which might impair the use of the Property; (vi) the making of the Loan and performance of the transaction contemplated in the Commitment does not violate any agreement to which Borrower or any Guarantor is a party; and (vii) the zoning of the Property permits its contemplated use.

SIGNS:
Borrower agrees that the Loan Documents shall contain language permitting First Union to post signs on the Property indicating that First Union has provided the construction financing for the Improvements.

ENTITY RESOLUTIONS:
As to any non-natural Borrower or Guarantor, Borrower will furnish to First Union, on or prior to Closing, appropriate resolutions and satisfactory evidence of authority documenting the right of the individuals acting for or on behalf of Borrower and each Guarantor to so act and bind them. Borrower will also furnish evidence that it and each Guarantor are duly organized, validly existing and in good standing and are duly qualified to transact business in the jurisdictions where Borrower and each Guarantor are organized and/or qualified, and where the Property is located, and certified true copies of organizational documents for Borrower and each Guarantor.

ADDITIONAL INFORMATION:
Borrower shall furnish to First Union any and all other information, documentation, opinions, and assurances with respect to the transactions contemplated hereby as First Union or its counsel shall reasonably require.

END OF SCHEDULE

Sources & Uses of Funds Budget

		Detail Budget		
Loan Amount	15,000,000	Borrower:	Collier Venture One, L.L.C.	Obligator #:
Interest Rate	8.60%	Project:	Hidden Lakes Apartments	Obligation #:
Construction Term (Months)	12	Project Address:	N.W. 21st Ave.	Underwriter: Susan Beaugrand
Est. Percent Q/S Interest Reserve Calculation	60%	Project City/St:	Gainesville, FL	Date: 11/14/2000

LINE-ITEM DESCRIPTION	PROJECT COSTS %	PROJECT COSTS $	UP-FRONT EQUITY DUE AT CLOSING	DEFERRED EQUITY	TOTAL EQUITY	LOAN PROCEEDS	FUNDS DISB AT CLOSING	CUMULATIVE CHANGE ORDERS +/-	ADDITIONAL EQUITY REQUIRED	REVISED LOAN BUDGET
LOAN COST:										
FUNB Commit Fees %	0.0%	$75,000.00	$19,683.00	$0.00	$19,683.00	$55,317.00	$0.00	$0.00	$0.00	$55,317.00
Atty/Legal: Borrower		$15,000.00	$0.00	$0.00	$0.00	$15,000.00	$0.00	$0.00	$0.00	$15,000.00
Closing Costs		$83,600.00	$0.00	$0.00	$0.00	$83,600.00	$0.00	$0.00	$0.00	$83,600.00
SUBTOTAL LOAN COSTS		$173,600.00	$19,683.00	$0.00	$19,683.00	$153,917.00	$0.00	$0.00	$0.00	$153,917.00
	Per Unit									
LAND COST:	$0	$3,575,000.00	$2,700,000.00	$0.00	$2,700,000.00	$875,000.00	$0.00	$0.00	$0.00	$875,000.00
HARD COSTS:										
Site Development		$85,000.00	$34,844.00	$0.00	$34,844.00	$50,156.00	$0.00	$0.00	$0.00	$50,156.00
Infrastructure		$0.00	$0.00	$0.00	$0.00	$0.00	$0.00	$0.00	$0.00	$0.00
Utilities		$0.00	$0.00	$0.00	$0.00	$0.00	$0.00	$0.00	$0.00	$0.00
Landscaping		$0.00	$0.00	$0.00	$0.00	$0.00	$0.00	$0.00	$0.00	$0.00
Other Site Work		$0.00	$0.00	$0.00	$0.00	$0.00	$0.00	$0.00	$0.00	$0.00
Sewer Outfall Line		$0.00	$0.00	$0.00	$0.00	$0.00	$0.00	$0.00	$0.00	$0.00
Underground Power		$0.00	$0.00	$0.00	$0.00	$0.00	$0.00	$0.00	$0.00	$0.00
Street Lights		$0.00	$0.00	$0.00	$0.00	$0.00	$0.00	$0.00	$0.00	$0.00
Sewer & Water Inspection Fees		$0.00	$0.00	$0.00	$0.00	$0.00	$0.00	$0.00	$0.00	$0.00
Other County Fees		$0.00	$0.00	$0.00	$0.00	$0.00	$0.00	$0.00	$0.00	$0.00
Sidewalks		$0.00	$0.00	$0.00	$0.00	$0.00	$0.00	$0.00	$0.00	$0.00
Entrance/Signage		$0.00	$0.00	$0.00	$0.00	$0.00	$0.00	$0.00	$0.00	$0.00
Amenity Area		$125,000.00	$0.00	$0.00	$0.00	$125,000.00	$0.00	$0.00	$0.00	$125,000.00
Construction		$11,950,000.00	$347,191.00	$0.00	$347,191.00	$11,602,809.00	$0.00	$0.00	$0.00	$11,602,809.00
Models/Misc.		$55,000.00	$0.00	$0.00	$0.00	$55,000.00	$0.00	$0.00	$0.00	$55,000.00
Renovation of Bailey Gardens		$406,100.00	$215,549.00	$0.00	$215,649.00	$190,551.00	$0.00	$0.00	$0.00	$190,551.00
HARD COST CONTINGENCY %	0.00%	$323,000.00	$0.00	$0.00	$0.00	$323,000.00	$0.00	$0.00	$0.00	$323,000.00
SUBTOTAL HARD COSTS		$12,944,100.00	$597,584.00	$0.00	$597,584.00	$12,346,516.00	$0.00	$0.00	$0.00	$12,346,516.00

		(G)	(F)	(E)	(D)	(C)	(B)	(A)
SOFT COSTS:								
Marketing		$130,000.00	$1,544.00	$1,544.00	$128,456.00	$0.00	$0.00	$128,456.00
Attorney/Legal		$0.00	$0.00	$0.00	$0.00	$0.00	$0.00	$0.00
Architect/Engineer/Design		$275,000.00	$224,580.00	$224,580.00	$50,420.00	$0.00	$0.00	$50,420.00
Accounting		$0.00	$0.00	$0.00	$0.00	$0.00	$0.00	$0.00
Title Insurance		$30,400.00	$0.00	$0.00	$30,400.00	$0.00	$0.00	$30,400.00
Insurance—Bldrs. Risk, etc.		$0.00	$0.00	$0.00	$0.00	$0.00	$0.00	$0.00
Environmental		$0.00	$0.00	$0.00	$0.00	$0.00	$0.00	$0.00
Appraisals		$0.00	$0.00	$0.00	$0.00	$0.00	$0.00	$0.00
Inspection Fees		$0.00	$0.00	$0.00	$0.00	$0.00	$0.00	$0.00
Real Estate Taxes		$50,000.00	$0.00	$0.00	$50,000.00	$0.00	$0.00	$50,000.00
Leasing Commissions	0.00%	$0.00	$0.00	$0.00	$0.00	$0.00	$0.00	$0.00
Developers Fee		$0.00	$0.00	$0.00	$0.00	$0.00	$0.00	$0.00
Developer's OH	4.51%	$675,919.00	$0.00	$675,919.00	$0.00	$0.00	$0.00	$0.00
Other Miscellaneous Costs—Est.		$0.00	$0.00	$0.00	$0.00	$0.00	$0.00	$0.00
Operating Reserve to Lease Up		$0.00	$0.00	$0.00	$0.00	$0.00	$0.00	$0.00
Fees and Surveys		$118,100.00	$0.00	$0.00	$118,100.00	$0.00	$0.00	$118,100.00
Performance Bond		$0.00	$0.00	$0.00	$0.00	$0.00	$0.00	$0.00
Tap Fees		$347,191.00	$0.00	$0.00	$347,191.00	$0.00	$0.00	$347,191.00
SOFT COST CONTINGENCY %	0.00%	$0.00	$0.00	$0.00	$0.00	$0.00	$0.00	$0.00
SUBTOTAL–SOFT COSTS		$1,626,610.00	$226,124.00	$902,043.00	$724,567.00	$0.00	$0.00	$724,567.00
EST. INTEREST RESERVE		$900,000.00	$0.00	$0.00	$900,000.00	$0.00	$0.00	$900,000.00
TOTAL SOFT COSTS		$2,526,610.00	$226,124.00	$902,043.00	$1,624,587.00	$0.00	$0.00	$1,624,567.00
TOTAL COST		$19,219,310.00	$3,543,391.00	$4,219,310.00	$15,000,000.00	$0.00	$0.00	$15,000,000.00

SUMMARY

After reviewing term sheets from various lenders, a developer will decide which lender to use. Once the application has been submitted and approved by the loan committee, the lender will then issue a *commitment letter* and *closing conditions schedule* to the developer. The commitment letter contains mostly the same items as the previously issued term sheet, but it describes each item in greater detail. One major difference between the term sheet and the commitment letter is that once signed, the commitment letter is a legally-binding contract whereas the term sheet is nonbinding. The commitment letter describes in detail such items as the name of the borrower, amount borrowed, interest rate, maturity of the loan, collateral, commitment fees, performance bonds, environmental and appraisal reports, and any other requirements the bank may have.

Along with the commitment letter comes a closing conditions schedule. This document describes in detail what needs to be done before the loan can close. The closing conditions schedule refers to the loan documents, required type and amount of hazard and title insurance, level of survey required and who it should be certified to, any lien searches that must be performed, closing certificates, opinions of counsel, and other requirements the lender may have regarding the loan.

While the contents of commitment letters and closing condition schedules may be the same across lenders, the actual forms used are different. The borrower(s) and their legal counsel should carefully review the commitment letter, the closing conditions schedule, and any other items provided by the bank regarding the loan. These documents may contain clauses that, if missed, can potentially harm the borrower and cause great legal or financial grief.

KEY TERMS AND DEFINITIONS

Closing conditions schedule: Attached to commitment letter, this describes in detail what must be completed before closing the loan.

Commitment fee: Fee charged by the lender for making a loan to a borrower. It covers the cost of making the loan, maintaining a real estate loan department, and processing the loan.

Commitment letter: Letter describing in detail terms for loan being offered. Once signed by the borrower, it becomes a binding contract.

Guarantor: Person or entity acting to guarantee that the lender will be repaid should the borrower default on the loan.

Phase I environmental report: Environmental assessment report required by lenders. This report details the history of the property and assesses the possibility of any environmental issues.

Personal property: Generally, items that can be removed from a building without causing damage to the building.

Real property: Items that are attached to a building and cannot be removed without causing damage to the building.

Title commitment: Commitment from a title insurance company that it will issue a title insurance policy for the property.

KEY LEARNING POINTS

- List and explain all items contained in the commitment letter.
- List and explain all items contained in the closing conditions schedule.

QUESTIONS

1. Explain what a commitment letter is and the items it contains.
2. What are some possible ways to reduce either the commitment fee or the loan interest rate?
3. Why would a borrower want to ensure that the commitment letter does not state that the commitment fee was earned at the time of acceptance of the commitment letter?
4. Are each of these items considered personal property or real property?

   Built-in range
   Free-standing refrigerator
   Television
   Chandelier hanging from ceiling
   Air-conditioning window unit

10

Closing the Loan: The Note, Mortgage, Construction Loan Agreement, and Unconditional Guaranty

A blizzard of papers are signed at closing for a major construction loan. We will deal with four major documents in detail: the Note, the Mortgage, the Construction Loan Agreement, and the Unconditional Guaranty, complete copies of which can be found in Appendix A. We will then briefly touch on some of the other types of documentation that may be required.

The two most important documents that a borrower will be required to sign are the note and the mortgage. The note is evidence of indebtedness and constitutes a pledge to pay back the amount borrowed. A note is transferable and can be given or sold by one party to another party. The mortgage creates the lien on the real property that is given as collateral to ensure repayment of the note. A lien is legal claim on property and can arise in many circumstances and against all types of property; a mortgage is a document that gives evidence of that claim when the claim arises as the result of a voluntary pledging of real estate as collateral for a loan. Occasionally in casual use or when speaking in a narrow context in which the meaning is clear, even professionals will interchange the terms *lien* and *mortgage*.

The terms *note* and *mortgage* are also often used loosely and interchanged freely; however, the precise legal meanings are even more distinct. The note is the IOU, the debt itself, and the mortgage is the pledge of an asset to secure the repayment of that debt. Without the mortgage, the note would be said to be unsecured. Simply because one borrows money to build a project does not automatically mean that the project is collateral for the loan. The mortgage is the legal instrument that creates that relationship between the debt and the asset used as security. Furthermore, in order to put third parties on notice to the existence of a lien on the real property, the mortgage *must* be recorded in the public records of the county or parish in which the real property is located. To record documents in the public records, the general rule is that an original must be presented and it must have at least two witnesses and be notarized. Although every state is free to adopt its own procedures, in most jurisdictions a copy of a court order or other court document that has been certified as a correct copy by the clerk of the court will be accepted in lieu of an original. The clerk stamps the original document with a book and page number, which become the reference points, makes a copy, and returns the original.

The public records are usually found in the county courthouse, and it seems as though they are always in the basement! In days past the public records consisted of huge, thick, dusty books. Now they are mostly on microfilm and many are converting to electronic databases. Although such a filing in the public records may seem like an elementary task, occasionally mortgages are filed in the wrong county or the legal description is incorrect, and havoc can ensue. Failure to file in the public records or to file correctly means that the property could be sold to an innocent third party, a bona fide purchaser for value who has no knowledge, actual or constructive, of the mortgage, and the new owner of the real property will not be bound by the mortgage. Such a sale would be fraud on the part of the seller who knew of the mortgage, but it would not be on the part of the buyer if that buyer were truly without knowledge of the lein and mortgage. It is the duty of the holder of the mortgage to put the world on notice, via a filing in the public record, of the existence of the debt and the pledge of the real estate as collateral for its repayment.

THE NOTE

The essential terms of a promissory note are the lender, the borrower, the principal sum, the interest rate, and the time(s) of repayment. Only the signature of the borrower is required, because it is only the borrower who has an active obligation—to pay and to do so in a timely manner. The lender has only to passively receive funds as they are tendered. Nor are witnesses or a notary required, as the note itself does not have to be recorded, only the mortgage. Some mortgages will contain or incorporate a copy of the note, but it is not a requirement. Most mortgages will simply reference the amount of the debt and the original date of the note, along with the due date of the final payment. Other terms such as the interest rate are usually omitted.

The Real Estate Promissory Note for $15,000,000 for the Hidden Lake apartment project is shown in Appendix A. The first words are "For Value Received," which are important because they state for the record that consideration has been given by the lender to the borrower in return for the promissory note. Nowhere in the note does it state that the bank will give the borrower $15,000,000, merely that the borrower agrees to pay (not even repay!) to the order of the bank the principal sum of $15,000,000. Thus, absent any issues with usury statutes, it is legally possible for a lender to actually lend a lesser sum than the face amount of the note received. The discount from the face value creates an implied interest rate, and, indeed, Treasury bills are sold this way. As long as the combination of the implied interest rate and the stated interest rate do not exceed any usury limit, it is a perfectly legal practice. In this case, the borrower actually received proceeds equal to the face amount of the note; however, it is important to know that this information is not contained in the Note itself and the face amount of the note cannot always be taken at face value.

Collier Venture One, L.L.C., a Florida limited liability company, is listed as the borrower, and First Union National Bank is listed as the bank/lender. The interest rate is given as LIBOR plus 1.90% per annum, as calculated over a 360-day year (which makes the actual interest rate slightly higher). The note is interest-only for two years and then has a one-year option with monthly payments of $121,289 principal and interest, provided that the borrower has provided evidence to the lender that the property has achieved and is capable of maintaining a minimum 1.25 debt service coverage ratio. The debt service coverage ratio is defined as "the annualized Net Operating Income of the Property divided by the aggregate annualized principal and interest payments due hereunder (after taking into account any applicable interest rate swaps) for the same period. 'Net Operating Income' shall mean all income from the Property minus all operating expenses (including a four percent (4%) management fee) and reasonable reserves for capital repairs and replacements."

There is a late fee of 5% of the payment due for any payment received after five days. During the construction period of the loan this is generally a moot point, inasmuch as part of the sources and uses of funds statement contains an account for interest expense and the bank simply draws down on the account and applies the funds to the interest due. This can be done as long as neither the total loan amount nor the interest reserve is exceeded.

The note contains a provision for the lender and the borrower to enter into a swap agreement that essentially fixes the interest rate for the period of the loan. From the lender's perspective, this reduces the amount of risk and thus increases the amount of money it was willing to lend, which was the borrower's motivation for entering into the swap agreement. The decision to float or to fix the interest rate is always a gamble; in this case the Federal Reserve cut interest rates six weeks after the loan agreement was entered into and the borrower would have been substantially better off, at least during the first six months of the loan, with a floating interest rate. The full picture can only be told in retrospect, and, of course, things could easily have gone the other way. Every day trader would sell his broker's soul in a flash for tomorrow's newspaper.

The note states that it can be prepaid at anytime. That is true, but a swap agreement can be expensive to unwind early, and although swap agreements can stand alone as a pure interest rate bet, they are typically tied to some underlying transaction and it may be difficult to bifurcate them.

The note cites the mortgage and unconditional guaranty taken to secure the repayment of the note. The note goes on to grant the bank a sweeping security interest: "a continuing security interest in *all property of Borrower, now or hereafter in the possession of Bank* [emphasis added], as security for the payment of this Note and any other liabilities of Borrower to Bank, which security interest shall be enforceable and subject to all the provisions of this Note, as if such property were specifically pledged hereunder."

The default interest rate is the "highest permissible rate under applicable usury law." The default interest rate frequently can be negotiated to something lower (e.g., akin to "4% points over the note rate") and in longer-term loans the borrower is more likely to negotiate that point. Longer-term loans are more likely to be sold out of the bank's portfolio, and the borrower may end up dealing with an institution that has no interest in an ongoing relationship and has no motivation to make any accommodation, reasonable or otherwise. As a practical matter, the borrower has no intention of defaulting, and of the wide range of negotiable issues to which limited time and energy can be devoted, the default rate ranks low.

The borrower makes substantial and significant representations, warranties, and covenants, which are three ways of saying pretty much the same thing. A representation is a statement of fact to which legal liability may attach if false. A warranty is a guarantee or assurance of some fact, truth, or reality, along with the obligation, implied or expressed, to do all in one's power to remedy or restore the situation or make the other party whole if the situation should change. A covenant is a formal agreement or promise. Covenants used to have to be under seal, a formal solemnity that was supposed to add extra weight to the promise. Few, if any, jurisdictions retain that requirement. In the context of a deed to real estate, the different types of covenants have very real meaning, and the term "usual covenants" has a very specific meaning, neither of which is particularly relevant in the context of a note.

In essence, the borrower swears that everything is true and correct, that everything has been done properly, that the borrower will pay for everything and anything if anything goes wrong, and that the borrower will continue to keep the bank fully informed. If the bank fails to exercise a right, it is not a waiver of that right, now or in the future; if the bank grants any concession, the bank has no obligation to continue granting that concession. There is a lengthy clause that, in essence, says that if anything in this note runs afoul of any usury law, oops, we are sorry, we did not mean it and the interest rate is "immediately reduced to such maximum legal rate and the portion of all prior interest payments in excess of such maximum legal rate shall be applied to and shall be deemed to have been payments in reduction of the outstanding principal balance." In the area of usury, much turns on what is interest and what is not. Is a late fee interest? Is a required fee interest? Although the rule varies by jurisdiction, the general rule is that reasonable late fees are not interest, but unreasonable ones are—which begs the question as to what is reasonable and what is not. Generally, if a fee is for a true expense reasonably related to the loan, it is not interest. If it is a fee the lender charges just because it can, then it is interest. Under this note, the borrower further agrees that in "determining whether or not any interest payable under this Note exceeds the highest rate permitted by law, any non-principal payment, including without limitation, late charges, shall be deemed to the extent permitted by law to be an expense, fee or premium rather than interest."

The bank reserves the right to sell the note, and the borrower grants any court in the State of Florida jurisdiction over the case and waives any defense based on improper venue or inconvenient forum. This is another example of a clause that could easily be negotiated to restrict jurisdiction to the county where the property is located, the most convenient place to the borrower for any litigation to occur. However, although the court in the county where the bank has its headquarters may accept jurisdiction, as a practical matter it is unlikely that any court other than one in a juridiction where the property is based would accept jurisdiction. The general rule of law is one of common sense: that a case should be filed in the jurisdiction where there is the greatest connection. Although that is frequently a value judgment, in the case of real property it is usually conceded to be the location of the real property. A judge can voluntarily accept jurisdiction if all the parties submit to the court's jurisdiction, but this is rare. Many judges have heavy workloads and see no reason to add to their caseload backlogs by accepting a case that does not have a meaningful nexus to their forum.

The note also contains an extensive arbitration clause designed to speed up the resolution of any disputes. The final clause is in boldface capitals and constitutes the borrower's waiver of the right to jury trial; it concludes with the borrower acknowledging and agreeing that the waiver is a "specific and material aspect of this Note and that Bank would not extend credit to Borrower if the waivers set forth in this section were not part of this Note." The clause represents the bank's concerns about the capriciousness of the American jury system and an awareness that banks rarely make sympathetic plaintiffs.

THE MORTGAGE

A mortgage is a document by which a borrower/mortgagor conveys an interest in real property to a lender/mortgagee as security for the payment of a debt. The note is the evidence of the debt, the mortgage is evidence of the security for the debt.

The mortgage, titled the Mortgage and Security Agreement, lists First Union National Bank as the mortgagee and Collier Venture One, L.L.C., as the mortgagor and then goes on to note that the "Mortgagor is justly indebted to the Mortgagee in the principal sum of Fifteen Million Dollars and No Cents ($15,000,000) (the "Loan"), which loan evidenced by a certain Real Estate Promissory Note of even date herewith."

The literal reading of the mortgage is akin to a deed with the mortgagor/borrower conveying fee simple title to the land to the mortgagee/lender:

"Therefore, in consideration of and to secure the Note, together with interest thereon and any and all sums due or which may become due from Mortgagor to Mortgagee, Mortgagor does grant, bargain, sell, alien, remise, release, convey and confirm unto Mortgagee, its successors and assigns, in fee simple, all of that certain tract of land of which Mortgagor is now seized and possessed and in actual possession, all of which situate in the County of Alachua, State of Florida and is more fully described in Exhibit 'A'.... To Have and to Hold all and singular the Mortgaged Property hereby conveyed, and the tenements, hereditaments and appurtenances thereunto belonging or in any way appertaining, and the reversion and reversions, remainder and remainders, rents, issues and profits thereof and also all the estate, right, title, interest property, possession, claim and demand whatsoever as well in law as in equity of Mortgagor in and to the same and every part and parcel thereof unto Mortgagee in fee simple."

However, immediately subsequent to the language of conveyance, the mortgage contains reversionary language: "Provided always that if Mortgagor shall pay to Mortgagee any and all indebtedness due by Mortgagor to Mortgagee... and shall perform, comply with and abide by each and every stipulation, agreement, condition, and covenant of the Note, the Loan Agreement and of this Mortgage, then this Mortgage and the estate hereby created shall cease and be null and void."

In spite of the literal reading of the language of a mortgage, both case law and the statutes of most, if not all, states hold that a mortgage is not a true conveyance of title and that a formal legal foreclosure proceeding is necessary to transfer title in the event of a default. Most states provide substantial legal procedural protection for mortgagors with a statutory right of redemption up until the traditional sale on the courthouse steps and, in many cases, for several days thereafter. A right of redemption in this case is the right, no matter how far along the foreclosure case, to pay all the monies owed (principal, default interest, costs, and attorneys' fees) and receive clear title to the land. This right is frequently extended by statute to several days after the "final" sale under the foreclosure proceedings, that is, a purchaser at a foreclosure sale must wait a period of time to see whether the sale remains valid. Typically, during this period of time, the prospective purchaser at a foreclosure sale will be required to deposit the necessary funds or a significant portion thereof in the registry of the clerk of the court.

In case of default, the lender files for foreclosure in the county in which the property is located, and if the court does not find to the contrary, a foreclosure judgment is obtained. The sheriff then takes possession of the property in the name of the court and, after public notice, auctions it off at public auction to the highest bidder. Anyone can bid, including the owner and the lender. The terms of the sale are typically cash, but in some jurisdictions a purchaser may put up a hefty binder and be given a short period of time to come up with the balance. Obviously, this greatly restricts the number of potential buyers and thus depresses the price obtained.

The proceeds of the sale are used to pay off the balance of the mortgage note. If there is any excess cash from the sale, after the note and legal fees and any other liens are paid, it would go to the original owner. If the foreclosure sale does not bring enough money to pay off the note, the borrower still owes the balance unless the note is a nonrecourse note.

It is rare for a property to actually go into foreclosure and even rarer to go to public sale. These odds further depress the price of the few properties that do go to sale. No intelligent investor purchases a property without significant due diligence. Meaningful due diligence is an expensive and time-consuming process, and because few properties in foreclosure actually make it to sale, most astute investors are reluctant to spend the resources on the many in order to bid on the few.

Furthermore, the odds at a public sale favor the insiders who already know the true value of the real estate. The lender is allowed to bid its lien as if it were cash, and the lender will not let the property go for much less than its true value, because that would increase the loss it suffers. It is not unheard of for the owner to be asked to be part of a consortium of bargain hunters (because of her intimate knowledge of the property and its value) bidding at the auction in case the lender is eager to wash its hands of the project and will take a bit less in order to get it off its books.

Most troubled real estate loans go through a workout process whereby the lender and the owner meet as professionals and attempt to devise a plan to guide the property back to prosperity. Most lenders do not want a foreclosed property on their books. Foreclosures and related legal fees are very expensive and wasteful, and generally both parties know the strengths of their respective hands and rarely overplay them. If the property truly lacks value, most owners would rather deed back the property to the lender in lieu of foreclosure. If a lender pushes too hard on a property that has promise, the owner can always file bankruptcy in an attempt to buy time.

Law and Equity

The conveyance clause of the mortgage contains the phrase "in law and in equity," and in that small phrase lies significant history. Most American law has its roots in England, and that is where we get most of our legal traditions. (The only significant exception is Louisiana, which is based on the French civil code dating from sweeping legal reformation instigated by Napoleon.) In late medieval times in England there evolved two parallel court systems. One system was based strictly on the law and was run by the state. The other was based on equity and was run by the church. In those times the law was very rigid, with few remedies, and at times arrived at outcomes that were patently unfair. The system of equity, which existed to balance the legal system, sprang from the feudal concept that in return for pledging your loyalty to your liege, the king, the king in return owed you both protection and justice (an abstract concept). Originally, that meant the right to appear before the king and plead your case. Obviously, as England grew, hearing such pleas became a time-consuming duty, and the king delegated the responsibility of ensuring that his subjects received justice to the church. Over time a formal system of equity courts run by the church emerged, which to a certain extent paralleled the legal system.

In those days, when you defaulted on a mortgage, that was it. You could have been only a day or two late, the lien might have been for only 20% of the value of the property—it did not matter: A default was a default. There was no opportunity to cure, no opportunity or time to raise the money necessary to redeem the land. You immediately lost title to the land upon default, and it became fully the property of the mortgagee. Obviously, this resulted in some outcomes that were unjust, all the more so in that the mortgagee was under no obligation to sell the land to settle the debt. Thus, if the value of the land exceeded the debt and related costs, the mortgagee was unjustly enriched. The courts of equity evolved to right such injustices, and that is where the concept of foreclosure began; that is, a formal legal proceeding to transfer the title to ensure that justice was done, as well as the implementation of a right of redemption. There was a period of time after the occurrence of the default during which the debtor could redeem the property by paying off the debt. We take such concepts of fairness for granted now, but in ancient England, they were somewhat novel. In the mid-1800s, England combined its courts of law and equity, and today most American courts are courts of both law and equity.

The treatment of Contracts for Deeds illustrates the level of procedural protection built into most states' statutes. Contracts for Deeds were popular for a time as a means of owner financing of the sale of real estate and were designed to provide greater protection for the seller/financier by structuring the sale as a contract to purchase a deed whereby the final title to the land did not pass until all the payments due under the contract to purchase the deed had been made. The idea was that in the event of a default, an expensive and time-consuming foreclosure could be avoided inasmuch as the seller had never transferred the title. Both the courts and the legislatures of most states have taken the position that regardless of its form, a Contract for Deed is in sum and substance a mortgage and that all the procedural protections available for a mortgage apply. As a result, Contracts for Deed have fallen out of favor as they provided little, if any, benefit.

Acceleration Clause

The mortgage has an acceleration clause, which provides that upon default "all monies due hereunder shall become immediately due and payable." This is a very important clause, because if the mortgagor defaults by missing a single payment, what are the remedies available to the mortgagee? Sue for the single payment? Without the acceleration clause, all that is due is the payments that have been missed and perhaps the related costs of collection and legal fees. A meaningful sum perhaps, but one that pales in consideration of the entire principal balance. In the absence of the acceleration clause, the lender would have to either file an individual suit to collect on each and every payment as it came due or wait until the end of the loan and file for the entire principal balance.

Suffer No Waste

The mortgagor promises to keep the Mortgaged Property in "good condition and repair," and not "commit nor permit to be committed waste thereon, shall not do nor permit to be done any act by which the Mortgaged Property shall become less valuable" and also promises to "operate ... the Mortgaged Property in compliance with all applicable laws, ordinances, regulations, covenants, conditions and restrictions." All of the preceeding requirements are simply good business; more restrictively, the mortgagor gives up significant rights as well as some operating flexibility: "Unless required by law ... Mortgagor shall not allow changes in the stated use of Mortgaged Property from that which was disclosed to Mortgagee" and "shall not initiate or acquiesce to a zoning change of the Mortgaged Property without the prior notice to and consent of Mortgagee."

Future Advances

The mortgage provides for future advances, that is, the lending of additional amounts under the mortgage, whether they are obligatory or at the option of the mortgagee. An obligatory advance is one the lender makes to protect its interest—for example, to pay property taxes or insurance or attorneys' fees and legal costs associated with collecting the debt. These are treated as advances under the mortgage, so they will be considered a secured debt. The mortgage specifically states that the mortgage is given not only to secure existing indebtedness, but also future advances "to the same extent as if such future advances are made on the date of the execution of this Mortgage." This is important, because the lender wants to preserve its place in line in case other creditors come calling. The wording of the future advance clause makes sure that any additional funds advanced are both secured by a lien on the property *and* that the lien is equal in time and in priority to the mortgage placed on the property. Because the lender made clear via a title search and title insurance that the title was clear of all liens at the time the mortgage was placed, the lender is assured that it has first priority claim on the property over all other creditors of the borrower. The only lien that can have a higher priority would be future property taxes. The mortgage's future advance clause limits the total amount secured to twice the face amount of the loan, so unless there is some principal paydown, the amount of future advances is limited, in this case, to $15 million. The future advance clause further provides that to be secured by the mortgage, the advances must be made within 20 years of the date of the mortgage. When it is time to satisfy the mortgage, that is, to record on the public record that the mortgage has been paid in full, a well-drawn satisfaction of mortgage makes specific reference to the fact that the satisfaction covers the future advance clause as well, and that said clause is void in the future and can no longer be used to securitize any future debt.

Liens and Title Searches

Because title searches are good for only a given point in time and title records always lag a few days behind the actual recording of documents, the bank does have a window of vulnerability in which a lien could be filed after the effective date of the title search and before the lender's mortgage is recorded. For that reason a prudent lender always has a follow-up title search done that shows that the lender's mortgage has been properly recorded *and* that no other lien was filed after the prior title search. If such a lien had been filed, the borrower would be under an immediate duty to remove the lien. That can be done by paying it off or, if the borrower wishes to dispute the lien, most jurisdictions allow a property owner to remove a lien from the public record by bonding it off. This may be done by posting adequate funds (principal amount owed plus one years' interest is a common statutorily required amount; some jurisdications require a provision for including an amount for legal costs and attorney's fees) in the registry of the court or, more likely, posting a bond issued by a registered surety. The fee for the posting varies according to the credit quality of the person guaranteeing payment to the surety, but it can be as low as a small percentage of the amount at risk.

Escrow Accounts

Because this a short-term construction loan, the bank merely reserves the right to require the mortgagor/borrower to escrow funds for insurance and property taxes as opposed to actually implementing the requirement that funds be escrowed.

An escrow account refers to funds that are held in trust for a dedicated purpose, in this case property taxes and insurance. Typically, in a longer-term permanent loan, the escrow paragraph would require the borrower to make the deposits for taxes and insurance with each installment. This means that every month, the owner, in addition to paying principal and interest on the mortgage, must pay a monthly amount sufficient to cover the taxes and the insurance when they come due. If, for example, the real estate taxes on this project are $240,000 per year, then $\frac{1}{12}$ of $240,000, or $20,000, in additional funds will have to be paid each month into an escrow account. In addition, if the insurance is $36,000 per year, the borrower will have to pay $\frac{1}{12}$ of $36,000, or $3,000, in additional funds each month into the escrow account for insurance. This total of $23,000 per month will be paid to the bank or its agent and put into a special escrow account. It is not unusual for the borrower in a permanent loan to be required to fund the escrow account up front with three months' payments in addition to having to begin making immediate monthly payments. Typically, no interest is paid to the borrower on funds in escrow, making them a cash cow for the lender, or for the loan servicer if a third party is hired to service the loan, as is usually the case in conduit loans.

Permanent loans frequently require an escrow account known as reserves for replacement for anticipated future expenditures such as for the replacement of carpets, refrigerators, ovens, hot water heaters, roofs, and parking lots, all elements of the project that will not last as long as the building shell. Although it may be decades before some of these items will be replaced on new construction, it is the norm in the financing industry to begin escrowing replacement reserves immediately. There is some minimal additional financial security in doing so for a new project, but the primary motivation is most likely that the escrow account represents interest-free funds for the lender/loan servicer.

Although it is exceedingly rare for it to occur, the mortgage does give the mortgagee the right to obtain an appraisal on the property *at the mortgagor's* expense if "required by the regulations of the Federal Reserve Board or the Office of the Comptroller of the Currency or at such other times as Mortgagee may reasonably require, but in any event, not more frequently than annually unless required by the regulations of the Federal Reserve Board or the Office of the Comptroller of the Currency."

Assignment of Leases, Subleases, Franchises, Rents, Sales Contracts, Issues, and Profits

As additional security, the mortgage provides for the mortgagor to transfer, assign, and set over all the mortgagor's interest in all leases, subleases, franchises, rents, sales contracts, issues, and profits. This is because the value of the project lies in its income stream, which is dependent on the leases. The leases of the property are a separate asset from the property itself, and the quickest way to take control of the income stream of the property is to have control of the leases. Owning the property can be of very limited benefit if the property is leased and the leases provide for the income to go to someone other than the owner of the property.

The assignment of leases clause appoints "Mortgagee as Mortgagor's true and lawful attorney-in-fact, to collect any and all rents from the Premises, expressly authorizing Mortgagee to receipt tenants therefor, and does by these presents ratify and confirm any and all acts of such attorney-in-fact in relation to the foregoing." Unlike an automatic transfer of title upon default, a material default can automatically validly trip the assignment of leases clause, and the provision for the appointment of the mortgagee as attorney-in-fact will hold up in court.

Security Agreement in Personal Property

The mortgage also contains a specific provision to give the mortgage holder a security interest in all the personal property on the premises.

CONSTRUCTION LOAN AGREEMENT

A construction loan is inherently more complex than a standard real estate loan. The asset—the project—that is to secure the loan, does not yet exist. The funds to create the project that is to secure the loan are to be released gradually, in draws, as the project progresses. The construction loan agreement, designed to cover many of the day-to-day details of the arrangement between the lender and the borrower during the construction period, is the workhorse of the documents executed at closing.

The Construction Loan Agreement begins with a litany of recitals, terms, and definitions that lay out the framework and details of the agreement between the borrower and the lender, restating the information contained in the note, the mortgage, and the commitment letter. The borrower repeats and reaffirms the representations and warranties made in the mortgage and the note.

Then the conditions precedent to the lender's obligation to make advances/draws under the loan are laid out:

- All provisions of the Loan Commitment shall have been complied with.
- Borrower's representations and warranties shall remain true and correct.
- No Event of Default shall have occurred under this Agreement or under any other Loan Document.
- Evidence shall be furnished to Lender, which evidence shall be satisfactory to Lender in its sole and absolute discretion, that Borrower's equity in an amount not less than $843,391.00 has previously been invested in the Premises or for approved uses as set forth on the Sources and Uses of Funds and satisfactory written proof of such input of Borrower's Equity has been furnished to Lender in the form of paid invoices.
- The requirements with respect to requests for advances (draws) shall have been complied with.

Normally, a lender looks for an amount of equity equal, as an absolute minimum, to 20% of cost, which in this case would be a number north of $3,000,000. Because the borrower owned the raw land free and clear prior to closing and had substantial equity in the existing 39 units, only $843,391 of additional borrower's equity was required. A substantial portion of that amount had already been invested in prior renovations of the existing 39 units and in the professional fees for the permitting and regulatory process necessary to get to the point of being ready to start construction, so the actual cash due to meet the borrower's equity requirement was minimal.

The Construction Loan Agreement goes on to provide that "[d]isbursements for the construction of the Improvements shall be made on application of Borrower, which applications shall not be more than once every month. Request for advances shall be submitted on AIA [American Institute of Architects] Forms G-702 and G-703 'Application and Certificate for Payment' signed by Borrower, Borrower's Contractor and Borrower's Architect and shall be received by Lender and the Inspecting Agent not less than ten (10) days prior to the date on which the payment is desired and shall set forth in detail the amounts expended or costs incurred for work done and materials incorporated on the Premises."

An issue that frequently arises is the treatment of supplies bought in bulk (i.e., lumber) and stored on the site for a time prior to being incorporated in the building. Does this represent an expenditure of funds that the borrower can include in the draw application? Lenders vary in their treatment. Some allow reimbursement for off-site storage at a lumberyard or truss assembly site, others require that the supplies be incorporated in the building prior to application for reimbursement. This lender takes the middle road: "No funds will be disbursed for materials stored on the Premises without the prior written consent of Lender and then only if such materials are, in Lender's sole opinion, adequately secured."

The lender also uses the Construction Loan Agreement to create the right to request that each request for an advance "be accompanied by a certificate of endorsement from the Title Insurer stating that a search of the public records has been made and that such search reveals no change in the state of title," that is, that no liens have been filed against the property. Like most states, Florida has an extensive Construction Lien statute, designed in part to protect suppliers of construction materials. Florida law provides for the filing of a Notice of Commencement in the public record at the start of a construction project; the filing is a requirement in order to obtain the first inspection. The notice lists the name of the contractor and the name of the owner and the lender, if any. Any contractor who wishes to preserve his lien rights and any supplier not in direct privy of contract with the owner or general contractor must send a Notice to Owner (NTO) with a copy to the lender within a certain number of days of first beginning work on the job. This puts the owner on notice that before or at the time of paying the general contractor, the owner must receive lien waivers for work and supplies furnished to date from those subcontractors and suppliers who have sent in NTOs, in order to avoid direct liability for payment and the possibility of paying for the same work or supplies twice.

The Construction Loan Agreement also specifies that $900,000 of loan funds have been set aside in order to create an undisbursed interest reserve. Because the project will not be generating funds during construction, this is the source of payment of the interest due on the loan during construction and lease up. It is a rather large interest reserve, or at least the developer hopes it is. The total loan amount outstanding will eventually be $15,000,000, and the first draw of just over $1 million was made on November 17, 2000; the developer plans to complete the project by July 30, 2001, eight and a half months later. The interest rate has been swapped out at about 8.5%. Although the total loan amount at the end of the project will be $15,000,000, the average loan amount will be significantly less during the construction period as the loan is gradually drawn out in monthly advances as the building progresses and costs are incurred. The developer calculates that, on average, 60% of the loan amount will be outstanding over the first nine months of the project. $15,000,000 × 60% × 8.5% × ¾ of a year (9 months) = $573,750 of interest, substantially less than the $900,000 interest reserve. Of course, this assumes that the project is completed in a timely manner and that it fills up at the start of the school year in late August and stabilizes virtually immediately. When fully drawn down, the interest on the entire loan is $106,250 per month, so the $325,000 of excess interest reserve could fund the project for three months even if no income were forthcoming. If the project comes in late or experiences trouble in leasing up, there is usually some rental income; even a troubled project should lease sufficiently to generate adequate income to allow the interest reserve to last a full year until the next leasing cycle—which was most likely the lender's intention.

Although lease up is not the general contractor's responsibility, like any business, a general contractor wants happy, repeat customers, and a developer whose project is not leasing is not a happy customer. There are many ways, large and small, in which the general contractor can assist in lease up: getting the leasing trailer set up as rapidly as possible, allowing potential customers to view construction in progress (limited area with hard hats and waivers a must), getting the clubhouse and amenities done quickly, having the first building completed swiftly in order to have models to show, maintaining a clean job site, and showing sensitivity to any neighborhood concerns.

The Construction Loan Agreement gives the lender the right to retain 10% of the amount applied for in each draw as retainage to ensure the full and correct completion of the job. This right is standard in the industry and is mirrored and repeated in the developer's contract with the general contractor, and the general contractor's contracts with the subcontractors. A bit of a cash flow issue can arise in regard to supplies, such as lumber, that are often purchased directly by the general contractor. Although suppliers will typically give 30 to 45 days' credit, they are not generally willing to accept a 10% retainage. Astute cash flow management can smooth over the issue, but the absence of financial acumen can have the developer (or general contractor, depending on the terms of the contract) unhappily having to fund the difference in float until the end of the project. The payment for supplies purchased directly by a subcontractor is the responsibility of the subcontractor. Typically, the retainage represents the subcontractor's profit, and the progress payments made during the job are sufficient to pay ongoing expenses. Of course, it is possible for the general contractor to purchase no supplies directly and contract in such a way as to have the subcontractors pay for all supplies; for example, the framer may supply the lumber. Sometimes a better price can be achieved by buying direct, sometimes not; a good general contractor will look at doing it both ways, and a sophisticated developer/project manager will monitor the process to ensure that the best possible project is built for the lowest possible cost. The lender may "at its sole discretion, release the ten percent (10%) Retainage held back on a particular subcontractor when said contractor's work is satisfactorily completed and is free and clear of all construction liens and unpaid bills."

The Construction Loan Agreement provides that the death of the guarantor is an event of default. Whereas this is a condition that is beyond the control of both the borrower and the guarantor, it was the subject of much discussion and negotiation. Because the guarantor and developer were one and the same, the lender's position was that while it respected and appreciated both the company the developer owned and the team he had put together, the personal presence and involvement of the guarantor/developer was a major factor in making the loan. The developer, although flattered that the lender considered his talents so crucial, opined in reply that the last thing the project needed in the event of the tragedy of his death was the additional trauma of loan default. Eventually, a compromise was reached that required a principal paydown of $3 million in the event of the death of the guarantor, and the developer assigned a life insurance policy to cover that eventuality.

The final clause of the Construction Loan Agreement once again has the borrower waiving that most fundamental of American rights, the right to a jury trial.

UNCONDITIONAL GUARANTY

The Borrower/Customer for this construction loan is Collier Venture One, L.L.C., a Florida-based limited liability company. Collier Venture One is a single-asset entity, i.e., it owns nothing more than the land the project is on and other related assets, such as the work product of the architect and site engineers. The market value of an ongoing construction project is at best minimal and generally significantly below cost. Full potential market value is not realized until the project is complete and stabilized. Since development and construction is a risky business, fraught with unseen peril, construction lenders generally require more security for the construction loan than the assets of the construction project itself.

This is where the Unconditional Guaranty comes in; it provides additional security in terms of the pledge of the assets of a high net worth individual(s) or entity. To quote from the Unconditional Guaranty on Hidden Lake, "Whereas, First Union National Bank is unwilling to extend or to continue to extend credit to and/or to engage in business transactions and enter into various contractual relationships with and otherwise deal with Customer unless it receives an unconditional and continuing, joint and several guaranty from the above identified, undersigned Guarantor." While underwriting guidelines vary, generally lenders look for a guarantor with a net worth of at least twice the loan amount with a meaningful portion of that net worth liquid, that is, easily convertible to cash.

Usually, the guarantor is the developer/investor/owner(s) behind the project who signs either as an individual or for the business entity or both, depending upon how the meaningful assets that provide the bank reassurance are titled. Too, the guarantor is generally the developer/investor/owner because he is the one willing to run the risk, as he is the one in a position to reap the upside gain. In addition to financial strength, the guarantor often possesses significant development, business, and project management skills that can be brought to bear if needed.

The Unconditional Guaranty is just that: an unconditional obligation that is sweeping in its terms, breadth, and scope: "Guarantor, jointly and severally, hereby absolutely and unconditionally guarantees to First Union National Bank and its successors and assigns, the full amount due, whether by acceleration or otherwise under the loan documents, plus all interest or finance charges, costs of court, penalty interest, late payment charges and the reasonable attorney's fees of First Union National Bank. This Guaranty is in addition to and is not intended to supersede any prior existing Guaranty of the guarantor." The clear intent of the unconditional guaranty is that the guarantor stands fully between the bank and any potential losses on the loan.

Any assets that the guarantor had on deposit with the lender bank may be seized to pay off amounts due: "As security for any and all liabilities of Guarantor hereunder, now existing or hereafter arising, or otherwise, Guarantor hereby grants to First Union National Bank the right to retain a security interest in any and all moneys or other property; also funds, investment securities, choses in action and any and all forms of property, whether real or personal or mixed, and any right, title, or interest of Guarantor therein or thereto or the proceeds thereof, which have been or may hereafter be deposited or left with First Union National Bank." As a result of this right to seize assets in the lender's possession, many guarantors choose not to keep large checking accounts, certificates of deposit, or investment portfolios at the same institution where they also are a guarantor. While the debt will still have to be dealt with, such segregation of assets allows a guarantor a bit more flexibility in maintaining normal operations and dealing with any situation. It can be very disrupting to a business to have its operating checking accounts frozen, and precipitous actions by a creditor can sometimes worsen a salvageable situation.

A portion of the Unconditional Guaranty quoted here uses the legal term "choses in action." A chose in action is akin to a legal right that has not been fully exercised. An owner does not have possession of it but does have a right of action for its possession. Examples of choses in action are rights to receive or recover a debt, or money, or damages for breach of contract or for a tort connected with a contract. These rights are assets but they cannot be enforced without action, thus the name choses in action.

While the financial assets that the Unconditional Guaranty represents are important, the value of the Unconditional Guaranty to the lender goes beyond monetary terms. The Unconditional Guaranty insures that the project has (or will have in the event of a crisis) the attention of an extremely motivated individual. The lender never wants to have to collect on the Unconditional Guaranty or take over operation of the project. The Unconditional Guaranty makes it highly unlikely that the Guarantor will ever walk away from a project.

OTHER CLOSING DOCUMENTS

Flood Insurance Information

Federal regulations and the Housing and Urban Development Act of 1968, Section 1365, require that the bank advise the borrower that according to FEMA Standard Flood Hazard Determination, the National Flood Insurance Rate Map No. 125107-008B dated January 19, 1983, reflects Flood Zone "C" and therefore flood insurance is not required.

Hazard and Title Insurance Acknowledgement Form

To protect consumers from inordinate pressure from lenders to do business with a hazard or title insurance company chosen by the lender, this form is required.

> THE FOLLOWING STATEMENT IS REQUIRED UNDER CHAPTER 4.3.002 OF THE RULES AND REGULATIONS PROMULAGTED BY THE INSURANCE COMMISSIONER RELATIVE TO ANTI-COERCION:
> The Insurance Laws of this State provide that the Lender may not require the Borrower to obtain insurance through any particular insurance agent or company to protect the mortgaged property. The Borrower, subject to the rules adopted by the Insurance Commissioner, has the right to have the insurance placed with an insurance agent or company of his choice provided the company meets the requirements of the Lender. The Lender has the right to designate reasonable financial requirements as to the company and the adequacy of the coverage.

In this case, the borrower chose Nationwide Insurance for the hazard insurance and First American Title Insurance Company to write the title insurance.

Certified Company Resolution for Borrowing Authorization

The powers and duties of corporate officers may be restricted by the articles of incorporation, bylaws, or board of directors. This resolution provides assurance to the lender that the corporate (or in this case, limited liability company) officer has the authority to bind the business entity and sign the loan documents.

> I, the undersigned, hereby certify to First Union National Bank ("Bank") that I am the managing member of Collier Venture One, L.L.C., a limited liability company duly organized and existing under the laws of the State of Florida and in good standing and fully authorized to transact business in the State of Florida and that the following is a true copy of the Resolutions duly adopted by the Manager (i.e., the developer/borrower) and Members of the Company at its meeting duly held on the 17th day of November 2000, at which a quorum was present and acted throughout and that such Resolutions are in full force and effect, have not been amended or rescinded and that there is no provision in the Articles of Organization, Operating Agreement, Charter or Bylaws of the Company limiting the power of the Manager and Members of the Company to pass the following Resolutions, which are in full conformity with the provisions of the Articles of Organization, Operating Agreement, Charter and Bylaws:

RESOLVED, that the present holder of the following office and/or positions of the company and their successors in office or position, to wit:

Nathan S. Collier, Managing Member

is hereby authorized on behalf of, in the name of and for the account of the Company, upon such terms and conditions as he deems desirable to borrow money and obtain credit (with or without security) from Bank, in such amounts as he deems desirable, to guarantee the obligations of others to the Bank, to engage in business transactions of all nature and kind and to enter into all manner and kinds of contractual relationships with Bank.

Certificate of the Members and Managers of Collier Venture One, LLC

This above Certified Company Resolution for Borrowing Authorization was signed by the managing member of Collier Venture One, L.L.C., i.e., an employee, this document is signed by the members and managers of Collier Venture One, L.L.C. (i.e., the owner/developer/borrower) and refers to and verifies the above document.

Compliance Agreement

Loan closings are complex and it's not unusual for errors to creep in or details to be overlooked. The Compliance Agreement survives closing and provides protection to the lender by compelling the borrower and guarantor to cooperate in correcting errors and omissions.

If requested by First Union National Bank ("Lender"), the undersigned borrower and Guarantor agree to cooperate fully and in a timely manner to assist in correcting errors and/or omissions which may be found in this loan's documents, exhibits or applications when correction is deemed by the Lender to be desirable or necessary.

Borrower and Guarantor understand that regulations of relevant government agencies and/or mortgage investors require the Lender to conduct regular post-closing reviews of loans. Loans chosen for such reviews are randomly selected and the reviews will in no way affect the integrity or specific terms of original loans. In the event that this loan is selected for a post-closing review the Borrower and Guarantor agree to give full cooperation to Lender in conducting said review.

Notice of Representation

Even though the borrower is paying the lender's attorney, the notice of representation makes it clear that the lender's attorney acts solely on behalf of the lender and has no duty to the borrower. Caveat Emptor is the rule.

The undersigned Borrower and Guarantor do hereby expressly confirm the fact that they knew and recognized at the time of closing of the above referenced real estate transaction that [lender's attorney] as Settlement Agent, was acting solely for and on behalf of the Lender. The undersigned acknowledge that the Borrower is paying the Lender's attorney's fees as a cost of the loan closing. Furthermore, the undersigned understand that they had the opportunity to employ counsel of their own choice in connection with this transaction.

Borrower's No Lien and Possession Affidavit

The borrower (the affiant) after having been duly sworn and deposed, says that the borrower is authorized to make this affidavit and states in accordance with Section 1445 of the Internal Revenue Code and under penalties of perjury that the borrower is not a foreign person as defined by Section 1445(f) of the Internal Revenue Code, that the borrower is the owner in fee simple of the property, and that there are no other parties other than the borrower and its tenants in possession thereof. The borrower further states that there have been no improvements or repairs made by the borrower in the past 90 days for which the cost or any part thereof remain unpaid, that there are no construction liens or claims, demands, contract rights, liens, or judgments outstanding against the property, and that there are no outstanding rights of dower, curtesy, or easements not shown of the public records of Alachua County, Florida.

Assignment of Borrower's Interest in Contract Documents

The borrower assigns to the lender all the borrower's "rights, title and interest" in the contracts necessary to construct the project. These include contracts with the general contractor, subcontractors, surveyors, materialmen, suppliers, and/or laborers, any agreement for architectural and engineering services, any drawings, plans, and specifications, any and all building permits, governmental permits, licenses, or other governmental licenses, and any and all utility service agreements.

The purpose is twofold: to provide additional security for the lender and to put the lender in a position to finish the project in the event of default.

Assignment of Management Agreement and Subordination of Management Fees

As is typical, the borrower has signed a management agreement with a property management firm to market and manage the property for a fee of 4% of gross rents received. This form assigns the management agreement to the lender, once again in order to provide additional security for the lender and to put the lender in position to take over management of the project in the event of default. As is frequently the case, the choice of the property management firm was not an arm's-length transaction. The property management firm is a 300-person company wholly owned by the developer, which manages the developer's other real estate holdings.

Environmental Indemnification Agreement

Basically, the borrower and guarantor agree to indemnify the lender against any possible environmental issues that may occur. The document cites various and numerous governmental rules, regulations, and federal statutes as well as several polysyllabled and unpleasant-sounding chemicals. The borrower and guarantor, in essence, state that the property is free of all nasty stuff and in compliance with all applicable standards and that if not, they will move heaven and earth and empty their wallets to make it so.

Conditional Assignment of Rents, Leases, and Revenues

The borrower assigns all its interest in the rents, leases, and revenues of the project to the lender. This document essentially duplicates what was in the mortgage; lenders and lawyers must come to closing wearing both belt and suspenders.

Financing Statement

There are two Financing Statements, one filed with the secretary of state in the state capital of Tallahassee, and the other with the clerk of the court in the public records of the county in which the property is located (more redundancy). These documents perfect the lender's security interest in the personal property on the premises under the Uniform Commercial Code (UCC).

The Notice of Commencement

The Notice of Commencement was referred to earlier in this chapter; it is filed with the clerk of the court in the public records of the county in which the property is located and is supposed to be posted on site. It lists the name and address of the owner, the lender, and the contractor and puts all interested parties on notice as to the parties involved.

Loan Closing Statement

The Loan Closing Statement is a summary of the finances of the closing; it lists the loan closing costs, which are normally deducted from the loan proceeds, and shows the remaining balance of the loan. See Figure 10.1. The largest item is the payoff of the mortgage on the existing 39 units: $878,461.98, including interest through three days after closing. The next largest amount is the $75,000, or half point loan commitment fee to First Union, a major contributor, one hopes, to year-end bonuses at the bank. The next largest item is the title insurance fee of $39,990, or just over a quarter point of the loan amount. This sum also covers the borrower's attorney's fee. The next two items are taxes: Documentary Stamp Tax on the note of $52,500, or .35 per $100, and an Intangible Tax on the note of .20 per $100, both charged by the State of Florida. These taxes occur every time a property is refinanced.

The lender's attorney's fee is $8,250, and there were two appraisals done, costing $4,800 and $4,300, respectively. There is a $1,500 plan review fee paid to the bank and a $1,400 Environmental Insurance fee, also paid to the bank.

Obviously, closing a loan is a rather expensive and time/energy-consuming process.

LOAN CLOSING STATEMENT

LENDER:	**First Union National Bank**
BORROWER:	**Collier Venture One, L.L.C.**
LOAN:	$15,000,000.00 Construction Loan
CLOSING DATE:	November 17, 2000

Loan Closing Costs:

1.	Title Fees & Borrower's Attorneys Fees & Costs (Clayton, Johnston et al.)	$ 39,990.00
2.	Documentary Stamp Taxes - Note	52,500.00
3.	Intangible Taxes	30,000.00
4.	Loan Commitment Fee	75,000.00
5.	Mortgage Loan Payoffs (Includes accrued interest thru 11/21/00)	878,461.98
6.	TRETS Fee	1,237.00
7.	Environment Insurance Fee	1,400.00
8.	Plan Review Fee (Reimburse Lender)	1,500.00
9.	Flood Certification Fee	10.00
10.	Appraisal Fee (Reimburse Lender)	4,300.00
11.	Appraisal Fee (Emerson Appraisal Company, Inc.)	4,800.00
12.	Lender's Attorneys Fees	8,250.00
13.	Recording and Filing Fees (estimate)	250.00
14.	Courier, FedEx, Facsimile, and Duplicating Expenses	250.00

Total Loan Closing Costs paid from Loan Proceeds: $ 1,097,948.98

Remaining Loan Proceeds: $13,902,051.01

The undersigned authorize Rogers, Towers, Bailey, Jones & Gay to disburse the closing costs as herein provided. The undersigned further authorize the sum of $82,750.00 to be deposited into the Clayton, Johnson Trust Account maintained with Lender in order to record the loan closing documents, which sum includes the documentary stamp tax, intangible tax and recording costs.

FIG. 10-1 Loan Closing Statement.

BORROWER: LENDER:

Collier Venture One, L.L.C.   **First Union National Bank**

By:_____   By: _____
Name: Nathan S. Collier   Name: _____
Its: Managing Member   Its: Assistant Vice President

FIG. 10-1 Continued.

SUMMARY

After a long process of negotiations, meetings, and analyses, a developer finally finds himself ready to close the loan. The paperwork associated with a loan is lengthy and extremely detailed. A developer should completely understand all the paperwork that will be signed at loan closing. The four major documents related to closing the construction loan are the *note*, the *mortgage*, the *construction loan agreement*, and the *unconditional guaranty*.

A *note* is evidence of indebtedness and constitutes a pledge to pay back the amount borrowed. Essential note terms are the lender, the borrower, the principal sum, the interest rate, and the time(s) of repayment. The borrower's signature is the only signature required on the note. The note only states the amount that the borrower is responsible for paying back, not the amount that was lent to the borrower. The details of how the interest rate is calculated are stated in the note, usually an underlying index plus a margin. Provisions are also included in the note regarding swap agreements, prepayments, and late fees. The final clause of the note waives the borrower's right to a jury trial.

The *mortgage* is a document by which a borrower *(mortgagor)* conveys an interest in real property to a lender *(mortgagee)* as security for the payment of a debt. The note is the evidence of debt; the mortgage is evidence of security for the debt. Without a mortgage, a loan would be labeled an "unsecured loan." In order to put third parties on notice to the existence of the mortgage, the document is recorded in the public records in the jurisdiction in which the real property is located. Failure to file in the public records can result in the property being sold to an innocent third party, in which case the new owner would not be bound by the mortgage. Mortgages contain numerous clauses regarding default, property condition, future advances, liens and title searches, escrow accounts, and assignments of leases and contracts.

The *construction loan agreement* is the workhorse of the documents executed at closing. This agreement describes the day-to-day details of the loan. Provisions include advances (or draws), required forms, notices to owner, and interest reserves.

The *unconditional guaranty* provides additional security to the lender in the form of assets from a high net worth individual or entity. The guarantor is guaranteeing that the lender will have its money repaid under the terms of the note.

Aside from the four major documents, other important papers must be signed at closing. These documents refer to flood insurance, hazard and title insurance, borrowing authorization, compliance, assignments, environmental issues, financing statements, and notices of commencement. The loan closing statement is a summary of the finances at closing; it lists each item and the amount charged to the borrower.

KEY TERMS AND DEFINITIONS

Acceleration clause: Clause in the mortgage that states that the mortgage shall become immediately due and payable should default occur.

Construction loan agreement: Workhorse of the documents executed at closing. This agreement covers the day-to-day details of the arrangement between the lender and borrower.

Contract for deed: Means of owner financing in which the final title of the land does not pass until all payments due under the contract to purchase the deed have been made.

Covenant: Formal agreement or promise.

Mortgage: Document by which a borrower conveys an interest in real property to a lender as security for payment of a debt.

Note: Document that acts as evidence of indebtedness and constitutes a pledge to pay back the amount of the note.

Notice of commencement: Notice filed in the public record at the start of a construction project. It lists the names of the contractor, owner, and lender.

Representation: Statement of fact to which legal liability may attach if false.

Suffer no waste clause: Clause in the mortgage where the borrower promises to keep the mortgaged property in "good condition and repair" and not commit or allow any waste on the property that will devalue it.

Unconditional guaranty: Unconditional obligation given by a guarantor to a lender that guarantor stands fully between the bank and any potential losses on the loan.

Unsecured loan: Loan to which there is no mortgage or collateral attached.

Warranty: Guarantee or assurance of some fact, truth, or reality, along with the obligation implied or expressed, to do all in one's power to remedy or to restore the situation or make the other party whole if the situation should change.

KEY LEARNING POINTS

- Understand the essential terms of a promissory note.
- Understand the numerous clauses and terminology of a mortgage.
- Explain the importance of the construction loan agreement.
- Understand the details of an unconditional guaranty.
- Understand all the other documents related to closing the loan.

QUESTIONS

1. What must be done to put third parties on notice to the existence of a mortgage (or lien) on a property?

2. Answer the following questions regarding the note:

   What are the five essential terms of a note?

   Is a witness or notary required to sign the note?

   Is the note required to be recorded in a public record?

3. Why is it important to know that the face amount of the note cannot always be taken at face value?

4. The literal reading of a mortgage is akin to a deed, with the borrower conveying a fee simple title to the land to the lender. In practice, is the mortgage actually conveying title? Explain.

5. Explain why, in the eyes of a lender, an acceleration clause is necessary in a mortgage.

6. Why is it necessary for the lender to perform a follow-up title search before the mortgage is recorded?

7. Why would a general contractor try to assist with the lease up of a project? In what ways does he assist?

8. Why would a guarantor of a loan not want to keep large amounts of assets in the institution giving the loan?

PART III
Evolution of the Development Process

11
Joint Ventures

In today's complex real estate market, more and more joint ventures (JVs) are being formed to marry capital and investment-management skills. The verb marry is used deliberately because, while the legal structure used for each investment is often technically a one-off joint venture, the intention frequently is to form an ongoing relationship, to create a platform capable of handling scale.

The investment world has changed drastically in the last decade. Globalization and the Internet have made it a much smaller, tighter community. Alliances, which would have been difficult in the past, are now increasingly the order of the day. Information is much more available. Unfamiliar with the site? A satellite view is instantly available on the Web. Digital pictures of a project in progress can be sent instantly from a cell phone in China to headquarters in Germany. Complex architectural and engineering documents can be emailed around the globe, allowing projects to be analyzed quickly and in detail.

ASSET ALLOCATION AND GEOGRAPHIC DIVERSIFICATION

Because of globalization, the reach of the Internet, and ease of alliances, capital is increasingly accumulated and invested on a worldwide basis. Most, if not all, long-term mega sources (institutions with billions of U.S. dollars to deploy) of investment capital practice asset allocation to spread their risk. Asset allocation reduces risk in a portfolio because historically we know that the returns on different asset classes tend to move differently and that some are more volatile than others. By investing in different asset classes that are negatively correlated, it is possible to smooth out returns over the long term, thus reducing volatility and risk.

Asset allocation typically occurs across asset classes and geography. At the highest level, the asset classes are debt, equity, cash, and real estate, and the geographic regions are the United States, Europe, and Asia. However, almost infinite subdivisions are possible. For example, debt may be broken down into government versus nongovernment; short-, intermediate-, or long-term, and secured versus nonsecured, with gradations going on virtually ad infinitum. Equity can be large, medium, or small cap, growth or value, domestic or international, developed country or emerging.

The diversification possibilities in real estate are almost as great in terms of class (office, retail, residential, or industrial), quality (A, B, C, or D), and geography. Many investors desire to invest in real estate as an asset class because of its long-term stability and the benefit it brings to their portfolios as a whole.

Furthermore, real estate in the United States tends to benefit from the desire of overseas investors both to have standard geographic diversification and to diversify political risk. The United States offers political and legal stability that is perceived as a tangible benefit to many overseas investors. This is a benefit that many Americans do not fully appreciate because they do not have direct experience of the potential vagaries of other political and legal systems and the havoc they can wreak on investment plans and business models. Even to investors in stable political and legal systems, in addition to the basic benefits of geographic diversification, the United States offers the additional benefit of a reduced regulatory environment with regard to labor and other markets.

TYPES OF JOINT VENTURE PARTNERS, UNION OF FINANCIAL AND INTELLECTUAL CAPITAL

Providers of capital, such as pension funds, investment funds, insurance companies, and banks, search the world over for good investment opportunities and for reliable local partners (investment advisors, developers, property managers, asset managers, and other real estate professionals) to assist in the deployment of that capital.

Providers of capital are not necessarily large companies or even institutions. As a young investor in my 20s and 30s, I bemoaned my lack of capital as I surveyed the myriad investment opportunities I saw before me. In short, I had more time and opportunity than I had capital. Now, decades later, I am awash in capital, and I bemoan the lack of appropriate investment opportunities. Now I have more capital than I have time and opportunity. Also, the desirable scale of investment has changed.

Some investments that might offer an acceptable return percentage are too small: The absolute return is too small to be attractive for the amount of time and energy required or the risk exposure. At other times, both the absolute and the percentage return are acceptable but the investment is too far outside our current scope, either geographically or by class, to make it worthwhile to devote the required managerial and entrepreneurial time and energy. When an investment is right in our "sweet spot," solidly in the core of what our organization is aligned to do, then generally the risk profile drops significantly.

Getting fully up to speed on investments that are in new fields and that represent new markets is time consuming. Often existing resources are fully committed, and the executive talent that could easily add a project or investment to an existing assembly-line process would be a stretch to fully and completely investigate and manage as a one-off. While new talent can be hired, that too is time consuming, and the process of fully integrating new talent into an organization often takes longer than anticipated.

It is hard to overemphasize how even small, seemingly insignificant changes can meaningfully increase risk. A major renovation project even just two hours from the home office is significantly more difficult to accomplish than one where one has a home-field advantage and well-known relationships and resources to call upon. Never underestimate the benefits of frequent in-person visits and the enhancement in rapport and problem solving that face-to-face relationships can bring. In complex projects, even small disadvantages can multiply and interact to create geometric increases in difficulty.

Back to the balance of capital available and investment opportunities in real estate: It is not the markets that have changed but, rather, my horizons and abilities. The financial capital was there when I was in my twenties, I just did not know how to find it and, then, once I found it, how to present proposals. And truth be told, even if I had found the capital, in many cases I might not have been willing to pay the price in terms of sharing the desired return, the loss of personal control, and the degree of reporting required, the paperwork, the red tape.

Still, there are many sources of capital—individual and institutional, large and small—searching for suitable, reliable, knowledgeable hands-on partners and operators to whom they can entrust their funds.

What I describe is the age-old balance between financial capital and intellectual capital.

Today, I have the organization and people to deal with reporting requirements that relationship management needs and, in effect, the size of my organization has forced me to give up many levels of personal control. The remaining issues of control between me and my new institutional partners can be handled via negotiation and buy and sell agreements.

The intention to create an ongoing relationship is often expressed in a nonbinding *Letter of Intent* (LOI).

ILLUSTRATIVE EXAMPLE OF A DEAL AND RELATED JV NEGOTIATIONS

Recently I made a $52 million, 348-unit apartment deal, and I looked at three JV proposals before accepting one and closing the deal. In addition to the apartments, the property also involved 32 acres of raw land suitable for future development. Here I will discuss one of the JV proposals in depth and contrast it on key terms with the other two JV proposals, emphasizing the proposal I ultimately accepted.

The development potential of the raw land complicated the deal. However, the treatment of the raw land turned out to be a critical component in the deal's success.

The following is a typical JV proposal from an investment fund, one we ended up not going further with for reasons I will explain. It is important to remember that this proposal is just that—a proposal. Some points are hard points, but many terms are open to negotiation, the normal give and take of any business agreement. This proposal is intended merely as a general outline, as a starting point for discussion.

The proposal provides the *potential* for preferred returns for the operating partner in order to compensate the operating partner for:

(a) finding and putting together the deal;
(b) running selected risks (the realistic extent of which make for an interesting debate relating to the adequacy of the compensation); and, last but certainly not least,

(c) motivating the operating partner to operate the asset so as to produce above-average returns.

My comments and thoughts follow the terms quoted from the proposal. Paradigm is my company, the operating partner. The names of all other parties have been changed to preserve privacy.

Proposed Acquisition Joint Venture Terms

Operating Partner and Minority Investor: *Paradigm Properties.*
Majority Investor: *Preferred Premium Properties, LLC.*
> The quality of your partner is of utmost importance in your decision to proceed with any joint venture. The experience level of your partner firm and of the person who will be your personal point of contact are vital, as is their ability to make timely decisions. Many opportunities can be lost if it takes too long for your partner to ramp up. Ask for references and complete lists of partners and customers, not just lists of satisfied ones. Everyone has someone who likes them, so make sure you get a comprehensive, 360-degree view of your potential partner. Speak to the people who are directly involved in the relationship. You are going to be spending a lot of time together over the next few years. Make sure you like your potential partner and that you can get along personally as well as professionally. It is challenging to do your best work when the relationship is rocky, and the last thing you need is distraction from the real work of insuring that a property performs well. In this case, this potential partner passed all our character and industry reputation checks with flying colors.

Investment Strategy: *Value-added acquisitions of existing student housing projects in college and university markets in close proximity to Gainesville, FL, including but not limited to Tampa (USF), Orlando (UCF), Tallahassee (FSU), Jacksonville (UNF), and Valdosta, GA (Valdosta State). The above constituting "Approved Markets."*
> This proposal is targeted at the student housing market that is one of Paradigm's areas of expertise. The student housing market is considered to be growing with the overall educational needs of the country and its economy, and the education industry is perceived as recession resistant. Paradigm has an excellent reputation as an experienced operator of student housing in the southern and eastern United States.

Stabilized Expected Returns: *Acquisitions will be targeted to deliver greater than 9% unleveraged returns on cost.*
> While not explicitly stated, the more than 9% desired return is a combination of the going-in capitalization rate (the cap rate is the net operating income, or NOI, generated by the property divided by all-in purchase price) and the expected appreciation. The in-excess of 9% desired return is exclusive of any benefits achieved by leveraging the property with debt. At the time of this proposal, cap rates were in the 6% to 7% range and expected to appreciate 2% to 3% annually. In the subsequent year, cap rates were to fall more, to the 5%

to 6% range with severe compression between cap rates on the A, B, and C asset classes. Normal spreads were coming close to disappearing.

Brokers attempt to focus on the pro forma, a generally rosy projection of future returns to be delivered by hoped-for operating results in a spreadsheet-created fantasy world where nothing ever goes wrong and rents march forever upward in perfect unison and costs stay tamely under control and never increase faster than revenue. I prefer to focus on the trailing 12 months and prior three years of operating results. Of course, these two points of view yield strikingly different cap rates. It is important that cap rate calculations also include closing costs and the amount of any capital expenditures required to bring the property up to par or to deliver the rent increases and cost reductions so blissfully promised in the pro forma. Also, even if the community does have the potential for substantial rent increases, realistic projections will take into account both the time required to implement any desired capital improvements *and* the time required for the benefits therefrom to roll through the rent structure. Rent adjustments for existing residents must generally be more moderate and spread out than increases to "street" rents. Otherwise a mass exodus may occur with corresponding increases in vacancy and turnover costs. Many investors and brokers lack experience in the operations management side of real estate and may need to have their views tempered by someone whose perspective includes having to actually deliver on the projections and assumptions.

This proposal was made at a time when the 10-year Treasury bill was bouncing around in the 3.8% to 4.2% range and 70% to 80% loan-to-value (LTV) debt was available at 90 to 120 basis points for a 10-year term, 30-year amortization loan. The property was eventually acquired by assuming an existing loan of $17 million on one phase at 6.95% and putting a 10-year, $22 million loan on the other phase at 5.415%, 30-year amortization, starting out with 3 years interest only. The existing loan was still in its original 3-year lockout period, so it could not be refinanced even if anyone wished to pay the defeasance costs.

Equity Investment Percentages: *Preferred will commit 80% of the project equity. Paradigm (and its principals) will commit 20% of the project equity. Paradigm shall not syndicate its equity investment.*

Investors GREATLY desire to have their operating party have some "skin" in the game, some capital at risk. It is truly important to have financial interests aligned, and when the entity or individual in charge of finding the investment asset and operating the asset has invested hard cash, the chances of success are significantly increased.

The requirement of nonsyndication of the operating partner's investment is to insure that the operator is personally committed and motivated. This requirement can sometimes be stretched a bit via negotiation to include contributions by close family members or trusts of which the operator is a beneficiary, or entities that the key principal of the operator controls, or investments from key associates of the operating entity.

I recently spoke with a representative of a small ($30-million) real estate equity fund that specialized in an interesting niche: They were providers of a "second slice" of equity for the operating partner. For example, in the above deal they would not be the first 80% of equity but rather furnish 80% of Paradigm's 20%. Of course, Preferred and others in their position might object to a third party providing a second slice of equity (see "Paradigm shall not syndicate its equity investment"), but the representative I spoke to claimed that they were frequently able to negotiate that point, in part because they typically required personal liability on their investment and they positioned themselves as being a valued-added player due to their real estate expertise and highly-leveraged motivation to ensure the deal succeeded.

When paired with an institutional investor interested in investing meaningful amounts of capital, a 20% investment by the minority or operating partner, as requested here, is a bit on the high side. Capital, after all, is what the capital partner is supposed to bring to the table. Too high a required capital contribution from the operating partner both reduces the operating partner's return and will limit the scalability of the joint venture; the JV can't "roll out" to any great scale. If the operating partner is required to put up 20% of the required equity for every deal, the number of deals that can be done will be severely limited because the operating partner could quickly run out of capital. If the operating partner had that kind of capital resources, it probably would not have gone looking for a capital partner to begin with.

What is more common is 5% to 10% of the required investment. It can even be in the form of a contribution of "bricks," existing real estate in which the operating partner has equity.

When a "land partner" and a developer/builder and/or operator come together, a 50-50 split is more common. The land partner contributes the land to the joint venture, the developer provides the needed cash and arranges and guarantees the financing.

The desire for 20% investment was flexible to a certain extent. In subsequent talks, they agreed to a 90-10 deal.

Leverage: *Project leverage not to exceed the greater of 75% of cost or value.*

Residential real estate is one of the most stable of the real estate sectors. Many investors are willing to go 80% LTV or even higher, particularly if the debt coverage ratio is 1.3 or better. Personally, I prefer 80% LTV. However, many institutional investors have particularly long-term horizons and prefer the ultimate protection against risk that lower loan-to-value ratios provide. I work with one overseas institution whose target portfolio LTV ratio is 50%.

It is possible that this potential JV partner might have agreed to 80% LTV as part of the negotiation process.

Program Capital: *$50 million when combined with Paradigm's $12.5 million of program capital can provide for $250 million of acquisitions. PPP will also receive an option to provide Paradigm an additional $50 million of program capital on same terms.*

This is the scalability factor. They are envisioning a $250-million portfolio with a potential of up to $500 million *at their option* if all goes well. Here is where the difference in LTV ratios comes in. At 80% LTV, the same amount of capital would control $300 million of real estate, not $250 million.

This particular proposal was sent on a $50 million investment. More typical would be a $15 million to $25 million investment per community, so a $300 million portfolio would be 12 to 15 communities or 3,000 to 4,000 apartment homes.

Options on future investments can be sticky. No one likes to have his hands tied and flexibility reduced. It is unclear how restrictive this "option" would be. Options can be as vague as a loose "agreement to agree" (a nonbinding statement of future intent) or as detailed as requiring a right of first refusal on all future investments. Limitations on product type (market vs. student, multifamily vs. commercial), geography (specified cities, states, and/or markets), and time (say 1 or 2 years from last closing) usually exist in such options. Geographic restrictions can even be project based (within five miles of any existing joint venture) to eliminate potential conflicts of interest.

We will touch more on options.

Expected Holding Period: *The targeted hold period for these assets shall be 1 year after asset stabilization (anticipated to be 3 years after initial investment). Exits will be explored after asset stabilization. Market-priced exit required.*

We are long-term investors. This partner has a shorter-term horizon. This is another reason we passed on this JV proposal. We liked the people, the company had an excellent reputation; but the fit was not right here. We determined that given the organizational nature of investment funds (they are usually formed with a 5- to 10-year, in-out, investment-liquidation horizon), the investment holding period was one of the harder points in the proposal.

In any partnership or joint venture, needs, interests, and organizational imperatives must be aligned. To state the obvious, long-term investors should not align themselves with a buy-and-flip perspective.

Also the preferred returns that Paradigm is eligible for under this proposal are driven by Internal Rate of Return (IRR). Since IRR is extremely sensitive to the length of the investment and the amount and timing of the returns, and is insensitive to risk, IRR is not the best method (or should not be the sole measure) of partner compensation when doing long-term value investing.

Among other things, IRR calculations assume that one can reinvest at the given IRR: Not always a viable proposition. Also, when comparing IRRs, people often fail to adjust for relative risk, meaning the details and income stream of the project you currently own are much better known (less risky) than of any prospective purchase. Also, people frequently underestimate or fail to take into account full transaction costs, both financial and organizational. Mobilizing your organization and personnel to properly market and sell a community is resource intensive, as is doing the required in-depth due diligence on multiple potential purchases until the proper investment is found. Income tax considerations should also be completely accounted for, including the possibility that the time pressures created by attempting a Section 1031 like-kind exchange may lead to a suboptimal investment. There also is a post-closing tendency upon the part of even seasoned professionals to regard the potential tax savings of a 1031 exchange as "free money," or as a discount on the purchase price of the next investment. Most investors would deny such a perspective, but I have seen it emerge in unguarded moments time after time. Tax policy has enormous potential to distort economic analysis.

First Look Rights: *Preferred will have a first look to enter into joint venture arrangements for all Paradigm's student housing acquisitions in Approved Markets.*

Nice try. No way. I am not giving up that kind of flexibility. Basically, the potential partner is asking for a no-cost option on Paradigm's deal flow. We did not consider their proposal to be a "sweet" enough deal to constitute compensation for granting an option. If the JV partner's deal is a good fit, we would naturally want to take deals to them. Our response to requests like this is a free market one: "Make us *want* to take deals to you. Don't try to *make* us take deals to you." No harm in asking though. If you don't ask for what you want, it's difficult to get what you want.

That said, we do have a three-mile notice requirement in one JV deal: We are required to notify them of any purchase or sale within three miles of our JV location.

We have only two major JV partners at the moment (plus two or three minor ones). By major, I refer to both the size of the partner and the potential for future deals.

We tend to give major JV partners a heads up when we move a significant piece around on Paradigm's financial chessboard. We are just being courteous and maintaining the relationship. We don't want them thinking that we are keeping all the good stuff for ourselves. If we thought it was a good fit, we would pitch it to them. Usually the deals are happening too fast or are too vague and unformed to work for an institution. Or the potential deals have too much "hair" on them, too many risks and unknowns.

For example, a fellow developer ran across 130 acres in a good location for just over $40,000 per acre. He put 50% down and took a 30-day note from the seller for the other half. He then called us (actually his CFO called one of our senior asset managers) to ask if we would join him in the deal. He needed someone to help cover the note. He is strong financially and could do it personally, but he has five or six projects under way, is a busy man, and would prefer to stay liquid. We took a look at the deal, and heck, it's good land, the price is excellent, and the title is clean. We have only the most general idea of how to develop it, but we figure we can't go too far wrong at the price, so Paradigm plunked money down next to his. All within a couple of weeks. Good deal (we hope), but it is not the type that works well for many institutions. And Paradigm didn't really put down its own money. We used land as collateral to borrow at LIBOR plus 200 basis points. Nothing like that ticking interest rate clock to motivate one to get busy developing a project.

It is important to mention deals up front to your partners when the unknowns are still unknown and still scary. It is amazing how major risks seem to appear minor in retrospect.

Pursuit Costs: *Soft money deposits provided by Paradigm. Hard money deposits on a 50-50 basis. Fifty-fifty sharing of preacquisition pursuit costs to be determined on a project-by-project basis subject to written agreement.*

Pursuit money is an interesting point. We look at a lot of deals for every one deal we do, and it is an expensive process in terms of intellectual capital, time, and energy. Other than the possibility of preferred returns, there is nothing in this proposal to compensate the operating partner for the costs of investigating the deals we do not do, which truly are part and parcel of the costs of the deals done, i.e., there are no acquisition fees to be earned.

Note also that the proposal is for deposits and preacquisition pursuit costs to be shared 50-50, even though the proposed equity investment is 80-20. They are asking us to put up half the preacquisition pursuit costs, even though we have only 20% of the equity. Presumably, this would be rebalanced at closing and the 50-50 is designed to insure that we are highly selective in the deals we pursue. Nonetheless, it is a significant point to be negotiated. Bad precedent.

We have done deals where we have received 50 basis points up front (at closing) as an acquisition fee for finding a deal. So it should come as no surprise that this partner gets first look at every good deal we run across. You get what you pay for. (Well, while true in this case, not always true in life or business. While it is rare in business to get something without paying, it is also quite possible to pay for something, such as quality, and not get it. That is why extensive and comprehensive due diligence is vital. Trust but verify. Expect the best and inspect for what you expect.)

This proposal calls for us to put up *all* the soft (refundable) deposits. In other words, our partner is using us as a bank. That can be acceptable if the promotes are good (these aren't that good), and you have the working capital to spare. But you have to be very careful that momentum does not build and you get busy and forget to collect your partner's portion of the funds before the deposits go hard. It can happen. Then you are potentially in a bad spot, because it is your money on the line. And if anything goes south before you collect your partner's share, well, it is a good partner who cheerfully and promptly makes you whole. However, those are the types of partners who usually get their portion of the funds in on time in the first place. So, unfortunately, if anything ever goes wrong, statistically speaking, you most likely are dealing with a partner who is looking for any way possible to avoid fulfilling its obligation to you.

Involvement breeds commitment. Make sure your potential partner's soft money deposit goes up simultaneously with yours. And it is a good idea to have a pursuit capital fund checking account set up that you both fund. The nature of the beast is that these things happen so fast that you will not have time to go to your partner to get one-off funding for each individual expense item. So one of two things happens: (a) you lose most of your deals because you cannot compete in real time, or (b) you end up funding most of the expenses and going back to your partner for reimbursement. Not only does this mean that you have become the de facto provider of working capital for the partnership, it also allows your partner to have the benefit of 20/20 hindsight from the perspective of the rear echelon while you are operating on the front lines. Some partners use this as an opportunity to nitpick decisions. Avoid those partners! If an ongoing partner does not trust you enough to set up a pursuit capital fund, question if you should be in business with him.

Due diligence preacquisition costs can and should be extensive and expensive, starting with a physical inspection of the property, everything from structural to survey to lease audits to physical inspection of 100% of the unit interiors. We recently sent a five-person team for four days to do a lease file audit and to walk every apartment of a 158-unit, approximately 550-bed student community in Charlotte, North Carolina. The total cost was in excess of $8,000 for airfare, car rental, hotel, and meals. That figure does not include salaries. We also shopped the competition and visited the university.

Zoning compliance letters and other elements of legal due diligence, including full examination of the title, is vital. We have found deed restrictions and zoning twists that have come close to being deal killers, including one where the local municipality owned the "streets" and "on-street" parking of a community. The idea is based on the new urbanism concept, but when you looked at the community, the streets and the parking appeared much more like normal parking lots than city streets. Practically speaking, it meant that we would lose control of the community's parking as well as the lot maintenance. Anyone can park on city streets and maintenance issues such as striping, seal coating, and repaving were controlled by the city.

I have seen six-figure legal bills run up just for drawing up a joint venture agreement. (I kid you not. It blew me away, and I had a hard time seeing the value-add. Thankfully, I was paying only 10% of the bill.) But it made my partners happy, and they are good partners, other than their preference for big-city lawyers.

Conditions Precedent to Preferred Funding: *(i) Completion of business plan and first year budget.*

Pro formas (a budget with a forecasted return) are interesting. A tremendous number of assumptions, forecasts, professional estimates, and outright guesses go into them. Typically a pro forma covers 10 years. Personally, I have a hard time forecasting next month, much less next year.

Pro formas are particularly difficult for new development when you must forecast rents and expenses for nonexistent buildings. Pro formas for existing projects are a bit easier in some respects, because you have historical information to base your assessments on. Or, you think you do. Getting accurate historical data out of the current owner can be more difficult than you might think, even when the owner is cooperative. Even cooperative people can be disorganized, overworked, and behind schedule. And let us not even think about the noncooperative types. The priorities of headquarters are not always the priorities of the field or of the clerk in the accounting department. And sometimes there are things that people do not want you *or* their bosses to know about—how money was spent or not spent, the condition of the property, or the lease files, or service contracts.

Also, coding standards for accounts are not uniform by any measure, and statements generally are not audited. Frequently, discounts or concessions given to entice renters, or to compensate for soft markets, or above-market rents, do not show up on the books. So a month's free rent may not be recorded as revenue in and concession out; it may not even be shown on the lease. Sometimes the only way to ascertain free rent concessions is to note discrepancies between move-in dates (sometimes verified via utility company records) and rent deposits in the bank.

So, too, it may be difficult to tell what was a true operating expense and what was coded as a capital expense but was a borderline operating expense. I generally ask for certified correct statements of all funds spent on or near the property, no matter what the justification, even if it was coded to the property's headquarters. Heck, if the owner came to visit from Timbuktu, I want to see where the expense was coded. Amazing what you find when you dig.

We recently looked at two communities in close proximity, both less than five years old, both touted as luxury properties with luxury rents. While neither had any structural deferred maintenance, one had some *marketing* deferred maintenance: It was showing a bit of wear and tear around the edges. The trim was looking faded and in need of touching up, the landscaping was a bit ragged, the clubhouse and pool furniture could have used replacement or refurbishment. You get the idea. The other property looked sharp. Landscaping was up to par, the clubhouse and workout area had been redone, and the hallways looked good. The second property also showed $1.3 million of capital expense (capex) expenditures on its books over the last 3 years.

We all know what a lot of that $1.3 million was—expenditures that kept the property looking sharp, that kept rents at the top of the market, occupancy in the high nineties, concessions low, and that made the leasing staff's job a lot easier. The first community had been coasting on its initial start-up good looks, and the free ride was about to end. Either a substantial investment needed to be made to spruce up the place or concessions would become a regular part of its marketing program. The alternative is to gracefully accept its aging and prepare for a fall from the top tier of rents.

We could have an interesting discussion of what the definition of capex is, bringing in all sorts of viewpoints from that of the Internal Revenue Service (anything that benefits more than the current year), to your lender (whatever is necessary to maintain the income stream and prevent physical deterioration), to your loan servicer who handles your replacement reserves (whatever the loan agreement says and not one thing more no matter how logical: You wanted it in, you should have asked for it when you got your loan).

I will tell you a property manager's definition of capex: "Anything the property needs that isn't in my operating budget."

In the final analysis, what the previous owner ran the property for is now history and is, at best, only a guide. The question that really matters is, what do you think *you* can run the property for?

To make sure we tell ourselves the truth when we ask that question, we always run three pro formas. Yes, three. Optimistic, conservative, and middle of the road. Because as much as people want to hear it, *there is no one NOI or IRR number*. There is no certainty in life, at least not beyond death and taxes. No one can tell you for certain exactly what a community is going to kick out in NOI next year, much less over the next 10 years. At best, they can give you the middle of a range, the average of the possible outcomes.

But people do not like risk and they particularly do not like to openly and repeatedly acknowledge that risk exists. People like certainty or at least the illusion of it. So folks tend to warm up to someone projecting confidence who breezes in and makes a presentation full of vim and vigor, laying out a pro forma as if the returns are as certain as the sun rising in the east. "Why, practically guaranteed. No, better than that, 100% warranted by the devotion and enthusiasm of your operating staff!"

Remember: Confidence is not the same as competence, and even competence is no guarantee of success.

A pro forma contains estimates of future rents, potential rent increases, future expenses including insurance rates, property tax increases, labor costs, health care costs, and implicit in all these are forecasts of future inflation rates, economic cycles, and GNP increases. Since most pro formas include a projected sale price, implicitly or explicitly, there is an attempt to forecast interest rates and cap rates at the time of sale. And since the sale price is potentially based on the property's performance over the new buyer's holding period, you are implicitly forecasting for perhaps another 10 years of results when you forecast what your exit price will be. One hopes that this will engender a bit of humility and caution into the process, at least among intelligent readers.

That said, we have ALWAYS (knock on wood) met or beaten our pro formas over a consolidated three-year horizon. (Sometimes it takes a bit of time. Sometimes you have to hang in there.) Rarely does a community's operating statement turn out exactly the way we anticipated. Income will be off, or come in ways we had not anticipated, such as corporate or furnished units, and some expenses will be higher, others lower). But by adapting to the market rather than attempting to dictate to the market, the savvy operator usually finds a way.

Conditions Precedent to Preferred Funding: *(ii) Acquisition loan closed with JV single-purpose entity with Paradigm or its principals as guarantor(s). Paradigm will sign on any recourse and nonrecourse carve-outs. The Loan Documents shall specifically provide for, in the event of an uncured loan default, Preferred rising to the role of sole managing member and assumption of the loan, but not the guarantees.*

This is the part I love. They want *me* to guarantee the loan personally. *and* if there are any problems ("uncured loan defaults"), they take over ("Preferred rising to the role of sole managing member") while leaving me on the hook ("but not the guarantees"). No thanks. If things go south, if I'm on the hook, I want to be the guy in charge trying to solve the problem. Everyone always says not to worry, nothing will ever go wrong. And, anyway, we will make sure we only get nonrecourse loans with only the carve-outs to sign for. Well, if it is no big deal (1) why do the lenders insist on loan guarantees that are signed by either a high net worth individual or an entity with lots of assets, and (2) why don't *they* sign as guarantor?

Well, the capital partner's reply is that they are not in charge of the asset, we are. And, as operating partner, we are in the best position to make sure nothing goes wrong. True enough. However, our reply is that we need to be paid and paid well to run this kind of disproportionate risk.

Guarantees can be avoided or negotiated away, generally by using low LTVs. Think 60% LTV. That plays havoc with your IRR and capital asset allocation models. Using 60% LTV eats up twice as much capital as 80% LTV. However, this only works with new loans. If you are trying to assume existing loans, you must generally take them as you find them.

Or you can have an entity signing the guarantee. However, many lenders want a higher net worth requirement for an entity than for an individual on the theory that an individual is more motivated to do whatever it takes to salvage a deal than a soulless legal fiction. Also, it is generally easier to transfer assets out of an entity than it is for an individual to legally shed net asset value.

And while most carve-outs are limited in nature, there are at least two factors that increase the risk:

(1) Frequently when a loan gets in serious trouble, the legal clock starts to run. The guarantor is liable for virtually all the lender's expenses, legal and otherwise. It is not unheard of for the legal and tertiary costs to rival the underlying economic costs.

(2) It is possible for the liability exposure on the carve-outs to be used as leverage. All the lender has to do is *allege* a violation and all sorts of bad things can happen (including lots of stress and potentially sleepless nights for the key principal who is personally liable and concerned about his family's future). The lender and/or servicer owes the key principal no duty of good faith. Quite the contrary, their fiduciary obligation is to the investors who provided the capital for the loan. All the lender or servicer has to do is allege a prima facie case under the carve-outs and the burden of proof can shift to the guarantor to prove they are wrong.

Occasionally Paradigm has been able to negotiate personal guarantees on loans that are confined in scope. This deal, on which we contributed 12% of the required cash, eventually ended up with about a $40 million loan on which I signed a $3 million guarantee on the loan carve-outs. Flat. My liability could never exceed that amount. I also received an indemnification from my partner for 88% of any amount I was forced to pay. The only exception was if I were "judicially determined" to be at fault. The original draft simply provided for nonpayment of the indemnity if I was "at fault." I requested the "judicially determined" language in order to have an objective, third-party standard.

(See Chapter 12, Condominiums and Condominium Conversions, for a more extensive discussion of carve-outs and liability.)

Conditions Precedent to Preferred Funding: *(iii) Environmental indemnification by Paradigm*

Environmental indemnification is a *huge* potential liability. It is rare, but when it happens it can be devastating. And if you do enough deals, the rare can become commonplace. Notice that the environmental indemnification usually is blanket (i.e., strict liability). The potential liability is in no way related to or limited to losses caused by any actions of ours, negligent or otherwise. Now, the loan carve-outs already include an environmental indemnification for the lender, which is bad enough. This implies that I cannot turn around and ask my partner to share in the loss. As written, this is a nonstarter.

Cash Flow/Residual Waterfall-Portfolio: *On an annual portfolio basis (all investments made during any given calendar year will be considered "a pool." If at least three investments are not made in any calendar year, they shall be pooled with the prior or next year's pool at Preferred's option):*

  (i) *Return of all capital including operating and debt service shortfalls previously funded*
 (ii) *Preferred return of 10.0% paid to equity, pari passu.*
(iii) *70% to Preferred and 30% to Paradigm until Preferred IRR of 15% has been achieved*
 (iv) *60% to Preferred and 40% to Paradigm until Preferred IRR of 20% has been achieved*
  (v) *50% to Preferred and 50% to Paradigm after Preferred IRR of 20% has been achieved.*

In theory, this is where the good stuff should be. The preferred return to the operating partner should be the motivation for all the risk and costs assumed previously. Unfortunately, it is not to be found in this proposal, at least not as presented.

This provision defines how income will be distributed: first to pay any debt and capital expenses. That's reasonable.

Then 10% to each partner according to each partner's equity investment (that's what pari passu means). Well, that is setting the bar a bit high. I've seen deals with the bar as low as 8%, though you see 8.5% or 8.75%, or even 9% more often.

The height of this bar is important, because above it is where the preferred returns start. The higher the bar, the harder it is to get to the preferred return.

It should be emphasized that the height of the bar should be measured not so much in absolute terms but relative to the amount of spread over the cap rate of the investment and, even more important, the spread over the rate of leveraged return given the chosen debt structure. If an investment had a going-in cap rate of 6.75% and a leveraged return of 8%, then the spread over the "promote" hurdle would be 200 basis points, using the above 10% preferred return scenario.

Creating a return above the going-in cap rate can only be achieved by increases in the NOI (raise rents, hold costs in line) and/or capital appreciation.

Capital appreciation occurs mainly by increases in NOI being valued at a constant cap rate or by the market applying a lower cap rate to the existing NOI, or some combination thereof. The leveraged return theoretically could also be increased by lower-cost debt or by more debt, as long as the interest rate was below the cap rate (return) of the property. If your interest rate is higher than your cap rate, you have negative leverage, and that is not a good position to be in.

Mortgage constants need to be addressed here as well. A mortgage constant is the annualized combined interest and principal payments of a mortgage divided by the current outstanding mortgage balance. For example, if the monthly principal and interest payment on a $12-million mortgage is $100,000, then the mortgage constant will be 10.

$$\$100,000 \times 12 \text{ months} = \$1.2\text{MM}, \$1.2\text{MM}/\$12\text{MM} = 10$$

Dependent upon the rate of amortization, it is possible to have a high mortgage constant even if the underlying interest rate is low. A high rate of amortization creates a high mortgage constant. If there is no amortization, if the financing is interest only, then the mortgage constant equals the interest rate.

Mortgage constants are important because they impact cash flow, thus Internal Rates of Return. When you make a principal payment on a loan, that principal payment represents cash flow that is not available to return to your investors. In effect, you are investing capital at the interest rate on the loan, and since that is generally significantly below your investor's overall desired rate of return, it represents a drag on their return, a reduction of the potential IRR.

Returning to the promote structure, once the 10% return on equity has been paid, the split goes to 70-30 until an IRR of 15% has been reached. Since the equity split is already 80-20, this represents a relatively small increase in the operating partner's return for the costs and risk incurred.

From 15% IRR to 20% IRR, the split is 40% Paradigm, 60% Preferred. This is starting to get motivational, but barely. Above a 20% IRR, a 50-50 split kicks in. This is the sweet spot, the pot of gold at the end of the rainbow. And for this deal, possible but not likely.

Return should always be measured in relation to the risk exposure required to earn the return. Not all ventures have equal probability of success, some even have a downside greatly in excess of the initial capital investment. I am always amazed how frequently people compare returns without comparing corresponding risk profiles.

This property was experiencing leasing and occupancy issues that we thought we could solve. We were buying a trailing cap rate of 6 to 6.5. We felt we could quickly (within 12 to 18 months) get the property to perform a good 100 basis points higher, say 7 to 7.5 unleveraged return, perhaps even 7.75% within 24 to 30 months. We were able to access three-year, interest-only new money, so we had high hopes of getting a leveraged cash-on-cash return north of 10%.

However, to get 15% IRR we would have to sell before the interest-only money ran out and do well on the sale, hoping the historically-low cap rates in effect at the time of the purchase did not move against us (did not become higher). We definitely felt we could hit 15%, some projections had returns north of 20%, and still others even north of 25%. We felt returns of that magnitude, north of 20%, were possible but not probable. I was expecting a return in the high teens, north of 15% IRR for sure, but how far north I was not sure. Anyone who projects IRRs on real estate that involve digits to the right of the decimal place (tenths and hundredths of a percent return) has a better crystal ball then most. Personally, I think you are doing well to get the second digit to the left of the decimal point correct, in the teens, the twenties, or the thirties.

In subsequent talks, 75% Preferred and 25% Paradigm over 14% IRR was offered along with 60-40 until 18% IRR to Preferred, and 50-50 above 20% IRR to Preferred.

A bit better perhaps, but I still thought the initial hurdle rate was too high and the cost and risk assumption requirements were a bit aggressive. The joint venture deal with this partner was doable but not attractive.

Governance, Control, Investment Committee:
- *The joint venture will have a four-person committee comprised of two representatives of each firm.*
- *The committee is responsible for annual business planning, material business decisions (leasing rates for upcoming year, major capex items, property-level budgets, marketing), financing (type, fixed/floating), sales and capital calls.*
  - *Refinance and sale decisions: joint approval with PPP holding tiebreaker*
  - *Asset operating budgets: require joint approval*
- *In situations where Paradigm and Preferred do not unanimously agree, the parties will vote their ownership interests, with the majority vote determining the outcome.*
- *Preferred and Paradigm shall be permitted to transfer their respective ownership interest in the joint venture to affiliates.*

We never like running anything by committee, especially when the other guy has the tie-breaking vote. Fair enough perhaps, as they are the majority investor, but we are the operating partner. We don't want to set leasing rates or marketing or property budgets via committee, particularly a committee composed of financial and operating types going against each other. Believe me, if it's got Paradigm's money in it and Paradigm's name on it, we are motivated to run it right. It's the only way we know how to do it. It is demotivating and counterproductive to have to run operating decisions by a committee. Either trust us as an operator, or get a partner you do trust.

We are good at what we do because we have a lean, flat organizational structure, we move fast, and we keep decisions close to the property level. Don't tell us you love our results and our track record and you want to do business with us and then, "Oh, by the way, would you mind changing the operating methods, corporate philosophy, and company culture that produced those results?"

Property Management: *Paradigm will be the property manager, will be responsible for all day-to-day operations at the property, and will be entitled to a property* *managemen: fee of 4% of effective gross revenue from property-level cash flows. Property management duties will include but not be limited to: leasing of apartments, day-to-day management, maintenance of property, payment of bills, hiring and management of property-level employees, managing contracts related to property, financial reporting, and all other matters related to the upkeep of property. Paradigm will have the right to earn a property management incentive fee of 10% of all cash flow from a pool once the pool generates a 10% cash-on-cash return to investors after debt service and reserves (emphasis added). Preferred will have the right to remove Paradigm from property management if budgets are missed by 15% for a period of more than one year.*

The property management incentive fee is nice. But since we are on both sides of the deal, as property manager and equity investor, the potential that helps us as a property manager could hurt us as an equity investor attempting to hit a preferred return hurdle. I meant to generate a spreadsheet to model it to see how it worked out under various scenarios, but I never found the time or energy.

Paradigm could be removed as operator for missing budgets for a period of more than one year. I can understand the need to remove a nonperforming operating partner, but any such performance criteria should have some reference to the performance of the surrounding market. For example, few if any New Orleans real estate investments made their budgets post-Katrina, and insurance costs doubled and tripled in Florida and other coastal regions. I generally go for a removal clause that references misfeasance, malfeasance, and nonfeasance.

Shortfalls: *Preferred and Paradigm will fund operating and debt service shortfalls on the following basis: Through the end of the first full school year of operation after acquisition, the partners will fund shortfalls pro rata. In subsequent years, Preferred and Paradigm will fund operating and debt service shortfalls on a 50-50 basis.*

I did find it interesting that after the first year, "operating and debt service shortfalls will be funded on a 50-50 basis," even though we are only 20% partners (and could potentially not be in operational charge under the prior clause). I think I like the hedge fund model better. The hedge fund operator gets 1% to 2% of the fund value annually just for existing, *plus* 20% of the upside and *nothing* of the downside. Maybe we are in the wrong business.

This is only a proposal for discussion purposes, and it is not intended to be binding upon either party.

This is standard disclaimer language.

We also were in conversation with two other potential joint venture partners; one was another real estate fund and the other a major institutional investor. One of my concerns was that I had personally contributed the soft money ($250,000), and when the time came for the deposit to go hard and an additional $250,000 was to be placed in nonrefundable escrow, I became more and more desirous of finding a joint venture partner who was willing to share the risk with me.

We had done a small deal with the real estate fund (we will call them Diamond Realty) that was one-quarter the size of this deal. They were fine guys, and they had a new partner who I knew and trusted, and they knew the market and were willing to put up deposit money and pursuit capital on the spot. That was the good news.

The bad news was that Diamond Realty drove a hard bargain. Too hard, I thought. The property was a by-the-bedroom student community. It kicked out great income on a per-unit basis. But while my friend, the new partner, was well-versed in student housing and comfortable with the business model, the senior partners at Diamond Realty were evidently not completely comfortable with the concept. Whether it was this lack of comfort, or just a different overall investment corporate philosophy, or the squeeze between promised returns to external investors and internally-desired bonuses, Diamond Realty's proposals made Preferred's look good.

Yet we ended up spending much more time negotiating with Diamond than with Preferred; even though, looking back on it, Diamond's proposals were never better than Preferred's, and frequently they were less attractive.

I attribute this misallocation of time and energy resources to several things. First, the power of a preexisting relationship. We genuinely liked the Diamond partner we knew personally and the previous deal was working out well, though that may have had more to do with the inherent high-profit potential of that deal than with the underlying deal structure itself.

Second, there is a tendency to respond. Preferred and the major institutional investor were there for us. They were interested in the deal. But it was up to us to carry the ball and provide the energy to move the deal forward. Diamond Realty was proactive. They put a lot of energy into pursuing the deal and we tended to always respond at some level to their proposals, maintaining or even adding energy to the dynamic.

This leads to the third and final reason we put so much time and energy into what was ultimately a fruitless endeavor. This is the least important reason, but it is far from unique to this encounter: Developers and real estate investors tend to be optimists. We think we can solve any problem and we get a kick out of doing it. We enjoy finding a way to solve complex problems. At the same time, we frequently can be extremely cautious and carefully examine the downside (hey, we didn't do the deal with Diamond, right?), but underlying that caution is a core belief that there is always a way and we are the ones who can find it.

The issue was complicated by the fact that Diamond Realty was very interested in the development potential of the land and the major institutional investor was not interested in the land at all. We were free to split it off and buy it. They did not bank land. Period. End of discussion. They did development, but they only came in when the bulldozers were ready to roll: full entitlement, full permits, construction loan in place, risk minimized as much as possible. Hey, who is to argue? They were very good at what they did and they were equally successful at it. Their people were top-notch professionals, very impressive in their industry knowledge, their dedication and commitment.

The flip side was they would only come in at the last minute on this deal as well. All the risk until closing was ours. They would show up at closing with fistfuls of cash (really, a bank wire out of an asset base so large that this investment was a rounding error to them), but it would be my half-million dollars on the line as a rock-hard deposit. They would reimburse me my share of actual out-of-pocket due diligence costs (survey, environmental, etc.), but only at closing.

More good news was that the final negotiated hurdle rate was lower than Preferred's (8.75%), and while once again I was to sign the carve-outs, they would indemnify me up to the value of their partnership interest. Ah, well, that was something. But the main issue was their lack of interest in the raw land. We thought the land price was fair, the location excellent, and a parcel that size difficult to find so close to major activity centers. We saw a lot of upside in the development potential of the land.

Diamond Realty continued to make a strong play for the deal, at least in terms of throwing various deal structures at us. I find it interesting how much of business—theoretically the realm exclusively of facts and hard analysis—turns on personalities and relationships. In part, this is because true facts, hard facts, verifiable facts, are hard to come by. But it also is largely due to businesspeople just being people, with all the strengths and weakness that come from being human.

I felt that the deal structures discussed between Paradigm and Diamond Realty were growing increasingly complex. This was due to an attempt to accommodate each other's interests as much as possible, but it was also because we were far apart in how we saw the deal—its upside potential and downside risk—and how the returns and risk should be shared.

Sometimes the more complex the deal structure, the more each side can see it turning out their way or, at least, convincing themselves that this is a possibility. However, greater complexity also increases the possibility of misunderstandings and future conflict over interpretation.

Diamond Realty really did put a lot of effort into the negotiation process. They were very IRR driven and produced complex spreadsheets driven by many assumptions that, in turn, seemed to drive their negotiation process. I also am fond of a good IRR, but I care much more about broad deal points and risk allocation. I am a healthy skeptic about spreadsheets because of the numerous assumptions built into them.

I tend to let one of my senior people handle the details of deal negotiations, getting briefed as necessary, giving feedback on what direction to proceed, what is acceptable, and what will not pass muster. The upside of this approach is that you can do more, have more deals cooking. The downside is that you do lose some of the "feel of the deal," some of the subtlety and nuance of the negotiation process. My associate had the personal relationship with the other side, not me. In effect, you are not as emotionally involved, and that has good points and bad points.

As I said before, because of the by-the-bed nature of the property, Diamond Realty considered this a risky deal and attempted to compensate by putting more of the risk on our side of the table. They wanted us to put up a whopping 23%, take full liability on the construction loan and carve-outs, and accept what I considered a minimal fee on the property management side.

From my perspective, the deal killer was that they were demanding priority distribution as the major equity partner. They would receive the full hurdle rate

(9%) return on their capital before we received one thin dime on ours. No pari passu here!

This lack of equal treatment was untenable to me and rather unusual in my understanding of industry norms. On cash contributions, partners tend to be treated as equals to the extent of their percentage of actual cash equity invested.

Diamond Realty's reply was something to the effect that if we believed in the deal it should not be a problem, because achieving the first hurdle rate should be almost a certainty. My reply was, "Perhaps so," but I do not like having to stand behind you to receive my return, and that this was a deal killer for me on an emotional level. What I saw were big trust factor and relationship issues: how they saw our relationship versus how I saw it.

Diamond Realty attempted to goose the returns to us on the higher end so if the deal hit the ball out of the park, we would do well. However, if the deal turned out to be so-so, or even just middle of the road, we would not do that well. Actually we would do rather poorly. Throughout the deal, it seemed we stood in line behind Diamond Realty to get paid. This would be the payoff for finding the deal, operating the deal, and putting up 23% of the cash. Thanks, but no.

I have a practice of going to Cambridge, Massachusetts, annually for a week of study at Harvard Business School. I find it an intellectually stimulating and refreshing experience. These negotiations reached a critical point during this week, and I have a vivid memory of two of the Diamond partners flying to Cambridge to meet with me for a late afternoon negotiating session. The senior man in my organization, the head of my asset management company, also flew out to join us, along with my wife. This was the first time we had all met in person and it was to be the final session to clear up all the points of the deal.

They said they had a proposal that they were sure I would like and that would address my concerns. I had asked for a preview and they demurred, saying that the changes were not complex and that they would prefer to present them in person. I did not push the point. Perhaps I should have, as it might have saved a lot of time.

We met for predinner drinks at a hotel that is a short walk across the Charles River from the business school campus. The meeting started off poorly and got worse. First, I'm a morning person, not a night person. Second, the dim light of a lobby bar with an audience looking on and waiting is no place to get comfortable with complex spreadsheets, review changes, confirm inputs, assumptions, and computations. Third, for whatever reason, I did not click on a personal level with the senior person from Diamond Realty.

As best I remember, their proposal was to give up a bit more on the back end of the deal and we would get more of the low-probability event outcome. They had sliced and diced the pro forma spreadsheet one more time, and under certain conditions and assumptions we did better than in their last proposal. I saw a lot of risk and uncertainty, many unknowns, so I was not much moved, particularly since it was my organization (and me) that would be sweating bullets to produce those outcomes. I did not want to be lying awake nights worrying about this deal just so I could be in a position to receive a few pennies after they had divvied-up the big bucks and pocketed their end-of-year bonuses. That may sound a bit extreme, but that is how I felt after reviewing their last proposal.

I responded by focusing on the broader deal points, the fact that our capital did not stand equally with theirs in terms of distributions and that I was not comfortable with the amount of personal liability I was assuming, particularly with the compensation I was receiving for running that risk. I distinctly remember that at a critical moment in explaining my concerns about my personal guarantee on the construction loan, the senior Diamond Realty representative shrugged his shoulders. I took that bit of body language to mean he was shrugging off my concerns and nothing said subsequently led me to believe differently.

Cutting to the chase: I thought I had made it clear prior to the meeting that a lack of pari passu treatment on equity contributions was a deal breaker. If they were not willing to address that, then there was no point in continuing the discussion. That pretty much ended it. My wife and I then had a pleasant dinner for two.

In any negotiation, it is important to have options. I was able to walk because I had options.

First, we could swing the deal by ourselves if we had to. It would be a major strain and tie up a lot of cash, but we could do it. It is important never to get yourself into a box you can't get out of on your own. Your exit on your own may be painful and not your preferred exit method, but at least it is yours to control, your ace in the hole. In this case, we were pretty sure the pain would be temporary. We could always look for a partner after purchasing the property to reduce our cash investment if we so desired. In fact, postclosing, with many unknowns removed, we might even get a better deal from another JV partner.

Secondly, we still had another joint venture partner in the works, the major institutional investor (with whom we subsequently did the deal).

Thirdly, there were and are many other real estate investment funds and sources of capital. We had deliberately limited ourselves to three sources, both to conserve our time and resources and also as a professional courtesy. Every real estate deal is different, and giving a meaningful indication of interest requires an investment of time and energy. The biggest issue in interesting others, at this point, would be the short time frame to closing to bring them up to speed on the deal.

Lastly, while it would be expensive, I had the option of going for mezzanine debt (think 5% to 7% *over* the underlying debt, in this case 10% to 12.5%. Ouch! But if the deal was a solid 15% IRR, this is still positive leverage). Debt usually can be arranged faster than equity.

In the final analysis, I had to get comfortable with going to the closing table funding 100% of the preclosing costs personally (including $500,000 of hard deposit money), but in the end it all worked out. The major institutional investor's final deal was only marginally better than the Preferred deal (perhaps even identical to what Preferred would have negotiated to if we had gotten serious about it with them), but it was pari passu *and* the major institutional investor was willing to let us split off the development land, which Preferred most likely would have wanted to participate in. Plus, there was meaningful prestige in doing business with the major institutional investor and the possibility of significant future deal flow.

SUMMARY

Joint ventures are formed to create a marriage of capital and management experience. The investment climate has changed drastically over the last decade. Globalization and the access to information through the Internet have created a platform for partnerships to take place over great distances. Investors also are looking to form joint ventures to spread their asset allocation among various types of investments and locations.

Providers of capital such as pension funds, insurance companies, banks, and private investment funds offer many alternatives for a *joint venture* (JV) deal. Depending on the entity's investment objectives and capital availability, an infinite number of JV structures can be created. In this chapter, we looked at a JV proposal in which there was a majority owner and a minority, operating owner.

When selecting a potential partner, the quality and experience of the companies will determine their ability to fit the proposed project. You must look at the potential partner's overall investment strategies for each project, plus the possibility of future projects, when analyzing the suitability of a partner. The two parties must set an investment objective for stabilized, expected returns. This is important because it is a crucial factor for both parties' investment objectives, and it will also dictate preferred returns under the waterfall distribution.

The JV proposal consists of an equity contribution level for each partner. To insure commitment, the smaller operating partner generally has between 5%–10% in the deal, and the majority investor usually prefers a nonsyndicated investment entity. The partners must also determine the amount of leverage to use. This will depend on the risk profiles of both sides. The level of program capital sets the stage for the overall investment strategy.

It is important in any partnership or joint venture that the needs, interests, and organizational imperatives be aligned. To state the obvious, long-term investors should not align themselves with partners with a shorter-term perspective.

Under the example proposal, a waterfall distribution method is used to provide a variety of distribution levels at different hurdle rates. The distributions are based on equity contributions up to the hurdle rate. From that point on, the operating partner is usually rewarded with comparably higher returns based on the success of the project. Both parties will have an idea of their potential or probable returns given conservative, realistic, and aggressive estimates. The difficulty, however, is that pro formas are filled with estimates and guesswork; no one can predict such numbers with great certainty. The key for both parties is to negotiate a required return based on their commitment to the project (time and resources) and their investment risk profile.

Negotiating these points can be challenging, as both parties may have very different interests. The ideal is a collaborative approach that satisfies both parties. All the while, investors must keep their options open for comparative purposes and must have an alternate plan in case no decision is reached.

KEY TERMS AND DEFINITIONS

Capitalization rate: Net operating income (NOI) generated by the property divided by all-in purchase price.

Mortgage constant: The annualized combined interest and principal payments of a mortgage divided by the current outstanding mortgage balance.

Pari passu: Distribution based on each partner's pro rata contribution.

Pro forma: A revenue and expense estimate with a forecasted return. Typically, a pro forma on an existing property forecasts up to 10 years into the future.

KEY LEARNING POINTS

- Understand how and why joint ventures are used in today's market.
- Know the various sources of joint venture capital.
- Understand the role and interests of the operating partner in a joint venture.
- Understand the roles of risk, return, and control in a joint venture proposal.
- Have an effective understanding of the criteria used in selecting a joint venture partner.

QUESTIONS

1. What are two reasons for the increased use of joint ventures over the last decade?
2. Why are operating partners rewarded with the potential for preferred returns?
3. Why do majority partners often require nonsyndication of the operating partner's investment?
4. What are two drawbacks of using one-off funding rather than an expense account for covering pursuit costs?
5. Although constructing pro formas for new projects can be difficult, finding historical information on existing developments also can be troublesome. Why?
6. While most carve-outs are limited in nature, there are at least two factors that increase the risk. What are they?
7. When does the mortgage constant equal the interest rate?
8. What is the upside and downside to assigning a deal to senior management in your company?

12
Condominiums and Condominium Conversions

Real estate, obviously the first and oldest of the asset classes, still continues to evolve and change, offering new and fascinating twists that impact the field of construction, financing, and development.

One of the latest trends in the field of real estate is the upsurge in condominium construction in general and, more specifically, condominium conversions, particularly in the United States, that occurred in the first half of the first decade of the twenty-first century.

CONDOMINIUM DEFINED

A condominium is merely a form of real estate ownership, and while condominiums are most often used in residential housing, condominiums can be used in any sector of real estate, including office, retail, or industrial.

A condominium is a type of joint ownership of real estate in which portions of the property are commonly owned and other portions are individually owned. The tremendous variety of condominium usage prevents a more concise definition. There are usually detailed rules governing the condominium as well as an owner's association that frequently hires third-party management. Condominiums can be bought and sold like any other form of real estate but instead of the traditional legal description describing the outlines of a parcel of land, condominiums are defined by their vertical and horizontal boundaries—a three-dimensional box of space. Most condominiums are residential and many are high rises.

Typically, the common areas (hallways, lobby, and driveways), the amenities (pool, spa, gym, etc.), and building shell are owned in common. The interiors of the individual units are owned individually. Balconies and terraces can be individually owned or can be "limited access common elements." Interesting variations can occur: On the lower levels of a high-rise condominium where several units may share access to the elevator, the hallway is a common element. On the top penthouse floors, where only one unit has access to the elevator (and access to the floor may be restricted electronically or via elevator key), the hallway may be individually owned and decorated to taste.

Often parking spots are also individually owned and they may either be permanently associated with a specific unit or bought and sold separately. Indeed, stand-alone parking garages can be condominiums. In some urban areas, the demand for parking is so great that owning your own parking space is touted not only as a time-saving convenience but also as an excellent financial investment, perhaps with appreciation potential outperforming the stock market. Boat-docking slips at marinas are another interesting type of real estate that have been sold as condominiums.

HOTEL CONDOMINIUMS

Hotel condominiums are also increasing in popularity and illustrate the many forms of legal rights that condominium owners can have (or not have). In a hotel condominium, owners have the option to rent their units as part of the hotel and receive a portion (often less than 50% after fees and expenses) of the rental revenue if and when the unit rents. Frequently, the developer will retain a certain minimum number of units to insure that there is a viable base for the hotel, or a pure hotel will be built as part of the same development to serve the same purpose. Many hotel franchises will not participate without the guarantee of a certain number of available units.

Zoning must be carefully considered prior to planning a condominium hotel. Zoning that will allow a residential building might not necessarily allow a hotel and vice versa.

Unless the condominium developers choose to register with the Securities and Exchange Commission (SEC), a long and arduous process, it is illegal in the United States to forecast financial benefits from renting one's condominium unit as part of the hotel. To do so would be to cross the line between selling real estate and selling a security. Some legal experts suggest the condominium sales personnel not even speak of the existence of the hotel rental option until a firm, signed contract exists to purchase the condominium. The theory is that this insures that the decision to buy is not influenced by the potential investment aspects of the hotel rental program. (On resales, it is permitted to reveal *past* economic performance.)

Any mention of rental possibilities, oral or written, should be limited to something such as "ownership may include the opportunity to place one's unit for rent." No mention of tax or economic benefits should be made. The challenge of monitoring the performance of myriad sales personnel to observe the letter of the law, particularly when their compensation is performance based, leads the most cautious legal advisors toward a total ban on any mention of rental potential. If a buyer is inappropriately sold a unit based upon its investment potential, the contract could be rescinded and the developer could be sued for securities fraud and potentially be legally liable for the buyer's losses. Such a significant downside risk argues for caution.

The SEC has a three-pronged approach for compliance:

- *No emphasis on the economic benefits to the purchaser:* During the sales process, economic benefits of the hotel rental program should not be addressed.
- *No rental program arrangement:* Unit owners can only receive the benefits from the rental of their specific units; income cannot be pooled and shared among rental unit owners.

- *Limits on restrictions:* A unit owner cannot be required to hold his unit available for rent or be required to use an exclusive rental agent or otherwise materially restrict the owner's occupancy or rental of his unit.

The rental management office may be located on site, but it should not be located within the condominium sales office.

Renting the condominium unit usually allows it to be treated as an investment for tax purposes, creating many financial benefits including depreciation and deductibility of any interest expense on debt used to purchase. (United States tax law generally limits home interest deduction to the interest on the first million dollars of debt on your first and second homes, and lower limits apply for home equity loans. No deductions are available for interest on additional homes. However, at today's real estate prices, it is hard to imagine having first and second homes that would not qualify for at least a million dollars of mortgage debt between them).

A certain minimum amount of personal use is allowed before one must begin prorating deductible expenses between rental and personal use: generally the *greater* of 14 days or 10% of the number of days it is rented out to arms-length third parties, i.e., if a unit was only rented 150 days during the year, then personal use would be limited to 15 days before proration would be required.

Personal use is any day that it is used by you or by any other person who has an interest in it or by a member of your family or by a member of the family of any other person who has an interest, or by anyone at less than fair rental price. As with any tax situation, there are many subtle variations, and it is always advisable to consult a tax professional.

The organizational documents of hotel condominiums tend to grant the hotel significantly greater legal rights and the unit owners meaningfully fewer. Often, the only building "unit" the hotel will own or be required to own will be the lobby itself. However, the hotel also will own or control all the common areas, amenities, and the shell of the buildings, areas typically owned by the condominium association. Fair enough, except that the condominium association often will still be required to maintain the common areas and the buildings' shells and pay both the operational (utility bills, property taxes, insurance, etc.) and all capital expenses. Hotel condominiums are typically structured for the benefit of the hotel, not the unit owner, a situation the marketplace has tolerated due to the rapid appreciation in the condominium market. Just as in the tech stock bubble of the late 1990s, people tend not to ask hard questions when there is plenty of profit to spread around.

Since condominium owners in hotel condominiums in the United States cannot be compelled to place their units for rent (absent registration of the condominium hotel as a security), developers often attempt to set up incentives to persuade participation. These incentives typically take the form of reduced or free access to the upgraded hotel amenity package, which can include concierge services, room and maid service, and upscale spa facilities. Remember that the amenities and common areas, normally owned by the condominium association in a nonhotel condominium, are typically owned by the hotel owner in a hotel condominium.

Hotel condominiums are usually *not* legally different from other condominiums from a statutory perspective. Typically, there is not a separate section of governing statutes that create hotel condominiums, separate from other types.

It is important to realize that a hotel condominium has certain physical requirements that differ from a standard residential building. Meeting space (100 sq. ft. per guest room is one rule of thumb), restaurants and set-up areas for caterers, concierge and valet areas, luggage storage rooms, and maid closets on every floor are just a few. Typically, room sizes are smaller; what is a small studio or one bedroom for an apartment unit is a large executive or full suite for a hotel. Closets tend to be smaller in hotel condominiums since they are used only for short stays. In condominium hotels, too, there is often an additional lockable closet for the unit owner's personal possessions or the hotel provides on-site storage as an alternative.

Meeting rooms must have unobstructed views. Any supporting columns that block the view of the speaker greatly reduce the value of the space. This can add to construction costs.

A condominium hotel will not succeed anywhere that a normal hotel would not. It is not a panacea for a badly located site (though it may be for an overpriced one). Condominium hotels are usually seen at vacation destination locations such as Las Vegas or Miami, and urban markets, such as Boston, Chicago, and New York City.

Condominium owners who agree to place their units for rent must agree to use a standard furniture rental package that often must be upgraded or replaced as needed, depending on usage. Hotels typically replace furniture on a 5- to 10-year cycle and linens, obviously, more frequently. The more upscale the hotel, the tighter the replacement cycle.

Having an upscale "flag" (well-known hotel brand), such as Ritz-Carlton, Four Seasons, or W, associated with a condominium can boost sales tremendously. Even a nonhotel brand name such as Trump or Hard Rock can sometimes help sales. Obviously, when a condominium is under development and is named after a hotel brand, the marketplace will be aware of the future existence of a hotel rental program, even though sales personnel cannot tout it without running afoul of SEC regulations. Independent hotel management firms are available and generally offer lower fees and greater flexibility than the major brands as a tradeoff for the reduced profile and cachet.

Why do developers build condominium hotels? Typically, condominium hotel units sell at a higher dollar price per square foot than surrounding condominium units, as much as 50% to 75% more. From the developer's perspective, the unit size is smaller, so the absolute dollar amount required is less per unit. While a portion of that profit is eaten up by the necessity for all the additional nonrevenue space a hotel requires (meeting rooms, etc.) and upgraded amenity packages, and smaller units do cost marginally more to construct than larger units, the net for the developer is usually positive. This still holds true even after the upscale hotel brand names take their cut for the use of their names.

Why does the marketplace buy units in condominium hotels? Typically, they are second or third homes for buyers who do not intend to use them full-time but who want to enjoy (or think they will) the prestige and other benefits of ownership versus renting. Most unit owners are sophisticated enough to realize that they are unlikely to make an operational profit on their unit. Their profit, if any, will come from appreciation and the hotel aspect will merely defray the cost of ownership. This would more likely be true if hotel condominium units frequently did not have a sharp built-in price per square foot premium over the surrounding condominium market.

GOVERNING LEGISLATION

In the United States and most other jurisdictions, condominiums are authorized and governed by legislation (generally at the state level in the United States), so details vary according to the enforcing jurisdiction. For instance, the State of Florida, due to its high number of condominiums, many of them occupied by politically-active retirees, has an extremely detailed and pro-consumer condominium statute. For example, to prevent high-pressure sales tactics and to relieve buyer's remorse, Florida's condominium statute provides for a 15-day right of recision by the buyer on *new* condominiums and a three-day right of recision on *previously-owned* condominiums.

Furthermore, upon condominium conversion of their rental community, Florida statutes give renters both the right to extend their leases and the right to cancel their leases. The right to extend is generally no more than 270 days and the right to cancel generally requires 30 days notice. Also, residents who have been renters for at least 180 days are given the right to buy their units at the lowest price offered to the market. Since these and similar pro-consumer provisions are not unique to Florida, potential condominium converters are well advised to learn the full impact of local regulations before proceeding. Hiring experienced local legal counsel is always a wise precaution.

Traditionally, most condominiums were "built to order," that is, a building was designed and constructed with the idea that it would be condominium. Historically, it was relatively rare for a real estate investor to choose to convert an existing building to condominiums.

However, at its most basic level, a condominium is nothing more than a form of real estate ownership. So, technically speaking, condominium conversion is primarily a legal process and mainly a matter of filing the proper documents with the proper authorities and having them reviewed and approved.

SPEED TO MARKET

It is possible to convert a building to condominiums much faster than it is to design, permit, and construct a building. This is particularly true given the dramatic increase in regulatory restrictions in the past decade and the greatly increased likelihood of opposition from surrounding neighborhoods and adjacent landowners.

The possibility of doing a condominium conversion of an existing property has always existed in the modern real estate market. As a result of the boom in home ownership and real estate investment in America, primarily driven by the low interest rates of the early to mid 2000s, the unique, speed-to-market condominium conversion blossomed as the construction of new condominiums could not be ramped up fast enough to satisfy consumer demand.

The speed to market a condominium conversion provides over a regular construction project creates many benefits, not the least of which are reduced risk and higher return. Because markets change, the longer it takes to get from concept to finished product (both physically and economically, e.g., sold out or leased up), the greater the risk that some important factor will move against the condominium developer. Interest rates and construction prices may go up, demand might falter, the economy can tank, and investors may lose interest. The list goes on ad infinitum. Of course, good things can happen, too, but never write a business plan in which good luck is a critical component.

It should be noted that the speed-to-market advantage of condominium conversion can be lost if substantial renovations are required. This should be a double caution: Renovations frequently take longer and cost more than even the most seasoned industry professional anticipates.

The speed-to-market advantage can also be lost if the project is mispriced or mismarketed, lingering in the marketplace too long while the costs of ownership, financing, and marketing mount. In traditional economic theory, the longer the exposure to market, the more buyers will be found. In reality, too long an exposure to the market can have a negative effect, as potential buyers begin to wonder why the project did not sell out quickly, and discounts or additional upgrades may be required to overcome their discomfort. Further, the longer the sellout, the higher the carrying costs and marketing expenses for the owner/promoter, creating a lower return.

PRESALES, RISK, AND REQUIRED DEVELOPER EQUITY

Many new condominiums have preconstruction sales efforts that allow them to fine tune their pricing and marketing approach prior to full investment. Indeed, many financing institutions will not provide financing without presales of between 30% to 60% of the units, the requirement typically varying according to the financial strength of the developers and how much capital they are willing to put at risk. One frequent exception to the presales requirement is in Manhattan, where the condominium market is so deep and comparables so ubiquitous that banks are comfortable underwriting financially strong developers who choose to forego presales to avoid the normal preconstruction price discount that the marketplace typically demands. However, even the most seasoned developer can misjudge a market.

Developer Scraps Plans for Luxury Condominium in Las Vegas

By Kathleen Hennessey, Associated Press
January 6, 2006

A high-profile developer is scrapping plans to build a 502-unit luxury con-dominium complex on 4.5 acres just off the Las Vegas Strip, the latest sign the city's high-rise craze is losing steam.

"It's a very painful decision for us to make," Related Las Vegas President Marty Burger told The Associated Press on Friday.

Burger and veteran Florida developer Jorge Perez led the Icon project, which initially was hailed as one of the stronger of dozens of high-rise condominiums planned in Las Vegas because of its solid financing and seasoned development team.

Company executives blamed the high cost of construction for Icon's demise. They said legal disputes with a local landowner delayed the project while con-struction costs skyrocketed.

"Basically we got delayed in construction," Burger said. "The incredibly escalating costs made it impossible to build Icon based on original pricing without seriously impacting the integrity of the development."

This is the second aborted Las Vegas project for Related. Last fall, talks with the city to build a mixed-use development on 61 downtown acres fell apart.

Icon was one of four Las Vegas projects still in the works for Related, the development arm of Related Cos. in New York and the Related Group in Miami. Related Cos. built the Time Warner Center in New York City.

In Las Vegas, the company is involved in the expansion of the World Market Center, a convention hall and mall for the furniture industry. It has plans to partner with actor George Clooney and Las Vegas-based Centra Properties to build a $3 billion hotel-casino complex called Las Ramblas. The company also is in a partnership with Centra on another development, but details have not been announced.

Related has no plans to scuttle those projects.

"We remain committed to the Las Vegas market," Burger said.

Icon, which was to be located on Convention Center Drive, included two 48-story glass towers filled with Strip-view units priced from about $500,000 to $1.5 million.

Analysts predict Icon is just one of several proposed luxury condominium projects that won't live to grace the Las Vegas skyline. Last year speculators, developers and celebrities were clamoring to cash in on a booming market, but recent months have seen that momentum cool.

A $600 million project involving Michael Jordan was canceled last July and the site was sold to Chicago investors. Australian developer Victor Altomare has sold the site of his proposed 21-story Liberty Tower, and last month he put the for sale sign on his Ivana Trump project, including presales.

In an announcement this week, Boyd Gaming executive Bob Boughner said the company considered adding condominiums to its plans for a $4 billion resort complex on the Strip, but ruled against it, in part, because the sales process was unpredictable and the market unstable.

Las Vegas Developer Sam Cherry called Las Vegas "its own market." He said casino construction tends to tie up laborers and the few general contractors capable of handling big projects. Add to that the rising cost of materials and you have an equation different from other condo-hubs like Miami, he said.

"I've heard of developers coming into Las Vegas thinking they're going to get their project off the ground for some amount of money and they wind up being $100 million dollars off," said Cherry, whose Soho Lofts in downtown Las Vegas is set to open its doors next month. "It's almost like Vegas is on an island in terms of getting labor and contractors."

With presales, buyers usually pay a 10% deposit at contract signing and another 10% at the start of construction. Start of construction is usually defined as the beginning of site work (which can be subject to varying interpretations, some as little as just beginning to move the dirt around a bit). Jurisdictions differ but usually a way can be found for the developer to use the deposit money for purposes of funding the construction––using the buyers' deposits as developer's equity. In Florida, the developer is required to post a bond to use the first 10% of deposited funds; beyond that, the deposit funds are generally freely accessible once construction begins.

Clearly, if a developer can get deposits equal to 20% of the *value* of a project (one hopes the project value will be a higher number than the project cost) and a 80% loan-to-*cost* mortgage, it may be possible to build a project with very little of the developer's funds at risk at that point. This is particularly true if the developer is able to buy the land, adding value for appraisal purposes during the regulatory and permitting process.

Of course, the developer must put seed capital at risk, money to tie up or buy the land, money to pay professionals to design and market the building, and start-up funds to get the project to the point of full entitlement. While the developer may be able to pull this money out once the project is under construction and especially if the building is 100% presold, the funds must still be available in the beginning and placed at risk for a substantial period of time.

And if the developer goes into the construction phase with less than full presales, the developer will have that much less deposit money to work with. Fifty percent presales with 20% down as deposits would amount to only 10% of the value of the building, and if the value add over cost was 20%, then that would equal only 12% of costs toward the 20% of costs that is a lender's typical minimum required equity investment.

It is true that developers may contribute their developer's fee as part of the equity of a project. However, some financing institutions may balk at allowing full credit up front (after all, the developer fee is not fully earned until the project is completed). Instead, some institutions may prefer to parcel out credit for the fee pro rata, draw by draw. And the developer's fee is not all profit, as there are significant overhead and personnel costs associated with being a developer, including some allocation of the costs for the projects that do not go forward and for maintaining an organization between projects.

A developer's fee is typically 4% to 5% of hard costs, though the only true constraints are what the financing entity and the investment community (the debt and equity sources) will accept. Developers can put any number they want in the pro forma for a developer's fee. Unbeknownst to the developer, however, unless he asks, the financing institution will probably substitute a number more akin to what they consider the industry norm when doing their internal underwriting. I recently saw a project proposed with a 12% developer's fee, a breathtaking number from an investor's point of view. Also, while the fee is generally on hard construction costs only (not land or soft costs, such as engineers and architects), this too can vary depending on the sophistication, interests, and negotiating skills of the parties involved.

A developer's fee is typically ordinary income, so it may not be the best way to take profit, particularly if there is any way to convert or restructure the fee as long-term capital gain. Achieving long-term capital gain is more difficult in condominiums than in other forms of development since condominiums are considered by the Internal Revenue Service the equivalent of inventory on a grocer's shelf, therefore, ordinary income. To qualify for long-term capital gains, real estate must be held as an investment.

Sometimes it is possible to convert a portion of the potential gain to long-term capital gain: If the land has been held for more than a year and has appreciated sufficiently to make it worthwhile, the land may be sold to a new entity to capture and differentiate the gain. The new entity will then go forward with the development plan with a new, higher current market basis in the land. The new entity should have sufficiently different ownership structure so as to pass a substance over form test. Since new partners and investors often come in at the time of commencement of construction, this can be easy to accomplish. The same benefit can be achieved in a condo conversion if the original owner wishes to stay in the deal with all or a portion of his equity. In this, as in all legal, tax, accounting, and related issues, consult competent professionals.

While it is relatively rare for a condominium project to fail during the construction phase, obviously any preconstruction buyer is playing a high-risk game, as he essentially is providing equity funding for a developer with his deposit.

RATES OF RETURN

So, the greater speed to market of a condominium conversion reduces risk over a build-to-order condominium project. Speed to market also can increase return because investment capital is at risk for a shorter period of time. Many condominium converters are in and out in 12 to 18 months.

Remember, it is not the total return that is most important; it is the *annualized* return *and* the amount of risk exposure.

Occasionally, I have heard some version of:

"I doubled my money on that piece of real estate."
"Oh? How long did you own it?"
"About 10 years."

Well, I'm happy for them, but doubling your money every 10 years works out to 7% compounded. While 7% may be fine in times of low inflation for a risk-free, no-hassle investment, it is rather mediocre for any investment with risk and the personal involvement required in owning real estate.

Some rules of thumb: A 20% compounded return will have you doubling your money in just under four years, 15% compounded return in about six and half years, 12% compounded in just over six years, 10% compounded in roughly a little over seven years, and 6% compounded in about 12 years.

No matter what anyone feels or says during the froth of a real estate boom, no real estate investment is risk free. I have been through three real estate downturns in thirty-five years of real estate investing, and I'm still standing. Fortunately, my portfolio, capital structure, and financing relationships were solid enough that I was not negatively impacted by the downturns that swamped others who were more financially extended.

Historically, real estate downturns drive many into foreclosure and bankruptcy. A lot of money can be made going full out, but there is much, much greater risk of losing it all as well. More importantly, those with solid financial structures and well thought-out portfolios tend to sleep soundly at night.

There are pundits who say that the increased transparency and financial discipline afforded by the ever-growing number of publicly-held real estate companies will bring an end to real estate cycles or, at least significantly reduce the intensity and duration of the cycles. There are those who claim that the increased amount of information available in our Internet-linked digital age will allow investors to trim their sails sooner, thus eliminating real estate cycles. Others say that the increased sophistication of financial markets, more seasoned investors, and the more advanced nature of today's complex financial instruments have greatly reduced the risks in real estate. While there is truth in all these statements, the wise investor will continue to plan on the market having its ups and downs, its cycles.

While many aspects of interacting with one's government may go well (in Florida, you can form a limited liability company virtually instantly online at the Secretary of State's Web site; making sure that the name you have chosen is unique is typically the greatest snag, so be creative), having documents drawn up and approved for a condominium can take several months.

There are several reasons for this. Since every piece of real estate is unique, the documentation for every condominium has some unique aspects. Also, the doctrine of freedom of contract (the principle that competent adults may contract for anything that is not expressly forbidden by statute or public policy) interacts with the statutory protections of the condominium legislation, requiring all documents to be vetted to insure that they fully comply with frequently complex statutes. This is where using competent, experienced professionals with good reputations can speed the process.

Since condominium converters are dealing with "used" buildings that were not specifically designed to be condominiums (the buildings may possess some sub-optimal features or structural obsolescence), they typically look for a price point far enough below (usually 20% at minimum) nearby entry-level, single-family housing or surrounding new condominium construction to be attractive to buyers or investors. Buildings constructed to be rental housing of economic necessity are designed differently than buildings designed to be owner-occupied housing, and some new paint, additional landscaping, and bath and kitchen cabinetry and flooring upgrades are often not enough to fully address these differences.

IMPACT OF CONDOMINIUM CONVERSION ON THE APARTMENT INDUSTRY

Since most, if not all, of the buildings that are converted are apartments (some hotels have been converted as well as some older office buildings with locations or floor plans obsolete for today's Internet commuting and cubicle culture), it is important to ask what the impact will be on the apartment industry.

Conversions of existing communities will generally help the apartment industry. First, unlike new condominium construction, conversion reduces the existing stock of apartment supply. Second, unlike apartments, many condominiums tend to be underoccupied—e.g., a professional single will frequently choose to occupy a two-bedroom condominium, using the extra space as an office or guest bedroom. Furthermore, because the purchase decision is a more permanent decision then renting, there is more of a tendency to "upsize" when buying to allow for potential future needs than when renting. Because renting is a year-to-year decision, someone who thinks she will need a two-bedroom apartment at some unknown time in the future but only a one bedroom now, will rent a one-bedroom apartment until she truly needs a two bedroom. Since buying is a much more permanent decision, that same person is more likely to buy a two bedroom in anticipation of future needs. From the perspective of the apartment industry, every unoccupied converted condominium bedroom is noncompeting space.

Third, many condominiums (conversion or new construction) are either second (vacation) homes or investments. Obviously, an apartment converted into a second home does not compete with the apartment industry, though it might displace an occasional stay at a resort hotel.

Condominiums used for rentals rarely compete effectively with apartments because they tend not to be professionally managed. It is hard to be all things to all people. Generally, condominium rentals are managed directly by the unit owner, condominium manager, or third-party real estate firm. None of these individuals or entities have as their sole purpose, rationale, or focus the rental of apartments at the location of the rental, and it is hard to compete with an organization that does.

Statistically, the large, professionally-managed apartment communities have an occupancy rate that is several percentage points higher than smaller, nonprofessionally managed rentals.

Lastly, the rental market occasionally gets a short-term boost if a condominium-conversion community is taken off-line for a while for renovations.

THE CONDOMINIUM CONVERSION PROCESS: THE GABLES

The Gables is a 168-unit apartment community that I owned in Gainesville, Florida, and listed with Dan Allen and Fred Marks of the Jacksonville, Florida, office of CB Richard Ellis (CBRE) in mid 2005 as a potential condo conversion. The sale closed in January 2006. CB Richard Ellis is a NYSE-listed firm with more than 300 offices in 50 countries and a 100-year tradition of service to the real estate industry.

Since I was the sole principal in this sale, I am able to give you a highly unusual, "behind the scenes" tour of the process, pulling back the curtain to show details rarely made public.

The Gables is a gated community, ideally suited by layout and location for condominium conversion. Relatively rare in rental communities, all the units are either single story or townhouses with private entrances and attached garages (see Figure 12-1). Thus the community has many of the privacy attributes of single-family residences as well as low site density of 7.9 units per acre. Furthermore, The Gables has excellent visibility on a major thoroughfare, near an interstate interchange, and with easy access to schools, shopping, dining, and major employers.

The offering stated that the sales price was to be determined by the marketplace and gave a due date for offers. Of course, the brokers were given authorization to convey a "whisper" price at their discretion. In this case, the whisper price was in the range of $150,000 per unit, or $25,200,000 in total.

The existing rent structure prior to closing was:

32 1-bedroom units, 790 square feet, at $929 per month

78 2-bedroom units, 1,131 square feet, at $1,089 per month

58 3-bedroom units, 1,629 square feet, at $1,299 per month

The agreement in Figures 12-2a–12-2e is for three months, from August 1 to November 1. In paragraph 2, the agreement is modified to state that a commission is earned for services rendered if during the term of the agreement "the property is sold to a purchaser procured by Broker, Owner or anyone else" or "any contract for sale of the property is entered into by the Owner." Note that the broker does NOT have to be the cause of procuring the sale, it is enough that the contract or sale occur during the term. Under this agreement, the owner could sell the property to his brother, best friend, or neighbor during the term and a commission might be due. This provision is not at all uncommon. Several other even more broker-friendly clauses were negotiated out, including a clause that a commission would be due if (1) the owner withdrew the property from the market or if (2) the

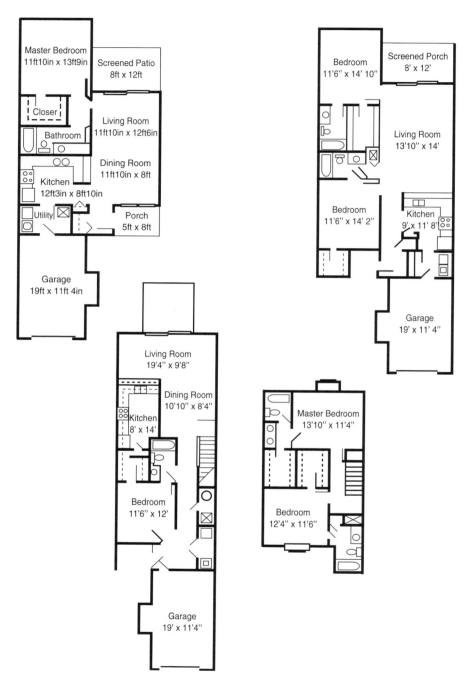

FIG. 12-1   Floor plans.

CBRE:
CB RICHARD ELLIS

ExcLusive Sales Listing Agreement
CB Richard Ellis
Brokerage and Management
Licensed Real Estate Broker

1. In consideration of the listing for sale of the real property hereinafter described (the "Property") by CB RICHARD ELLIS, INC. ("Broker"), and Broker's agreement to use its best efforts to effect a sale of same, the undersigned ("Owner") hereby grants to Broker the exclusive right to sell the Property for a period commencing ___August 1___, 20_05_, and ending midnight ___November 1___, 20_05_ (the "Term"), at a price of _____ Dollars ($ _Price Acceptable to Owner_) upon the following terms:___Cash_____

The Property is situated in the City of ___Gainesville___, County of ___Alachua___, State of _Florida___, and is further described as _____The Gables (168 units), 4700 S.W. Archer Road, Gainesville, FL 32608_____.

References herein to the Property shall be understood to include portions of the Property.

[handwritten right margin: OR AS EXTENDED IAW PARAGRAPH 10.]

2. Owner agrees to pay Broker a sales commission in accordance with Broker's Schedule of Sale and Lease Commissions (the "Schedule"), a copy of which is executed by Owner, attached hereto and hereby made a part hereof. This commission shall be earned for services rendered if, during the Term: (a) the Property is sold to a purchaser procured by Broker, Owner, or anyone else; ~~(b) a purchaser is procured by Broker, Owner, or anyone else who is ready, willing and able to purchase the Property at the price and on the terms above stated, or on any other price and terms agreeable to Owner;~~ (c) any contract for the sale of the Property is entered into by Owner; (d) ~~Owner removes the Property from the market or the Property is transferred due to eminent domain or the threat thereof, foreclosure, or conveyance in lieu of foreclosure; (e) Owner contributes or conveys the Property to a partnership, joint venture or other business entity; (f) Owner is a corporation, partnership or other business entity and an interest in such corporation, partnership or other business entity is transferred, whether by merger, outright purchase or otherwise, in lieu of a sale of the Property.~~ Broker is authorized to cooperate with and to share its commission with other licensed real estate brokers, regardless of whether said brokers represent prospective purchasers or act as Broker's subagents. *[handwritten: AND ENCOURAGED]*

3. As used in this Agreement, the term "sale" shall include an exchange of the Property, and also the granting of an option to purchase the Property. Owner agrees that in the event such an option is granted, Owner shall pay Broker a sales commission in accordance with the Schedule on the price paid for the option and for any extensions thereof. This commission shall be paid upon receipt by Owner of any such payment(s). In the event such an option is exercised, whether during the Term or thereafter, Owner shall also pay Broker a sales commission on the gross sales price of the Property in accordance with the Schedule. Notwithstanding the foregoing, to the extent that all or part of the price paid for the option or any extension thereof is applied to the sales price of the Property, then any commission previously paid by Owner to Broker on account of such option payments shall be credited against the commission payable to Broker on account of the exercise of the option.

4. Owner further agrees that Owner shall pay Broker a commission in accordance with the Schedule if, within ~~one hundred twenty (120)~~ *NINETY (90)* calendar days after the expiration or termination of the Term, the Property is sold to, or Owner enters into a contract of sale of the Property with, or negotiations continue, resume or commence and thereafter continue leading to a sale of the Property to any person or entity (including his/her/its successors, assigns or affiliates) with whom Broker has negotiated (either directly or through another broker or agent) or to whom the ~~Property has been submitted~~ prior to the expiration or termination of the Term. Broker is authorized to continue negotiations with such persons or entities. Broker agrees to submit a list of such persons or entities to Owner no later than fifteen (15) calendar days following the expiration or termination of the Term, provided, however, that if a written offer has been submitted then it shall not be necessary to include the offeror's name on the list. *[handwritten right margin: BROKER CAN BE IDENTIFIED AS the procuring cause.]*

5. ~~OWNER FURTHER AGREES THAT (a) IF A LEASE OF THE PROPERTY IS ENTERED INTO DURING THE TERM TO ANYONE, OR (b) IF, WITHIN ONE HUNDRED TWENTY (120) CALENDAR DAYS AFTER THE EXPIRATION OR TERMINATION OF THE TERM, THE PROPERTY IS LEASED TO, OR OWNER ENTERS INTO A CONTRACT TO LEASE THE PROPERTY WITH, OR NEGOTIATIONS CONTINUE, RESUME OR COMMENCE AND THEREAFTER CONTINUE LEADING TO THE LEASE OF THE PROPERTY TO ANY PERSON OR ENTITY AS DESCRIBED IN PARAGRAPH 4 ABOVE, OWNER SHALL PAY BROKER A LEASING COMMISSION IN ACCORDANCE WITH THE SCHEDULE.~~

6. Commissions shall be payable hereunder when earned or at the earliest of closing, close of escrow, recordation of a deed, lease execution, or taking of possession by the purchaser or tenant.

7. Unless otherwise provided herein, the terms of sale shall be, at the option of the purchaser, either cash or cash to any existing loan. Any offer may contain normal and customary contingencies such as those relating to the condition of the Property, title report, and timing of closing.

8. Owner and Broker agree that the Property will be offered in compliance with all applicable anti-discrimination laws.

1

U:\Roo\CB FORMS\Ex Sale Listing Agmt\THE GABLES.doc

FIG. 12-2a   Exclusive sales-listing agreement.

9.   Owner agrees to cooperate with Broker in bringing about a sale of the Property and to refer immediately to Broker all inquiries of anyone interested in the Property. All negotiations are to be through Broker. Broker is authorized to accept a deposit from any prospective purchaser and to handle it in accordance with the instructions of the parties unless contrary to applicable law. Broker is exclusively authorized to advertise the Property and, exclusively, to place a sign(s) on the property if, in Broker's opinion, such would facilitate the sale of the Property. Owner and its counsel will be responsible for determining the legal sufficiency of a purchase and sale agreement and other documents relating to any transaction contemplated by this Agreement.

10. In the event the Property is removed from the market due to the opening of an escrow or acceptance of an offer to purchase the Property during the Term, or any extension thereof, and the sale is not consummated for any reason then, in that event, the Term shall be extended for a period of time equal to the number of days that the escrow had been opened and/or the Property had been removed from the market, whichever is longer, provided that, in no event shall such extension(s) exceed one hundred eighty (180) calendar days in the aggregate.

11. Owner agrees to disclose to Broker and to prospective purchasers and tenants any and all information which Owner has regarding present and future zoning and environmental matters affecting the Property and regarding the condition of the Property, including, but not limited to structural, mechanical and soils conditions, the presence and location of asbestos, PCB transformers, other toxic, hazardous or contaminated substances, and underground storage tanks, in, on, or about the Property. Broker is authorized to disclose any such information to prospective purchasers or tenants.

12. Owner represents that it is the owner of the Property and that, except as may be set forth in an addendum attached hereto, no person or entity who has an ownership interest in the Property is a foreign person as defined in the Foreign Investment in Real Property Tax Act (commonly known as "FIRPTA").

13. ~~If earnest money or similar deposits made by a prospective purchaser or tenant are forfeited, in addition to any other rights of Broker pursuant to this Agreement, Broker shall be entitled to one-half (1/2) thereof, but not to exceed the total amount of the anticipated commission.~~

14. To the extent permitted by applicable law, Broker is authorized to deduct its commissions from any deposits, payment or other funds, including proceeds of sale or rental payments, paid by a purchaser or tenant in connection with a transaction contemplated by this Agreement, and Owner hereby irrevocably assigns said funds and proceeds to Broker to the extent necessary to pay said commissions. Broker is authorized to provide a copy of this Agreement to any escrow or closing agent working on such transaction, and such escrow or closing agent is hereby instructed by Owner to pay Broker's commissions from any such funds or proceeds available. Owner shall remain liable for the entire amount of said commissions regardless of whether Broker exercises its rights under this paragraph.

15. Owner acknowledges that Broker is a national brokerage firm and that in some cases it may represent prospective purchasers or tenants. Owner desires that the Property be presented to such persons and entities and hereby consents to Broker acting, in such event, as a transaction broker for both Owner and a prospective purchaser or tenant if the same licensee representing Owner should represent such prospective purchaser or tenant. If a licensee of Broker different from ____ CB Richard Ellis, Inc. ___ the licensee(s) representing Owner should represent such prospective purchaser or tenant, then Owner consents to Designated Agency created thereby. Broker shall not disclose the confidential information of one principal to the other. In the event that the licensee(s) named above becomes incapacitated or terminates his/her employment with Broker, Broker shall have the right to substitute a licensee of similar skill and experience, subject to Owner's approval, which approval shall not be unreasonably withheld.

16. In the event that the Property comes under the jurisdiction of a bankruptcy court, Owner shall immediately notify Broker of the same, and shall promptly take all steps necessary to obtain court approval of Broker's appointment, unless Broker shall elect to terminate this Agreement upon said notice.

17. In the event that the Property becomes the subject of foreclosure proceedings prior to the expiration of this Agreement then this Agreement shall be deemed suspended until such time as Owner may reacquire the Property within the Term. If this Agreement is suspended pursuant to this paragraph, Broker shall be free to enter into a listing agreement with any receiver, the party initiating the foreclosure, the party purchasing the Property at a foreclosure sale, or any other person having an interest in the Property.

18. In the event of any dispute between Owner and Broker relating to this Agreement, the Property or Owner's or Broker's performance hereunder, Owner and Broker agree that such dispute shall be resolved by means of binding arbitration in accordance with the commercial arbitration rules of the American Arbitration Association, and judgment upon the award rendered by the arbitrator(s) may be entered in any court of competent jurisdiction. Depositions may be taken and other discovery obtained during such arbitration proceedings to the same extent as authorized in civil judicial proceedings in the state where

FIG. 12-2b   Continued.

the office of Broker executing this Agreement is located. The arbitrator(s) shall be limited to awarding compensatory damages and shall have no authority to award punitive, exemplary, or similar type damages. The prevailing party in the arbitration proceeding shall be entitled to recover its expenses, including the costs of the arbitration proceeding, and reasonable attorneys' fees. Should Broker become due a commission hereunder, Owner hereby consents to Broker filing a claim for lien with the Recorder of Deeds for the county in which the Property is located, satisfying the requirements of Sec. 475-42(j), Florida Statutes Annotated. Upon payment of the commission described in the claim for lien, Broker shall provide Owner with a recordable release therefor.

19. In the event that Owner lists the Property with another broker after the expiration or termination of this Agreement, Owner agrees to provide in the subsequent listing agreement that a commission will not be payable to the new broker with respect to transactions for which Owner remains obligated to pay a commission to Broker under paragraph 4 or 5 hereof. Owner's failure to do so, however, shall not affect Owner's obligation to Broker under paragraphs 4 or 5.

20. Each signator to this Agreement represents and warrants that he or she has full authority to sign this Agreement on behalf of the party for whom he or she signs and that this Agreement binds such party.

21. This Agreement constitutes the entire agreement between Owner and Broker and supersedes all prior discussions, negotiations and agreements, whether oral or written. No amendment, alteration, cancellation or withdrawal of this Agreement shall be valid or binding unless made in writing and signed by both Owner and Broker. This Agreement shall be binding upon, and shall benefit, the heirs, successors and assignees of the parties. In the event any clause, provision, paragraph or term of this Agreement shall be deemed to be unenforceable or void based on any controlling state or federal law, the remaining provisions hereof, and each part, shall remain unaffected and shall continue in full force and effect.

22. The parties hereto agree to comply with all applicable federal, state and local laws, regulations, codes, ordinances and administrative orders having jurisdiction over the parties, property or the subject matter of this Agreement, including, but not limited to, the 1964 Civil Rights Act and all amendments thereto, the Foreign Investment In Real Property Tax Act, the Comprehensive Environmental Response Compensation and Liability Act, and The Americans With Disabilities Act.

The undersigned Owner hereby acknowledges receipt of a copy of this Agreement and the Schedule.

a(n): *The Gables Apartments of Gainesville, LTD.*

Accepted:

CB Richard Ellis, Inc.
Licensed Real Estate Broker

By: _James P. Cirano_

Title: Managing Director

Address: 225 Water Street, Suite 110

Jacksonville, FL 32202

Date: 9/9/05

Telephone: (904) 644-1200

By: _(signature)_

Title: *Authorized Signature*

By: _____

Title: _____

Address: 220 N. Main St.

Gainesville FL 32601

Date: August 3rd, 2005

Telephone: 352-375-2152

CONSULT YOUR ADVISORS – This document has legal consequences. No representation or recommendation is made by Broker as to the legal or tax consequences of this Agreement or the transaction(s) which it contemplates. These are questions for your attorney and financial advisors.

C:\DATA\CB FORMS\Exclusive Listing Agmt\THE GABLES.doc   EXCLUSIVE SALES LISTING AGREEMENT

FIG. 12-2c   Continued.

Schedule of Sale Commissions
CB Richard Ellis
Brokerage and Management
Licensed Real Estate Broker

FOR PROPERTY AT _____ 4700 S.W. Archer Road, Gainesville, Florida (The Gables – 168 units).

Broker's commission shall be __*__ of the gross sales price. Gross sales price shall include any and all consideration received or receivable, in whatever form, including but not limited to assumption or release of existing liabilities. This commission shall be paid when earned or at the close of escrow through escrow, or if there is no escrow, then upon recordation of the deed; provided, however, if the transaction involves an installment contract, then payment shall be made upon execution of such contract. In the event Owner contributes or conveys the Property or any interest therein to a joint venture, a partnership, or other business entity, the commission shall be calculated on the fair market value of the Property, less the value of the interest in the Property retained by or transferred, whether by merger, outright purchase, or otherwise, in lieu of a sale of the Property, and applicable law does not prohibit the payment of a commission in connection with such sale or transfer, the commission shall be calculated on the fair market value of Property, rather than the gross sales price, multiplied by the percentage of interest so transferred, and shall be paid at the time of the transfer.

Broker agrees to reduce the commission by Ten Thousand Dollars ($10,000) to be allocated to the on-site staff.

The provisions hereof are subject to the terms and provisions of any Exclusive Sales Listing Agreement or other agreement to which this Schedule may be attached and which is executed by the parties hereto.

In the event Owner fails to make payments within the time limits set forth herein, then from the date due until paid the delinquent amount shall bear interest at the maximum rate permitted in the state in which the office of the Broker executing this Schedule is located. If Broker is required to institute legal action against Owner relating to this Schedule or any agreement of which it is a part, Broker shall be entitled to reasonable attorneys' fees and costs.

Owner hereby acknowledges receipt of a copy of this Schedule and agrees that it shall be binding upon its heirs, successors and assignees. In the event Owner sells or otherwise disposes of its interest in the Property, Owner shall remain liable for payment of the commissions provided for in this Schedule and any agreement of which it is a part. The term "Owner" as used herein shall be deemed to include the owner of the Property, a party under contract to acquire the Property and a tenant under a ground lease.

APPROVED this 3rd day of August, 2005

The Gables Apartments of Gainesville LTD.
              Owner

By: _____

Title: Authorized Signatory

By: _____

Title: _____

CB Richard Ellis, Inc.
Licensed Real Estate Broker

James P. Civano

FIG. 12-2d Continued.

CB RICHARD ELLIS

SCHEDULE OF SALE COMMISSIONS
CB RICHARD ELLIS
BROKERAGE AND MANAGEMENT
LICENSED REAL ESTATE BROKER

*Commission Structure:

Fee	If Sales Price is:
.60%	$25,000,000
5%	Above $25,000,000

FOR EXAMPLE, IF THE PURCHASE WERE $26,500,000:

THE COMMISSION WOULD BE CALCULATED AS FOLLOWS:

$150,000 (60 bp × $25,0MM); PLUS, 5% × $1,500,000

OR

$150,000 + $75,000 = $225,000

2

Form No. 8328 Rev 6/30 (Investment Properties)
C:\Data\CB FORMS\Schedule of Sale Commissions The Gables.doc

08/03/05
SCHEDULE OF SALE COMMISSIONS
8/4/05

FIG. 12-2e   Continued.

broker found a buyer willing and able to sell on "the terms stated above or any other price and terms agreeable to the owner." Brokers usually stand very firm on these terms simply because the time and expense of marketing a property are so great. In this case, the removal of the terms was in recognition of the length and strength of the relationship and the broker's faith in the seriousness of the seller.

In paragraph 13, another standard clause, a provision calling for a fifty-fifty split between the broker and owner of any deposits forfeited, was removed. In the absence of such a clause, the broker would only obtain his normal percentage commission.

Page 3 documents an insightful and professional act upon the part of CBRE. They agree to allocate $10,000 of their commission to the Gables on-site staff. This motivates and energizes the property personnel who otherwise might be concerned about all the upcoming changes and unhappy about potential loss of employment under the new owner. This was less an issue at this community since we own multiple communities within the same market and could offer convenient transfers. But the gesture illustrates one of the many reasons we chose CBRE.

CB Richard Ellis "Gables Marketing Report" to Owner

Figure 12-3 is the marketing report provided by the broker to show the marketing progress being made. It gives contact information and the names and companies of those who have responded or made inquires. Some 66 contacts are listed as of the date of this report, representing the excellent job of exposure to the market being done by the broker. "CA" refers to a Confidentiality Agreement that everyone must sign prior to receiving an "OM" (or Offering Memorandum) e-mail (or access to a password protected Web site) or physical package.

Taking a property tour (the fifth captioned column in Figure 3) is an important indication of interest, as it requires a meaningful investment of time and money since most buyers are from out of town. The organizational level of those making the tour is also an indicator: Are they decision makers or information gatherers? A second visit or multiple persons making a single visit also can give clues to level of interest. Be wary of a *Letter of Intent* (LOI) from someone who has not made a site visit. It may very well be an attempt to tie up the property and take it off the market while the alleged buyer decides if he has any serious interest at all. Most buyers are serious when they submit a LOI, and they close at a high percentage. However, some are not. Remember, Letters of Intent are generally *not* legally binding and most explicitly say so in their terms.

One can always put a property back on the market after a failed LOI and usually there is no serious taint (though there might be after multiple failed attempts). Recently, we were second in line in a best and final bid for a 300-unit community and elected not to sweeten our offer when given the hint of a chance. While the property was an excellent one, well-maintained and in our home market, I felt the lead offer was a bit aggressive, a bit frothy. The "winner" of the best and final offer on this 300-unit community commenced the 45-day due-diligence period and at the end of that time elected to pass. The broker's story was that the offering party attempted to retrade the deal, going back to the seller for a negotiation "nibble"

Company	Signed CA/ Offer?	Date OM sent	OM / E / PKG	Property Tour	Interest Level	Comments
C-001	Y	8/30/2005	OM	Y	10	9-29 Made offer today. 8-24 Drove the property/ Reviewing, but says will make offer. Expect to make offer.
C-002	Y	8/31/2005	EMAIL	Y	10	9-23 Made strong pre-emptive offer. 9-19 Working on submitting offer. Toured and expect to make offer.
C-003	Y	8/30/2005	EMAIL	Y	10	9-22 Made strong pre-emptive offer. Property tour Fri, Sept 2nd
C-004	Y	8/30/2005	EMAIL/OM		10	9-26 Made offer today. 8-26 Not in office today ,call on Tuesday.
C-005	Y	8/30/2005	EMAIL/OM	Y	10	9-19 Submitted offer today. 8-30 Expect to make offer. Touring Wed, Aug 31st
C-006	Y	9/9/2005	EMAIL	Y	10	9-14 Submitted pre-emptive offer.

FIG. 12-3 Gables marketing report.

Company	Signed CA/ Offer?	Date OM sent	OM / E / PKG	Property Tour	Interest Level	Comments
C-007	Y	8/30/2005	EMAIL	Y	10	9-16 Submitted pre-emptive offer. 9-7 Will tour tomorrow 8-30 Wants to tour week of Sept 5th. 8-26 Will tour, needs to review the OM.
C-008	Y	8/30/2005	EMAIL	Y	10	9-26 Made offer today. 9-17 Toured. Lifestyles. 9-16 Will tour tomorrow Call re: tour week of Sept 5th.
C-009	Y	8/30/2005	EMAIL/OM	Y	10	9-29 Submitted offer today. 9-16 Will tour tomorrow. Will be in town Wed, Sept 14th. Converting Links at
C-010	Y	8/30/2005	EMAIL	Y	9	9-26 Finishing market study / working on submitting offer/8-8-26 Have driven the property. Will tour Friday,
C-011	Y	8/30/2005	EMAIL/OM		7	9-21 Reviewing information. 8-29 LM w/assistant. 825 LVM
C-012	Y	8/30/2005	OM		6	9-26 Seeing if can submit offer. 8-29 Discussing with partners. 8-26 LVM

FIG. 12-3 Continued.

C-013	Y	8/30/2005	EMAIL	6	9-22 LVM -29 Will review information. 8-24 LVM
C-014	Y	8/30/2005	EMAIL/OM	5	9-9 No answer, VM full. 8-26 VM full. Will call back Monday.
C-015	Y	8/30/2005	EMAIL	5	9-27 LVM 9-6 LVM re: tour 8-29 LVM 8-24 LVM
C-016	Y	9/7/2005	EMAIL/OM	5	9-16 LVM
C-017	Y	9/7/2005	EMAIL	5	9-16 LVM w/ Hal Hultquist.
C-018	Y	9/7/2005	EMAIL	5	9-27 LVM 9-16 LVM
C-019	Y	9/7/2005	EMAIL/OM	5	9-20 LVM 9-16 LVM
C-020	Y	9/7/2005	EMAIL/OM	5	9-14 LVM
C-021	Y	9/7/2005	OM	5	9-20 LVM 9-14 LVM
C-022	Y	9/7/2005	EMAIL	5	9-20 LVM
C-023	Y	9/14/2005	OM	5	9-20 LVM

FIG. 12-3 Continued.

Company	Signed CA/ Offer?	Date OM sent	OM / E / PKG	Property Tour	Interest Level	Comments
C-013	Y	8/30/2005	EMAIL		6	9-22 LVM -29 Will review information. 8-24 LVM
C-014	Y	8/30/2005	EMAIL/OM		5	9-9 No answer, VM full. 8-26 VM full. Will call back Monday.
C-024	Y	9/14/2005	EMAIL		5	9-14 LVM
C-025	Y	9/14/2005	OM		5	9-20 LVM 9-14 LVM
C-026	Y	9/16/2005	EMAIL		5	9-20 LVM 9-14 LVM
C-027	Y	9/14/2005	EMAIL/OM		5	9-20 LVM 9-16 LVM
C-028	Y	9/14/2005	OM		5	9-22 LM w/ assistant. 9-14 LVM
C-029	Y	9/16/2005	EMAIL / OM		5	9-14 LVM
C-030	Y	9/14/2005	EMAIL		5	9-14 LVM
C-031	Y	9/16/2005	EMAIL / OM		5	9-16 LVM

FIG. 12-3 Continued.

C-032	Y	9/14/2005	EMAIL	5		9-20 LVM 9-16 LVM
C-033	Y	9/14/2005	OM	5		9-20 LVM 9-14 LVM
C-034	Y	9/16/2005	OM	5		9-16 LVM
C-035	Y	9/9/2005	EMAIL	5		9-16 LVM
C-036	Y	9/14/2005	EMAIL	5		9-14 LVM
C-037	Y	8/30/2005	EMAIL / OM	5		9-20 LM w/assistant
C-038	Y	8/30/2005	OM	3		8-24 will review info, but currently not looking in Gainesville to convert.
C-039	Y	8/30/2005	OM	3		8-25 will review, but only starting conversions. Not a strong player.
C-040	Y	8/30/2005	EMAIL	0	Y	9-25 Passed, due to small Gainesville market. 8-24 conducting market study on Gainesville before.

FIG. 12-3 Continued.

Company	Signed CA/ Offer?	Date OM sent	OM / E / PKG	Property Tour	Interest Level	Comments
C-041	Y	8/30/2005	OM		0	9-28 Pass on deal, declined to bid due to full plate with core assets, no converstions.
C-042	Y	9/14/2005	EMAIL		0	9-19 Not a major converter, but did like the opportunity. Passing due to timing. 8-29 LVM
C-043	Y	8/30/2005	EMAIL / OM		0	9-23 Pass, full plate with conversion in Orlando area (and passed on Oviedo, liked the property but can't act at this time. 9-20 underwriting the deal.
C-044	Y	8/30/2005	OM		0	9-20 Pass on Gainesville to convert. 8-26 LVM
C-045	Y	8/30/2005	EMAIL	Y	0	9-26 Pass, due to full plate with purchase of existing multi-family and retail in Gainesville.
C-046	Y	8/30/2005	EMAIL / OM		0	9-26 Pass, due to location. Outside their market. 8-29 deciding on tour date.
C-047	Y	9/14/2005	OM		0	9-22 Not buying in Gainesville currently. 8-26 Will review the information and then decide about touring

FIG. 12-3 Continued.

C-048	Y	8/30/2005	OM	0	9-26 Pass on Gainesville due to smaller market, will continue to convert in Jacksonville, Orlando, Tampa.
C-049	Y	9/14/2005	EMAIL / OM	0	9-20 Pass on Gainesville marketplace, sticking to Tampa, Jacksonville and Orlando instead.
C-050	Y	9/14/2005	OM	0	9-20 Not converting at this time. 9-16 LVM
C-051	Y	9/16/2005	EMAIL	0	9-20 Pass, not converting in Gainesville at this time.
C-052	Y	8/30/2005	EMAIL	0	9-20 Not converting in Florida
C-053	Y	9/14/2005	EMAIL / OM	0	8-25 LVM
C-054	Y	8/30/2005	OM	0	9-19 Pass on Gainesville Market. 9-14 LVM
C-055	Y	8/30/2005	EMAIL	0	9-19 Pass , not converting in Gainesville. 8-24 LVM
C-056	Y	8/30/2005	EMAIL	0	9-20 Can't make the numbers work. 9-9 Underwriting the deal now / studying the market.
C-057	Y	9/14/2005	EMAIL	0	9-20 Pass on deal, plate is currently full

FIG. 12-3 Continued.

Company	Signed CA/ Offer?	Date OM sent	OM / E / PKG	Property Tour	Interest Level	Comments
C-058	Y	8/30/2005	OM	Y	0	9-20 Pass, due 9-2 Toured the property.
C-059	Y	9/14/2005	EMAIL / OM		0	9-20 Pass on deal, not currently converting in Gainesville, not sure of viabilitiy. 9-6 Reviewing
C-060	Y	8/30/2005	EMAIL / OM		0	9-18 Likes to convert older properties and does not pay high prices
C-061	Y	8/30/2005	EMAIL		0	9-16 Pass on deal to due unfamiliarity with Gainesville market. 9-6 LVM. 8-29 LVM.
C-062	Y	8/30/2005	EMAIL		0	9-7 Pass, not converting and can't compete. 8-25 LVM
C-063	Y	9/14/2005	EMAIL		0	8-29 Not actively converting at this time
C-064	Y	9/14/2005	EMAIL		0	Broker
C-065	Y	9/14/2005	OM		0	9-26 Pass on Gainesville market - too small
C-066	Y	9/16/2005	EMAIL		0	9-28 Pass on deal, only looking at 300 + units to convert.

FIG. 12-3 Continued.

that equaled or exceeded the spread between his offer and ours. The prospective buyer's story was that the rent roll was not as strong as promised, and he had concerns about the strength of the local market. Who knows for sure? Transactions are complex, and there often are multiple motives and many points of view. The upshot is that we were willing to honor our original offer on the property, though we did stiffen up slightly in the negotiation of the terms, knowing that no seller and broker want to take a property back to the market a third time. The property has performed well, and we are happy buyers.

In the marketing report, note that the broker assigns a number grade to the interest level and that the comments section includes information that two potential buyers made strong preemptive offers, hoping to take the deal off the table and avoid the auction process. We did respond at one point to a bidder from Las Vegas with a $160,000 per unit offer, and while it was a tempting offer and a serious buyer, the offer never went hard. Perhaps the Las Vegas market offered too many alternatives.

The broker eventually received nine Letters of Intent worthy of consideration. In an effort to screen and prequalify potential buyers as genuine prospects capable of closing, bidders were asked to complete two questionnaires: *Transactional Qualifications* (see three examples in Figure 12-4) and *Underwriting Qualifications* (see three examples in Figure 12-5).

Transactional Qualifications

The Transactional Qualification form is an attempt to get a feel for the qualifications of the potential buyers, their geographic focus, their internal approval process, and entity structure, whether they are under any potential IRS 1031 exchange time pressures, what financial resources they have available including the sources of their debt and equity capital, their recent deal history, their overall business plan, and how this deal relates tactically to their strategic focus, that is, how important this deal is to them. Buyers vary on the amount of detail and information they feel comfortable providing. They obviously want to be taken seriously and be able to pass muster sufficiently to provide enough certainty of closing to be competitive. At the same time, some private companies balk at providing data they feel is proprietary, and some larger private entities or listed public companies can take the position (and with some justification) that their names and reputations constitute sufficient references.

Underwriting Qualifications

The Underwriting Qualifications questionnaire gives an opportunity to determine how much financial analysis the bidder has done, indicating how seriously the accompanying Letter of Intent can be viewed. The questionnaire also gives the seller and broker market feedback, insight into the valuation perspective of sellers, and the ability to monitor trends and evaluate the different approaches that sellers may take to the process.

Also, any outliers in terms of underwriting numbers (including occasional out-and-out math errors) can expose potentially weak bidders who are more likely

Property: The Gables
Number of units: 168
Prepared for: Nathan Collier, David Materna, The Paradigim Group
Purchaser:
Price: $23,520,000
Date: September 29th, 2005

TRANSACTIONAL QUALIFICATIONS

Please comment in writing on the following questions relating to the deal structure and sources of debt and equity for the transaction The Gables Apartments.

1. What type of ownership entity are you proposing to acquire the property with?
    With a single asset LLC.

2. How much equity will be used in acquiring the asset and what are the major sources for this equity? Please be specific as to the amounts or percentages of equity from each source and whether or not that equity is readily available.
    30–35% equity

3. What approvals must be obtained in order to invest this equity in this asset?
    None.

4. Are you using a 1031 exchange in this transaction? If so, please provide the name of the exchange company and a contact name.
    There may be some 1031 money used in this purchase, but probably not the entire amount of the purchase.

5. What was the most recent transaction that you have closed and how large was it?
    $15MM closing in September 2005, 168 units conversion in Las Vegas.

6. How many deals have you closed during the last 12 months?
    12-14 deals in the past 12 months, $80MM total.

7. Please provide transactional references, including contact names and phone numbers.

8. What other multi-family assets do you own and operate? Where are these assets located? Do you use a third party management company? If so, please provide a contact name and phone number.
    Own multi-family land for new ground construction condos and have sold 2 multi-family projects recently, $15MM and $40MM.

    FIG. 12-4a The Gables, Transactional Qualifications.

Property: The Gables
Number of units: 168
Prepared for: Nathan Collier, David Materna, The Paradigim Group
Purchaser:
Price: $23,520,000
Date: September 29th, 2005

9.   Aside from the due diligence process, are there any contingencies that you may seek in order to complete the transaction?
       None.

10.   If you are planning to use new financing to complete the transaction, please identify your lender, a lender contact and attach the terms.
       2/3 debt, 1/3 equity

11.   What approvals must be obtained to complete the financing?
       None.

12.   How much business have you done with this particular lender in the last year?
       $15MM

13.   Have you defaulted on any of your loans or declared bankruptcy within the past year?
       No.

14.   How many deals are you currently working on? (Please identify the number of contracts and letters of intent that are under negotiations).
       8–10 deals under contract to close, most are smaller transactions.

15.   Briefly describe your due diligence process.
       Engineers, attorneys, contractors etc.

16.   What is your current business plan and how does it relate to this asset?
       Condo conversions in Florida and Las Vegas.

FIG. 12-4a Continued.

Property: The Gables
Number of units: 168
Prepared for: Nathan Collier, David Materna, The Paradigm Group
Purchaser:
Price: $23,520,000
Date: September 29th, 2005

TRANSACTIONAL QUALIFICATIONS

Please comment in writing on the following questions relating to the deal structure and sources of debt and equity for the transaction The Gables Apartments.

1.   What type of ownership entity are you proposing to acquire the property with?
     LLC

2.   How much equity will be used in acquiring the asset and what are the major sources for this equity? Please be specific as to the amounts or percentages of equity from each source and whether or not that equity is readily available.
     $500,000 in deposit and this will be specific to the lender.

3.   What approvals must be obtained in order to invest this equity in this asset?
     None.

4.   Are you using a 1031 exchange in this transaction? If so, please provide the name of the exchange company and a contact name.
     No.

5.   What was the most recent transaction that you have closed and how large was it?
     $12MM, which is a lease deal.

6.   How many deals have you closed during the last 12 months?
     Closed $260MM worth of loans since January 2005.

7.   Please provide transactional references, including contact names and phone numbers.

8.   What other multi-family assets do you own and operate? Where are these assets located? Do you use a third party management company? If so, please provide a contact name and phone number.
     Equity partner currently owns 2 hotels in Vegas, 200 acres in Washington D.C., warehousing in San Francisco, millions in Dallas/Fort Worth.

FIG. 12-4b The Gables, Transactional Qualifications.

Property: The Gables
Number of units: 168
Prepared for: Nathan Collier, David Materna, The Paradigm Group
Purchaser:
Price: $23,520,200
Date: September 29th, 2005

9. Aside from the due diligence process, are there any contingencies that you may seek in order to complete the transaction?
    None.

10. If you are planning to use new financing to complete the transaction, please identify your lender, a lender contact and attach the terms.
    LJ Melody.

11. What approvals must be obtained to complete the financing?
    None.

12. How much business have you done with this particular lender in the last year?
    None, although the equity partner has acquired over $260MM in assets since January 2005.

13. Have you defaulted on any of your loans or declred bankruptcy within the past year?
    No.

14. How many deals are you currently working on? (Please identify the number of contracts and letters of intent that are under negotiations).
    1 under LOI at $60MM

15. Briefly describe your due deligence process.
    Mechanical inspection and building inspection.

16. What is your current business plan and how does it relate to this asset?
    Expanding in Florida with condo conversions.

FIG. 12-4b Continued.

Property: The Gables
Number of units: 168
Prepared for: Nathan Collier, David Materna, The Paradigm Group
Purchaser:
Price: $25,183,200
Date: October 3rd, 2005

TRANSACTIONAL QUALIFICATIONS

Please comment in writing on the following questions relating to the deal structure and sources of debt and equity for the transaction The Gables Apartments.

1. What type of ownership entity are you proposing to acquire the property with?
    LLC

2. How much equity will be used in acquiring the asset and what are the major sources for this equity? Please be specific as to the amounts or percentages of equity from each source and whether or not that equity is readily available.
    Equity will be internal and the deposit will be $150,000 hard day one, subject to title, environmental as well as no structural defects.

3. What approvals must be obtained in order to invest this equity in this asset?
    None.

4. Are you using a 1031 exchange in this transaction? If so, please provide the name of the exchange company and a contact name.
    No.

5. What was the most recent transaction that you have closed and how large was it?
    Closed 260 units in Sarasota, $48,880,000 within past 2 months.

6. How many deals have you closed during the last 12 months?
    2 deals, with a third set to close in November.

7. Please provide transactional references, including contact names and phone numbers.

8. What other multi-family assets do you own and operate? Where are these assets located? Do you use a third party management company? If so, please provide a contact name and phone number.
    Conversion in Jacksonville, 260 units in Sarasota and will close on a 3rd this November in the Tampa area. Have also converted in Miami for over two decades.

FIG. 12-4c The Gables, Transactional Qualifications.

Property: The Gables
Number of units: 168
Prepared for: Nathan Collier, David Materna, The Paradigm Group
Purchaser:
Price: $25,183,200
Date: October 3rd, 2005

9.   Aside from the due diligence process, are there any contingencies that you may seek in order to complete the transaction?
        None.

10.   If you are planning to use new financing to complete the transaction, please identify your lender, a lender contact and attach the terms.
        Will provide full contact information upon request.

11.   What approvals must be obtained to complete the financing?
        None.

12.   How much business have you done with this particular lender in the last year?
        In excess of $50MM in 2005.

13.   Have you defaulted on any of your loans or declared bankruptcy within the past year?
        No, and have borrowed over $500MM combined and have never missed a payment.

14.   How many deals are you currently working on? (Please identify the number of contracts and letters of intent that are under negotiations).
        Just closed the 260 unit, $48,800,000 conversion in Sarasota and will begin selling in October. Will close one other conversion in November.

15.   Briefly describe your due diligence process.
        Walk units, engineer to inspect the buildings, etc.

16.   What is your current business plan and how does it relate to this asset?
        Converting in Jacksonville, Tampa, Sarasota and would like to move into Gainesville. Principal is a University of Florida alumnus.

FIG. 12-4c Continued.

Property: The Gables
Number of Units: 168
Prepared for: Nathan Collier, David Materna, The Paradigm Group
Purchaser:
Price: $23,520,000
Date: September 29th, 2005

UNDERWRITING QUALIFICATIONS

Please comment in writing to each of the following questions relating to your underwriting of The Gables Apartments.

1.   REAL ESTATE TAXES

a.) What is your assumption as it relates to any potential adjustments to the real estate taxes?
Used the proforma.

b.) Specifically, what number are you using in your underwriting?
$194,268

2.   REPLACEMENT RESERVES/CAPITAL

a.) What are your underwriting assumptions for replacement reserves (this would include carpets, appliances, HVAC, etc.)?
The buyer will convert the property upon closing. $200/unit.

b.) What are your up-front capital assumptions?
Working with _____ and this up-front captial assumption will be as requested by _____.

3.   UTILITY EXPENSES

What are your assumptions regarding utility expenses at the property? Are you projecting any cost savings or expense recovery?
Will have this part of the home owners association.

4.   INTEREST RATE RISKS

Please comment on your underwriting of interest rate risks.
While there is upward pressure with interest rates, the buyer aims to have these units sold out as condos in 12–18 months.

5.   GENERAL ISSUES

Please comment below on any other items that you would like the owner to be aware of, relative to your acquistions underwriting or interest level in acquiring this asset.
None.

6.   YEAR ONE PROFMA

Please provide your year one proforma for this transaction.
_____ has provided a proforma for the sellout

FIG. 12-5a The Gables, Underwriting Qualifications.

Property: The Gables
Number of Units: 168
Prepared for: Nathan Collier, David Materna, The Paradigm Group
Purchaser:
Price: $23,520,000
Date: September 29th, 2005

UNDERWRITING QUALIFICATIONS

Please comment in writing to each of the following questions relating to your underwriting of The Gables Apartments.

1.   REAL ESTATE TAXES

a.) What is your assumption as it relates to any potential adjustments to the real estate taxes?
The real estate taxes will be paid by the buyer only until the units are converted.

b.) Specifically, what number are you using in your underwriting?
The proforma number, which is $194,268.

2.   REPLACEMENT RESERVES/CAPITAL

a.) What are your underwriting assumptions for replacement reserves (this would include carpets, appliances, HVAC, etc.)?
$250/unit but will convert immediately.

b.) What are your up-front capital assumptions?
$3,000–$4,000 per unit.

3.   UTILITY EXPENSES

a.) What are your assumptions regarding utility expenses at the property? Are you projecting any cost savings or expense recovery?
The home owners association will pay once established.

4.   INTEREST RATE RISKS

Please comment on your underwriting of interest rate risks.
Using LJ Melody and are having them underwrite the interest rate risk currently and may hedge their risks.

5.   GENERAL ISSUES

Please comment below on any other items that you would like the owner to be aware of, relative to your acquisitions underwriting or interest level in acquring this asset.
None.

6.   YEAR ONE PROFMA

Please provide your year one proforma for this transaction.
Convert to condos immediately and sell out roughly within 1 year or so.

FIG. 12-5b The Gables, Underwriting Qualifications.

Property: The Gables
Number of units: 168
Prepared for: Nathan Collier, David Materna, The Paradigm Group
Purchaser:
Price: $25,183,200
Date: October 3rd, 2005

UNDERWRITING QUALIFICATIONS

Please comment in wrting to each of the following questions relating to your underwriting of The Gables Apartments.

1.   REAL ESTATE TAXES

   a.) What is your assumption as it relates to any potential adjustments to the real estate taxes?
   The real estate taxes will be paid by the buyer only until the units are converted.

   b.) Specifically, what number are you using in your underwriting?
   The proforma number, which is $194,268.

2.   REPLACEMENT RESERVES/CAPITAL

   a.) What are your underwriting assumptions for replacement reserves (this would include carpets, appliances, HVAC, etc.)?
   $250/unit but will convert immediately.

   b.) What are your up-front capital assumptions?
   As necessary, perhaps $2,000–$4,000 per unit.

3.   UTILITY EXPENSES
   What are your assumptions regarding utility expenses at the property? Are you projecting any cost savings or expense recovery?
   Will build in to the home owners association once established.

4.   INTEREST RATE RISKS
   Please comment on your underwriting of interest rate risks.
   Lender is currently underwriting the risk.

5.   GENERAL ISSUES
   Please comment below on any other items that you would like the owner to be aware of, relative to your acquisitions underwriting or interest level in acquiring this asset.
   None.

6.   YEAR ONE PROFMA
   Please provide your year one proforma for this transaction.
   Convert to condos immediately and sell using _____.

FIG. 12-5c The Gables, Underwriting Qualifications.

to drop out during the due-diligence process. All sellers want the highest price possible but high contracts that do not close result in a tremendous waste of time and money. The mere act of putting a community up for sale, or even serious consideration of a sale, consumes meaningful organizational resources, time, and energy, representing real opportunity cost. And it can disrupt the property being sold and unsettle on-site personnel as they begin to wonder about their job security.

Letters of Intent

Letters of Intent can be as simple as a single page or rival a Purchase and Sale Agreement (PSA) in complexity. Numerous Letters of Intent are included in Appendix C to give the reader a sense of the tremendous variation that exists. More important, these letters show how LOIs stack up and compare to each other, allowing the reader to create a more impressive and competitive LOI.

To put these offers in perspective, we purchased this community just a few years earlier for what I thought (then) was the astronomical price of $95,000 per unit. Paying the commission and defeasing (paying off) the mortgage to deliver the property free and clear would add another $7,000 or so to my per-unit cost.

Exhibit C-1 is a simple, single-page, unsigned LOI dated 9/22/05 for $23,520,000, or $140,000 a door. It calls for a 30-day due diligence period, a 30-day closing period, and $250,000 earnest money deposit with an additional $100,000 after the feasibility period expires. The start of the feasibility period is not specified. A place is provided at the end for the Seller to sign, presumably to signify acceptance.

Exhibit C-2 is another one-page LOI *from the same bidder* dated 10 days later, 10/3/05, this time with a much more attractive $160,000 per unit price for $26,880,000 in total.

The bidder's $20,000 per door offering price increase is made possible by an attempt at innovative financial structures. Three options are given on how to do the transaction, all involving the seller retaining significant financial involvement postclosing.

In Option 1, the LOI asks the Seller to *finance* the transaction by carrying back 40% of the purchase price as debt at 6% interest for two years. Option 2 is the same terms but in a *joint venture* format instead of debt. Option 3 sweetens the terms on the prior option: "previous offer with hard money on day one subject to all inspections."

Stating that the deposit is "hard" and subject to all inspections leaves a lot open to interpretation and brings into question the definition of hard money. Presumably it means that they must have a valid reason to demand a refund. The truth of the matter is that no property is perfect, and you can always find a way to find fault and demand a refund. Hard money generally means a nonrefundable deposit versus "soft" money, which is refundable and put up as evidence of good faith and seriousness of intent. Soft money can be refundable at will or under certain circumstances. Even "hard" money can generally be refunded if the *seller* defaults.

In the final analysis, no deposit is truly "hard" until the escrow agent has released it. Even if a deposit is hard, if there are competing claims on a deposit an escrow agent will generally refuse to release funds absent a court order (and then even only after the period for filing an appeal to a higher court has expired, generally 10 to 30 days) or a waiver from all parties. It is common for a cautious escrow agent, seeking to protect himself from any possible charge of breach of fiduciary duty, to request a waiver from the nonreceiving party, even if no dispute has arisen. This can create a delay that can be an unpleasant surprise for someone anticipating a rapid refund and redeployment of working capital. To protect against this eventuality, a clause may be included in the escrow agreement or the PSA that provides for specific indemnification of the escrow agent and a waiver of claims by the seller if a refund is made to the potential purchaser under certain clearly-defined circumstances, such as receipt of written notice from the purchaser of termination of the PSA during the inspection period.

The reality is that no contract can be written to cover every eventuality, and it is too easy to waste time and energy (and legal fees) negotiating the "perfect" contract instead of doing the underlying deal. Good faith, strong relationships, ethical business practices, and strong references and reputation are perhaps one's best protection. Most problems can be resolved by getting in front of the true decision maker and listening to his concerns, interests, and goals and then forging a creative solution that respects both his needs and yours.

The LOI provides for a 30-day due-diligence period to run from "acceptance," presumably acceptance of the LOI. This starts the due-diligence clock running immediately and creates a significantly shorter effective due-diligence period than one that runs from execution of the PSA, since negotiating and completing the PSA can easily take one to three weeks. The shorter the due-diligence period, the more competitive the offer. A condo converter needs a shorter due-diligence period than an income buyer since the condo converter does not really care about the leases (other than rapid expiration and none greater than one year) and operational expenses.

Exhibit C-3 is a three-page LOI for $25,183,200, or $149,900 per unit, and calls for a $100,000 earnest money deposit "within two business days of the execution of a binding contract of purchase and sale," with an additional $100,000 due at the end of the due-diligence period. The LOI specifically calls for the PSA to state that "receipt of the Earnest Money as liquidated damages shall be Seller's sole and exclusive remedy in event of Purchaser's default." In other words, no specific performance. A reasonable term from a purchaser's perspective, but while several LOIs referred to the liquidated damages function of the deposit, this was the only LOI to further state that liquidated damages were seller's sole and exclusive remedy versus an available option.

The LOI states that:

> Purchaser shall have (30) days from the effective date of the contract or (30) days from the Purchaser receiving the last of the following items: plans and specs used to build the building, as-builts if any, all surveys, all environmental studies and approvals, copies of the past title commitments, current P&L statements, copies of all service agreements, including cable television, security, water and sewer agreements, if any, surface water and storm management agreements if any, insurance policies, certificates

of occupancy for all units including all common elements, legal descriptions and all governmental approvals.

The wording of the LOI is unclear as to whether the due diligence runs from the earlier or later of the two events. The general rule of law is that ambiguities in a contract are interpreted against the drafting party under the theory that they had the best chance to create clarity. That is why you will so often see a "joint work product" clause in a contract stating that the contract is the result of the joint work of both parties and shall not be construed in favor of either party. Of course, since the LOI is generally not a binding contract (this one so states in paragraph 8 on page 3, and such declarations are common), it may be a moot point in a LOI.

This LOI also states closing period terms: "Closing to be 30 days from the end of due diligence and Purchaser shall have the option to extend the closing period for an additional Thirty (30) days if Purchaser deposits an additional $100,000 in Earnest Money." Unique among all the LOIs received, this one states, "It is the intent of the Buyer and Seller to close on either the last or the first day of a calendar month." It is unclear how that would impact the closing period: Shorten it to the first available end of month? Lengthen to the next? Clarity and brevity often are at odds.

The LOI is dated September 29, and it states that "this offer is conditioned upon acceptance by Seller by 5 PM, October 7, 2005."

Exhibit C-4 is for $23,520,000, or $140,000 per unit. The LOI calls for $500,000 in deposits, payable $250,000 at execution of the PSA and another $250,000 at the end of due diligence. Due diligence is to be 40 days from execution of the PSA and closing 40 days from the end of due diligence. A bit unusually, this LOI calls for seller (versus the purchaser) to "provide a new survey, staked on the ground, showing all wetlands, easements and protected trees" as well as a "Phase 1 environmental study/report that shows the property to be free of contamination." While the language does not specify a new environmental study, virtually every owner has a Phase 1 on file (no intelligent buyer has bought land without one for decades and a commercial loan is practically impossible to get without one). However, the owner's Phase 1 may not be current and certainly would not be certified to the new owner.

The LOI further states that "the Seller will immediately cease marketing the property to other buyers and will negotiate in good faith exclusively with the Buyer" and then continues "*except as set forth in the preceding sentence*, no binding agreement shall exist unless a formal Agreement, mutually acceptable to the Seller and Buyer, has been executed by both parties" (italic emphasis added). Interesting twist to make the marketing stop and good-faith negotiation contractually binding terms but nothing else. I do not think I would want to agree, complicates matters too much.

The LOI concludes that it will terminate on a given date, which is four days from the date the LOI is dated on its first page. The LOI is signed with a personal signature with no entity block or title, and it provides a space for the seller to acknowledge, agree, and sign.

Exhibit C-5 contains a much more detailed LOI (but only $135,850 per unit, or $22,823,000) and provides at the top of page 2, under "Investigation Period," for a 30-day due-diligence period running from the latter of "1) a bilaterally executed formal contract or 2) delivery of a current survey." This is excellent contract language, and I have frequently used a similar version expressing the same terms, often conditioning the start upon a receipt of all or substantially all of the requested due-diligence material. It is difficult to do proper due diligence without the full packet of information from the seller. In this LOI, "current survey" is not defined. Banks generally like a survey to be no more than 90 days old, but for purposes of beginning due diligence, a survey done in the last few years is generally acceptable. Practically speaking, one presumes that the purchaser does not require a 90-day "current survey," as it would take 4 to 6 weeks to order and complete one from scratch. I would clarify expectations and wording before proceeding, but then everyone has a different world view.

The LOI provides for 30 days due diligence and a 30-day close period. There are standard terms in a heated marketplace, 30 days and 30 days. In more purchaser-oriented markets, 45 days and 45 days would be seen more frequently. It is hard to know how much time will be required for satisfactory due diligence. The easier the site is to access (geographically, hours of operation, cooperation level of owner's and on-site staff, degree of structure, order of lease files, etc.), the more complete, organized, and quickly delivered the due-diligence package, the better the shape the property is in (physically and organizationally), the faster due diligence will go.

The length of time required to close can vary tremendously as well. Major factors are processing any required loan assumptions (the Department of Housing and Urban Development, HUD, may take a while) and lining up any new capital structure, debt, or equity.

Also under "Investigation Period," this LOI provides for a 15-day extension of the due-diligence period upon payment of an additional *nonrefundable* (except upon seller default) $50,000 deposit. The buyer is wise to plan ahead for unforeseen contingencies and the nonrefundable nature of the additional deposit makes the clause palatable to a seller.

The total escrow deposit is $300,000, payable in equal installments of $100,000 after (1) signing of the PSA, (2) expiration of the Title Review Period, and (3) expiration of the Inspection Period.

The LOI provides under "Purchaser's Obligations: A. Work Product," that if the purchaser fails to close the sale, the seller will be provided "with original copies of the studies, plans and permits that have been sanctioned during the contractual period." These documents contain useful information that is valuable to the seller and the provision for "original copies" insures that the documents received will be high-quality reproductions.

Important Note: Possession of "original copies of the studies, plans and permits" usually does *not* mean that the seller or others have the legal right to rely upon or use the documents in a formal manner. The seller is not typically in "privity of contract" (a party to the original contract for services, etc.) with the providers of the documents, generally professionals such as appraisers, structural or environmental engineers, surveyors, accountants, attorneys, contractors, and providers of marketing data. A clause stating that in addition to providing original copies, the "Purchaser will also assign all rights and interests in said studies, plans and permits and any contracts, agreements, understandings, etc. if the providers of same shall allow such assignment," should create substantially more legal rights. However, the providers of said services might be understandably reluctant to agree to such expansion of services and potentially greater liability, and the purchaser may not want to take the time and trouble to go back and negotiate with each provider. We have negotiated such clauses in specific cases where I foresaw a need, but we do not do so generally. In any case, if there is a need for a specific service or document, the original provider will usually be glad to redo it in the name of the seller or new purchaser for a nominal or reduced fee.

Page 4, last paragraph, of the LOI has an unusual clause, providing for the LOI to be a legally-binding contract, and it was the only LOI to so stipulate. I would appreciate such a clause being more prominently featured, perhaps capitalized like the phrase "TIME IS OF THE ESSENCE." The phrase, "time is of the essence," as well as the phrase, "good faith," are both legal terms, and it is important to understand their implications.

Time Is of the Essence: Generally speaking, the dates in a contract are only approximate, that is, the parties only have to make a reasonable attempt to adhere to them. Coming within three or four business days of a closing date is usually quite acceptable, absent some extenuating circumstances creating urgency. Phrases such as "date certain" and "time is of the essence" mean that the dates are absolute. They must be met or consequences will occur, such as the contract is terminated or the deposit is forfeited.

Good Faith: The general American rule of law, absent some specific statute to the contrary, is "Caveat Emptor," or "Let the buyer beware." One does not owe a duty of fair dealing to the other party, rather each side looks out for themselves. Many statutes have been enacted in the consumer area (and even some case law has evolved) to increase protections in the marketplace, but these are much less prevalent on the commercial side, where it is presumed that parties are more knowledgeable and more equally matched. Fraud is definitely and always illegal, lying is prohibited, and one cannot actively conceal or misrepresent, but neither does one have a duty to disclose facts unknown or perhaps even those unknowable to the other party, or to point out mistakes the other side may have made.

Inserting an obligation of good faith into a contract or agreement changes that balance, injecting equitable concepts of fairness and disclosure. Good faith could be interpreted to include avoidances of onerous but technically correct interpretations of a contract that might fly against a reasonable person's understanding of the agreement. Good faith could also perhaps include an obligation not to take advantage of excessive leverage or a significantly stronger bargaining position.

Good faith behavior is a standard I strongly urge everyone to aspire to in both their professional and personal lives. As a legal concept, it can get dicey. Concepts of fairness vary from individual to individual, and where normal bargaining ends and intimidation begins can be difficult to ascertain. The possibilities for increased litigation abound.

There is a story told in contract law class in many law schools that illustrates good faith. It is *The Three-Legged Cow Rule: Balancing the Obligation Not to Conceal v. the Absence of a Duty to Disclose*. Farmer Brown has a cow for sale, and Farmer Smith comes to Farmer Brown's farm and views the cow grazing contently at pasture. Farmer Smith walks around the cow, pats her sides, asks about her milk production capacity, and evidently receives satisfactory answers because at the end of the conversation he proclaims, "I'll take her!" and loads the cow into a trailer and drives off.

At dawn the next day, Farmer Smith pounds on Farmer Brown's door, loudly proclaiming that Farmer Brown is a liar and a thief because, "That cow you sold me had three legs, and you never told me." Well, assuming that Farmer Brown had not affixed a realistic-looking prosthetic on the cow (a possible attempt at prohibited concealment), Farmer Smith is plain wrong. Farmer Brown had no duty to disclose, particularly that which is obvious to any buyer taking any reasonable level of care.

This LOI also provides for a 15-business day period (three calendar weeks) for the negotiation of the PSA, during which time "Purchaser will not negotiate to purchase land from any other competing property owner and Seller will not negotiate to sell Property to any other prospective purchaser." With this language, the seller is most likely giving up more than the prospective purchaser. The seller, having spent a good deal of time churning up interest in the property, usually has several serious purchasers and has a vested interest in taking backup offers if only to stiffen his bargaining position. The purchaser is not going to give up pursuing all other deals, only deals on "competing property," and the definition of competing property is interesting to speculate about. Competing, meaning physically adjacent? Geographically proximate? In the same marketplace? Rental marketplace or condo sales marketplace? Or competing in the sense of being an alternative use of the purchaser's capital, both financial and human/intellectual? While I doubt the last is the intended definition, it is the one most relevant to the seller, because it relates most closely to the seller's interests. While on the subject of definitions and crystal-clear legal drafting, I'm not sure the terminology prohibits the seller from taking backup offers, as long as they are patently defined as such. The language obviously does not explicitly so state, and if the negotiations, offers, or contracts were unambiguously backups, where is the true harm to the purchaser? Reduced bargaining leverage?

The document provides a specific expiration date, presumably to address the general legal principle that, absent specific terms to the contrary, offers remain good until revoked (or at least for a reasonable period).

The LOI is signed and provides a place for the Seller to sign, signifying acceptance. Two exhibits are attached: Exhibit A for the Legal Description (not provided here) and Exhibit B, which is a comprehensive 21-point list of due-diligence items to be provided by the seller, including any construction documents in seller's possession or reasonably obtainable by seller; most current title policy and survey;

environmental Phase 1 report; last two years' operating statements; any market analysis, appraisals, engineering, environmental and other studies that seller possesses; a schedule or inventory of personal property owned or leased and used in connection with the operation of the property; tangible and intangible property list; all capital improvements made during seller's ownership; current rent roll and standard lease; copies of utility and tax bills; copies of all service, employment, or other agreements; copies of all insurance contracts (including list of recent casualty losses), licenses, permits, maps, certificates of occupancy, building inspection approvals, covenants and restrictions; copy of current payroll; copies of the records of the security deposit trust account; owner's organizational documents; list of any current, pending, or threatened litigation or arbitration; plus all documentation concerning terms of the negotiated escrow agreement.

This is very professional Letter of Intent.

Exhibit C-6 is for $21,000,000, or $135,950 per unit, and calls for an impressive deposit of $1,000,000, half "under the P&S" (Purchase and Sale) and half at the end of due diligence The due-diligence period requested is "twenty one (21) *business* days" (emphasis added). The importance of careful reading of LOIs and other documents cannot be overemphasized. Most of the LOIs received implicitly refer to calendar days (by not making a specific reference to business days). In my first reading, I read the due-diligence period as being calendar days in part because when the number of days is denominated in sevens, it usually refers to calendar days, and I assumed 21 days meant three calendar weeks. It was only when I read that the closing period was 30 *business* days that I went back and double-checked the due-diligence period. Of course, 21 business days is slightly more than four weeks or the virtual equivalent of 30 calendar days.

You can build trust with the other party by clearly drawing attention to anything unusual or nonstandard about your terms or contract.

A business day generally is any day the Federal Reserve is open. If the expiration of a calendar day falls on a weekend or holiday, the general rule is that the date advances to the next business day. A calendar day generally ends at midnight, a business day generally ends at 5 PM. in the time zone of the jurisdiction under which it is stated the contract is to be interpreted; failing any specificity on the point, then the time zone of the property itself is the determiner. Case law and statutes vary. These are only guidelines and this text is not intended to be legal advice. Remember, obtain private legal counsel.

It should be further noted that under this LOI, the due-diligence period does not run until the delivery of the specified due-diligence documents. A reasonable position and a well drawn PSA will stipulate that (1) delivery of "*materially* all documents" will trigger the start of the due-diligence clock to prevent the time frame from being drawn out untenably over minor issues, and (2) the purchaser must acknowledge in writing receipt of said documents and the start of the due-diligence period. Having the due-diligence period start upon a disputable date is a sure recipe for disagreements down the road.

Closing is to occur 30 *business* days (i.e., 6 weeks) after the end of due diligence, and the purchaser may obtain an additional 30 *business* days extension by placing an additional $500,000 up as a nonrefundable deposit. A potential three-month period from the end of due diligence to closing is a bit daunting, and the desire for so long a period of time raises the issue of why. Is the purchaser unable to close with in-house equity and must shop for partners? Or is he merely cautious? The longer a deal hangs fire, the more likely something, somewhere, will go off track. Nonrefundable deposits totaling $1.5 million can be sweet compensation, but it is only 7% of the value of the deal, which is not much consolation if you miss the top of a market cycle and suffer a 10% or 15% drop in short-term value, or if you were counting on the liquidity to move forward in other areas.

Furthermore, to get to the end of the closing period, the seller will have invested enormous amounts of top-level executive and support staff time and energy, human capital that represents a very real opportunity cost in terms of other potential deals not pursued. In addition, substantial billings will have been incurred by attorneys, accountants, and other professionals in preparation for closing. In short, forfeited deposits are far from a windfall.

The LOI provides that "after the expiration of the Due Diligence Period, Seller will not enter into, modify or terminate any lease without first obtaining the Purchaser's approval." A well-drawn PSA will often have a clause to the effect that the seller shall continue to lease, maintain, and operate the property in a normal business manner consistent with past practices, as no purchaser wants to walk into sweetheart leases or a wave of concessions, deferred maintenance, unturned units, or excessive vacancies that have occurred between the end of due diligence and closing. At the same time, sellers do not like to have their hands tied. Note that a literal reading of the language prohibits the Seller from entering into *any* lease without the purchaser's approval and gives no standards by which the purchaser is required to grant said approval. Many condo converters *want* vacancies to speed the selling process. On the other hand, increased vacancies prior to closing represent a loss of income to the seller and an even greater potential loss of income if closing does not occur.

Because of a confidentiality clause in this LOI, the exhibit C-6 has been edited. Since the seller did not agree to the terms of the LOI, the confidentiality clause is not binding, but my aim is to further obscure the identity of the bidder as a matter of professional courtesy.

Exhibit C-7 is another LOI at $21,000,000, providing for $200,000 at the signing of a "Definitive Agreement" (a PSA), which shall be increased to $400,000 at the end of the "Study Period." The LOI calls for entering into a binding contract within 10 days of the acceptance of the LOI and further provides that the LOI is "terminable at will by either party and is not binding except that for ten (10) days after the date hereof, Owner will not sell, offer for sale or negotiate with respect to the sale of the Property with parties other than the Buyer unless Owner has first terminated this Letter of Intent."

LOIs often will give the seller an idea of the buyer's "hot buttons," issues that are important to him and that he may negotiate strongly to have included in the PSA. In this case, this buyer is one of the few to touch on the issue of disclosure in the LOI. The LOI calls for the seller to disclose, in the *Definitive Agreement*,

"Owner's knowledge about the structural or mechanical defects and petroleum products, underground storage tanks, asbestos or hazardous materials at or affecting the Property. Owner will also disclose any known issues related to zoning and code compliance, historic designation, condemnation and pending or threatened legal proceedings. Claims of misrepresentation must be raised within one year after Closing." The extent of the duty of disclosure, if any, is a highly-negotiated area, and PSAs can devote pages and pages to the issue.

Sellers prefer to sell "as is, where is" with no representations or warrants. Buyers would love to have complete disclosure and fully-guaranteed representations and warranties. Sellers are concerned about spurious litigation, whereas buyers take the view that no one knows more about the property than the seller and due diligence should not be a game of hide and seek.

One major issue is "whose knowledge" is being repped and warranted? In the extreme, buyers can take the position that it includes not only the personal knowledge of the seller but of all his agents and employees (current, former, even vendors?), as well. And if the seller is a legal entity, does it include just the knowledge of the chief executive? What about the board of directors, officers, all employees? Knowledge they currently remember or knowledge they once had and have since forgotten? Knowledge they do not have but should have known? It is easy to see how complex it can quickly get, and such ambiguities provide fertile ground for legal fees. As a general rule, sellers refuse to accept a duty to disclose and expressly provide for no or very limited representations and warranties beyond title.

An area not often addressed if reps and warrants are granted and create post-closing liability, is what stands behind those guarantees. If the real estate itself is sold (versus the legal entity owning the real estate), and the legal entity owns no other assets, and the proceeds of the sale are distributed to the owners of the legal entity (such as shareholders or LLC members), then the legal entity that made the representations and warrants no longer has any assets to back them up. Absent intentional fraud on the part of the owners themselves, based upon their personal knowledge and actions (very unlikely and equally difficult to prove), it would virtually be impossible to pierce the corporate veil.

This LOI also includes another term not present in many others that addresses the operation of the property during the Study Period ("operate as has been operated heretofore"), and at the end of the Study Period, "the Owner will cooperate with Buyer in allowing the Buyer a right of first refusal to lease any apartment units that come available for lease during the Study Period." Here the buyer is trying to get a leg up on the condo sales process by creating an inventory of apartments immediately available. Such attention to detail speaks of an experienced and knowledgeable professional.

Exhibit C-8 is a short LOI with a low $19,000,000, or $113,095 per unit price, and a low $100,000 earnest money deposit, with no call for an additional deposit after the Inspection Period. Inspection period and close period are 30/30.

Exhibit C-9 shows a two-page LOI for an even lower $18,480,000 or $110,000 per unit, with a $100,000 deposit upon "contract execution" and a $400,000 additional deposit at the end of the due-diligence period. A 30-day due-diligence period is called for, running from execution of the contract, and a 60-day closing period is suggested. The agreement calls for the purchaser to deliver a PSA to the seller within five business days of mutual execution of the LOI and complete execution of the PSA to occur within 15 business days of the same date.

The LOI language also states that the "Seller shall not offer the Property for sale to, or negotiate with anyone other than the Purchaser until such time that the due diligence and subsequent PSA preparation period has been completed." The LOI is signed and explicitly provides that it is nonbinding and that the LOI shall expire if not signed and returned within 10 days.

This is another very professional LOI, especially given its brevity.

A final LOI of $16,531,200, or $98,400 per unit, also was received but it is not reproduced here. It called for a 45-day due-diligence period and a 30-day close, and provided for an initial $25,000 earnest money deposit with an additional $75,000 to follow. Even if the price were not far out of the running, the low earnest money offered indicated the possibility that the bidder either was not serious, was undercapitalized, or was an infrequent maker of deals of this size. Note also that the price offered was below seller's cost structure.

Simplified Pro Forma

Figure 12-6 is a highly simplified pro forma for a condominium conversion based on the sales price of $25,000,000 or $148,810 per unit for The Gables. While I am not privy to the purchaser's internal financial statements nor their cost structure, the following represents my estimates and can serve as a rough guide. The pro forma uses a range of three different potential sales prices—*conservative, middle of the road*, and *home run*—to convey the magnitude of uncertainty and potential returns.

Interestingly, built into the clubhouse building are a complete two-bedroom unit and a complete three-bedroom unit. Both are attractive poolside units that should command a premium price. Intended as easy-to-show model units for the rental community, they are included in the unit counts.

Setting the Sale Prices

Remember that all units come with an attached garage, which is not included in the square-footage given (i.e., heated and cooled only), and property amenities include a pool and hot tub, tennis courts, guardhouse, and clubhouse.

For the 32 one bedrooms ($929 per month rental value, 790 square feet), the potential prices range from $119,000 to $149,000, or from $152 per square foot to $189 per square foot.

For the 79 two bedrooms ($1,089 per month rental value, 1,131 square feet), the potential prices range from $179,900 to $215,000, or from $159 per square foot to $190 per square foot.

For the 59 three bedrooms ($1,299 per month rental value, 1,629 square feet), the potential prices range from $229,900 to $265,000, or from $141 per square foot to $165 per square foot.

SAMPLE CONDO CONVERSION PRO FORMA

Purchase Price: 168 units	$25,000,000		
Marketing and Carrying Costs @ $20,000/unit	$3,360,000		
	$28,360,000		
Senior Mortage @ 85% of Cost, LIBOR + 300 bp	($24,106,000)		
Mezzanine Debt @ 95% of Cost @ 18%	($2,836,000)		
Required Equity	$1,418,000		

	Conservative	Middle	Home run
Potential Sales Price			
One Bedrooms	$119,900	$135,000	$149,000
Price per Sq Ft	$152	$171	$189
Two Bedrooms	$179,900	$195,000	$215,000
Price per Sq Ft	$159	$172	$190
Three Bedrooms	$229,900	$249,000	$269,000
Price per Sq Ft	$141	$153	$165
Potential Sales Proceeds			
One Bedrooms	$3,836,800	$4,320,000	$4,768,000
Two Bedrooms	$14,212,100	$15,405,000	$16,985,000
Three Bedrooms	$13,564,100	$14,691,000	$15,871,000
Total Gross Sales Proceeds	$31,613,000	$34,416,000	$37,624,000
Less 6% Sales Commission	($1,896,780)	($2,064,960)	($2,257,440)
Purchase Price	($28,360,000)	($28,360,000)	($28,360,000)
Potential Profit	$1,356,220	$3,991,040	$7,006,560
Mezzanine Debt (1 yr @ 75% av. outstanding balance, 3% fees, closing costs)	($467,940)	($467,940)	($467,940)
	$888,280	$3,523,100	$6,538,620
Return on Required Equity	63%	248%	461%
Potential Net Profit per Unit	$5,287	$20,971	$38,920

FIG. 12-6 Sample condo-conversion pro forma.

The converter's *initial* offering to the *current residents* was:

1-bedroom units from $139,900 to $142,900, or $177 to $181 per square foot (variances location dependent)

2-bedroom units from $188,900 to $191,400, or $167 to $169 per square foot (again, location dependent)

3-bedroom units at $262,900 or $161 per square foot

Current residents who wished to purchase their units "as is," going to contract immediately using a preferred lender, were offered a $5,000 discount (later advertisements mentioned as much as a $10,000 discount). The preferred lender was offering 100% financing with a first and second mortgage at 6.5% to "qualified purchasers."

Six percent price increases for sale to the *public* were anticipated at:

1-bedroom units from $148,294 to $151,474, or $188 to $192 per square foot

2-bedroom units from $200,234 to $202,884, or $177 to $180 per square foot

3-bedroom units at $278,674 or $171 per square foot

The one bedrooms sold well, the two bedrooms so-so, and the three bedrooms required a meaningful price adjustment. This is an interesting variance in market acceptance, since the price per square foot was highest on the one bedroom units. Presumably, the lesson is that absolute price can be as important as per square foot pricing.

It is not the least unusual for a converter (or anyone else) to vary pricing depending on market response. Subsequent marketing literature stated that the units were offered at:

1-bedroom units from $156,400 to $159,400

2-bedroom units from $188,400 to $196,900

3-bedroom units from $234,900 to $249,900

Note that the one bedroom units' new pricing reflects a smart upward adjustment, the two bedrooms' a very modest reduction, and the three bedrooms' new pricing is a 10% to 12% reduction. See Exhibit C-10 for a January 2007 newspaper article on The Gables.

Acquisition Costs, Fix-Up Costs, Carrying Costs

The cost of a condominium conversion is much more than just the purchase price of the community. Acquisition costs, including due-diligence costs, loan costs, survey, legal, environmental, and other closing costs can be substantial.

If a community is older and in need of repairs or sprucing up, or it needs additions or modifications to be successfully marketed, there can be meaningful hard renovation costs in addition to normal soft costs.

There also may be meaningful carrying costs during the transition from a rental community to a fully-sold condominium. Even if efforts are made to maximize revenue from the operation of the community as an ongoing rental during the transition period and to perfectly match lease terminations with new sales, the primary purpose of the venture is condominium sales and a good inventory of different floor plans in different locations must be maintained in order to attract and satisfy buyers.

It is a rare condominium converter whose community breaks even during the condominium conversion phase, especially given that a significant premium is generally paid for the community over its investment value and the converter often may be using relatively expensive short-term high loan-to-value (or cost) debt. The intelligent investor attempting a condominium conversion would do well to plan for considerable carrying costs. Most condo converters are quite rightly focused on selling units as rapidly as possible at the highest possible market price, not managing an apartment community efficiently.

Indeed, some communities undergo such heavy renovation that they are completely depleted of income-producing occupants—i.e., renters. Of course, this results in significant carrying costs as the meter continues to run on such expenses as interest on the acquisition loan, property taxes, and insurance. On the plus side, as condominium units are sold, owners become responsible for property taxes, and the monthly condominium maintenance fees help pay for operating costs.

Marketing, Sales Commissions, Overhead

Marketing costs and sales commissions tend to be major costs. Often, the condominium converter or his agent acts as listing broker, leaving a typical 2.5% to 3% commission for the selling broker. Even when the converter is the broker, there are substantial on-site costs and the converter must compensate his own sales and support people and pay for marketing, so the benefit is more one of control than of cost savings. For the purposes of simplicity, a 6% sales commission was used across the board.

Furthermore, for ease of calculation, combined marketing and carrying costs were assumed to be $20,000 a unit.

Closing Costs

The condominium documents for the Gables state, "at time of closing, each purchaser shall reimburse the developer a closing fee in the amount of 1.75% of the total purchase price of the unit to defray developer's cost of closing." As a result, no closing costs were included in cost estimates.

The condominium documents also state:

> At closing each purchaser shall contribute a sum equal to two months assessment toward the working capital fund to be used by the Condominium Association to defray common expenses as may be permitted by law. Restrictions on short-term leasing: limited to leases of 3 months or more and not more than twice a year. Animals limited to not more than two household pets. Use of unit limited to single-family residential use; children may not play on or about the condominium property.

Finance Options

Figure 12-7 shows a possible financial structure suggested by CBRE in conjunction with RJ Melody. The capital stack (structure) involves using a senior (first) mortgage conversion loan combined with mezzanine financing.

Senior (First) Mortgage

- *Loan to Cost:* The senior mortgage would be 80%–85% of cost. Cost would include the acquisition price plus any capital improvement budget, soft costs, and marketing expense; this is a generous, inclusive definition of cost. Realize that this dollar amount may come close to and perhaps even exceed the actual purchase price of the community; it could represent 100% financing of the purchase price. Soft costs might include an interest and/or carrying cost

FINANCE OPTIONS

Financing option available for the purchase and condo conversion of The Gables Apartments in Gainesville, Florida through L.J. Melody Capital Markets:

POTENTIAL STRUCTURE OF 1ST MORTGAGE (CONVERSION LOAN) AND MEZZANINE FINANCE

Senior (1st) Mortgage

LOAN TO COST: 80-85% conversion loan (cost includes acquisition price plus capital improvement budget, soft costs and sales and marketing expense)

PRICING: 325-375 basis points (over 30 day libor); Interest Only

RECOURSE: Non Recourse (except for standard carve-outs)

TERM: 18-36 months

PRESALE REQUIREMENT: 20-30% of units to be pre-sold at which time a mass closing will occur; thereafter units may be closed on a one off basis

LOAN REPAYMENT: 80-100% of sales proceeds (minus cost of sales) will go to pay-down of the loan (negotiable)

FEES: 1% of loan amount to lender at loan closing; .05%-1% of loan amount exit fee to lender at payoff of loan (negotiable)

LOAN TO VALUE: Not to exceed 65% of the total sell out as condominiums

Mezzanine Finance

LOAN TO COST: Non participating equity (mezzanine finance) available up to 80-85% of the equity gap. Total loan capitalization up to 95 - 98% of cost. Sponsor does not have to share the profits with a partner as the mezzanine finance acts simply as an additional loan and lender collects their yield.

PRICING: 16 – 22% (interest only)

RECOURSE: Non Recourse (except for standard carve-outs)

FEES: 1.5% - 2% of loan amount to lender at loan closing

Full or partial Recourse options also available for a lower cost of capital (Call for details)

CONTACT FOR MORE DETAILS

J. Mark Gibson | Vice President
CBRE | L.J. Melody & Company
225 Water Street, Suite 110 | Jacksonville, FL 32202
T 904.633.2606 | F 904.791.8953 | C 904.477.3841
mark.gibson@ljmelody.com | www.ljmelody.com

FIG. 12-7 Finance options. (L.J. Melody & Company)

reserve. Such amounts, along with any capital improvement budget, may not be fully disbursed at closing. Instead, such funds are more typically available to be drawn down as costs are actually incurred. The interest rate (see below) on the loan will reflect the generous loan terms.

- *Loan to Value:* Not to exceed 65% of the total projected sellout as a condominium. This 65% loan-to-*value* ratio limitation would not be a constraint on the 85% loan-to-*cost* ratio at the home run valuation, but it would be at the lower valuations, middle and conservative.

- *Pricing would be 325 to 375 basis points (3.25% to 3.75%) over 30-day LIBOR, interest only:* Current 30-day LIBOR is 5.75%, yielding a current interest rate of 9.25%, using the midpoint of the given range. A typical construction loan would be priced at 175 to 225 basis points over LIBOR, so this pricing is 150 basis points over construction lending, making it an attractive loan for the lender. The inclusive definition of costs allows a borrower to perhaps obtain 20% more funds, or $5,000,000, than would be available under a standard loan on the rental community as a straight income-producing investment asset. If the loan were $25,000,000, the extra 1.5% of interest would represent a total annual interest carrying cost of $375,000. If the sole or main reason for the extra 1.5% of interest charge was the higher loan-to-cost ratio (the extra $5,000,000), then it can be said that the interest cost of the extra $5 million is 16.75%: $375,000/$5,000,000 = 7.5% + 9.25% = 16.75%. Expensive debt, but reasonably-priced equity, which is what it really is.

- *Nonrecourse except for standard carve-outs:* The term "standard carve-outs" is a bit on a misnomer. Carve-outs are vigorously negotiated by sophisticated borrowers. A pure nonrecourse loan involves no personal liability to the borrower or to any guarantor or guarantor entity. Actually, a pure nonrecourse entity needs no guarantor. What would be the point? What lenders like to call nonrecourse usually involves extensive carve-outs to nonrecourse that end up creating substantial liability, especially for the unwary borrower or guarantor. Lenders like to call carve-outs "bad-boy" provisions, with the explicit implication that they kick in only if the borrower or guarantor has done some intentionally and willfully bad act. The truth is that most carve-outs are far more extensive in their potential impact.

    A list of common carve-outs: Bankruptcy, any environmental issues, failure to pay rent into the proper account, misapplication of rent, failure to pay taxes, insurance or make repairs, failure to insure or fully insure against all required risks, contesting lender's enforcement of rights, misapplication of insurance or condemnation proceedings, unauthorized transfer of the property, misapplication of security deposits, violation of single-asset entity provisions, wrongful removal or destruction of property or intentional waste, voluntary liens, misrepresentation in the application or reporting requirements. Many carve-outs are worded so as to include acts or failures to act of the borrower, guarantor, *and* related entities.

Obviously, the list is extensive and includes many acts about which the borrower-guarantor may not have personal knowledge or may only inadvertently trigger. It is a rare borrower-guarantor who wakes up one morning and decides: "What a beautiful day! I think I will go violate my loan covenants and trigger personal liability." More commonly, something was overlooked, an employee forgot to renew an insurance policy, an accountant misapplied funds, or an agent committed fraud for which the borrower-guarantor must answer.

First, it is important to remember that the *environmental* liability carve-out is usually *strict liability*. No act or failure to act is required upon the part of the borrower-guarantor. It is not a requirement that the borrower-guarantor to have done a bad thing or even a negligent thing. It is enough that environmental liability exists. Under most carve-outs, if environmental liability exists, the borrower-guarantor is personally liable. Period. End of story. No debate. It may have come from the prior owner or an adjacent property owner or fallen from the sky. It makes no difference. You may obtain environmental insurance, but unless the lender agrees in advance, you are still liable if the insurance company finds a way to deny coverage, or goes out of business, or delays payment. The lender will look directly to the borrower-guarantor for payment. The fact that the borrower-guarantor may have claims for reimbursement or compensation by others is of no interest to the lender. The lender wants to be paid by the borrower-guarantor and will not wait—and does not have to wait—until the borrower-guarantor is paid by an insurance company or successfully pursues a claim against a third party.

Second, it is important to realize that in most carve-out provisions, *there need not be any causal link between the carve-out violated and the economic loss* for which the lender wishes to be paid. The loan may be nonperforming for purely economic reasons—e.g., the condominium market collapsed—but if the lender can find ANY carve-out that the borrower-guarantor might have violated, then the lender can claim liability on the part of the borrower-guarantor regardless of the lack of a link between the alleged violation and the economic loss.

Third, generally no required standard of proof is articulated in the loan documents or guarantee for the lender to make an allegation that a carve-out has been violated. The standard of proof required to allege a carve-out violation is certainly not beyond a reasonable doubt (criminal) or clear predominance of the evidence (civil). Presumably, it is enough that the lender can make a mere prima facie (a presumption of fact) case against the borrower-guarantor to create liability. That is an exceedingly low standard to trigger such potentially overwhelming financial consequences.

Fourth, it is vital to understand that by the time carve-outs are in play, things are bad and unfortunate, regrettable things have occurred, if only inadvertently. There is generally plenty of blame to go around. Relationships are strained at best, trust is generally nonexistent, and the nice, friendly folks who sold you on giving the lender your business are long gone. Indeed, your loan has probably been sold and is being administered by a servicer who has no interest in your well-being whatsoever. The servicer's sole and exclusive concern is its fiduciary duty to its bondholders. Or, even worse, your loan may have been sold at a steep discount to a hedge fund that has turned your loan over to a big-city lawyer anxious get a whopping bonus and to impress her new multibillion dollar client with how well she can squeeze dollars out of the borrower-guarantor. In such circumstances, it is not inconceivable that a violation of carve-outs may be alleged simply as a negotiating tactic. It may be completely untrue, but to defend yourself will cost huge legal fees and consume years worth of your time and energy. And the ultimate Catch-22 may be that contesting a lender's enforcement of its rights may be a carve-out violation in and of itself, and you will certainly be liable for the lender's legal fees, quite possibly even if you win.

Hedge Funds Play Hardball with Firms Filing Late Financials

By Peter Lattman and Karen Richardson
The Wall Street Journal, August 29, 2006, Page A1
Hedge funds looking to extract bigger returns from the companies they invest in have come up with a new game of hardball: Fail to file a quarterly report on time, and they'll try to make you pay off your debt immediately.

Traditionally, when companies missed a deadline for filing their financial statements, bondholders would look the other way and let the company work out the kinks—even though, technically, the company was in default and bondholders could demand repayment.

But return-hungry hedge funds and other big investors have found an opportunity to profit, thanks in part to a spreading scandal over the practice at many companies of backdating stock options that were granted to employees as a form of compensation. That practice has come under scrutiny by regulators, and dozens of companies are having to review whether their earnings statements accurately accounted for such compensation—which, in some cases, is delaying their filings.

In one of the largest recent examples, a group of UnitedHealth Group Inc. bondholders last week formally warned the Minnetonka, Minn., insurance company in a letter dated Aug. 25 that it is in default for failing to file its second-quarter report with the U.S. Securities and Exchange Commission. If it doesn't file the paperwork within 60 days, the group says it has the right to declare the bonds due and payable immediately.

The amount UnitedHealth would have to pay: $800 million, not otherwise due until 2036. Investors would stand to make a quick profit because UnitedHealth's bonds are trading below face value; if the company is forced to pay full value to redeem them, the bondholders who bought at below par would make a tidy return on their investment.

Other companies that have been targeted by bondholders for missing their filing deadlines include department store Saks Inc., truck and engine maker Navistar International Corp. and software maker Mercury Interactive Corp.

UnitedHealth's filing schedule was tripped up after the company was caught in the continuing options-backdating scandal in which executives at a number of companies allegedly doctored the prices of stock options to boost the pay packages of insiders. In May, UnitedHealth said it was the subject of a criminal probe by federal prosecutors in the U.S. related to the company's past stock-option grants. And on Aug. 10, it said it was delaying its filing with the SEC, citing the investigation.

"The company believes it is not in default and intends to defend itself vigorously," Mark Lindsay, a spokesman for UnitedHealth, said yesterday.

The backdating controversy, which so far has spread to more than 120 companies, has led to a record number of late filings. Some 138 companies with market values of more than $75 million each filed late reports for the second quarter, according to research firm Glass, Lewis & Co. Of those, 48 blamed investigations related to stock-options practices.

More bondholders are declaring technical default and either demanding immediate payment of debt or extracting substantial fees from the issuers in exchange for an extension of their default deadlines. Lawyers say acceleration of payment in one group of bonds could lead to a cross-default—the forced acceleration of all of a company's bonds—putting some cash-strapped companies at risk of bankruptcy.

"There used to be a kind of brotherhood of bond investors, where you didn't want to be the guy who turned the kid in to the teacher because he wasn't wearing a shirt with a collar," said Kirk Davenport, a partner at law firm Latham & Watkins in New York. But now, it is "outweighed by the desire to make a lot of money."

Andrew Redleaf is chief executive at Whitebox Advisors LLC, a $1.6 billion group of hedge funds that use the technical-default tactic. "Bondholders used to be extremely lazy," says Mr. Redleaf, whose firm holds bonds for both UnitedHealth and BearingPoint Inc., a consulting firm that also missed its filing deadline. "Part and parcel of what investors do is assert their rights, whether they're shareholders, bondholders or otherwise."

In the bond business, a standard indenture—a detailed contract between an issuer and investors—requires a company to file quarterly and annual reports with bondholders at or around the same time it files with the SEC. A company usually has 60 days to meet its missed filing deadline. Since a late filing is a technical default, so-called vulture investors, who typically buy bonds that trade at a discount to their face values, see a chance for a fast profit if a company can be forced to redeem at full value. The option-backdating probe, which has knocked down the bond prices of many of the companies being investigated, has provided a fresh opening for these investors.

Hedge funds, or private investment partnerships that cater to the wealthy investors, are fast becoming the dominant players in distressed-debt markets. But as they have proliferated, they are facing increasing pressure to generate outsized returns amid a sideways market.

With the number of delinquent filers on the rise, the trend could heat up. At least 25 companies during the past 18 months had their bonds accelerated in this way, or were forced to pay multimillion-dollar fees to bondholders, according to research by Merrill Lynch.

In a worst-case scenario for the companies being targeted, as part of the process for filing for Chapter 11 bankruptcy-court protection, bondholders and other lenders could end up taking over ownership, says Dan Arbess, head of Xerion Partners, a hedge fund that invests in distressed assets.

Vitesse Semiconductor Corp., for example, is in such a precarious position, analysts say. The company, which makes networking and telecommunications equipment, has less than $30 million in cash. That is far less than the $96.7 million payment that on Aug. 21 bondholders demanded to be accelerated.

The Camarillo, Calif., Vitesse, whose shares have fallen to about 85 cents from more than $3 in March, lapsed into technical default after failing to file its financial statements on time. Once a high-flyer, with a share price of more than $100 in 2000, it's been fending off activist shareholders who want to put it up for sale. Now, analysts are concerned that the company is in jeopardy from bondholder demands.

"We believe Vitesse does not have the financial strength to make these payments," and it could suffer a serious cash crunch "if this dispute is not resolved," says Allan Mishan, an analyst at investment bank CIBC World Markets.

Chris Gardner, Vitesse's chief executive officer, was quoted in a prepared statement as saying that the bond investors' demands "have exceeded anything that we would consider reasonable under the circumstances." Vitesse, which is currently in negotiations with bondholders, didn't return calls for comment.

In order to avoid default, some delinquent issuers have offered concessions to bondholders in the form of extra fees or better terms on the bonds. These include retailer Saks, Connetics Corp. and Bausch & Lomb Inc., according to the companies themselves.

The concessions can be costly. In July, software maker Mercury Interactive, one of the first companies caught up in the options investigation, said in a July 3 regulatory filing that because it failed to file financial results, Mercury had to pay $7.1 million to creditors, and grant them an option to redeem their notes at a premium, to ward off default. It may have to pay as much as an extra $40.2 million if creditors exercise the option.

Other companies that have missed filing deadlines as a result of backdating issues have begun negotiating with their bondholders. On Aug. 21, Sanmina-SCI Corp. asked its bondholders for an extension, offering financial concessions of $12.5 million. On Aug. 11, Amkor Technology Inc. announced that trustees for a group of its bondholders warned that if the company didn't meet an upcoming filing deadline it would be considered in default of its bond indenture.

In January, a trustee representing BearingPoint bondholders filed a lawsuit against the consulting firm claiming that it was in default on two of its bond issues because it missed an SEC filing deadline due to accounting issues. BearingPoint disputed the claim and said in a statement: "This is a cynical attempt to extract leverage, and we intend to contest this every step of the way."

Jeff Ross of Anthony, Ostlund & Baer, the lawyer representing the trustee against BearingPoint, says bond funds have a legal obligation to their own investors to enforce their rights. "Someone lending hundreds of millions of dollars to companies is entitled to accurate financial information."

By now the reader should understand that there is potentially more liability than not in carve-outs and the phrase "nonrecourse" should not be taken literally. Indeed, it might be more appropriate to call them recourse loans with some nonrecourse carve-outs. Carve-out provisions have not yet been extensively tested via a significant real estate downturn. The legal system has yet to produce extensive case law on point, and it remains to be seen how ethically lenders will behave when there are real dollars at stake.

Caveat: As a developer or promoter or converter, do not sign disproportionately on the carve-outs. If you are the 10% or 20% minority "human" partner doing business with an entity equity partner, do not sign for *all* the carve-outs, by which you would be assuming carve-out liability for 100% of the loan. The ratio of liability to return should always be balanced. Majority equity partners prefer to have the active-managing, sweat-minority partner sign on the carve-outs under the theory that carve-outs are only for bad acts, and it would be the minority partner's bad acts that would trigger the carve-outs, as it is the minority partner who has actual knowledge and control over the situation. Unfortunately, the actual situation is much more complex and nuanced. Equity partners often take the position that assuming disproportionate liability for the minority partner goes hand in hand with the possibility of receiving disproportionate return. My response is that the carve-outs represent a very real and current contingent liability and the disproportionate return is a mere future possibility.

You make your money on the deals that you do, you keep your money on the deals you don't do. All returns are not equal, so always evaluate potential returns on a risk-adjusted basis. A 12% low-risk return is probably a much better investment than a high-risk 30% return. If you keep bellying up to the high-risk table, sooner or later the wheel turns against you. It may take years, but sooner or later you roll snake eyes. And if you have been pushing all your chips back onto the table time after time, you lose it all. It is easy to say that you will be disciplined enough to pull some back, to take a meaningful amount off the table, but the very risk-taking personality that is a component of every developer, the very personality that makes a certain developer go for high-risk projects, the very personality that makes many developers always want to push the edge of the envelope and build the biggest, best, highest-profile development that their dreams and resources can conceivably support, mitigate against being disciplined enough to take sufficient protective measures to guard against the inevitable arrival of the downside.

While a strong balance sheet is always the ultimate preference, lenders often like to have an individual entrepreneur type on the carve-outs, because frequently the best salvation of a project lies in having a savvy, high-energy individual take direct control of the helm and steer the property to safety.

A classic example of an entrepreneur steering a troubled project to a safe harbor occurred in 1991 when Warren Buffet become chief executive officer of the major investment bank Salomon Brothers for nine months, following irregularities in Treasuries trading. The willingness of Warren Buffet, the quintessential, high-level strategic player, to take on day-to-day operational responsibilities was an incredible act of personal commitment (he had never before and has not since assumed operational responsibility for any significant investment) and a unique demonstration of faith that sent a tremendously strong signal to the markets, allowing Salomon Brothers the breathing room to recover.

- *Term of the loan would be 18 to 36 months:* If a condominium conversion has not sold out in this time frame, there most likely are big problems.
- *Presale requirement:* Twenty to thirty percent of units to be presold prior to mass closing, closings thereafter on a one-off basis. It is important to establish the viability of the market and the project before starting closings. The nightmare is to sell 5% or 10% of a conversion and then be unable to move the balance. Tremendous value destruction occurs in that circumstance, because the community is then neither beast nor fowl, rather a dysfunctional hybrid. It cannot be resold as a normal, income-producing rental community investment, as no owner wants to deal with a dozen or so minor "partners" (the unit owners). Nothing is more difficult to manage than something half condo, half rental.
- *Loan repayment and release clause:* Eighty to one hundred percent of the sales proceeds (less costs of sales) are intended to pay down the loan. The lender knows that the only meaningful source of income to pay off the loan is the sale of condominiums. Each sale requires a release from the underlying master mortgage. Typically, some flexibility exists in this clause, particularly after the mass closing and as the loan-to-value ratio drops. The 325 to 375 basis points spread attached to this financing is a profitable, desirable loan especially when performing well with solid underlying financials. Once the high-risk portion of the loan has been paid, the financing entity would be in no particular hurry to lose this lucrative revenue stream.
- *Fees:* One percent of the loan amount to the lender at loan closing, exit fee to the lender of .05% to 1% of the loan amount at payoff. The lender wishes to receive fees both entering and exiting the loan.

Mezzanine Financing

- *Loan to cost:* Nonparticipating equity available for up to 80% to 85% of the equity gap, or the difference between the required cash to do the deal and the first level of debt, which is the senior (or first) mortgage. Total of first and second loans is not to exceed 95% to 98% of cost. Converter is not required to share profits with the mezzanine lender, as the lender under this program is content to simply act as a provider of additional debt.

To illustrate, if this is a $31,000,000 deal with a $25,000,000 first mortgage, requiring $6,000,000 of equity, the converter can have as little as $600,000 to $1,500,000 (2%–5%) in the deal. Potentially the converter's equity could also include the contribution of some of his fees—but the thinner the equity, the less likely it would be permitted.

- *Pricing:* Sixteen to twenty-two percent, interest only. If the converter borrowed $5,000,000 at 20%, the annual carrying cost would be $1,000,000.
- *Recourse:* Nonrecourse except for standard carve-outs (see previous discussion on carve-outs).
- *Fees:* Loan amount to lender at closing is 1.5% to 2%. The fee on a $5,000,000 loan would be $75,000 to $100,000. While many third-party reports could be used from the senior mortgage, additional closing costs would no doubt arise, potentially including recording costs and the ever-present attorney's fees.

The pricing is stiff but certainly within market. If you do not have the money to do the deal on your own, such equity sources are quite welcome. If you do have the money, most would prefer to capture such rich returns themselves, saving the time and fees as well. While this particular source is structured as debt, it truly is more akin to preferred equity. Given the infinite permutations that can be created by the human mind, the line between debt and equity can at times be difficult to discern, as the gradations at the margin grow finer and finer.

Profitability

The key to profit in a condominium conversion is a fast sellout. Too long a sellout and your marketing and carrying costs begin to cut deeply into any potential profit. This can be particularly true if any expensive mezzanine debt is used or an equity partner with a double-digit preferred return exists. Long sellouts indicate a loss of momentum and potential buyers can take that as a sign that the project is not a premium one or properly priced, resulting in a possible death spiral from which it can be difficult to pull out. At the extreme, a too-long sellout results in the condominium converter's sales competing with resales from the original wave of sales.

Figure 12-6 calculates the total cost of $2,836,000 of mezzanine debt at 18% as $467,940 based upon a one-year sellout, 3% closing costs and fees, and an average outstanding balance over the year of 75%. The presumption is that 100% of the loan is outstanding during the first six months and then the mezzanine debt is paid off pro rata over the next six months.

The key to a fast sellout is proper pricing, responding to the marketplace, raising prices rapidly if sales are going well, quickly adding discounts and specials if sales lag. The potential profit in condominium conversions is meaningful and worthy of some risk taking. If a sellout is going slowly or the market is trending sideways or down, it is not unusual for a converter to "wholesale out" the 10 or 20 remaining units of a project, selling them at a steep discount to an entrepreneur who is willing to take the risk in return for 20% or more off the retail price. The entrepreneur is often local and generally has a lower cost structure than the converter, and frequently he will manage and market the units personally. The converter is happy to be able to cease paying for marketing efforts and on-site staff, and the converter's time, energy, and attention is now available for other transactions.

The given prices per floor plan yield potential gross sales proceeds for the entire Gables community ranging from $31,613,000 on the low side to $37,624,000 on the high side. Costs of a conversion tend to vary more with time than with unit sales price, so I implicitly assumed a one-year sellout and kept cost estimates on the optimistic side. As a result, potential profit projections range from $888,280 on the conservative side to in excess of $6.5 million on the home run side, providing potential returns on a fully-leveraged $1,418,000 hypothetical investment of from 63% to 460%, a most pleasing prospect for any investor.

Remember, The Gables is presented for illustration and educational purposes only, and I have no knowledge of the converter's actual equity investment, costs, or real return.

SUMMARY

The latest trend of condominium construction and condo conversion has shown how real estate continues to evolve and change, offering new and fascinating twists that impact the field of construction, financing, and development. A condominium is a type of joint ownership of real estate in which portions of the property are commonly owned and other portions are individually owned. This mix of ownership interests leads to a variety of legal requirements and selling conditions that set the condo industry apart from other property classes.

Hotel condominiums are an example of this complexity. The project must meet several SEC requirements under certain marketing circumstances and has several physical requirements that differ from a standard residential building.

For condo construction and conversions, speed to market is an important factor. Managing cash flows is essential, because holding costs can quickly rise from interest payments, marketing costs, and the loss of revenue from idle units. To minimize this exposure, it is important for the developer to have a significant level of presales and deposits. This money up front can help reduce the investor's equity commitment to the project.

The Gables case study illustrates the sale of a rental property for condominium conversion. The property was listed and marketed by a trusted commercial broker. Before any offers are received, the seller must prequalify the potential buyers to determine their transactional and underwriting qualifications. Although

9 LOIs (Letters of Intent) were received, each offer had unique aspects that affected the attractiveness of the proposed deal. Although the sale price is usually the most important factor, the seller must also consider the credibility and intentions of the buyer, as well as the possible legal outcomes given the contract language.

In converting rentals to condominium ownership, the investor must set a price that will achieve the optimal sales velocity. If sales are moving too quickly, a higher price may yield more profit. If sales are moving at a slower than expected pace, a reduction in price may be warranted. The investor must also consider acquisition costs, fix-up costs, carrying costs, marketing, sales commissions, and overhead in his pro forma analysis. If financing is required, there are numerous ways to structure it. One thing to remember with debt financing is the effect of carve-outs on nonrecourse loans. Under certain conditions, even those events beyond the control of the investor can lead to full recourse status.

KEY TERMS AND DEFINITIONS

Carve-outs: Contract clauses that "carve out" exceptions creating liability in what otherwise would be nonrecourse loans.

Condominium: A type of joint ownership of real estate in which portions of the property are commonly owned and other portions are individually owned.

Doctrine of freedom of contract: The principle that competent adults may contract for anything that is not expressly forbidden by statute or public policy.

Good faith: A legal term that stipulates fairness, but which can be very subjective.

LOI: Letter of Intent.

Hard money: Nonrefundable deposit.

Personal use: Days that a condo unit is used by the owner or a member of the owner's family, any other person who has an interest in the unit or a member of that person's family, or anyone using the unit at less than fair rental price.

PSA: Purchase and sale agreement.

Soft money: Refundable deposit that is put up as evidence of good faith and seriousness of intent.

Wholesale out: The act of selling the remaining units in a condominium at a significant discount.

KEY LEARNING POINTS

- Understand how condominiums differ from other real estate investments.
- Understand the legal and operational challenges of hotel condominiums.
- Explain the important steps and challenges of a condo conversion.
- Determine the importance of various clauses in a letter of intent.

QUESTIONS

1. In the United States, what is required prior to the condominium developer forecasting financial benefits to a buyer who may rent his condominium unit as part of a hotel?

2. Name two ways the speed-to-market advantages of condo conversions can be lost?

3. How are condo conversions usually taxed and why?

4. What is the impact of condo conversions on the rental apartment market? Explain.

5. What is a potential problem the project owner may face with "hard money"?

6. Why does a condo converter require a shorter due-diligence period than an income buyer?

7. What is a good rule of thumb for determining what is a business day?

8. What are some other condo-conversion costs, other than the purchase price of the community?

9. Why are carve-outs sometimes called "bad-boy" provisions by lenders?

10. When an environmental liability occurs, what is the effect on a nonrecourse loan?

11. What is the key to a fast sellout?

PART IV
Cash Forecasts and the Time Value of Money

This section is taken almost directly from the previous edition of *Construction Funding* by Courtland A. Collier and Don A. Halperin. These basic mathematical principles remain unchanged by time. As such, Nathan S. Collier, author of the current edition, chooses to allow the previous authors' work to speak for them.

13

How to Forecast Cash Needs During Construction

PLANNING EXPENDITURES

A well-managed company keeps its initial capital as intact as possible, and in fact tries to accumulate additional capital. This additional capital is leveraged and used to obtain more work and larger jobs, and thus earn more return. However, only a small percentage of total income can be added to company capital since most of the income is spent on payroll and other current expenses. It is essential to plan each job carefully to avoid borrowing from the company capital to meet short-term cash flow needs any more than is absolutely necessary. The same careful thought and planning must go into the expenditure of money as go into the planning and coordination of the actual work of construction, which involves the scheduling of personnel, materials, and specialty contractors. Thus, before each job starts, the prudent contractor forecasts just how much cash will be needed each month and determines how to obtain that money without utilizing any more company capital than is necessary.

BAR CHARTS

Tentative money draw schedules can be estimated before the job starts if enough time is set aside for planning. Most knowledgeable contractors make use of critical path method (CPM) diagrams to establish the length of the job and to speed up the process of construction. From a good CPM diagram it is not at all difficult to draw a *bar chart*. The actual drawing of the bar chart takes very little time, and the chart itself makes it easy to see at a glance just what percentage of each item on the draw schedule should be completed each month.

EXAMPLE OF A BAR CHART

Of course it is not necessary to formulate a CPM diagram and then reduce it to a bar chart, but this is a more accurate process than drawing a bar chart based on intuition or experience. In either case the final drawing will resemble Figure 13-1.

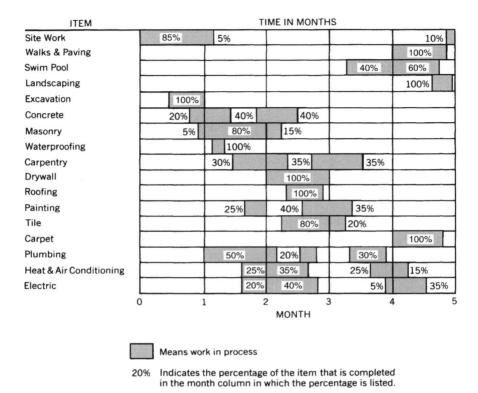

FIG. 13-1   Bar chart.

This example (Figure 13-1) is not complete and is given merely for purpose of illustration. To simplify and clarify the example, the construction time period has been cut down to 5 months. Notice that at the end of the first month all the excavation will have been completed, 85% of the site work will have been accomplished, and 20% of the concrete work will be finished; however, it is estimated that only 5% of the masonry will be in place, if all goes according to schedule.

COST PER MONTH

Estimated percentages of completion can be applied against dollar values to obtain a good idea of the amount of cash required during each month, as shown in Table 13-1. These are the amounts that will actually have been spent on the job. A similar estimate could be made for each month of the job. All of these several estimates would then be combined into a summary of totals, as shown at the bottom row of Table 13-1 and repeated in Table 13-2.

TABLE 13.1 List of Monthly Expenditures by Item for a $3.5 Million Project

	Expenditures Incurred Before Construction Starts 0	1	2	3	4	5	Total
	100%						
Land	700,000						$700,000
Closing, loan brokerage, tax during construction	*72%*	*28%*					
	77,393	30,097					107,490
Construction loan interest		*7%*	*13%*	*20%*	*27%*	*33%*	
		9,544	17,724	27,268	36,812	44,992	136,340
	22%	*18%*	*15%*	*15%*	*15%*	*15%*	
Overhead & bond	66,117	54,096	45,080	45,080	45,080	45,080	300,533
		85%	*5%*			*10%*	
Site work		101,046	5,944			11,888	118,878
						100%	
Walks & paving						74,317	74,317
					40%	*60%*	
Swim pool					13,630	20,446	34,076
						100%	
Landscaping						13,678	13,678
		100%					
Excavation		19,928					19,928
		20%	*40%*	*40%*			
Concrete		65,254	130,507	130,507			326,268
		5%	*80%*	*15%*			
Masonry		7,751	124,020	23,254			155,025
			100%				
Waterproofing			1,928				1,928
			30%	*35%*	*35%*		
Rough carpentry ⎫ Finish carpentry ⎬			77,555	90,481	90,480		⎰ 83, 130 ⎱ 175, 386
			30%	*35%*	*35%*		
Metalwork			896	1,047	1,047		2,990
				100%			
Drywall				136,485			136,485
				100%			
Roofing				62,893			62,893
				25%	*40%*	*35%*	
Painting				26,483	42,372	37,076	105,931
				80%	*20%*		
Tile				108,554	27,138		135,692

Continued

TABLE 13.1 (*Continued*)

	Expenditures Incurred Before Construction Starts 0	1	2	3	4	5	Total
Carpet					*100%* 94,861		94,861
Cabinets						*100%* 66,406	
Plumbing			*50%* 85,879	*20%* 34,352	*30%* 51,527		171,758
Heat & air conditioning			*25%* 53,602	*35%* 75,043	*25%* 53,602	*15%* 32,161	214,408
Electric			*20%* 46,067	*40%* 92,134	*5%* 11,517	*35%* 80,616	230,334
Miscellaneous		*20%* 3,874	*20%* 3,874	*20%* 3,874	*20%* 3,874	*20%* 3,874	19,369
Ranges & refrigerators						*100%* 66,960	66,960
Totals	843,510	291,590	619,559	873,344	466,644	460,417	3,555,064

TABLE 13.2   Estimated Summary of Monthly Expenditures for a $3.5 Million Project

Month	Monthly Value	Running Total
Before construction	$843,510	$ 843,510
1	291,590	1,135,100
2	619,559	1,754,659
3	873,344	2,628,003
4	466,644	3,094,647
5	460,417	3,555,064

PURPOSE OF BAR CHARTS

The purpose of the bar charts is to graphically display the anticipated percentages of completion of each item in the job for each month during the duration of the job. These percentages are applied against the dollar values of the items, so as to obtain an estimated total of the dollars required each month as the job progresses. Most of these dollars will come from the monthly draws. The rest will have to come from operating capital, or else the difference will have to be borrowed as front money at the beginning of the job, or as short-term loans as the job progresses.

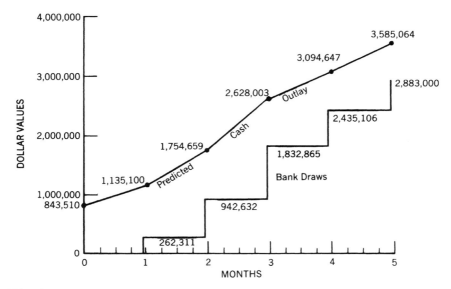

FIG. 13-2 S-curve. The time has been shortened to 5 months simply to make the explanation easier. The same principles apply if the job takes much longer.

The differences can best be seen if the two totals (actual cost vs. draws) are plotted on a graph, as shown in Figure 13-2.

S-CURVE

The graph has as an ordinate (vertical axis)—dollar values—and it has as an abscissa (horizontal axis)—the time in days, weeks, or, as shown here, months. When the predicted cash outlay is plotted on the graph, it will be a series of points. The first point will show the amount of money spent before construction starts, which would be $843,510 for this example, and will be placed above time zero. The prediction was that at the end of the first month of work $1,135,100 would have been spent, so that point is plotted, and so forth. When all six points of the predicted actual cost have been plotted in Figure 13-2, they can be connected either with straight lines or with a smooth curve. In either event, at this stage the shape of the drawing will look roughly like an elongated or tilted letter "S," and therefore is called the S-curve of cost versus time.

PLOTTING BANK DRAWS

The predicted bank draws can be plotted on the same graph. Each of these draws is based on an estimated draw schedule, which has been calculated using the schedule illustrated by the bar chart of Figure 13-1. The resulting monthly draw schedule is shown in Table 13-3 and illustrated graphically in Figure 13-2.

TABLE 13.3 List of Monthly *Draws* and Income by Item

	Expenditures Investment Before Construction Starts 0	1	2	3	4	5	Total
Developer's equity	672,064						
		85%	*5%*			*10%*	
Site work		136,417	8,024			16,049	160,490
						100%	
Walks & paving						102,760	160,490
					40%	*60%*	
Swim pool					15,836	23,754	39,590
						100%	
Landscaping						15,890	15,890
		100%					
Excavation		27,340					27,340
		20%	*40%*	*40%*			
Concrete		83,342	166,684	166,684			416,710
		5%	*80%*	*15%*			
Masonry		10,708	171,328	32,124			214,160
			100%				
Waterproofing			2,240				2,240
			30%	*35%*	*35%*		
Rough carpentry			34,500	40,250	40,250		115,000
			30%	*35%*	*35%*		
Finish carpentry			72,876	85,022	85,022		242,920
				100%			
Metalwork				3,480			3,480
				100%			
Drywall				158,580			158,580
			25%	*40%*	*35%*		
Roofing			18,273	29,236	25,581		73,090
				80%	*20%*		
Painting				148,240	37,060		185,300
					100%		
Tile					154,570		154,570
					100%		
Carpet					110,650		110,650
						100%	
Cabinets						77,160	77,160
			50%	*20%*	*30%*		
Plumbing			90,175	36,070	54,105		180,350
			25%	*35%*	*25%*	*15%*	

Continued

TABLE 13.3 (*Continued*)

	Expenditures Investment Before Construction Starts 0	1	2	3	4	5	Total
Heat & air conditioning			62,285	87,199	62,285	37,371	249,140
			20%	40%	5%	35%	
Electric			49,432	98,864	12,358	86,506	247,160
		20%	20%	20%	20%	20%	
Miscellaneous		4,504	4,504	4,504	4,504	4,504	22,520
						100%	
Ranges & refrigerators						83,900	83,900
Totals		262,311	680,321	890,353	602,221	447,894	2,883,000

THE FIRST DRAW

In a few instances the first draw might occur at the initial closing, that is, at time zero, when construction is just about to start. Such would be the case with certain FHA loans, but in general the first draw does not occur until after the first month has gone by. In the example of Figure 13-2 it is assumed that conventional financing is used, so the estimated first draw of $262,311 is plotted just above the point that indicates the end of the first month.

STEP CURVES

The several points representing the bank draws should not be connected with a curve because the funds are received at monthly intervals and no additional money comes in between these monthly payments. In the case of the actual construction expenditures a curve was drawn as an approximation of the money that is actually spent from day to day on the job, keeping up with the constantly increasing actual cost until the job is completed. However, since the level of each bank draw does not change during any given month, straight horizontal and vertical lines are drawn stepwise to connect the five points shown in Figure 13-2.

CASH FORECASTING

Now the additional cash necessary at the beginning of each month, and also the cash necessary on any given day of the month, can be predicted. At the start of the job $843,510 will have been spent. If front money is borrowed to cover this expenditure, then interest will have to be paid on that front money. During the first month an additional sum of $262,311 will have been spent (as shown in Table 13-3), and the contractor must figure out the best way to finance this amount. A good part of that money is needed to meet the payroll during the first month, since most of the work done during this month is the general contractor's responsibility.

NET ACTUAL COST

At the end of the first month the first draw of $262,311 will be obtained from the bank (see Table 13-3), but the first draw amount will not be enough to cover all costs up to that date. There will be a net difference of $1,135,100 spent by end of month 1, minus $262,311 drawn at the end of month 1, which equals $872,789. Of course, if the costs of land and closing plus loan and tax costs were omitted, the actual cost at the end of the first month would be reduced by $700,000 (land) + $107,490 (closing, etc.) = $807,490, leaving a net actual cost of only $872,789 − $807,490 = $65,299. (The starting figure of $843,510 shown on the graph in Figure 13-2 is less than $872,789 because it assumes some loan and tax costs will be paid after construction starts.) In fact, the net actual cost of construction only (excluding closing, interest, and overhead) during the first month will be less than $263,311 because the draw schedule has been front-end loaded. The true total costs to the general contractor from the time construction starts until the first draw is received should not be very much more than the first draw if the schedule has been arranged properly (actually $197,853 according to the figure in this example). The actual total of all of the developer's costs, which includes land and fees, will be considerably greater than the draw, however, and this differential will remain large throughout the job.

EFFECT OF TIME LAG

During the construction period the time of payments of bank draws, as represented in Figure 13-2, may not conform to the dates of actual receipt of the funds by the developer. If the request for draw is not submitted until the last day of the month, the money may not be received until about the tenth day of the following month. Therefore the contractor should forecast an estimate of the amount of work to be accomplished during the last few days of the month, and submit a bill about 3 days before the end of the month. If all goes well, the owner's architect or engineer will be able to check the bill, authorize payment, and submit it to the lender bank by the first of the month, in which case the money may be forthcoming as early as the fifth. The time lag will have been shortened as much as possible, but it will still exist and interest costs will continue to mount up. Therefore, the entire set of step lines illustrating the bank draws should be shifted to the right, along the time scale, by about 5 days or one-sixth of 1 month. The gap between draws and actual cost has now become greater, but reflects a more accurate forecast for working out the financial planning for the project.

TABLE 13.4 Calculation of Interest Due on the Construction Loan to Cover Construction Draws

Draw Number	Amount of Draw, P	Number of Months on Loan, n	Interest Only $P[(F/P\ 1\%\ n) - 1]$
1	$262,311	5	0.0510 = $13,378
2	680,321	4	0.0406 = 27,621
3	890,253	3	0.0303 = 26,975
4	602,221	2	0.0201 = 12,105
5	447,894	1	0.0100 = 4,479
	$2,883,000		$84,558

PREDICTING CONSTRUCTION INTEREST

Another important point is that the predicted actual cost must include interest on the construction loan, particularly if the contractor is also the developer. If the first draw is $262,311, and if the job duration is 5 months, then this money will have been held for 4 months. If the interest rate is 12% (per annum is understood), or 1% per month effective interest, the interest during the 4 months will amount to $262,311 \times (1.01^4 - 1) = \$10,650$ on the first draw. Each draw will have interest charged to it for the time during which that draw is held. For the example shown in Figure 13-2 the second draw will be held for 3 months, the third draw will be held for 2 months, and the fourth draw will have interest charged to it for only 1 month. Theoretically, the fifth draw will not have any interest charge, because the permanent financing will take effect at the time. However, there is usually a time lag of 1 month before the permanent financing takes over the construction loan, so that every one of the interest computations for each predicted draw should be increased by 1 month to account for this time lag. The first draw, therefore, will probably be held for a total of 5 months until the construction loan has been paid off by the permanent lender's mortgage. In that case, the total interest due on the first draw of $262,311 will amount to $262,311 \times (1.01^5 - 1) = \$13,378$, and the total interest is calculated as shown in Table 13-4.

The total construction interest of over $84,000 is equal to more than half of the contractor's profit (assuming the work actually proceeds according to schedule and a profit is earned). We assume that an origination fee of 2 points must also be paid to the construction lender. This 2 points amounts to $0.02 \times \$2,883,000 = \$57,660$ in the example of Figure 13-2. Thus, the construction lender will be getting total true interest of $84,588 + $57,660 = $142,218, and this figure must be included in the computation of predicted actual cost.

SUMMARY

One measure of a well-managed construction project is an ability to accurately predict how much cash will be needed at regular intervals throughout the job, and then to secure those funds by the time they are actually required. An S-curve can be drawn based upon estimated *actual* costs to the contractor. The draw schedule can then be adjusted to a reasonable extent by a modest amount of front-end loading so that the cash draw requested will come closer to covering the contractor's actual out-of-pocket costs each month. Front-end loading must not be carried beyond a reasonable point nor beyond any contractually agreed-upon limits. The greatest percentage of the estimated surcharge of overhead and profit is placed quite properly on the contractor's own work, and smaller percentages are placed on the various subcontractors' work. All of the percentages are adjusted so as not to violate the terms of the agreement or any standards of reasonableness. These percentages can be applied only one time, and that is when the first schedule of values for completed work is presented to the owner's agent for approval. After the owner's agent approves these values, they become fixed. Therefore, to ensure a valid schedule of values, sufficient time should be spent in financial preplanning, using a CPM, a bar chart, and the S-curve and step curve.

KEY TERMS AND DEFINITIONS

Bar chart: Graphical display of the anticipated percentage of completion of each job item per month during the duration of the job.

S-curve: Graphical display of total project expenses per month; often includes monthly bank draws on same chart.

KEY LEARNING POINTS

- Understand why project scheduling is important.
- Explain how bar charts are created and their role in project scheduling.
- Identify the relationships between S-curves and bank draws and monthly project costs.
- Understand the effect of a time lag on project cost.

QUESTIONS

1. What is the first step often taken in preparing a bar chart?
2. What is the purpose of bar charts? Why are they important?
3. On an S-curve, why are bank draws plotted as "step curves?"
4. Explain how project delays can significantly impact the financing of a construction project.
5. Assuming the following construction loan, calculate the total amount of interest charged on the first loan draw during the duration of the project:

Project duration: 12 months

Draw amount: $450,000

Annual interest rate: 12% (1% per month)

6. Using the figures in Question 5, assume that the project has been delayed five months. Calculate the additional interest that will be charged during the five months.

14

Basic How-to-Do-It Time Value of Money Calculations

*KEY EXPRESSIONS IN THIS CHAPTER**

A = Uniform series of n end-of-period payments or receipts, with interest compounded at rate, i, on the balance in the account at the end of each period.

F = Future value. A single lump sum cash payment occurring in the future at the end of the *last* of n time periods. The future balance of all payments under consideration, together with accrued interest at rate i.

G = Arithmetic gradient increase, or decrease, in funds flow at the end of each period (except the first period) for n periods.

P = Present value of all payments under consideration. Present value may be thought of as an equivalent single lump sum cash payment now, at time zero, the beginning of the first of n time periods. No interest has accrued. The amount of the present value differs from an equivalent future value by the amount of interest compounded on the present value in the intervening period.

i = Interest rate, assumed to be the annual rate unless otherwise specified. This is the rate at which the balance of the account is charged for use of the funds. Or, in nonfinancial problems, i is the growth or decline of the base number. It is assumed as annual and compounded unless otherwise noted or obvious from the problem.

n = Numbers of compounding time periods, frequently years, but may be quarters, months, days, minutes, or as otherwise specified.

EQUATIONS USED IN THIS CHAPTER

$$F = P(1+i)^n \qquad (1a)$$

$$P = \frac{F}{(1+i)^n} \qquad (1b)$$

---

*The words *value, worth, sum, amount*, and *payment* are used interchangeably. For instance, *present value, present worth, present sum*, and so forth, all mean the same

$$F = A \frac{(1+i)^n - 1}{i} \tag{2a}$$

$$A = F \frac{i}{(1+i)^n - 1} \tag{2b}$$

$$A = P \frac{i(1+i)^n}{(1+i)^n - 1} \tag{3a}$$

$$P = A \frac{(1+i)^n - 1}{i(1+i)^n} \tag{3b}$$

$$F = \frac{G}{i} \left[\frac{(1+i)^n - 1}{i} - n \right] \tag{4}$$

$$P = \frac{G}{i} \left[\frac{(1+i)^n - 1}{i(1+i)^n} - \frac{n}{(1+i)^n} \right] \tag{5}$$

$$A = G \left[\frac{1}{i} - \frac{n}{(1+i)^n - 1} \right] \tag{6}$$

CASH FLOW

As the words imply, cash flow occurs whenever cash or its equivalent "flows," or changes hands from one party to another. When you pay money to the cashier at the lunch counter or at the store, cash flows from you to the cashier. If you pay by check, the check is considered an equivalent to cash, so "cash" still flows when you hand over the check. If you pay by credit card, you owe the money as soon as you sign the charge slip, but the cash flow does not occur until the credit card firm receives your check in lieu of cash.

CASH FLOW DIAGRAM

Information on cash flow can be communicated quickly and easily by use of a line diagram called a cash flow diagram, a type of graph used extensively because of its simplicity and ease of construction. It consists of two basic parts: the horizontal time line, and the vertical cash flow lines. The horizontal time line is subdivided into n compounding periods, with each compounding period representing whatever unit of time duration is specified for the problem under consideration, such as a year, month, day, and so on. The vertical lines represent cash flow and are placed along the time line at points corresponding to the timing of the cash flow. The vertical lines are not necessarily to scale, although a large cash flow is usually represented by a longer line than a small cash flow.

Example 14.1. Draw the cash flow diagram from the *borrower's* viewpoint, showing a loan of $1,000 for 1 year at 10% interest.

Solution: The cash flow diagram from the viewpoint of the borrower is shown in Figure 14-1.

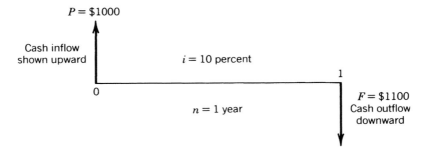

FIG. 14-1   Borrower's cash flow line diagram.

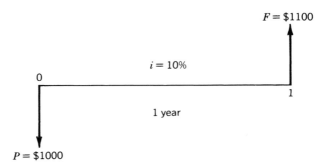

FIG. 14-2   Lender's cash flow line diagram.

Normally, receipts or incomes are represented by upward-pointed arrows since they represent cash flow in and an increase in the balance in the account. Conversely, costs, disbursements, or expenditures are usually represented by downward-pointed arrows, indicating a decrease in account balance due to a cash flow out.

Notice that when the cash flow diagram is drawn for the lender's point of view, the arrows point in the opposite directions than for the borrower. In lending you the $1000, the lender has a cash flow *out* (arrow downward), and upon repayment the lender has a cash flow *in* (arrow upward), as demonstrated in Example 14.2.

Example 14.2. Draw the cash flow diagram from the *lender's* viewpoint showing a loan of $1,000 for 1 year at 10% interest.

Solution: The cash flow diagram is drawn as shown in Figure 14-2.

BALANCE-IN-THE-ACCOUNT DIAGRAM

Additional information on project financing can be communicated by use of the balance-in-the account diagram. As the name suggests, this graph simply depicts the balance accumulated or left in the account at all points in time. Whereas the

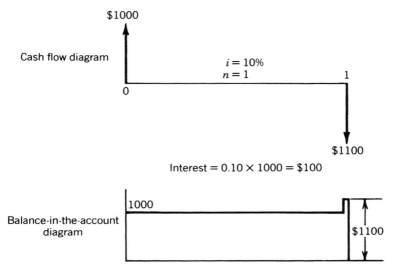

FIG. 14-3   Cash flow diagram and corresponding balance-in-the-account diagram.

cash flow diagram shows all transfers, except interest payments, into or out of the account, the balance-in-the-account diagram shows both the interest payments and the balance before and after the interest payments.

Example 14.3. Draw the cash flow diagram and corresponding balance-in-the-account diagram for a loan of $1,000 for 1 year at 10%, from the borrower's viewpoint.

Solution: Both diagrams are shown in Figure 14-3.

MONEY AS A BUILDER'S TOOL

To the builder, money is just as important an ingredient of construction as labor, equipment, and material. Money to finance the project is acquired in much the same way as other essential tools—it is either owned or rented (borrowed). When the builder already owns the needed funds, they must be withdrawn from the builder's accumulated savings (out of liquid capital funds). These funds then become tied up in the project and can no longer earn interest, so interest is lost or foregone for these funds. The lost interest should be charged as an added cost to the project. When the funds needed to finance the project are rented (borrowed), the lender expects some compensation for doing without the borrowed funds, so rent (interest) is charged for every time period (months, years, etc.) that the funds are on loan, and this interest cost also should be charged as an added cost to the project. So regardless of whether the project is funded with the owner's money or with money borrowed from a bank, interest costs should be charged against the project for all funds invested therein.

Money has a time value, and the dollar amount of interest paid is proportional to the time the money is on loan. If you borrow $1,000 from Bank A for 6 months, and borrow another $1,000 from Bank B for 12 months, you expect to pay about twice as many total dollars of interest to Bank B because you will hold the funds for twice as much time. The dollar amounts of interest payments are very similar to rent payments in that both are charged to enable a nonowner to acquire use of someone else's property for a limited amount of time. Both interest and rent are charged per unit of time and both are based on the value of the amount loaned or item rented.

INTEREST DEFINED

More formally, interest may be defined as money paid for the use of borrowed money. Or, in a broad sense, interest can be said to be the return obtainable by the productive investment of capital. The rate of interest is the ratio between the interest chargeable or payable at the end of a period of time and the money owed at the beginning of that period. The rate is usually based on a 1-year period, unless a shorter time is stipulated, such as 1% per month. Thus, if $10 of interest is payable on a debt of $100, the interest rate is $10/\$100 = 0.10$ per year. This is described as an interest rate of 10%, with the "per year" being understood.

RATE OF INTEREST

Sometimes interest is payable more often than once each year, but the interest rate per year is almost always what is meant when the interest rate is quoted, unless specifically stated otherwise. In this way, 0.833% payable monthly, 2½% payable quarterly, or 5% payable semiannually are all described as 10%. If $1,000 were deposited in each of four accounts with each account representing one of these four interest rates, there would be a small difference in the account balances at the end of 1 year, due to the differences in compounding. However, the difference between the nominal rate of 10% and the effective rate produced by each of the others is not large enough to affect a decision in the economic analysis of any construction project. (More accurately, the 10% nominal rate reflects a rate of 0.00833 compounded monthly = 10.47% effective annual rate; 0.025 compounded quarterly = 10.38% annual; and 0.05 compounded semiannually = 10.25% annual.)

PLANS FOR PAYING BACK A LOAN

Consider the four plans shown in Table 14-1 and illustrated by cash flow diagrams in Figure 14-4 by which a loan of $10,000 is paid back in 10 years with interest at 10%. The date at which the loan is made is considered time 0, and the time periods are measured in years from that date. The $10,000 amount of the loan is called the *principal* of the loan.

TABLE 14.1   Four Plans for Repayment of 10,000 in 10 Years with Interest at 10%

End of Year	Interest Due (10% of Money Owed at Start of Year)	Total Money Owed Before Year-End Payment	Year-End Payment	Money Owed After Year-End Payment
Plan 1				
0				$10,000.00
1	$1,000.00	$11,000.00	$1,000.00	10,000.00
2	1,000.00	11,000.00	1,000.00	10,000.00
3	1,000.00	11,000.00	1,000.00	10,000.00
4	1,000.00	11,000.00	1,000.00	10,000.00
5	1,000.00	11,000.00	1,000.00	10,000.00
6	1,000.00	11,000.00	1,000.00	10,000.00
7	1,000.00	11,000.00	1,000.00	10,000.00
8	1,000.00	11,000.00	1,000.00	10,000.00
9	1,000.00	11,000.00	1,000.00	10,000.00
10	1,000.00	11,000.00	11,000.00	0
Plan 2				
0				$10,000.00
1	$1,000.00	$11,000.00	$ 2,000.00	9,000.00
2	900.00	9,900.00	1,900.00	8,000.00
3	800.00	8,800.00	1,800.00	7,000.00
4	700.00	7,700.00	1,700.00	6,000.00
5	600.00	6,600.00	1,600.00	5,000.00
6	500.00	5,500.00	1,500.00	4,000.00
7	400.00	4,400.00	1,400.00	3,000.00
8	300.00	3,300.00	1,300.00	2,000.00
9	200.00	2,200.00	1,200.00	1,000.00
10	100.00	1,100.00	1,100.00	0
Plan 3				
0				$10,000.00
1	$1,000.00	$11,000.00	$1,627.45	9,372.55
2	937.24	10,309.79	1,627.45	8,682.34
3	868.23	9,550.57	1,627.45	7,923.12
4	792.31	8,715.43	1,627.45	7,087.98
5	708.80	7,796.78	1,627.45	6,169.33
6	616.93	6,786.26	1,627.45	5,158.81
7	515.88	5,674.67	1,627.45	4,047.24
8	404.72	4,451.96	1,627.45	2,824.51
9	282.45	3,106.96	1,627.45	1,479.51
10	147.95	1,627.45	1,627.45	0
Plan 4				
0				$10,000.00
1	$1,000.00	$11,000.00	$0.00	11,000.00
2	1,100.00	12,100.00	0.00	12,100.00
3	1,210.00	13,310.00	0.00	13,310.00
4	1,331.00	14,641.00	0.00	14,641.00
5	1,464.10	16,105.10	0.00	16,105.10
6	1,610.51	17,715.61	0.00	17,715.61

Continued

TABLE 14.2 (*Continued*)

End of Year	Interest Due (10% of Money Owed at Start of Year)	Total Money Owed Before Year-End Payment	Year-End Payment	Money Owed After Year-End Payment
7	1,771.56	19,487.17	0.00	19,487.17
8	1,948.72	21,435.89	0.00	21,435.89
9	2,143.59	23,579.48	0.00	23,579.48
10	2,357.95	25,937.43	25,937.43	0

SHORT-TERM NOTES

Plan 1 is typical of a method of repayment often used with renewable short-term notes. Suppose that you borrow some money on a 30-day note in order to meet your payroll. At the end of the month you could pay back the principal and the interest out of your draw, but then you would find that you had to borrow the same amount again. To save bookkeeping and certain other finance charges, the bank offers to let you continue the note if you will pay only the interest due at the end of every year. This process is continued until the end of the job, at which time you agree to pay off the note plus the interest for the last month. Notice that in Plan 1 no money is paid on the principal until the very end of the total time period, but interest is paid at the end of each year.

UNIFORM PRINCIPAL PAYMENTS

Plan 2 is another method often used in repaying short-term notes. It differs from Plan 1 in that periodic payments are made on the principal in addition to paying the interest due at the end of each period of time. But in this case, because the principal amount is being steadily reduced, each of the interest payments is less than the preceding one. Thus, the amount of dollars paid on each installment is a steadily decreasing number. In fact, the total number of dollars paid in Plan 1 is $20,000, but the total number of dollars paid in Plan 2 is $15,000.

EQUAL PERIODIC PAYMENTS

The method used in Plan 3 is the usual way of paying off a mortgage note. The amount of $1,627.45 is called the *equal periodic payment*. Out of this payment first comes all the interest due at that time, then the remainder is applied toward reducing the principal. For example, out of the first payment of $1,627.45, the first $1,000 is used to pay the interest, and the remaining ($1,627.45 − $1,000.00 =) $627.45 is paid on the principal, reducing it from $10,000 to $9,372.55. From the second $1,627.45 payment, the first $937.24 is paid on interest, leaving ($1,627.45

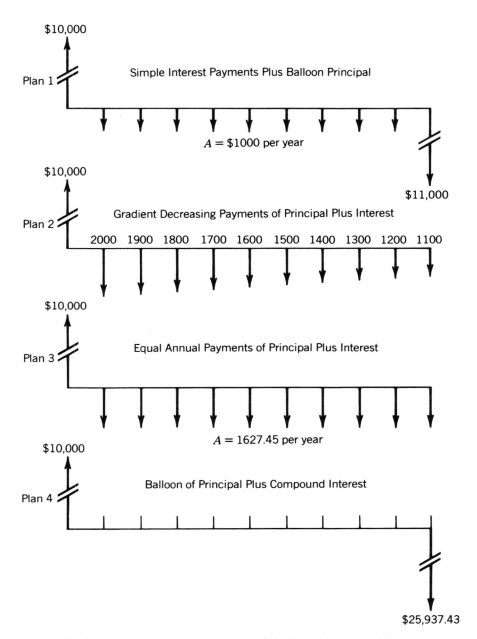

FIG. 14-4 Cash flow diagram for repayment of $10,000 in 10 years with interest at 10%.

− $937.24) = $690.21 to be paid on the principal. This reduces the principal balance from $9,372.55 to $8,682.34. Notice that at first more than half of the equal periodic payment is used to pay interest, but as time goes on more is applied to the principal and less to the interest, until at the end only $147.95 is due on interest, while $1,479.50 is applied to the principal. But the number of dollars paid each time remains the same. The total number of dollars actually paid back is 10 × $1,627.56 = $16,274.50, which includes $10,000 for repayment of principal and $6,274.50 for the total of the interest payments.

PAYING OFF A LOAN

One last observation should be made concerning Plan 3. Unless a penalty clause is included in the terms of the loan, the principal balance amount can be paid off at any time, thus discharging your debt. For example, after making the fifth payment of $1,627.45 there remains an unpaid balance of $6,169.33. At that time, if an additional payment of $6,169.33 is made, the debt will be canceled. No further interest is owed. Interest is paid only on money that is in the borrower's possession for the time during which it is held. No interest is owed on money not received, nor is interest owed on money already paid back.

COMPOUND INTEREST

Plan 4 is an example of what is called *compound interest*. It is typical of what happens to a sum of money left untouched in a bank account. If considered as a debt, it is often called a *balloon note* because the lump sum "balloon" is there at the end of the loan period. (Plan 1 is another form of balloon note.) Because no payments whatsoever are made between the time the money is borrowed (or placed in the bank) and the end of a specified time period, interest is paid on the interest already accumulated in the account. For instance, at the end of the first year, because no payments are made out of the account, the total amount owed is the principal of $10,000 plus the interest of $1,000 for a total of $11,000. At the beginning of the second year, then, $11,000 is owed and the interest is charged against this amount during the course of the year. At the end of the second year the interest due is $1,100 instead of $1,000, the additional $100 being the interest on the interest (0.10 × $1,000 = $100). This means that interest is compounding. In the third year interest will be charged on $11,000 + $1,100 = $12,100, and so on. At the end of 10 years the total compound amount of $25,937.43 must be paid to discharge the debt. If the debt is paid off sooner, say at the end of 5 years, the total amount due at that time must be paid ($16,105.10 for 5 years).

EQUIVALENCE

Surprisingly, all of the four plans of repayment are equivalent, one to the other, with respect to the time period and the rate of interest. This is true because all four plans provide for payment of 10 cents of interest for every one dollar still owed at the end of each year. The dollar amounts are different because each plan has a different repayment schedule. For example, compare Plan 1 with Plan 4. At the end of the first year the lender bank receives a $1,000 interest payment, which it can immediately lend to some third party (call her Jones) at the same rate of interest. During the second year that $1,000 will earn $0.10 \times \$1,000 = \$100$ for the bank. At the end of the second year the bank receives $1,000 from the borrower using Plan 1, plus an additional $100 from Jones, for a total of $1,100, the same as the interest shown in Plan 4. The bank, having lent $1,000 to Jones, now lends $1,100 to Smith, and receives as interest at the end of the third year $1,000 from the first borrower, $100 from Jones, and $0.10 \times \$1,100 = \$110.00$ from Smith, for a total of $\$1,000 + \$100 + \$110 = \$1,210.00$, the same amount as shown in Plan 4. This process can be repeated all the way down the line for 10 years, so that Plan 1 is equivalent to Plan 4.

WHAT DO ALL FOUR PLANS HAVE IN COMMON?

It is not difficult to see that the same line of reasoning can be applied when comparing Plan 2 with Plan 4, and that it will also hold true when considering Plan 3 in relation to Plan 4. In other words, each one of the first three plans is equivalent to Plan 4 from the lender's viewpoint, and thus they are all equivalent to each other provided that all funds earn interest at the same rate. The bank will make the same amount of money on the loan no matter which one of the four plans is adopted for repayment. There are three things common to each one of the plans: the principal of $10,000, the interest rate of 10%, and the total time of 10 years.

THE BORROWER'S VIEWPOINT

From the borrower's viewpoint also, the plans are equivalent. Again consider Plan 1 versus Plan 4. The money you have to work with should make money for you, or you should not have borrowed it in the first place. In fact, it must earn at least as much as it costs to borrow. Therefore, the borrowed $10,000 should earn at least $1,000 for you during the first year. At the end of that year, if you do not pay $1,000 to the bank, you should be able to put the money to work so that it earns at least $0.10 \times \$1,000 = \$100$ for you during the second year. Simultaneously, the original $10,000 is earning at least $1,000 for you during the second year, so that at the end of that year you should have a capital of $\$10,000 + \$1,000 + \$100 + \$1,000 = \$12,100$, the same as the amount shown in Plan 4. It is simply a question of which pocket the money goes into. Therefore, Plan 1 is equivalent to Plan 4 from the borrower's viewpoint, and it can be seen that, in a similar way, all the plans are equivalent to one another.

SUPERIORITY OF PLANS

There is no single answer as to which plan is superior. In practice the lender usually requires one specific method of repayment. Therefore, if the borrower wants the money, he will have to agree to the terms. If the option is with the borrower, the decision depends on how he thinks he will best be able to pay the money back, and what use he has for the money. In these examples, the actual true cost to the borrower and the total income to the bank are the same, no matter which plan is adopted. The total number of dollars changing hands is not the same, because of the timing of the repayments:

$20,000	for Plan 1
$15,000	for Plan 2
$16,274.50	for Plan 3
$25,937.43	for Plan 4

However, under each of the four plans for lending out $10,000, if all of the principal and interest payments received by the bank are immediately reinvested at 10%, then the bank would accumulate $25,937.43 by the end of year 10 in all four cases.

PRESENT WORTH

All four plans discussed in the preceding paragraph were equivalent because they were based on the same loan amount (that is $10,000) at the beginning of the loan period (time zero), and yielded the same interest (10%) on the unpaid balance. Measured at the time the loan is made (or at the time the funds are invested), the amount of principal is called the Present Worth of the money and is designated as *PW*, or sometimes just *P* for short.

Example 14.4. Find *P*, given *F, i, n*.

   A particular loan specifies a promise to repay a lump sum of $25,937 at a time 10 years from now, with 10% interest on the unpaid balance. Find the present worth of that future $25,937 lump sum payment.

Solution:
$$P = F(P/F, \ 10\%, \ 10)$$
$$= \$25{,}937 \times 0.38554$$
$$= \$10{,}000$$
$$\text{where } F = \$25{,}937$$

and $(P/F, \ 10\%, \ 10) = 0.38554$ found either from solving equation 1b, or from finding the value in Appendix D, the 10% table, column headed *P/F*, line $n = 10$.

The present worth is $10,000. In other words $10,000 could be loaned at 10% interest compounded annually on this promise to repay $25,937 at end of year (EOY) 10.

Example 14.5. Find P, given A, i, n.

Another loan specifies a promise to repay $1,627.45 annually for each of the next 10 years, and the interest is 10% on the unpaid balance. Find the present worth of all ten of those repayments.

Solution:
$$P = A(P/A, \ 10\%, \ 10)$$
$$= \$1627.45 \times 6.1445$$
$$= \$10,000$$
where $A = \$1,627.45$ the annual payment

and $(P/A, 10\%, 10) = 6.1445$ found either from solving equation 3b, or by finding the value in Appendix D, the 10% table, column headed *P/A*, line $n = 10$.

Again the present worth is $10,000. Or the amount that could be loaned with this promise to repay is $10,000 also. The method of calculating the sums involved is presented a few paragraphs further on.

MEANING OF "PRESENT"

The word "present" in "present worth" refers to the date on which the loan is made, sometimes called problem-time-zero or PTZ for short. Thus, if money had been borrowed in the year 1426 with a promise to pay it back in 1492, then for purposes of computation 1426 becomes the "present" or PTZ, even though that date is more than 500 years ago. Or, if a loan is going to be made in the year 2437, to be paid back by 2447, the loan amount of PTZ in 2437 is its present worth. The rules of interest computation are concerned with accrued interest and are not to be confused with inflation or deflation.

FUTURE VALUE OF PRESENT WORTH, F/P

The rules of compound interest lead to the useful equations shown at the beginning of this chapter. The first of these can be derived fairly simply.

Suppose that a loan has a principal amount P. If the interest rate is i, then at the end of the first year the amount of interest owed will be iP. For instance, if the principal, P, $= \$100$, and interest is at 10%, or $i = 0.10$, then the amount of interest owed is iP, or $0.10 \times \$100 = \$10$ interest at EOY 1. The total amount owed will be $P + iP = P(1 + i)$ or $\$100 \times 1.10 = \$110$ principal plus interest. If none of this is paid, at the end of the second year the amount of interest owed will be the rate of interest times the total amount owed at the beginning of the second year, which comes to $iP(1 + i)$. The total amount owed at the end of the second year will be the total owed at the beginning of the year plus the accrued interest for the year, which is

$$
\begin{aligned}
P(1 + i) + iP(1 + i) &= (P + iP)(1 + i) \\
&= P(1 + i)(1 + i) \\
&= P(1 + i)^2 \\
&= \$100 \times 1.10^2 \\
&= \$121 \text{ principal plus accrued interest compounded}
\end{aligned}
$$

At the end of the third year the interest owed will be $iP(1 + i)^2$. Add this to the amount owed at the beginning of the third year, and you get

$$
\begin{aligned}
P(1 + i)^2 + iP(1 + i)^2 &= (P + iP)(1 + i)^2 \\
&= P(1 + i)(1 + i)^2 \\
&= P(1 + i)^3 \\
&= \$100 \times 1.10^3 \\
&= \$133.10 \text{ principal plus accrued} \\
&\quad\ \text{interest compounded}
\end{aligned}
$$

By extension, the rule now becomes obvious. If F is the total sum owed at the end of n years, then

$$
F = P(1 + i)^n \tag{1a}
$$

The expression $(1 + i)^n$ may be called the *single payment compound amount factor*, SPCAF, but more often is referred to as $(F/P, i, n)$, or just F/P, the ratio of future value F to present value P(see Appendix D). For example, if the interest is 10% and $10,000 is borrowed for a period of 10 years, then

$$
\begin{aligned}
F &= \$10,000(1 + 0.10)^{10} \\
&= \$10,000 \times 2.593743 \\
&= \$25,937.43
\end{aligned}
$$

will be the total amount owed at the end of 10 years, if no payments are made before then (see Plan 4, Table 14-1). Notice that the interest rate must be put into decimal form to use in the formula. By dividing both sides of equation 1 by $(1 + I) n$, P in terms of F is obtained.

$$
P = \frac{F}{(1 + i)^n} \tag{1b}
$$

The term $1/(1 + i)^n$ is sometimes called the *single payment present worth factor*, SPPWF, but more often is referred to as $(P/F, i, n)$, or just P/F, where P/F is the ratio of present value P to future value F for any given values of i and n. For convenience of notation, this factor may be designated by the notation $(F/P, i, n)$. Using this notation equations 1a and 1b would be expressed as

$$F = P(F/P, i, n) \tag{1a}$$

$$P = F(P/F, i, n) \tag{1b}$$

Example 14.6. Find P, given F, i, n.

If 10 years from now a proposed investment will repay you a lump sum amount of \$25,937.43, how much can you afford to invest now (Present Worth) if an acceptable interest rate is 10%? In other words, how much would you have to invest in an account drawing 10% interest compounded annually in order to accumulate \$25,937.43 in 10 years?

Solution: Using equation 1b, the following solution is obtained.

$$
\begin{aligned}
P &= \frac{\$25{,}937.43}{(1 + 0.10)^{10}} \\
&= \frac{\$25{,}937.43}{2.593743} \\
&= \$10{,}000.00
\end{aligned}
$$

Or using the 10% table and the P/F column from Appendix D,

$$
\begin{aligned}
P &= F(P/F, 10\%, 10) \\
&= \$25{,}937.43 \times 0.38554 \\
&= \$10{,}000
\end{aligned}
$$

EQUAL PERIODIC PAYMENTS, A DERIVATION OF THE F/A EQUATION

Suppose that you want to have F dollars in the bank at the end of n years, and you want to make a deposit of A dollars at the end of each year such that the deposits will compound to F. No deposit is made at the beginning of the time period, at time 0, and the first deposit is made at the end of the first year (EOY 1). Then that first deposit will accumulate interest, not for n years, but for $(n - 1)$ years; that is, it earns no interest during the first year because it was deposited not at time 0, but rather at the end of the first year. At the end of n years, if the interest rate is i, the first deposit will amount to

$$A(1 + i)^{n-1}$$

The second deposit is of the same amount of A dollars, but it is made at the end of the second year (EOY 2), so that it will amount to

$$A(1+i)^{n-2}$$

The third year's deposit will accumulate to

$$A(1+i)^{n-3}$$

and so on. The deposit just before the last one will be

$$A(1+i)$$

and the last deposit will earn no interest—it will simply be equal to A dollars.
The total in the bank will be the sum of all the future sums:

$$F = A(1+i)^{n-1} + A(1+i)^{n-2} + A(1+i)^{n-3} + \cdots + A(1+i) + A$$

Reversing the order and factoring gives

$$F = A[1 + (1+i) + (1+i)^2 + \cdots + (1+i)^{n-3} + (1+i)^{n-2} + (1+i)^{n-1}]$$

Now multiply both sides of the equation by $(1+i)$ to get

$$F + iF = A[(1+i) + (1+i)^2 + \cdots + (1+i)^{n-3} \\ + (1+i)^{n-2} + (1+i)^{n-1} + (1+i)^n]$$

Subtract the first equation from the second, and the only terms remaining are

$$iF = A[-1 + (1+i)^n]$$

or

$$iF = A[(1+i)^n - 1]$$

and

$$F = A\frac{(1+i)^{n-1}}{i} \tag{2a}$$

The expression $F/A = \frac{(1+i)^n - 1}{i}$ is called the *uniform annual series compound amount factor*, UACAF, or just *F/A*, or (*F/A, i, n*).
Then

$$A = F\left[\frac{i}{(1+i)^n - 1}\right] \tag{2b}$$

The quantity $i/[(1+i)^n - 1]$ is sometimes called the *sinking fund deposit factor*, SFF, or just *A/F*. For convenience of notation this factor may be designated by the notation (*A/F, i, n*). Using this notation, equation 2(a,b) is expressed as:

$$F = A(F/A, i, n) \quad \text{or} \quad A = F(A/F, i, n)$$

Example 14.7. Find *A*, given *F, i, n.*

Determine how much must be deposited at the end of each year for 10 years in order to accumulate $25,937.43 if the interest is 10%.

Solution:
$$A = F \left[\frac{i}{(1+i)^n - 1} \right]$$
$$= \$25,937.43 \left[\frac{0.10}{(1+0.10)^{10} - 1} \right]$$
$$= \$25,937.43 \times \frac{0.10}{(2.158924) - 1}$$
$$= \$25,937.43 \times 0.06274539$$
$$= \$1,627.45$$

or alternatively, using Appendix D, the 10% table and the *A/F* column on the line n = 10:

$$A = F(A/F, 10\%, 10)$$
$$= \$25,937.43 \times 0.06275$$
$$= \$1,627.57$$

The difference of $0.12 is due to a rounding error of course. (See Plan 3, Table 14-1, and note that it is indeed equivalent to Plan 4.)

CAPITAL RECOVERY FACTOR, A/P

Because $F = P(1+i)^n$, it is possible to substitute in equation 2(a, b) and get

$$A = P(1+i)^n \left[\frac{i}{(1+i)^n - 1} \right]$$

or

$$A = P \left[\frac{i(1+i)^n}{(1+i)^n - 1} \right] \tag{3a}$$

Another form of equation 3a that gives exactly the same answer is

$$A = P \left[\frac{i}{(1+i)^n - 1} + i \right]$$

358   *Basic How-to-Do-It Time Value of Money Calculations*

For convenience of notion, equation 3(a, b) may be expressed as

$$A = P(A/P, i, n) \quad \text{and} \quad P = A(P/A, i, n)$$

Equation 3(a, b) answers the question: How much must be paid at the end of each year so as to pay off a debt of P dollars in n years if interest is at rate i? Alternatively, the question can be asked as follows: How much must I get at the end of each year for n years to justify an investment of P dollars if I want an i rate of return on my investment? As used with mortgages, the expression

$$A/P = \frac{i(1+i)^n}{(1+i)^n - 1}$$

is referred to as the *capital recovery factor* or just *A/P*. Because both forms of equation 3(a, b) produce exactly the same answer, the capital recovery factor is always equal to the sinking fund factor plus the interest rate:

$$\frac{i(1+i)^n}{(1+i)^n - 1} = \frac{i}{(1+i)^n - 1} + i$$

or

$$A/P = A/F + i$$

Example 14.8. Find A, given P, i, n.

What are the annual payments on a 10-year mortgage of $10,000 if the interest is 10%?

Solution: The yearly payment would be

$$A = P\left[\frac{i(1+i)^n}{(1+i)^n - 1}\right]$$
$$= \$10,000\left[\frac{0.10(1+0.10)^{10}}{(1+0.10)^{10} - 1}\right]$$
$$= \$10,000\left(\frac{0.10 \times 2.593743}{2.593743 - 1}\right)$$
$$= \$10,000 \times 0.162745$$
$$= \$1,627.45$$

or, alternatively, using the 10% table and the *A/P* column:

$$A = P(A/P, 10\%, 10)$$
$$= \$10,000 \times 0.16275$$
$$= \$1,627.50$$

If monthly payments are specified, then the 10% interest becomes a nominal annual interest rate, and the actual i is found as

$$i = \frac{0.10}{12} = 0.008333/\text{month}$$

Equation 3a can be inverted to obtain

$$P = A\left[\frac{(1+i)^n - 1}{i(1+i)^n}\right] \tag{3b}$$

designated as $P = A(P/A, i, n)$

The expression $P/A = \frac{(1+i)^n - 1}{i(1+i)^n}$ is the *uniform annual series present worth factor*, UAPWF, or just *P/A* or $(P/A, i, n)$.

Example 14.9. Find P, given A, i, n.

Find how large a loan can be obtained upon a promise to pay \$1,627.45 per year for 10 years if the interest is 10%.

Solution: Using equation 3b, we have:

$$\begin{aligned} P &= A\left[\frac{(1+i)^n - 1}{i(1+i)^n}\right] \\ &= \$1,627.45\left[\frac{(1+0.10)^{10} - 1}{0.10(1+0.10)^{10}}\right] \\ &= \$1,627.45\left(\frac{2.593743 - 1}{0.10 \times 2.593743}\right) \\ &= \$1,627.45 \times 6.144568 \\ &= \$10,000 \end{aligned}$$

or, alternatively, turning to Appendix D, the 10% tables, and the *P/A* column and line n = 10:

$$\begin{aligned} P &= A(P/A, 10\%, 10) \\ &= \$1,627.45 \times 6.1446 \\ &= \$10,000 \end{aligned}$$

To facilitate the solution of problems, tables of all six factors are given in Appendix D.

ARITHMETIC GRADIENT, G

Periodic payments that increase or decrease are encountered frequently. For instance, operating and maintenance costs for equipment or structures may increase every year, productivity of equipment may decrease with age, rental incomes or expenditures may increase every year. These increases or decreases may be reasonably predictable and may be approximated by an arithmetic gradient, *G*.

For example, annual maintenance costs on a proposed mechanical unit are estimated at

Year	Maintenance ($)
1	0
2	1,000
3	2,000

The growth increment in this example is *G* = $1,000/year and is termed a "gradient." Since the increment is a *constant amount* at $1,000, the progression is described as arithmetic (compared to geometric if the growth increased by the same *percent* each year).

This situation occurs often enough to warrant the use of special equivalence factors relating the arithmetic gradient, *G*, to other cash flows. The gradient *G* can be related to the future value, *F*, the uniform series value, *A*, and the present value, *P*.

FUTURE VALUES OF GRADIENT AMOUNTS, F/G

Notice that the maintenance table above starts with a value of $0 at year 1 and then increases by a gradient *G* of $1,000/year. The cash flow for such a series is shown in Figure 14-5.

The gradient amount, designated as *G* in the generalized problem, can be either positive or negative, but always increases in absolute value with increasing time (the values grow larger from left to right on the cash flow diagram) as shown in Figure 14-5.

The equations for *F/G, A/G,* and *P/G* are derived in a manner similar to the time value equations derived previously, resulting in the relationships shown in Figure 14-6.

The use of equations 4, 5, and 6 is shown in the following examples.

Example 14.10. Find *F*, given *G, i,* and *n*.

A contractor is putting money aside to purchase some equipment, deciding to invest $2,000 at EOY 2 and increasing the investment amount by an additional $2,000 each year until EOY 5, as shown in Figure 14-7. The investment will earn 10% compounded annually. Find the balance in the account after 5 years.

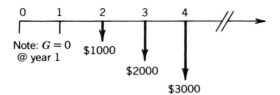

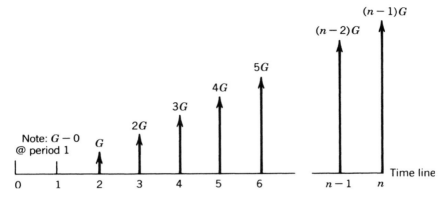

FIG. 14-5   Cash flow diagram for $G = -\$1000$ and $r = 4$.

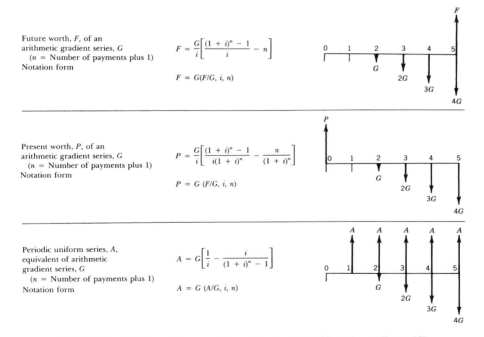

Future worth, F, of an arithmetic gradient series, G (n = Number of payments plus 1) Notation form	$F = \dfrac{G}{i}\left[\dfrac{(1 + i)^n - 1}{i} - n\right]$ $F = G(F/G, i, n)$
Present worth, P, of an arithmetic gradient series, G (n = Number of payments plus 1) Notation form	$P = \dfrac{G}{i}\left[\dfrac{(1 + i)^n - 1}{i(1 + i)^n} - \dfrac{n}{(1 + i)^n}\right]$ $P = G\,(F/G, i, n)$
Periodic uniform series, A, equivalent of arithmetic gradient series, G (n = Number of payments plus 1) Notation form	$A = G\left[\dfrac{1}{i} - \dfrac{i}{(1 + i)^n - 1}\right]$ $A = G\,(A/G, i, n)$

FIG. 14-6   Cash flow diagrams illustrating typical arithmetic gradients (G).

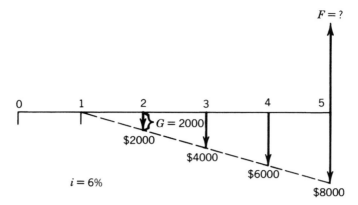

FIG. 14-7   Cash flow diagram for Example 14.10.

Solution: The problem may be solved by either of the following methods:

(a) Solution by equation 4.

$$F = \frac{G}{i}\left[\frac{(1+i)^n - 1}{i} - n\right]$$
$$= \frac{\$2,000}{0.10}\left[\frac{(1+0.10)^5 - 1}{0.10} - 5\right]$$
$$= \$22,102$$

(b) Solution by factors from the tables.

$$F = G(F/G, 10\%, 5)$$
$$= \$2,000 \times 11.051$$
$$= \$22,102$$

CASH FLOW DIAGRAM AND GRAPH OF INCREASE IN F AS N INCREASES

The graph in Figure 14-8 illustrates the timing of the cash flows of G, as well as the relationships between G, F, i, and n, as illustrated by Example 14.10. Note that the first deposit of G ($2,000 in this example) occurs at the *end* of the *second* period. Therefore, the first interest is not earned until the end of the third period. Gradient deposits are made at the end of every year except the first year, so there are a total of $(n-1)$ deposits in the G series (as contrasted with n deposits in all of the A series). Deposits are increased by the amount G ($2,000 in this case) for each period (year, for this example). Therefore, the amount of the last deposit is $G(n-1)$, or in this example $\$2,000(5-1) = \$8,000$. An ability to determine the

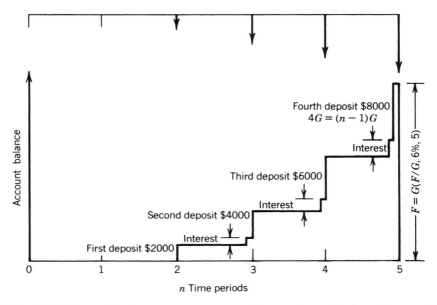

FIG. 14-8 Balance in the account, corresponding to the cash flow diagram for Example 14.10.

correct value of n is essential in solving many problems commonly encountered. Since there are always $(n - 1)$ gradient deposits in the G series, the value of n may be determined as the number of deposits plus one.

Example 14.11. Find decreasing gradient G and A, in terms of dollars per cubic yard, given F, i, and, n, with G and A in terms of cubic yards per year.

A contractor estimates that 10 years from today he will need a total of $80,000 in order to replace a dragline he now owns. He expects to move about 100,000 cubic yards of earth this year with the dragline, but because of its age and increasing downtime he expects this amount to decrease by about 5,000 cubic yards per year each year over the 10-year period. His other operating and maintenance (O & M) costs run about $0.50 per cubic yard. He needs to determine the additional charge per cubic yard required to accumulate the $80,000 in 10 years if he can invest the amount earned from the additional charge at the end of each year and earn 10% interest compounded.

Solution: This problem is approached by separating it into simple components, solving each component, and summing the results. First identify the A series and separate it from the G series. Then solve each series independently and add up the total. The variables are identified as:

$$F = \$80,000$$
$$n = 10 \text{ years}$$
$$A = (100,000 \text{ cubic yards per year}) \times (\text{dollars per cubic yard})$$
$$G = (-5,000 \text{ cubic yards per year}) \times (\text{dollars per cubic yard})$$
$$i = 10\%$$

The other O & M costs of $0.50/cubic yard is extraneous information not needed to solve the problem. The inclusion of such information here simulates the real world where much useless information is often available to confuse the problem.

One basic problem here is translating cubic yards/year into dollars/year. This may be done by letting y represent the extra charge in terms of dollars per cubic yard. Then find how many dollars/cubic yard $\times$ cubic yards/year are needed to accumulate the $80,000.

$$A = (100,000 \text{ cubic yards}) \times (y), \text{ the annual base income}$$
$$G = (-5,000 \text{ cubic yards}) \times (y) \text{ the declining gradient}$$
$$F = A(F/A, i, n) - G(F/G, i, n)$$
$$\$80,000 = (100,000y)(F/A, 10\%, 10) - \frac{(5,000\ y)}{0.10}\left[\frac{(1.10^{10} - 1)}{0.10} - 10\right]$$
$$\$80,000 = 1,593,740y - 296,871y$$
$$y = \frac{80,000}{1,296,869}$$
$$= \$0.0617$$
$$= \$0.062/\text{cubic yard}$$

By charging an extra 6.2 cents per cubic yard and investing the resulting funds at the end of each year at 10% compounded, the contractor will accumulate $80,000 at the end of 10 years to purchase a new dragline.

UNIFORM SERIES VALUES OF GRADIENT AMOUNTS, A/G

Many times the problem involves finding an equivalent uniform series A that is equivalent to the gradient series G. The cash flow diagram for this problem is given in Figure 14-9.

The example that follows illustrates the A/G relationship.

Example 14.12. Find G, given P, A, and n.

Construction of an apartment project is estimated to cost $40,000 per apartment unit. Financing is available at 11% for 25 years on the full cost. Due to competition in the area, rents must begin at $300 per month but may be raised some every year.

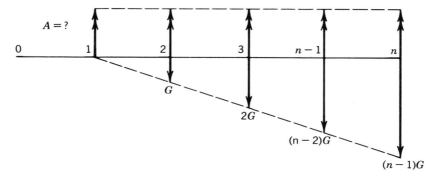

FIG. 14-9 A typical *A/G* equivalency.

Operating costs, taxes, and insurance amount to $100 per month, leaving $200 per month to meet principal and interest on the mortgage payments at the start. What annual increase in rents is necessary to pay off the 11%, 25-year mortgage, assuming the lender is willing to take arithmetic gradient payments with 11% interest on the unpaid balance. To simplify the calculations, use an annual basis instead of monthly.

Solution: The annual mortgage payments to amortize the $40,000 cost are found as:

$$A_1 = \$40,000(A/P, 11\%, 25) = \$4,748 \text{ per year } 0.1187$$

The initial rental income available to pay the mortgage is:

$$A_2 = \$200 \times 12 \text{ months} = \$2,400 \text{ per year}$$

The equivalent annual payment deficit to be made up by periodic rent increase is:

$$\text{Deficit} = A_1 - A_2 = \$4,748 - 2,400 = \$2348 \text{ per year}$$

The required annual gradient increase in rent is found as:

$$G = \$2,348(G/A, 11\%, 25) = \$330.50 \text{ per year}$$

(Equivalent to raising the rent approximately $330.50 per year = $27.54 per month each year from a base of $300 per month the first year.)

PRESENT WORTH VALUES OF GRADIENT AMOUNTS, P/G

This *P/G* series provides for solution of problems involving a payment (cost or income) that changes (increase or decreases) by *G* dollars per period for *n* periods.

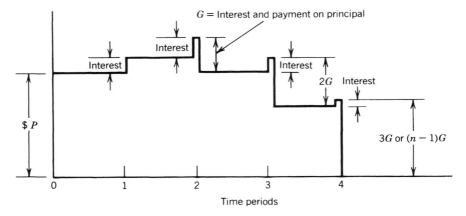

FIG. 14-10   Graph of balance in the account for a loan P with $(n-1)$ repayments periodically increasing by amount G.

Interest is earned on any balance that remains in the loan or deposit. The equation is derived by finding the present sum required to finance this G series for n periods and results in a balance-in-the-account diagram as shown in Figure 14-10.

Example 14.13. Find P, given g, i, and n.

The repair costs on a water pump are expected to be zero the first year and to increase $100 per year over the 5-year life of the pump. A fund bearing 6% on the remaining balance is set up in advance to pay for these costs. How much should be in the fund? Costs are billed to the fund at the end of the year.

Solution: The cash flow diagram appears in Figure 14-11.

(a) Solution by equation 5:

$$P = \frac{G}{i}\left[\frac{(1+i)^n - 1}{i(1+i)^n} - \frac{n}{(1+i)^n}\right]$$
$$= \frac{100}{0.06}\left[\frac{(1+0.06)^5 - 1}{0.06(1+0.06)^5} - \frac{5}{(1+0.06)^5}\right]$$
$$= 100 \times 7.9345$$
$$= \$793.45$$

(b) Alternative solution by use of the tables:

$$P = G(P/G, 6\%, 5)$$
$$= 100(7.9345)$$
$$= \$793.45$$

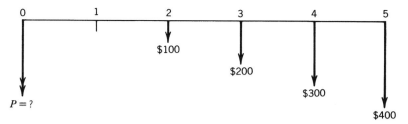

FIG. 14-11   Cash flow diagram for Example 14.13.

PERIODS SHORTER THAN ONE YEAR

All six equations (1(a, b) through 6) assume that n is the number of compounding periods, whether months, quarters, years, or whatever, while i is the interest rate at which interest is compounded on the unpaid balance. To use the equation for any compounding periods, whether longer or shorter than a year, simply make the following substitutions:

n = number of compounding periods

i = interest rate per compounding period

A = amount paid at end of each period

F = sum of money at end of the total number of periods

P remains the present worth, to be measured at the beginning of the reckoning.

Example 14.14. Find how much must be paid back at the end of 1 year, if $10,000 is borrowed at the beginning of that year and interest is 10% compounded *semiannually* (every 6 months).

Solution: Here $n = 2$; therefore, $i = 0.10/2 = 0.05$, and

$$F = P(1 + i)^n$$
$$= \$10{,}000(1 + 0.05)^2$$
$$= \$10{,}000 \times 1.1025$$
$$= \$11{,}025$$

or

$$F = P(F/P, 5\%, 2)$$
$$= \$10{,}000(1.1025)$$
$$= \$11{,}025$$

Example 14.15. Find how much must be paid back at the end of 10 years, given the same terms and conditions as in Example 14.14.

Solution: We have $n = 10 \times 2 = 20$, $i = 0.10/2 = 0.05$, and

$$
\begin{aligned}
F &= \$10,000(1 + 0.05)^{20} \\
&= \$10,000 \times 2.653298 \\
&= \$26,532.98
\end{aligned}
$$

or

$$
\begin{aligned}
F &= P(F/P, 5\%, 20) \\
&= \$10,000(2.6533) \\
&= \$26,533
\end{aligned}
$$

This is \$595.55 more than the \$25,937.43 determined by compounding at 10% for 10 years, since the compounding occurs twice as often but for an interest rate only one-half as much each time.

EFFECTIVE RATE

The effective rate of interest can be found by using the equation

$$
i_e = (1 + i)^n - 1
$$

where i and n are the numbers obtained from the procedure used in Examples 14.14 and 14.15. For instance, the effective rate of interest for 10% compounded semiannually becomes

$$
i_e = (1 + 0.05)^2 - 1 = 1.1025 - 1 = 0.1025
$$

or 10.25%. Similarly, the true annual rate corresponding to 1% per month would be

$$
i_e = (1 + 0.01)^{12} - 1 = 1.1268 - 1 = 0.1268 \text{ or } 12.68\%, \text{ not } 12\%.
$$

There are no tables for these odd rates of interest, so the calculations must be run by solving the equation, or by interpolation of the tables.

EXAMPLES OF TYPICAL APPLICATIONS

Example 14.16. Find F, given P, i, and n.

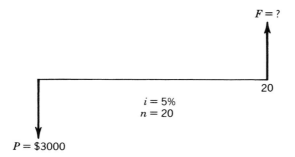

FIG. 14-12 Cash flow diagram for Example 14.16.

Three typical examples of situations involving this approach are the following: (1) If \$3,000 is invested now at 5%, how much will it accumulate to in 20 years? Or (2) What is the compound amount of \$3,000 for 20 years with interest at 5%? Or (3) How much must be saved 20 years from now in order to justify a present expenditure of \$3,000 if money is worth 5%?

Solution: The cash flow diagram is shown in Figure 14-12.

$$i = 0.05$$
$$n = 20$$
$$P = \$3,000$$
$$F = ?$$
$$F = P(1 + i)^n$$
$$= \$3,000(1 + 0.05)^{20}$$

The compound amount factor $(1.05)^{20}$ is given in the 5% table (Appendix D) as 2.653, so that

$$F = \$3,000 \times 2.653$$
$$= \$7,950$$

or, using the table for i = 5%, the F/P column, and the row where n = 20, then

$$F = (F/P, 5\%, 20)$$
$$= \$3,000 \times 2.6533$$
$$= \$7,950$$

Example 14.17. Find F, given several P, i, and n values.

If \$3,000 is invested now, \$2,000 is invested 3 years from now, and \$1,000 is invested 6 years from now, all at 6%, what will be the total amount 15 years from now?

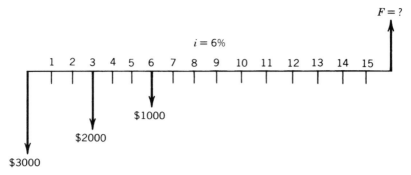

FIG. 14-13   Cash flow diagram for Example 14.17.

Solution: The cash flow diagram is shown in Figure 14-13.

The formulas involving A cannot be used because the amounts are not all the same, the time intervals are not 1 year or less, and the first investment was made at the beginning of the time instead of at the end of the first time interval. The solution therefore requires three separate calculations involving P and F. The first "present" is now, the second "present" starts 3 years from now, and the third "present" begins 6 years from now.

$$P_1 = \$3,000, P_2 = \$2,000, P_3 = \$1,000$$
$$n_1 = 15, n_2 = 12, n_3 = 9$$
$$i_1 = 0.06, i_2 = 0.06, i_3 = 0.06$$
$$
\begin{aligned}
F &= F_1 + F_2 + F_3 \\
&= P_1(1+i)^{n_1} + P_2(1+i)^{n_2} + P_3(1+i)^{n_3} \\
&= \$3,000(1.06)^{15} + \$2,000(10.6)^{12} + \$1,000(1.06)^{9} \\
&= \$3,000 \times 2.379 + \$2,000 \times 2.012 + \$1,000 \times 1.689 \\
&= \$7,191 + \$4,024 + \$1,689 \\
&= \$12,904
\end{aligned}
$$

Example 14.18. Find F, given P, i, and n, semiannual compounding.

If \$500 is deposited in an account now and the account bears interest at 12% (nominal) compounded semiannually, find the balance of accrued interest plus principal at the end of 10 years.

Solution: The cash flow diagram is shown in Figure 14-14.

The interest rate period is $12\%/2 = 6\%$. The number of periods is $10 \times 2 = 20$. From the 6% table (Appendix D) the compound amount factor is found to be 3.2071.

$$i = 0.06$$
$$n = 20$$
$$P = \$500$$
$$F = ?$$
$$F = P(F/P, 6\%, 20)$$
$$= \$500 \times 3.2071$$
$$= \$1,603.60$$

Example 14.19. Find P, given F, i, and n, compounded quarterly.

What is the present worth of $5,800 due 8 years from now if interest is 10% compounded quarterly?

Solution: The cash flow diagram is drawn in Figure 14-15.

$$i = 0.025$$
$$n = 32$$
$$F = \$5,800$$
$$P = ?$$
$$P = F \left[\frac{1}{(1+i)^n} \right]$$
$$= \$5,800 \left[\frac{1}{(1.025)^{32}} \right]$$
$$= \$5,800 \times 0.4538$$
$$= \$2,632.04 \text{ or } \$2,632$$

Example 14.20. Find n, given F/P and i.

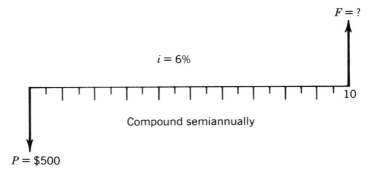

FIG. 14-14 Cash flow diagram for Example 14.18.

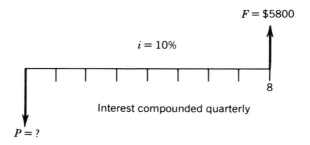

FIG. 14-15   Cash flow diagram for Example 14.19.

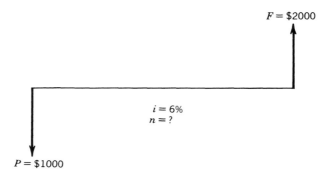

FIG. 14-16   Cash flow diagram for Example 14.20.

How long will it take an investment of $1,000 to increase to $2,000 if the interest is 6%? In other words, how many years will it take for money to double itself with the interest at 6%?

Solution: The cash flow diagram is shown in Figure 14-16.

$$i = 0.06$$
$$\frac{F}{P} = \frac{\$2,000}{\$1,000} = 2$$
$$n = ?$$
$$F = P(1+i)^n$$
$$\frac{F}{P} = (1+i)^n$$
$$2 = (1.06)^n$$

From the 6% column (Appendix D) the compound amount factors that bracket the derived value of $F/P = 2$ are:

F/P	n
1.898	11
2.000	?
2.012	12

The answer can be found by interpolation as

$$n = 11 \text{ years} + \frac{2.000 - 1.898}{2.012 - 1.898} \times 1 \text{ year}$$

$$n = 11.89 \text{ years}$$

and many pocket calculators will solve directly for

$$n = \frac{\ln 2}{\ln 1.06} = 11.90 \text{ years}$$

RULE OF 70

An approximate solution can also be found for the preceding problem by applying the rule of 70. The number 70 divided by the interest rate in percent will give the approximate number of years required for capital to double at that rate. If the interest is 6%.

$$\frac{70}{6} = 11.7 \text{ years (approximate)}$$

If the interest is 3%

$$\frac{0.70}{0.03} = \frac{70}{3} = 23.3 \text{ years, and so forth}$$

Conversely, if the number of years is given over which any investment has doubled in value, the interest rate may be approximated.

Example 14.21. Find F, given P, i, and n, using the approximate rule of 70.

Land was purchased 5 years ago for $10,000 and is now worth $20,000. Find the compounded interest rate at which the value of the land increased each year.

Solution:

$$\frac{70}{5 \text{ years}} = 14\% \text{ compounded}$$

OTHER TYPICAL CALCULATIONS

Example 14.22. Find i, given F, P, and n.

A savings certificate that costs \$75 now will pay \$100 in 6 years. What is the interest rate?

Solution: The cash flow diagram is drawn in Figure 14-17.

$$\frac{F}{P} = \frac{100}{75} = 1.333$$
$$n = 6$$
$$i = ?$$
$$\frac{F}{P} = (1+i)^n$$
$$\text{Since } \frac{F}{P} = \frac{100}{75} = 1.333$$
$$\text{Then } 1.333 = (1+i)^6$$
$$1+i = 1.333^{1/6}$$
$$i = 1.333^{1/6} - 1$$
$$i = 0.0491$$
$$i = 4.91\%$$

Example 14.23. Find A, given F, i, and n.

Three situations to which these conditions would apply are the following: (1) It is desired to establish a sinking fund that will accumulate to \$600,000 in 25 years. If interest is at 12% how much must be deposited in equal annual payments at the end of each of those 25 years? OR (2) What uniform annual expenditure, such as on the preventive maintenance, is justifiable for each of 25 years in order to avoid spending \$600,000 at the end of that time, if money is worth 12%? OR (3) What annual deposits must be made at 12% to save up enough to replace a structure that will cost \$600,000 just 25 years from now?

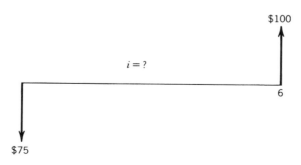

FIG. 14-17   Cash flow diagram for Example 14.22.

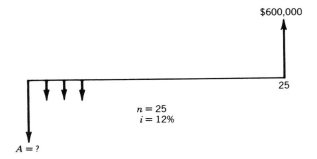

FIG. 14-18   Cash flow diagram for Example 14.23.

Solution: The cash flow diagram is shown in Figure 14-18.

$$i = 0.12$$
$$n = 25$$
$$F = \$600,000$$
$$A = ?$$

The 12% table (Appendix D) gives the *A/F* factor as 0.00750 for $n = 25$.

$$A = F(A/F, 5\%, 25)$$
$$= \$600,000 \ (0.00750)$$
$$= \$4,500 \text{ per year}$$

Example 14.24. Find *F*, given *A*, *i*, and *n*.

How much would be accumulated in the sinking fund in Example 14.23 at the end of 15 years?

Solution: The cash flow diagram is drawn as shown in Figure 14-19.

$$i = 0.12$$
$$n = 15$$
$$A = \$4,500/\text{year}$$
$$F = ?$$

The 12% table gives the uniform series *F/A* factor for $n = 15$ as 37.279:

$$F = A(F/A, 5\%, 15)$$
$$= \$4,500 \ (37.279)$$
$$= \$167,755$$

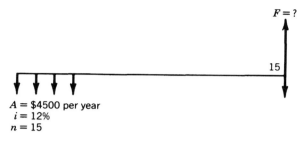

FIG. 14-19   Cash flow diagram for Example 14.24.

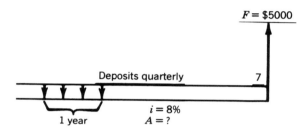

FIG. 14-20   Cash flow diagram for Example 14.25.

Example 14.25. Find *A*, given *F*, *i*, *n* with quarterly compounding.

What quarterly deposit must be made into a sinking fund to amount to $5,000 in 7 years if interest is at 8% compounded quarterly?

Solution: The cash flow diagram is drawn in Figure 14-20.

$$i = 1/4 \times 0.08 = 0.02$$
$$n = 4 \times 7 = 28$$
$$F = \$5,000$$
$$A = ?$$

From the 2% table (Appendix D) the *A/E* factor for $n = 28$ is found to be 0.02699.

$$A = F(A/F, 2\%, 28)$$
$$= \$5,000 \ (0.02699)$$
$$= \$134.95$$

Notice that this is a quarterly, not a yearly deposit.

Example 14.26. Find *A*, given *P*, *i*, and *n*.

What equal annual year-end payment of principal plus interest for 10 years is necessary to repay a loan of $10,000 if interest is 8%?

or

If $10,000 is deposited now at 8% interest, what uniform amount could be withdrawn at the end of each year for 10 years to have nothing left in the account at the beginning of the eleventh year?

Solution:
$$P = \$10,000$$
$$i = 0.08$$
$$n = 10 \text{ years}$$
$$Find \ A = ?$$
$$A = P(A/P, 8\%, 10)$$
$$= \$10,000 \ (0.1490)$$
$$= \$1,490.30 \text{ per year}$$

Example 14.27. Find the balance due on an installment loan. Find P, given A, i, and n.

How much will be owed on the loan in Example 14.26 after three payments have been made?

As previously explained, only the remaining principal of the loan is owed at that point. No further interest is owed if the loan is paid off in one lump sum at this time. Therefore, it is necessary to find the present worth of the loan at that time, which equals the present worth of the remaining payments.

Solution: The solution to Example 14.27 is the answer to this question: "What is the present worth of $1,490.30 for 7 years with interest at 8%?"

The cash flow diagram is drawn as shown in Figure 14-21.

$$i = 0.08$$
$$n = 7$$
$$A = \$1,490.30$$
$$P = ?$$
$$P = A\left[\frac{(1+i)^n - 1}{i(1+i)^n}\right]$$

From the 8% table (Appendix D), the uniform annual series P/A factor is seen to be 5.206, so that

$$P = A(P/A, 9\%, 7)$$
$$= \$1,490.30 \ (5.206)$$
$$= \$7,758.50$$

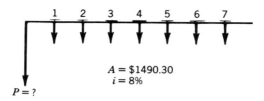

FIG. 14-21   Cash flow diagram for Example 14.27.

Example 14.28. Find the cost of financing a loan. Find *P*, given *A, i,* and *n*.

A construction manager has completed a certain job on which his fee was to have been $100,000. The owner offers to pay him $30,000 at once, and the remaining $70,000 in five yearly installments of $14,000 each. If the construction manager has to pay 12% interest on any money he borrows, how much is he losing by accepting the owner's offer?

Solution: The cash flow diagram is drawn in Figure 14-22.

The loss must be computed on the basis of what is owed now, not on what might happen in the future. True, the construction manager will have to pay 12% interest if the money must be borrowed, but if the money had been on hand, it could have been invested so as to earn 12%. Therefore,

$$i = 0.12$$
$$n = 5$$
$$A = \$14{,}000$$
$$P = ?$$

From the 12% table (Appendix D), the uniform annual series *P/A* factor is found to be 3.60478

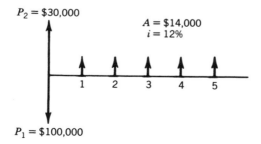

FIG. 14-22   Cash flow diagram for Example 14.28.

$$P = A(P/A, 12\%, 5)$$
$$= \$14,000 \ (3.60478)$$
$$= \$50,467$$

Therefore, the loss would be $\$70,000 - \$50,467 = \$19,533$, in terms of present worth dollars.

Example 14.29. Find A, given P, i, and n.

What would be the proper payments for the owner to make under the conditions of Example 14.28?

Solution: The cash flow diagram is drawn in Figure 14-23.

$$i = 0.12$$
$$n = 5$$
$$P = \$70,000$$
$$A = ?$$

From the 12% table, the A/P factor is found to be 0.27741, so the payments should be as follows:

$$A = P(A/P, 12\%, 5)$$
$$= \$70,000 \ (0.27741)$$
$$= \$19,419$$

instead of the $14,000 offered.

Example 14.30. Find the total P, given A, F, and n.

A certain builder takes back a second mortgage note for $10,000 amortized at 12% over a 10-year period. That is, the mortgage holder receives sufficient monthly payments to pay out the mortgage over a 120-month (10 year) period with interest on the unpaid balance at 1% per month compounded (12% nominal). After 4 months

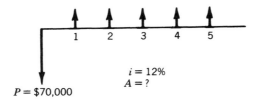

FIG. 14-23 Cash flow diagram for Example 14.29.

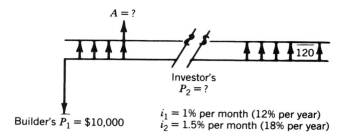

$A = ?$

$\boxed{120}$

Investor's
$P_2 = ?$

Builder's $P_1 = \$10,000$

$i_1 = 1\%$ per month (12% per year)
$i_2 = 1.5\%$ per month (18% per year)

FIG. 14-24   Cash flow diagram for Example 14.30.

the builder wants to sell the second mortgage, but a prospective investor–buyer wants to receive an 18% return on her money. How much will the investor–buyer pay for the mortgage?

Solution: The cash flow diagram is drawn in Figure 14-24.

The builder's second mortgage calls for monthly payments of

$$A = P_1(A/P, i, n)$$
$$= \$10,000 \ (A/P, 1\%, 120)$$
$$= \$10,000 \ (0.01434)$$
$$= \$143.47 \text{ per month}$$

The investor is purchasing a mortgage that is 4 months old and has only 116 payments left. Furthermore, the investor insists on $1\frac{1}{2}\%$/month (18% nominal), so to the investor the mortgage is worth:

$$P_2 = A(P/A, i, n)$$
$$= \$143.47 \ (P/A, 1.5\%, 116)$$
$$= \$143.47 \ (54.8135)$$
$$= \$7,864.09$$

The investor therefore is willing to pay only $7,864 for the remaining 114 payments in order to earn 18% on the investment.

Example 14.31. Find *P, A, F*, given *G, i,* and *n*.

This example illustrates applications of all three arithmetic gradient equations to the same problem situation.

To operate, maintain, and repair a motor grader costs $1,000 the first year and increases $500 per year thereafter, so that the second year's costs are $1,500, the third year's $2,000, and so on, for 5 years. For this example *i* = 8%.

Find:

1. The present worth of these costs
2. The equivalent uniform annual cost
3. The future worth of these costs

Solution:

1. $P = A(P/A, i, n) + G(P/G, i, n)$
    $= \$1,000(P/A, 8\%, 5) + \$500(P/G, 8\%, 5)$
    $= \$1,000(3.993) + \$500(7.372)$
    $= \$3,993 + \$3,686 = \$7,679$

To further illustrate this concept, if $7,679 were put into an account drawing 8% interest on the balance left in the account, and $1,000 were drawn out at the end of the first year to pay for operation and maintenance, $1,500 the second year, and so on, the account would be drawn down to zero at the end of the fifth year.

2. $A = A + G(A/G, i, n)$
    $= \$1,000 + \$500(1.846)$
    $= \$1,000 + \$923$
    $= \$1,923$

Or, in other words, if every year $1,923 were paid into an account drawing 8% interest, $1,000 could be drawn out the first year, $1,500 the second year, and so on, until the fifth year the account balance would be zero.

3. $F = A(F/A, i, n) + G(F/G, i, n)$
    $= \$1,000(5.867) + \$500(10.83)$
    $= \$5,867 + \$5,415$
    $= \$11,282$

To look at this solution another way, if at the end of the first year $1,000 were borrowed at 8% to pay for operating and maintenance expenses, $1,500 borrowed for the second year, and so on, at the end of the fifth year the amount owed would be $11,282.

SUMMARY

The understanding of money and cash flow is crucial in planning a successful construction project. Recognizing how time, interest, and the nature of repayment affect cash flow helps define total project financing and cash requirements. Multiple tools can be used to display this information; cash flow diagrams graphically display monetary inflows and outflows while balance-in-the-account diagrams depict account balances throughout a project's duration. Through the use of time value of money equations (or interest tables), the present value, future value, and periodic payment at different times can be determined.

KEY TERMS AND DEFINITIONS

Balance-in-the-account diagram: A graph that depicts the balance accumulated or left in the account at all points in time.

Capital recovery factor: A/P; the sinking fund deposit factor plus the interest rate. The amount that must be paid at the end of each year to pay off a debt of P dollars in n years at interest rate i.

Cash flow diagram: A graph that displays cash inflows and outflows over time.

Compound interest: The fee accumulated for borrowing money over the course of the loan term.

Effective rate: True interest rate charged on borrowed funds, depending on the compounding period involved.

Equal periodic payment: Usual way of paying off a mortgage note that involves a fixed periodic payment. All interest due at that time is paid, and the remainder of the payment is applied toward principal. Over time, the amount applied toward the interest decreases as the amount applied toward the principal increases.

Rule of 70: Tool used for determining the approximate number of years required for capital to double at a given interest rate; involves dividing the number 70 by the interest rate.

Single payment compound amount factor: $(1 = i)^n$ or F/P; the ratio of future value F to present value P.

Single payment present worth factor: $1/(1 + i)^n$ or P/F; the ratio of present value P to future value F.

Sinking fund deposit factor: $i/(1 + i)^n - 1$ or A/F; the ratio of periodic payment A to future value F in equal periodic payment scenarios.

Uniform annual series compound amount factor: $(1 + i)^n - 1/I$ or F/A; the ratio of future value F to periodic payment A in equal periodic payment scenarios.

Uniform annual series present worth factor: $[(1 + i)^n - 1]/i(1 + i)^n$ or P/A; the ratio of present worth P to periodic payment A in equal periodic payment scenarios.

KEY LEARNING POINTS

- Create and interpret cash flow diagrams.
- Calculate key expressions in time value of money calculations.
- Understand different methods of loan repayment.
- Know the concepts of arithmetic gradient, effective interest rates, and rule of 70.

QUESTIONS

1. What is a cash flow diagram? How is it constructed?

2. What type of repayment scenario is considered the "usual way" of paying off a mortgage note?

3. In the context of repayment plans 1–4, explain the concept of equivalence. Since these plans have different repayment amounts, how are they equivalent?

4. A loan specifies a promise to repay a lump sum of $53,600 at a time 20 years from now, with 10% interest on the unpaid balance. Find the present worth of that future $53,600 lump sum payment.

5. A loan specifies a promise to repay $2,500 annually for each of the next 15 years, and the interest is 8% on the unpaid balance. Find the present worth of all ten of those repayments.

6. Determine how much must be deposited at the end of each year for 20 years in order to accumulate $50,000 if the interest rate is 8%.

7. Determine the annual payment amount on a 30-year mortgage of $50,000 if the interest is 10%.

Appendix A

EXHIBIT A-1

REAL ESTATE PROMISSORY NOTE

$15,000,000.00

November 17, 2000
Jacksonville, Florida

FOR VALUE RECEIVED, **COLLIER VENTURE ONE, L.L.C.**, a Florida limited liability company (the **"Borrower"**), jointly and severally, hereby promises to pay to the order of **FIRST UNION NATIONAL BANK** (the **"Bank"**), at its offices at 225 Water Street, Third Floor, F0016, Jacksonville, Florida 32202, or such other place as Bank shall designate in writing from time to time, the principal sum of Fifteen Million and No/100 Dollars ($15,000,000.00) (the "Loan"), together with interest thereon as hereinafter provided.

1.   **INTEREST RATE.** Interest shall be charged on the outstanding principal balance from the date hereof until the full amount of principal due hereunder has been paid at a rate equal to 1-month LIBOR plus one and 90/100s percent (1.90%) per annum (**"LIBOR-Based Rate"**), as determined by Bank prior to the commencement of each Interest Period. Interest shall be calculated daily on the basis of the actual number of days elapsed over a 360 day year. The LIBOR-Based Rate shall remain in effect, subject to the provisions hereof, from and including the first day of the Interest Period to and excluding the last day of the Interest Period for which it is determined.

"LIBOR" means, with respect to each day during each Interest Period, the rate for U.S. dollar deposits of one month maturity as reported on Telerate page 3750 as of 11:00 a.m., London time, on the second London business day before the relevant Interest Period begins (or if not so reported, then as determined by the Bank from another recognized source or interbank quotation).

"Interest Period" means, initially, the period commencing on (and including) the date hereof and ending on (but excluding) the first Payment Date (as hereinafter defined), and thereafter, each period commencing on (and including) the last day of the immediately preceding Interest Period and ending on (but excluding) the next Payment Date, provided, (i) any Interest Period that would otherwise end on (but exclude) a day which is not a New York business day shall be extended to the next succeeding New York business day, unless such extension would carry such Interest Period into the next month, in which event such Interest Period shall end on (but exclude) the preceding New York business day; (ii) any Interest Period that ends in a month for which there is no day which numerically corresponds to the Payment Date shall end on (but exclude) the last New York business day of such month, and (iii) any Interest Period that would otherwise extend past the Maturity Date shall end on (but exclude) the Maturity Date.

2.   **PAYMENT OF PRINCIPAL AND INTEREST.**

2.1   Interest only on the outstanding principal balance accrued from and after the date hereof shall be payable monthly, commencing on the tenth (10th) day of January, 2001, and continuing on the same day of each month thereafter (each such date, a **"Payment Date"**) until and including November 10, 2002 (the "Conversion Date").

2.2   In the event Borrower satisfies each of the requirements set forth below in Section 2.4, payments of principal and interest in the amount of $121,289.90, shall be due and payable monthly, commencing on the 10th day of December, 2002, and continuing on the same day of each successive month next thereafter ensuing until the Maturity Date.

2.3   In the event Borrower satisfies each of the requirements set forth below in Section 2.4, the entire unpaid principal amount hereof, together with accrued and unpaid interest thereon and all other amounts payable hereunder shall be due and payable on November 10, 2003 (the **"Maturity Date"**).

2.4   The foregoing notwithstanding, the entire unpaid principal balance hereunder, together with any accrued and unpaid interest, is due and payable on the Conversion Date unless each of the following requirements is met on or before the Conversion Date: (i) no event of default has occurred hereunder or under any other loan document executed in connection with the loan evidenced hereby, (ii) Borrower has provided to Bank all items required for the final advance under the Loan Agreement (as hereinafter defined), and (iii) Borrower has provided to Bank satisfactory evidence that the Property (as hereinafter defined) has achieved and is capable of maintaining a minimum 1.25:1.0 Debt Service Coverage Ratio. For purposes of this Note, "Debt Service Coverage Ratio" shall mean the annualized Net Operating Income of the Property divided by the aggregate annualized principal and interest payments due hereunder (after taking into account any applicable interest rate swaps) for the same period. "Net Operating Income" shall mean all income from the Property minus all operating expenses (including a four percent (4%) management fee) and reasonable reserves for capital repairs and replacements.

3. **APPLICATION OF PAYMENTS.** Except as otherwise specified herein, each payment or prepayment, if any, made under this Note shall be applied to pay late charges, accrued and unpaid interest, principal, escrows (if any), and any other fees, costs and expenses which Borrower is obligated to pay under this Note, in such order as Bank may elect from time to time in its sole discretion.

4. **TENDER OF PAYMENT.** All payments on this Note are payable on or before 2:00 p.m. on the due date thereof, at the office of Bank specified above and shall be credited on the date the funds become available in lawful money of the United States. All sums payable to Bank which are due on a day on which Bank is not open for business shall be paid on the next succeeding business day and such extended time shall be included in the computation of interest.

5. **LATE CHARGE.** In the event that any installment of principal or interest required to be made by Borrower under this Note shall not be received by Bank within five (5) days after its due date, Borrower shall pay to Bank, on demand, a late charge of five percent (5%) of such delinquent payment. The foregoing right is in addition to, and not in limitation of, any other rights which Bank may have upon Borrower's failure to make timely payment of any amount due hereunder.

6. **SWAP AGREEMENT.** Borrower and Bank have entered into that certain ISDA Master Agreement (with accompanying schedules and confirmations) dated as of November 17, 2000 (the "SWAP Agreement"), contemplating an exchange of interest rate payments based on a notional amount equal to the principal balance of this Note. All payments of interest and principal due under this Note are intended to coincide with interest payments due with reductions of the notional principal amount as contemplated in the SWAP Agreement. Any sums due Borrower from Bank under the SWAP Agreement by reason of an "Early Termination" thereof, as defined therein, shall be applied to the unpaid balance of this Note. Any prepayment of this Note as set forth in the following paragraph shall not affect Borrower's obligations to continue making payments under the Swap Agreement, which Swap Agreement shall remain in full force and effect notwithstanding such prepayment. Borrower is liable for any breakage costs associated with the SWAP Agreement as a result of any prepayment.

7. **PREPAYMENT.** The Loan may be prepaid, in whole or in part, at any time and from time to time without penalty or premium. Any prepayment shall include accrued and unpaid interest to the date of prepayment on the principal amount prepaid and all other sums due and payable hereunder. Nothing herein shall be deemed to alter or affect any obligations that Borrower may have to Bank under any interest rate swap agreements.

8. **SECURITY FOR THE NOTE.**

8.1 This Note is executed and delivered in accordance with a commercial transaction described herein. As security for the payment of the monies owing under this Note, Borrower has delivered or has caused to be delivered to Bank the following (each a **"Loan Document"** and collectively with this Note, and any other guaranty, document, certificate or instrument executed by Borrower or any other obligated party in connection with the Loan, together with all amendments, modifications, renewals or extensions thereof, the **"Loan Documents"**): (a) a Mortgage and Security Agreement (the "**Mortgage**") encumbering certain real and personal property and the improvements situated thereon in the City of Gainesville, County of Alachua, State of Florida, as more fully described in the Mortgage (the **"Property"**); (b) a Construction Loan Agreement (the **"Loan Agreement"**) providing for the development and construction of certain improvements on the Property; (c) an Assignment of Borrower's Interest in Contract Documents; (d) a Conditional Assignment of Rents, Leases and Revenues; (e) an Environmental Indemnification Agreement; and a Real Estate Unconditional Guaranty (the **"Guaranty"**) by Nathan S. Collier.

8.2   Borrower hereby grants to Bank a continuing security interest in all property of Borrower, now or hereafter in the possession of Bank, as security for the payment of this Note and any other liabilities of Borrower to Bank, which security interest shall be enforceable and subject to all the provisions of this Note, as if such property were specifically pledged hereunder.

9.   **DEFAULT RATE.** From and after the Maturity Date or from and after the occurrence of an Event of Default hereunder, irrespective of any declaration of maturity, all amounts remaining unpaid or thereafter accruing hereunder, shall, at Bank's option, bear interest at the highest permissible rate under applicable usury law (the **"Default Rate"**). Such default rate of interest shall be payable upon demand, but in no event later than when scheduled interest payments are due, and shall also be charged on the amounts owed by Borrower to Bank pursuant to any judgments entered in favor of Bank with respect to this Note.

10.   **REPRESENTATIONS AND WARRANTIES.** Borrower represents and warrants to Bank as follows:

10.1   **Organization, Powers.** Borrower is a limited liability company duly organized, validly existing and in good standing under the laws of the state of its organization, and is authorized to do business in each other jurisdiction wherein its ownership of property or conduct of business legally requires such authorization; (ii) has the power and authority to own its properties and assets and to carry on its business as now being conducted and as now contemplated; and (iii) has the power and authority to execute, deliver and perform, and by all necessary action has authorized the execution, delivery and performance of, all of its obligations under each Loan Document to which it is a party.

10.2   **Execution of Loan Documents.** Each of the Loan Documents to which Borrower is a party has been duly executed and delivered by Borrower.

Execution, delivery and performance of each of the Loan Documents to which Borrower is a party will not: (i) violate any of its organizational documents, provision of law, order of any court, agency or other instrumentality of government, or any provision of any indenture, agreement or other instrument to which it is a party or by which it or any of its properties is bound; (ii) result in the creation or imposition of any lien, charge or encumbrance of any nature, other than the liens created by the Loan Documents; and (iii) require any authorization, consent, approval, license, exemption of, or filing or registration with, any court or governmental authority.

10.3   **Obligations of Borrower.** Each of the Loan Documents to which Borrower is a party is the legal, valid and binding obligation of Borrower, enforceable against it in accordance with its terms, except as the same may be limited by bankruptcy, insolvency, reorganization or other laws or equitable principles relating to or affecting the enforcement of creditors' rights generally. Borrower is obtaining the Loan for commercial purposes.

10.4   **Litigation.** There is no action, suit or proceeding at law or in equity or by or before any governmental authority, agency or other instrumentality now pending or, to the knowledge of Borrower, threatened against or affecting Borrower or any of its properties or rights which, if adversely determined, would materially impair or affect: (i) the value of any collateral securing this Note; (ii) Borrower's right to carry on its business substantially as now conducted (and as now contemplated); (iii) its financial condition; or (iv) its capacity to consummate and perform its obligations under the Loan Documents to which Borrower is a party.

10.5   **No Defaults.** Borrower is not in default in the performance, observance or fulfillment of any of the obligations, covenants or conditions contained herein or in any material agreement or instrument to which it is a party or by which it or any of its properties is bound.

10.6   **No Untrue Statements.** No Loan Document or other document, certificate or statement furnished to Bank by or on behalf of Borrower contains any untrue statement of a material fact or omits to state a material fact necessary in order to make the statements contained herein and therein not misleading. Borrower acknowledges that all such statements, representations and warranties shall be deemed to have been relied upon by Bank as an inducement to make the Loan to Borrower.

11.   **COVENANTS.**

11.1   **No Encumbrances.** Borrower shall not create or permit to exist any mortgage, lien, security interest or other encumbrance upon the Property except the Mortgage.

11.2   **<u>Documentary and Intangible Taxes.</u>** Borrower shall be liable for all documentary stamp and intangible taxes assessed at the closing of the Loan or from time to time during the life of the Loan.

11.3   **<u>Financial Statements: Compliance Certificate.</u>**

11.3.1   Borrower shall furnish to Bank the financial information, in each instance prepared in accordance with generally accepted accounting principles consistently applied, as set forth in the loan commitment from Bank to Borrower and the Mortgage and shall provide such other information respecting the operations of Borrower, the Property or the Guarantor as Bank may from time to time reasonably request.

11.3.2   Borrower shall furnish to Bank, with each set of financial statements described herein, a compliance certificate signed by Borrower's chief financial officer certifying that: (i) all representations and warranties of Borrower set forth in this Note or any other Loan Document remain true and correct as of the date of such compliance certificate; (ii) none of the covenants of Borrower contained in this Note or any other Loan Document has been breached; and (iii) to its knowledge, no event has occurred which constitutes an Event of Default (or which, with the giving of notice or the passage of time, or both, would constitute an Event of Default) under this Note or any other Loan Document. In addition, Borrower shall promptly notify Bank of the occurrence of any default, Event of Default, adverse litigation or material adverse change in its financial condition.

11.4   **<u>Indemnification.</u>**

11.4.1   Borrower hereby indemnifies and agrees to defend and hold harmless Bank, its officers, employees and agents, from and against any and all losses, damages, or liabilities and from any suits, claims or demands, including reasonable attorneys' fees incurred in investigating or defending such claim, suffered by any of them and caused by, arising out of, or in any way connected with the Loan Documents or the transactions contemplated therein (unless determined by a final judgment of a court of competent jurisdiction to have been caused solely by the gross negligence or willful misconduct of any of the indemnified parties) including, without limitation: (i) disputes with any architect, general contractor, subcontractor, materialman or supplier, or on account of any act or omission to act by Bank in connection with the Property; (ii) losses, damages (including consequential damages), expenses or liabilities sustained by Bank in connection with any environmental inspection, monitoring, sampling or cleanup of the Property required or mandated by any applicable environmental law; (iii) claims by any tenant or any other party arising under or in connection with any lease of all or any portion of the Property; (iv) any untrue statement of a material fact contained in information submitted to Bank by Borrower or the omission of any material fact necessary to be stated therein in order to make such statement not misleading or incomplete;

(v) the failure of Borrower to perform any obligations herein required to be performed by Borrower; and (vi) the ownership, construction, occupancy, operation, use or maintenance of the Property.

11.4.2   In case any action shall be brought against Bank, its officers, employees or agents, in respect to which indemnity may be sought against Borrower, Bank or such other party shall promptly notify Borrower and Borrower shall assume the defense thereof, including the employment of counsel selected by Borrower and satisfactory to Bank, the payment of all costs and expenses and the right to negotiate and consent to settlement. Bank shall have the right, at its sole option, to employ separate counsel in any such action and to participate in the defense thereof, all at Borrower's sole cost and expense. Borrower shall not be liable for any settlement of any such action effected without its consent (unless Borrower fails to defend such claim), but if settled with Borrower's consent, or if there be a final judgment for the claimant in any such action, Borrower agrees to indemnify and hold harmless Bank from and against any loss or liability by reason of such settlement or judgment.

11.4.3   The provisions of this Section 11.4 shall survive the repayment or other satisfaction of the Liabilities.

12.   **EVENTS OF DEFAULT.** Subject to the notice and cure periods set forth in the Loan Documents, each of the following shall constitute an event of default hereunder (an **"Event of Default"**): (a) the failure of Borrower to pay any amount of principal or interest hereunder when due and payable; (b) should there occur an event of default under the SWAP Agreement, or should any event occur thereunder which results in an "Early Termination" of the SWAP Agreement (as defined therein) not expressly permitted by the terms of this Note; or (c) the occurrence of any other default in any term, covenant or condition hereunder or any Loan Document.

13.   **REMEDIES.** If an Event of Default exists, Bank may exercise any right, power or remedy permitted by law or as set forth herein or in the Mortgage, the Loan Agreement, the Guaranty or any other Loan Document including, without limitation, the right to declare the entire unpaid principal amount hereof and all interest accrued hereon, and all other sums secured by the Mortgage or any other Loan Document, to be, and such principal, interest and other sums shall thereupon become, immediately due and payable.

14.   **MISCELLANEOUS.**

14.1   **Disclosure of Financial Information.** Bank is hereby authorized to disclose any financial or other information about Borrower to any regulatory body or agency having jurisdiction over Bank and to any present, future or prospective participant or successor in interest in any loan or other financial accommodation made by Bank to Borrower. The information provided may include, without limitation, amounts, terms, balances, payment history, return item history and any financial or other information about Borrower.

14.2   **Integration.** This Note and the other Loan Documents constitute the sole agreement of the parties with respect to the transaction contemplated hereby and supersede all oral negotiations and prior writings with respect thereto.

14.3   **Attorneys' Fees and Expenses.** If Bank retains the services of counsel by reason of a claim of a default or an Event of Default hereunder or under any of the other Loan Documents, or on account of any matter involving this Note, or for examination of matters subject to Bank's approval under the Loan Documents, all costs of suit and all reasonable attorneys' fees and such other reasonable expenses so incurred by Bank shall be paid by Borrower, on demand, and shall be deemed part of the obligations evidenced hereby.

14.4   **No Implied Waiver.** Bank shall not be deemed to have modified or waived any of its rights or remedies hereunder unless such modification or waiver is in writing and signed by Bank, and then only to the extent specifically set forth therein. A waiver in one event shall not be construed as continuing or as a waiver of or bar to such right or remedy in a subsequent event. After any acceleration of, or the entry of any judgment on, this Note, the acceptance by Bank of any payments by or on behalf of Borrower on account of the indebtedness evidenced by this Note shall not cure or be deemed to cure any Event of Default or reinstate or be deemed to reinstate the terms of this Note absent an express written agreement duly executed by Bank and Borrower.

14.5   **Waiver.** Borrower, jointly and severally, waives demand, notice, presentment, protest, demand for payment, notice of dishonor, notice of protest and diligence of collection of this Note. Borrower consents to any and all extensions of time, renewals, waivers, or modifications that may be granted by Bank with respect to the payment or other provisions of this Note, and to the release of any collateral, with or without substitution. Borrower agrees that makers, endorsers, guarantors and sureties may be added or released without notice and without affecting Borrower's liability hereunder. The liability of Borrower shall not be affected by the failure of Bank to perfect or otherwise obtain or maintain the priority or validity of any security interest in any collateral. The liability of Borrower shall be absolute and unconditional and without regard to the liability of any other party hereto.

14.6   **No Usurious Amounts.** Anything herein contained to the contrary not withstanding, it is the intent of the parties that Borrower shall not be obligated to pay interest hereunder at a rate which is in excess of the maximum rate permitted by law. If by the terms of this Note, Borrower is at any time required to pay interest at a rate in excess of such maximum rate, the rate of interest under this Note shall be deemed to be immediately reduced to such maximum legal rate and the portion of all prior interest payments in excess of such maximum legal rate shall be applied to and shall be deemed to have been payments in reduction of the outstanding principal balance, unless Borrower shall notify Bank, in writing, that Borrower elects to have such excess sum returned to it forthwith. Borrower agrees that in determining whether or not any interest payable under this Note exceeds the highest rate permitted by law, any non-principal payment, including without limitation, late charges, shall be deemed to the extent permitted by law to be an expense, fee or premium rather than interest. In addition, Bank may, in determining the maximum rate of interest allowed under applicable law, as amended from time to time, take advantage of: (i) the rate of interest permitted by Section 687.12 Florida Statutes ("Interest rates; parity among licensed lenders or creditors") and 12 United States Code, Sections 85 and 86, and (ii) any other law, rule or regulation in effect from time to time, available to Bank which exempts Bank from any limit upon the rate of interest it may charge or grants to Bank the right to charge a higher rate of interest than allowed by Florida Statutes, Chapter 687.

14.7 **Partial Invalidity.** The invalidity or unenforceability of any one or more provisions of this Note shall not render any other provision invalid or unenforceable. In lieu of any invalid or unenforceable provision, there shall be added automatically a valid and enforceable provision as similar in terms to such invalid or unenforceable provision as may be possible.

14.8 **Binding Effect.** The covenants, conditions, waivers, releases and agreements contained in this Note shall bind, and the benefits thereof shall inure to, the parties hereto and their respective heirs, executors, administrators, successors and assigns; provided, however, that this Note cannot be assigned by Borrower without the prior written consent of Bank, and any such assignment or attempted assignment by Borrower shall be void and of no effect with respect to Bank.

14.9 **Modifications.** This Note may not be supplemented, extended, modified or terminated except by an agreement in writing signed by the party against whom enforcement of any such waiver, change, modification or discharge is sought.

14.10 **Sales or Participations.** Bank may from time to time pledge, sell or assign, in whole or in part, or grant participations in, the Loan, this Note and/or the obligations evidenced thereby. The holder of any such sale, assignment or participation, if the applicable agreement between Bank and such holder so provides, shall be: (a) entitled to all of the rights, obligations and benefits of Bank; and (b) deemed to hold and may exercise the rights of setoff or banker's lien with respect to any and all obligations of such holder to Borrower, in each case as fully as though Borrower were directly indebted to such holder. Bank may in its discretion give notice to Borrower of such sale, assignment or participation; however, the failure to give such notice shall not affect any of Bank's or such holder's rights hereunder.

14.11 **Jurisdiction.** Borrower irrevocably appoints each and every owner, partner and/or officer of Borrower as its attorneys upon whom may be served, by regular or certified mail at the address set forth below, any notice, process or pleading in any action or proceeding against it arising out of or in connection with this Note or any other Loan Document; and Borrower hereby consents that any action or proceeding against it be commenced and maintained in any court within the State of Florida by service of process on any such owner, partner and/or officer; and Borrower agrees that the courts of such State shall have jurisdiction with respect to the subject matter hereof and the person of Borrower and all collateral securing the obligations of Borrower. Borrower agrees not to assert any defense to any action or proceeding initiated by Bank based upon improper venue or inconvenient forum.

14.12 **Notices.** All notices and communications under this Note shall be in writing and shall be given by either (a) hand-delivery, (b) first class mail (postage prepaid), or (c) reliable overnight commercial courier (charges prepaid), to the addresses listed in the Mortgage. Notice shall be deemed to have been given and received: (i) if by hand delivery, upon delivery; (ii) if by mail, three (3) calendar days after the date first deposited in the United States mail; and (iii) if by overnight courier, on the date scheduled for delivery. A party may change its address by giving written notice to the other party as specified herein.

14.13 **Governing Law.** This Note shall be governed by and construed in accordance with the substantive laws of the State of Florida without reference to conflict of laws principles.

14.14 **Joint and Several Liability.** If Borrower consists of more than one person or entity, the word **"Borrower"** shall mean each of them and their liability shall be joint and several.

14.15 **Continuing Enforcement.** If, after receipt of any payment of all or any part of this Note, Bank is compelled or agrees, for settlement purposes, to surrender such payment to any person or entity for any reason (including, without limitation, a determination that such payment is void or voidable as a preference or fraudulent conveyance, an impermissible setoff, or a diversion of trust funds), then this Note and the other Loan Documents shall continue in full force and effect or be reinstated, as the case may be, and Borrower shall be liable for, and shall indemnify, defend and hold harmless Bank with respect to, the full amount so surrendered. The provisions of this Section shall survive the cancellation or termination of this Note and shall remain effective notwithstanding the payment of the obligations evidenced hereby, the release of any security interest, lien or encumbrance securing this Note or any other action which Bank may have taken in reliance upon its receipt of such payment. Any cancellation, release or other such action shall be deemed to have been conditioned upon any payment of the obligations evidenced hereby having become final and irrevocable.

14.16 **Arbitration.** Upon demand of either Borrower or Bank, whether made before or after institution of any judicial proceeding, any claim or controversy arising out of or relating to the Loan Documents (a **"Dispute"**) shall be resolved by binding arbitration conducted under and governed by the Commercial Financial Disputes Arbitration Rules (the **"Arbitration Rules"**) of the American Arbitration Association (the **"AAA"**) and the Federal Arbitration Act. Disputes may include, without limitation, tort claims, counterclaims, a dispute as to whether a matter is subject to arbitration, claims brought as class actions, or claims arising from documents executed in the future. A judgment upon the award may be entered in any court having jurisdiction. Notwithstanding the foregoing, this arbitration provision does not apply to disputes under or related to swap agreements. **Special Rules**. All arbitration hearings shall be conducted in the city named in the address of Bank first stated above. A hearing shall begin within 90 days of demand for arbitration and all hearings shall conclude within 120 days of demand for arbitration. These time limitations may not be extended unless a party shows cause for extension and then for no more than a total of 60 days. The expedited procedures set forth in Rule 51 *et seq.* of the Arbitration Rules shall be applicable to claims of less than $1,000,000.00. Arbitrators shall be licensed attorneys selected from the Commercial Financial Dispute Arbitration Panel of the AAA. The parties do not waive applicable Federal or state substantive law except as provided herein. **Preservation and Limitation of Remedies**. Notwithstanding the preceding binding arbitration provisions, Borrower and Bank agree to preserve, without diminution, certain remedies that any party may exercise before or after an arbitration proceeding is brought. The parties shall have the right to proceed in any court of proper jurisdiction or by self-help to exercise or prosecute the following remedies, as applicable: (i) all rights to foreclose against any real or personal property or other security by exercising a power of sale or under applicable law by judicial foreclosure including a proceeding to confirm the sale; (ii) all rights of self-help including peaceful occupation of real property and collection of rents, set-off, and peaceful possession of personal property; (iii) obtaining provisional or ancillary remedies including injunctive relief, sequestration, garnishment, attachment, appointment of receiver and filing an involuntary bankruptcy proceeding; and (iv) when applicable, a judgment by confession of judgment. Any claim or controversy with regard to any party's entitlement to such remedies is a Dispute.

14.17 **Waiver of Jury Trial.** BORROWER AND BANK AGREE THAT, TO THE EXTENT PERMITTED BY APPLICABLE LAW, ANY SUIT, ACTION OR PROCEEDING, WHETHER CLAIM OR COUNTERCLAIM, BROUGHT BY BANK OR BORROWER, ON OR WITH RESPECT TO THIS NOTE OR ANY OTHER LOAN DOCUMENT OR THE DEALINGS OF THE PARTIES WITH RESPECT HERETO OR THERETO, SHALL BE TRIED ONLY BY A COURT AND NOT BY A JURY. BANK AND BORROWER EACH HEREBY KNOWINGLY, VOLUNTARILY, INTENTIONALLY AND INTELLIGENTLY, AND WITH THE ADVICE OF THEIR RESPECTIVE COUNSEL, WAIVE, TO THE EXTENT PERMITTED BY APPLICABLE LAW, ANY RIGHT TO A TRIAL BY JURY IN

ANY SUCH SUIT, ACTION OR PROCEEDING. FURTHER, BORROWER **WAIVES ANY RIGHT IT MAY HAVE TO CLAIM OR RECOVER, IN ANY SUCH SUIT, ACTION OR PROCEEDING, ANY SPECIAL, EXEM-PLARY, PUNITIVE, CONSEQUENTIAL OR OTHER DAMAGES OTHER THAN, OR IN ADDITION TO, ACTUAL DAMAGES. BORROWER AC-KNOWLEDGES AND AGREES THAT THIS SECTION IS A SPECIFIC AND MATERIAL ASPECT OF THIS NOTE AND THAT BANK WOULD NOT EXTEND CREDIT TO BORROWER IF THE WAIVERS SET FORTH IN THIS SECTION WERE NOT A PART OF THIS NOTE.**

IN WITNESS WHEREOF, Borrower, intending to be legally bound, has duly executed and delivered this Note as of the day and year first above written.

> **COLLIER VENTURE ONE, L.L.C.**, a Florida limited liability company
>
>
> By: _____
> Name: Nathan S. Collier
> Title: Managing Member

PROPER FLORIDA DOCUMENTARY STAMP TAX HAS BEEN PAID ON THIS NOTE AND EVIDENCE THEREOF APPEARS ON THE MORTGAGE SECUR-ING THIS NOTE.

EXHIBIT A-2

Prepared by and Record and Return to:
C. Davis Ely, Esquire
Rogers, Towers, Bailey, Jones & Gay, P.A.
1301 Riverplace Boulevard, Suite 1500
Jacksonville, FL 32207

MORTGAGE AND SECURITY AGREEMENT

THIS MORTGAGE AND SECURITY AGREEMENT ("Mortgage") is executed this 17th of November, 2000 by and between **FIRST UNION NATIONAL BANK**, a national banking association, whose address is Real Estate Portfolio Management, 225 Water Street, 3rd Floor, FL0016, Jacksonville, Florida 32202 (hereinafter referred to as the "Mortgagee"), and **COLLIER VENTURE ONE, L.L.C.,** a Florida limited liability company, whose address for notice under this Mortgage is P.O. Box 13116, Gainesville, Florida 32604 (hereinafter referred to as "Mortgagor").

W I T N E S S E T H :

A.   Mortgagor is justly indebted to Mortgagee in the principal sum of Fifteen Million Dollars and No Cents ($15,000,000.00) (the "Loan"), which Loan is evidenced by a certain Real Estate Promissory Note of even date herewith, with the payment of any and all outstanding principal and accrued interest being due no later than November 10, 2003 (hereinafter, together with any and all extensions, renewals, modifications, replacements, substitutions, and any and all other certificates of evidence of indebtedness evidenced by said Real Estate Promissory Note, referred to as the "Note"), which Note is by reference made a part hereof.

B.   That certain Construction Loan Agreement of even date herewith (the "Loan Agreement") provides for periodic advances of loan proceeds by Mortgagee to Mortgagor to facilitate the construction of improvements by Mortgagor on the Premises, as said term is defined herein.

C.   To evidence and secure the Loan, Mortgagor has executed and delivered to Mortgagee the Note, this Mortgage, the Loan Agreement, UCC-1 Financing Statements, an Assignment of Borrower's Interest in Contract Documents and a Conditional Assignment of Rents, Leases and Revenues, all of even date herewith and other documentation related to the Loan, which documents and any modification, extension and amendments thereof are herein referred to as the "Loan Documents."

D.   This Mortgage shall secure the Loan outstanding from time to time under the Loan Agreement and indebtedness referred to herein and the observance and performance by Mortgagor of the terms and conditions and covenants and agreements of Mortgagor in the Loan Documents.

THEREFORE, in consideration of and to secure the Note, together with interest thereon and any and all sums due or which may become due from Mortgagor to Mortgagee, Mortgagor does grant, bargain, sell, alien, remise, release, convey and confirm unto Mortgagee, its successors and assigns, in fee simple, all of that certain tract of land of which Mortgagor is now seized and possessed and in actual possession, all of which is situate in the County of Alachua, State of Florida and is more fully described in Exhibit ("A") attached hereto and made a part hereof, together with the buildings and improvements thereon erected or to be erected (hereinafter referred to as the "Premises");

TOGETHER with:

(i)   all leasehold estate, and all right, title and interest of Mortgagor in and to all leases or subleases covering the Premises or any portion thereof now or hereafter existing or entered into, and all right, title and interest of Mortgagor thereunder, including, without limitation, all cash or security deposits, advance rentals, and deposits or payments of similar nature;

(ii)   all right, title and interest of Mortgagor in and to all options to purchase or lease the Premises or any portion thereof or interest therein, and any greater estate in the Premises owned or hereafter acquired;

(iii)   all easements, streets, ways, alleys, rights-of-way and rights used in connection therewith or as a means of access thereto, and all tenements, hereditaments and appurtenances thereof and thereto, and all water rights;

(iv)   any and all buildings, structures and improvements now or hereafter erected thereon, including, but not limited to the fixtures, attachments, appliances, equipment, machinery, and other articles attached to said buildings, structures and improvements (sometimes hereinafter referred to as the "Improvements");

(v)   all fixtures, appliances, machinery, equipment, furniture, furnishings and articles of personal property now or hereafter affixed to, placed upon or used in connection with the operation of any of said properties and all gas, steam, electric, water and other heating, cooking, refrigerating, lighting, plumbing, ventilating, irrigating and power systems, machines, appliances, fixtures, and appurtenances which are now or may hereafter pertain to or be used with, in or on said premises, even though they may be detached or detachable and all building improvement and construction materials, supplies and equipment hereafter delivered to said land contemplating installation or use in the constructions thereon and all rights and interests of Mortgagor in building permits and architectural plans and specifications relating to contemplated constructions or Improvements on said Premises and all rights and interests of Mortgagor in present or future mortgage loan commitments pertaining to any of said Premises or Improvements thereon (sometimes hereinafter referred to as the "Personal Property");

(vi)   all proceeds of insurance for the Premises or any part thereof to which Mortgagor is entitled and all awards and proceeds of condemnation for the Premises or any part thereof to which Mortgagor is entitled for any taking of all or any part of the Premises by condemnation or exercise of the right of eminent domain. All such awards and proceeds are hereby assigned to Mortgagee and Mortgagee is hereby authorized, subject to the provisions contained in this Mortgage, to apply such awards and proceeds or any part thereof, after deducting therefrom any expenses incurred by Mortgagee in the collection or handling thereof, toward the payment, in full or in part, of the Note, notwithstanding the fact that the amount owing thereon may not then be due and payable;

(vii)   all rents, issues and profits of the Premises and all the estate, right, title and interest of every nature whatsoever of Mortgagor in and to the same;

(viii)   all accounts (including contract rights) and general intangibles pertaining to or arising from or in connection with all or any part of the Mortgaged Property, as hereinafter defined, including without limitation, all proceeds and choses in action arising under any insurance policies maintained with respect to all or any part of the Mortgaged Property;

(ix)   all building permits, governmental permits, licenses or other governmental authorizations in favor of or in the name of Mortgagor now existing or hereafter executed, including, but not limited to, stormwater permits, water distribution system permits, utility reservation and service agreements, concurrency reservations, department of transportation permits, and sewage collection system permits; and

(x)   all proceeds, products, replacements, additions, substitutions, renewals and accessions of any of the foregoing items.

All of the foregoing real and personal property, and all rights, privileges and franchises are collectively referred to as the "Mortgaged Property."

TO HAVE AND TO HOLD all and singular the Mortgaged Property hereby conveyed, and the tenements, hereditaments and appurtenances thereunto belonging or in anyway appertaining, and the reversion and reversions, remainder and remainders, rents, issues and profits thereof and also all the estate, right, title, interest property, possession, claim and demand whatsoever as well in law as in equity of Mortgagor in and to the same and every part and parcel thereof unto Mortgagee in fee simple.

PROVIDED ALWAYS that if Mortgagor shall pay to Mortgagee any and all indebtedness due by Mortgagor to Mortgagee (including the indebtedness evidenced by the Note and any and all renewals of the same) and shall perform, comply with and abide by each and every stipulation, agreement, condition, and covenant of the

Note, the Loan Agreement and of this Mortgage, then this Mortgage and the estate hereby created shall cease and be null and void. Provided, it is further covenanted and agreed by the parties hereto that this Mortgage also secures the payment of and includes all future or further advances as hereinafter set forth, to the same extent as if such were made on the date of the execution of this Mortgage, and any disbursements made for the payment of tax, levies or insurance on the Mortgaged Property, with interest on such disbursements at the Default Rate as hereinafter defined.

To protect the security of this Mortgage, Mortgagor further covenants, warrants and agrees with Mortgagee as follows:

ARTICLE 1
COVENANTS AND AGREEMENTS OF MORTGAGOR

1.1   **Payment of Secured Obligations.** Mortgagor shall pay when due the principal of, and the interest on, the indebtedness evidenced by the Note, and the charges, fees and the principal of, and interest on, any future advances secured by this Mortgage and shall otherwise comply with all the terms of the Note, the Loan Agreement and this Mortgage.

1.2   **Warranties and Representations.** Mortgagor hereby covenants with Mortgagee that Mortgagor is indefeasibly seized of the Mortgaged Property; that Mortgagor has full power and lawful right to convey the same in fee simple as aforesaid; that it shall be lawful for Mortgagor at all times peaceably and quietly to enter upon, hold, occupy and enjoy the Mortgaged Property and every part thereof; that Mortgagor will make such further assurances to perfect the lien interest in the Premises in Mortgagee, as may reasonably be required; and that Mortgagor does hereby fully warrant the title to the Mortgaged Property and every part thereof and will defend the same against the lawful claims of all persons whomsoever.

Mortgagor further represents and warrants to Mortgagee that all information, reports, paper, and data given to Mortgagee with respect to Mortgagor, and to the Loan evidenced by the Note and Mortgage are accurate and correct in all material respects and complete insofar as may be necessary to give Mortgagee a true and accurate knowledge of the subject matter.

1.3   **Ground Leases, Leases, Subleases, Declaration of Covenants and Restrictions and Easements.** Mortgagor, at Mortgagor's sole cost and expense, shall maintain and cause to be performed all of the covenants, agreements, terms, conditions and provisions on its part to be kept, observed and performed under any ground lease, lease, sublease, declaration of covenants and restrictions or easements which may constitute a portion of or an interest in the Premises, shall require its tenants or subtenants to keep, observe and perform all the covenants, agreements, terms, conditions and provisions on their part to be kept, observed or performed under any and all ground leases, leases, subleases, declaration of covenants and restrictions or easements; and shall not suffer or permit any breach or default to occur with respect to the foregoing; and in default thereof, Mortgagee shall have the right to perform or to require performance of any such covenants, agreements, terms, conditions or provisions of any such ground lease, lease, sublease, declaration of covenants and restrictions or easements and to add any expense incurred in connection therewith to the debt secured hereby, which such expense shall bear interest from the date of payment to the date of recovery by Mortgagee at the Default Rate. Any such payment by Mortgagee with interest thereon shall be immediately due and payable. Mortgagor shall not, without the consent of Mortgagee, consent to the modification, amendment, cancellation, termination or surrender of any such ground lease, lease, sublease, declaration of covenants and restrictions or easement.

No release or forbearance of any of Mortgagor's obligations under any such ground lease, lease, sublease, declaration of covenants and restrictions or easement shall release Mortgagor from any of its obligations under this Mortgage.

1.4   **Required Insurance.** Mortgagor will, at Mortgagor's sole cost and expense, maintain or cause to be maintained with respect to the Mortgaged Property, and each part thereof, the following insurance:

(a)   Liability and builder's risk insurance and where applicable, insurance against loss or damage to the Improvements by fire and any of the risks covered by insurance of the type now known as "fire and extended coverage," in an amount not less than the greater of the original amount of the Note or the full replacement cost of the Improvements; and

(b)   Such other insurance and in such amounts, as may from time to time be required by Mortgagee against the same or other hazards.

All policies of insurance required by the terms of this Mortgage shall contain an endorsement or agreement by the insurer that any loss shall be payable in accordance with the terms of such policy notwithstanding any act or negligence of Mortgagor which might otherwise result in forfeiture of said insurance and the further agreement of the insurer waiving all rights of set-off, counterclaim or deductions against Mortgagor.

Mortgagor may effect for its own account any insurance not required under this Section 1.4, but any such insurance effected by Mortgagor on the Premises, whether or not so required, shall be for the mutual benefit of Mortgagor and Mortgagee and shall be subject to the other provisions of this Mortgage.

1.5   **Delivery of Policies, Payment of Premiums.** All policies of insurance shall be issued by companies and in amounts in each company satisfactory to Mortgagee. All policies of insurance shall have attached thereto a lender's loss payment endorsement for the benefit of Mortgagee in form satisfactory to Mortgagee. Mortgagor shall furnish Mortgagee with an original policy of all policies of required insurance. If Mortgagee consents to Mortgagor providing any of the required insurance through blanket policies carried by Mortgagor and covering more than one location, then Mortgagor shall furnish Mortgagee with a certificate of insurance for each such policy setting forth the coverage, the limits of liability, the name of the carrier, the policy number, and the expiration date. At least thirty (30) days prior to the expiration of each such policy, Mortgagor shall furnish Mortgagee with evidence satisfactory to Mortgagee of the payment of premium and the reissuance of a policy continuing insurance in force as required by this Mortgage. All such policies shall contain a provision that such policies will not be canceled or materially amended, which term shall include any reduction in the scope or limits of coverage, without at least thirty (30) days prior written notice to Mortgagee. In the event Mortgagor fails to provide, maintain, keep in force or deliver and furnish to Mortgagee the policies of insurance required by this Section, Mortgagee may procure such insurance or single-interest insurance for such risks covering Mortgagee's interest, and Mortgagor will pay all premiums thereon promptly upon demand by Mortgagee together with interest thereon at the Default Rate.

1.6 **Insurance Proceeds.** After the happening of any casualty to the Mortgaged Property or any part thereof, Mortgagor shall give prompt written notice thereof to Mortgagee.

(a) In the event of any damage to or destruction of the Mortgaged Property, Mortgagee shall have the option in its sole discretion of applying or paying all or part of the insurance proceeds (i) to any indebtedness secured hereby and in such order as Mortgagee may determine, or (ii) to the restoration of the Improvements, or (iii) to Mortgagor.

(b) In the event of such loss or damage, all proceeds of insurance shall be payable to Mortgagee, and Mortgagor hereby authorizes and directs any affected insurance company to make payment of such proceeds directly to Mortgagee. Mortgagee is hereby authorized and empowered by Mortgagor to settle, adjust or compromise any claims for loss, damage or destruction under any policy or policies of insurance.

(c) Except to the extent that insurance proceeds are received by Mortgagee and applied to the indebtedness secured hereby, nothing herein contained shall be deemed to excuse Mortgagor from repairing or maintaining the Mortgaged Property as provided in this Mortgage or restoring all damage or destruction to the Mortgaged Property, regardless of whether or not there are insurance proceeds available or whether any such proceeds are sufficient in amount, and the application or release by Mortgagee of any insurance proceeds shall not cure or waive any default or notice of default under this Mortgage or invalidate any act done pursuant to such notice.

(d) The provisions of this Paragraph 1.6 to the contrary notwithstanding, in the event of any loss or damage to the Mortgaged Property due to such casualty, Mortgagor shall be entitled to use all insurance proceeds payable as the result of such loss or damage in order to repair and/or restore the Mortgaged Property provided the following conditions are satisfied:

(i)   Mortgagor is not in default under any obligations secured hereby or under the terms of any other Loan Document;

(ii)   the Proceeds are paid into an escrow account maintained with Mortgagee;

(iii) Mortgagor deposits into the escrow account described in (ii) above, a sum necessary to complete the repairs and/or restoration (as determined by Mortgagee in its reasonable opinion) in the event the Proceeds are insufficient to complete such repairs and/or restoration prior to commencing such repairs and/or restoration;

(iv) all repairs and/or restorations are carried out pursuant to plans and specifications approved by Mortgagee;

(v)   the repairs and/or restoration can be completed prior to the Maturity Date of the Note; and

(vi) the proceeds held in escrow (both the insurance proceeds and Mortgagor's proceeds) are disbursed in accordance with Mortgagee's standard construction loan administration procedures.

1.7   **Assignment of Policies Upon Foreclosure.** In the event of foreclosure of this Mortgage or other transfer of title or assignment of the Mortgaged Property in extinguishment, in whole or in part, of the debt secured hereby, all right, title and interest of Mortgagor in and to all policies of insurance required by this Section shall inure to the benefit of and pass to the successor in interest to Mortgagor or the purchaser or grantee of the Mortgaged Property. Mortgagor hereby appoints Mortgagee its attorney-in-fact to endorse any checks, drafts or other instruments representing any proceeds of such insurance, whether payable by reason of loss thereunder or otherwise.

1.8   **Taxes, Utilities and Impositions.** Mortgagor will pay, or cause to be paid and discharged, on or before the last day on which they may be paid without penalty or interest, all such duties, taxes, sewer rents, charges for water, or for setting or repairing of meters, and all other utilities on the Mortgaged Property or any part thereof, and any assessments and payments, usual or unusual, extraordinary or ordinary, which shall be imposed upon or become due and payable or become a lien upon the Premises or any part thereof and the sidewalks or streets in front thereof and any vaults therein by virtue of any present or future law of the United States or of the State, County, or City wherein the Premises are located (all of the foregoing being herein collectively called "Impositions"). In event of default of any such payment of any Imposition, Mortgagee may pay the same and the amount so paid by Mortgagee shall, at Mortgagee's option, become immediately due and payable with interest at the Default Rate and shall be deemed part of the indebtedness secured by this Mortgage.

If at any time there shall be assessed or imposed (i) a tax or assessment on the Premises in lieu of or in addition to the Impositions payable by Mortgagor pursuant to this Section or (ii) a license fee, tax or assessment imposed on Mortgagee and measured by or based in whole or in part upon the amount of the outstanding obligations secured hereby, then all such taxes, assessments or fees shall be deemed to be included within the term "Impositions" as defined in this Section, and Mortgagor shall pay and discharge the same as herein provided with respect to the payment of Impositions or, at the option of Mortgagee, all obligations secured hereby, together with all accrued interest thereon, shall immediately become due and payable. Anything to the contrary herein notwithstanding, Mortgagor shall have no obligation to pay any franchise, estate, inheritance, income, excess profits or similar tax levied on Mortgagee or on the obligations secured hereby.

Mortgagor will pay all mortgage recording taxes and fees payable with respect to this Mortgage or other mortgage or transfer taxes due on account of this Mortgage or the Note secured hereby.

Mortgagor will exhibit to Mortgagee the original receipts or other reasonably satisfactory proof of the payment of all Impositions which may affect the Mortgaged Property or any part thereof or the lien of the Mortgage promptly following the last date on which each Imposition is payable hereunder.

Notwithstanding the foregoing, Mortgagor shall have the right, after prior written notice to Mortgagee, to contest at its own expense the amount and validity of any Imposition affecting the Mortgaged Property by appropriate proceedings conducted in good faith and with due diligence and to postpone or defer payment thereof, if and so long as:

(a)   Such proceedings shall operate to suspend the collection of such Imposition from Mortgagor or the Mortgaged Property;

(b)   Neither the Mortgaged Property nor any part thereof would be in immediate danger of being forfeited or lost by reason of such proceedings, postponement or deferment; and

(c)   In the case of any Imposition affecting the Mortgaged Property which might be or become a lien, encumbrance or charge upon or result in any forfeiture or loss of the Mortgaged Property or any part thereof, or which might result in loss or damage to Mortgagor or Mortgagee, Mortgagor, prior to the date such Imposition would become delinquent, shall have furnished Mortgagee with security satisfactory to Mortgagee, and, in the event that such security is furnished, Mortgagee shall not have the right during the period of the contest to pay, remove or discharge the Imposition.

1.9   **Tax and Insurance Deposits.** Upon an event of default hereunder and if required by Mortgagee, Mortgagor shall pay to Mortgagee, each month until the Note is fully paid, a sum equal to the premiums that will next become due and payable on policies of insurance required under this Mortgage, plus the taxes, assessments and other charges next due upon the Premises, all as estimated by Mortgagee, less all sums already paid therefor, divided by the number of months to elapse before one (1) month prior to the date when each of such items will become payable. Such sums shall be held by Mortgagee in escrow in an interest-bearing account to pay such insurance premiums, taxes, assessments, and other charges. The failure by Mortgagor to make any such monthly payment as and when required under this numbered Paragraph shall constitute a default under the Mortgage.

Mortgagor shall furnish to Mortgagee, not later than fifteen (15) days after receipt by Mortgagor, an official statement of the amount of all insurance premiums, taxes, assessments, and other charges next payable. Mortgagee shall pay such items to the extent of the then unused escrowed funds on hand therefor, as and when they become severally due and payable. An official receipt therefor shall be conclusive evidence of such payment and of the validity of such expenses.

If the total of the payments made by Mortgagor under this numbered Paragraph shall exceed the amount of expenses actually paid by Mortgagee for the purposes set forth herein, Mortgagee shall credit such excess on subsequent payment to be made under this numbered Paragraph by Mortgagor or shall refund such excess to Mortgagor at the option of Mortgagee. If, however, the monthly payments to be made under this numbered Paragraph by Mortgagor shall not be sufficient to pay such items when the same shall become payable, then Mortgagor shall pay to Mortgagee any amount necessary to make up the deficiency five (5) days on or before the date when payment of such insurance premiums, taxes, assessments and other charges shall become due and payable. If at any time Mortgagor shall tender to Mortgagee, in accordance with the provisions of the Mortgage Note secured hereby, full payment of the entire indebtedness represented thereby, Mortgagee, in computing the amount of such indebtedness, and at its option, may credit to the account of Mortgagor any balance remaining in the funds so accumulated in escrow. The amount of the existing credit under this numbered Paragraph at the time of any transfer of the Premises shall, without the necessity for a separate assignment thereof or agreement relating thereto inure to the benefit of the successor-owner of the Premises and shall be applied under and be subject to all of the provisions of this numbered Paragraph. If there shall be a default under any of the provisions of this Mortgage resulting in a public sale of the Premises, or if Mortgagee acquires the Premises otherwise after default, Mortgagee may apply, at the time of the commencement of such a proceeding or at the time the Premises are otherwise acquired, the balance then remaining in escrow accumulated hereunder as a credit against the indebtedness remaining unpaid under the Note.

1.10 **Maintenance, Repairs, Alterations.** Mortgagor shall keep the Mortgaged Property, or cause the same to be kept, in good condition and repair and fully protected from the elements to the satisfaction of Mortgagee; Mortgagor shall not commit nor permit to be committed waste thereon and shall not do nor permit to be done any act by which the Mortgaged Property shall become less valuable; Mortgagor will not remove, demolish or structurally alter any of the Improvements (except such alterations as may be required by laws, ordinances or regulations) without the prior written permission of Mortgagee; Mortgagor shall complete promptly and in good and workmanlike manner any building or other improvement which may be constructed on the Premises and promptly restore in like manner any Improvements which may be damaged or destroyed thereon and will pay when due all claims for labor performed and materials furnished therefor; Mortgagor shall use and operate, and shall require its lessees or licensees to use or operate, the Mortgaged Property in compliance with all applicable laws, ordinances, regulations, covenants, conditions and restrictions, and with all applicable requirements of any ground lease, lease or sublease now or hereafter affecting the Premises or any part thereof. Unless required by law or unless Mortgagee has otherwise agreed in writing, Mortgagor shall not allow changes in the stated use of Mortgaged Property from that which was disclosed to Mortgagee at the time of execution hereof. Mortgagor shall not initiate or acquiesce to a zoning change of the Mortgaged Property without the prior notice to and consent of Mortgagee. Mortgagee and its representatives shall have access to the Premises at all reasonable times to determine whether Mortgagor is complying with its obligations under this Mortgage, including, but not limited to, those set out in this Section.

1.11 **Eminent Domain.** Should the Mortgaged Property, or any part thereof or interest therein, be taken or damaged by reason of any public use or improvement or condemnation proceeding, or in any other manner ("Condemnation"), or should Mortgagor receive any notice or other information regarding such Condemnation, Mortgagor shall give prompt written notice thereof to Mortgagee.

(a) Mortgagee shall be entitled to all compensation, awards and other payments or relief granted in connection with such Condemnation, and shall be entitled, at its option, to commence, appear in and prosecute in its own name any action or proceedings relating thereto. Mortgagee shall also be entitled to make any compromise or settlement in connection with such taking or damage. All such compensation, awards, damages, rights of action and proceeds awarded to Mortgagor (the "Proceeds") are hereby assigned to Mortgagee and Mortgagor agrees to execute such further assignments of the Proceeds as Mortgagee may require.

(b) In the event any portion of the Mortgaged Property is so taken or damaged, Mortgagee shall have the option in its sole and absolute discretion, to apply all such Proceeds, after deducting therefrom all costs and expenses (regardless of the particular nature thereof and whether incurred with or without suit), including attorneys' fees, incurred by it in connection with such Proceeds, upon any indebtedness secured hereby, or to apply all such Proceeds, after such deductions, to the restoration of the Mortgaged Property upon such conditions as Mortgagee may determine. Such application or release shall not cure or waive any default or notice of default hereunder or invalidate any act done pursuant to such notice.

(c) Any amounts received by Mortgagee hereunder (after payment of any costs in connection with obtaining same), shall, if retained by Mortgagee, be applied in payment of any accrued interest and then in reduction of the then outstanding principal sum of the Note, notwithstanding that the same may not then be due and payable. Any amount so applied to principal shall be applied to the payment of installments of principal on the Note in inverse order of their due dates.

(d) The provisions of this Paragraph 1.11 to the contrary notwithstanding, in the event of any loss or damage to the Mortgaged Property due to such Condemnation proceeding, Mortgagor shall be entitled to use all Proceeds payable as the result of such loss or damage in order to repair and/or restore the Mortgaged Property provided the following conditions are satisfied:

(i) Mortgagor is not in default under any obligations secured hereby or under the terms of any other Loan Document;

(ii) the Proceeds are paid into an escrow account maintained with Mortgagee;

(iii) Mortgagor deposits into the escrow account described in (ii) above, a sum necessary to complete the repairs and/or restoration (as determined by Mortgagee in its reasonable opinion) in the event the Proceeds are insufficient to complete such repairs and/or restoration prior to commencing such repairs and/or restoration;

(iv) all repairs and/or restorations are carried out pursuant to plans and specifications approved by Mortgagee;

(v) the repairs and/or restoration can be completed prior to the Maturity Date of the Note; and

(vi) the proceeds held in escrow (both the condemnation Proceeds and Mortgagor's proceeds) are disbursed in accordance with Mortgagee's standard construction loan administration procedures.

1.12   **Actions by Mortgagee to Preserve the Security of this Mortgage.**
If Mortgagor fails to make any payment or to do any act as and in the manner
provided for in this Mortgage or the Note, Mortgagee, in its own discretion, without
obligation so to do and without notice to or demand upon Mortgagor and without
releasing Mortgagor from any obligation, may make or do the same in such manner
and to such extent as Mortgagee may deem necessary to protect the security hereof.
Mortgagor will pay upon demand all expenses incurred or paid by Mortgagee
(including, but not limited to, attorneys' fees and court costs, including those in
all appellate and bankruptcy proceedings) on account of the exercise of any of the
aforesaid rights or privileges or on account of any litigation which may arise in
connection with this Mortgage or the Note or on account of any attempt, without
litigation, to enforce the terms of this Mortgage or the Note. In case the Mortgaged
Property or any part thereof shall be advertised for foreclosure sale and not sold,
Mortgagor shall pay all costs in connection therewith.

In the event that Mortgagee is called upon to pay any sums of money
to protect this Mortgage and the Note as aforesaid, all monies advanced or due
hereunder shall become immediately due and payable, together with interest at the
Default Rate, computed from the date of such advance to the date of the actual
receipt of payment thereof by Mortgagee.

1.13   **Cost of Collection.** In the event this Mortgage is placed in the hands
of an attorney for the collection of any sum payable hereunder, Mortgagor agrees
to pay all costs of collection, including reasonable attorney's fees including those
in all appellate and bankruptcy proceedings, incurred by Mortgagee, either with
or without the institution of any action or proceeding, and in addition to all costs,
disbursements and allowances provided by law. All such costs so incurred shall be
deemed to be secured by this Mortgage.

1.14   **Survival of Warranties.** All representations, warranties and covenants
of Mortgagor contained herein or incorporated by reference shall survive funding
of the Loan evidenced by the Note and shall remain continuing obligations, warranties and representations of Mortgagor during any time when any portion of the
obligations secured by this Mortgage remain outstanding.

1.15   **Additional Security.** In the event Mortgagee at any time holds additional security for any of the obligations secured hereby, it may enforce the
sale thereof or otherwise realize upon the same, at its option, either before or
concurrently herewith or after a sale is made hereunder.

1.16   **Inspections.** Mortgagee, or its agents, representatives or workmen, are
authorized to enter at any reasonable time upon or on any part of the Premises for
the purpose of inspecting the same, and for the purpose of performing any of the
acts it is authorized to perform under the terms of this Mortgage.

1.17 **Liens.** Mortgagor shall pay and promptly discharge, at Mortgagor's cost and expense, all liens, encumbrances and charges upon the Mortgaged Property or any part thereof or interest therein. Mortgagor shall have the right to contest in good faith the validity of any such lien, encumbrance or charge, provided Mortgagor shall first deposit with Mortgagee a bond or other security satisfactory to Mortgagee in such amounts as Mortgagee shall reasonably require, and provided further that Mortgagor shall thereafter diligently proceed to cause such lien, encumbrance or charge to be removed and discharged. If Mortgagor shall fail to discharge any such lien, encumbrance or charge, then, in addition to any other right or remedy of Mortgagee, Mortgagee may, but shall not be obligated to, discharge the same, either by paying the amount claimed to be due, or by procuring the discharge of such lien by depositing in court a bond for the amount claimed or otherwise giving security for such claim, or in such manner as is or may be prescribed by law. Any amount so paid by Mortgagee shall, at Mortgagee's option, become immediately due and payable with interest at the Default Rate, and shall be deemed part of the indebtedness secured by this Mortgage.

1.18 **Future Advances.** This Mortgage is given to secure not only existing indebtedness, but also future advances, whether such advances are obligatory or are to be made at the option of Mortgagee, or otherwise, as are made within twenty (20) years from the date hereof, to the same extent as if such future advances are made on the date of the execution of this Mortgage. The total amount of indebtedness that may be so secured may decrease to a zero amount from time to time, or may increase from time to time, but the total unpaid balance so secured at one time shall not exceed twice the face amount of the Note, plus interest thereon, and any disbursements made for the payment of taxes, levies or insurance on the Mortgaged Property, with interest on such disbursements at the Default Rate.

1.19 **No Limitation of Future Advance Rights.** Mortgagor covenants and agrees with Mortgagee that:

(a) Mortgagor waives and agrees not to assert any right to limit future advances under this Mortgage, and any such attempted limitation shall be null, void and of no force and effect. Any correspondence by Mortgagor regarding the future advances must be sent to Mortgagee at the address set forth above and to Mortgagee's counsel: C. Davis Ely, Rogers, Towers, Bailey, Jones & Gay, P.A., 1301 Riverplace Boulevard, Suite 1500, Jacksonville, Florida 32207.

(b) An Event of Default, as said term is hereinafter defined, under this Mortgage shall automatically exist (i) if Mortgagor executes any instrument which purports to have or would have the effect of impairing the priority of or limiting any future advance which might ever be made under the Mortgage or (ii) if Mortgagor takes, suffers, or permits any action or occurrence which would adversely affect the priority of any future advance which might ever be made under the Mortgage.

1.20   **Appraisals.** Mortgagor covenants and agrees that Mortgagee may obtain an appraisal of the Mortgaged Property when required by the regulations of the Federal Reserve Board or the Office of the Comptroller of the Currency or at such other times as Mortgagee may reasonably require, but in any event, not more frequently than annually unless required by the regulations of the Federal Reserve Board or the Office of the Comptroller of the Currency. Such appraisals shall be performed by an independent third party appraiser selected by Mortgagee. The cost of such appraisal shall be borne by Mortgagor. If requested by Mortgagee, Mortgagor shall execute an engagement letter addressed to the appraiser selected by Mortgagee. Mortgagor's failure or refusal to sign such an engagement letter however shall not impair Mortgagee's right to obtain such an appraisal. Mortgagor agrees to pay the cost of such appraisal within ten (10) days after receiving an invoice for such appraisal.

ARTICLE 2
ASSIGNMENT OF LEASES, SUBLEASES,
RENTS, SALES CONTRACTS, ISSUES AND PROFITS

2.1   **Assignment of Rents and Sales Contracts.** As additional security, Mortgagor does hereby transfer, assign, and set over to Mortgagee all of Mortgagor's interest as lessor in any and all present and future leases, and any and all rents, issues and profits arising out of or accruing from the Mortgaged Property, now due or to become due from the Premises or any separate rental premises therein contained, including all contracts, binders or other agreements between Mortgagor and a buyer of the Mortgaged Property for the purchase and sale of the Mortgaged Property or a portion thereof, including such contract binders or other agreements which may hereafter come into existence with respect to any future Mortgaged Property and including all deposits and other monies paid or payable thereunder. Upon an Event of Default hereunder, this assignment shall be absolute and become operative upon written demand from Mortgagee. Such rents, issues and profits shall be collected by or at the direction and under the control of Mortgagee and the net proceeds thereof (net after payment of collection costs) shall be applied to the indebtedness secured hereby in such manner as Mortgagee elects, as and when the same shall become due and payable. For the purpose of carrying out the provisions of this numbered paragraph, Mortgagor does by these presents constitute and appoint Mortgagee as Mortgagor's true and lawful attorney-in-fact, to collect any and all rents from the Premises, expressly authorizing Mortgagee to receipt tenants therefor, and does by these presents ratify and confirm any and all acts of such attorney-in-fact in relation to the foregoing.

2.2   **Collection Upon Default.** Upon any Event of Default under this Mortgage, Mortgagee may, at any time without notice, either in person, by agent or by a receiver appointed by a court, and without regard to the adequacy of any security for the indebtedness hereby secured, enter upon and take possession of the Mortgaged Property, or any part thereof, in its own name, sue for or otherwise collect such rents, issues and profits, including those past due and unpaid, and apply the same, less costs and expenses of operation and collection, including attorneys' fees, upon any indebtedness secured hereby, and in such order as Mortgagee may determine. The collection of such rents, issues and profits, or the entering upon and taking possession of the Mortgaged Property, or the application thereof as aforesaid, shall not cure or waive any default or notice of default hereunder or invalidate any act done in response to such default or pursuant to such notice of default.

2.3   **Restriction on Further Assignments, etc.** Except as hereinafter specifically provided, Mortgagor shall not, without the prior written consent of Mortgagee, assign the rents, issues or profits, sales contracts, or any part thereof, from the Mortgaged Property or any part thereof; and shall not consent to the modification, cancellation or surrender of any lease or sublease covering the Mortgaged Property. An action of Mortgagor in violation of the terms of this Section shall be void as against Mortgagee in addition to being a default under this Mortgage.

Mortgagor shall not, without the consent of Mortgagee, consent to the cancellation or surrender or, accept prepayment of rents, issues or profits, other than rent paid at the signing of a lease or sublease, under any lease or sublease now or hereafter covering the Mortgaged Property or any part thereof, nor modify any such lease or sublease so as to shorten the term, decrease the rent, accelerate the payment of rent, or change the terms of any renewal option; and any such purported assignment, cancellation, surrender, prepayment or modification made without the written consent of Mortgagee shall be void as against Mortgagee. Mortgagor shall, upon demand of Mortgagee, enter into an agreement with Mortgagee with respect to the provisions contained in the preceding provision regarding any lease or sublease covering the Mortgaged Property or any part thereof, and Mortgagor hereby appoints Mortgagee attorney-in-fact of Mortgagor to execute and deliver any such agreement on behalf of Mortgagor and deliver written notice thereof to the tenant to whose lease such agreement relates.

Not later than fifteen (15) days after execution, Mortgagor agrees to furnish to Mortgagee a copy of any modification of any lease presently in effect and copies of all future leases affecting the Mortgaged Property covered by this Mortgage, and failure to timely furnish to Mortgagee a copy of any modification of a lease or a copy of any future lease affecting the Mortgaged Property shall be deemed a default under this Mortgage and the Note, for which the holder of this Mortgage may, at its option, declare the entire unpaid balance of the subject Mortgage and Note to be immediately due and payable.

All leases or subleases hereafter entered into by Mortgagor with respect to the Mortgaged Property or any part thereof, shall be subordinate to the lien of this Mortgage unless expressly made superior to this Mortgage in the manner hereinafter provided. At any time or times Mortgagee may execute and record in the appropriate Office of the Register or County Clerk of the County where the

Premises are situated, a notice of subordination reciting that the lease or leases therein described shall be superior to the lien of this Mortgage. From and after the recordation of such Notice of Subordination, the lease or leases therein described shall be superior to the lien of this Mortgage and shall not be extinguished by any foreclosure sale hereunder.

ARTICLE 3
ENVIRONMENTAL CONDITION OF PREMISES

3.1   **Environmental Condition of Property.** Mortgagor hereby warrants and represents to Mortgagee after thorough investigation that:

(a)   the Premises are now and at all times hereafter will continue to be in full compliance with all Federal, State and local environmental laws and regulations, including but not limited to, the Comprehensive Environmental Response, Compensation and Liability Act of 1980 (CERCLA), Public Law No. 96-510, 94 Stat. 2767, and the Superfund Amendments and Reauthorization Act of 1986 (SARA), Public Law No. 99-499, 100 Stat. 1613, and

(b)   (i) as of the date hereof there are no hazardous materials, substances, waste or other environmentally regulated substances (including without limitation, any materials containing asbestos) located on, in or under the Premises or used in connection therewith, or (ii) Mortgagor has fully disclosed to Mortgagee in writing the existence, extent and nature of any such hazardous material, substance, waste or other environmentally regulated substance, currently present or which Mortgagor is legally authorized and empowered to maintain on, in or under the Premises or use in connection therewith, Mortgagor has obtained and will maintain all licenses, permits and approvals required with respect thereto, and is and will remain in full compliance with all of the terms, conditions and requirements of such licenses, permits and approvals. Mortgagor further warrants and represents that it will promptly notify Mortgagee of any change in the environmental condition of the Premises or in the nature or extent of any hazardous materials, substances or wastes maintained on, in or under the Premises or used in connection therewith, and will transmit to Mortgagee copies of any citations, orders, notices or other material governmental or other communication received with respect to any other hazardous materials, substances, waste or other environmentally regulated substance affecting the Premises.

Mortgagor hereby indemnifies and holds harmless Mortgagee from and against any and all damages, penalties, fines, claims, suits, liabilities, costs, judgments and expenses (including attorneys', consultants' or experts' fees) of every kind and nature incurred, suffered by or asserted against Mortgagee as a direct or indirect result of:

(a)   any warranty or representation made by Mortgagor in this paragraph being or becoming false or untrue in any material respect, or

(b) any requirement under the law, regulation or ordinance, local, state or federal, regarding the removal or elimination of any hazardous materials, substances, waste or other environmentally regulated substances.

Mortgagor's obligations hereunder shall not be limited to any extent by the term of the Note, and, as to any act or occurrence prior to payment in full and satisfaction of the Note which gives rise to liability hereunder, shall continue, survive and remain in full force and effect notwithstanding foreclosure of this Mortgage, where Mortgagee is the purchaser at the foreclosure sale, or delivery of a deed in lieu of foreclosure to Mortgagee.

ARTICLE 4
SECURITY AGREEMENT

4.1   **Creation of Security Interest.** Mortgagor hereby grants to Mortgagee a security interest in the Personal Property. This instrument is a self-operative security agreement with respect to the above described property, but Mortgagor agrees to execute and deliver on demand such other security agreements, financing statements and other instruments as Mortgagee may request.

4.2   **Warranties, Representations and Covenants of Mortgagor.** Mortgagor hereby warrants, represents and covenants as follows:

(a) Except for the security interest granted hereby, Mortgagor is, and as to portions of the Personal Property to be acquired after the date hereof will be, the sole owner of the Personal Property, free from any adverse lien, security interest, encumbrance or adverse claims thereon of any kind whatsoever. Mortgagor shall notify Mortgagee of, and shall defend the Personal Property against, all claims and demands of all persons at any time claiming the same or any interest therein.

(b) Mortgagor shall not lease, sell, convey or in any manner transfer the Personal Property without the prior written consent of Mortgagee.

(c) The Personal Property is not and shall not be used or bought for personal, family or household purposes.

(d) The Personal Property shall be kept on or at the Premises and Mortgagor will not remove the Personal Property from the Premises without the prior written consent of Mortgagee, except such portions or items of Personal Property which are consumed or worn out in ordinary usage, all of which shall be promptly replaced by Mortgagor.

(e) Mortgagor maintains a place of business in the State of Florida and Mortgagor shall immediately notify Mortgagee in writing of any change in its place of business as set forth in the beginning of this Mortgage.

(f)   At the request of Mortgagee, Mortgagor shall join Mortgagee in executing one or more financing statements and renewals and amendments thereof pursuant to the Uniform Commercial Code of Florida in form satisfactory to Mortgagee, and will pay the cost of filing the same in all public offices wherever filing is deemed by Mortgagee to be necessary or desirable.

(g)   All covenants and obligations of Mortgagor contained herein relating to the Mortgaged Property shall be deemed to apply to the Personal Property whether or not expressly referred to herein.

(h)   This Mortgage constitutes a Security Agreement as that term is used in the Uniform Commercial Code of Florida.

ARTICLE 5
EVENTS OF DEFAULT AND REMEDIES UPON DEFAULT

5.1   **Events of Default.** The occurrence of any one or more of the following shall constitute a default (an "Event of Default") under this Mortgage and the Note hereby secured:

(a)   Failure of Mortgagor to make one or more payments required by the Note within ten (10) days from the date such payments are due.

(b)   Failure of Mortgagor to pay the amount of any costs, expenses or fees (including counsel fees) of Mortgagee, with interest thereon, as required by any provision of this Mortgage and such failure to comply continues for a period of thirty (30) days after written notice is delivered to Mortgagor by Mortgagee.

(c)   Failure to exhibit to Mortgagee, within ten (10) days after demand, receipts showing payment of real estate taxes and assessments.

(d)   Except as permitted herein, the actual or threatened alteration, demolition or removal of any building on the Premises without written consent of Mortgagee.

(e)   Failure to maintain the Improvements on the Premises as herein required, free of any liens placed or threatened during the term hereof.

(f)   Failure to comply with any requirements or order or notice of violation of law or ordinance issued by any governmental department claiming jurisdiction over the Mortgaged Property within three (3) months from the issuance thereof, or before any such violation becomes a lien against the Mortgaged Property, whichever first occurs.

(g)   Failure of Mortgagor or others to comply with or perform any other warranty, covenant or agreement contained herein, in the Note, in the Loan Commitment Letter, as said term is defined herein, or in any other Loan Document executed by Mortgagor in conjunction with this transaction and such failure to comply continues for a period of thirty (30) days after written notice is delivered to Mortgagor by Mortgagee, or, if such failure is not capable of being cured within thirty (30) days, Mortgagor fails to diligently and continuously pursue such cure to completion after receipt of notice. Notwithstanding the foregoing, it shall be a default if a cure has not been completed within sixty (60) days after notice thereof.

(h)   Any breach of any covenant or warranty or material untruth of any representation of Mortgagor contained in this Mortgage, or the Note or any guaranty executed in conjunction herewith.

(i)   The institution of any bankruptcy, reorganization or insolvency proceedings against the then owner or Mortgagor in possession of the Mortgaged Property, or any guarantor, or the appointment of a receiver or a similar official with respect to all or a substantial part of the properties of the then owner or Mortgagor in possession of the Mortgaged Property and a failure to have such proceedings dismissed or such appointment vacated within a period of ninety (90) days.

(j)   The institution of any voluntary bankruptcy, reorganization or insolvency proceedings by the then owner or Mortgagor in possession of the Mortgaged Property, or any guarantor, or the appointment of a receiver or a similar official with respect to all or a substantial part of the properties of the then owner or Mortgagor in possession of the Mortgaged Property at the instance of the then owner or Mortgagor in possession of the Mortgaged Property.

(k)   The assertion or making of any levy, seizure, forfeiture action, construction lien or attachment on the Mortgaged Property or any part thereof and a failure to provide to Mortgagee a bond acceptable to Mortgagee or a failure to have such proceedings dismissed within a period of thirty (30) days.

(l)   If default shall occur in any loan now or hereafter in existence between Mortgagee and Mortgagor or any mortgage which Mortgagor or any guarantor has any interest whatsoever, and, conversely, the occurrence of an Event of Default hereunder shall also constitute a default under any such other loan.

(m) The occurrence of any Event of Default under the Note, under any swap agreement which may be entered into as of the date hereof or in the future, or any loan agreement or guaranty, whether or not such event is specifically set forth herein.

(n)   The failure of Mortgagor to maintain its existence in good standing or the death of guarantor. The foregoing notwithstanding, death of the guarantor shall not be an event of default provided (i) the apartment project being constructed upon the Premises reaches "stabilization" (which, for purposes hereof, means such project meets the conditions set forth in Section 2.4 of the Note) and (ii) the indebtedness evidenced by the Note is reduced by a minimum of $3,000,000.00 subsequent to stabilization.

5.2   **Default Rate.** The Default Rate shall be the highest rate allowable by law at the time of default, provided, however, that at no time shall any interest or charges in the nature of interest be taken, exacted, received or collected which would exceed the maximum rate permitted by law.

5.3   **Acceleration Upon Default, Additional Remedies.** In the event that one or more defaults as above provided shall occur, the remedies available to Mortgagee shall include, without limitation, any one or more of the following:

(a)   Mortgagee may declare the entire unpaid balance of the Note immediately due and payable without notice.

(b)   Mortgagee may take immediate possession of the Mortgaged Property or any part thereof (which Mortgagor agrees to surrender to Mortgagee) and manage, control or lease the same to such person or persons and at such rental as it may deem proper and collect all rents, issues and profits therefrom, including those past due as well as those thereafter accruing, with the right of Mortgagee to cancel any lease or sublease for any cause which would entitle Mortgagor to cancel the same; to make such expenditures for maintenance, repairs and costs of operation as it may deem advisable; and after deducting the cost thereof and a commission of five (5%) percent upon the gross amount of rents collected, to apply the residue to the payment of any sums which are unpaid hereunder or under the Note. The taking of possession under this paragraph shall not prevent concurrent or later proceedings for the foreclosure sale of the Mortgaged Property as provided elsewhere herein.

(c)   Mortgagee may apply to any court of competent jurisdiction for the appointment of a receiver or similar official to manage and operate the Mortgaged Property, or any part thereof, and to apply the net rents and profits therefrom to the payment of the interest and/or principal of the Note and/or any other obligations of Mortgagor to Mortgagee hereunder. In event of such application, Mortgagor agrees to consent to the appointment of such receiver or similar official, and agrees that such receiver or similar official may be appointed without notice to Mortgagor, without regard to the adequacy of any security for the debts and without regard to the solvency of Mortgagor or any other person, firm or corporation who or which may be liable for the payment of the Note or any other obligation of Mortgagor hereunder.

(d)   Without declaring the entire unpaid principal balance due, Mortgagee may foreclose only as to the sum past due, without injury to this Mortgage or the displacement or impairment of the remainder of the lien thereof, and at such foreclosure sale the property shall be sold subject to all remaining items of indebtedness; and Mortgagee may again foreclose, in the same manner, as often as there may be any sum past due.

(e)   Mortgagee may bring such action or actions to compel performance by Mortgagor of its obligations hereunder or under the Note, Loan Agreement or any other Loan Document executed in conjunction with the Loan secured hereby, including without limitation, the institution of proceedings at law for damages and/or in equity for injunctive relief and/or specific performance.

Mortgagee shall have all remedies available under Florida law, which remedies may be exercised to the maximum extent permitted by then applicable law and shall be cumulative and may be pursued, separately, concurrently or successively. No delay by Mortgagee in exercising any such remedy shall operate as a waiver thereof or preclude the exercise thereof during the continuance of that or any subsequent Event of Default. The obtaining of a judgment or decree on the Note, whether in the State of Florida or elsewhere, shall not in any manner affect the lien of this Mortgage upon the Mortgaged Property and any judgment or decree so obtained shall be secured hereby to the same extent as the Note is now secured.

5.4   **Additional Provisions.** Mortgagor expressly agrees, on behalf of itself, its successors and assigns and any future owner of the Mortgaged Property, or any part thereof or interest therein, as follows:

(a)   All remedies available to Mortgagee with respect to this Mortgage shall be cumulative and may be pursued concurrently or successively. No delay by Mortgagee in exercising any such remedy shall operate as a waiver thereof or preclude the exercise thereof during the continuance of that or any subsequent default.

(b)   The obtaining of a judgment or decree on the Note, whether in the State of Florida or elsewhere, shall not in any manner affect the lien of this Mortgage upon the Mortgaged Property covered hereby, and any judgment or decree so obtained shall be secured to the same extent as the Note is now secured.

(c)   In the event of any foreclosure sale hereunder, all net proceeds shall be available for application to the indebtedness hereby secured (whether or not such proceeds may exceed the value of the Mortgaged Property) and for unpaid taxes, liens, assessments and any other costs related to the Mortgaged Property.

(d)   The only limitation upon the foregoing agreements as to the exercise of Mortgagee's remedies is that there shall be but one full and complete satisfaction of the indebtedness secured hereby.

(e)   Mortgagor shall duly, promptly and fully perform each and every term and provision of the Loan Agreement which has been executed and delivered by the parties hereto simultaneously with the execution and delivery hereof, the terms of which Loan Agreement are incorporated herein by reference. The lien of this Mortgage secures the payment of all sums payable to Mortgagee and the performance of all covenants and agreements of Mortgagor under the terms of the Loan Agreement.

5.5   **Remedies Not Exclusive.** Mortgagee shall be entitled to enforce payment and performance of any indebtedness or obligations secured hereby and to exercise all rights and powers under this Mortgage or the Note or under any other agreement or any laws now or hereafter in force, notwithstanding some or all of the said indebtedness and obligations secured hereby may now or hereafter be otherwise secured, whether by mortgage, deed of trust, pledge, lien, assignment or otherwise. Neither the acceptance of this Mortgage nor its enforcement shall prejudice or in any manner affect Mortgagee's right to realize upon or enforce any other security now or hereafter held by Mortgagee, it being agreed that Mortgagee shall be entitled to enforce this Mortgage and any other security now or hereafter held by Mortgagee in such order and manner as Mortgagee may in its absolute discretion determine. No remedy herein conferred upon or reserved to Mortgagee is intended to be exclusive of any other remedy herein or by law provided or permitted, but each shall be cumulative and shall be in addition to every other remedy given hereunder or now or hereafter existing at law or in equity or by statute. Every power or remedy given to Mortgagee or to which it may be otherwise entitled, may be exercised, concurrently or independently, from time to time and as often as may be deemed expedient by Mortgagee and it may pursue inconsistent remedies.

ARTICLE 6
MISCELLANEOUS

6.1   **Entity Existence.** So long as the Mortgaged Property shall be owned or held by a limited liability company, such entity shall at all times maintain its existence in good standing and shall be fully authorized to do business in the State of Florida and shall maintain in the State of Florida a duly authorized registered agent for the service of process. Failure to comply with such obligations shall be a default under this Mortgage. Within ninety (90) days after the expiration of the time for filing its annual report and the payment of the appropriate taxes in the State of Florida, Mortgagor will furnish to Mortgagee a certificate of good standing or other evidence satisfactory to Mortgagee to show compliance with the provisions of this Section.

6.2   **Statements by Mortgagor.** Mortgagor, within three (3) days after request in person or within ten (10) days after request by mail, will furnish to Mortgagee or any person, firm or corporation designated by Mortgagee, a duly acknowledged written statement setting forth the amount of the debt secured by this Mortgage, and stating either that no offsets or defenses exist against such debt, or, if such offsets or defenses are alleged to exist, full information with respect to such alleged offsets and/or defenses.

6.3 **Successors and Assigns.** The provisions hereof shall be binding upon and shall inure to the benefit of Mortgagor, its successors and assigns, including without limitation subsequent owners of the Premises or the leasehold estate of the Premises or any part thereof; shall be binding upon and shall inure to the benefit of Mortgagee, its successors and assigns and any future holder of the Note, and any successors or assigns of any future holder of the Note. In the event the ownership of the Mortgaged Property or any leasehold estate that may be covered by this Mortgage, becomes vested in a person other than Mortgagor, Mortgagee may, without notice to Mortgagor, deal with such successor or successors in interest with reference to this instrument and the Note in the same manner as with Mortgagor, and may alter the interest rate and/or alter or extend the terms of payments of the Note without notice to Mortgagor hereunder or under the Note hereby secured or the lien or priority of this Mortgage with respect to any part of the Mortgaged Property covered hereby, but nothing herein contained shall serve to relieve Mortgagor of any liability under the Note or this Mortgage (or any other agreement executed in conjunction therewith) unless Mortgagee shall expressly release Mortgagor in writing. Mortgagor and any transferee or assignee shall be jointly and severally liable for any documentary or intangible taxes imposed as a result of any transfer or assumption.

6.4 **Notices.** All notices, demands and requests given by either party hereto to the other party shall be in writing. All notices, demands and requests by Mortgagee to Mortgagor shall be deemed to have been properly given if sent by United States registered or certified mail, postage prepaid, addressed to Mortgagor at the address as Mortgagor may from time to time designate by written notice to Mortgagee, given as herein required. All notices, demands and requests by Mortgagor to Mortgagee shall be deemed to have been properly given if sent by United States registered or certified mail, postage prepaid, addressed to Mortgagee, or to such other address as Mortgagee may from time to time designate by written notice to Mortgagor given as herein required. Notices, demands and requests given in the manner aforesaid shall be deemed sufficiently served or given for all purposes hereunder at the time such notice, demand or request shall be deposited in any post office or branch post office regularly maintained by the United States Government.

Mortgagor shall deliver to Mortgagee, promptly upon receipt of same, copies of all notices, certificates, documents and instruments received by it which materially affect any part of the Mortgaged Property covered hereby, including, without limitation, notices from any lessee or sublessee claiming that Mortgagor is in default under any terms of any lease or sublease and notices from any purchaser claiming that Mortgagor is in default under any terms of any contract for the sale of all or any portion of the Mortgaged Property.

    6.5   **Modifications in Writing.** This Mortgage may not be changed, terminated or modified orally or in any other manner than by an instrument in writing signed by the party against whom enforcement is sought.

    6.6   **Captions.** The captions or headings at the beginning of each Section hereof are for the convenience of the parties and are not a part of this Mortgage.

    6.7   **Invalidity of Certain Provisions.** If the lien of this Mortgage is invalid or unenforceable as to any part of the debt, or if the lien is invalid or unenforceable as to any part of the Mortgaged Property, the unsecured portion of the debt shall be completely paid prior to the payments of the secured portion of the debt, and all payments made on the debt, whether voluntary or otherwise, shall be considered to have been first paid on and applied to the full payment of that portion of the debt which is not secured or fully secured by the lien of this Mortgage.

    6.8   **No Merger.** If both the lessor's and lessee's estates under any lease or any portion thereof which constitutes a part of the Mortgaged Property shall at any time become vested in one owner, this Mortgage and the lien created hereby shall not be destroyed or terminated by application of the doctrine of merger and, in such event, Mortgagee shall continue to have and enjoy all of the rights and privileges of Mortgagee as to the separate estates. In addition, upon the foreclosure of the lien created by this Mortgage on the Mortgaged Property pursuant to the provisions hereof, any leases or subleases then existing and created by Mortgagor shall not be destroyed or terminated by application of the law of merger or as a result of such foreclosure sale shall so elect. No act by or on behalf of Mortgagee or any such purchaser shall constitute a termination of any lease or sublease unless Mortgagee or such purchaser shall give written notice thereof to such tenant or subtenant.

    6.9   **Governing Law and Construction of Clauses.** This Mortgage shall be governed and construed by the laws of the State of Florida. No act of Mortgagee shall be construed as an election to proceed under any one provision of the Mortgage or of the applicable statutes of the State of Florida to the exclusion of any other such provision, anything herein or otherwise to the contrary notwithstanding.

    6.10   **Transfer.** In the event all or any part of the property encumbered by this Mortgage, or any interest therein, is sold, conveyed, encumbered or otherwise transferred by Mortgagor, without Mortgagee's prior written consent, or any change in the ownership of Mortgagor, then, and in the event any of the foregoing events occur, Mortgagee may, in its sole discretion, require a modification of the terms of the Loan secured hereby (including without limitation those related to the rate of interest and terms or schedule of repayment) in a manner satisfactory to Mortgagee, and may charge an "assumption fee" or similar fee in consideration of such modification or approval; or accelerate the indebtedness secured hereby and declare the then outstanding balance, with all accrued interest to be immediately due and payable.

6.11   **Books and Records.** Mortgagor will furnish to Mortgagee (or cause to be furnished to Mortgagee in the case of the guarantor of the loan secured hereby) the financial statements, tax returns and other financial information required by the Loan Commitment Letter and as set forth below. Mortgagor shall maintain full and correct books and records showing in detail the income, expenses and earnings relating to the Premises, and to permit Mortgagee's representative to examine such books and records and all supporting vouchers and data at any time and from time to time as Mortgagee may reasonably request at such place within the United States of America as such books and records are customarily kept. In addition to the foregoing provisions of this numbered paragraph, Mortgagor will furnish or cause to be furnished to Mortgagee all of the below described documents:

(a)   Mortgagor shall deliver to Mortgagee, not later than ninety (90) days after the end of each fiscal year during the term hereof, a balance sheet of Mortgagor as of the close of each year and statements of income and retained earnings and sources and application of funds for the fiscal year then ended, prepared in conformity with generally accepted accounting principles, applied on a basis consistent with that of the preceding period or containing disclosure of the effect on the financial position or results of operations of any change in the application of generally accepted accounting principles during the period;

(b)   Mortgagor shall cause to be delivered to Mortgagee, not later than ninety (90) days after the end of each fiscal year during the term hereof, complete financial statements of guarantor, in form and content satisfactory to Mortgagee;

(c)   Mortgagor shall deliver or cause to be delivered to Mortgagee, within ten (10) days after Mortgagor's issuance or receipt thereof, copies of all reports submitted to Mortgagor or guarantor by their independent public accountants that contain an opinion rendered in connection with an examination of any financial statements of Mortgagor or guarantor by such accountants;

(d)   Mortgagor shall deliver or cause to be delivered to Mortgagee, within fifteen (15) days after filing, complete copies of the annual income tax returns of Mortgagor and guarantor, including all supporting schedules;

(e)   Mortgagor shall deliver or cause to be delivered to Mortgagee, not later than ninety (90) days after the end of each fiscal year during the term hereof, a rent schedule of the Premises, certified by an accounting officer of Mortgagor, showing the name of each tenant and the space occupied, the lease expiration date and the rent paid;

(f)   Mortgagor shall deliver or cause to be delivered to Mortgagee, promptly upon Mortgagee's written request, such other information about the financial condition and operations of Mortgagor or guarantor in a format as Mortgagee, from time to time, may require; and

(g)   Mortgagor shall notify Mortgagee of any change in its fiscal year, indicating such new fiscal year, within fifteen (15) days of the date such change is made.

6.12   **Financial Statements.** If requested by Mortgagee, Mortgagor will within ninety (90) days after the end of each fiscal year, furnish to Mortgagee a complete financial statement including profit and loss and income and expense statements, balance sheet and reconciliation of surplus which statement shall be certified by an accounting officer of Mortgagor. The cost of such audit shall be paid by Mortgagor.

6.13   **Other Indebtedness Secured.** This Mortgage is also given as security for any and all other sums, indebtedness, obligations and liabilities of any and every kind now or hereafter during the term hereof owing and to become due from Mortgagor to Mortgagee, however created, incurred, evidenced, acquired or arising, whether under the Note or this Mortgage, or any other instrument, obligation, contract, agreement or dealing of any and every kind now or hereafter existing or entered into between Mortgagor and Mortgagee, or otherwise, as amended, modified or supplemented from time to time, and whether direct, indirect, primary, secondary, fixed or contingent, and any and all renewals, modifications or extensions of any or all of the foregoing.

6.14   **Loan Commitment Letter.** The Note evidences a loan made pursuant to that certain Loan Commitment Letter from Mortgagee to Mortgagor, dated November 15, 2000 (the "Loan Commitment Letter"). The terms of the Loan Commitment Letter are hereby incorporated by reference herein. However, in the event of any conflict between the terms of this Mortgage and the terms of the Loan Commitment Letter, the terms of this Mortgage shall control.

6.15   **Arbitration.** Upon demand of any party hereto, whether made before or after institution of any judicial proceeding, any dispute, claim or controversy ("Disputes") arising out of, connected with or relating to this Mortgage, the Note, and other Loan Documents between or among parties to the Mortgage, as modified, shall be resolved by binding arbitration as provided herein. Institution of a judicial proceeding by a party does not waive the right of that party to demand arbitration hereunder. Disputes may include, without limitation, tort claims, counterclaims, disputes as to whether a matter is subject to arbitration, claims brought as class actions, claims arising from Loan Documents executed in the future, or claims arising out of or connected with the transaction reflected in the Mortgage, as modified.

Arbitration shall be conducted under and governed by the Commercial Financial Disputes Arbitration Rules (the "Arbitration Rules") of the American Arbitration Association (the "AAA") and Title 9 of the U.S. Code. All arbitration hearings shall be conducted in the city in which the office of Mortgagee first stated above is located. The expedited procedures set forth in Rule 51 *et seq.* of the Arbitration Rules shall be applicable to claims of less than $1,000,000.00. All applicable statutes of limitations shall apply to any Dispute. A judgment upon the award may be entered in any court having jurisdiction. The panel from which all arbitrators are selected shall be comprised of licensed attorneys. The single arbitrator selected for expedited procedure shall be a retired judge from the highest court of general jurisdiction, state or federal, of the state where the hearing will be conducted or if such person is not available to serve, the single arbitrator may be a licensed attorney. Notwithstanding the forgoing, the arbitration procedure does not apply to disputes under or related to swap agreements.

6.16 **Waiver of Jury Trial.** MORTGAGOR HEREBY KNOWINGLY, VOLUNTARLY AND INTENTIONALLY WAIVES ANY RIGHT IT MAY HAVE TO A TRIAL BY JURY IN RESPECT OF ANY LITIGATION BASED ON THIS MORTGAGE, OR ARISING OUT OF, UNDER OR IN CONNECTION WITH THIS MORTGAGE OR ANY AGREEMENT CONTEMPLATED TO BE EXE-CUTED IN CONNECTION WITH THIS MORTGAGE, OR ANY COURSE OF CONDUCT, COURSE OF DEALING, STATEMENTS (WHETHER VERBAL OR WRITTEN) OR ACTIONS OF ANY PARTY WITH RESPECT HERETO. THIS PROVISION IS A MATERIAL INDUCEMENT FOR MORTGAGEE ACCEPT-ING THIS MORTGAGE FROM MORTGAGOR.

IN WITNESS WHEREOF, Mortgagor has hereunto set hand and seal all done as of the day and year first hereinbefore written.

Signed, sealed and delivered
in the presence of:

COLLIER VENTURE ONE, L.L.C.,
a Florida limited liability company

Name: _____

By: _____
Name: Nathan S. Collier
Its: Managing Member

Name: _____

Address: P.O. Box 13116
Gainesville, Florida 32604

STATE OF FLORIDA
COUNTY OF ALACHUA

The foregoing instrument was acknowledged before me this 17th day of November, 2000, by Nathan S. Collier, the Managing Member of Collier Venture One, L.L.C., a Florida limited liability company, on behalf of the company. He [CHECK ONE] is personally known to me or has proved to me on basis of satisfactory evidence to be the person who executed this instrument.

_____

(Print Name) _____
Notary Public, State of Florida
My Commission expires:

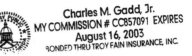

Charles M. Gadd, Jr.
MY COMMISSION # CC857091 EXPIRES
August 16, 2003
BONDED THRU TROY FAIN INSURANCE, INC.

EXHIBIT "A"

Parcel 1:

Commence at the Northwest corner of Section 32, Township 9 South, Range 20 East, and thence South 00 deg. 07 min. 43 sec. West along the West line of Section 32, Township 9 South, Range 20 East, a distance of 665.89 feet to the Northwest corner of the South 1/2 of the Northwest 1/4 of the Northwest 1/4 of said Section; thence run South 89 deg. 33 min. 47 sec. East along the North line of the South 1/2 of the Northwest 1/4 of the Northwest 1/4 of said Section a distance of 990 feet to a concrete monument and the Point of Beginning; then continue South 89 deg. 33 min. 47 sec. East along the North line of the South 1/2 of the Northwest 1/4 of the Northwest 1/4 (the South right of way line of NW 21st Avenue) of said Section a distance of 357.04 feet to a concrete monument; thence run South 00 deg. 00 min. 33 sec. East, a distance of 200 feet to a concrete monument; thence run South 89 deg. 33 min. 47 sec. East, a distance of 672.99 feet to a concrete monument on the West line of Pine Park Subdivision; thence run South 00 deg. 00 min. 33 sec. East along the West line of Pine Park Subdivision a distance of 467.22 feet to a concrete monument on the North right of way of NW 19th Lane; thence run North 89 deg. 31. min. 27 sec. West along the North right of way line of NW 19th Lane, a distance of 43.42 feet to a concrete monument; thence run South 00 deg. 28 min. 33 sec. West along the West right of way line of NW 8th Street a distance of 114 feet to a concrete monument; thence run North 89 deg. 18 min. 28 sec. West along the North lines of Ingleside Subdivision and Haythorne Heights Annex a distance of 713.09 feet to a concrete monument; thence run North 00 deg. 05 min. 18 sec. East a distance of 117.41 feet to a concrete monument; thence run North 89 deg. 40 min. 36 sec. West along the North line of Howard's Subdivision Unit II a distance of 274.36 feet to a concrete monument; thence run North 00 deg. 07 min. 43 sec. East a distance of 661.14 feet to the Point of Beginning, all lying and being in Section 32, Township 9 South, Range 20 East, Alachua County, Florida.

LESS and EXCEPT, a tract of land situated in Section 32, Township 9 South, Range 20 East, Alachua County, Florida, said tract of land being more particularly described as follows: Commence at the Northwest corner of Section 32, Township 9 South, Range 20 East, and run South 00 deg. 07 min. 43 sec. West, along the West line of said Section 32, 665.89 feet; thence run South 89 deg. 33 min. 47 sec. East, 1,347.04 feet; thence run South 00 deg. 00 min. 33 sec. East, 200.00 feet; thence run South 89 deg. 33 min. 47 sec. East, 672.99 feet; thence run South 00 deg. 00 min. 33 sec. East, 232.22 feet to the Point of Beginning; thence continue South 00 deg. 00 min. 33 sec. East, 235.00 feet; thence run North 89 deg. 31 min. 27 sec. West, 40.72 feet; thence run North 02 deg. 43 min. 30 sec. East, 184.87

feet; thence run North 08 deg. 58 min. 10 sec. East 50.62 feet; thence run North 89 deg. 59 min. 27 sec. East, 24.00 feet to the Point of Beginning.

Parcel 2:

A parcel of land situated in the Northwest 1/4 of Section 32, Township 9 South, range 20 East, Alachua County, Florida, being more particularly described as follows:

For a point of reference commence at a railroad spike at the Northwest corner of said Section 32, and run on an assumed bearing of South 00 deg. 12 min. 35 sec. East along the West line of said Northwest 1/4, a distance of 667.37 feet; thence run North 90 deg. 00 min. 00 sec. East, a distance of 310.05 feet to a 4″ × 4″ concrete monument stamped R.L.S. 509 on the South right of way line of Northwest 21st Avenue and the Point of Beginning; thence continue North 90 deg. 00 min. 00 sec. East along said right of way line a distance of 680.10 feet to a 4″ × 4″ concrete monument stamped R.L.S. 509; thence run South 00 deg. 10 min. 34 sec. East, a distance of 444.94 feet to a 4″ × 4″ concrete monument stamped R.L.S. 509; thence run South 89 deg. 59 min. 43 sec. West, a distance of 679.95 feet to a 4″ × 4″ concrete monument stamped R.L.S. 509; thence run North 00 deg. 11 min. 45 sec. West, a distance of 445.00 feet to the Point of Beginning.

LESS and EXCEPT:

A tract of land situated in the Northwest 1/4 of Section 32, Township 9 South, Range 20 East, Alachua County, Florida being more particularly described as follows:

For a point of reference commence at a railroad spike at the Northwest corner of said Section 32 and run on an assumed bearing of South 00 deg. 12 min. 35 sec. East along the West line of said Northwest 1/4, a distance of 667.37 feet; thence run North 90 deg. 00 min. 00 sec. East, a distance of 310.05 feet to a 4″ × 4″ concrete monument stamped R.L.S. 509 on the South right-of-way line of Northwest 21st Avenue and the Point of Beginning; thence continue North 90 deg. 00 min. 00 sec. East, along said right-of-way line, a distance of 100.00 feet to a 1/2 inch rebar and cap stamped P.S.M. 5582; thence run South 00 deg. 11 min. 45 sec. East, a distance of 444.99 feet to a ½ inch rebar and cap stamped P.S.M. 5582; thence run South 89 deg. 59 min. 43 sec. West, a distance of 100.00 feet to a 4″ × 4″ concrete monument stamped R.L.S. 509; thence run North 00 deg. 11 min. 45 sec. West, a distance of 445.00 feet to the Point of Beginning.

EXHIBIT A-3

CONSTRUCTION LOAN AGREEMENT

THIS CONSTRUCTION LOAN AGREEMENT (this "Agreement") is made and entered into as of the 17th day of November, 2000 by and between **FIRST UNION NATIONAL BANK**, a national banking association, its successors or assigns (the "Lender"); and **COLLIER VENTURE ONE, L.L.C.**, a Florida limited liability company (the "Borrower").

R E C I T A L S:

A.   Borrower and Lender desire to enter into this Agreement for the purpose of evidencing a construction loan (the "Loan") in the maximum principal amount of $15,000,000.00 for the construction of improvements on real property situate in Gainesville, Alachua County, Florida now and hereafter encumbered by the Mortgage (as hereinafter defined).

B.   The Loan will be evidenced by a Real Estate Promissory Note in the amount of $15,000,000.00 and will be secured by the Mortgage.

NOW, THEREFORE, in consideration of the mutual covenants and agreements contained herein, Lender agrees to make and Borrower agrees accept the Loan in accordance with and subject to the terms and conditions set forth herein.

ARTICLE 1
PARTICULAR TERMS AND DEFINITIONS

1.1   For purposes of this Agreement, the following terms shall have the respective meanings specified in this Article 1 (such meanings to be equally applied to both the singular and plural forms of the terms defined):

1.2   Account to Receive Advances: Construction Draw Account of Borrower established with Lender.

1.3   Agent to Request Advances: Nathan S. Collier, David Materna, or any agent of Borrower, appointed by Borrower and approved by Lender.

1.4   Borrower and Address: Collier Venture One, L.L.C.
                                        P.O. Box 13116
                                        Gainesville, Florida 32604

1.5   Borrower's Architect: Andrew Kaplan.

1.6   Borrower's Contractor: Charles Perry Construction, Inc.

1.7   Closing: The time of the execution and delivery hereof by Borrower and Lender.

1.8   Commencement Date: On or before thirty (30) days from Closing.

1.9   Completion Date: On or before ten (10) months from Closing.

1.10   Sources and Uses of Funds Document: The document attached hereto as **Exhibit** ("A") which has been certified by Borrower as accurate and sufficient to complete the Improvements.

1.11   Governmental Authority: The United States, the state in which the Premises are located, the state under the laws of which Borrower is organized, any state in or to residents of which offers to sell or lease any portion of the Premises or Improvements will be made, and any political subdivision thereof and any agency, department, commission, board, bureau or instrumentality of any of them.

1.12   Guarantor and Address: Nathan S. Collier
P.O. Box 13116
Gainesville, Florida 32604

1.13   Improvements: Construction of two hundred twenty-one (221) "Class A" apartment units in five (5) separate buildings to be known as the "Hidden Lake Apartments" located on N.W. 21st Avenue in Gainesville, Florida, including amenities, parking areas, appurtenances and related improvements. Certain proceeds of the Loan will also be used to provide financing for the land and the improvements consisting of a thirty-nine (39) unit apartment complex known as "Bailey Gardens" but the Loan will not be used to fund the construction of any other Improvements except as described herein.

1.14   Inspecting Agent: The agent selected by Lender to inspect the construction of the Improvements.

1.15   Interest Rate: The interest rate applicable from time to time to principal outstanding under the Note.

1.16   Lender and Address: First Union National Bank
Real Estate Portfolio Management
225 Water Street, 3rd Floor
FL0016
Jacksonville, Florida 32202.

1.17   Loan Amount: Fifteen Million Dollars and No Cents ($15,000,000.00).

1.18   Loan Commitment: The Loan Commitment Letter from Lender to Borrower dated November 15, 2000.

1.19 Loan Documents: Those items required by the Loan Commitment, together with any other document or instrument executed or submitted in connection with this Loan, including but not limited to this Agreement; Note; Mortgage; Assignment of Borrower's Interest in Contract Documents; Conditional Assignment of Rents, Leases and Revenues; Guaranty of Guarantor, Environmental Indemnity Agreement, No Lien Affidavit; Company Resolution; Title Insurance Binder or Policy; Survey; Site Plan; Plans and Specifications; Sources and Uses of Funds Document; insurance policies; Opinion(s) of counsel; letters of any Governmental Authority, provider of utilities, architect, engineer or other consultant; and Loan Commitment.

1.20 Mortgage: The Mortgage and Security Agreement dated of even date herewith to be recorded in the public records of Alachua County, Florida, securing the repayment of the Note from Borrower to Lender.

1.21 Note: The Real Estate Promissory Note dated of even date herewith in the Loan Amount executed and delivered by Borrower to Lender.

1.22 Plans and Specifications: Those plans and specifications prepared by Borrower's Architect for the construction of the Improvements and all amendments thereto, approved by Lender and the Inspecting Agent.

1.23 Premises: The real property described in and encumbered by the Mortgage.

1.24 Requirement of Governmental Authority: Any law, ordinance, order, rule or regulation of a Governmental Authority.

1.25 Title Insurer: First American Title Insurance Company.

ARTICLE 2
REPRESENTATIONS AND WARRANTIES OF BORROWER

Borrower represents and warrants that:

2.1 The Financial Statements heretofore delivered to Lender by Borrower and Guarantor are true and correct in all respects, have been prepared in accordance with generally accepted accounting principles, consistently applied, and fairly present the respective financial conditions of the subjects thereof as of the respective dates thereof, no materially adverse change has occurred in the financial conditions reflected therein since the respective dates thereof and no additional borrowings have been made by Borrower or Guarantor since the date thereof other than the borrowing contemplated thereby or approved by Lender. Borrower shall provide to Lender the financial statements required by the Loan Commitment and the Mortgage. Additional financial statements may be requested when deemed necessary by

Lender. All other information submitted by Borrower or Guarantor in support of the application for the Loan is true and correct as of the date of this Agreement, and no material adverse change has occurred.

2.2   There are no actions, suits or proceedings pending or, to the knowledge of Borrower, threatened against or affecting it or the Premises or Guarantor, or involving the validity or enforceability of the Mortgage or the priority thereof, at law or in equity, or before or by any Governmental Authority except actions, suits and proceedings fully covered by insurance or which, if adversely determined, would not substantially impair the ability of Borrower or Guarantor to pay when due any amounts which may become payable in respect of the Note; and to Borrower's knowledge it is not in default with respect to any order, writ, injunction, decree or demand of any court or any Governmental Authority.

2.3   The consummation of the transaction hereby contemplated and performance of this Agreement will not result in any breach of, or constitute a default under, any deed to secure debt, mortgage, deed of trust, indenture, security agreement, lease, bank loan or credit agreement, partnership agreement, joint venture agreement, company charter, articles of incorporation, articles of organization, operating agreement, by-laws, covenants or use restrictions applicable to the Premises or other instruments to which Borrower is a party or by which it or the Premises may be bound or affected.

2.4   Borrower has made no contract or arrangement of any kind, the performance of which by the other party thereto would give rise to a lien or claim of lien on the Premises.

2.5   At the time of the execution and delivery of the Loan Documents and at the time of the recording of the Mortgage and at the time of the execution and delivery of this Agreement, no work has been done on Improvements or on the Premises by Borrower or anyone else acting for, in behalf of or under Borrower, and no materials have been placed on the Premises by any materialmen or by anyone else; or if any work shall have been done on the Improvements or the Premises, or any materials furnished thereto, all work done and all materials furnished have been paid for in full. If required by Lender, Borrower shall evidence such payment by releases, receipts and waivers satisfactory to Lender.

2.6   All roads necessary for insurable ingress and egress to the Premises have been completed and all conditions precedent to the use of any easements have been met.

2.7   There is no default on the part of Borrower under this Agreement, the Note, the Mortgage, the permanent loan commitment, if any, or any other Loan Document, and no event has occurred and is continuing which with notice or the passage of time or either would constitute a default under any whereof.

2.8   The following utility services are available to the Premises in adequate supply: water, sewer, electricity and telephone.

2.9   All governmental permits, licenses and approvals necessary for the construction and sale of the Improvements, including but not limited to those specified in Borrower's Architect's and Engineer's Certificates attached hereto as **Exhibit "B,"** have been obtained or are obtainable without restriction, limitation or delay upon any necessary application and payment of the required fees and that there are no conditions which would prohibit, impede or delay issuance of any such permits.

2.10   The Improvements shall be constructed and be wholly within the Premises so that Lender shall at all times have an insurable first mortgage on all of the Improvements.

ARTICLE 3
CONDITIONS PRECEDENT TO
LENDER'S OBLIGATION TO MAKE ADVANCES

Lender's obligation to make advances shall be subject to the satisfaction of the time of each advance of the following conditions:

3.1   All provisions of the Loan Commitment shall have been complied with.

3.2   Borrower's representations and warranties shall remain true and correct.

3.3   No Event of Default shall have occurred under this Agreement or under any other Loan Document.

3.4   Evidence shall be furnished to Lender, which evidence shall be satisfactory to Lender in its sole and absolute discretion, that Borrower's equity in an amount not less than $843,391.00 ("Borrower's Equity") has been previously invested in the Premises or for approved uses as set forth on the Sources and Uses of Funds and satisfactory written proof of such input of Borrower's Equity has been furnished to Lender in the form of paid invoices.

3.5   The requirements of Article 4 with respect to requests for advances shall have been complied with.

ARTICLE 4
ADVANCES

The Loan funds shall be disbursed by Lender at the times and under the terms and conditions as follows:

4.1   Loan funds will be disbursed in accordance with the Sources and Uses of Funds attached hereto as **Exhibit** "A" and the conditions contained in this Agreement.

4.2   Disbursements for the construction of the Improvements shall be made on application of Borrower, which applications shall not be more than once every month. Request for advances shall be submitted on AIA Forms G-702 and G-703 "Application and Certificate for Payment" signed by Borrower, Borrower's Contractor and Borrower's Architect and shall be received by Lender and the Inspecting Agent not less than ten (10) days prior to the date on which the payment is desired and shall set forth in detail the amounts expended or costs incurred for work done and materials incorporated on the Premises.

4.3 $900,000.00 of the Loan funds have been allocated to create an un-disbursed interest reserve. Said sums shall be disbursed periodically for the exclusive purpose of paying accrued interest on the Loan as it comes due under the Note. Said sums shall be so used until such time as said reserve has been extinguished so long as Borrower is not in default under the terms of the Note, Mortgage, this Agreement or the Loan Documents. However, the creation of said reserve shall not release Borrower from its contractual obligation to pay interest under the terms of the Note to the extent said reserve is insufficient to pay all of the interest under the Note or should Lender not be obligated under the terms of this Agreement or the Loan Documents to use said reserve for the payment of accrued interest.

4.4   No funds will be disbursed for materials stored on the Premises without the prior written consent of Lender and then only if such materials are, in Lender's sole opinion, adequately secured.

4.5   If requested by Lender, each request for an advance shall be accompanied by a certificate of endorsement from the Title Insurer stating that a search of the public records has been made and that such search reveals no change in the state of title since the preceding advance and there are no survey exceptions not theretofore approved by Lender, and that the amount of the requested Advance will be covered by the Title Insurance Policy.

4.6   With each application for periodic Loan disbursements, Borrower shall furnish to Lender a certified statement or bill of the particular contractor or subcontractor to whom the monies are due, together with such evidence as Lender shall require (including the certificate of Borrower's Architect and the Inspecting Agent) to evidence and establish that the work has been satisfactorily done, that the particular contractor or subcontractor is entitled to the said progress payment as billed, that the amount of the particular request plus the amount previously disbursed under the Loan do not exceed the percentage of completion as of the requisition date and that the un-disbursed portion of the direct costs is sufficient to complete the Improvements in accordance with the approved Plans and Specifications.

4.7   Each such request by Borrower for a Loan advance shall constitute its certification that the work has been done and that the particular contractor or subcontractor is entitled to the said progress payment requested by it.

4.8   Each application for advance made by Borrower, including the initial advance at Closing, shall constitute a reaffirmation that all representations and warranties hereunder and under all other instruments executed in conjunction with the Loan remain true and correct, and a certificate binding upon Borrower that Borrower is in compliance with all provisions of this Agreement; that there exists no default hereunder or under the Note, Mortgage or any other Loan Documents; that all bills for labor, materials and services (including engineering services, survey and land planning) incurred and payable in connection with the Improvements will be paid from the Loan advance then requested; that all funds received through previous requisitions have been properly applied to bills for labor and materials used on the Premises; and that the un-disbursed Loan proceeds are sufficient to pay in full the costs of all work remaining to be done to complete the Improvements. Lender, however, may nevertheless require further evidence of such payments and remaining costs in the form of receipts, releases, certifications or otherwise.

4.9   All requests for construction and development disbursements will be subject to an on-site inspection by Lender and/or the Inspecting Agent, and shall be at the expense of Borrower, in the amount of $550.00 per inspection. In addition, Borrower shall pay at Closing a $1,500.00 fee for the review of the Plans and Specifications for the benefit of Lender, the budget for this project and other matters relating to the design, construction, operation and use of the Improvements.

4.10   Based upon the information supplied by Borrower to Lender and as set out in the Sources and Uses of Funds Document furnished to Lender by Borrower and as attached hereto as **Exhibit** "A" Lender shall allocate the Loan between costs which relate to the Loan and the Improvements other than direct costs of construction of the Improvements (the "Indirect Costs") and direct costs of construction of the Improvements (the "Direct Costs"), provided, however, that in no event shall Lender be obligated to make disbursements hereunder in excess of Verified Project Costs. For purposes hereof, "Verified Project Costs" shall mean, in the aggregate and from time to time, of (a) Indirect Costs actually incurred by Borrower, and (b) Direct Costs actually incurred by Borrower for work in place as part of the Improvements, as certified by Lender's inspector, minus the aggregate of (y) the portion of Borrower's Equity which Borrower is required to have invested in the Improvements and (z) the Retainage (as hereinafter defined). The amount of each advance for the Direct Costs shall be equal to the amount of the Loan allocated for Direct Costs multiplied by the percentage of completion of the Improvements as certified by the Inspecting Agent, less ten percent (10%) ("Retainage") and less all advances previously made on account of Direct Costs.

4.11   By execution of this Agreement, Borrower authorizes Lender, at Lender's option, to make advances directly to any contractor or subcontractor and to advance to itself sums required to pay interest for the preceding month. No further direction or authorization from Borrower shall be necessary to warrant such direct advances and all such advances shall satisfy *pro tanto* the obligations of Lender hereunder and shall be secured by the Mortgage as fully as if made to Borrower.

4.12   The balance not disbursed as aforesaid shall be disbursed when all the Improvements have been completed and all work and materials incorporated therein and Lender has received: (i) certification from the Inspecting Agent that the Improvements have been acceptably completed, (ii) the affidavit conforming to the lien laws of the State of Florida, (iii) full and complete releases of lien from each and every party who performed any work or supplied any materials towards the construction and installation of the Improvements, or otherwise, upon the Premises, (iv) the acceptance of the Improvements by the county and any other Governmental Authority having jurisdiction, including, without limitation, a certificate of occupancy, (v) a final as-built survey of the Premises, locating all of the Improvements thereon, and (vi) such other documents and papers as may reasonably be required by Lender to satisfy itself that the Improvements have been properly and fully completed, that all costs of the work done and materials supplied in connection therewith have been fully paid, and that no person has any right or claim of lien upon the said Premises for any work done or materials supplied. Lender may, at its sole discretion, release the ten percent (10%) Retainage held back on a particular subcontractor when said subcontractor's work is satisfactorily completed and is free and clear of all construction liens and unpaid bills.

4.13   Lender shall be entitled to withhold any disbursements or advance of Loan proceeds at any time when Borrower is in default either under any of the terms of this Agreement or of said Note or Mortgage. Lender will at all times have final determination as to the amounts to be advanced.

4.14   After the initial disbursement, Lender may disburse to itself from the un-disbursed Loan proceeds any sums payable to Lender on account of origination or commitment fees, interest, costs, documentary stamp taxes, intangible taxes, charges, fees including attorneys' fees, brokerages, commissions or expenses owing to Lender by Borrower, and any such disbursement shall be considered with like effect as if same had been made to Borrower. Likewise, Lender may apply un-disbursed Loan proceeds to the satisfaction of Borrower's obligations hereunder and under the Mortgage and other Loan Documents, and amounts so applied shall be part of the Loan, shall bear interest at the Interest Rate set forth in the Note, and shall be secured by the Mortgage.

4.15   Borrower will receive the advances to be made hereunder and will hold the same as a trust fund for the purpose of paying the costs as shown on the Sources and Uses of Funds Document submitted to Lender and for no other purpose.

4.16   The terms of this Agreement notwithstanding, no disbursements shall be made under this Agreement for any of the budget items described in the Sources and Uses of Funds Document relating to the Direct Costs of the construction of the Improvements until Borrower has provided Lender with a copy of an executed contract between Borrower and a contractor acceptable to Lender for the construction of the particular budget items which Lender is being requested to fund. Such contract must provide that the work to be performed under that contract can be completed for an amount equal to or less than the amount(s) budgeted in **Exhibit** "A" for the particular budget item(s). If the contract amount exceeds the amount(s) budgeted in **Exhibit** "A" for the work in question, then at Lender's option, Borrower shall deposit with Lender, in cash, an amount equal to the contract amount less the budgeted amount in **Exhibit** "A" for the budget item(s) in question. If at any time during the course of construction Lender determines that the un-disbursed Loan reserve for any budget line item is insufficient to complete the work contemplated by the line item, then the Loan shall be considered "out of balance." Borrower, within three (3) days after notice from Lender that the Loan is out of balance, shall deposit sufficient funds, in cash, with Lender to bring the Loan in balance and shall submit a revised Sources and Uses of Funds Document reflecting the additional costs and showing the Loan to be in balance. The amount so deposited by Borrower shall equal the cost to complete the work contemplated by the particular budget line item minus the un-disbursed Loan reserve for such budget item. The amount(s) so deposited shall be disbursed by Lender before any additional Loan proceeds are advanced. In the event of default, any moneys deposited under this paragraph and not previously disbursed may be applied by Lender against the amount of indebtedness then outstanding.

4.17   Borrower shall disclose to Lender and the Inspecting Agent on AIA Document G-805 and on a current and ongoing basis, the names of all persons with whom Borrower has contracted or intends to contract for any construction or for the furnishing of labor or materials therefor, and when required by Lender, obtain the approval by Lender of all such persons. All such contracts and subcontracts shall be covered by payment and performance bonds furnished to and acceptable to Lender and which bonds meet all requirements of the Loan Commitment. If Borrower requests that this bonding requirement be waived, Borrower shall submit to Lender such financial information and description of previous experience as to each such contractor for which a waiver is sought. Lender shall review this submitted information and promptly notify Borrower if the bonding requirement is waived as to each particular contractor. The decision to waive any bonding requirement shall be within the sole discretion of Lender.

4.18   Total advances made under this Agreement shall not exceed the Loan Amount. It is the intent of the parties that this Agreement not evidence a revolving line of credit.

ARTICLE 5
COVENANTS OF BORROWER

Borrower covenants with Lender as follows:

5.1   Borrower will not convey or encumber the Premises in any way without the prior written consent of Lender. All easements to be executed after the date of this Agreement affecting the Premises shall be submitted to Lender for its approval prior to the execution thereof by Borrower, accompanied by a drawing or survey showing the location thereof.

5.2   Borrower will comply promptly with any Requirement of a Governmental Authority.

5.3   Borrower will pay all costs and expenses required to satisfy the conditions of this Agreement; without limitation of the generality of the foregoing, Borrower will pay: (a) all taxes and recording expenses, including all intangible and documentary stamp taxes, if any; (b) all fees and commissions lawfully due to brokers in connection with this transaction; (c) all legal fees and expenses of Lender's Counsel; (d) all title insurance premiums; and (e) all fees and expenses of the Inspecting Agent.

5.4   Borrower will cause all conditions hereof to be satisfied to the extent it is within its power to do so. Borrower will commence work on the Improvements by the Commencement Date and will diligently pursue said work on the Improvements to completion in accordance with the Loan Documents on or before the Completion Date.

5.5   Borrower will receive the advances to be made hereunder and will hold the same as a trust fund for the purpose of paying the costs as shown on the Sources and Uses of Funds Document submitted to Lender and for no other purpose.

5.6   Borrower will indemnify and hold Lender harmless from any loss or liability arising out of claims of third parties by reason of the execution hereof or the consummation of the transaction contemplated hereby.

5.7   Borrower shall disclose to Lender and the Inspecting Agent, upon demand, the names of all persons with whom Borrower has contracted or intends to contract for any construction or for the furnishing of labor or materials therefor and, when required by Lender, obtain the approval by Lender of all such persons.

5.8   Borrower will comply with all restrictive covenants affecting the Premises.

5.9   Lender may apply amounts due hereunder to the satisfaction of the conditions hereof, and amounts so applied shall be part of the Loan and shall be secured by the Mortgage.

5.10   Borrower will maintain Builder's Risk Insurance in the amount of Borrower's general contract with Borrower's Contractor or the full insurable value of the Improvements whichever is greater; and public liability insurance with Two Million and 00/100 Dollars ($2,000,000.00) coverage. Borrower shall furnish Lender with evidence of worker's compensation insurance and shall obtain such other insurance coverage as may reasonably be required by Lender. All insurance policies shall name Lender as first mortgagee, shall be written on companies satisfactory to Lender and shall not be cancelable unless thirty days prior written notice is given to Lender.

5.11   Borrower will comply with all land use, building, subdivision, zoning, condominium and similar Requirements of Governmental Authority applicable to the use of the Premises, the construction of any Improvements and the operation thereof. Borrower shall obtain and deliver to Lender the originals or true copies of all subdivision, building, zoning, use, condominium and other government permits, licenses or approvals required for the construction of the Improvements, including those described in **Exhibit "B"** hereto. In the event any such permits, licenses or approvals are revoked or subjected to attack by action before any court, administrative agency or other body having jurisdiction, Borrower agrees to notify Lender of such action and to defend against such action, and Lender may refuse to make further advances under this Agreement, and at its discretion, all advances previously made shall become payable and in default and Lender may exercise all of the remedies available for default in this Agreement.

5.12   Borrower will not (i) seek to rezone all or any portion of the Premises, (ii) seek to amend any development order which directly affects the Premises or (iii) impose or modify any covenants which affect the Premises without the prior written consent of Lender.

5.13   Authority for approval, any site plan for the Improvements or which would affect the Premises without Lender's prior written consent.

5.14   Borrower covenants to construct all of the Improvements within the Premises. At Lender's request, Borrower will obtain a certificate from a surveyor certifying that all of the Improvements are in fact being constructed within the Premises.

5.15   Borrower agrees to allow Lender to erect and maintain signs on the Premises which indicate financing by Lender during the period of this Loan.

ARTICLE 6
EVENTS OF DEFAULT AND REMEDIES

6.1   The occurrence of any one of the following events shall constitute an Event of Default hereunder:

(a)   Borrower fails to make any payment due under the Note, Mortgage, or any of the Loan Documents, within ten (10) days from the date such payment is due;

(b)   Borrower fails to comply with any of the covenants made by it in this Agreement and such failure to comply continues for a period of thirty (30) days after written notice of such default is delivered to Borrower by Lender;

(c)   Borrower or Guarantor commits a non-monetary default under the Note, Mortgage, or any other Loan Document or any event of default occurs under any swap agreement which may be entered into as of the date hereof or in the future and such non-monetary default continues for a period of thirty (30) days after written notice of such default is delivered to Borrower or Guarantor by Lender, or, if such default is not capable of being cured within thirty (30) days, Borrower or Guarantor fails to diligently and continuously pursue such cure to completion after receipt of notice. Notwithstanding the foregoing, it shall be a default if a cure has not been completed within sixty (60) days after notice thereof;

(d)   Any representations, warranty or statement made by Borrower herein or in any certificate, report or other writing delivered pursuant hereto shall be untrue as of the date made;

(e)   Borrower is unable to satisfy any condition of its right to the receipt of an advance hereunder for a period in excess of thirty (30) days;

(f)   A lien or claim of lien for the performance of work or the supply of materials be filed against the Premises and remain unsatisfied or unbonded at the time of any request for any advance or for a period of thirty (30) days after the date of filing thereof;

(g)   Borrower or Guarantor makes an assignment for the benefit of creditors, files a petition in bankruptcy, is adjudicated insolvent or bankrupt, petitions or applies to any tribunal for any receiver of or trustee for it or any substantial part of its property, commences any proceeding relating to Borrower or Guarantor under any reorganization, arrangement, readjustment of debt, dissolution or liquidation law or statute of any jurisdiction, whether now or hereafter in effect, or if there is commenced against Borrower or Guarantor by any such act proceeding which remains undismissed for a period of ninety (90) days, or Borrower or Guarantor by any act indicates its consent to, approval of, or acquiescence in any such proceeding or the appointment of any receiver of or trustee for it or any substantial part of its property, or suffers any such receivership or trusteeship to continue undischarged for a period of ninety (90) days;

(h)   Any change in the legal or equitable ownership of a controlling interest in Borrower or the Premises, or any change in the management of Borrower, if in Lender's sole judgment such change materially and adversely affects the ability of Borrower to perform in accordance with the terms of this Agreement;

(i)   The failure of Borrower to maintain its existence in good standing or the death of the Guarantor. The foregoing notwithstanding, death of the Guarantor shall not be an event of default provided (i) the apartment project being constructed upon the Premises reaches "stabilization" (which, for purposes hereof, means such project meets the conditions set forth in Section 2.4 of the Note) and (ii) the indebtedness evidenced by the Note is reduced by a minimum of $3,000,000.00 subsequent to stabilization;

(j)   Any legal or equitable action shall be commenced against Borrower which, if adversely determined, could reasonably be expected to impair substantially the ability of Borrower to perform each and every obligation under the Loan Documents and this Agreement;

(k)   The priority or security of the Mortgage or any other security for the Loan is in jeopardy; or

(l)   The validity of any permit, approval or consent by any Governmental Authority relating to the Premises, the Improvements, or the operation thereof is questioned by a proceeding before any board, commission, agency, court, or other authority having jurisdiction and such proceeding is not satisfactorily resolved, in the reasonable opinion of Lender, within thirty (30) days of the commencement of proceedings.

6.2   Upon the occurrence of an Event of Default, Lender may, at its option and in addition to any remedies specifically provided for such default under the Note and Mortgage, do all or any of the following:

(a)   declare all sums evidenced by the Note and all sums secured by the Mortgage and all sums due hereunder to Lender to be immediately due and payable, and may foreclose said Mortgage and in so doing shall be entitled to reasonable attorney's fees (including attorney's fees through any appeals and in the bankruptcy court) and other foreclosure expenses;

(b)   pursue any and all remedies granted under the Note and/or the Mortgage for default and/or the remedies granted under any and all laws and statutes, all remedies therein and contained in this Agreement being deemed cumulative so that the exercise of no remedy or combination of remedies in whatever sequence shall be deemed to exclude the subsequent exercise of any other remedy whatsoever; and

(c)   enter upon and take possession of the Premises and make secure the property and all uncompleted construction of said Improvements and may complete, or enter into a contract with another to complete said Improvements. Borrower agrees to pay to Lender, on demand, all costs and expenses of completion of the Improvements, including all sums disbursed by Lender incident to said completion and reasonable attorneys' fees incurred by Lender incident to said default and the completion of said construction or incident to the enforcement of any provision hereof, and all such sums, even though they may, when added to the construction moneys advanced and disbursed under this Agreement, exceed the principal amount of the Note, shall be secured by the lien of the Mortgage as though the same were a part of the debt originally described in and secured thereby. If said sums are not paid by Borrower immediately on demand, Lender may declare all such sums, and all other sums secured by the Mortgage, immediately due and payable and nonpayment thereof by Borrower shall constitute a default under the Mortgage.

ARTICLE 7
GENERAL CONDITIONS

The following conditions shall be applicable throughout the term of this Agreement:

7.1   No advance of Loan proceeds hereunder shall constitute a waiver of any of the provisions, conditions or obligations set forth in the Loan Commitment, this Agreement or any other Loan Document, nor, in the event Borrower is unable to satisfy any such provision or condition, shall any such waiver have the effect of precluding Lender from thereafter declaring such inability to be an Event of Default as hereinabove provided.

7.2   All proceedings taken in connection with the transaction provided for herein, all surveys, appraisals and documents required or contemplated by the Loan Commitment, or this Agreement, and the persons responsible for the execution and preparation thereof; the insurers and the form of all policies of insurance shall be satisfactory to Lender and Borrower shall promptly furnish to Lender's counsel copies of all documents which they may request in connection therewith.

7.3   All conditions of the obligations of Lender to make advances hereunder are imposed solely and exclusively for the benefit of Lender and its assigns and no other person shall have standing to require satisfaction of such conditions in accordance with their terms or be entitled to assume that Lender will refuse to make advances in the absence of strict compliance with any or all thereof and no other person shall, under any circumstances, be deemed to be beneficiary of such conditions, any or all of which may be freely waived in whole or in part by Lender at any time if in its sole discretion it deems it advisable to do so.

7.4   All notices shall be in writing and shall be deemed to have been sufficiently given or served for all purposes when presented personally or sent by express mail or courier service or by registered or certified mail to any party hereto at its address above-stated or at such other address of which it shall have been notified by the party giving such notice in writing.

7.5   Neither this Agreement nor any provision hereof may be changed, waived, discharged or terminated orally, but only by an instrument in writing signed by the party against whom enforcement of the change, waiver, discharge or termination is sought.

7.6   The remedies herein provided shall be in addition to and not in substitution for the rights and remedies which would otherwise be vested in Lender in any Loan Document or in law or equity, all of which rights and remedies are specifically reserved by Lender. The remedies herein provided or otherwise available to Lender shall be cumulative and may be exercised concurrently. The failure to exercise any of the remedies herein provided shall not constitute a waiver thereof; nor shall use of any of the remedies hereby provided prevent the subsequent or concurrent resort to any other remedy or remedies. It is intended that this clause shall be broadly construed so that all remedies herein provided for or otherwise available to Lender shall continue and each and all available to Lender until all sums due it by reason of this Agreement have been paid to it in full and all obligations incurred by it in connection with the construction or operation of any Improvements have been fully discharged without loss or damage to Lender.

7.7   A default by Borrower in this Agreement shall constitute a default by Borrower in the Note, Mortgage and every other Loan Document.

7.8   Lender is not a partner with Borrower or any other party in the development of the Premises. Lender shall not in any way be liable or responsible by reason of the provisions hereof, or otherwise, for the payment of any claims growing out of the operation.

7.9   The Mortgage shall constitute security for all moneys advanced by Lender and all obligations incurred by Lender under this Agreement including funds advanced and obligations incurred by Lender in excess of the Loan Amount, advanced or incurred shall constitute a lien upon the Premises secured by said Mortgage, and recovery therefor may be had by Lender upon the Mortgage, in addition to all other remedies herein granted to Lender.

7.10   In this Agreement, whenever the context so requires, the neuter gender includes the feminine and/or masculine, as the case may be, and the singular number includes the plural.

7.11   The terms, conditions, covenants, agreements, powers, notices and authorization herein contained shall extend to, be binding upon and available to the heirs, executors, administrators, successors and, to the extent permitted hereunder, to the assigns of each of the respective parties hereto. Notwithstanding the foregoing, Borrower shall not assign or transfer voluntarily or by operation of law, or otherwise dispose of this Agreement, or any rights in Lender's commitment, or any moneys, property or funds deposited with Lender. An assignment or transfer in violation of this provision shall be invalid, and an assignment or transfer by operation of law shall be deemed to be an invalid transfer.

7.12 This Agreement may be executed in any number of counterparts, all of which taken together shall constitute one and the same instrument and any of the parties or signatories hereto may execute this Agreement by signing any such counterpart.

7.13 This Agreement and each transaction consummated hereunder shall be deemed to be made under the laws of the State of Florida and shall be construed in accordance with and governed by the laws of said State.

7.14 BORROWER AND LENDER, JOINTLY AND SEVERALLY, HEREBY KNOWINGLY, VOLUNTARILY AND INTENTIONALLY WAIVE THE RIGHT EITHER MAY HAVE TO A TRIAL BY JURY IN RESPECT OF ANY LITIGATION BASED HEREON, OR ARISING OUT OF, UNDER OR IN CONNECTION WITH THIS AGREEMENT AND ANY AGREEMENT CON-TEMPLATED TO BE EXECUTED IN CONJUNCTION HEREWITH, OR ANY COURSE OF CONDUCT, COURSE OF DEALING, STATEMENTS, WHETHER VERBAL OR WRITTEN, OR ACTIONS OF EITHER PARTY. THIS PROVI-SION IS A MATERIAL INDUCEMENT FOR LENDER MAKING THE LOAN.

IN WITNESS WHEREOF, Lender and Borrower have hereunto set their hands and seals this 17th day of November, 2000.

Signed, sealed and delivered
in the presence of:

"BORROWER"

COLLIER VENTURE, L.L.C.,
a Florida limited liability company

_____

By: _____

_____

Name: Nathan S. Collier
Its: Managing Member

As to Borrower

"LENDER"

FIRST UNION NATIONAL BANK

_____

By: _____

_____

Name: _____
Title: Assistant Vice President

As to Lender

The form and content of all Loan Documents is approved.

"GUARANTOR"

_____

NATHAN S. COLLIER

EXHIBIT A-4

November 17, 2000
**DATE OF EXECUTION
AND DELIVERY**

**REAL ESTATE
UNCONDITIONAL GUARANTY**

CUSTOMER: **Collier Venture One, L.L.C.,**
a Florida limited liability company
P.O. Box 13116
Gainesville, Florida 32604

GUARANTOR(S):   **Nathan S. Collier**
P.O. Box 13116
Gainesville, Florida 32604

FUNB: **First Union National Bank**
Real Estate Portfolio Management
225 Water Street, 3rd Floor, FL0016
Jacksonville, Florida 32202

WHEREAS, the above Customer desires to obtain extensions of credit and enter into various contractual relationships and otherwise to deal with FIRST UNION NATIONAL BANK (hereinafter termed "FUNB") and

WHEREAS, FUNB is unwilling to extend or continue to extend credit to and/or to engage in business transactions and enter into various contractual relationships with, and otherwise to deal with Customer unless it receives an unconditional and continuing, joint and several guaranty from the above identified, undersigned GUARANTOR (hereinafter termed "Guarantor"), covering all "Obligations of Customer," as hereinafter defined.

NOW, THEREFORE, in consideration of the premises and of other good and valuable consideration, and in order to induce FUNB to extend or continue to extend credit to Customer in the principal amount of Fifteen Million Dollars and No Cents ($15,000,000.00), plus interest, as evidenced by that certain Real Estate Promissory Note dated of even date herewith in favor of FUNB (the "Note"), to enter into that certain Construction Loan Agreement of even date therewith executed in conjunction with this transaction (the "Loan Agreement"), which Note and Loan Agreement are secured by that certain Mortgage and Security Agreement encumbering the real and personal property described therein dated of even date herewith to be recorded in the public records of Alachua County, Florida (the "Mortgage") (the Note, Loan Agreement, Mortgage and all other agreements, documents and instruments evidencing or securing the obligations of Customer being herein collectively called the "Loan Documents"), pursuant to which Customer is liable as maker or otherwise, and to otherwise deal with Customer, Guarantor, jointly and severally, hereby absolutely and unconditionally guarantees to FUNB and its successors and assigns, (i) the full and prompt payment of principal, interest and any other amounts due or to become due, whether by acceleration or otherwise, under the Loan Documents; (ii) the performance of any and all obligations of Customer under the Loan Documents including, without limitation, obligations for the payment of insurance premiums and taxes, assessments and other impositions with respect to or against the Property; and (iii) the full payment and performance of all Obligations of Customer (as hereinafter defined), now or hereafter existing, to any person who shall heretofore or hereafter deposit any sum of money with Customer or any agent or escrow agent designated by Customer, on account of any contract of agreement regarding the lease or purchase of any portion of the property, including all renewals, extensions and/or modifications thereof (all liabilities and obligations of the Customer to FUNB, pursuant to the foregoing, being hereinafter termed "Obligations of Customer"), plus all interest or finance charges, costs of court, penalty interest, late payment charges and the reasonable attorney's fees of FUNB.

This Guaranty is in addition to and is not intended to supersede any prior existing Guaranty of Guarantor.

Further, whether or not suit is brought by FUNB to acquire possession of any collateral of Guarantor or Customer or to enforce collection of any unpaid balance(s) hereunder, Guarantor expressly hereby agrees to pay all legal expenses and the reasonable attorney's fees (including those relative to appellate proceedings, if any) actually incurred by FUNB.

In order to implement the foregoing and as additional inducements to FUNB, Guarantor further covenants and agrees:

1.   This Guaranty is and shall remain an unconditional and continuing guaranty of payment and not of collection, shall remain in full force and effect irrespective of any interruption(s) in the business or other dealings and relations of Customer with FUNB and shall apply to and guarantee the due and punctual payment of all "Obligations of Customer" due by Customer to FUNB. To that end, Guarantor hereby expressly waives any right to require FUNB to bring any action against any Customer or any other person(s) or to require that resort be had to any security or to any balance(s) of any deposit or other account(s) or debt(s) or credit(s) on the books of FUNB in favor of Customer or any other person(s). Guarantor acknowledges that its liabilities and obligations hereunder are primary rather than secondary. To that end and without limiting the generality of the foregoing, undersigned Guarantor herewith expressly waives any rights he otherwise might have had under provisions of the law of the State of Florida to require FUNB to attempt to recover against Customer and/or to realize upon any securities or collateral security which FUNB holds for the obligation evidenced or secured hereby. Notwithstanding the satisfaction or performance of the "Obligations of Customer" Guarantor's liability shall continue to exist for so long as the satisfaction of the "Obligations

of Customer" could be set aside or such "Obligations of Customer" otherwise be reinstated under the bankruptcy, insolvency, fraudulent conveyance, debtor relief, or other similar laws of any Federal, State or other competent jurisdiction.

2. **TIME IS OF THE ESSENCE HEREOF**. Any notice(s) to Guarantor shall be sufficiently given, if mailed to the first above stated address(es) of Guarantor.

3. If any process is issued or ordered to be served upon FUNB, seeking to seize Customer's and/or Guarantor's rights and/or interests in any deposit or other account(s) maintained with FUNB, the balance(s) in any such account(s) shall immediately be deemed to have been and shall be set-off against any and all "Obligations of Customer" and/or all obligations and liabilities of Guarantor hereunder as of the time of the issuance of any such writ or process; whether or not Customer, Guarantor and/or FUNB shall then have been served therewith.

4. All moneys available to and/or received by FUNB for application toward payment of (or reduction of) the "Obligations of Customer" may be applied by FUNB to such individual debt(s) in such manner and apportioned in such amount(s) and at such time(s) as FUNB, in its sole discretion, may deem suitable or desirable.

5. As security for any and all liabilities of Guarantor hereunder, now existing or hereafter arising, or otherwise, Guarantor hereby grants FUNB the right to retain a security interest in any and all moneys or other property (*i.e.*, goods and merchandise, as well as all documents relative thereto); also, funds, Investment Securities, choses in action and any and all other forms of property, whether real, personal or mixed, and any right, title, or interest of Guarantor therein or thereto and/or the proceeds thereof, which have been or may hereafter, be deposited or left with FUNB (or with any agent or other third party acting on FUNB's behalf) by or for the account or credit of undersigned Guarantor, including (without limitation of the foregoing), any property in which Guarantor may have any interest. Further where any money is due FUNB hereunder, FUNB is herewith authorized to exercise its right of set-off or "bank lien" as to any moneys deposited in demand, checking, time, savings, or other accounts of any nature maintained in and with it by any of the undersigned, without advance notice. Said right of set-off shall also be applicable and exercised by FUNB, in its sole discretion, where FUNB is indebted to any Guarantor by reason of any certificate(s) of deposit, bond(s), note(s) or otherwise.

6. Guarantor agrees that his liability hereunder shall not be diminished by any failure on the part of FUNB to perfect (by filing, recording, or otherwise) any security interest(s) it may have in any property securing this Guaranty and/or the "Obligations of Customer" secured hereby and hereunder.

7. Guarantor further hereby consents and agrees that FUNB may at any time, or from time to time, in its sole discretion: (i) extend or change the time

of payment, and/or the manner, place or terms of payment of any or all of the "Obligations of Customer"; (ii) exchange, release and/or surrender all or any of the collateral security, or any part(s) thereof, by whomsoever deposited, which is or may hereafter be held by it in connection with all or any of the "Obligations of Customer" and/or any liabilities or obligations of Guarantor hereunder; (iii) sell or otherwise dispose of and/or purchase all or any of such collateral at public or private sale, or to or through any investment securities broker and after deducting all costs and expenses of every kind for collection, preparation for sale, sale or delivery, the net proceeds of any such sale(s) or other disposition may be applied by FUNB upon all or any of the "Obligations of Customer"; (iv) release any endorser of the "Obligations of Customer" or any Guarantor thereof, with or without consideration and without notice to or further consent from any Guarantor and such release shall not in any way affect the liability of the undersigned; (v) settle or compromise with the Customer (and/or any other person(s) liable thereon) any and all of the "Obligations of Customer" (including, but not limited to, any insurance applicable to the "Obligations of Customer"), and/or subordinate the payment of all or any part of same, to the payment of any other debts or claims, which may at any time(s) be due or owing to FUNB and/or any other person(s); and (vi) alter, extend, change, modify, release, waive or cancel any covenant, agreement, condition, obligation or provision contained in any or all Loan Documents; all in such manner and upon such terms as FUNB may deem proper and/or desirable, and without notice to or further assent from Guarantor, it being agreed that Guarantor shall be and remain bound upon this Guaranty, irrespective of the existence, value or condition of any collateral, and notwithstanding any such change, exchange, settlement, compromise, surrender, release, foreclosure, sale or other disposition, application, renewal or extension and notwithstanding also that the "Obligations of Customer" may at any time(s) exceed the aggregate principal sum hereinabove prescribed (if any such limiting sum appears). Further this Guaranty shall not be construed to impose any obligation of FUNB to extend or continue to extend credit or otherwise deal with Customer at any time.

8.   If Customer is an organization, this Guaranty covers all "Obligations of Customer" purporting to be created or undertaken on behalf of such organization by any officer, partner, manager or agent of such organization, without regard to the actual authority of any such officer, partner, manager or agent, whether or not corporate resolutions, proper or otherwise, are given by any corporate Customer to FUNB, and/or whether or not such purported organizations are legally chartered or organized.

9.   In consideration of FUNB's extension of credit to Customer, in FUNB's sole discretion, Guarantor hereby agrees:

(a)   To subordinate, and by this Agreement does subordinate, debts now or hereafter owed by Customer to Guarantor to any and all debts of Customer to FUNB now or hereafter existing while this Agreement is in effect.

(b)   Every note evidencing any part of the subordinated debt and every ledger page relating thereto will bear a legend which will indicate this subordination.

(c)   Guarantor will not request or accept payment of or any security for any part of the subordinated debt, and if all or any part of it should be paid to Guarantor, through error or otherwise, Guarantor will immediately forward every such payment to FUNB in the form received, properly endorsed to the order of FUNB, to apply on any debt then owing to FUNB by the Customer. This subordination shall continue in full force and effect as long as this Agreement is in effect.

(d)   Guarantor further agrees that it will not assert any right to which it may be or become entitled, whether by subrogation, contribution or otherwise against Customer or any of the other guarantors or any of their respective properties, by reason of the performance of the undersigned of his obligations under this Guaranty, except after payment in full of all amounts (including costs and expenses) which may become payable in respect of or under the "Obligations of Customer." The Guarantor hereby subordinates any and all indebtedness of Customer now or hereafter owed to the undersigned, to all indebtedness of Customer to FUNB and agrees with FUNB that the undersigned shall not demand or accept any payment of principal or interest from Customer, shall not claim any offset or other reduction of the Guarantor's obligations hereunder because of such indebtedness and shall not take any action to obtain any of the security described in and encumbered by any instruments securing payment of the "Obligations of Customer."

(e)   Guarantor, to the best of its knowledge, warrants and represents to FUNB after thorough investigation, that: (a) the Property described in the Mortgage is now, and at all times hereafter, will continue to be in full compliance with all federal, state and local environmental laws and regulations including, but not limited to, the Comprehensive Environmental Response, Compensation and Liability Act of 1980 (CERCLA), Public Law No. 96-510, 94 Stat. 2767, 42 U.S.C. 9601 *et seq*., and the Superfund Amendments and Reauthorization Act of 1986 (SARA), Public Law No. 99-499, 100 Stat. 1613; and (b) (i) as of the date hereof there are no hazardous materials, substances, wastes or other environmentally regulated substances (including, without limitation, any materials containing asbestos) located on, in or under the Property or used in connection therewith, or (ii) Guarantor has fully disclosed to FUNB, in writing, the existence, extent and nature of any such hazardous materials, substances, wastes or other environmentally regulated substances which Guarantor is legally authorized and empowered to maintain on, in or under the Property or use in connection therewith; and Guarantor has caused the Customer to obtain, and will cause to be maintained, all licenses, permits and approvals required with respect thereto, and is in full compliance with all of the terms, conditions and requirements of such licenses, permits and approvals. Guarantor further warrants and represents that it will promptly notify FUNB of any change in the nature or extent of any hazardous materials, substances, or wastes maintained on, in or under the Property or used in connection therewith, and will transmit to FUNB copies of any citations, orders, notices or other material, governmental or other, received with respect to any other hazardous materials, substances, wastes or other environmentally regulated substances affecting the Property.

Guarantor hereby indemnifies and holds FUNB harmless from and against any and all damages, penalties, fines, claims, liens, suits, liabilities, costs (including cleanup costs), judgment and expenses (including attorneys', consultants' or experts' fees and expenses), of every kind and nature, suffered by or asserted against FUNB as a direct or indirect result of any warranty or representations made by Guarantor in the preceding paragraph being false or untrue in any material respect, or any requirement under any law, regulation or ordinance, local, state or federal which requires the elimination or removal of any hazardous materials, substances, wastes or other environmentally regulated substances by FUNB, Guarantor or any other transferee of Guarantor or FUNB.

10.   This Guaranty shall be binding upon Guarantor, and the heirs, executors, administrators, successors and assigns of Guarantor, and it shall inure to the benefit of, and be enforceable by FUNB, and its successors, transferees and assigns. It further shall be deemed to have been made under and shall be governed by the Laws of the State of Florida in all respects, including matters of construction, validity and performance.

11.   Further, all terms or expressions contained herein which are defined in the Uniform Commercial Code of the State of Florida shall have the same meaning herein as in said Articles of said Code.

12.   No waiver by FUNB or any default(s) by Guarantor or Customer shall operate as a waiver of any other default or of the same default on a future occasion. If more than one person has signed this Guaranty, such parties are jointly and severally obligated hereunder. Further use of the masculine or neuter pronoun herein shall include the masculine, feminine and neuter, and also the plural. The term "Guarantor", as used herein, shall (if signed by more than one person) mean the "Guarantors and each of them." If any Guarantor shall be a partnership, the obligations, liabilities and agreements on the part of such Guarantor shall remain in full force and effect and fully applicable notwithstanding any changes in the individuals composing the partnership. Further, the term "Guarantor" shall include in such event any altered or successive partnerships, it being also understood that the predecessor partnership(s) and their partners shall not thereby be released from any obligations or liabilities hereunder. FUNB, or any other holder hereof, may correct patent errors in this Agreement.

13.   Guarantor hereby waives: (i) notice of acceptance of this Guaranty; (ii) notice(s) of extensions of credit and/or continuations of credit extensions to

Customer by FUNB; (iii) notice(s) of entering into and engaging in business transactions and/or contractual relationships and any other dealings between Customer and FUNB; (iv) presentment and/or demand for payment of any of the "Obligations of Customer"; (v) protest or notice of dishonor or default to Guarantor or to any other person with respect to any of the "Obligations of Customer"; and (vi) any demand for payment under this Guaranty.

14.   Anything contained herein to the contrary notwithstanding, if for any reason the effective rate of interest on any of the "Obligations of Customer", should exceed the maximum lawful rate, the effective rate of such obligation(s) shall be deemed reduced to and shall be such maximum lawful rate, and any sums of interest which have been collected in excess of such maximum lawful rate shall be applied as a credit against the unpaid principal balance due hereunder.

15.   Guarantor hereby acknowledges that FUNB has suggested that Customer and Guarantor obtain independent legal counsel to represent their interest in the transaction evidenced hereby and by the Loan Documents.

16.   **WAIVER OF JURY TRIAL. BY THE EXECUTION HEREOF, GUARANTOR KNOWINGLY, VOLUNTARILY AND INTENTIONALLY HEREBY AGREES, THAT:**

(A) NEITHER THE GUARANTOR, NOR ANY ASSIGNEE, SUCCESSOR, HEIR, OR LEGAL REPRESENTATIVE OF THE SAME SHALL SEEK A JURY TRIAL IN ANY LAWSUIT, PROCEEDING, COUNTERCLAIM, OR ANY OTHER LITIGATION PROCEDURE ARISING FROM OR BASED UPON THIS GUARANTY OR ANY OF THE LOAN DOCUMENTS EVIDENCING, SECURING, OR RELATING TO THE "OBLIGATIONS OF CUSTOMER" WHICH ARE SECURED HEREBY, OR TO THE DEALINGS OR RELATIONSHIP BETWEEN OR AMONG THE PARTIES THERETO;

(B) NEITHER THE GUARANTOR, CUSTOMER, NOR FUNB WILL SEEK TO CONSOLIDATE ANY SUCH ACTION, IN WHICH A JURY TRIAL HAS BEEN WAIVED, WITH ANY OTHER ACTION IN WHICH A JURY TRIAL HAS NOT BEEN OR CANNOT BE WAIVED;

(C) THE PROVISIONS OF THIS PARAGRAPH HAVE BEEN FULLY NEGOTIATED BY THE PARTIES HERETO, AND THESE PROVISIONS SHALL BE SUBJECT TO NO EXCEPTIONS;

(D) NEITHER THE GUARANTOR, CUSTOMER, NOR FUNB HAS IN ANY WAY AGREED WITH OR REPRESENTED TO ANY OTHER PARTY THAT THE PROVISIONS OF THIS PARAGRAPH WILL NOT BE FULLY ENFORCED IN ALL INSTANCES; AND

(E) THIS PROVISION IS A MATERIAL INDUCEMENT FOR FUNB TO ACCEPT THIS GUARANTY.

17.   EVENTS OF DEFAULT. Guarantor shall be in default under this Guaranty, upon the happening of any of the following events, circumstances or conditions; namely:

(a) Default in the payment or performance of any of the obligations or of any covenant, warranty or liability contained or referred to herein, or contained in any loan agreement, collateral assignment agreement or in the mortgage securing this Guaranty or in the Mortgage securing any "Obligation of Customer," or in any other contract or agreement of Customer or Guarantor with FUNB, whether now existing or hereafter arising; or

(b) Any warranty, representation or statement made or furnished to FUNB by or on behalf of Customer or Guarantor, in connection with this Guaranty or to induce FUNB to extend credit or otherwise deal with either Customer or Guarantor proving to have been false in any material respect when made or furnished; or

(c) Death, dissolution, termination of existence, insolvency, business failure, appointment of a Receiver of any part of the property of, Assignment for the Benefit of Creditors by, or the commencement of any proceeding under any State or Federal Bankruptcy or Insolvency Laws by or against Guarantor or Customer and a failure to have such proceeding dismissed or such appointment vacated within a period of ninety (90) days. The foregoing notwithstanding, death of the Guarantor shall not be an event of default provided (i) the apartment project being constructed upon the property secured by the Mortgage reaches "stabilization" (which, for purposes hereof, means such project meets the conditions set forth in Section 2.4 of the Note) and (ii) the indebtedness evidenced by the Note is reduced by a minimum of $3,000,000.00 subsequent to stabilization; or

(d) Failure of the Customer or its corporate general partner to maintain its respective existence in good standing; or a sale of all or substantially all of the assets of Customer or Guarantor or the control of primary ownership of the Customer, or sale or transfer of a material portion of its assets outside of the ordinary course of business without the prior written consent of FUNB, which consent shall not be unreasonably withheld; or

(e) The assertion or making of any seizure, vesting or intervention by or under authority of any government by which the management of Customer or Guarantor is displaced or their authority in the conduct of their business(es) is curtailed; or

(f) Upon the entry of any monetary judgment or the assessment and/or filing of any tax lien against either Customer or Guarantor or upon the issuance of any writ of garnishment or attachment against any property of, debts due or rights of Customer or Guarantor, to specifically include the commencement of any action of proceeding to seize moneys of either Customer or Guarantor on deposit in any bank account with FUNB.

18. REMEDIES ON DEFAULT. Upon the occurrence of any of the fore-going events, circumstances, or conditions of default, all of the obligations evidenced herein and secured or guaranteed hereby shall immediately be due and payable without notice. Further, FUNB shall then have all of the rights and remedies granted hereunder, all of the rights and remedies of a secured party and/or holder-in-due-course under the Uniform Commercial Code as adopted and other Laws of the State of Florida.

WITNESS the Hand(s) and Seal(s) of the undersigned, this Guaranty being executed and delivered on the date first above written. Each Guarantor has adopted as his seal the word "SEAL" appearing beside his signature.

WITNESS: _____   _____(SEAL)
Name: _____ **Nathan S. Collier**

WITNESS: _____
Name: _____

STATE OF FLORIDA
COUNTY OF ALACHUA

The foregoing instrument was acknowledged before me this 17th day of November, 2000, by Nathan S. Collier. He [CHECK ONE] is personally known to me or has proved to me on basis of satisfactory evidence to be the person who executed this instrument.

_____

Notary Public, State of Florida

Name: _____

My Commission Expires: _____

My Commission Number is: _____

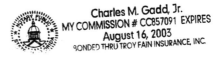

Charles M. Gadd, Jr.
MY COMMISSION # CC857091 EXPIRES
August 16, 2003
BONDED THRU TROY FAIN INSURANCE, INC.

EXHIBIT A-5

Market reports come in many forms, including brief summaries; for example, here are synopses prepared by REIS, Inc. (Used with permission from reis.com, © 2001 Reis, Inc. All rights reserved.) of four sectors of the Orlando, Florida market as of September 30, 2000:

Orlando Apartments: The Orlando apartment market has experienced a reversal in the occupancy trend, as active new construction drove average vacancy upward. While the degree of threat posed by the new trend seems an open question, some observers appear concerned that the market is now in "grave danger" of oversupply. Construction, in any event, does not appear ready to slow: Multifamily building permit data for 1999 indicate a rise in the number of units approved for construction from the level reported for the previous year. Still, this is not a market withering under the stresses of overbuilding—not yet, at any rate. Vacancy was reported at 5.2% at the beginning of both 1997 and 1998. By year-end 2000, a gain to 6.9% is projected, which would qualify as the highest average vacancy reported since 1995. Over the past five years, growth in the average asking rent has averaged 4.1% per year. As of January 2000, average asking and effective rents of $662 and $654 per month were reported, each up 4.3% from a year earlier; average gross revenue of $625.59 is also reported, up from $598.17. Despite the rising vacancy, a 4.1% gain in the average asking rent this year is expected.

Orlando Industrial: This is a market that has been hot and has remained hot as strong leasing activity in recent years resulted in successively lower levels of average vacancy. But a steep rise in construction completions in 1998 resulted in a vacancy increase in early 1999. As speculative construction continues, additional gains in vacancy seem likely, at least in some areas. Still, average vacancy has remained acceptably low and rental increases continue. By the beginning of 1999 the vacancy rate had slipped to 7.5%, the lowest level reported since 1983. However, amid the higher construction totals attending a new industrial building cycle, a rise in the vacancy to 8.8% was reported as of January 2000. Rental performance has been erratic in recent years. For 1995 and 1996, net rent increases of 3.9% and 9.7% were reported. Nineteen ninety-seven and 1998 followed, respectively, with a 4.4% net loss and a small, sub-inflationary 0.2% gain. As of January 2000, average asking and effective rents of $4.64 per square foot and $4.56 per square foot were reported, up 2.4% and 2.5% respectively. An asking rent gain of 3.0% is projected for this year.

Orlando Office: The market charged by rapid economic growth and related development now faces significant challenges in the supply arena. Sources report rapid rises in vacancy, either under way or about to be. While good rental growth is generally indicated, some portion of it is purely statistical phenomenon, reflecting the large volumes of new Class A* space with their higher asking rents;

Class A: Buildings are always the highest-quality space in a given market. Finishes, services and amenities, and systems are top of the line. Rents are above market. *Class B:* Buildings with average services, appearance, image, location, and rents for a given market. *Class C:* Generally older buildings with minimal services, frequently with structural obsolescence, in secondary locations.

a slowing in rental growth is commonly anticipated. The pace of construction is expected to decline, albeit not immediately. Still, despite clear warning signs, there appears to be a substantial reservoir of optimism. Vacancy fell slightly to 7.5% in 1999. However, a January 2001 vacancy rate of 11.1% is predicted—a large gain of 3.6 percentage points. This rise will be accompanied by a gain in the volume of vacant stock of close to 1.3 million square feet as the volume of completed construction races ahead of net absorption. Additional rises in the vacancy rate are anticipated for a period thereafter. Gains in the average asking rent averaged 4.2% per year from 1994 through 1999. As of January 2000, average asking and effective office rents of $19.21 per square foot and $18.17 per square foot were reported, up 2.2% and 2.0%, respectively, from a year earlier—the smallest rates of gain reported since 1993.

Orlando Retail: Rapid gains in population and strong residential development are ingredients for a very strong retail market. Oversupply has been virtually unknown here, although the combination of the conclusion of a heavy development cycle and the onset of an economic recession did push the vacancy rate close to 10% in 1991. Since then, the vacancy trend has tended to be favorable. Rental growth is slowing but stays positive. A number of major mixed-use projects with substantial retail components, including a new regional mall, are being developed. Notably, with a new construction cycle under way, the vacancy rate continues to decline. Since 1996, vacancy rates have fluctuated in the vicinity of 8%, some years slightly higher, some slightly lower. As of January 2000, a vacancy rate of 7.4% was reported, below the January 1999 estimate of 7.8%—and the lowest vacancy level reported since 1986. A new spurt in rental growth, beginning in 1996, occurred. Thereafter, gains in average rent ran from 3.0% to 6.6% up until last year. As of January 2000, average asking and effective non-anchor space lease rates of $18.81 per square foot and $17.94 per square foot were reported, up 1.5% and 1.6%, respectively, from a year earlier—the lowest rates of gain reported by this source since 1995. Rental growth is expected to remain in the vicinity of 2% per year.

Markets also can be ranked on a national scale. Figure A5-1 shows the Orlando market's rankings, as of the fourth quarter of 2000, among the top 50 markets in the country according to one researcher. The development climate in Orlando does not appear very favorable at the moment. The rate of rent growth for apartments is 36 of 50, that is, two-thirds of the top 50 apartment markets in the United States are forecasted to have higher rent growth. It is forecasted to have the highest vacancy rate of any of the top 50 markets, and the growth in the inventory of apartments (i.e., more product is coming on line as more apartment communities are built) is forecasted to be the highest in America. The rankings for the other sectors are similarly dismal.

The following snapshots of the San Jose, California market, also provided by REIS, Inc. (used with permission from reis.com, © 2001 Reis, Inc. All rights reserved.), provide an excellent contrast to the Orlando market and illustrate the amount of regional diversity that can exist within the national market.

ORLANDO, FLORIDA

Sector	National Ranking
APARTMENT	
Rent Growth:	36
Vacancy Rate:	50
Inventory Growth:	1
INDUSTRIAL	
Rent Growth:	36
Vacancy Rate:	32
Inventory Growth:	3
OFFICE	
Rent Growth:	45
Vacancy Rate:	42
Inventory Growth:	2
RETAIL	
Rent Growth:	45
Vacancy Rate:	36
Inventory Growth:	3

FIG. A5-1 Orlando market ranking, September 30, 2000. (Used with permission from reis.com, © 2001 Reis, Inc. All rights reserved.)

San Jose Apartment: Housing in this highly affluent region is dominated by the single-family sector. Despite strong demand for affordable housing, high land and development costs along with community resistance to high-density housing make development generally difficult and, unless tax credits are available, virtually impossible for all but luxury projects. These long-embedded factors combine with the region's strong economic performance in recent years to produce a market with exceedingly high levels of occupancy and strong rental trends, making this a market in which virtual full occupancy has been the norm. As per January 1999, a vacancy rate of 2.5% was reported, up from 1.9% a year earlier and the highest rate reported since 1995. As of January 2000 no change in vacancy from the prior year had occurred. Very high average rents are the norm, as are strong rental gains. As of January 2000, average asking and effective rents were reported at $1,379 and $1,372 per month, respectively, each up 7.5% from a year earlier.

Note the strong contrast with the Orlando apartment market, with average asking rents of $1,379 in San Jose versus $662 for Orlando, with rents up 7.5% in San Jose versus 4.3% rent growth in Orlando. Thus, not only are the average residential rents higher in California, the rate of rent growth is higher as well. Furthermore, the occupancy rate is lower: 2.5% versus a projected 6.9%. Why are

San Jose's rents so much higher? Higher costs, starting with per-unit land costs in California which are easily double and triple Orlando's land costs, account for some of the difference. The scarcity of developable sites and the restrictive regulatory climate also restrain development activity no matter how attractive the return. The result drives up rents as consumer demand bids up the price of the limited available supply of housing stock.

San Jose Industrial: With Silicon Valley as the centerpiece, the San Jose industrial market is heavily oriented toward research and development and computer-related manufacturing, with well above half of all industrial space countywide falling into the R&D category. In addition, the affordable land prices typically required for the development of speculative warehousing and other lower-rent industrial property types are in short supply. The vacancy rate was 9.2% as per January 2000, up from 7.9% a year earlier, and from 5.2% at the beginning of 1998 (the lowest level reported since 1980). For the industrial market overall, as of January 2000 average asking and effective rents were reported at $7.48 per square foot and $7.37 per square foot, up 2.7% and 2.6%, respectively, from a year earlier. This source expects the rate of gain to fall to about 1.3% this year.

Once again, note the higher prices per square foot in San Jose, $7.48 versus $4.64 for Orlando, this time for industrial space. However, while Orlando is forecasting a gain of 3% in rent growth in the next year, San Jose is expected to gain only 1.3% rent growth. Furthermore, the San Jose vacancy rate has been rising and, at 9.2%, surpasses Orlando's.

San Jose Office The Asian economic crisis that emerged in 1998, much feared in this region for its putative potential to stymie the local economy and its office real estate markets, came and went with barely a ripple. Although strong demand is expected to persist, concerns that heavy construction could compromise strong market fundamentals have also surfaced. The heavy orientation of the market toward computer-related business constitutes long-term risk. Vacancy during 1998 rose a mere half point, from 5.8% at the beginning of the year to 6.3% in January 1999. A downward movement resumed immediately thereafter. By January 2000, a vacancy rate of 4.5% was reported, the lowest reported since 1980. A small rise, to 5.6%, is projected for year-end. This is a high-end area and a high-end market, replete with prime high-tech tenants. Rents, accordingly, are quite high by national norms. Extraordinary gains of 18.4% and 10.9% were reported for 1997 and 1998. As of January 2000, average asking and effective rents were reported at $33.11 and $32.14 per square foot, up 9.3% and 9.4%, respectively, from a year earlier. However, a steady decline in rental rate growth is anticipated with a forecast for future market imbalances.

San Jose's office rents are about 60% higher than Orlando's, with very strong rent growth in the 9% range as versus 2% for Orlando, and Orlando's 11% office vacancy rate is more than double San Jose's projected 5.6%.

San Jose Retail: Very high levels of disposable income and a vigorous local economy have made this a strong market for retail real estate. Indeed, Santa Clara County has been the recent leader in retail sales totals among counties in the greater San Francisco Bay area. The market remains vibrant and very tight, with low levels of new supply. Occupancy is high and rents are high and rising amid strong demand and a less than robust pace of development. The favorable trend of declining average vacancy that we reported in our previous coverage of this market has continued. As of January 2000, average vacancy was reported at 3.6%, down from 4.5% a year earlier and the lowest rate reported since 1985. An insignificant tenth-of-a-point rise is expected by year-end 2000. Moreover, the volume of vacant stock, slightly above 1.2 million square feet, is at its lowest level since 1986. With its high levels of household and disposable income and high costs of development, the San Jose market has evolved as a prime locale for upscale retailing. These factors result in high average rents. As of January 2000 average asking and effective non-anchor space lease rates were reported at $28.69 and $27.83 per square foot, each up 4.6% from a year earlier; an average gross revenue of $27.66 is indicated, up from $26.21.

Once again, San Jose's retail rents are about 50% higher than Orlando's. At 4.6%, the rent growth is more than double Orlando's 1.5% to 2% rent growth rate, and at 3.6%, San Jose's vacancy rate is one-half Orlando's 7% plus vacancy. Figure A5-2 shows San Jose's national market rankings as of the fourth quarter of 2000. We have briefly looked at the amount of variation that occurs in rents,

SAN JOSE, CALIFORNIA

Sector	National Ranking
APARTMENT	
Rent Growth:	2
Vacancy Rate:	20
Inventory Growth:	9
INDUSTRIAL	
Rent Growth:	37
Vacancy Rate:	30
Inventory Growth:	22
OFFICE	
Rent Growth:	3
Vacancy Rate:	4
Inventory Growth:	15
RETAIL	
Rent Growth:	16
Vacancy Rate:	3
Inventory Growth:	23

FIG. A5-2 San Jose market ranking, September 30, 2000. (Used with permission from reis.com, © 2001 Reis, Inc. All rights reserved.)

SUBMARKET	CENTER TYPE	SUBTYPE	VACANCY	LOW	HIGH	AVERAGE
North County	Community	Non-Anchor	3.5%	$18.00	$43.61	$24.78
	Neighborhood	Non-Anchor	2.9%	$16.80	$45.59	$23.87
	Regional	Non-Anchor	3.5%	$27.90	$41.85	$35.83
West County	Community	Non-Anchor	.9%	$21.96	$36.00	$27.46
	Neighborhood	Non-Anchor	2.2%	$17.34	$28.50	$23.86
	Regional	Non-Anchor	4.0%	$27.00	$37.00	$30.34
San Jose/S. County	Community	Non-Anchor	5.3%	$13.71	$29.53	$22.66
	Neighborhood	Non-Anchor	5.1%	$12.79	$30.99	$20.33
	Regional	Non-Anchor	1.6%	$23.86	$40.00	$31.33

Quarter Ending 9/30/00

FIG. A5-3   Retail submarkets, San Jose, September 30, 2000. (Used with permission from reis.com, © 2001 Reis, Inc. All rights reserved.)

vacancy, and rent growth rates that occur on the national level; it is important to understand that a similar amount of variation can occur even within a given metro market. Figure A5-3 shows the retail submarkets in the San Jose area. Even with a given submarket and subtype, the variation between the high and low rents can be substantial. Factors such as age, design, trends, and micro-location all play major roles.

Appendix B

EXHIBIT B-1

THURSDAY, NOVEMBER 4,1999

The Gainesville Sun

Hidden Lake

The controversial Lake Meta development will put the city to test on how seriously it supports the concept of "infill."

Developer Nathan Collier's new Gainesville project is to be named Hidden Lake Apartments. And that seems appropriate; when finished, occupants probably won't even be able to see, let alone access, nearby Lake Meta.

Nonetheless, this 221-unit apartment project has been the source of considerable controversy. A handful of residents who live right on that lake, not far from Gainesville High School, worry that it will destroy the peace and tranquility of their secluded neighborhood. For his part, Collier argues that he is doing exactly what the city commission wants builders to do ... "urban infill," which will increase densities within the city as opposed to strewing growth out into the suburbs.

Increased densities within city limits make for a more efficient and affordable delivery of transportation, public safety and other essential services. Mixed-used neighborhoods also make for more livable and interesting cities.

All of the controversy aside, it's hard to see how the city can turn Collier down. The land in dispute is zoned for multi-family use. The proposed density, at 13 units per acre, does not seem excessive. Collier has even agreed to fence off access to the lake to keep residents happy.

Collier summed up the dilemma facing both himself and city officials in a recent e-mail to a city commissioner: "It became a classic case of 'Yes, we want infill, just not here, even if it is zoned multi-family,' and 'Yes, we want infill, just so long as it is perfect and makes everybody happy'."

"Well, in the real world there is no such thing as a perfect development," he added, "and there are not too many parcels left inside the city limits zoned multi-family that are large enough to develop and are in a marketable location."

Is the city serious about encouraging infill development as an antidote to urban sprawl? Or is Gainesville's commitment to that principle as hidden as the view of Lake Meta?

Reprinted with permission from the Gainesville Sun.

EXHIBIT B-2

Saturday, November 6, 1999

Apartment complex put on hold
By RAY WASHINGTON
Gainesville Sun writer

A proposed 262 apartment development was put on hold early Friday as the city's Development Review Board for the second time failed to conclude a public hearing on site plan approval for developer Nathan Collier's Hidden Lake Apartments.

"The delay is unfortunate but we will continue on as fast a timeline as possible," said Collier, who had hoped to have construction complete by July and most apartments leased by August.

That timeline might still be possible, "but this sure doesn't help," Collier said.

Hidden Lake opponent Paul Wheeler said the delay could help board members focus on the issues, but "it is really hard for me to judge what is going on at this point," Wheeler said.

The board first considered the project last month, but had to continue consideration of the project largely as a result of questions raised by opponents of the project.

More than 50 residents—most from nearby neighborhoods and most opposed to the project—showed up Thursday, arguing against Collier's plans in a hearing that continued past midnight.

City planners already have recommended approval of the project on two parcels controlled by Collier north of Lake Meta, a secluded five-acre lake a few blocks east of NW 13th Street, near NW 23rd Avenue. The proposed project will consist of clusters of two- and three-story buildings next to Collier's existing one-story Bailey Gardens apartment complex, which fronts NW 21st Avenue.

Opponents of the project object to a recommendation by planners that Collier be allowed to add extra units under a complex bonus points system that can allow more dense development than existing zoning ordinarily allows. They also object to the placement of two- and three-story apartment buildings near single-family houses in adjacent neighborhoods, and to Collier's plans to direct stormwater runoff from the project into nearby Lake Meta.

Arguments and public comments on the site plan are now complete, but rebuttal arguments and final consideration by the board has been continued to the board's next regular meeting, scheduled for Nov. 16 at 5 p.m. in the city hall auditorium.

EXHIBIT B-3

Thursday, November 18, 1999

Hidden Lake gets approval
by RAY WASHINGTON
Gainesville Sun staff writer

Developer Nathan Collier's proposed $14 million Hidden Lake Apartment complex was approved 2–1 by the city's Development Review Board early Wednesday morning at the end of a third heated late night meeting attended by dozens of opponents.

The 260-unit complex, to be built near NW 13th Street just north of secluded Lake Meta, had been praised by city planners as ideal "infill" favored by city officials intent on combatting urban sprawl west of the city.

"It's going to put people this side of 34th Street," Collier said after the vote. "There's not too many projects doing that. And I really think that's best for the entire city."

But opponents of the 626-bedroom, 626-parking space development predicted the board's action would turn into a rallying cry for re-examining the city's infill policies.

"They are destroying beauty and calling it saving beauty," said Lake Meta resident Paul Wheeler. "I think as a community we have to stand up now real quick and begin to scream."

Lake Meta and nearby residents around the development have been fighting the project since last year, when Collier acquired a long-term lease on land south of NW 21st Avenue and east of NW 13th Street. That land, next to Collier's existing low-density Bailey Gardens apartment complex, is being merged with Bailey Gardens land to create a 20-acre higher density development to be called Hidden Lake.

Concerns about the effects on Lake Meta dominated much of Tuesday night's debate.

In the past, Collier had maintained the lake itself should not be part of the site approval process since neither the lake nor its shore are on project land. But Collier engineer Stuart Cullen on Tuesday argued that if Lake Meta were considered, it should not be consideration as a lake.

"It's artificially maintained," said Cullen, presenting research he said proved that for decades the lake's water level has been the result of a 200-foot-deep well and a pumping system "installed in the 1970s because the lake had dried up."

An environmental expert hired last week by the city said Lake Meta without pumping "likely would behave like a wetland with varying water levels."

But Lake Meta residents said that regardless of Lake Meta's water level, runoff from Collier's development would hurt water quality and adversely affect plant and animal life in and around it.

Panel members made approval of the project contingent on Collier's agreement to provide a dry stormwater retention system with no overflow and no discharge into Lake Meta.

Opponents also objected to setbacks, height and building configurations planned for the mostly three-story development, and said added traffic would cause problems for the surrounding neighborhoods.

The panel did not require any changes to those aspects of the project, but did require Collier to alter his plans to include a fence on part of the northern edge of the property and more trees on part of the southern edge for greater visual buffer. Members also concluded that traffic generated by the development would not excessively affect the surrounding neighborhoods, but at the same time required Collier to maintain a break in the fence to encourage bicycle and pedestrian transportation.

Members were in less agreement over how to respond to opponents' objections to Hidden Lake's proposed density of about 13 units an acre, which they said was incompatible with the lower density neighborhood surrounding it. The two members voting in favor of the project agreed with planning staff recommendations that most of the requested density furthered city policies encouraging infill.

But member Alice Bojanowski, who voted against the plan, said she believed the project was inconsistent with elements of the city's comprehensive plan.

"If this is infill, I think it's giving infill a bad name," she said.

Collier disagreed.

"I really do think the project is going to benefit the community," he said. Construction of Hidden Lake will not begin until September, Collier said.

Reprinted with permission from the Gainesville Sun.

Appendix C

EXHIBIT C-1

Letter of Intent to Purchase

[Buyer] hereby expresses its interest in purchasing the property called "the Gables" located at 4700 SW Archer Rd in Gainesville, Florida 32608 utilizing Mr. Dan Allen from CB Richard Ellis as our representing agent in the transaction. The terms of said purchase shall be as follows:

1. Purchase price to be $23,520,000. ($140,000 per door.)
2. Earnest money deposit to be $250,000. With an additional $100,000 after feasibility expires.
3. Buyer to have a contingent feasibility period of 30 days from acceptance.
4. Close of escrow to be on or before 30 days thereafter.
5. Purchase agreement will be executed upon agreement of the above terms. Said Purchase agreement will include these and other mutually agreed upon terms.

Date: 9/22/05

Buyer: ＿＿＿＿＿＿

Date: ＿＿＿＿＿

Seller: ＿＿＿＿＿＿＿

Exhibit C-2   **465**

EXHIBIT C-2

Letter of Intent to Purchase

[Buyer] hereby expresses its interest in purchasing the property called "the Gables" located at 4700 SW Archer Rd in Gainesville, Florida 32608 utilizing Mr. Dan Allen from CB Richard Ellis as our representing agent in the transaction. The terms of said purchase shall be as follows:

Option 1:

1. Purchase price to be $26,880,000. ($160,000 per door.)
2. Earnest money deposit to be $250,000. With an additional $100,000 after feasibility expires.
3. Terms of said purchase shall be.
   a. Down payment $350,000.
   b. Owner carry 40%
   c. Interest rate 6% for two (2) years
   d. Interest payments (annually) $645,120
   e. Effective sales price $28,170,240.
4. Buyer to have a contingent feasibility period of 30 days from acceptance.
5. Close of escrow to be on or before 30 days thereafter.
6. Purchase agreement will be executed upon agreement of the above terms. Said Purchase agreement will include these and other mutually agreed upon terms.

Option 2: Joint Venture
Seller to obtain full asking price plus profits from the condo conversion. Ask for details
Option 3: previous offer with hard money on day 1 subject to all inspections

Date: 10/03/05

Buyer:

EXHIBIT C-3

September 29, 2005   Via Telefax

Mr. Daniel V. Allen
Mr. Fred Marks
CB Richard Ellis
225 Water Street, Suite 110
Jacksonville, Florida 32202

Re: **The Gables, 168 Units, Gainesville, Florida**

Dear Mr. Allen & Mr. Marks:

This letter will serve to set forth the terms and conditions upon which the under-signed and/or assigns ("Purchaser") intends to purchase the rights and interests in the properties described above and all improvements thereon, all tenant leases, all equipment and any other personal property related to the operation of the prop-erty located thereon, and any other rights, benefits, or intangibles owned or used by Seller in connection with the operation of the improvements (collectively the "Property")

1. PURCHASE PRICE: The Purchase Price will be $25,183,200.00 cash to seller at closing. Seller to be responsible to pay any sales commissions as well as any penalty or charges to pay off current mortgages.

2. EARNEST MONEY: Within two (2) business days after the execution of a binding contract of purchase and sale, Purchaser will place the sum of One Hundred Thousand Dollars ($100,000.00) as an earnest money deposit to be credited towards purchase price. The contract evidencing the transaction described in this letter shall provide that receipt of the Earnest Money, as liquidated damages shall be the Seller's sole and exclusive remedy in the event of Purchaser's default. At end of feasibility period as stated below, Purchaser will deposit $100,000.00 as additional earnest money. All of the escrow deposits shall be credited towards purchase price.

3. DUE DILIGENCE PERIOD: Purchaser shall have (30) days from the effec-tive date of the contract or (30) days from Purchaser receiving the last of the following items: plans & specs used to build the buildings, as-builts if any, all surveys, all environmental studies & approvals, copies of the past title commitments, current P&L statements, copies of all service agreements, including cable television, security, water & sewer agreements if any, sur-face water & storm water management agreements if any, insurance policies, certificates of occupancy for all units including all common elements, legal descriptions and all governmental approvals. Purchaser shall have (30) days to

Exhibit C-3   **467**

conduct such due diligence activities, inspections, and studies of the Property as it deems necessary or appropriate, and examine and investigate to its full satisfaction all facts, circumstances, and matters relating to the Property (including the physical condition and use, compliance with applicable laws, environmental conditions, engineering and structural matters), survey matters, and any other matters it deems necessary or appropriate for purposes of consummating this transaction. The Due Diligence shall be at Buyer's sole cost and expense.

4. CLOSING: The Closing will be held Thirty (30) days after expiration of the (30) day Feasibility period, unless such date falls upon a holiday or weekend, in which event the Closing will take place on the next ensuing business day, provided that the Purchaser shall have the right to accelerate the Closing to an earlier business day selected by the Purchaser. Purchaser shall have an option to extend the closing period for an additional Thirty (30) days, if Purchaser deposits an additional $100,000.00 in Earnest Money. It is the intent of the Buyer and Seller to close on either the last day or the first day of a calendar month.

5. TITLE INSURANCE: Sellers will furnish and pay for a commitment for title insurance ("Title Commitment") and an Owner's Policy of Title Insurance in the amount of the Purchase Price issued by the Title Company to Purchaser and insuring good and indefeasible title to the Property subject to no exceptions other than (a) exceptions contained in the Title Commitment and approved by Purchaser prior to Closing, and (b) any liens placed on the Property in connection with Purchaser's financing of its purchase of the property. Within ten (10) days after the effective date of the contract, Seller shall deliver to Purchaser a commitment for an owner's policy of title insurance, and legal copies of any instruments of record creating exceptions to title to any property. Seller will pay for document stamps.

6. PRORATIONS AND OTHER COSTS: Any interest, ad valorem taxes, rents, operating expenses, etc., will be prorated as of the Closing. Seller will pay all Florida transfer taxes. All other costs, including recording fees, will be allocated between Seller and Purchaser in the manner customary for transactions of this nature.

7. CONDEMNATION: In the event that all or any portions of the Property is condemned or destroyed or damaged by fire or other casualty prior to the Closing, Purchaser shall have the option to either (i) terminate the Contract and receive back the Earnest Money, or (ii) consummate the Contract and receive any proceeds arising from said condemnation or casualty.

8. LETTER OF INTENT: It is understood that this instrument constitutes only a letter of intent and that neither Seller nor Purchaser shall have any liability in connection with the transaction described above until such time as a Contract relating to such transaction has been prepared and executed by both parties.

Upon full execution of this letter by the Seller, Purchaser will proceed to prepare the Contract in accordance with the terms of this letter. If the foregoing correctly reflects your understanding of our mutual intentions, please execute and return a copy of this letter to the undersigned. This offer is conditioned upon acceptance by Seller by 5:00 pm, October 7, 2005. All notifications to the buyer shall be e-mailed to [address].

Agreed and Accepted:

By

Date: September 29, 2005

By: _____

Title: _____
      Owner

Date: _____

Exhibit C-4   **469**

EXHIBIT C-4

September 22, 2005   Via Facsimile

Mr. Daniel V. Allen
Senior Vice President
CB Richard Ellis
225 Water Street
Suite 110
Jacksonville, Florida 32202

    Re: LETTER OF INTENT- The Gables Apartments
                              4700 SW Archer Road, Gainesville, Florida

Dear Dan;

Please accept this "Letter of Intent" to purchase the above-referenced project located on 4700 SW Archer Road in Gainesville, Florida.

If these terms are acceptable to the Seller we will prepare a Purchase and Sale Agreement based on the following terms and conditions:

BUYER:

SELLER: Recorded title holder

PROPERTY DESCRIPTION: 168 unit apartment project and all personal property and improvements on 21.19 acres.

PRICE: $23,520,000

TERMS: Cash at closing.

EARNEST MONEY DEPOSIT: $250,000 will be deposited as a refundable down payment into an escrow account upon execution of the Purchase and Sale Agreement. An additional deposit of $250,000 will be deposited into the escrow account at the end of the Due Diligence period. Deposits become non-refundable after the expiration of the Due Diligence period, and are credited against the purchase price.

DUE DILIGENCE: Buyer will have 40 days from Purchase and Sale Agreement execution to perform all necessary inspections of the property. Seller will provide a new survey, staked on the ground, showing all wetlands, easements, and protected trees; title insurance commitment; and a Phase I environmental study/report that shows the property to be free of contamination. Buyer must accept the property in writing on or before the end of the Due Diligence period.

CLOSING: On or before 40 days following the end of the due diligence period.

CLOSING COSTS: Normal and customary.

BROKER: Any and all broker fees to be paid by Seller at closing.

This Letter of Intent is not intended to articulate every detail of the proposed transaction and is subject to the negotiation and execution by Buyer and Seller of the Purchase and Sale Agreement except for the provisions hereof dealing with (i) Buyer's right to perform inspections and its due diligence activities, (ii) confidentiality and (iii) further offers. If the forgoing is acceptable to you, please execute below to signify acceptance of the terms hereof. It is understood that Seller will immediately cease marketing the property to other buyers and will negotiate in good faith exclusively with Buyer to enter into the Agreement. Except as set forth in the preceding sentence, no binding agreement shall exist unless a formal Agreement, mutually acceptable to Seller and Buyer, has been executed by both parties.

TERMINATION: This offer will terminate on September 26, 2005, unless accepted by Seller where indicated below.

Thank you for your consideration. If you have any questions please call me at [phone].

Sincerely;

ACKNOWLEDGED AND AGREED TO BY:

_____

_____

Title

Dated: _____

Exhibit C-5 **471**

EXHIBIT C-5

September 27th, 2005

Gables Apartments of Gainesville Ltd.
c/o Daniel V. Allen
CB Richard Ellis   VIA EMAIL:

    RE: The Gables Apartments
           4700 Southwest Archer Rd.
           Gainesville, FL 32608
           Tax ID: 06819-000-000 & 06935-000-000

Ladies and Gentlemen:

The following letter sets forth the general terms and conditions under which ("Purchaser") will enter into an agreement for purchase and sale of the above referenced properties.

The Property, defined as the above-mentioned property (see Exhibit "A" for a more detailed property description), shall be sold and acquired for Purchaser's intended use, which is to convert the existing 168 apartment dwellings into condominiums (the "Intended Use").

The purchase price will be Twenty Two Million Eight Hundred Twenty Three Thousand Dollars ($22,823,000).

The purchase price shall be payable as follows:

$100,000	to be deposited in escrow within 48 hours of bilateral execution of a purchase and sale agreement as an initial good faith refundable deposit.
$100,000	An additional deposit of One Hundred Thousand Dollars ($100,000.00) shall be made pursuant to the above terms upon the expiration of the Title Review Period;
$100,000	to be deposited in escrow within 48 hours of the expiration of the Investigation Period.

Deposits shall be in the form of cash and shall <u>not</u> be subject to financing and shall only be subject to Conditions Precedent. The balance of the purchase monies shall be paid in cash at closing.

INVESTIGATION PERIOD:

The Investigation Period shall run 30 days from the latter of: (1) a bilaterally executed formal contract or (2) the "...delivery of a current survey of the Property boundaries identifying total acreage, wetland jurisdictional boundaries,...." as described herein under SELLER'S OBLIGATIONS (A.).

During the Inspection Period the Purchaser reserves the right, for any reason, to find the Subject unsuitable for its purposes and demand return of deposits. Buyer may extend the Investigation Period for an additional fifteen days, at Buyer's election, by notifying Seller and depositing an additional fifty thousand dollars ($50,000.00) ("hereinafter referred to as the "Investigation Extension Deposit") on or before the scheduled expiration of the Investigation Period. The Investigation Extension Deposit shall be non-refundable, except in the event of Seller default.

PURCHASER'S OBLIGATIONS:

A. WORK PRODUCT: In the event Purchaser fails to close the purchase and sale agreement, Purchaser will provide Seller with original copies of studies, plans, permits, etc... that have been sanctioned during the contractual period.

B. TITLE COMMITMENT: Purchaser will provide, at Closing Expense of the Purchaser, a title insurance commitment (Form ALTA B) within 14 days of bilateral contract execution. Customary cure periods shall apply.

C. ENVIRONMENTAL STUDIES: During the Investigation Period, Buyer shall cause to have undertaken a Phase I Environmental Study of the Property (the "Phase I Study"). In the event the Phase I Study suggests or requires a Phase II Environmental Study (the "Phase II Study"), Buyer shall cause to have such study undertaken. The cost of the such studies shall be borne solely by Buyer.

SELLER'S OBLIGATIONS:

A. Within two (2) business days of the execution of this Contract Seller shall deliver to Buyer the items described on Exhibit "B" as well as the most current Property survey. Seller shall provide to Purchaser copies of any **existing** leases, permits, applications, soil test analysis, environmental reports, engineering plans and calculations, zoning and utility letters, title policies, evidence of concurrency vesting, or other information that may be useful in Purchaser's investigation of the Property. To the extent that Seller's delivery of said information is delayed beyond two (2) business days, the Investigation Period shall be extended a like number of days.

B. TITLE: Seller has, and at the time of closing will have and deliver good and marketable fee simple title to the property free and clear of encumbrances

Exhibit C-5   **473**

of any kind or nature except as otherwise accepted by Purchaser. In the event encumbrances exist which are considered unacceptable by Purchaser, the Seller shall have an amount of time, which is considered "customary" and reasonable, in which to cure said defects.

C. CONVEYANCE: Seller shall convey title to the Property by General or Special Warranty Deed, free and clear of all liens, qualifications, and encumbrances, except those specifically permitted by the Contract.

D. CLOSING COSTS: Unless otherwise stated, Seller shall be responsible for those closing costs customarily paid by sellers, including documentary stamps, recording fees and document preparation (excluding title insurance).

CURE OF TITLE OR SURVEY DEFECTS:

Buyer shall have a period of fifteen (15) days after receipt of the Current Survey and Title Commitment in which to notify Seller of any defects or matters revealed by either the Current Survey or Title Commitment that are unacceptable to Buyer. In such event, Seller shall, at its sole cost and expense, promptly undertake to eliminate all such unacceptable matters to the reasonable satisfaction of Buyer and the Title Company. Seller agrees to use its best efforts to satisfy promptly any such objection (for the purposes of this paragraph, best efforts shall not include the filing of a lawsuit to cure an objection or the expenditure of $50,000.00 in the aggregate to cure an objection, unless such defect is a monetary lien capable of being bonded off or paid at Closing), but in the event Seller is unable with the exercise of its best efforts to satisfy said objections within thirty (30) days after said notice, Buyer may, at its option, (a) accept title subject to the objections raised by Buyer in which event said objections shall be deemed to be waived for all purposes or (b) cancel this Agreement, whereupon the Deposit shall be returned to Buyer and this Agreement shall be of no further force and effect. It is expressly agreed that Buyer, in its sole discretion, may elect to accept or reject any proposed affirmative title insurance as a satisfaction of a title objection. It is further specifically understood that Buyer hereby objects to and will require the deletion of all standard exceptions including, without limitation:

(a) rights or claims or parties in possession not shown by public records;

(b) easements or claims of easements not shown by public records;

(c) discrepancies, conflicts in boundary lines, shortage in area, encroachments and any items which a correct survey and inspection of the Property would disclose and which are not shown by public records;

(d) any lien, or right to a lien, for services, labor or material heretofore or hereafter furnished, imposed by law and not shown by public records; and

(e) defects and liens first appearing subsequent to the effective date of the title commitment but prior to the Closing Date.

CONDITIONS PRECEDENT:

Purchaser's obligations to close the initial purchase and sale agreement shall be conditioned upon the following items:

A. Absent of any condemnation, moratoriums, or other proceedings that would materially affect Purchaser's Intended Use of the property.

B. There shall be no breach by Seller and that all representations of Seller (including absence of toxic waste) are true and correct, and all obligations of Seller provided for in the purchase and sale agreement have been performed or waived by Purchaser.

CLOSING:

Closing shall occur on or before 30 days following the expiration of the investigation period.

BROKER:

The parties hereto represent each to the other that neither has employed a real estate broker in connection with the consummation of the purchase and sale agreement contemplated herein except for Daniel V. Allen of CB Richard Ellis, who were engaged as brokers by Seller, respectively (hereafter referred to as "Brokers").

Real estate brokerage commissions/fees shall be a reduction in the amount due Seller on the closing statement.

In the event that there is a claim against one of the parties arising out of an act or actions by the other party giving rise to a claim for commission with respect to any broker (other than the named Brokers who shall be treated as set forth in the previous paragraph), then said party which committed such acts or actions which gave rise to said claim shall indemnify, defend, save and hold the other party harmless from and against said claim for commission, including but not limited to reasonable attorney's fees and costs.

There is a sincere interest in the property founded by its ability to develop the intended use described herein and agrees to enter into negotiations to purchase the property.

If the general terms and conditions set forth herein are acceptable, please indicate so by dating and signing the enclosed duplicate copy of this letter and return same to Purchaser. The heresodescribed Letter of Intent is a binding agreement between both Seller and Purchaser. TIME IS OF THE ESSENCE. Upon acceptance of both parties, Purchaser shall instruct council to immediately begin drafting a final purchase and sale agreement. Thereafter, both parties agree to negotiate in good

Exhibit C-5   **475**

faith, for a period not to exceed 15 business days, wherein Purchaser will not negotiate to purchase land from any other competing property owner and Seller will not negotiate to sell Property to any other prospective purchaser until such time as both parties concur that a satisfactory purchase and sale agreement cannot be consummated as contemplated herein, at which time the parties hereto hereby release each other from any further liability.

If we do not receive a copy of this letter signed by an authorized signatory on or before 5:00 P.M. September 29th, 2005 we will consider the general terms and conditions set forth herein are unacceptable.

Sincerely,

Project Partner

Terms as set forth accepted:

SELLER

By: _____   Title: _____

   _____   Dated: _____

Entity: _____

EXHIBIT "A"

Legal Description to be provided by Seller

Exhibit C-5   **477**

EXHIBIT "B"

1. To the extent that the following is in the Seller's possession (or could be obtained with minimal effort and expense), a full set of construction documents, including but not limited to building plans and specifications, site plans, engineering, certified as-built surveys for the entire property, topographical surveys and landscaping plans;

2. Most current title policy;

3. Copy of phase-one environmental report for the property;

4. Copy of the most current survey of the Property in Seller's possession;

5. 2004 and 2005 Year to date operating statements;

6. All market analyses, appraisals, engineering, environmental and other studies in Seller's possession that relate to this property;

7. A schedule or inventory of all personal property and fixtures owned or leased by Property's entity and used in connection with the operation of the Property;

8. A list of tangible personal property and intangible property of Property;

9. A list of all capital improvements made to the Property during Seller's ownership term;

10. A copy of the standard Lease for the Property and any exception thereto and a current Rent Roll;

11. Copies of the utility bills, property tax assessments and tax bills with respect to the Property since January 1, 2004;

12. Copies of all service and employment contracts and any other agreements relating to the Property;

13. Copies of all present property, fire, extended risk, liability and other insurance policies covering the Property and a schedule of the premiums thereof;

14. Copies of all licenses, permits, maps, certificates of occupancy, building inspection approvals and covenants and restrictions with respect to the Property;

15. A report of all casualty losses suffered by or affecting the Property since January 1, 2004;

16. A copy of the current employee payroll for the Property;

17. Audited, or if not available, unaudited monthly and annual income and operating statements for the Property since January 1, 2004;

18. Copies of all records with respect to the Property's security deposit trust account;

19. Owner's organizational documents including all exhibits and amendments thereto; and

20. A list of matters, current, pending or threatened, involving litigation or arbitration proceedings affecting the Property or Seller;

21. All documentation detailing the terms of the Negotiated Escrow Agreement.

EXHIBIT C-6

Mr. Daniel V. Allen
CB Richard Ellis, Inc
225 Water Street, Suite 110
Jacksonville, FL 32202

RE: The Gables

Dear Mr. Allen:

The purpose of this Letter of Intent is to indicate the basis which Purchaser is prepared to purchase the following property located at:

4700 Southwest Archer Road
Gainesville, Florida
Residential Property Containing 168 Units
207,482 A/C Square Feet

If this Letter of Intent is acceptable, it shall serve as a basis Purchaser and Seller to negotiate a mutually acceptable binding agreement with respect to the Property.

Purchase Price: $21,000,000

Purchase and Sale Agreement (the "P&S"): The Parties shall move forward to enter into a P&S mutually satisfactory to both parties. The P&S will be prepared by the Seller's counsel and submitted to the Purchaser for review. Purchaser and Seller shall in good faith, negotiate, endeavor to agree upon the terms of, and execute the P&S.

Deposit: The Deposit under the P&S shall be $500,00 followed by another $500,000 at the end of the due diligence period to be held by a mutually acceptable escrow agent. The is Deposit will serve as liquidated damages in the event of a default by Purchaser. The Deposit shall be nonrefundable to Purchaser upon expiration of the Due Diligence Period, defined below, except upon a breach by the Seller under the P&S.

Due Diligence: All due diligence documents referenced in Exhibit A will be de-livered with the P&S to Purchaser. Purchaser shall have twenty-one (21) business days from the receipt of Due Diligence documents to conduct its due diligence (the "Due Diligence Period"). During the Due Diligence Period, Purchaser may perform such physical inspections, surveys and studies, and review such other matter related to the Property as it deems appropriate. Purchaser shall not unreasonably interfere with ordinary operations of the Property. Purchaser shall give Seller reasonable advance notice prior to entry by Purchaser or its representatives or independent

Exhibit C-6   **479**

contractors on the Property. Purchaser is buying the Property in "as is physical condition," without Seller representations or warranties.

Closing Date: It is the intent of the parties to close no later than thirty (30) business days after the expiration of the Due Diligence Period. Purchaser may extend the closing by an additional thirty (30) business days upon the deposit of an additional non-refundable amount of $500,000.

Environmental: Purchaser may request a Phase I Environmental study at its expense, and if warranted, and with Seller's written approval, a Phase II study as well. Seller knows of no environmental conditions affecting the Property that would necessitate a Phase II study.

Seller shall be responsible for:

— All transferred taxes;
— All cost incurred to repay any monetary liens created by Seller; and
— All other customary Seller's expenses due or incurred in connection with the transaction

Purchaser shall be responsible for:

— Costs associated with Phase I and/or Phase II environmental studies;
— Title Insurance (Basic and extended coverage);
— All survey expenses;
— All other due diligence costs and financing;
— All other customary Buyer's expenses due or incurred in connection with the transaction.

Seller and Purchaser each shall be responsible for the fees and expenses of their legal counsel incurred in connection with the transaction.

Prorations: The P&S shall provide that real estate taxes, property insurance, rents, income and expense items relating to the property, and other typical closing costs shall be pro-rated to the day of closing. Said amounts shall be due and payable by the respective parties at or prior to closing.

Brokerage: Seller and Purchaser hereby acknowledge that no other broker or agent have been involved in this transaction other than CB Richard Ellis (as "Broker"). Purchaser and Seller agree that Seller will pay a commission to Broker with respect to the proposed transaction.

Leases: After expiration of the Due Diligence Period, Seller will not enter into, modify or terminate any leases without first obtaining the Purchaser's written approval.

The terms and provisions of this Letter of Intent shall remain confidential and shall not be disclosed to any third party other than select lenders, accountants and other experts working on behalf of the sale or purchase.

We look forward to the successful completion of this transaction.

Very truly yours,

By ————————

ACCEPTED BY:

————————————

Exhibit C-6   ***481***

EXHIBIT A
DUE DILIGENCE DOCUMENTS TO BE DELIVERED BY SELLER

Tenant Information:

1. Rent Roll as of the execution date of the Letter of Intent.
2. All leases, subleases, amendments, lease modifications, tenant improvement construction agreements, Commencement letter and other letter agreements related thereto.
3. Any letters of intent (executed or otherwise) with prospective tenants.

Operating Information:

1. Historical financial statements for the Property, including balance sheets and income statements, for the prior three (3) years.
2. Year-to-date financial statements for the Property.
3. Listing of capital expenditures for the Property for the prior three (3) years.
4. Accounts receivable report as of the date of this Agreement.
5. Copies of all service, maintenance, leasing, management or other contracts and all other agreements, warranties and guaranties relating to the operating, use, management or maintenance of the Property, including any amendments and/or letter agreements pertaining to each.
6. Copies of real estate tax bills (including special assessments) for the Property for the period for the prior three (3) years.
7. Copies of the utility bills for the last thirty-six (36) months.
8. Copies of insurance bills and certificate.

Building Information:

1. Final "as built" shelf, electrical, mechanical and structural plans and specifications for the Property, including for all tenant improvements, and, to the extent that any portion of the Property is under construction as of the Closing Date, any and all plans, specifications and construction contracts or agreements related thereto shall be available at the on-site management office.
2. Architect's calculations of the gross leaseable area of the improvements.
3. List of personal property to be transferred to Purchaser.

Miscellaneous:

1. Most recent boundary and title survey of the Property, including a legal description and copies of any title exceptions noted thereon.
2. Copies of Seller's most current title policy, including copies of all exceptions listed thereon.
3. Copies of any easements/parking agreements with adjoining property owners.
4. Copies of Certificates of Occupancy and other documents indicating compliance with all applicable governmental requirements, if available.

EXHIBIT C-7

September 19, 2005

Mr. Daniel V. Allen
CB Richard Ellis
225 Waters Street, Suite 110
Jacksonville, Florida 32202

Re: The Gables

Dear Daniel,

Please be advised that [Buyer] a Michigan limited liability company ("**Buyer**") or assignee proposes to acquire The Gables ("**Property**") referred to above on the terms set forth in this letter (the "**Letter of Intent**").

Property:	The Property contains 168 apartments with 207,482 square feet of rentable area, 166 garage parking spaces and 194 surface parking spaces located on approximately 21.19 acres of land at 4700 SW Archer Road, Gainesville, Florida, known as The Gables. The Property includes all land, parking, easement rights, and all amenities and fixtures. The property includes all personal property at the Property except property that belongs to apartment tenants.
Price:	Buyer will pay Twenty One Million Dollars ($21,000,000) in immediately available funds at closing.
Deposit:	When the Definitive Agreement is signed, Buyer will deposit Two Hundred Thousand Dollars ($200,000) with Chicago Title Company as escrow agent. This aggregate deposit (including interest, the "**Deposit**") will be in the form of cash. The Deposit will be increased to Four Hundred Thousand Dollars ($400,000) at the end of the Study Period.
Definitive Agreement:	This Letter of Intent is meant to express the terms on which the parties propose to enter into a binding contract (the "**Definitive Agreement**"). The Seller and Buyer will use their best efforts to negotiate and complete the Definitive Agreement within ten (10) days from acceptance of the Letter of Intent by Seller. This Letter of Intent is terminable at will by either party and is not binding except that for ten (10) days after the date hereof, Owner will not sell, offer for sale or negotiate with respect to the sale of the Property, with parties other than Buyer unless Owner has first terminated this Letter of Intent.

Exhibit C-7   *483*

Disclosure: Owner will be required to disclose, in the Definitive Agreement, Owner's knowledge about structural or mechanical defects and petroleum products, underground storage tanks, asbestos or hazardous materials at or affecting the Property. Owner will also disclose any known issues related to zoning and code compliance, historic designation, condemnation and pending or threatened legal proceedings. Claims of misrepresentation must be raised within one year after Closing.

Operation of Property: Owner will maintain, repair, replace, operate and lease the Property through the Study Period in the same manner and condition as the Property has been maintained, operated and leased heretofore, subject to such ordinary wear and tear as may, in the ordinary course of business, remain uncorrected at Closing. At the end of the Study Period the Owner will cooperate with Buyer in allowing the Buyer a right of first refusal to lease any apartment units that come available for lease during the Study Period. All fixtures and appliances and all utilities required for the normal operation of all apartments must be present and in good working condition at Closing.

Closing: Closing will be held within thirty (30) days after the end of the study period. Owner will convey the Property by special warranty deed, subject only to exceptions accepted by Buyer during the Study Period. Real estate taxes will be prorated on an accrual basis. Utility charges and rents will be adjusted through the day prior to the date of Closing and will then be Buyer's. Other closing costs will be apportioned between Buyer and Owner as per custom in Florida.

Study Period: Promptly after signing the Definitive Agreement, Owner will provide Buyer with information listed in Schedule A. Starting when the Definitive Agreement is fully executed, Buyer will have thirty (30) business days (the "**Study Period**") in which to study the Property. Buyer may terminate the Definitive Agreement during the Study Period for any reason in Buyer's absolute discretion.

Default: Owner will receive the Deposit as liquated damages if Buyer fails to close as required by the Definitive Agreement. If Owner defaults under the Definitive Agreement, Buyer may pursue all legal and equitable remedies available, including specific performance, provided that Buyer may not recover consequential damages for Owner's failure to close unless specific performance is not available. Except for specific performance and liquidated damages, all remedies will be reciprocal.

Brokers: Each party represents that it has not employed any broker in con-
                      nection with this transaction, except that Owner has engaged CB
                      Richard Ellis, whose compensation will be the Owner's respon-
                      sibility. Each party will indemnify the other for the indemnifying
                      party's breach of this representation.

If these terms are satisfactory, please sign and date a copy of this letter and return
it to us within five (5) business days after the date hereof.

Sincerely,

Multifamily Acquisition Manager

READ AND ACCEPTED BY OWNER:

By:

Name:

Title:

Exhibit C-7   **485**

EXHIBIT "A"

BASIC INFORMATION REQUIREMENTS

To the extent that they are available, copies of the following documents with respect to the Property will be delivered by Owner to Buyer at Owner's expense.

Monthly Operating Statements for 2004 and 2005

Current Property Survey

As-Built Plans and Specifications, including Layouts

All Service Contracts, Warranties and Guarantees

List of Personal Property

Current Title Insurance Policy with documents evidencing each exception.

Insurance Claim Information for 2004–2005

Real Estate Tax Bills 2004–2005

Permits and Licenses

All Environmental and Engineering Reports and Studies

Current Rent Roll

List of Employees at Property and their compensation

EXHIBIT C-8

September 29, 2005

Mr. Fred Marks
CB Richard Ellis
225 Water Street, Suite 110
Jacksonville, Florida 32202

VIA FAX:

Re: The Gables

Dear Fred,

[Buyer] is prepared to enter into a Purchase and Sale Agreement (the "Agreement") for the purchase of The Gables under the following terms and conditions:

Purchaser:

Property:	The Gables, a 168-unit multifamily community located in Gainesville, Florida.
Purchase Price:	$19,000,000; cash due at closing.
Escrow Deposit:	Purchaser shall deposit $100,000 into an Interest Bearing Escrow Account. All funds in the Escrow Account will be applied to the Purchase Price at Closing.
Inspection Period:	Purchaser shall have thirty (30) days to perform necessary due diligence with respect to the physical qualities and economic prospects of the Property ("Inspection Period"). Purchaser shall have the right to terminate the Agreement in its sole discretion if, within the Inspection Period, its review is not satisfactory. The Escrow Deposit and interest earned thereon will he returned to Purchaser if Agreement is terminated prior to the expiration of the Inspection Period. **All funds in the Escrow Account shall be considered "at risk" and non-refundable upon expiration of the Inspection Period.**
Closing:	The Closing shall take place thirty (30) days following the expiration of the Inspection Period.

Exhibit C-8   **487**

Expenses: Seller shall be responsible for its normal closing expenses, including any brokerage fees, the owner's title insurance premium, deed stamps, and any conveyance or transfer taxes.

Property Records: Within five (5) days from the execution of the Agreement, Seller shall provide copies of all available data pertaining to the Property that is in possession of the Seller, including rent rolls, financial reports, service contracts, environmental reports, surveys, building plans, etc.

If the terms of this Letter of Intent are acceptable, please arrange for the execution of this letter as provided for below. Upon execution, Purchaser will immediately begin drafting a Purchase and Sale Agreement to be submitted to the Seller. This letter is an expression of interest only and shall be non-binding on either party until both parties execute a definitive, mutually acceptable Purchase and Sale Agreement.

Sincerely,

Vice President

Agreed and accepted this _____ **day of** _____ **2005.**

SELLER:

_____

_____

EXHIBIT C-9

September 13, 2005

Via E-mail:

Daniel V. Allen
CBRE

RE: The Gables
  Gainsville, Florida

Dear Dan:

[Buyer] and/or its assigns ("Purchaser") has a strong interest in purchasing the above referenced Property. Our group is privately capitalized and has the ability to close on this transaction. We have visited the property and are very familiar with the market area. The terms under which we would consider moving forward with a purchase of the Property are as follows:

1. PURCHASE   PRICE: Eighteen Million Four Hundred Eighty Thousand Dollars ($18,480,000) all cash.

2. EARNEST MONEY DEPOSIT: Upon the execution of a mutually acceptable purchase agreement, Buyer shall deposit $500,000.00 in cash with Leopold, Korn & Leopold, PA, as escrow agent, in the following manner: $100,000.00 will be deposited upon contract execution and at the end of the Due Diligence Period an additional $400,000.00 will be deposited. The $500,000.00 (Full Deposit) will be applied to the purchase price at closing.

3. DUE DILIGENCE PERIOD: Buyer shall complete its Due Diligence in Thirty (30) days from execution of a contract and the delivery to the Buyer of all due diligence materials requested as part of the Contract. During this period, Buyer may terminate the contract at its sole discretion and receive a refund of the carnest money deposit. It is agreed that the $500,000 will remain in escrow until closing and become non-refundable only after the expiration of the Due Diligence period.

4. CLOSING: Closing shall take place 60 Days after the Expiration of the Due Diligence Period.

5. CLOSING COSTS: Transfer taxes and documentary stamps shall be paid by the Seller. Title insurance premiums, costs to record the deed and costs relating to the survey will be paid by the Buyer.

6. PRO-RATIONS: All income and expenses and other customarily prorated items shall be prorated as of the date of closing.

Exhibit C-9 **489**

7. ASSIGNMENT: The contract may only be assigned to an entity affiliated with the Buyer.

8. BROKERS: It is understood that Seller shall be responsible to pay at closing, for any and all Commissions that may be due and payable.

9. PURCHASE AND SALE AGREEMENT: A Purchase & Sale Agreement shall be prepared by the Purchaser and delivered to the Seller, within Five (5) business days after mutual execution of this Letter of Intent. Buyer and Seller agree to negotiate, in good faith, and execute a mutually acceptable Purchase and Sale Agreement within Fifteen (15) business days after execution of this Letter of Intent.

Commencing on the execution date of this Letter of Intent, Seller shall not offer the Property for sale to, or negotiate with, anyone other than the Purchaser until such time that the due diligence and subsequent Purchase and Sale Agreement preparation period has been completed.

This letter is not intended as, and does not constitute a binding agreement by any party, nor an agreement by any party to enter into a binding agreement, but is merely intended to specify some of the proposed terms and conditions of the contemplated transaction. Neither party may claim any legal rights against the other by reason of the signing of this letter of intent or by taking any action in reliance thereon.

If a signed copy of this letter is not so returned within ten days from today, the letter shall expire and become void.

Sincerely,   Agreed to and accepted by Seller:

By: _____

Its: _____

Date: _____

Converted condos offer additional space, storage areas

By MICHELLE HARRIS
Special to the Sun

TRACY WILCOX/The Gainesville Sun

Above: A bedroom in the Preakness model, a 3-bedroom townhome at The Gables on Archer Road. At left: An external view of the Gables Townhome Condominiums. Prices range from $159,900 to $261,900 for 1- to 3-bedroom townhomes.

EXHIBIT C-10

Scott Denardo had his eye out for a college town when he decided to trade private practice in Pinehurst, N.C., for teaching and research.

"I've always wanted to settle in a university town in Florida," said Denardo, 48.

So when the opportunity arose, the cardiologist and his wife, Shirley, chose Gainesville. The people are friendly and the weather is like the "California of the South," said the San Francisco native.

Scott said The Gables Townhome Condominiums is ideally situated — near his offices at Shands HealthCare Center but not in the center of town. He also likes the easy access for getting out of the city and onto the open road.

"We love bicycle riding," he said, "my wife and I are hoping to cycle to Cedar Key."

Built as apartments in 1998, The Gables is now a 168-unit condominium conversion. On Archer Road just west of Interstate 75, the gated community is a short distance from shopping and dining, the University of Florida and the Shands HealthCare Center and the Veterans Administration Center.

Refurbished models include The Derby with 1 bedroom/1 bath, The Belmont with 2 bedrooms/2 baths and The Preakness with 3 bedrooms/3 baths, each with an attached garage. Square footage ranges from 790 to 1,629 and models are priced from $159,900 to $261,900.

Monthly Home Owner Association

fees are $158.18 to $295.57 and include cable TV with premium channels, monitoring for condominium alarm system, evening attendant for front entryway and all maintenance.

The Gables is set amid 21 acres of mature pine and oak trees with fully landscaped greenways between each building. The townhomes feature a brick and vinyl siding exterior with private covered entryway.

The one-story townhomes feature 13-foot vaulted ceilings in the great room and all models are concrete-block construction designed to reduce noise.

Refurbished models include ceramic-tile flooring in the foyer, kitchen and bath, screened porch with ceiling fan, new smooth-top stove, under-cabinet mounted microwave, monitored security system and lighted ceiling fans in the bedrooms and living room. In addition, each model includes generous closet space and an inside laundry room with

PREVIEW on Page 2F

The Gables Townhome Condominiums

AT A GLANCE

■ **WHERE:**
4700 SW Archer Road

■ **MODELS:**
1, 2 and 3 bedrooms with 1, 2 and 3 baths; 790 sq. ft. to 1,629 sq. ft.

■ **PRICES:**
$159,900 to $261,900

■ **SCHOOLS:**
Idylwild or Kimball Wiles Elementary, Kanapaha Middle and Gainesville High.

PREVIEW: Condos offer proximity to the university, activities

Continued from 1F

washer, dryer and additional shelving. Bedroom window seats and built-in book shelves are also standard in the two- and three-bedroom models.

Kitchen and bath upgrades include cabinetry in a choice of five wood grains, granite counter tops in three colors, stainless steel appliances, bathroom fixtures and new bathroom lighting. New kitchen lighting is also available for the 3-bedroom model only. Upgrade packages are priced at $12,000 and can be installed within 30-45 days.

The community clubhouse has been fully refurbished and now features a floor-to-ceiling stone fireplace, 20-foot vaulted ceiling and kitchenette. A billiard table with high-top seating areas has been added and the room is furnished with over-stuffed couches and leather club chairs. The clubhouse will also feature a business center with high-speed Internet access, computer, copy and fax

machines.

The fitness room is available 24 hours and features a full line of cardiovascular equipment including treadmills, elliptical, stair master and universal machines. Free weights, cable TV and full-sized sauna are also available.

The adjacent 3,200-square-foot pool area features a 30-by-50 foot pool with separate hot tub. Additional recreation facilities include lighted basketball and tennis courts.

The Denardo's purchased a 2-bedroom/2-bath model at The Gables, while they await the sale of their North Carolina home, said Denardo. They'll eventually use the condominium as a rental property investment.

As diehard college sports enthusiasts in general, and Gator fans in particular, being in Gainesville these last two weeks has been heaven, said Denardo.

"Watching the Ohio State game — What a win!"

The kitchen in the Preakness model, a 3-bedroom townhome at The Gables on another Road. The 3-bedroom is 1,629 square feet.

TRACY WILCOX/The Gainesville Sun

EXHIBIT C-10 **Continued.**

Reprinted with permission from the Gainesville Sun.

491

Appendix D*
Interest Tables

*Appendix D is taken from *Engineering Cost Analysis* by Courtland A. Collier and William B. Ledbetter. Copyright 1982 by Courtland A. Collier and William B. Ledbetter. Reprinted by permission of Harper & Row, Publishers, Inc.

	$i=0.5\%$			$i=0.5\%$			$i=0.5\%$			
	PRESENT SUM, P			UNIFORM SERIES, A			FUTURE SUM, F			
n	P/F	P/A	P/G	A/F	A/P	A/G	F/P	F/A	F/G	n
1	0.99502	0.9950	0.0000	1.00000	1.00500	0.0000	1.0050	1.0000	0.0000	1
2	0.99007	1.9851	0.9900	0.49875	0.50375	0.4987	1.0100	2.0050	1.0000	2
3	0.98515	2.9702	2.9603	0.33167	0.33667	0.9966	1.0150	3.0150	3.0050	3
4	0.98025	3.9505	5.9011	0.24813	0.25313	1.4937	1.0201	4.0301	6.0200	4
5	0.97537	4.9258	9.8026	0.19801	0.20301	1.9900	1.0252	5.0502	10.050	5
6	0.97052	5.8963	14.655	0.16460	0.16960	2.4854	1.0303	6.0755	15.100	6
7	0.96569	6.8620	20.449	0.14073	0.14573	2.9800	1.0355	7.1058	21.175	7
8	0.96089	7.8229	27.175	0.12283	0.12783	3.4738	1.0407	8.1414	28.281	8
9	0.95610	8.7790	34.824	0.10891	0.11391	3.9667	1.0459	9.1821	36.423	9
10	0.95135	9.7304	43.386	0.09777	0.10277	4.4588	1.0511	10.228	45.605	10
11	0.94661	10.677	52.852	0.08866	0.09366	4.9501	1.0564	11.279	55.833	11
12	0.94191	11.618	63.213	0.08107	0.08607	5.4405	1.0616	12.335	67.112	12
13	0.93722	12.556	74.460	0.07464	0.07964	5.9301	1.0669	13.397	79.448	13
14	0.93256	13.488	86.583	0.06914	0.07414	6.4189	1.0723	14.464	92.845	14
15	0.92792	14.416	99.574	0.06436	0.06936	6.9069	1.0776	15.536	107.31	15
16	0.92330	15.339	113.42	0.06019	0.06519	7.3940	1.0830	16.614	122.84	16
17	0.91871	16.258	128.12	0.05651	0.06151	7.8803	1.0884	17.697	139.46	17
18	0.91414	17.172	143.66	0.05323	0.05823	8.3657	1.0939	18.785	157.15	18
19	0.90959	18.082	160.03	0.05030	0.05530	8.8504	1.0994	19.879	175.94	19
20	0.90506	18.987	177.23	0.04767	0.05267	9.3341	1.1049	20.979	195.82	20
21	0.90056	19.888	195.24	0.04528	0.05028	9.8171	1.1104	22.084	216.80	21
22	0.89608	20.784	214.06	0.04311	0.04811	10.299	1.1159	23.194	238.88	22
23	0.89162	21.675	233.67	0.04113	0.04613	10.780	1.1215	24.310	262.09	23
24	0.88719	22.562	254.08	0.03932	0.04432	11.261	1.1271	25.432	286.39	24
25	0.88277	23.445	275.26	0.03765	0.04265	11.740	1.1328	26.559	311.82	25
26	0.87838	24.324	297.22	0.03611	0.04111	12.219	1.1384	27.691	338.38	26
27	0.87401	25.198	319.95	0.03469	0.03969	12.697	1.1441	28.830	366.07	27
28	0.86966	26.067	343.43	0.03336	0.03836	13.174	1.1498	29.974	394.90	28
29	0.86533	26.933	367.66	0.03213	0.03713	13.651	1.1556	31.124	424.87	29
30	0.86103	27.794	392.63	0.03098	0.03598	14.126	1.1614	32.280	456.00	30
32	0.85248	29.503	444.76	0.02889	0.03389	15.075	1.1730	34.608	521.72	32
34	0.84402	31.195	499.75	0.02706	0.03206	16.020	1.1848	36.960	592.11	34
36	0.83564	32.871	557.56	0.02542	0.03042	16.962	1.1966	39.336	667.22	36
48	0.78710	42.580	959.91	0.01849	0.02349	22.543	1.2704	54.097	1219.5	48
60	0.74137	51.725	1448.6	0.01433	0.01933	28.006	1.3488	69.770	1954.0	60
120	0.54963	90.073	4823.5	0.00610	0.01110	53.550	1.8194	163.87	8775.8	120
180	0.40748	118.50	9031.3	0.00344	0.00844	76.211	2.4540	290.81	22163.	180
240	0.30210	139.58	13415.	0.00216	0.00716	96.113	3.3102	462.04	44408.	240
300	0.22397	155.20	17603.	0.00144	0.00644	113.41	4.4649	692.99	78598.	300
360	0.16604	166.79	21403.	0.00100	0.00600	128.32	6.0225	1004.5	128903.	360
INF	0.00000	200.00	43000.	0.0000	0.00500	200.00	INF	INF	INF	INF

i = 0.75%

	PRESENT SUM, P			UNIFORM SERIES, A			FUTURE SUM, F			
n	P/F	P/A	P/G	A/F	A/P	A/G	F/P	F/A	F/G	n
1	0.99256	0.9925	0.0000	1.00000	1.00750	0.0000	1.0075	1.0000	0.0000	1
2	0.98517	1.9777	0.9851	0.49813	0.50563	0.4981	1.0150	2.0075	1.0000	2
3	0.97783	2.9555	2.9408	0.33085	0.33835	0.9950	1.0226	3.0225	3.0075	3
4	0.97055	3.9261	5.8525	0.24721	0.25471	1.4906	1.0303	4.0452	6.0300	4
5	0.96333	4.8894	9.7058	0.19702	0.20452	1.9850	1.0380	5.0755	10.075	5
6	0.95616	5.8456	14.486	0.16357	0.17107	2.4782	1.0458	6.1136	15.150	6
7	0.94904	6.7946	20.180	0.13967	0.14717	2.9701	1.0537	7.1594	21.264	7
8	0.94198	7.7366	26.774	0.12176	0.12926	3.4607	1.0616	8.2131	28.424	8
9	0.93496	8.6715	34.254	0.10782	0.11532	3.9501	1.0695	9.2747	36.637	9
10	0.92800	9.5995	42.606	0.09657	0.10417	4.4383	1.0775	10.344	45.911	10
11	0.92109	10.520	51.817	0.08755	0.09505	4.9252	1.0856	11.421	56.256	11
12	0.91424	11.434	61.874	0.07995	0.08745	5.4109	1.0938	12.507	67.678	12
13	0.90743	12.342	72.763	0.07352	0.08102	5.8954	1.1020	13.601	80.185	13
14	0.90068	13.243	84.472	0.06801	0.07551	6.3786	1.1102	14.703	93.787	14
15	0.89397	14.137	96.987	0.06324	0.07074	6.8605	1.1186	15.813	108.49	15
16	0.88732	15.024	110.29	0.05906	0.06656	7.3412	1.1269	16.932	124.30	16
17	0.88071	15.905	124.38	0.05537	0.06287	7.8207	1.1354	18.059	141.23	17
18	0.87416	16.779	139.24	0.05210	0.05960	8.2989	1.1439	19.194	159.29	18
19	0.86765	17.646	154.86	0.04917	0.05667	8.7759	1.1525	20.338	178.49	19
20	0.86119	18.508	171.23	0.04653	0.05403	9.2516	1.1611	21.491	198.82	20
21	0.85478	19.362	188.32	0.04415	0.05165	9.7261	1.1698	22.652	220.32	21
22	0.84842	20.211	206.14	0.04198	0.04948	10.199	1.1786	23.822	242.97	22
23	0.84210	21.053	224.66	0.04000	0.04750	10.671	1.1875	25.001	266.79	23
24	0.83583	21.889	243.89	0.03818	0.04568	11.142	1.1964	26.188	291.79	24
25	0.82961	22.718	263.80	0.03652	0.04402	11.611	1.2053	27.384	317.98	25
26	0.82343	23.542	284.38	0.03498	0.04248	12.080	1.2144	28.590	345.36	26
27	0.81730	24.359	305.63	0.03355	0.04105	12.547	1.2235	29.804	373.96	27
28	0.81122	25.170	327.54	0.03223	0.03973	13.012	1.2327	31.028	403.76	28
29	0.80518	25.975	350.08	0.03100	0.03850	13.477	1.2419	32.260	434.79	29
30	0.79919	26.775	373.26	0.02985	0.03735	13.940	1.2512	33.502	467.05	30
32	0.78733	28.355	421.46	0.02777	0.03527	14.863	1.2701	36.014	535.31	32
34	0.77565	29.912	472.07	0.02593	0.03343	15.781	1.2892	38.564	608.61	34
36	0.76415	31.446	524.99	0.02430	0.03180	16.694	1.3086	41.152	687.02	36
48	0.69861	40.184	886.84	0.01739	0.02489	22.069	1.4314	57.520	1269.4	48
60	0.63870	48.173	1313.5	0.01326	0.02076	27.266	1.5656	75.424	2056.5	60
120	0.40794	78.941	3998.5	0.00517	0.01267	50.652	2.4513	193.51	9801.9	120
180	0.26055	98.593	6892.6	0.00264	0.01014	69.909	3.8380	378.40	26454.	180
240	0.16641	111.14	9494.1	0.00150	0.00900	85.421	6.0091	667.88	57051.	240
300	0.10629	119.16	11636.	0.00089	0.00839	97.654	9.4084	1121.6	109483.	300
360	0.06789	124.28	13312.	0.00055	0.00805	107.11	14.730	1830.7	196099.	360
INF	0.00000	133.33	17777.	0.0000	0.00750	133.33	INF	INF	INF	INF

i = 1%

n	P/F	P/A	P/G	A/F	A/P	A/G	F/P	F/A	F/G	n
		PRESENT SUM, P			UNIFORM SERIES, A			FUTURE SUM, F		
1	0.99010	0.9901	0.0000	1.00000	1.01000	0.0000	1.0100	1.0000	0.0000	1
2	0.98030	1.9704	0.9803	0.49751	0.50751	0.4975	1.0201	2.0100	1.0000	2
3	0.97059	2.9409	2.9215	0.33002	0.34002	0.9933	1.0303	3.0301	3.0100	3
4	0.96098	3.9020	5.8044	0.24628	0.25628	1.4875	1.0406	4.0604	6.0401	4
5	0.95147	4.8534	9.6102	0.19604	0.20604	1.9801	1.0510	5.1010	10.100	5
6	0.94205	5.7954	14.320	0.16255	0.17255	2.4709	1.0615	6.1520	15.201	6
7	0.93272	6.7281	19.916	0.13863	0.14863	2.9602	1.0721	7.2135	21.353	7
8	0.92348	7.6516	25.381	0.12069	0.13069	3.4477	1.0828	8.2856	28.567	8
9	0.91434	8.5660	33.695	0.10674	0.11674	3.9336	1.0936	9.3685	36.852	9
10	0.90529	9.4713	41.843	0.09558	0.10558	4.4179	1.1046	10.462	46.221	10
11	0.89632	10.367	50.806	0.08645	0.09645	4.9005	1.1156	11.566	56.683	11
12	0.88745	11.255	60.568	0.07885	0.08885	5.3814	1.1268	12.682	68.250	12
13	0.87866	12.133	71.112	0.07241	0.08241	5.8607	1.1380	13.809	80.932	13
14	0.86996	13.003	82.422	0.06690	0.07690	6.3383	1.1494	14.947	94.742	14
15	0.86135	13.865	94.481	0.06212	0.07212	6.8143	1.1609	16.096	109.69	15
16	0.85282	14.717	107.27	0.05794	0.06794	7.2886	1.1725	17.257	125.78	16
17	0.84438	15.562	120.78	0.05426	0.06426	7.7613	1.1843	18.430	143.04	17
18	0.83602	16.398	134.99	0.05098	0.06098	8.2323	1.1961	19.614	161.47	18
19	0.82774	17.226	149.89	0.04805	0.05805	8.7016	1.2081	20.810	181.09	19
20	0.81954	18.045	165.46	0.04542	0.05542	9.1693	1.2201	22.019	201.90	20
21	0.81143	18.857	181.69	0.04303	0.05303	9.6354	1.2323	23.239	223.91	21
22	0.80340	19.660	198.56	0.04086	0.05086	10.099	1.2447	24.471	247.15	22
23	0.79544	20.455	216.06	0.03889	0.04889	10.562	1.2571	25.716	271.63	23
24	0.78757	21.243	234.18	0.03707	0.04707	11.023	1.2697	26.973	297.34	24
25	0.77977	22.023	252.89	0.03541	0.04541	11.483	1.2824	28.243	324.32	25
26	0.77205	22.795	272.19	0.03387	0.04387	11.940	1.2952	29.525	352.56	26
27	0.76440	23.559	292.07	0.03245	0.04245	12.397	1.3082	30.820	382.08	27
28	0.75684	24.316	312.50	0.03112	0.04112	12.851	1.3212	32.129	412.91	28
29	0.74934	25.065	333.48	0.02990	0.03990	13.304	1.3345	33.450	445.03	29
30	0.74192	25.807	355.03	0.02875	0.03875	13.755	1.3478	34.784	478.48	30
32	0.72730	27.269	399.58	0.02667	0.03667	14.653	1.3749	37.494	549.40	32
34	0.71297	28.702	446.15	0.02484	0.03484	15.544	1.4025	40.257	625.77	34
36	0.69892	30.107	494.62	0.02321	0.03321	16.428	1.4307	43.076	707.68	36
48	0.62026	37.974	820.14	0.01633	0.02633	21.597	1.6122	61.222	1322.2	48
60	0.55045	44.955	1192.8	0.01224	0.02224	26.533	1.8167	81.669	2166.9	60
120	0.30299	69.700	3334.1	0.00435	0.01435	47.834	3.3003	230.03	11003.	120
180	0.16678	83.321	5330.0	0.00201	0.01201	63.969	5.9958	499.58	31958.	180
240	0.09181	90.819	6878.6	0.00101	0.01101	75.739	10.892	989.25	74925.	240
300	0.05053	94.946	7978.6	0.00053	0.01053	84.032	19.788	1878.8	157885.	300
360	0.02782	97.218	8720.4	0.00000	0.01000	89.699	35.949	3494.9	313496.	360
INF	0.00000	100.00	10000.	0.0000	0.01000	100.00	INF	INF	INF	INF

Interest factor tables — $i = 1.5\%$

n	P/F	P/A	P/G	A/F	A/P	A/G	F/P	F/A	F/G
1	0.98522	0.9852	0.0000	1.00000	1.01500	0.0000	1.0150	1.0000	0.0000
2	0.97066	1.9558	0.9706	0.49628	0.51128	0.4962	1.0302	2.0150	1.0000
3	0.95632	2.9122	2.8833	0.32838	0.34338	0.9900	1.0456	3.0452	3.0150
4	0.94218	3.8543	5.7098	0.24444	0.25944	1.4813	1.0613	4.0909	6.0602
5	0.92826	4.7826	9.4228	0.19409	0.20909	1.9702	1.0772	5.1522	10.151
6	0.91454	5.6971	13.995	0.16053	0.17553	2.4565	1.0934	6.2295	15.303
7	0.90103	6.5982	19.401	0.13656	0.15156	2.9404	1.1098	7.3229	21.532
8	0.88771	7.4859	25.615	0.11858	0.13358	3.4218	1.1264	8.4328	28.855
9	0.87459	8.3605	32.612	0.10461	0.11961	3.9007	1.1433	9.5593	37.288
10	0.86167	9.2221	40.367	0.09343	0.10843	4.3772	1.1605	10.702	46.848
11	0.84893	10.071	48.856	0.08429	0.09929	4.8511	1.1779	11.863	57.550
12	0.83639	10.907	58.057	0.07668	0.09168	5.3226	1.1956	13.041	69.414
13	0.82403	11.731	67.945	0.07024	0.08524	5.7916	1.2135	14.236	82.455
14	0.81185	12.543	78.499	0.06472	0.07972	6.2582	1.2317	15.450	96.592
15	0.79985	13.343	89.697	0.05994	0.07494	6.7223	1.2502	16.682	112.14
16	0.78803	14.131	101.51	0.05577	0.07077	7.1839	1.2689	17.932	128.82
17	0.77639	14.907	113.94	0.05208	0.06708	7.6430	1.2880	19.201	146.75
18	0.76491	15.672	126.96	0.04881	0.06381	8.0997	1.3073	20.489	165.95
19	0.75361	16.426	140.50	0.04588	0.06088	8.5539	1.3269	21.796	186.44
20	0.74247	17.168	154.61	0.04325	0.05825	9.0056	1.3468	23.123	208.24
21	0.73150	17.900	169.24	0.04087	0.05587	9.4549	1.3670	24.470	231.36
22	0.72069	18.620	184.38	0.03870	0.05370	9.9018	1.3875	25.837	255.83
23	0.71004	19.330	200.00	0.03673	0.05173	10.346	1.4083	27.225	281.67
24	0.69954	20.030	216.09	0.03492	0.04992	10.788	1.4295	28.633	308.90
25	0.68921	20.719	232.63	0.03326	0.04826	11.227	1.4509	30.063	337.53
26	0.67902	21.398	249.60	0.03173	0.04673	11.664	1.4727	31.514	367.59
27	0.66899	22.067	267.00	0.03032	0.04532	12.099	1.4948	32.986	399.11
28	0.65910	22.726	284.79	0.02900	0.04400	12.531	1.5172	34.481	432.09
29	0.64936	23.376	302.97	0.02778	0.04278	12.961	1.5399	35.998	466.58
30	0.63976	24.015	321.53	0.02664	0.04164	13.388	1.5630	37.538	502.57
32	0.62099	25.267	359.69	0.02458	0.03958	14.235	1.6103	40.688	579.21
34	0.60277	26.481	399.16	0.02276	0.03776	15.073	1.6590	43.933	662.20
36	0.58509	27.660	439.83	0.02115	0.03615	15.900	1.7091	47.276	751.73
48	0.48936	34.042	703.54	0.01437	0.02937	20.666	2.0434	69.565	1437.6
60	0.40930	39.380	988.16	0.01039	0.02539	25.093	2.4432	96.214	2414.3
120	0.16752	55.498	2359.7	0.00302	0.01802	42.518	5.9693	331.28	14085.
180	0.06857	62.095	3316.9	0.00110	0.01610	53.352	14.584	905.62	48375.
240	0.02806	64.795	3870.6	0.00043	0.01543	59.737	35.632	2308.8	137924.
300	0.01149	65.900	4310.7	0.00017	0.01517	63.180	87.058	5737.2	362484.
360	0.00470	66.353	4310.7	0.00007	0.01507	64.966	212.70	14113.	916906.
INF	0.00000	66.666	4444.4	0.0000	0.01500	66.666	INF	INF	INF

i = 2%

n	P/F	P/A	P/G	A/F	A/P	A/G	F/P	F/A	F/G	n
	PRESENT SUM, P			UNIFORM SERIES, A			FUTURE SUM, F			
1	0.98039	0.9803	0.0000	1.00000	1.02000	0.0000	1.0200	1.0000	0.0000	1
2	0.96117	1.9415	0.9611	0.49505	0.51505	0.4950	1.0404	2.0200	1.0000	2
3	0.94232	2.8838	2.8458	0.32675	0.34675	0.9868	1.0612	3.0604	3.0200	3
4	0.92385	3.6077	5.6173	0.24262	0.26262	1.4752	1.0824	4.1216	6.0804	4
5	0.90573	4.7134	9.2402	0.19216	0.21216	1.9604	1.1040	5.2040	10.202	5
6	0.88797	5.6014	13.680	0.15853	0.17853	2.4422	1.1261	6.3081	15.406	6
7	0.87056	6.4719	18.903	0.13451	0.15451	2.9208	1.1486	7.4342	21.714	7
8	0.85676	7.3254	24.877	0.11651	0.13651	3.3960	1.1716	8.5829	29.148	8
9	0.83676	8.1622	31.572	0.10252	0.12252	3.8680	1.1950	9.7546	37.731	9
10	0.82035	8.9825	38.955	0.09133	0.11133	4.3367	1.2189	10.949	47.486	10
11	0.80426	9.7868	46.997	0.08218	0.10218	4.8021	1.2433	12.168	58.435	11
12	0.78849	10.575	55.671	0.07456	0.09456	5.2642	1.2682	13.412	70.604	12
13	0.77303	11.348	64.947	0.06812	0.08812	5.7230	1.2936	14.680	84.016	13
14	0.75788	12.106	74.799	0.06260	0.08260	6.1786	1.3194	15.973	98.696	14
15	0.74301	12.849	85.202	0.05783	0.07783	6.6309	1.3458	17.293	114.67	15
16	0.72845	13.577	96.128	0.05365	0.07365	7.0799	1.3727	18.639	131.96	16
17	0.71416	14.291	107.55	0.04997	0.06997	7.5256	1.4002	20.012	150.60	17
18	0.70016	14.992	119.45	0.04670	0.06670	7.9681	1.4282	21.412	170.61	18
19	0.68643	15.678	131.81	0.04378	0.06378	8.4073	1.4568	22.840	192.02	19
20	0.67297	16.351	144.60	0.04116	0.06116	8.8432	1.4859	24.297	214.86	20
21	0.65978	17.011	157.79	0.03878	0.05878	9.2759	1.5156	25.783	239.16	21
22	0.64684	17.658	171.37	0.03663	0.05663	9.7054	1.5459	27.299	264.94	22
23	0.63416	18.292	185.33	0.03467	0.05467	10.131	1.5769	28.845	292.24	23
24	0.62172	18.913	199.63	0.03287	0.05287	10.554	1.6084	30.421	321.09	24
25	0.60953	19.523	214.25	0.03122	0.05122	10.974	1.6406	32.030	351.51	25
26	0.59758	20.121	229.19	0.02970	0.04970	11.391	1.6734	33.670	383.54	26
27	0.58586	20.706	244.43	0.02829	0.04829	11.804	1.7068	35.344	417.21	27
28	0.57437	21.281	259.93	0.02699	0.04699	12.214	1.7410	37.051	452.56	28
29	0.56311	21.844	275.70	0.02578	0.04578	12.621	1.7758	38.792	489.61	29
30	0.55207	22.396	291.71	0.02465	0.04465	13.025	1.8113	40.568	528.40	30
32	0.53063	23.468	324.40	0.02261	0.04261	13.823	1.8845	44.227	611.35	32
34	0.51003	24.498	357.88	0.02082	0.04082	14.608	1.9606	48.033	701.69	34
36	0.49022	25.488	392.04	0.01923	0.03923	15.380	2.0398	51.994	799.71	36
48	0.38654	30.673	605.96	0.01260	0.03260	19.755	2.5870	79.353	1567.6	48
60	0.30478	34.760	823.69	0.00877	0.02877	23.696	3.2810	114.05	2702.5	60
120	0.09289	45.355	1710.4	0.00205	0.02205	37.711	10.765	488.25	18412.	120
180	0.02831	48.584	2177.8	0.00058	0.02058	44.755	35.320	1716.0	76802.	180
240	0.00863	49.568	2374.8	0.00017	0.02017	47.911	115.88	5744.4	275322.	240
300	0.00263	49.868	2483.9	0.00005	0.02005	49.208	380.23	18961.	933086.	300
360	0.00080	49.959	2483.5	0.00002	0.02002	49.711	1247.5	62328.	>10*6	360
INF	0.00000	50.000	2500.0	0.0000	0.02000	50.000	INF	INF	INF	INF

		i = 2.5%			i = 2.5%			i = 2.5%		
		PRESENT SUM, P			UNIFORM SERIES, A			FUTURE SUM, F			
n	P/F	P/A	P/G	A/F	A/P	A/G	F/P	F/A	F/G	n
1	0.97561	0.9756	0.0000	1.00000	1.02500	0.0000	1.0250	1.0000	0.0000	1
2	0.95181	1.9274	0.9518	0.49383	0.51883	0.4938	1.0506	2.0250	1.0000	2
3	0.92860	2.8560	2.8090	0.32514	0.35014	0.9835	1.0768	3.0756	3.0250	3
4	0.90595	3.7619	5.5268	0.24082	0.26582	1.4691	1.1038	4.1525	6.1006	4
5	0.88385	4.6458	9.0622	0.19025	0.21525	1.9506	1.1314	5.2563	10.253	5
6	0.86230	5.5081	13.373	0.15655	0.18155	2.4280	1.1596	6.3877	15.509	6
7	0.84127	6.3493	18.421	0.13250	0.15750	2.9012	1.1886	7.5474	21.897	7
8	0.82075	7.1701	24.166	0.11447	0.13947	3.3704	1.2188	8.7361	29.444	8
9	0.80073	7.9708	30.572	0.10046	0.12546	3.8355	1.2488	9.9545	38.180	9
10	0.78120	8.7520	37.603	0.08926	0.11426	4.2964	1.2800	11.203	48.135	10
11	0.76214	9.5142	45.224	0.08011	0.10511	4.7533	1.3120	12.483	59.338	11
12	0.74356	10.257	53.403	0.07249	0.09749	5.2061	1.3448	13.795	71.822	12
13	0.72542	10.983	62.108	0.06605	0.09105	5.6549	1.3785	15.140	85.617	13
14	0.70773	11.690	71.309	0.06054	0.08554	6.0995	1.4129	16.519	100.75	14
15	0.69047	12.381	80.975	0.05577	0.08077	6.5401	1.4483	17.931	117.27	15
16	0.67362	13.055	91.080	0.05150	0.07660	6.9766	1.4845	19.380	135.20	16
17	0.65720	13.712	101.59	0.04793	0.07293	7.4091	1.5216	20.864	154.58	17
18	0.64117	14.353	112.49	0.04467	0.06967	7.8375	1.5596	22.386	175.45	18
19	0.62553	14.978	123.75	0.04176	0.06676	8.2619	1.5986	23.946	197.84	19
20	0.61027	15.589	135.35	0.03915	0.06415	8.6823	1.6386	25.544	221.73	20
21	0.59539	16.184	147.25	0.03679	0.06179	9.0986	1.6795	27.183	247.33	21
22	0.58086	16.765	159.45	0.03465	0.05965	9.5100	1.7215	28.862	274.51	22
23	0.56670	17.332	171.92	0.03270	0.05770	9.9193	1.7646	30.584	303.37	23
24	0.55288	17.885	184.63	0.03091	0.05591	10.323	1.8087	32.349	333.96	24
25	0.53939	18.424	197.58	0.02928	0.05428	10.724	1.8539	34.157	366.31	25
30	0.47674	20.930	265.12	0.02278	0.04778	12.666	2.0975	43.902	556.10	30
35	0.42137	23.145	335.88	0.01821	0.04321	14.512	2.3732	54.928	797.12	35
36	0.41109	23.556	350.27	0.01745	0.04245	14.869	2.4325	57.301	852.05	36
40	0.37243	25.102	408.22	0.01484	0.03984	16.262	2.6850	67.402	1096.1	40
48	0.30567	27.773	524.03	0.01101	0.03601	18.868	3.2714	90.859	1714.3	48
50	0.29094	28.362	552.60	0.01026	0.03526	19.483	3.4371	97.484	1899.3	50
60	0.22728	30.908	690.86	0.00735	0.03235	22.351	4.3997	135.99	3039.6	60
100	0.08465	36.614	1125.9	0.00231	0.02731	30.752	11.813	432.54	13301.	100
120	0.05166	37.933	1269.3	0.00136	0.02636	33.463	19.358	734.32	24573.	120
180	0.01174	39.530	1496.6	0.00030	0.02530	37.861	85.171	3366.8	127475.	180
240	0.00267	39.893	1570.1	0.00007	0.02507	39.357	374.73	14949.	583381.	240
300	0.00061	39.975	1591.7	0.00002	0.02502	39.817	1648.7	65910.	>10**6	300
360	0.00014	39.994	1597.7	0.00000	0.02500	39.950	7254.2	290129	>10**6	360
INF	0.00000	40.000	1600.0	0.0000	0.02500	40.000	INF	INF	INF	INF

	i = 3% PRESENT SUM, P			i = 3% UNIFORM SERIES, A			i = 3% FUTURE SUM, F			
n	P/F	P/A	P/G	A/F	A/P	A/G	F/P	F/A	F/G	n
1	0.97087	0.9708	0.0000	1.00000	1.03000	0.0000	1.0300	1.0000	0.0000	1
2	0.94260	1.9134	0.9426	0.49261	0.52261	0.4926	1.0609	2.0300	1.0000	2
3	0.91514	2.8286	2.7728	0.32353	0.35353	0.9803	1.0927	3.0909	3.0300	3
4	0.88849	3.7171	5.4383	0.23903	0.26903	1.4630	1.1255	4.1836	6.1209	4
5	0.86261	4.5797	8.8887	0.18835	0.21835	1.9409	1.1592	5.3091	10.304	5
6	0.83748	5.4171	13.076	0.15460	0.18460	2.4138	1.1940	6.4684	15.613	6
7	0.81309	6.2302	17.954	0.13051	0.16051	2.8818	1.2298	7.6624	22.082	7
8	0.78941	7.0196	23.480	0.11246	0.14246	3.3449	1.2667	8.8923	29.744	8
9	0.76642	7.7861	29.611	0.09843	0.12843	3.8031	1.3047	10.159	38.636	9
10	0.74409	8.5302	36.308	0.08723	0.11723	4.2565	1.3439	11.463	48.796	10
11	0.72242	9.2526	43.533	0.07808	0.10808	4.7049	1.3842	12.807	60.259	11
12	0.70138	9.9540	51.248	0.07046	0.10046	5.1485	1.4257	14.192	73.067	12
13	0.68095	10.635	59.419	0.06403	0.09403	5.5872	1.4685	15.617	87.259	13
14	0.66112	11.296	68.014	0.05853	0.08853	6.0210	1.5125	17.086	102.87	14
15	0.64186	11.937	77.000	0.05377	0.08377	6.4500	1.5579	18.598	119.96	15
16	0.62317	12.561	86.347	0.04961	0.07961	6.8742	1.6047	20.156	138.56	16
17	0.60502	13.166	96.028	0.04595	0.07595	7.2935	1.6528	21.761	158.72	17
18	0.58739	13.753	106.01	0.04271	0.07271	7.7081	1.7024	23.414	180.48	18
19	0.57029	14.323	116.27	0.03981	0.06981	8.1178	1.7535	25.116	203.89	19
20	0.55368	14.877	126.79	0.03722	0.06722	8.5228	1.8061	26.870	229.01	20
21	0.53755	15.415	137.55	0.03487	0.06487	8.9230	1.8602	28.676	255.88	21
22	0.52189	15.936	148.50	0.03275	0.06275	9.3185	1.9161	30.536	284.55	22
23	0.50669	16.443	159.65	0.03081	0.06081	9.7093	1.9735	32.452	315.09	23
24	0.49193	16.935	170.97	0.02905	0.05905	10.095	2.0327	34.426	347.54	24
25	0.47761	17.413	182.43	0.02743	0.05743	10.476	2.0937	36.459	381.97	25
26	0.46369	17.876	194.02	0.02594	0.05594	10.853	2.1565	38.553	418.43	26
28	0.43708	18.764	217.53	0.02329	0.05329	11.593	2.2879	42.930	497.69	28
30	0.41199	19.600	241.36	0.02102	0.05102	12.314	2.4272	47.575	585.84	30
35	0.35538	21.487	301.50	0.01654	0.04654	14.037	2.8138	60.462	848.73	35
36	0.34503	21.832	313.70	0.01580	0.04580	14.368	2.8982	63.275	909.19	36
40	0.30656	23.114	351.75	0.01326	0.04326	15.650	3.2620	75.401	1180.0	40
45	0.26444	24.518	420.63	0.01079	0.04079	17.155	3.7816	92.719	1599.6	45
48	0.24200	25.266	455.02	0.00958	0.03958	18.006	4.1322	104.40	1880.2	48
50	0.22811	25.729	477.48	0.00887	0.03887	18.557	4.3839	112.79	2093.2	50
60	0.16973	27.675	583.05	0.00613	0.03613	21.067	5.8916	163.05	3435.1	60
70	0.12630	29.123	676.08	0.00434	0.03434	23.214	7.9178	230.59	5353.1	70
80	0.09398	30.200	756.08	0.00311	0.03311	25.035	10.640	321.36	8045.4	80
90	0.06993	31.002	823.63	0.00226	0.03226	26.566	14.300	443.34	11778.	90
100	0.05203	31.598	879.85	0.00165	0.03165	27.844	19.218	607.28	16909.	100
120	0.02881	32.373	963.86	0.00089	0.03089	29.773	34.711	1123.7	33456.	120
180	0.00489	33.170	1076.3	0.00015	0.03015	32.448	204.50	6783.4	220115.	180
240	0.00083	33.305	1103.5	0.00002	0.03002	33.134	1204.8	40128.	>10**6	240
INF	0.00000	33.333	1111.1	0.0000	0.03000	33.333	INF	INF	INF	INF

n	i=4% PRESENT SUM, P			i=4% UNIFORM SERIES, A			i=4% FUTURE SUM, F			n
	P/F	P/A	P/G	A/F	A/P	A/G	F/P	F/A	F/G	
1	0.96154	0.9615	0.0000	1.00000	1.04000	0.0000	1.0400	1.0000	0.0000	1
2	0.92456	1.8860	0.9245	0.49020	0.53020	0.4902	1.0816	2.0400	1.0000	2
3	0.88900	2.7750	2.7025	0.32035	0.36035	0.9738	1.1248	3.1216	3.0400	3
4	0.85480	3.6299	5.2669	0.23549	0.27549	1.4510	1.1698	4.2464	6.1616	4
5	0.82193	4.4518	8.5546	0.18463	0.22463	1.9216	1.2166	5.4163	10.408	5
6	0.79031	5.2421	12.506	0.15076	0.19076	2.3857	1.2653	6.6329	15.824	6
7	0.75992	6.0020	17.065	0.12661	0.16661	2.8433	1.3159	7.8982	22.457	7
8	0.73069	6.7327	22.180	0.10853	0.14853	3.2944	1.3685	9.2142	30.355	8
9	0.70259	7.4353	27.801	0.09449	0.13449	3.7390	1.4233	10.582	39.569	9
10	0.67556	8.1109	33.881	0.08329	0.12329	4.1772	1.4802	12.006	50.152	10
11	0.64958	8.7604	40.377	0.07415	0.11415	4.6090	1.5394	13.486	62.158	11
12	0.62460	9.3850	47.247	0.06655	0.10655	5.0343	1.6010	15.025	75.645	12
13	0.60057	9.9856	54.454	0.06014	0.10014	5.4532	1.6650	16.626	90.670	13
14	0.57748	10.563	61.961	0.05467	0.09467	5.8658	1.7316	18.291	107.29	14
15	0.55526	11.118	69.735	0.04994	0.08994	6.2720	1.8009	20.023	125.59	15
16	0.53391	11.652	77.744	0.04582	0.08582	6.6720	1.8729	21.824	145.61	16
17	0.51337	12.165	85.958	0.04220	0.08220	7.0656	1.9479	23.697	167.43	17
18	0.49363	12.659	94.349	0.03899	0.07899	7.4530	2.0258	25.645	191.13	18
19	0.47464	13.133	102.89	0.03614	0.07614	7.8341	2.1068	27.671	216.78	19
20	0.45639	13.590	111.56	0.03358	0.07358	8.2091	2.1911	29.778	244.45	20
21	0.43883	14.029	120.34	0.03128	0.07128	8.5779	2.2787	31.969	274.23	21
22	0.42196	14.451	129.20	0.02920	0.06920	8.9406	2.3699	34.248	306.19	22
23	0.40573	14.856	138.12	0.02731	0.06731	9.2972	2.4647	36.617	340.44	23
24	0.39012	15.247	147.10	0.02559	0.06559	9.6479	2.5633	39.082	377.06	24
25	0.37512	15.622	156.10	0.02401	0.06401	9.9925	2.6658	41.645	416.14	25
26	0.36069	15.982	165.12	0.02257	0.06257	10.331	2.7724	44.311	457.79	26
28	0.33348	16.663	183.14	0.02001	0.06001	10.990	2.9987	49.967	549.19	28
30	0.30832	17.292	201.06	0.01783	0.05783	11.627	3.2434	56.084	652.12	30
35	0.25342	18.664	244.87	0.01358	0.05358	13.119	3.9460	73.652	966.30	35
36	0.24367	18.908	253.40	0.01289	0.05289	13.401	4.1039	77.598	1039.9	36
40	0.20829	19.792	286.53	0.01052	0.05052	14.476	4.8010	95.025	1375.6	40
45	0.17120	20.720	325.40	0.00826	0.04826	15.704	5.8411	121.02	1900.7	45
48	0.15219	21.195	347.24	0.00718	0.04718	16.383	6.5705	139.26	2281.5	48
50	0.14071	21.482	361.16	0.00655	0.04655	16.812	7.1066	152.66	2566.6	50
55	0.11566	22.108	393.68	0.00523	0.04523	17.807	8.6463	191.15	3403.9	55
60	0.09506	22.623	422.99	0.00420	0.04420	18.697	10.519	237.99	4449.7	60
70	0.06422	23.394	472.47	0.00275	0.04275	20.196	15.571	364.29	7357.2	70
80	0.04338	23.915	511.11	0.00181	0.04181	21.371	23.049	551.24	11781.	80
90	0.02931	24.267	540.73	0.00121	0.04121	22.282	34.119	827.98	18449.	90
100	0.01980	24.505	563.12	0.00081	0.04081	22.980	50.504	1237.6	28440.	100
120	0.00904	24.774	592.24	0.00036	0.04036	23.905	110.66	2741.5	65539.	120
180	0.00086	24.978	620.59	0.00003	0.04003	24.845	1164.1	29078.	724456.	180
INF	0.00000	25.000	625.00	0.0000	0.04000	25.000	INF	INF	INF	INF

	PRESENT SUM, P			UNIFORM SERIES, A			FUTURE SUM, F			
	$i = 5\%$			$i = 5\%$			$i = 5\%$			
n	P/F	P/A	P/G	A/F	A/P	A/G	F/P	F/A	F/G	n
1	0.95238	0.9523	0.0000	1.00000	1.05000	0.0000	1.0500	1.0000	0.0000	1
2	0.90703	1.8594	0.9070	0.48780	0.53780	0.4878	1.1025	2.0500	0.0000	2
3	0.86384	2.7232	2.6347	0.31721	0.36721	0.9674	1.1576	3.1525	3.0500	3
4	0.82270	3.5459	5.1028	0.23201	0.28201	1.4390	1.2155	4.3101	6.2025	4
5	0.78353	4.3294	8.2369	0.18097	0.23097	1.9025	1.2762	5.5256	10.512	5
6	0.74622	5.0756	11.968	0.14702	0.19702	2.3579	1.3401	6.8019	16.038	6
7	0.71068	5.7863	16.232	0.12282	0.17282	2.8052	1.4071	8.1420	22.840	7
8	0.67684	6.4632	20.970	0.10472	0.15472	3.2445	1.4774	9.5491	30.982	8
9	0.64461	7.1078	26.126	0.09069	0.14069	3.6757	1.5513	11.026	40.531	9
10	0.61391	7.7217	31.652	0.07950	0.12950	4.0990	1.6288	12.577	51.557	10
11	0.58468	8.3064	37.498	0.07039	0.12039	4.5144	1.7103	14.206	64.135	11
12	0.55684	8.8632	43.624	0.06283	0.11283	4.9219	1.7958	15.917	78.342	12
13	0.53032	9.3935	49.987	0.05646	0.10646	5.3215	1.8856	17.713	94.259	13
14	0.50507	9.8986	56.553	0.05102	0.10102	5.7132	1.9799	19.598	111.97	14
15	0.48102	10.379	63.288	0.04634	0.09634	6.0973	2.0789	21.578	131.57	15
16	0.45811	10.837	70.159	0.04227	0.09227	6.4736	2.1828	23.657	153.15	16
17	0.43630	11.274	77.140	0.03870	0.08870	6.8422	2.2920	25.840	176.80	17
18	0.41552	11.689	84.204	0.03555	0.08555	7.2033	2.4066	28.132	202.64	18
19	0.39573	12.085	91.327	0.03275	0.08275	7.5569	2.5269	30.539	230.78	19
20	0.37689	12.462	98.488	0.03024	0.08024	7.9029	2.6533	33.066	261.31	20
21	0.35894	12.821	105.66	0.02800	0.07800	8.2416	2.7859	35.719	294.38	21
22	0.34185	13.163	112.84	0.02597	0.07597	8.5729	2.9252	38.505	330.10	22
23	0.32557	13.488	120.00	0.02414	0.07414	8.8970	3.0715	41.430	368.61	23
24	0.31007	13.798	127.14	0.02247	0.07247	9.2139	3.2251	44.502	410.04	24
25	0.29530	14.093	134.22	0.02095	0.07095	9.5237	3.3863	47.727	454.54	25
26	0.28124	14.375	141.25	0.01956	0.06956	9.8265	3.5556	51.113	502.26	26
28	0.25509	14.898	155.11	0.01712	0.06712	10.411	3.9201	58.402	608.05	28
30	0.23138	15.372	168.62	0.01505	0.06505	10.969	4.3219	66.438	728.77	30
35	0.18129	16.374	200.58	0.01107	0.06107	12.249	5.5160	90.320	1106.4	35
36	0.17266	16.546	206.62	0.01043	0.06043	12.487	5.7918	95.836	1196.7	36
40	0.14205	17.159	229.54	0.00828	0.05828	13.377	7.0399	120.80	1616.0	40
45	0.11130	17.774	255.31	0.00626	0.05626	14.364	8.9850	159.70	2294.	45
48	0.09614	18.077	269.24	0.00532	0.05532	14.894	10.401	188.02	2800.5	48
50	0.08720	18.255	277.91	0.00478	0.05478	15.223	11.467	209.34	3186.9	50
55	0.06833	18.633	297.51	0.00367	0.05367	15.966	14.635	272.71	4354.2	55
60	0.05354	18.929	314.34	0.00283	0.05283	16.606	18.679	353.58	5871.6	60
70	0.03287	19.342	340.84	0.00170	0.05170	17.621	30.426	588.52	10370.	70
80	0.02018	19.596	359.64	0.00103	0.05103	18.352	49.561	971.22	17824.	80
90	0.01239	19.752	372.74	0.00063	0.05063	18.871	80.730	1594.6	30092.	90
100	0.00760	19.847	381.74	0.00038	0.05038	19.233	131.50	2610.0	50200.	100
120	0.00287	19.942	391.97	0.00014	0.05014	19.655	348.91	6958.2	136765.	120
INF	0.00000	20.000	400.00	0.0000	0.05000	20.000	INF	INF	INF	INF

| | $i=6\%$ | | | $i=6\%$ | | | $i=6\%$ | | | |
| | PRESENT SUM, P | | | UNIFORM SERIES, A | | | FUTURE SUM, F | | | |
n	P/F	P/A	P/G	A/F	A/P	A/G	F/P	F/A	F/G	n
1	0.94340	0.9434	0.0000	1.00000	1.06000	0.0000	1.0600	1.0000	0.0000	1
2	0.89000	1.8333	0.8900	0.48544	0.54544	0.4854	1.1236	2.0600	1.0000	2
3	0.83962	2.6730	2.5692	0.31411	0.37411	0.9611	1.1910	3.1836	3.0600	3
4	0.79209	3.4651	4.9455	0.22859	0.28859	1.4272	1.2624	4.3746	6.2436	4
5	0.74726	4.2123	7.9345	0.17740	0.23740	1.8836	1.3382	5.6370	10.618	5
6	0.70496	4.9173	11.459	0.14336	0.20336	2.3304	1.4185	6.9753	16.255	6
7	0.66506	5.5823	15.449	0.11914	0.17914	2.7675	1.5036	8.3938	23.230	7
8	0.62741	6.2097	19.841	0.10104	0.16104	3.1952	1.5938	9.8974	31.624	8
9	0.59190	6.8016	24.576	0.08702	0.14702	3.6133	1.6894	11.491	41.521	9
10	0.55839	7.3600	29.602	0.07587	0.13587	4.0220	1.7908	13.180	53.013	10
11	0.52679	7.8868	34.870	0.06679	0.12679	4.4212	1.8983	14.971	66.194	11
12	0.49697	8.3838	40.336	0.05928	0.11928	4.8112	2.0122	16.869	81.165	12
13	0.46884	8.8526	45.962	0.05296	0.11296	5.1919	2.1329	18.882	98.035	13
14	0.44230	9.2949	51.712	0.04758	0.10758	5.5635	2.2609	21.015	115.91	14
15	0.41727	9.7122	57.554	0.04296	0.10296	5.9259	2.3965	23.276	137.93	15
16	0.39365	10.105	63.459	0.03895	0.09895	6.2794	2.5403	25.672	161.20	16
17	0.37136	10.477	69.401	0.03544	0.09544	6.6239	2.6927	28.212	186.88	17
18	0.35034	10.827	75.356	0.03236	0.09236	6.9597	2.8543	30.905	215.09	18
19	0.33051	11.158	81.306	0.02962	0.08962	7.2867	3.0256	33.760	246.00	19
20	0.31180	11.469	87.230	0.02718	0.08718	7.6051	3.2071	36.785	279.76	20
21	0.29416	11.764	93.113	0.02500	0.08500	7.9150	3.3995	39.992	316.54	21
22	0.27751	12.041	98.941	0.02305	0.08305	8.2166	3.6035	43.392	356.53	22
23	0.26180	12.303	104.70	0.02128	0.08128	8.5099	3.8197	46.995	399.93	23
24	0.24698	12.550	110.38	0.01968	0.07968	8.7950	4.0489	50.815	446.92	24
25	0.23300	12.783	115.97	0.01823	0.07823	9.0722	4.2918	54.864	497.74	25
26	0.21981	13.003	121.46	0.01690	0.07690	9.3414	4.5493	59.156	552.60	26
27	0.20737	13.210	126.86	0.01570	0.07570	9.6029	4.8223	63.705	611.76	27
28	0.19563	13.406	132.14	0.01459	0.07459	9.8568	5.1116	68.528	675.46	28
29	0.18456	13.590	137.31	0.01358	0.07358	10.103	5.4183	73.639	744.99	29
30	0.17411	13.764	142.35	0.01265	0.07265	10.342	5.7434	79.058	817.63	30
35	0.13011	14.498	165.74	0.00897	0.06897	11.431	7.6860	111.43	1273.9	35
40	0.09722	15.046	185.95	0.00646	0.06646	12.359	10.285	154.76	1912.7	40
45	0.07265	15.455	203.11	0.00470	0.06470	13.141	13.764	212.74	2795.7	45
50	0.05429	15.761	217.45	0.00344	0.06344	13.796	18.420	290.33	4005.6	50
55	0.04057	15.990	229.32	0.00254	0.06254	14.341	24.650	394.17	5652.8	55
60	0.03031	16.161	239.04	0.00188	0.06188	14.790	32.987	533.12	7885.4	60
65	0.02265	16.289	246.94	0.00139	0.06139	15.145	44.145	719.08	10901.	65
70	0.01693	16.384	253.32	0.00103	0.06103	15.461	59.075	967.93	14965.	70
80	0.00945	16.509	262.54	0.00057	0.06057	15.903	105.79	1746.6	27776.	80
90	0.00528	16.578	268.39	0.00032	0.06032	16.189	189.46	3141.0	50851.	90
100	0.00295	16.617	272.04	0.00018	0.06018	16.371	339.30	5638.3	92306.	100
120	0.00092	16.651	275.68	0.00005	0.06006	16.556	1088.1	18119.	299997.	120
INF	0.00000	16.666	277.77	0.0000	0.06000	16.666	INF	INF	INF	INF

	i=7%			i=7%			i=7%			
	PRESENT SUM, P			UNIFORM SERIES, A			FUTURE SUM, F			
n	P/F	P/A	P/G	A/F	A/P	A/G	F/P	F/A	F/G	n
1	0.93458	0.9345	0.0000	1.00000	1.07000	0.0000	1.0700	1.0000	0.0000	1
2	0.87344	1.8080	0.8734	0.48309	0.55309	0.4830	1.1449	2.0700	1.0000	2
3	0.81630	2.6243	2.5060	0.31105	0.38105	0.9549	1.2250	3.2149	3.0700	3
4	0.76290	3.3872	4.7947	0.22523	0.29523	1.4155	1.3108	4.4399	6.2849	4
5	0.71299	4.1002	7.6466	0.17389	0.24389	1.8649	1.4025	5.7507	10.724	5
6	0.66634	4.7665	10.978	0.13980	0.20980	2.3032	1.5007	7.1532	16.475	6
7	0.62275	5.3892	14.714	0.11555	0.18555	2.7303	1.6057	8.6540	23.628	7
8	0.58201	5.9713	18.788	0.09747	0.16747	3.1465	1.7181	10.259	32.282	8
9	0.54393	6.5152	23.140	0.08349	0.15349	3.5517	1.8384	11.978	42.542	9
10	0.50835	7.0235	27.715	0.07238	0.14238	3.9460	1.9671	13.816	54.520	10
11	0.47509	7.4986	32.466	0.06336	0.13336	4.3296	2.1048	15.783	68.337	11
12	0.44401	7.9426	37.350	0.05590	0.12590	4.7025	2.2521	17.888	84.120	12
13	0.41496	8.3576	42.330	0.04965	0.11965	5.0648	2.4098	20.140	102.00	13
14	0.38782	8.7454	47.371	0.04434	0.11434	5.4167	2.5785	22.550	122.15	14
15	0.36245	9.1079	52.446	0.03979	0.10979	5.7582	2.7590	25.129	144.70	15
16	0.33873	9.4466	57.527	0.03586	0.10586	6.0896	2.9521	27.888	169.82	16
17	0.31657	9.7632	62.592	0.03243	0.10243	6.4110	3.1588	30.840	197.71	17
18	0.29586	10.059	67.621	0.02941	0.09941	6.7224	3.3799	33.999	228.55	18
19	0.27651	10.335	72.599	0.02675	0.09675	7.0241	3.6165	37.379	262.55	19
20	0.25842	10.594	77.509	0.02439	0.09439	7.3163	3.8696	40.995	299.93	20
21	0.24151	10.835	82.339	0.02229	0.09229	7.5990	4.1405	44.865	340.93	21
22	0.22571	11.061	87.079	0.02041	0.09041	7.8724	4.4304	49.005	385.79	22
23	0.21095	11.272	91.720	0.01871	0.08871	8.1368	4.7405	53.436	434.80	23
24	0.19715	11.469	96.254	0.01719	0.08719	8.3923	5.0723	58.176	488.23	24
25	0.18425	11.653	100.67	0.01581	0.08581	8.6391	5.4274	63.249	546.41	25
26	0.17220	11.825	104.98	0.01456	0.08456	8.8773	5.8073	68.676	609.66	26
27	0.16093	11.986	109.16	0.01343	0.08343	9.1072	6.2138	74.483	678.34	27
28	0.15040	12.137	113.22	0.01239	0.08239	9.3289	6.6488	80.697	752.82	28
29	0.14056	12.277	117.16	0.01145	0.08145	9.5427	7.1142	87.346	833.52	29
30	0.13137	12.409	120.97	0.01059	0.08059	9.7486	7.6122	94.460	920.86	30
35	0.09366	12.947	138.13	0.00723	0.07723	10.668	10.676	138.23	1474.8	35
40	0.06678	13.331	152.29	0.00501	0.07501	11.423	14.974	199.63	2280.5	40
45	0.04761	13.605	163.75	0.00350	0.07350	12.036	21.002	285.74	3439.2	45
50	0.03395	13.800	172.90	0.00246	0.07246	12.528	29.457	406.52	5093.2	50
55	0.02420	13.939	180.12	0.00174	0.07174	12.921	41.315	575.92	7441.8	55
60	0.01726	14.039	185.76	0.00123	0.07123	13.232	57.946	813.52	10764.	60
65	0.01230	14.109	190.14	0.00087	0.07087	13.476	81.272	1146.7	15453.	65
70	0.00877	14.160	193.51	0.00062	0.07062	13.666	113.98	1614.1	22059.	70
80	0.00446	14.222	198.07	0.00031	0.07031	13.927	224.23	3189.0	44415.	80
90	0.00227	14.253	200.70	0.00016	0.07016	14.081	441.10	6287.1	88531.	90
100	0.00115	14.269	202.20	0.00008	0.07008	14.170	867.71	12381.	175452.	100
120	0.00030	14.281	203.51	0.00002	0.07002	14.250	3357.7	47954.	683345.	120
INF	0.00000	14.285	204.08	0.0000	0.07000	14.285	INF	INF	INF	INF

	i = 8% PRESENT SUM, P			i = 8% UNIFORM SERIES, A			i = 8% FUTURE SUM, F			
n	P/F	P/A	P/G	A/F	A/P	A/G	F/P	F/A	F/G	n
1	0.92593	0.9259	0.0000	1.00000	1.08000	0.0000	1.0800	1.0000	0.0000	1
2	0.85734	1.7832	0.8573	0.48077	0.56077	0.4807	1.1664	2.0800	1.0000	2
3	0.79383	2.5771	2.4450	0.30803	0.38803	0.9487	1.2597	3.2464	3.0800	3
4	0.73503	3.3121	4.6500	0.22192	0.30192	1.4039	1.3604	4.5061	6.3264	4
5	0.68058	3.9927	7.3724	0.17046	0.25046	1.8464	1.4693	5.8666	10.832	5
6	0.63017	4.6228	10.523	0.13632	0.21632	2.2763	1.5868	7.3359	16.699	6
7	0.58349	5.2063	14.024	0.11207	0.19207	2.6936	1.7138	8.9228	24.035	7
8	0.54027	5.7466	17.806	0.09401	0.17401	3.0985	1.8509	10.636	32.957	8
9	0.50025	6.2468	21.808	0.08008	0.16008	3.4910	1.9990	12.487	43.594	9
10	0.46319	6.7100	25.976	0.06903	0.14903	3.8713	2.1589	14.486	56.082	10
11	0.42888	7.1389	30.265	0.06008	0.14008	4.2395	2.3316	16.645	70.568	11
12	0.39711	7.5360	34.633	0.05270	0.13270	4.5957	2.5181	18.977	87.214	12
13	0.36770	7.9037	39.046	0.04652	0.12652	4.9402	2.7196	21.495	106.19	13
14	0.34046	8.2442	43.472	0.04130	0.12130	5.2730	2.9371	24.214	127.68	14
15	0.31524	8.5594	47.885	0.03683	0.11683	5.5944	3.1721	27.152	151.90	15
16	0.29189	8.8513	52.264	0.03298	0.11298	5.9046	3.4259	30.324	179.05	16
17	0.27027	9.1216	56.588	0.02963	0.10963	6.2037	3.7000	33.750	209.37	17
18	0.25025	9.3718	60.842	0.02670	0.10670	6.4920	3.9960	37.450	243.12	18
19	0.23171	9.6036	65.013	0.02413	0.10413	6.7696	4.3157	41.446	280.57	19
20	0.21455	9.8181	69.089	0.02185	0.10185	7.0369	4.6609	45.762	322.02	20
21	0.19866	10.016	73.062	0.01983	0.09983	7.2940	5.0338	50.422	367.78	21
22	0.18394	10.200	76.925	0.01803	0.09803	7.5411	5.4365	55.456	418.20	22
23	0.17032	10.371	80.672	0.01642	0.09642	7.7786	5.8714	60.893	473.66	23
24	0.15770	10.528	84.299	0.01498	0.09498	8.0066	6.3411	66.764	534.55	24
25	0.14602	10.674	87.804	0.01368	0.09368	8.2253	6.8484	73.105	601.32	25
26	0.13520	10.810	91.184	0.01251	0.09251	8.4351	7.3963	79.954	674.43	26
27	0.12519	10.935	94.439	0.01145	0.09145	8.6362	7.9880	87.350	754.38	27
28	0.11591	11.051	97.568	0.01049	0.09049	8.8288	8.6271	95.338	841.73	28
29	0.10733	11.158	100.57	0.00962	0.08962	9.0132	9.3172	103.96	937.07	29
30	0.09938	11.257	103.45	0.00883	0.08883	9.1897	10.062	113.28	1041.0	30
35	0.06763	11.654	116.09	0.00580	0.08580	9.9610	14.785	172.31	1716.4	35
40	0.04603	11.924	126.04	0.00386	0.08386	10.569	21.724	259.05	2738.2	40
45	0.03133	12.108	133.73	0.00259	0.08259	11.044	31.920	386.50	4268.8	45
50	0.02132	12.233	139.59	0.00174	0.08174	11.410	46.901	573.77	6547.1	50
55	0.01451	12.318	144.00	0.00118	0.08118	11.690	68.913	848.92	9924.0	55
60	0.00988	12.376	147.30	0.00080	0.08080	11.901	101.25	1253.2	14915.	60
65	0.00672	12.416	149.73	0.00054	0.08054	12.060	148.77	1847.2	22278.	65
70	0.00457	12.442	151.53	0.00037	0.08037	12.178	218.60	2720.0	33126.	70
80	0.00212	12.473	153.80	0.00017	0.08017	12.330	471.95	5886.9	72586.	80
90	0.00098	12.487	154.99	0.00008	0.08008	12.411	1018.9	12723.	157924.	90
100	0.00045	12.494	155.61	0.00004	0.08004	12.454	2199.7	27484.	342306.	100
120	0.00010	12.498	156.08	0.00001	0.08001	12.488	10253.	128150.	>10**6	120
INF	0.00000	12.500	156.25	0.0000	0.08000	12.500	INF	INF	INF	INF

| | i = 9% | | | i = 9% | | | i = 9% | | | |
| | PRESENT SUM, P | | | UNIFORM SERIES, A | | | FUTURE SUM, F | | | |
n	P/F	P/A	P/G	A/F	A/P	A/G	F/P	F/A	F/G	n
1	0.91743	0.9174	0.0000	1.00000	1.09000	0.0000	1.0900	1.0000	0.0000	1
2	0.84168	1.7591	0.8416	0.47847	0.56847	0.4784	1.1881	2.0900	1.0000	2
3	0.77218	2.5312	2.3860	0.30505	0.39505	0.9426	1.2950	3.2781	3.0900	3
4	0.70843	3.2397	4.5113	0.21867	0.30867	1.3925	1.4115	4.5731	6.3681	4
5	0.64993	3.8896	7.1110	0.16709	0.25709	1.8282	1.5386	5.9847	10.941	5
6	0.59627	4.4859	10.092	0.13292	0.22292	2.2497	1.6771	7.5233	16.925	6
7	0.54703	5.0329	13.374	0.10869	0.19869	2.6574	1.8280	9.2004	24.649	7
8	0.50187	5.5348	16.887	0.09067	0.18067	3.0511	1.9925	11.028	33.649	8
9	0.46043	5.9952	20.571	0.07680	0.16680	3.4312	2.1718	13.021	44.678	9
10	0.42241	6.4176	24.372	0.06582	0.15582	3.7977	2.3673	15.192	57.699	10
11	0.38753	6.8051	28.248	0.05695	0.14695	4.1509	2.5804	17.560	72.892	11
12	0.35553	7.1607	32.159	0.04965	0.13965	4.4910	2.8126	20.140	90.452	12
13	0.32618	7.4869	36.073	0.04357	0.13357	4.8181	3.0658	22.953	110.59	13
14	0.29925	7.7861	39.963	0.03843	0.12843	5.1326	3.3417	26.019	133.54	14
15	0.27454	8.0606	43.806	0.03406	0.12406	5.4346	3.6424	29.360	159.56	15
16	0.25187	8.3125	47.584	0.03030	0.12030	5.7244	3.9703	33.003	188.92	16
17	0.23107	8.5436	51.282	0.02705	0.11705	6.0023	4.3276	36.973	221.93	17
18	0.21199	8.7556	54.886	0.02421	0.11421	6.2686	4.7171	41.301	258.90	18
19	0.19449	8.9501	58.386	0.02173	0.11173	6.5236	5.1416	46.018	300.20	19
20	0.17843	9.1285	61.777	0.01955	0.10955	6.7674	5.6044	51.160	346.22	20
21	0.16370	9.2922	65.050	0.01762	0.10762	7.0005	6.1088	56.764	397.38	21
22	0.15018	9.4424	68.204	0.01590	0.10590	7.2232	6.6586	62.873	454.14	22
23	0.13778	9.5802	71.235	0.01438	0.10438	7.4357	7.2578	69.531	517.02	23
24	0.12640	9.7066	74.143	0.01302	0.10302	7.6384	7.9110	76.789	586.55	24
25	0.11597	9.8225	76.926	0.01181	0.10181	7.8316	8.6230	84.700	663.34	25
26	0.10639	9.9289	79.586	0.01072	0.10072	8.0155	9.3991	93.324	748.04	26
27	0.09761	10.026	82.124	0.00973	0.09973	8.1906	10.245	102.72	841.36	27
28	0.08955	10.116	84.541	0.00885	0.09885	8.3571	11.167	112.96	944.09	28
29	0.08215	10.198	86.842	0.00806	0.09806	8.5153	12.172	124.13	1057.0	29
30	0.07537	10.273	89.028	0.00734	0.09734	8.6656	13.267	136.30	1181.1	30
35	0.04899	10.566	98.359	0.00464	0.09464	9.3082	20.414	215.71	2007.9	35
40	0.03184	10.757	105.37	0.00296	0.09296	9.7957	31.409	337.88	3309.8	40
45	0.02069	10.881	110.55	0.00190	0.09190	10.160	48.327	525.85	5342.8	45
50	0.01345	10.961	114.32	0.00123	0.09123	10.429	74.357	815.08	8500.9	50
55	0.00874	11.014	117.03	0.00079	0.09079	10.626	114.40	1260.0	13389.	55
60	0.00568	11.048	118.96	0.00051	0.09051	10.768	176.03	1944.7	20942.	60
65	0.00369	11.070	120.33	0.00033	0.09033	10.870	270.84	2998.2	32592.	65
70	0.00240	11.084	121.29	0.00022	0.09022	10.942	416.73	4619.2	50546.	70
80	0.00101	11.099	122.43	0.00009	0.09009	11.029	986.55	10950.	120784.	80
90	0.00043	11.106	122.97	0.00004	0.09004	11.072	2335.5	25939.	287213.	90
100	0.00018	11.109	123.23	0.00002	0.09002	11.093	5529.0	61422.	681363.	100
120	0.00003	11.110	123.41	0.00000	0.09000	11.107	30987.	344289.	>10**6	120
INF	0.00000	11.111	123.45	0.0000	0.09000	11.111	INF	INF	INF	INF

n	PRESENT SUM, P			UNIFORM SERIES, A			FUTURE SUM, F			n
	$i=10\%$			$i=10\%$			$i=10\%$			
	P/F	P/A	P/G	A/F	A/P	A/G	F/P	F/A	F/G	
1	0.90909	0.9090	0.0000	1.00000	1.10000	0.0000	1.1000	1.0000	0.0000	1
2	0.82645	1.7355	0.8264	0.47619	0.57619	0.4761	1.2100	2.1000	1.0000	2
3	0.75131	2.4868	2.3290	0.30211	0.40211	0.9365	1.3310	3.3100	3.1000	3
4	0.68301	3.1698	4.3781	0.21547	0.31547	1.3811	1.4641	4.6410	6.4100	4
5	0.62092	3.7907	6.8618	0.16380	0.26380	1.8101	1.6105	6.1051	11.051	5
6	0.56447	4.3552	9.6841	0.12961	0.22961	2.2235	1.7715	7.7156	17.156	6
7	0.51316	4.8684	12.763	0.10541	0.20541	2.6216	1.9487	9.4871	24.871	7
8	0.46651	5.3349	16.028	0.08744	0.18744	3.0044	2.1435	11.435	34.358	8
9	0.42410	5.7590	19.421	0.07364	0.17364	3.3723	2.3579	13.579	45.794	9
10	0.38554	6.1445	22.891	0.06275	0.16275	3.7254	2.5937	15.937	59.374	10
11	0.35049	6.4950	26.396	0.05396	0.15396	4.0640	2.8531	18.531	75.311	11
12	0.31863	6.8136	29.901	0.04676	0.14676	4.3884	3.1384	21.384	93.842	12
13	0.28966	7.1033	33.377	0.04078	0.14078	4.6987	3.4522	24.522	115.22	13
14	0.26333	7.3666	36.800	0.03575	0.13575	4.9955	3.7975	27.975	139.75	14
15	0.23939	7.6060	40.152	0.03147	0.13147	5.2789	4.1772	31.772	167.72	15
16	0.21763	7.8237	43.416	0.02782	0.12782	5.5493	4.5949	35.949	199.49	16
17	0.19784	8.0215	46.581	0.02466	0.12466	5.8071	5.0544	40.544	235.44	17
18	0.17986	8.2014	49.639	0.02193	0.12193	6.0525	5.5599	45.599	275.99	18
19	0.16351	8.3649	52.582	0.01955	0.11955	6.2861	6.1159	51.159	321.59	19
20	0.14864	8.5135	55.406	0.01746	0.11746	6.5080	6.7275	57.275	372.75	20
21	0.13513	8.6486	58.109	0.01562	0.11562	6.7188	7.4002	64.002	430.02	21
22	0.12285	8.7715	60.689	0.01401	0.11401	6.9188	8.1402	71.402	494.02	22
23	0.11168	8.8832	63.146	0.01257	0.11257	7.1084	8.9543	79.543	565.43	23
24	0.10153	8.9847	65.481	0.01130	0.11130	7.2880	9.8497	88.497	644.97	24
25	0.09230	9.0770	67.696	0.01017	0.11017	7.4579	10.834	98.347	733.47	25
26	0.08391	9.1609	69.794	0.00916	0.10916	7.6186	11.918	109.18	831.81	26
27	0.07628	9.2372	71.777	0.00826	0.10826	7.7704	13.110	121.10	940.99	27
28	0.06934	9.3065	73.649	0.00745	0.10745	7.9137	14.421	134.21	1062.1	28
29	0.06304	9.3696	75.414	0.00673	0.10673	8.0489	15.863	148.63	1196.3	29
30	0.05731	9.4269	77.076	0.00608	0.10608	8.1762	17.449	164.49	1344.9	30
35	0.03558	9.6441	83.987	0.00369	0.10369	8.7086	28.102	271.02	2360.2	35
40	0.02209	9.7790	88.952	0.00226	0.10226	9.0962	45.259	442.59	4025.9	40
45	0.01372	9.8628	92.454	0.00139	0.10139	9.3740	72.890	718.90	6739.0	45
50	0.00852	9.9148	94.888	0.00086	0.10086	9.5704	117.39	1163.9	11139.	50
55	0.00529	9.9471	96.561	0.00053	0.10053	9.7075	189.05	1880.5	18255.	55
60	0.00328	9.9671	97.701	0.00033	0.10033	9.8022	304.48	3034.8	29748.	60
65	0.00204	9.9797	98.470	0.00020	0.10020	9.8671	490.37	4893.7	48287.	65
70	0.00127	9.9873	98.987	0.00013	0.10013	9.9112	789.74	7887.4	78174.	70
80	0.00049	9.9951	99.560	0.00005	0.10005	9.9609	2048.+	20474.	203940.	80
90	0.00019	9.9981	99.811	0.00002	0.10002	9.9830	5313.0	53120.	530302.	90
100	0.00007	9.9992	99.920	0.00001	0.10001	9.9927	13780.	137796.	>10**6	100
120	0.00001	9.9998	99.986	0.00000	0.10000	9.9987	92709.	927081.	>10**6	120
INF	0.00000	10.000	100.00	0.0000	0.10000	10.000	INF	INF	INF	INF

	$i = 11\%$			$i = 11\%$			$i = 11\%$			
	PRESENT SUM, P			UNIFORM SERIES, A			FUTURE SUM, F			
n	P/F	P/A	P/G	A/F	A/P	A/G	F/P	F/A	F/G	n
1	0.90090	0.9009	0.0000	1.00000	0.11000	0.0000	1.1100	1.0000	0.0000	1
2	0.81162	1.7125	0.8116	0.47393	0.58393	0.4739	1.2321	2.1100	1.0000	2
3	0.73119	2.4437	2.2740	0.29921	0.40921	0.9305	1.3676	3.3421	3.1100	3
4	0.65873	3.1024	4.2502	0.21233	0.32233	1.3699	1.5180	4.7097	6.4521	4
5	0.59345	3.6959	6.6502	0.16057	0.27057	1.7922	1.6850	6.2278	11.161	5
6	0.53464	4.2305	9.2972	0.12638	0.23638	2.1976	1.8704	7.9128	17.389	6
7	0.48166	4.7122	12.187	0.10222	0.21222	2.5863	2.0761	9.7832	25.302	7
8	0.43393	5.1461	15.224	0.08424	0.19432	2.9584	2.3045	11.859	35.085	8
9	0.39092	5.5370	18.352	0.07060	0.18060	3.3144	2.5580	14.164	46.945	9
10	0.35218	5.8892	21.521	0.05980	0.16980	3.6544	2.8394	16.722	61.109	10
11	0.31728	6.2065	24.694	0.05112	0.16112	3.9788	3.1517	19.561	77.831	11
12	0.28584	6.4923	27.838	0.04403	0.15403	4.2879	3.4984	22.713	97.392	12
13	0.25751	6.7498	30.929	0.03815	0.14815	4.5821	3.8832	26.211	120.10	13
14	0.23199	6.9818	33.944	0.03323	0.14323	4.8618	4.3104	30.094	146.31	14
15	0.20900	7.1908	36.870	0.02907	0.13907	5.1274	4.7845	34.405	176.41	15
16	0.18829	7.3791	39.695	0.02552	0.13552	5.3793	5.3108	39.189	210.81	16
17	0.16963	7.5487	42.409	0.02247	0.13247	5.6180	5.8950	44.500	250.00	17
18	0.15282	7.7016	45.007	0.01984	0.12984	5.8438	6.5435	50.395	294.50	18
19	0.13768	7.8392	47.485	0.01756	0.12756	6.0573	7.2633	56.939	344.90	19
20	0.12403	7.9633	49.842	0.01558	0.12558	6.2589	8.0623	64.202	401.84	20
21	0.11174	8.0750	52.077	0.01384	0.12384	6.4491	8.9491	72.265	466.04	21
22	0.10067	8.1757	54.191	0.01231	0.12231	6.6282	9.9335	81.214	538.31	22
23	0.09069	8.2664	56.186	0.01097	0.12097	6.7969	11.026	91.147	619.52	23
24	0.08170	8.3481	58.065	0.00979	0.11979	6.9555	12.239	102.17	710.67	24
25	0.07361	8.4217	59.832	0.00874	0.11874	7.1044	13.585	114.41	812.84	25
26	0.06631	8.4880	61.490	0.00781	0.11781	7.2443	15.079	127.99	927.26	26
27	0.05974	8.5478	63.043	0.00699	0.11699	7.3753	16.738	143.07	1055.2	27
28	0.05382	8.6016	64.496	0.00626	0.11626	7.4981	18.579	159.81	1198.3	28
29	0.04849	8.6501	65.854	0.00561	0.11561	7.6131	20.623	178.39	1358.1	29
30	0.04368	8.6937	67.121	0.00502	0.11502	7.7205	22.892	199.02	1536.5	30
35	0.02592	8.8552	72.253	0.00293	0.11293	8.1594	38.574	341.59	2787.1	35
40	0.01538	8.9510	75.778	0.00172	0.11172	8.4659	65.000	581.82	4925.6	40
45	0.00913	9.0079	78.155	0.00101	0.11101	8.6762	109.53	986.63	8560.3	45
50	0.00542	9.0416	79.734	0.00060	0.11060	8.8185	184.56	1668.7	14716.	50
55	0.00322	9.0616	80.771	0.00035	0.11035	8.9134	311.00	2818.2	25120.	55
60	0.00191	9.0735	81.446	0.00021	0.11021	8.9762	524.05	4755.0	42682.	60
65	0.00113	9.0806	81.881	0.00012	0.11012	9.0172	883.06	8018.7	72307.	65
70	0.00067	9.0848	82.161	0.00007	0.11007	9.0438	1488.0	13518.	122258.	70
INF	0.00000	9.3909	82.644	0.0300	0.11000	9.0909	INF	INF	INF	INF

	i = 12%			i = 12%			i = 12%			
	PRESENT SUM, P			UNIFORM SERIES, A			FUTURE SUM, F			
n	P/F	P/A	P/G	A/F	A/P	A/G	F/P	F/A	F/G	n
1	0.89286	0.8928	0.0000	1.00000	1.12000	0.0000	1.1200	1.0000	0.0000	1
2	0.79719	1.6900	0.7971	0.47170	0.59170	0.4717	1.2544	2.1200	1.0000	2
3	0.71178	2.4018	2.2207	0.29635	0.41635	0.9246	1.4049	3.3744	3.1200	3
4	0.63552	3.0373	4.1273	0.20923	0.32923	1.3588	1.5735	4.7793	6.4944	4
5	0.56743	3.6047	6.3970	0.15741	0.27741	1.7745	1.7623	6.3528	11.273	5
6	0.50663	4.1114	8.9301	0.12323	0.24323	2.1720	1.9738	8.1151	17.626	6
7	0.45235	4.5637	11.644	0.09912	0.21912	2.5514	2.2106	10.089	25.741	7
8	0.40388	4.9676	14.471	0.08130	0.20130	2.9131	2.4759	12.299	35.830	8
9	0.36061	5.3282	17.356	0.06768	0.18768	3.2574	2.7730	14.775	48.130	9
10	0.32197	5.6502	20.254	0.05698	0.17698	3.5846	3.1058	17.548	62.906	10
11	0.28748	5.9377	23.128	0.04842	0.16842	3.8952	3.4785	20.654	80.454	11
12	0.25668	6.1943	25.952	0.04144	0.16144	4.1896	3.8959	24.133	101.10	12
13	0.22917	6.4235	28.702	0.03568	0.15568	4.4683	4.3634	28.029	125.24	13
14	0.20462	6.6281	31.362	0.03087	0.15087	4.7316	4.8871	32.392	153.27	14
15	0.18270	6.8108	33.920	0.02682	0.14682	4.9803	5.4735	37.279	185.66	15
16	0.16312	6.9739	36.367	0.02339	0.14339	5.2146	6.1303	42.753	222.94	16
17	0.14564	7.1196	38.697	0.02046	0.14046	5.4353	6.8660	48.883	265.69	17
18	0.13004	7.2496	40.903	0.01794	0.13794	5.6427	7.6899	55.749	314.58	18
19	0.11611	7.3657	42.997	0.01576	0.13576	5.8375	8.6127	63.439	370.33	19
20	0.10367	7.4694	44.967	0.01388	0.13388	6.0202	9.6462	72.052	433.77	20
21	0.09256	7.5620	46.818	0.01224	0.13224	6.1913	10.803	81.698	505.82	21
22	0.08264	7.6446	48.554	0.01081	0.13081	6.3514	12.100	92.502	587.52	22
23	0.07379	7.7184	50.177	0.00956	0.12956	6.5010	13.552	104.60	680.02	23
24	0.06588	7.7843	51.692	0.00846	0.12846	6.6406	15.178	118.15	784.62	24
25	0.05882	7.8431	53.104	0.00750	0.12750	6.7708	17.000	133.33	902.78	25
26	0.05252	7.8956	54.417	0.00665	0.12665	6.8921	19.040	150.33	1036.1	26
27	0.04689	7.9425	55.436	0.00590	0.12590	7.0049	21.324	169.37	1186.4	27
28	0.04187	7.9844	56.767	0.00524	0.12524	7.1097	23.883	190.69	1355.3	28
29	0.03738	8.0218	57.814	0.00466	0.12466	7.2071	26.749	214.58	1546.5	29
30	0.03338	8.0551	58.782	0.00414	0.12414	7.2974	29.959	241.33	1761.1	30
35	0.01894	8.1755	62.605	0.00232	0.12232	7.6577	52.799	431.66	3305.5	35
40	0.01075	8.2437	65.115	0.00130	0.12130	7.8987	93.051	767.09	6059.1	40
45	0.00610	8.2825	66.734	0.00074	0.12074	8.0572	163.98	1358.2	10943.	45
50	0.00346	8.3045	67.762	0.00042	0.12042	8.1597	289.00	2400.0	19583.	50
55	0.00196	8.3169	68.408	0.00024	0.12024	8.2251	509.32	4236.0	34841.	55
60	0.00111	8.3240	68.810	0.00013	0.12013	8.2664	897.59	7471.6	61763.	60
65	0.00063	8.3280	69.058	0.00008	0.12008	8.2922	1581.8	13173.	109241.	65
70	0.00036	8.3303	69.210	0.00004	0.12004	8.3082	2787.8	23223.	192944.	70
INF	0.00000	8.3333	69.444	0.0000	0.12000	8.3333	INF	INF	INF	INF

	$i = 13\%$ PRESENT SUM, P			$i = 13\%$ UNIFORM SERIES, A			$i = 13\%$ FUTURE SUM, F			
n	P/F	P/A	P/G	A/F	A/P	A/G	F/P	F/A	F/G	n
1	0.88496	0.8849	0.0000	1.00000	1.13000	0.0000	1.1300	1.0000	0.0000	1
2	0.78315	1.6681	0.7831	0.46948	0.59948	0.4694	1.2769	2.1300	1.0000	2
3	0.69305	2.3611	2.1692	0.29352	0.42352	0.9187	1.4429	3.4069	3.1300	3
4	0.61332	2.9744	4.0092	0.20619	0.33619	1.3478	1.6304	4.8498	6.5369	4
5	0.54276	3.5172	6.1802	0.15431	0.28431	1.7571	1.8424	6.4802	11.386	5
6	0.48032	3.9975	8.5818	0.12015	0.25015	2.1467	2.0819	8.3227	17.867	6
7	0.42506	4.4226	11.132	0.09611	0.22611	2.5171	2.3526	10.404	26.189	7
8	0.37616	4.7987	13.765	0.07839	0.20839	2.8685	2.6584	12.757	36.594	8
9	0.33288	5.1316	16.428	0.06487	0.19487	3.2013	3.0040	15.415	49.351	9
10	0.29459	5.4262	19.079	0.05429	0.18429	3.5161	3.3945	18.419	64.767	10
11	0.26070	5.6869	21.686	0.04584	0.17584	3.8134	3.8358	21.814	83.187	11
12	0.23071	5.9176	24.224	0.03899	0.16899	4.0935	4.3345	25.650	105.00	12
13	0.20416	6.1218	26.674	0.03335	0.16335	4.3572	4.8980	29.984	130.65	13
14	0.18068	6.3024	29.023	0.02867	0.15867	4.6050	5.5347	34.882	160.63	14
15	0.15989	6.4623	31.261	0.02474	0.15474	4.8374	6.2542	40.417	195.51	15
16	0.14150	6.6038	33.384	0.02143	0.15143	5.0552	7.0673	46.671	235.93	16
17	0.12522	6.7290	35.387	0.01861	0.14861	5.2589	7.9860	53.739	282.60	17
18	0.11081	6.8399	37.271	0.01620	0.14620	5.4491	9.0242	61.725	336.34	18
19	0.09806	6.9379	39.036	0.01413	0.14413	5.5265	10.197	70.749	398.07	19
20	0.08678	7.0247	40.685	0.01235	0.14235	5.7917	11.523	80.946	468.82	20
21	0.07680	7.1015	42.221	0.01081	0.14081	5.9453	13.021	92.469	549.76	21
22	0.06796	7.1695	43.648	0.00948	0.13948	6.0880	14.713	105.49	642.23	22
23	0.06014	7.2296	44.971	0.00832	0.13832	6.2204	16.626	120.20	747.73	23
24	0.05323	7.2828	46.196	0.00731	0.13731	6.3430	18.788	136.83	867.93	24
25	0.04710	7.3299	47.326	0.00643	0.13643	6.4565	21.230	155.62	1004.7	25
26	0.04168	7.3716	48.368	0.00565	0.13565	6.5614	23.990	176.85	1160.3	26
27	0.03689	7.4085	49.327	0.00498	0.13498	6.6581	27.109	200.84	1337.2	27
28	0.03264	7.4412	50.209	0.00439	0.13439	6.7474	30.633	227.95	1538.0	28
29	0.02889	7.4700	51.017	0.00387	0.13387	6.8296	34.615	258.58	1766.0	29
30	0.02557	7.4956	51.759	0.00341	0.13341	6.9052	39.115	293.19	2024.6	30
35	0.01388	7.5855	54.614	0.00183	0.13183	7.1998	72.068	546.68	3936.0	35
40	0.00753	7.6343	56.408	0.00099	0.13099	7.3887	132.78	1013.7	7490.0	40
45	0.00409	7.6608	57.514	0.00053	0.13053	7.5076	244.64	1874.1	14070.	45
50	0.00222	7.6752	58.187	0.00029	0.13029	7.5811	450.73	3459.5	26227.	50
55	0.00120	7.6830	58.590	0.00016	0.13016	7.6260	830.4	6380.4	48656.	55
60	0.00065	7.6872	58.831	0.00009	0.13009	7.6530	1530.0	11761.	90015.	60
65	0.00035	7.6895	58.973	0.00005	0.13005	7.6692	2819.0	21677.	165247.	65
70	0.00019	7.6908	59.056	0.00003	0.13003	7.6788	5193.8	39945.	306732.	70
INF	0.00000	7.6923	59.171	0.0000	0.13000	7.6923	INF	INF	INF	INF

i = 14%

	PRESENT SUM, P			UNIFORM SERIES, A			FUTURE SUM, F			
n	P/F	P/A	P/G	A/F	A/P	A/G	F/P	F/A	F/G	n
1	0.87719	0.8771	0.0000	1.00000	1.14000	0.0000	1.1400	1.0000	0.0000	1
2	0.76947	1.6466	0.7694	0.46729	0.60729	0.4672	1.2996	2.1400	1.0000	2
3	0.67497	2.3216	2.1194	0.29073	0.43073	0.9129	1.4815	3.4396	3.1400	3
4	0.59208	2.9137	3.8956	0.20320	0.34320	1.3370	1.6889	4.9211	6.5796	4
5	0.51937	3.4330	5.9731	0.15128	0.29128	1.7398	1.9254	6.6101	11.500	5
6	0.45559	3.8886	8.2510	0.11716	0.25716	2.1218	2.1949	8.5355	18.110	6
7	0.39964	4.2883	10.648	0.09319	0.23319	2.4832	2.5022	10.730	26.646	7
8	0.35056	4.6388	13.102	0.07557	0.21557	2.8245	2.8525	13.232	37.376	8
9	0.30751	4.9463	15.562	0.06217	0.20217	3.1463	3.2519	16.085	50.609	9
10	0.26974	5.2161	17.990	0.05171	0.19171	3.4490	3.7072	19.337	66.695	10
11	0.23662	5.4527	20.356	0.04339	0.18339	3.7333	4.2262	23.044	86.032	11
12	0.20756	5.6602	22.639	0.03667	0.17667	3.9997	4.8179	27.270	109.07	12
13	0.18207	5.8423	24.824	0.03116	0.17116	4.2490	5.4924	32.088	136.34	13
14	0.15971	6.0020	26.900	0.02661	0.16661	4.4819	6.2613	37.581	168.43	14
15	0.14010	6.1421	28.862	0.02281	0.16281	4.6990	7.1379	43.842	206.01	15
16	0.12289	6.2650	30.705	0.01962	0.15962	4.9011	8.1372	50.980	249.86	16
17	0.10780	6.3728	32.430	0.01692	0.15692	5.0888	9.2764	59.117	300.84	17
18	0.09456	6.4674	34.038	0.01462	0.15462	5.2629	10.575	68.394	359.95	18
19	0.08295	6.5503	35.531	0.01266	0.15266	5.4242	12.055	78.969	428.35	19
20	0.07276	6.6231	36.913	0.01099	0.15099	5.5734	13.743	91.024	507.32	20
21	0.06383	6.6869	38.190	0.00954	0.14954	5.7111	15.667	104.76	598.34	21
22	0.05599	6.7429	39.365	0.00830	0.14830	5.8380	17.861	120.43	703.11	22
23	0.04911	6.7920	40.446	0.00723	0.14723	5.9549	20.361	138.29	823.55	23
24	0.04308	6.8351	41.437	0.00630	0.14630	6.0623	23.212	158.65	961.84	24
25	0.03779	6.8729	42.344	0.00550	0.14550	6.1610	26.461	181.87	1120.5	25
26	0.03315	6.9060	43.172	0.00480	0.14480	6.2514	30.166	208.33	1302.3	26
27	0.02908	6.9351	43.928	0.00419	0.14419	6.3342	34.389	238.49	1510.7	27
28	0.02551	6.9606	44.617	0.00366	0.14366	6.4099	39.204	272.88	1749.2	28
29	0.02237	6.9830	45.244	0.00320	0.14320	6.4791	44.693	312.09	2022.1	29
30	0.01963	7.0026	45.813	0.00280	0.14280	6.5422	50.950	356.78	2334.1	30
35	0.01019	7.0700	47.951	0.00144	0.14144	6.7824	98.100	693.57	4704.0	35
40	0.00529	7.1050	49.237	0.00075	0.14075	6.9299	188.88	1342.0	9300.1	40
45	0.00275	7.1232	49.996	0.00039	0.14039	7.0188	363.67	2590.5	18182.	45
50	0.00143	7.1326	50.437	0.00020	0.14020	7.0713	700.23	4994.5	35318.	50
55	0.00074	7.1375	50.691	0.00010	0.14010	7.1020	1348.2	9623.1	68343.	55
60	0.00039	7.1401	50.835	0.00005	0.14005	7.1197	2595.9	18535.	131965.	60
65	0.00020	7.1414	50.917	0.00003	0.14003	7.1298	4998.2	35694.	254496.	65
70	0.00010	7.1421	50.963	0.00001	0.14001	7.1355	9623.6	68733.	490451.	70
INF	0.00000	7.1428	51.020	0.0000	0.14000	7.1428	INF	INF	INF	INF

n	PRESENT SUM, P			UNIFORM SERIES, A			FUTURE SUM, F			n
	P/F	P/A	P/G	A/F	A/P	A/G	F/P	F/A	F/G	
1	0.86957	0.8695	0.0000	1.00000	1.15000	0.0000	1.1500	1.0000	0.0000	1
2	0.75614	1.6257	0.7561	0.46512	0.61512	0.4651	1.3225	2.1500	1.0000	2
3	0.65752	2.2832	2.0711	0.28798	0.43798	0.9071	1.5208	3.4725	3.1500	3
4	0.57175	2.8549	3.7864	0.20027	0.35027	1.3262	1.7490	4.9933	6.6225	4
5	0.49718	3.3521	5.7751	0.14832	0.29832	1.7228	2.0113	6.7423	11.615	5
6	0.43233	3.7844	7.9367	0.11424	0.26424	2.0971	2.3130	8.7537	18.358	6
7	0.37594	4.1604	10.192	0.09036	0.24036	2.4498	2.6600	11.066	27.112	7
8	0.32690	4.4873	12.480	0.07285	0.22285	2.7813	3.0590	13.726	38.178	8
9	0.28426	4.7715	14.754	0.05957	0.20957	3.0922	3.5178	16.785	51.905	9
10	0.24718	5.0187	16.979	0.04925	0.19925	3.3832	4.0455	20.303	68.691	10
11	0.21494	5.2337	19.128	0.04107	0.19107	3.6549	4.6523	24.349	88.995	11
12	0.18691	5.4206	21.184	0.03448	0.18448	3.9082	5.3502	29.001	113.34	12
13	0.16253	5.5831	23.135	0.02911	0.17911	4.1437	6.1527	34.351	142.34	13
14	0.14133	5.7244	24.972	0.02469	0.17469	4.3624	7.0757	40.504	176.69	14
15	0.12289	5.8473	26.693	0.02102	0.17102	4.5649	8.1370	47.580	217.20	15
16	0.10686	5.9542	28.296	0.01795	0.16795	4.7522	9.3576	55.717	264.78	16
17	0.09293	6.0472	29.782	0.01537	0.16537	4.9250	10.761	65.075	320.50	17
18	0.08081	6.1279	31.156	0.01319	0.16319	5.0843	12.375	75.836	385.57	18
19	0.07027	6.1982	32.421	0.01134	0.16134	5.2307	14.231	88.211	461.41	19
20	0.06110	6.2593	33.582	0.00976	0.15976	5.3651	16.366	102.44	549.62	20
21	0.05313	6.3124	34.644	0.00842	0.15842	5.4883	18.821	118.81	652.06	21
22	0.04620	6.3586	35.615	0.00727	0.15727	5.6010	21.644	137.63	770.87	22
23	0.04017	6.3988	36.498	0.00628	0.15628	5.7039	24.891	159.27	908.50	23
24	0.03493	6.4337	37.302	0.00543	0.15543	5.7978	28.625	184.16	1067.5	24
25	0.03038	6.4641	38.031	0.00470	0.15470	5.8834	32.919	212.79	1251.9	25
26	0.02642	6.4905	38.691	0.00407	0.15407	5.9612	37.856	245.71	1464.7	26
27	0.02297	6.5135	39.289	0.00353	0.15353	6.0319	43.535	283.56	1710.4	27
28	0.01997	6.5335	39.828	0.00306	0.15306	6.0960	50.065	327.10	1994.0	28
29	0.01737	6.5508	40.314	0.00265	0.15265	6.1540	57.575	377.17	2321.1	29
30	0.01510	6.5659	40.752	0.00230	0.15230	6.2066	66.211	434.74	2698.3	30
35	0.00751	6.6166	42.358	0.00113	0.15113	6.4018	133.17	881.17	5641.1	35
40	0.00373	6.6417	43.283	0.00056	0.15056	6.5167	267.86	1779.0	11593.	40
45	0.00186	6.6543	43.805	0.00028	0.15028	6.5829	538.76	3585.1	23600.	45
50	0.00092	6.6605	44.095	0.00014	0.15014	6.6204	1083.6	7217.7	47784.	50
55	0.00046	6.6636	44.255	0.00007	0.15007	6.6414	2179.6	14524.	96461.	55
60	0.00023	6.6651	44.343	0.00003	0.15003	6.6529	4384.0	29220.	194400.	60
65	0.00011	6.6659	44.390	0.00002	0.15002	6.6592	8817.7	58778.	391424.	65
INF	0.00000	6.6666	44.444	0.0000	0.15000	6.6666	INF	INF	INF	INF

| | i = 20% | | | i = 20% | | | i = 20% | | |
| | PRESENT SUM, P | | | UNIFORM SERIES, A | | | FUTURE SUM, F | | |
n	P/F	P/A	P/G	A/F	A/P	A/G	F/P	F/A	F/G	n
1	0.83333	0.8333	0.0000	1.00000	1.20000	0.0000	1.2000	1.0000	0.0000	1
2	0.69444	1.5277	0.6944	0.45455	0.65455	0.4545	1.4400	2.2000	1.0000	2
3	0.57870	2.1064	1.8518	0.27473	0.47473	0.8791	1.7280	3.6400	3.2000	3
4	0.48225	2.5887	3.2986	0.18629	0.38629	1.2742	2.0736	5.3680	6.8400	4
5	0.40188	2.9906	4.9061	0.13438	0.33438	1.6405	2.4883	7.4416	12.208	5
6	0.33490	3.3255	6.5806	0.10071	0.30071	1.9788	2.9859	9.9299	19.649	6
7	0.27908	3.6045	8.2551	0.07742	0.27742	2.2901	3.5831	12.915	29.579	7
8	0.23257	3.8371	9.8830	0.06061	0.26061	2.5756	4.2998	16.499	42.495	8
9	0.19381	4.0309	11.433	0.04808	0.24808	2.8364	5.1597	20.798	58.994	9
10	0.16151	4.1924	12.887	0.03852	0.23852	3.0738	6.1917	25.958	79.793	10
11	0.13459	4.3270	14.233	0.03110	0.23110	3.2892	7.4300	32.150	105.75	11
12	0.11216	4.4392	15.466	0.02526	0.22526	3.4841	8.9161	39.580	137.90	12
13	0.09346	4.5326	16.588	0.02062	0.22062	3.6597	10.699	48.496	177.48	13
14	0.07789	4.6105	17.600	0.01689	0.21689	3.8174	12.839	59.195	225.98	14
15	0.06491	4.6754	18.509	0.01388	0.21388	3.9588	15.407	72.035	285.17	15
16	0.05409	4.7295	19.320	0.01144	0.21144	4.0851	18.488	87.442	357.21	16
17	0.04507	4.7746	20.041	0.00944	0.20944	4.1975	22.186	105.93	444.65	17
18	0.03756	4.8121	20.680	0.00781	0.20781	4.2975	26.623	128.11	550.58	18
19	0.03130	4.8435	21.243	0.00646	0.20646	4.3860	31.948	154.74	678.70	19
20	0.02608	4.8695	21.739	0.00536	0.20536	4.4643	38.337	186.68	833.44	20
21	0.02174	4.8913	22.174	0.00444	0.20444	4.5333	46.005	225.02	1020.1	21
22	0.01811	4.9094	22.554	0.00369	0.20369	4.5941	55.206	271.03	1245.1	22
23	0.01509	4.9245	22.886	0.00307	0.20307	4.6475	66.247	326.23	1516.1	23
24	0.01258	4.9371	23.176	0.00255	0.20255	4.6942	79.496	392.48	1842.4	24
25	0.01048	4.9475	23.427	0.00212	0.20212	4.7351	95.396	471.98	2234.9	25
26	0.00874	4.9563	23.646	0.00176	0.20176	4.7708	114.47	567.37	2706.8	26
27	0.00728	4.9636	23.835	0.00147	0.20147	4.8020	137.37	681.85	3274.2	27
28	0.00607	4.9696	23.999	0.00122	0.20122	4.8291	164.84	819.22	3956.1	28
29	0.00506	4.9747	24.140	0.00102	0.20102	4.8526	197.81	984.06	4775.3	29
30	0.00421	4.9789	24.262	0.00085	0.20085	4.8730	237.37	1181.8	5759.4	30
35	0.00169	4.9915	24.661	0.00034	0.20034	4.9406	590.66	2948.3	14566.	35
40	0.00068	4.9966	24.846	0.00014	0.20014	4.9727	1469.7	7343.8	36519.	40
45	0.00027	4.9986	24.931	0.00005	0.20005	4.9876	3657.2	18281.	91181.	45
50	0.00011	4.9995	24.969	0.00002	0.20002	4.9945	9100.4	45497.	227236.	50
55	0.00004	4.9998	24.986	0.00001	0.20001	4.9975	22644.	113219.	565820.	55
60	0.00002	4.9999	24.994	0.00000	0.20000	4.9989	56347.	281733	>10**6	60
INF	0.00000	5.0000	25.000	0.0000	0.20000	5.0000	INF	INF	INF	INF

n	P/F	P/A	P/G	A/F	A/P	A/G	F/P	F/A	F/G	n
	PRESENT SUM, P			UNIFORM SERIES, A			FUTURE SUM, F			
1	0.80000	0.8000	0.0000	1.00000	1.25000	0.0000	1.2500	1.0000	0.0000	1
2	0.64000	1.4400	0.6400	0.44444	0.69444	0.4444	1.5625	2.2500	1.0000	2
3	0.51200	1.9520	1.6640	0.26230	0.51230	0.8524	1.9531	3.8125	3.2500	3
4	0.40960	2.3616	2.8928	0.17344	0.42344	1.2249	2.4414	5.7656	7.0625	4
5	0.32768	2.6892	4.2035	0.12185	0.37185	1.5630	3.0517	8.2070	12.828	5
6	0.26214	2.9514	5.5142	0.08882	0.33882	1.8683	3.8147	11.258	21.035	6
7	0.20972	3.1611	6.7725	0.06634	0.31634	2.1424	4.7683	15.073	32.293	7
8	0.16777	3.3289	7.9469	0.05040	0.30040	2.3872	5.9604	19.841	47.367	8
9	0.13422	3.4631	9.0206	0.03876	0.28876	2.6047	7.4505	25.802	67.209	9
10	0.10737	3.5705	9.9870	0.03007	0.28007	2.7971	9.3132	33.252	93.011	10
11	0.08590	3.6564	10.846	0.02349	0.27349	2.9663	11.641	42.566	126.26	11
12	0.06872	3.7251	11.602	0.01845	0.26845	3.1145	14.551	54.207	168.83	12
13	0.05498	3.7801	12.261	0.01454	0.26454	3.2437	18.189	68.759	223.03	13
14	0.04398	3.8240	12.833	0.01150	0.26150	3.3559	22.737	86.949	291.79	14
15	0.03518	3.8592	13.326	0.00912	0.25912	3.4529	28.421	109.68	378.74	15
16	0.02815	3.8874	13.748	0.00724	0.25724	3.5366	35.527	138.10	488.43	16
17	0.02252	3.9099	14.108	0.00576	0.25576	3.6083	44.408	173.63	626.54	17
18	0.01801	3.9279	14.414	0.00459	0.25459	3.6697	55.511	218.04	800.17	18
19	0.01441	3.9423	14.674	0.00366	0.25366	3.7221	69.388	273.55	1018.2	19
20	0.01153	3.9538	14.893	0.00292	0.25292	3.7667	86.736	342.94	1291.7	20
21	0.00922	3.9631	15.077	0.00233	0.25233	3.8045	108.42	429.68	1634.7	21
22	0.00738	3.9704	15.232	0.00186	0.25186	3.8364	135.52	538.10	2064.4	22
23	0.00590	3.9763	15.362	0.00148	0.25148	3.8634	169.40	673.62	2602.5	23
24	0.00472	3.9811	15.471	0.00119	0.25119	3.8861	211.75	843.03	3276.1	24
25	0.00378	3.9848	15.561	0.00095	0.25095	3.9051	264.69	1054.7	4119.1	25
26	0.00302	3.9879	15.637	0.00076	0.25076	3.9211	330.87	1319.4	5173.9	26
27	0.00242	3.9903	15.700	0.00061	0.25061	3.9345	413.59	1650.3	6493.4	27
28	0.00193	3.9922	15.752	0.00048	0.25048	3.9457	516.98	2063.9	8143.8	28
29	0.00155	3.9938	15.795	0.00039	0.25039	3.9550	646.23	2580.9	10207.	29
30	0.00124	3.9950	15.831	0.00031	0.25031	3.9628	807.79	3227.1	12788.	30
35	0.00041	3.9983	15.936	0.00010	0.25010	3.9858	2465.1	9856.7	39287.	35
40	0.00013	3.9994	15.976	0.00003	0.25003	3.9946	7523.1	30088.	120195.	40
45	0.00004	3.9998	15.991	0.00001	0.25001	3.9980	22958.	91831.	367146.	45
INF	0.00000	4.0000	16.000	0.0000	0.25000	4.0000	INF	INF	INF	INF

	i = 30%			i = 30%			i = 30%			
	PRESENT SUM, P			UNIFORM SERIES, A			FUTURE SUM, F			
n	P/F	P/A	P/G	A/F	A/P	A/G	F/P	F/A	F/G	n
1	0.76923	0.7692	0.0000	1.00000	1.30000	0.0000	1.3000	1.0000	0.0000	1
2	0.59172	1.3609	0.5917	0.43478	0.73478	0.4347	1.6900	2.3000	1.0000	2
3	0.45517	1.8161	1.5020	0.25063	0.55063	0.8270	2.1970	3.9900	3.3000	3
4	0.35013	2.1662	2.5524	0.16163	0.46163	1.1782	2.8561	6.1870	7.2900	4
5	0.26933	2.4355	3.6297	0.11058	0.41058	1.4903	3.7129	9.0431	13.477	5
6	0.20718	2.6427	4.6656	0.07839	0.37839	1.7654	4.8268	12.756	22.520	6
7	0.15937	2.8021	5.6218	0.05687	0.35687	2.0062	6.2748	17.582	35.276	7
8	0.12259	2.9247	6.4799	0.04192	0.34192	2.2155	8.1573	23.857	52.859	8
9	0.09430	3.0190	7.2343	0.03124	0.33124	2.3962	10.604	32.015	76.716	9
10	0.07254	3.0915	7.8871	0.02346	0.32346	2.5512	13.785	42.619	108.73	10
11	0.05580	3.1473	8.4451	0.01773	0.31773	2.6832	17.921	56.405	151.35	11
12	0.04292	3.1902	8.9173	0.01345	0.31345	2.7951	23.298	74.327	207.75	12
13	0.03302	3.2232	9.3135	0.01024	0.31024	2.8894	30.287	97.625	282.08	13
14	0.02540	3.2486	9.6436	0.00782	0.30782	2.9685	39.373	127.91	379.70	14
15	0.01954	3.2682	9.9172	0.00598	0.30598	3.0344	51.185	167.28	507.62	15
16	0.01503	3.2832	10.142	0.00458	0.30458	3.0892	66.541	218.47	674.90	16
17	0.01156	3.2948	10.327	0.00351	0.30351	3.1345	86.504	285.01	893.38	17
18	0.00889	3.3036	10.478	0.00269	0.30269	3.1718	112.45	371.51	1178.3	18
19	0.00684	3.3105	10.601	0.00207	0.30207	3.2024	146.19	483.97	1549.9	19
20	0.00526	3.3157	10.701	0.00159	0.30159	3.2275	190.05	630.16	2033.8	20
21	0.00405	3.3198	10.782	0.00122	0.30122	3.2479	247.06	820.21	2664.0	21
22	0.00311	3.3229	10.848	0.00094	0.30094	3.2646	321.18	1067.2	3484.2	22
23	0.00239	3.3253	10.900	0.00072	0.30072	3.2781	417.53	1388.4	4551.5	23
24	0.00184	3.3271	10.943	0.00055	0.30055	3.2890	542.80	1806.0	5940.0	24
25	0.00142	3.3286	10.977	0.00043	0.30043	3.2978	705.64	2348.8	7746.0	25
26	0.00109	3.3297	11.004	0.00033	0.30033	3.3049	917.33	3054.4	10094.	26
27	0.00084	3.3305	11.026	0.00025	0.30025	3.3106	1192.5	3971.7	13149.	27
28	0.00065	3.3311	11.043	0.00019	0.30019	3.3151	1550.2	5164.3	17121.	28
29	0.00050	3.3316	11.057	0.00015	0.30015	3.3189	2015.3	6714.6	22285.	29
30	0.00038	3.3320	11.068	0.00011	0.30011	3.3218	2620.0	8729.9	29000.	30
35	0.00010	3.3329	11.098	0.00003	0.30003	3.3297	9727.8	32422.	107960.	35
INF	0.00000	3.3333	11.111	0.0000	0.30000	3.3333	INF	INF	INF	INF

| | i = 40% | | | i = 40% | | | i = 40% | | | |
| | PRESENT SUM, P | | | UNIFORM SERIES, A | | | FUTURE SUM, F | | | |
n	P/F	P/A	P/G	A/F	A/P	A/G	F/P	F/A	F/G	n
1	0.71429	0.7142	0.0000	1.00000	1.40000	0.0000	1.4000	1.0000	0.0000	1
2	0.51020	1.2244	0.5102	0.41667	0.81667	0.4166	1.9600	2.4000	1.0000	2
3	0.36443	1.5889	1.2390	0.22936	0.62936	0.7798	2.7440	4.3600	3.4000	3
4	0.26031	1.8492	2.0199	0.14077	0.54077	1.0923	3.8416	7.1040	7.7600	4
5	0.18593	2.0351	2.7637	0.09136	0.49136	1.3579	5.3782	10.945	14.864	5
6	0.13281	2.1679	3.4277	0.06126	0.46126	1.5811	7.5295	16.323	25.809	6
7	0.09486	2.2628	3.9969	0.04192	0.44192	1.7663	10.541	23.853	42.133	7
8	0.06776	2.3306	4.4712	0.02907	0.42907	1.9185	14.757	34.394	65.986	8
9	0.04840	2.3790	4.8584	0.02034	0.42034	2.0422	20.661	49.152	100.38	9
10	0.03457	2.4135	5.1696	0.01432	0.41432	2.1419	28.925	69.813	149.53	10
11	0.02469	2.4382	5.4165	0.01013	0.41013	2.2214	40.495	98.739	219.34	11
12	0.01764	2.4559	5.6106	0.00718	0.40718	2.2845	56.693	139.23	318.08	12
13	0.01260	2.4685	5.7617	0.00510	0.40510	2.3341	79.371	195.92	457.32	13
14	0.00900	2.4775	5.8787	0.00363	0.40363	2.3728	111.12	275.30	653.25	14
15	0.00643	2.4839	5.9687	0.00259	0.40259	2.4029	155.56	386.42	928.55	15
16	0.00459	2.4885	6.0376	0.00185	0.40185	2.4262	217.79	541.98	1314.9	16
17	0.00328	2.4918	6.0901	0.00132	0.40132	2.4440	304.91	759.78	1856.9	17
18	0.00234	2.4941	6.1300	0.00094	0.40094	2.4577	426.87	1064.7	2616.7	18
19	0.00167	2.4958	6.1600	0.00067	0.40067	2.4681	597.63	1491.5	3681.4	19
20	0.00120	2.4970	6.1827	0.00048	0.40048	2.4760	836.68	2089.2	5173.0	20
21	0.00085	2.4978	6.1998	0.00034	0.40034	2.4820	1171.3	2925.8	7262.2	21
22	0.00061	2.4984	6.2126	0.00024	0.40024	2.4865	1639.9	4097.2	10188.	22
23	0.00044	2.4989	6.2222	0.00017	0.40017	2.4899	2295.8	5737.1	14285.	23
24	0.00031	2.4992	6.2293	0.00012	0.40012	2.4925	3214.2	8033.0	20022.	24
25	0.00022	2.4994	6.2347	0.00009	0.40009	2.4944	4499.8	11247.	28055.	25
INF	0.00000	2.5000	6.2500	0.0000	0.40000	2.5000	INF	INF	INF	INF

	$i = 50\%$ PRESENT SUM, P			$i = 50\%$ UNIFORM SERIES, A			$i = 50\%$ FUTURE SUM, F			
n	P/F	P/A	P/G	A/F	A/P	A/G	F/P	F/A	F/G	n
1	0.66667	0.6666	0.0000	1.00000	1.50000	0.0000	1.5000	1.0000	0.0000	1
2	0.44444	1.1111	0.4444	0.40000	0.90000	0.4000	2.2500	2.5000	1.0000	2
3	0.29630	1.4074	1.0370	0.21053	0.71053	0.7368	3.3750	4.7500	3.5000	3
4	0.19753	1.6049	1.6296	0.12308	0.62308	1.0153	5.0625	8.1250	8.2500	4
5	0.13169	1.7366	2.1563	0.07583	0.57583	1.2417	7.5937	13.187	16.375	5
6	0.08779	1.8244	2.5953	0.04812	0.54812	1.4225	11.390	20.781	29.562	6
7	0.05853	1.8829	2.9465	0.03108	0.53108	1.5648	17.085	32.171	50.343	7
8	0.03902	1.9219	3.2196	0.02030	0.52030	1.6751	25.628	49.257	82.515	8
9	0.02601	1.9479	3.4277	0.01335	0.51335	1.7596	38.443	74.886	131.77	9
10	0.01734	1.9653	3.5838	0.00882	0.50882	1.8235	57.665	113.33	206.66	10
11	0.01156	1.9768	3.6994	0.00585	0.50585	1.8713	86.497	170.99	319.99	11
12	0.00771	1.9845	3.7841	0.00388	0.50388	1.9067	129.74	257.49	490.98	12
13	0.00514	1.9897	3.8458	0.00258	0.50258	1.9328	194.62	387.23	748.47	13
14	0.00343	1.9931	3.8903	0.00172	0.50172	1.9518	291.92	581.85	1135.7	14
15	0.00228	1.9954	3.9223	0.00114	0.50114	1.9656	437.89	873.78	1717.5	15
16	0.00152	1.9969	3.9451	0.00076	0.50076	1.9756	656.84	1311.6	2591.3	16
17	0.00101	1.9979	3.9614	0.00051	0.50051	1.9827	985.26	1968.5	3903.0	17
18	0.00068	1.9986	3.9729	0.00034	0.50034	1.9878	1477.8	2953.7	5871.5	18
19	0.00045	1.9991	3.9810	0.00023	0.50023	1.9914	2216.8	4431.6	8825.3	19
20	0.00030	1.9994	3.9867	0.00015	0.50015	1.9939	3325.2	6648.5	13257.	20
21	0.00020	1.9996	3.9907	0.00010	0.50010	1.9957	4987.8	9973.7	19905.	21
22	0.00013	1.9997	3.9935	0.00007	0.50007	1.9970	7481.8	14961.	29879.	22
23	0.00009	1.9998	3.9955	0.00004	0.50004	1.9979	11222.	22443.	44841.	23
24	0.00006	1.9998	3.9969	0.00003	0.50003	1.9985	16834.	33666.	67284.	24
25	0.00004	1.9999	3.9978	0.00002	0.50002	1.9990	25251.	50500.	100951.	25
INF	0.00000	2.0000	4.0000	0.0000	0.50000	2.0000	INF	INF	INF	INF

Appendix E
Answers to End-of-Chapter Questions

CHAPTER 1

1. Phase I is economic expansion, characterized by robust construction, rising occupancy, and increasing rents. The result is overbuilding and oversupply of real estate, which is Phase II. Robust construction continues, but occupancy decreases and rents level off. In Phase III the real estate cycle is in recession. There is no new construction, although projects already in the pipeline are coming to completion and beginning operations. Occupancy and rents continue to fall as the market struggles to absorb oversupply. Phase IV is recovery: There is still no new construction, but occupancy and rents rise as oversupply is gradually worked off.

2. Liquidity cycles reflect fluctuations in the availability of capital, while interest rate cycles reflect fluctuations in the cost of capital.

3. 5.00 T-note + 1.25 spread = 6.25% stated interest rate.

4. The three primary real estate sectors are:

   - *Institutional:* Schools, museums, city halls, police stations, public hospitals
   - *Private:* Owner-occupied houses
   - *Commercial:* Offices, retail centers, industrial warehousing and manufacturing, multifamily

5. The primary driver of occupancy cycles are rental-growth rate cycles.

6. Real estate is considered illiquid because:

   - Each real estate site and structure is unique in age, design, maintenance, location, and market.
   - Financing usually is required and the dollar amounts tend to be relatively large.
   - Tax consequences may be significant.
   - Ownership can be complex.

- Environmental liability issues must be carefully investigated, as the current owner of real estate can be liable for the cleanup of environmental contamination caused by prior owners.
- Due diligence must be performed.
- On income-producing property, existing leases must be analyzed and verified, credit reports run on tenants, and expenses verified.

7. Factors that may create upward pressure on prices, when reversed, tend to create less downward pressure.

CHAPTER 2

1. The businesses that best describe the business forms, itemized from a through h, are:

   a. Limited Liability Company
   b. Sole Proprietorship
   c. REIT (Real Estate Investment Trust)
   d. Limited Liability Company
   e. Joint Venture
   f. C Corporation
   g. Partnership
   h. S Corporation

2. 75

3. C Corporations

4. The changes in tax laws that have greatly reduced the tax benefits of owning real estate include the following:

   - The time period over which assets may be depreciated has greatly increased.
   - Accelerated depreciation is no longer allowed, only straight-line depreciation may be used.
   - The Alternative Minimum Tax limits the total amount of tax benefits any one taxpayer can obtain.
   - The top tax bracket has been lowered from up to 70% to the current maximum of 35%, making tax shelters less attractive.

5. Some common fees sometimes collected by syndicators or general partners in putting together real estate deals include:

   - Promotes for putting deals together
   - Brokering purchases of land
   - Arranging financing
   - Overseeing the construction process
   - Overseeing property lease ups
   - Management of the real estate
   - Janitorial, landscaping, and other maintenance services

6. The general partner has unlimited liability while the limited partners have limited liability.

CHAPTER 3

1. *The Fading Offer.* The best way to counter this situation is to assert that the fishing poles were offered as part of a fair deal yesterday, and no new information has been introduced that justifies removing them from the deal.
2. *The Nibble.* Assert that you struck a fair deal last week that was mutually beneficial. The time for negotiation is over, and you look forward to him becoming one of the leading contributors to your team.
3. *Points of Personal Privilege.* In this deal, the use of a single parking spot is trivial, and it is no large concession on your part to grant this point of personal privilege. Happily agree to provide parking for the seller's son.
4. *The Missing Person Stall.* Insist that it is important for both parties that the negotiations remain productive and all interested people should be present and prepared for any meeting.

CHAPTER 4

1. Architects, engineers, land planners, landscape architects, surveyors, attorneys, and general contractors all will be part of a developer's external team.
2. The bond provides assurances from a third-party insurer, guarantor, or surety that funds will be available to complete the project for the contracted price if the builder does not perform as agreed.
3. Normally, an investor would not commit money to a project until it is fully vested with development rights and all entitlements necessary to launch the project.
4. The prevailing theory is that one would choose the best site because markets can recover but sites cannot move.
5. Institutional investors prefer to be in markets with other institutional investors, because it creates a sense of security and assures them of an exit strategy.
6. The developer should research the current vacancy rate, the current construction activity, and a forecast of growth in demand.
7. The option contract gives the developer control of the land while performing necessary due diligence. If he finds the proposed project is infeasible, his losses are limited to the option price, an amount significantly less than the money usually advanced under a purchase and sale agreement.
8. Zoning laws are deemed to protect property values by separating and regulating incompatible land uses, such as keeping heavy industrial property away from residential properties. Some claim zoning laws are exclusionary, designed by the "haves" to keep out the "have-nots." Another criticism

suggests that zoning grants special status to one group over another. Still another criticism is that zoning favors those who are politically well connected and understand how a particular political system works. A final criticism is that zoning has eliminated many mixed-use projects and has increased the need for motor vehicles.

9. A site plan depicts how a project will conform (or vary from) governmental guidelines pertaining to a particular site and the proposed development. The site plan addresses building locations, parking, and utility connections, along with how the project will meet governmental regulations such as height restrictions, site-coverage ratios, floor-area ratios, environmental, and other prescribed guidelines.

10. If a bank uses the 360-day year method, it makes more money over the term of the loan, because the interest payment will be calculated based on 360 days in a year but payments cover 365 actual days. Using the example in the text: If you borrowed $10,000,000 for exactly one year at 10%, you would assume you owe $1,000,000 in interest, calculating the daily interest payment to be $1,000,000/360 = $2,777.78 per day. But payments are made for all 365 days of the year. So the total interest paid for the year is $2,777.78 × 365 + $1,013,888.89. Due to the 360-day rule, the bank is making an additional $13,900 in interest income.

CHAPTER 5

1. No. Courts have ruled that restrictive covenants against public policy—e.g., race, religion, and national origin—are not enforceable.

2. Place the land under an option to buy and hire a firm to conduct test borings and/or test pits to ascertain topographical conditions and the extent of any adverse site conditions.

3. Shopping and retail centers, schools, churches, recreation facilities, and entertainment centers.

4. Travel time.

5. Location, adaptability, accessibility, transportation and commuting time, proximity to essential services, proximity to recreation, public improvements, and environmental amenities.

CHAPTER 6

1. Four assumptions a pro forma makes to forecast how a project will perform are:
   - Future rental rates
   - Anticipated occupancy levels
   - Operating expenses
   - Future interest rates

2. Construction costs are difficult to estimate because they are highly dependent on the current supply-and-demand environment, changes in the project's architectural renderings, and the contractor bidding process, all of which cannot be easily controlled by the developer.

3. The two primary methods employed to determine the maximum amount of development that can be constructed on a site are:
   • Site-coverage ratio
   • Floor-area ratio

4. Maximizing a site is not always the best alternative because higher densities often result in higher costs that accompany stricter building codes.

5. Apartment development is considered less risky because its shorter-term leases (typically one year or less) can be more easily adjusted to reflect increasing inflation rates. Retail and office leases are typically longer in duration and, therefore, must be indexed to ensure inflation protection over the term of the lease.

6. Auxiliary income can be generated by charging a higher rate for units with favorable views, charging for tenant application and redecoration fees, and by providing tenant services including laundry and vending.

7. The seven groups of operating expenses that are deducted from effective gross income to yield net operating income are:
   • Utility expenses
   • On-site leasing and management staff
   • Maintenance, supplies, and repairs
   • Replacement reserves
   • Management expenses
   • Taxes
   • Miscellaneous expenses

8. The debt coverage ratio equals the project's net operating income divided by the debt service payment. The debt coverage ratio (DCR) is the primary way for a lender to determine if there is enough cash flow to sufficiently cover the required debt service payments.

9. Value engineering is the name of this process. Its goal is to reduce construction costs but not to reduce the project's anticipated income in the process.

10. The developer must carefully assess the value of a site because it is highly dependent on outside forces, including future land use and transportation plans, as well as regulatory and zoning conditions.

11. These fees typically include construction interest, the developer's fee, and utility fees.

12. Additional costs that need to be considered include interim property taxes, marketing and lease-up costs, common-area furnishings, and construction interest.

CHAPTER 7

1. The appraised value largely defines the amount of financing that a lending institution is willing to provide toward a project. If the appraised value is higher, so is the amount that could likely be lent.

2. An appraisal attempts to define a probable sales price, the "market value" for a property that a willing buyer and seller would reach in an arm's-length transaction in a competitive, open market.

3. The six sections included in a typical appraisal are General Organization, General Appraisal Information, Background Information, Property Data, Value Conclusion, and Addenda. Whether or not a site is included in a floodplain could be found on a floodplain map, located in the Property Data section.

4. Found within an appraisal, these items can be described as follows:

   • *Site location map:* Depicts the size of the subject property as well as the sizes of adjacent parcels.
   • *Site plan:* Shows new construction, existing on-site structures, roadways, and necessary water retention basins.
   • *Floor plan:* Displays the general space layout as well as detailed information about unique building features.

5. The cost approach estimates value based on the cost to duplicate the project today; it is equal to the current value of the land plus the cost of improvements less depreciation.

6. The value of depreciation is estimated three ways in the cost approach and can be described as follows:

   • *Physical depreciation:* General wear and tear of the improvements; structural decay. An example would be a roof that needs to be replaced.
   • *Functional obsolescence:* Physical defects due to changes in market demands and/or customer tastes over time. An example would be a three bedroom house with only one bathroom.
   • *External obsolescence:* Loss in value due to conditions outside the property, such as the neighborhood environment; this form of depreciation is largely incurable.

7. The five typical operating expenses that are subtracted from a project's income stream include real estate taxes and insurance, maintenance, utilities expenses, administrative expenses, and reserves for replacement.

8. The market approach estimates the value of a property by comparing recent open-market sales of similar projects. The analysis is usually done by using either a gross income multiplier (GIM) or by direct physical comparison.

CHAPTER 8

1. Mortgage brokers bring together a lender and a borrower and facilitate the transaction for a fee. They typically screen the borrower and property for financial strength, gather and analyze necessary documents and reports related to borrower and property, and act as a connection point and conduit of information.

2. The two loan types are short-term financing (construction loans) and long-term financing (permanent financing). Commercial banks, with their vast amount of short-term deposits, are generally the institution to issue construction loans. Life insurance companies and pension funds are major sources of permanent financing. Commercial banks also may originate permanent financing, but they will quickly sell the loan to another institution.

3. A mortgage banker originates loans that it plans to sell at a later date. These institutions normally have short-term deposits on hand and cannot take the risk of making long-term loans. Portfolio lenders make loans that they intend to hold for the life of the loan.

4. The point at which a development would be considered stabilized is when it is fully leased up to the market level of occupancy and has been in operation long enough to have a solid track record of income and expenses on which a lender can rely in making a permanent, long-term loan.

5. The primary reasons that the term for permanent financing is often shorter than amortization are:
   - Lenders wish to avoid lending too far into a distant and murky future.
   - Borrowers frequently expect their properties to appreciate and believe that significant tax-free capital may be obtained by refinancing at periodic intervals.
   - The owners intend to sell within the 10-year time period and are aware that new owners typically refinance properties anyway.

6. The five major sources of commercial real estate lending are: commercial mortgage backed securities (CMBS)/conduit loans, insurance companies, governmental agencies and quasi-governmental corporations, commercial banks, and pension funds.

7. A lender will look to the three fundamental C's. The first C is *character*, which tells if the borrower has repaid his debt in the past. The second C is *competence*, which signifies whether the borrower will be able to put the loaned funds to good use to generate a profit to repay the loan. The third C is *collateral*, which ensures the lender that the borrower will invest in a solid property that will encourage preservation and appreciation of value. This ensures the lender that in the case of foreclosure, the buyer's property will be sufficient to cover the defaulted loan.

8. A complete loan application should include full project plans, engineering specifications, cost estimates, artist's rendering of the completed project, marketing and feasibility studies, maps and aerials, estimates of income and

operating expenses, as well as the qualifications and financial statements of the borrower.

9. A term sheet is a nonbinding letter from a prospective lender stating the terms under which it would make a loan. The term sheet typically includes information regarding borrower's name, estimated loan amount, purpose, collateral, term, interest rate, fees, guarantors, equity required, and additional requirements.

CHAPTER 9

1. A commitment letter is an expanded version of the term sheet issued by a lender. The commitment letter states in more detail the terms on which the loan will be made. Once signed by both parties, the commitment letter is a legally-binding contract. The items it contains are information regarding loan type, loan amount, borrower, guarantor, purpose and property, interest rate, required hedge, prepayment, repayment, maturity, collateral, commitment fee, construction period, initial equity requirement, payment and performance bonds, general contract, closing, environmental reports, appraisals, costs, and closing conditions.

2. It is possible for a borrower to roll the commitment fee into the loan via a higher interest rate, so the borrower does not have to come up with more cash out of pocket. On the other hand, the borrower can reduce the loan interest rate by paying a higher commitment fee at closing.

3. Many things can go wrong between commitment and loan closing that would prevent it from closing. If the loan is not closed, but it is stated that the commitment fee was earned at the time of acceptance, the borrower will still be required to pay this commitment fee without any loan.

4. The following items are considered either personal or real property:
   - Built-in range: Real property
   - Free-standing refrigerator: Personal property
   - Television: Personal property
   - Chandelier hanging from ceiling: Real property
   - Air-conditioning window unit: Personal property

CHAPTER 10

1. The mortgage or lien must be recorded in the public record in the jurisdiction in which the property is located. The general rule is that the original must be presented to the clerk of the court along with a notary stamp and signatures of two witnesses. Failure to file in the public record can result in a sale to an innocent third party who would not be bound by the mortgage.

2. The five essential terms of a note are lender, borrower, principal sum, interest rate, and time of repayment.

The note must be signed by only the borrower—and not the witnesses or notary.

Only the mortgage should be filed in the public record.

3. The face amount of the note is the amount that the borrower promises to repay, not the amount borrowed. If there is a difference between the face amount of the note and the amount borrowed, it creates an implied interest rate.

4. Immediately after the language of the conveyance, there is language stating that if the borrower complies with all stipulations and agreements of the note and mortgage, then the mortgage and conveyance of title shall be null and void. Also, most states hold that a mortgage is not a true conveyance of title and a formal foreclosure proceeding must take place to transfer title in the event of default.

5. An acceleration clause is important because if a borrower defaults by missing a single payment, the lender does not have many remedies. The lender can sue for the missed payment, but the time and money involved with doing that does not make it worthwhile. With the acceleration clause, the lender can automatically put pressure on the borrower to produce the late payment.

6. Due to the lag in time between the times liens are filed and the time they are recorded, a lender is vulnerable. A lien could be filed after the title search was completed but before the mortgage was recorded. This is the reason why a lender will perform a follow-up search before the mortgage is recorded.

7. It is in the general contractor's best interest to keep his client happy. If the project is not leasing up as fast as the developer would like, there is a chance the developer would not use the contractor again for the next project. Ways the general contractor can assist with lease-up are: setting up a leasing trailer quickly, allowing potential customers to view construction in progress, have a show unit available quickly, finish amenities (pool and clubhouse, etc.) early to show to potential renters and buyers.

8. Assets that the guarantor has on deposit with the lending bank may be seized to pay off amounts due to the lender. Guarantors choose not to keep large amounts of assets at the lending institution so that in case of default, their assets are not automatically depleted. Even though the payment still must be made, it will give the guarantor more flexibility in maintaining operation of her business.

CHAPTER 11

1. There has been an increased use of joint ventures in the last decade due to improved accessibility to information through the Internet and the need for diversification in investments and asset allocation strategies.

2. The operating partner is usually offered preferred returns for:

   • Finding and putting together the deal.
   • Running selected risks.
   • Motivating the operating partner to operate the asset so as to produce above-average returns.

3. To insure that the operator is personally committed and motivated.

4. You lose additional deal opportunities because you cannot compete in real time. You end up funding most of the expenses and going back to your partner for reimbursement.

5. Owners may not be cooperative, or they may be disorganized, overworked, and behind schedule. Discounts or concessions given to entice renters, or to compensate for soft markets, or above-market rents, often do not show up on the books.

6. Frequently when a loan gets in serious trouble, the legal clock starts to run. The guarantor is liable for virtually all the lender's expenses, legal and otherwise. It is not unheard of for the legal and tertiary costs to rival the underlying economic costs. It is possible for the liability exposure on the carve-outs to be used as leverage. All the lender has to do is allege a violation and all sorts of bad things can happen.

7. The mortgage constant equals the interest rate when there is no amortization period (when it is interest only).

8. The upside of this approach is that you can do more, have more deals cooking. The downside is that you lose some of the "feel of the deal," the subtlety and nuances of the negotiation process.

CHAPTER 12

1. The developer must register the project with the U.S. Securities and Exchange Commission (SEC).

2. If substantial renovations are required or the project is mispriced.

3. Condo conversions are taxed as ordinary income, similar to the inventory on a grocer's shelf, because the investment is usually only on the investor's books for a short period of time (less than 1 year).

4. In general, a condo conversion often helps the local rental apartment market. There are four possible reasons for this:

   • Conversion reduces the existing stock of rental apartment supply
   • Condominiums tend to be underoccupied
   • Condominiums are usually either second or vacation homes or investment homes
   • The community under conversion is taken off-line for renovations

5. If there are competing claims on a deposit, an escrow agent will generally refuse to release funds absent a court order or a waiver from all parties.

This can create delay, which can be an unpleasant surprise for someone anticipating a rapid refund and redeployment of working capital.

6. The condo converter does not really care about the existing leases (other than rapid expiration and none greater than one year) and operational expenses.
7. A business day generally is any day the Federal Reserve is open.
8. Costs of acquisition (due diligence, closing, loan, survey, legal, environmental), renovation, carrying, marketing and selling.
9. Carve-outs are supposed to kick in only if the borrower-guarantor has done some intentional and willfully bad act. In reality, they may also kick in under certain unintentional circumstances.
10. Under most carve-outs, if environmental liability exists, the borrower-guarantor is personally liable.
11. The key to a fast sellout is proper pricing, responding to the marketplace, raising prices rapidly if sales are going well, quickly adding discounts and specials if sales lag.

CHAPTER 13

1. The creation of a Critical Path Method (CPM) diagram is often the first step. CPM diagrams are used to establish the length of project.
2. A Bar Chart graphically displays the anticipated percentage of completion of each job item per month during the duration of the job. Estimated percentages of completion can be applied against dollar values to obtain a good idea of the amount of cash required each month. Most of the amount will be paid using bank draws of the construction loan; any deficiencies will need to be paid through operating capital or other borrowed funds.
3. Bank draws are plotted as step curves because funds are only received at monthly intervals. This is in contrast to construction expenditures (represented by the S-curve), where a smooth curve is drawn between points as an approximation of the money that is actually spent from day to day on the job.
4. Project delays increase interest costs. Funds drawn from a construction loan are charged interest from the point at which they are disbursed until permanent loan financing is in place. Delaying project completion—and subsequent permanent loan financing—increases the amount of time that funds are drawn from the construction lender and, subsequently, interest charges.
5. Total interest charged $= \$450,000 \times (1.01^{11} - 1) = \$52,050$
6. Total interest now charged $= \$450,000 \times (1.01^{16} - 1) = \$77,660$
   Less interest based on a 12-month schedule: $52,050.
   Additional interest collected due to five-month delay $= \$25,610$.

CHAPTER 14

1. A cash flow diagram is a graph that displays cash inflows and outflows over time. The diagram consists of two parts: the horizontal time line and the vertical cash flow lines. The time line is subdivided into n compounding periods, with each compounding period representing the unit of time duration; the vertical lines represent cash inflows and outflows.

2. Equal periodic payment

3. Plans 1–4 are equivalent because each plan provides for the payment of ten cents of interest per one dollar still owed the bank at the end of each year. The payment amounts are different because each plan has a different repayment schedule. Regardless, the bank will make the same amount of money on each loan no matter which of the four plans is adopted for repayment, because each plan includes a principal amount of $10,000, an interest rate of 10%, and a total time period of ten years.

4. Using the 10% interest tables in Appendix D, column heading P/F, line $n = 20$,

$$P = F(P/F, 10\%, 20) = \$53,600 \times 0.14864 = \$7,967.10$$

   This can also be solved using equation 1b, where $P = F / (1 + i)^n$,

$$P = \$53,600/(1.10)^{20} = \$7,967.30$$

5. Using the 8% interest tables in Appendix D, column heading P/A, line $n = 15$,
$$P = A(P/A, 8\%, 15) = \$2,500 \times 8.5594 = \$21,398.50$$

   This can also be solved using equation 3b, where $P = A \times [(1 + i)^n - 1]/[i(1 + i)^n]$

$$P = \$2,500 \times [(1.08)^{15} - 1]/[.08(1.08)^{15}] = \$21,398.70$$

6. Using the 8% interest tables in Appendix D, column heading A/F, line $n = 20$,
$$A = F(A/F, 8\%, 20) = \$50,000 \times 0.02185 = \$1,092.50$$

   This can also be solved using equation 2b, where $A = F \times \{ i/[(1 + i)^n - 1]\}$

$$A = \$50,000 \times \{0.08/[(1.08)^{20} - 1]\} = \$1,092.61$$

7. Using the 10% interest tables in Appendix D, column heading A/P, line $n = 30$,
$$A = P(A/P, 10\%, 30) = \$50,000 \times 0.10608 = \$5,304.00$$

   This can also be solved using equation 3a, where $A = P \times \{[i(1 + i)^n]/[(1 + i)^n - 1]\}$
$$A = \$50,000 \times \{[.10(1.10)^{30}]/[(1.10)^{30} - 1]\} = \$5,303.96$$

INDEX

AFRICA

World of New Men

Also by John J. Considine

ACROSS A WORLD

CALL FOR FORTY THOUSAND

WHEN THE SORGHUM WAS HIGH